CW01654848

CINEMAS
A FRENCH HERITAGE

A PHOTOGRAPHIC STUDY BY

SIMON EDELSTEIN

PREFACE BY

JACK LANG

JONGLEZ PUBLISHING

For Elisabeth, my faithful accomplice in this photographic adventure.

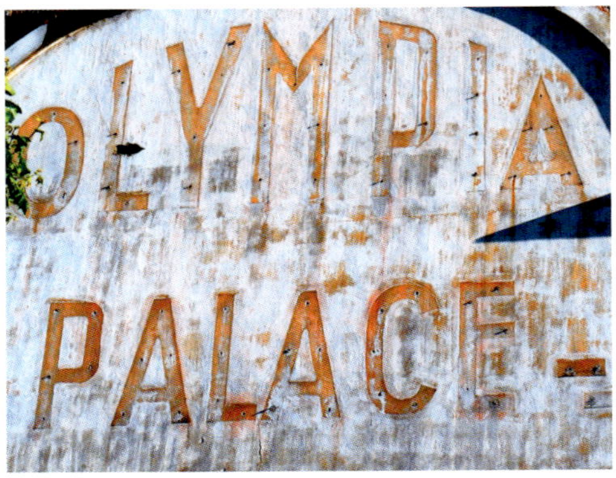
OLYMPIA
PALACE

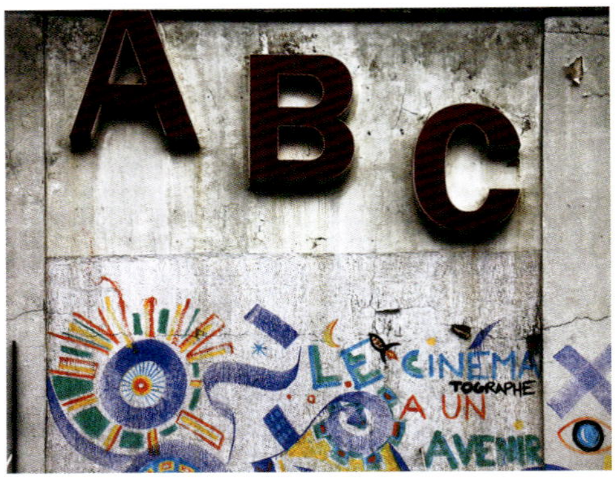
ABC
LE CINÉMA
TOGRAPHE
A UN
AVENIR

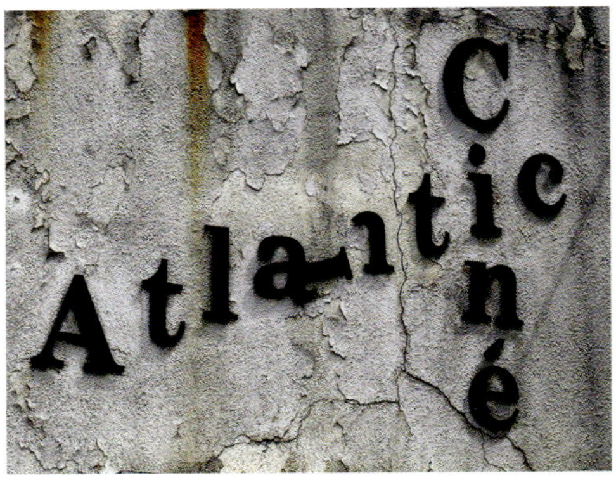
Atlantic
Ciné

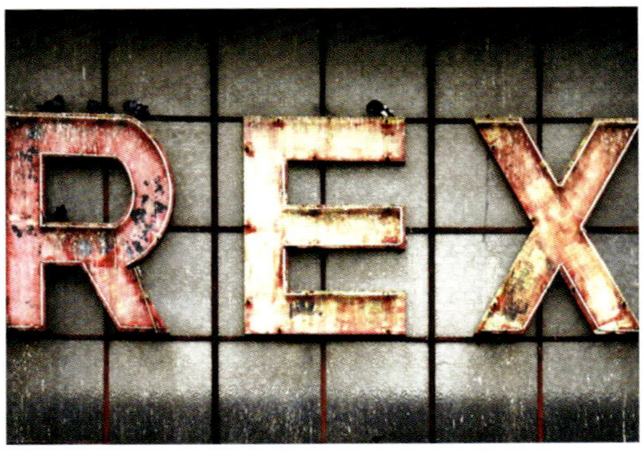
REX

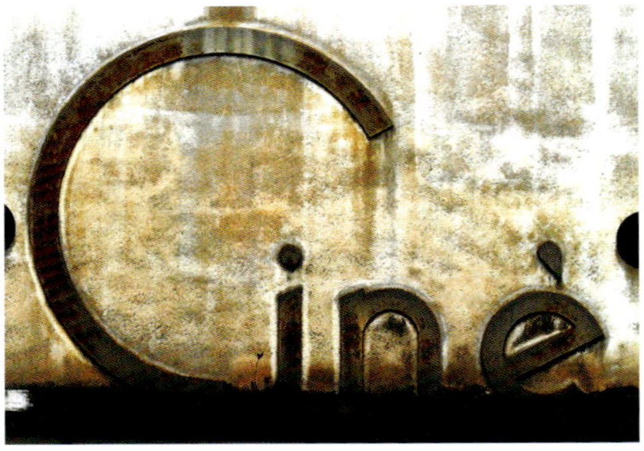
Ciné

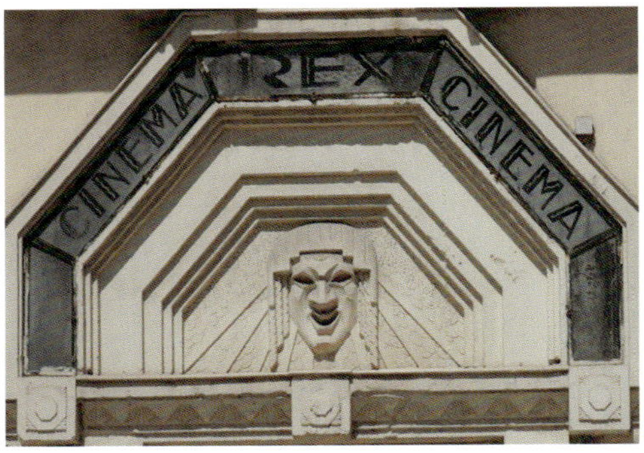
CINEMA
REX
CINEMA

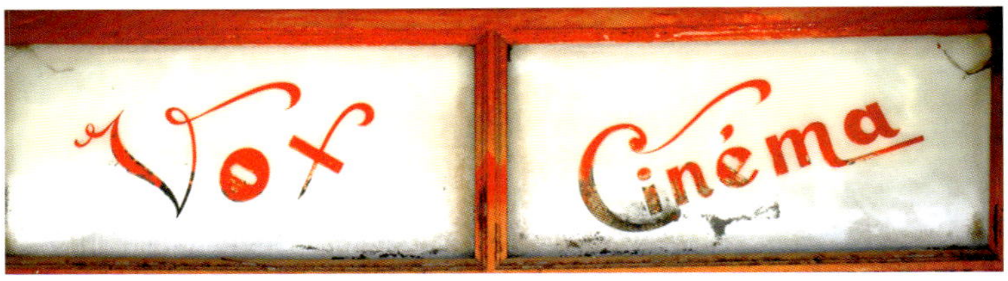
Vox
Cinéma

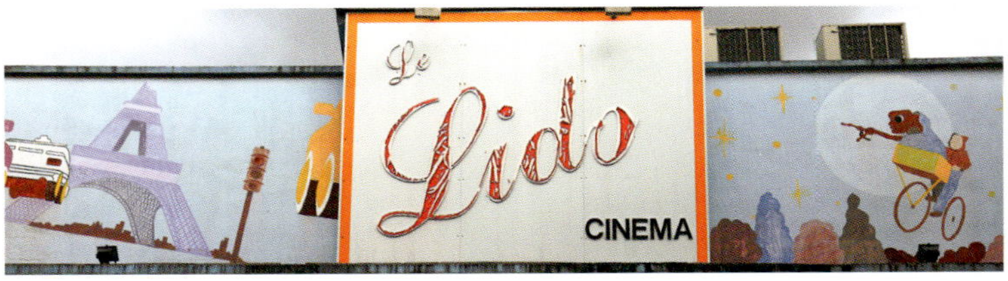
Le
Lido
CINEMA

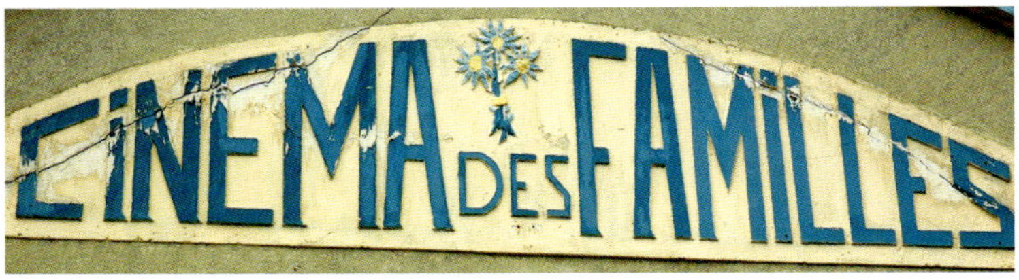
CINEMA DES FAMILLES

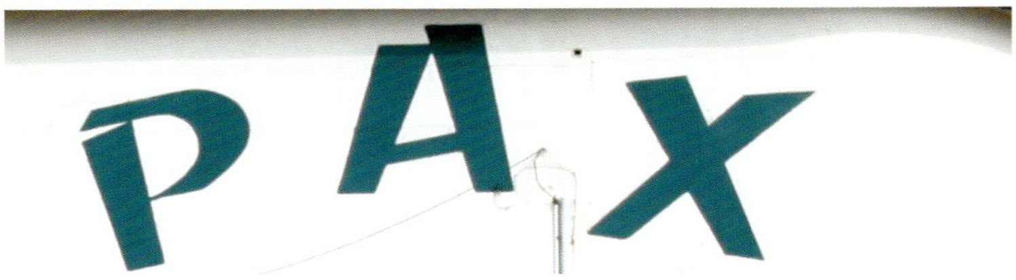
PAX

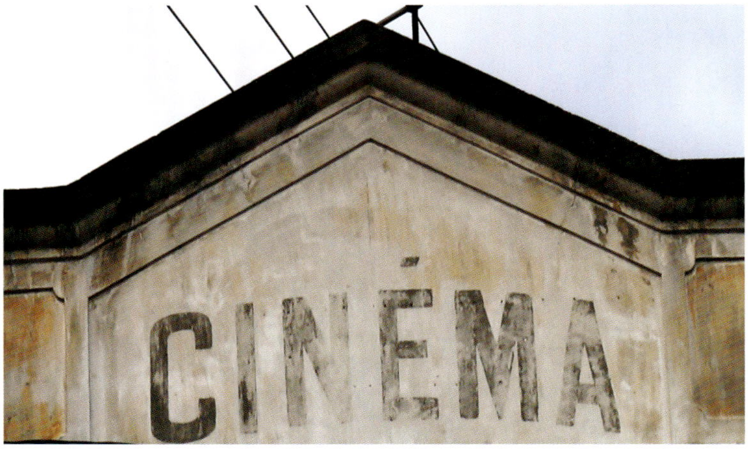
CINÉMA

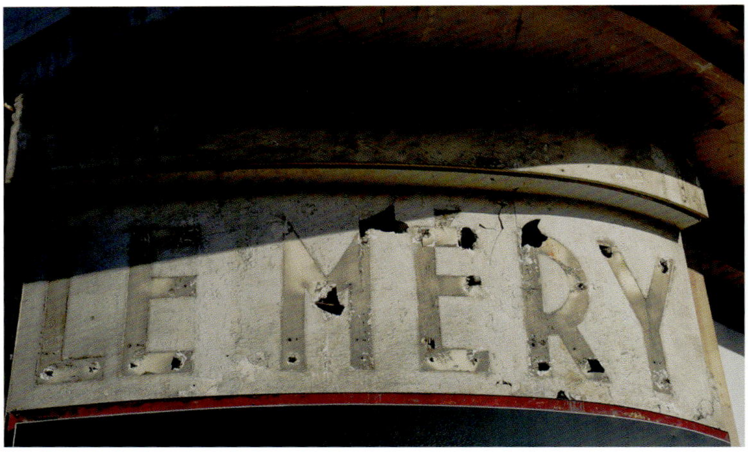
LE MERY

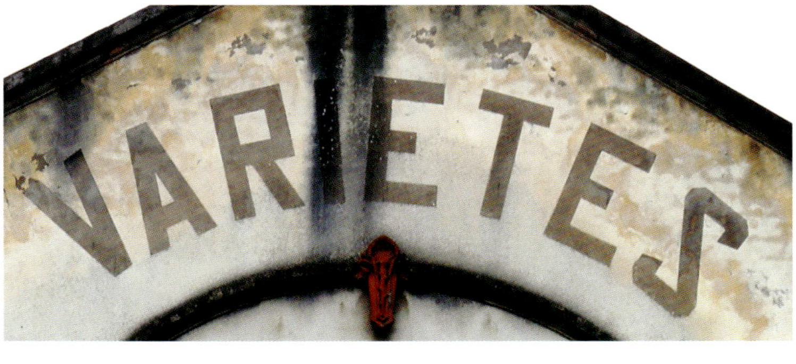
VARIETES

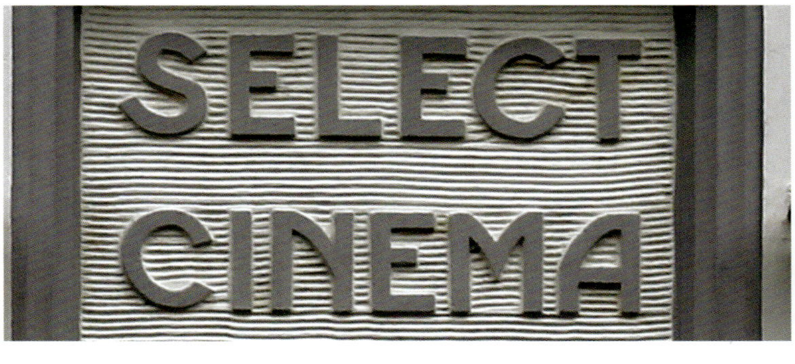
SELECT
CINEMA

MAGIC OF THE BIG SCREEN

Of all inequalities, the most tenacious, perverse and destructive is geographical inequality. It goes hand in hand with the social disparities whose ravages it accentuates. As a provincial Frenchman, I felt this extreme injustice long before I became a politician, fighting passionately so that one day the whole country could experience a cultural infusion. The expression 'French cultural desert', common at that time, crudely describes the abnormal Parisian centralisation leaving tens of millions to their cultural isolation throughout the rest of France.

In the 1970s, along with friends at the Nancy Festival, I organised a gathering of cultural activists with the deliberately striking title: *L'inacceptable sous-développement français* (The unacceptable French underdevelopment). Our tangible ideal was to cover the countryside with a dense network of lively cultural venues: arts centres, bookstores, libraries, artists' training schools. Increasing the number of cinemas was part of this dynamic. The Délégation à l'Aménagement du Territoire et à l'Attractivité Régionale (DATAR), a valuable and irreplaceable project manager, was already involved by supporting itinerant cinemas. The idea of this network was running through my mind. In 1981 it translated into an ambitious plan. As soon as we took office, the law on a minimum sale price for books gave life and hope to independent booksellers. Meanwhile, department by department, city by city, in close connection with creators and elected officials we planned the establishment of musical and theatrical venues. In short, the 1970's dream was gradually becoming living reality.

The situation was more complex for cinema. At the Festival International du Jeune Cinéma de Hyères of 1980, we launched the slogan 'Save national cinemas in Europe'. Film-makers from other countries (Volker Schlöndorff, Francesco Rosi, Théo Angelopoulos, Ettore Scola, Marguerite Duras, etc.) joined us. President François Mitterrand announced a major plan. Hopes were soon dashed – the cinemas of Europe, especially in Italy, Germany and the UK, collapsed, cannibalised by commercial television and abandoned by the authorities.

France refused this toxic fate and took the bull by the horns. A radical overhaul of the system was planned on the basis of a report entrusted to Jean-Denis Bredin and Bertrand Tavernier in May 1981. The many stimulus measures included the doubling of budget credits, regularisation of relations with television, creation of the Institut pour le Financement du Cinema et des Industries (IFCIC), appointment of a film ombudsman, direct grant aid, and a little later Sociétés de Financement de l'Industrie Cinématographique et de l'Audiovisuel (SOFICA) and the support of television companies.

Above all, a collective fervour seized the professionals and populations who restored the influence and power of cinema.

Key decisions included the safeguarding of movie theatres and their proliferation across

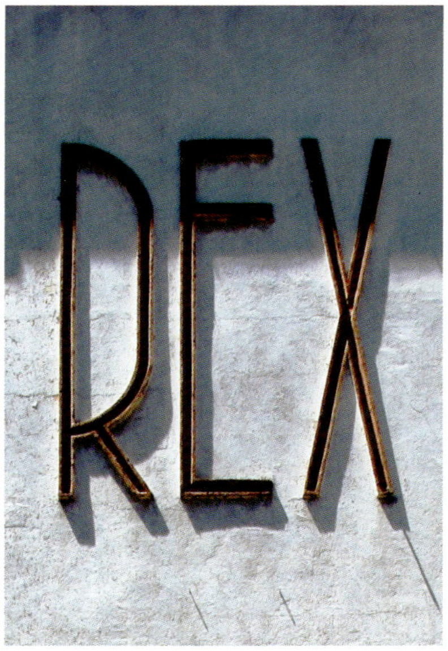
REX
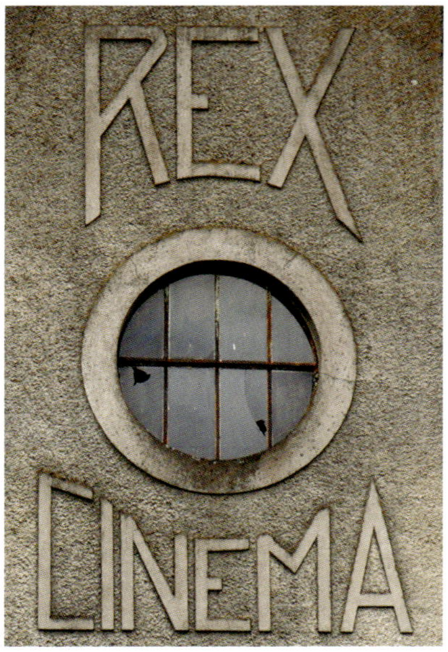
REX
CINEMA
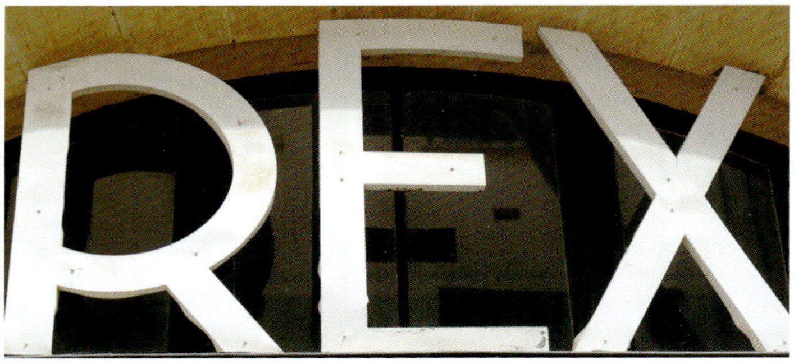
REX
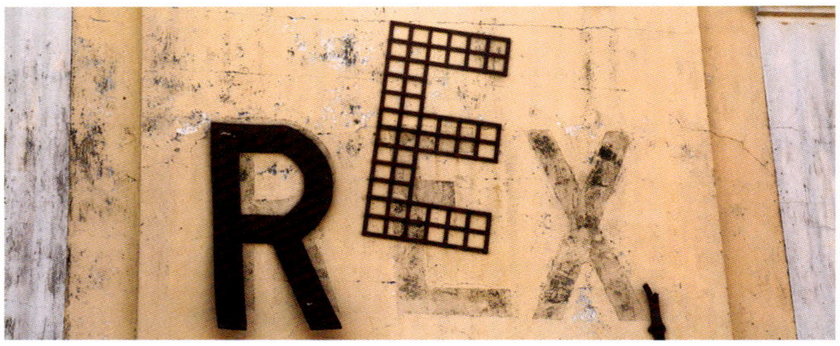
REX
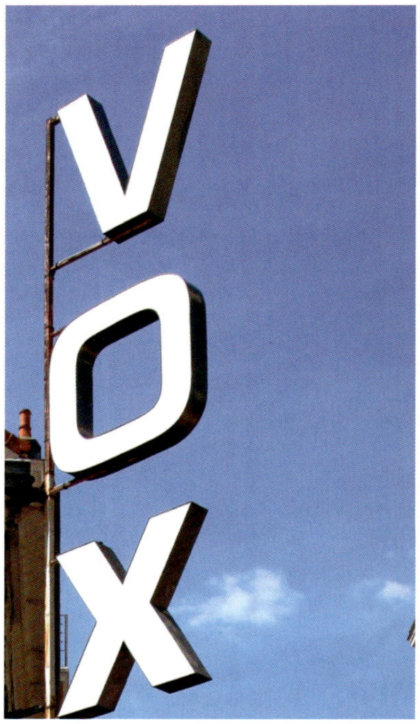
VOX
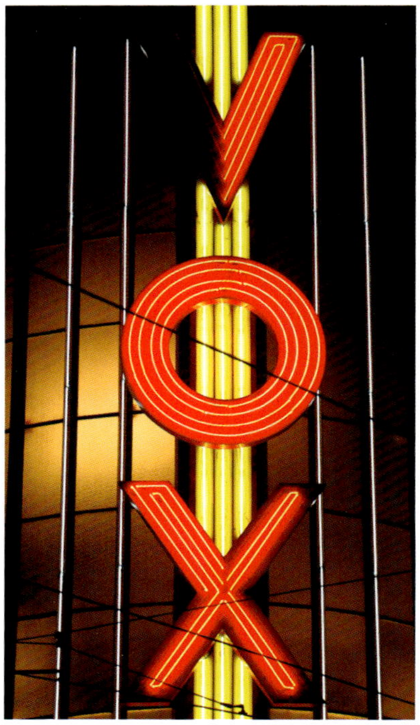
VOX
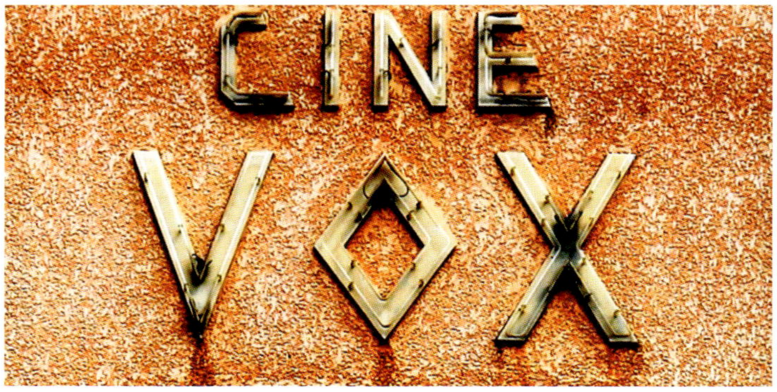
CINE
VOX
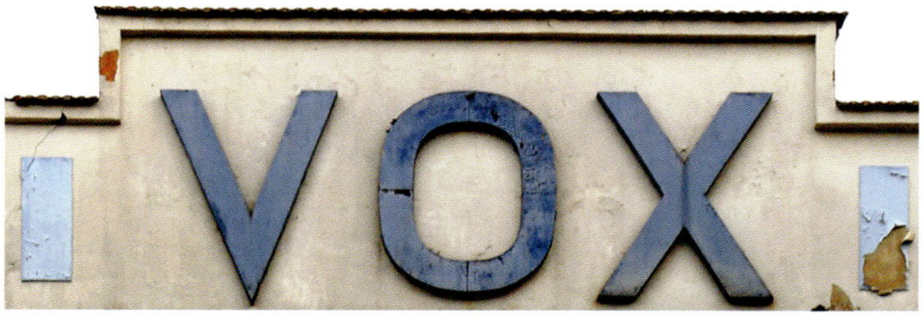
VOX
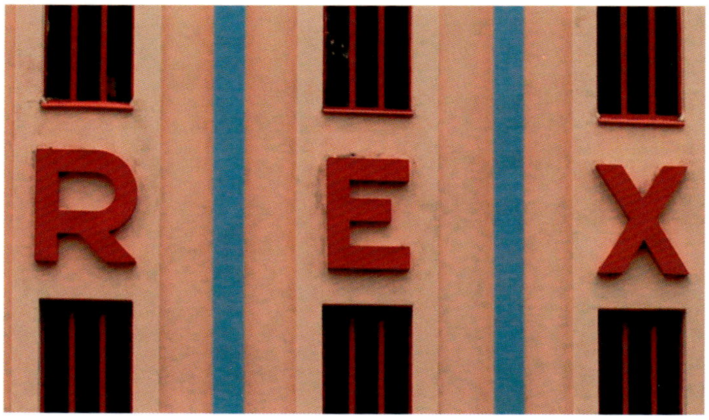
REX
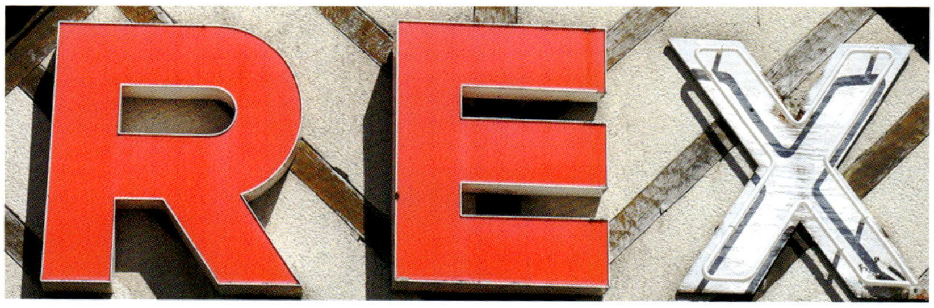
REX
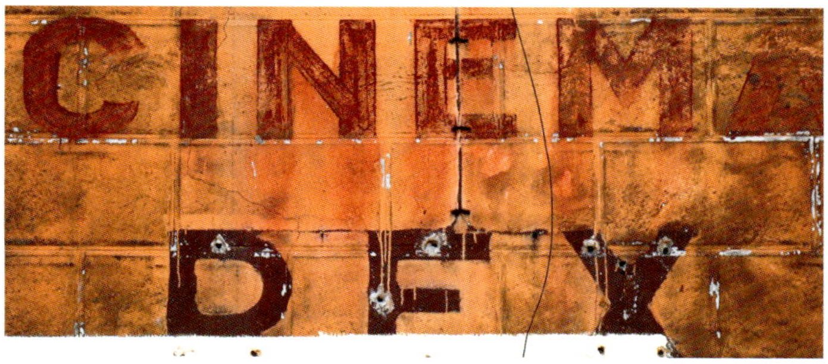
CINEMA
REX
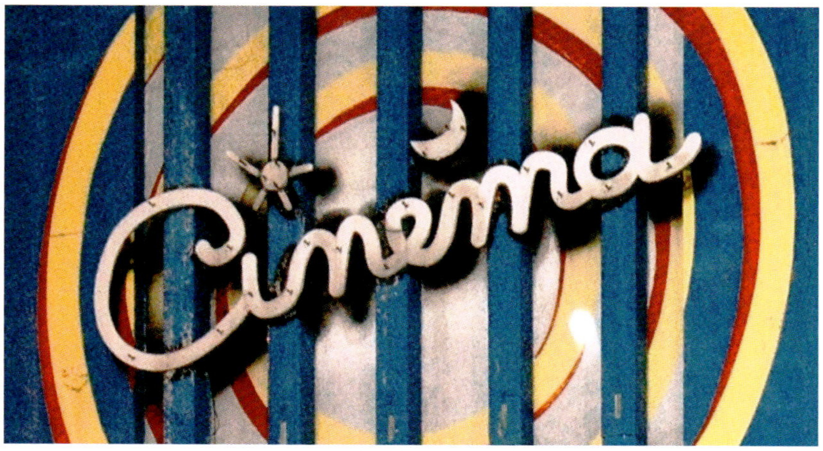
Cinéma

the country, in rural areas, small towns and local neighbourhoods.
To give strength and effectiveness to this project, on 11 February 1983 we set up the Agence pour le Développement Régional du Cinéma (ADRC), the direction of which was entrusted to a key figure, Jack Gajos. He was an enlightened builder, generous inventor and erudite film buff. Before his sudden death he helped us with the groundwork for the future Fondation Européenne pour les Métiers de l'Image et du Son (FEMIS). His team was a small commando unit on alert, enthusiastic, hands-on and supported by the French Ministry of Culture's National Centre for Cinema (CNC) bosses Pierre Viot, Gérard de Senneville and Bernard Vidal. The usual army of sceptics stood in their way, but they didn't care. They saved old cinemas, they promoted the construction of new venues. They took over forgotten places: religious buildings, railway stations, official buildings. At their request, as Minister of Culture I classified unique architecture as historic monuments, notably Le Grand Rex and Pagoda cinemas in Paris.
People involved with the cinema who felt strongly about this venture gave their personal sponsorship, in particular Louis Malle, Patrice Leconte, Bertrand Tavernier, Claude Miller, Philippe Noiret, Richard Bohringer, Bernadette Laffont, Jean-Paul Rappeneau, Pierre Arditi. At the same time, we launched the Colleges in Cinema and High Schools in Cinema projects and invited students to discover the magic of the so-called 7th art in theatres, on the big screen. The agency is today a permanent lever of the continuous conquest of the movie-going public and the love of cinema permeating the depths of French society. The work accomplished by Jack Gajos and his successors is unparalleled. Christian Landais brilliantly carries out this exceptional task today. France occupies a unique spot in the world of projection rooms.
Simon Edelstein's book, fruit of a vigorous passion and tireless curiosity, offers a striking image of this. Initially a travelling cinephile, over time he has seen movie theatres disappear. At first indifferent, then anxiously noting the displacement of cinemas, often taking inventive forms, replaced by hideous buildings, he finally revolted against the authorities and soulless real-estate developers. Killers of beauty in places of life, culture, joy, in short everything that helps us to live. All this experienced with a sense of mourning every time he saw a cinema disappear from the landscape – hence his desire to inventory the heritage of cinemas in France, beautiful, less than beautiful, abandoned, converted. For him, to photograph them is to immortalise them. Edelstein's route is remarkable – thanks to him we have an irreplaceable source of information. He invites us to stubbornly pursue the preservation and enrichment of this unique treasure: the joy of dreaming together.

Jack Lang
Former Minister of Education and Culture

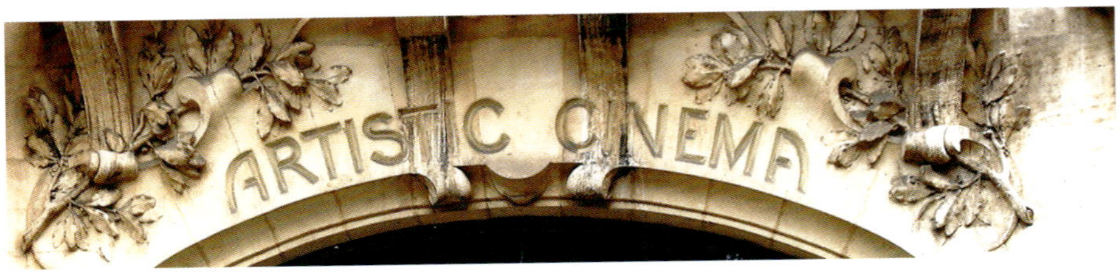
ARTISTIC CINEMA

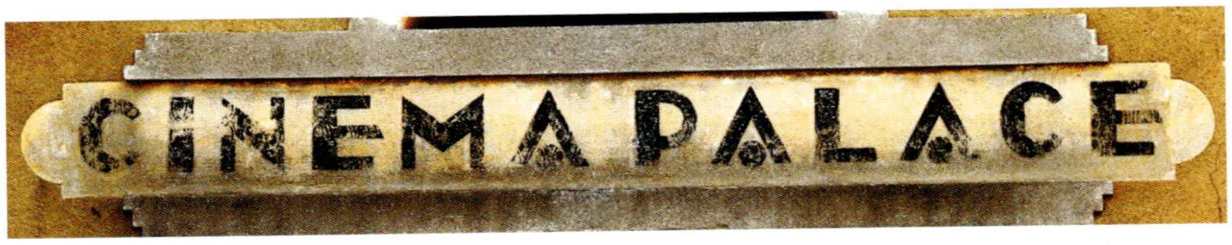
CINEMA PALACE

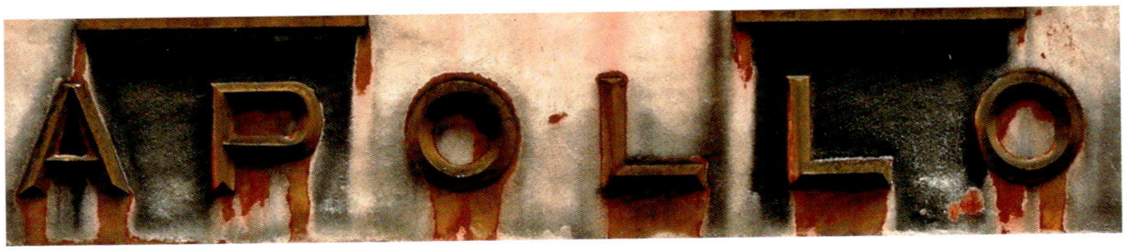
APOLLO

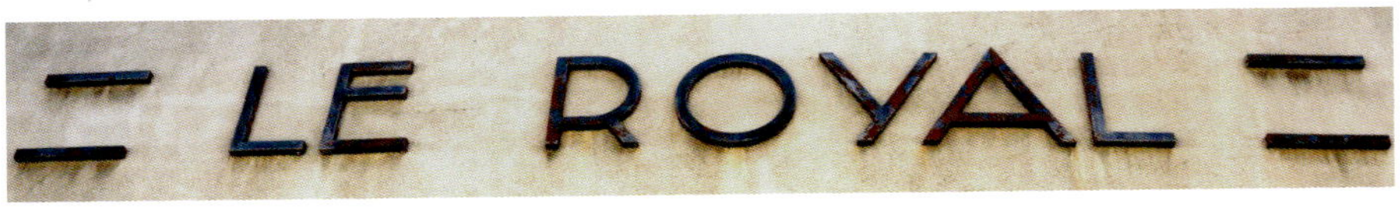
LE ROYAL

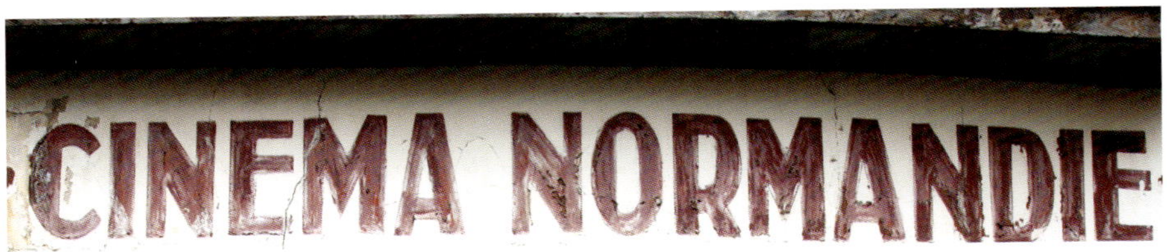
CINEMA NORMANDIE

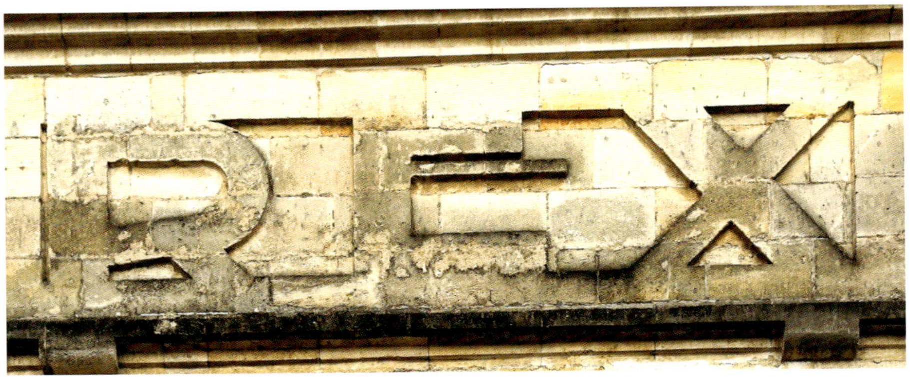
REX

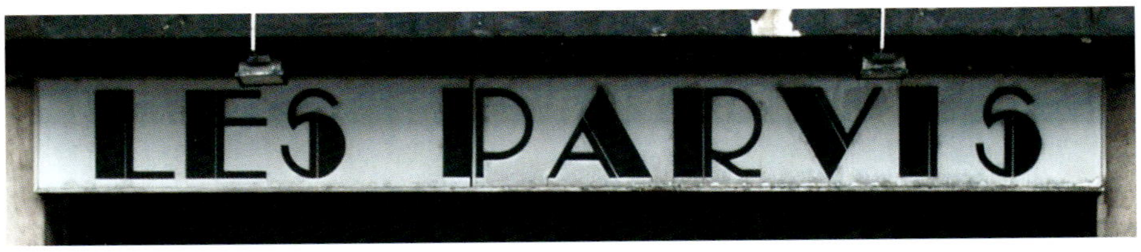
LES PARVIS

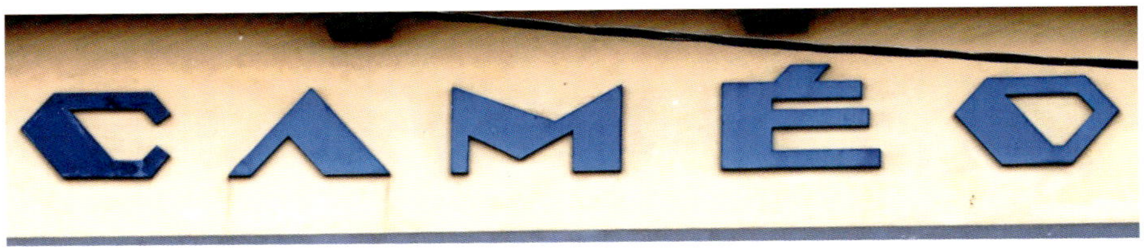
CAMÉO

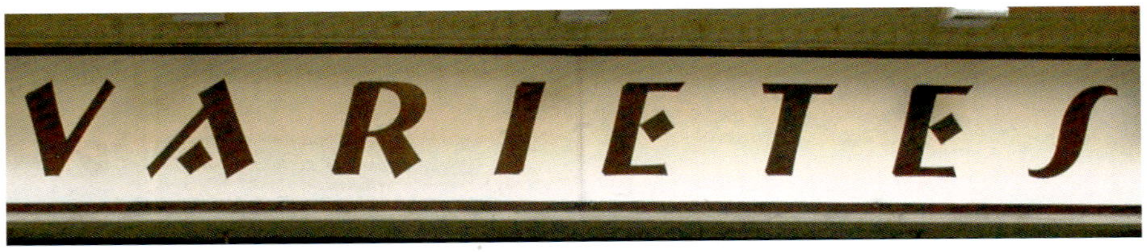
VARIETES

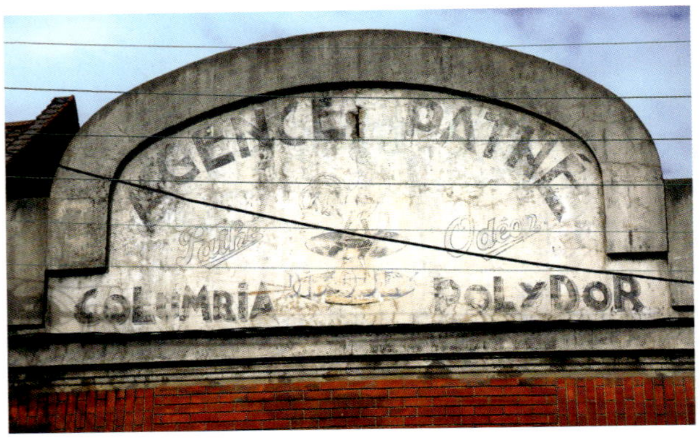
AGENCE PATHE
COLUMBIA
POLYDOR

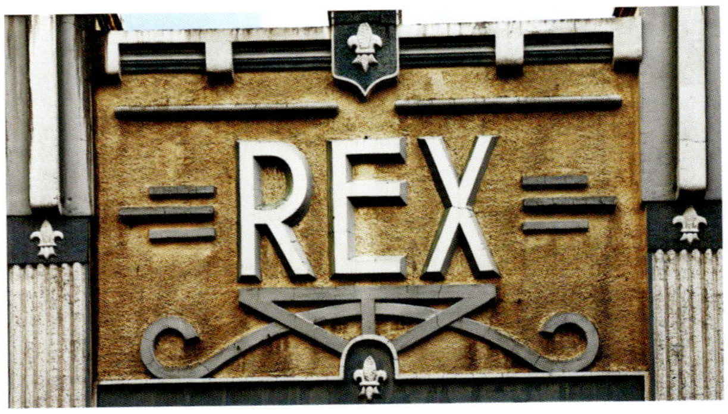
REX

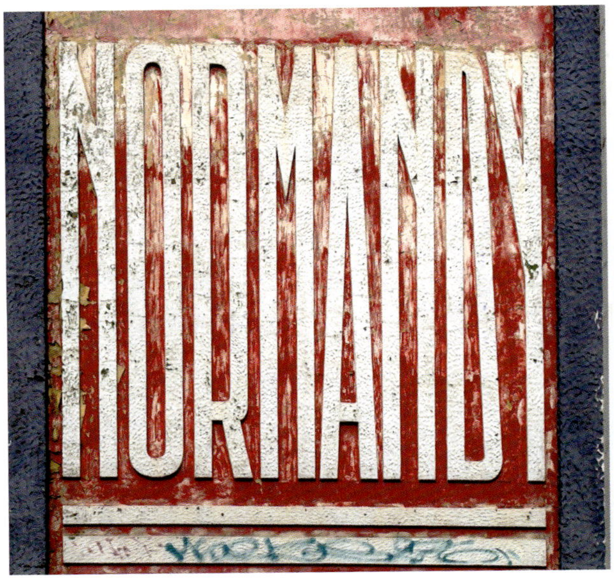
NORMANDY

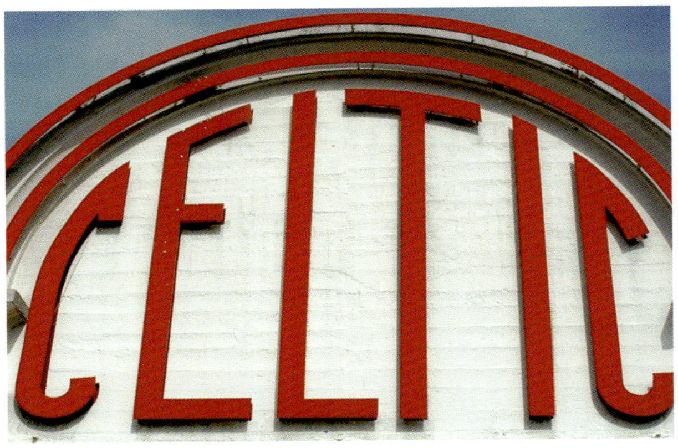
CELTIC

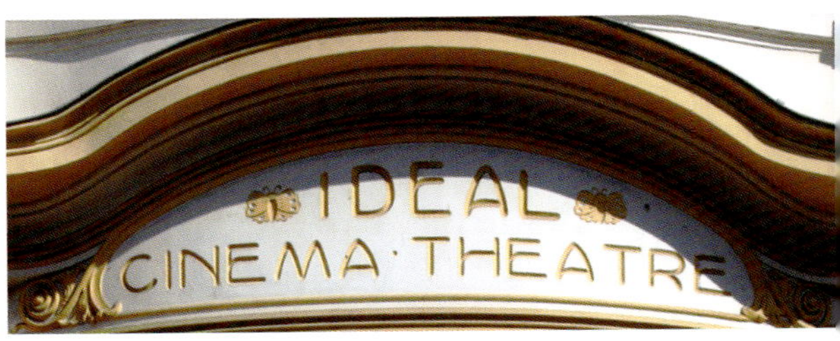
IDEAL
CINEMA·THEATRE

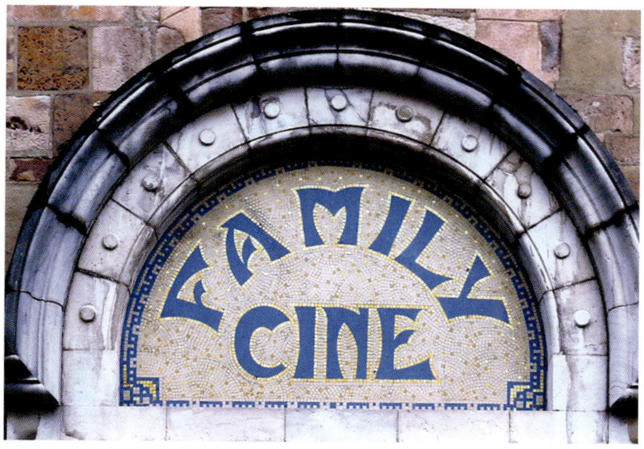
FAMILY
CINE

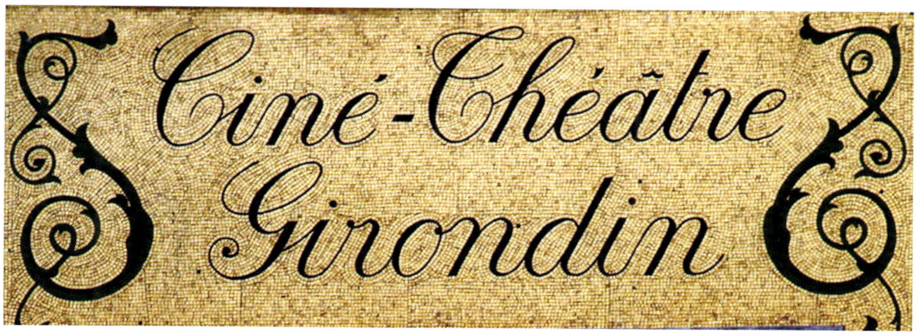
Ciné-Théâtre
Girondin

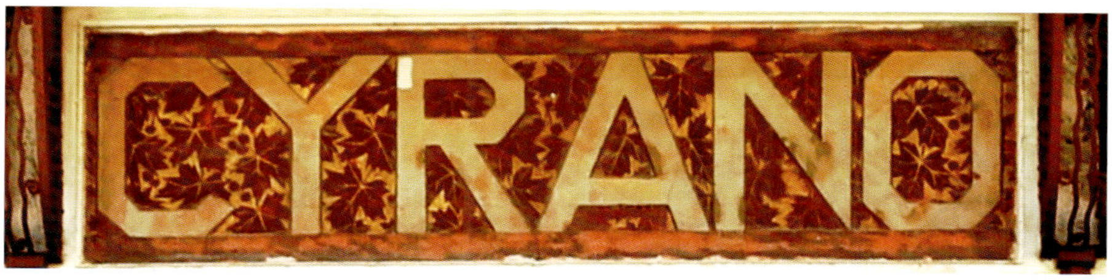
CYRANO

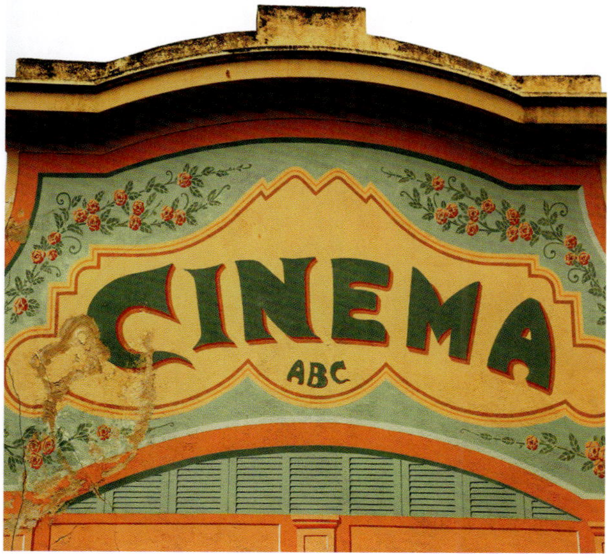
CINEMA
ABC

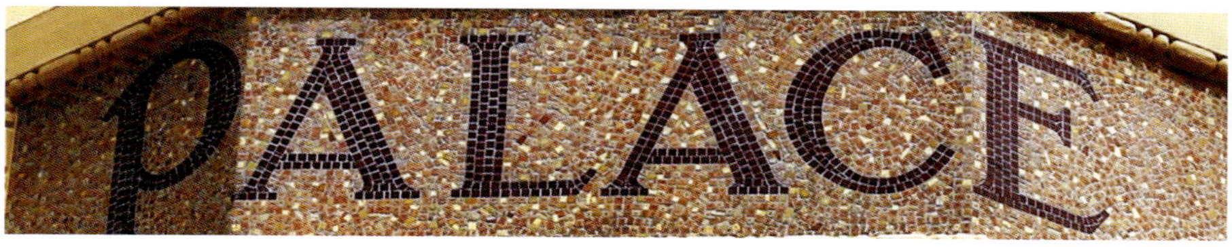
PALACE

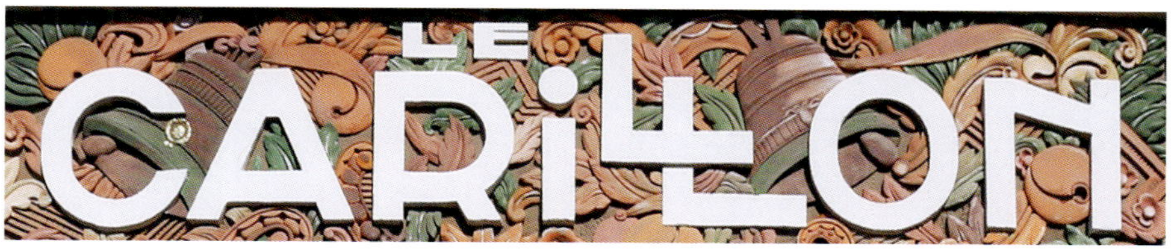
LE
CARILLON

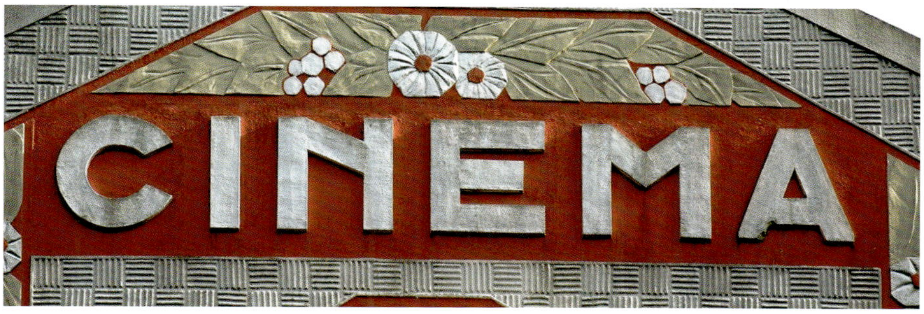
CINEMA

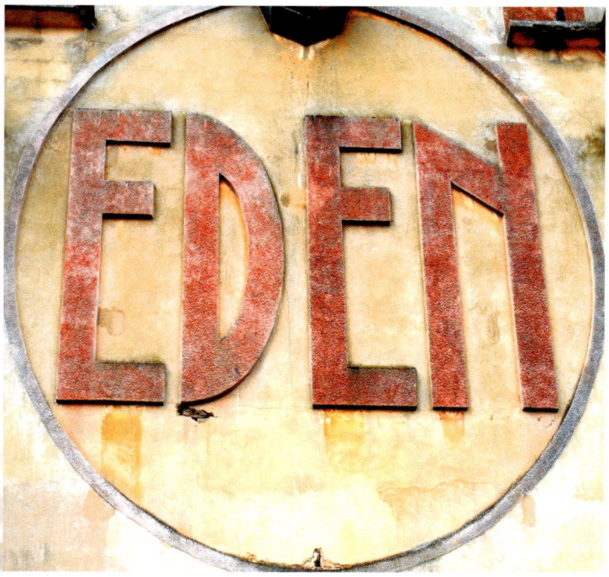
EDEN

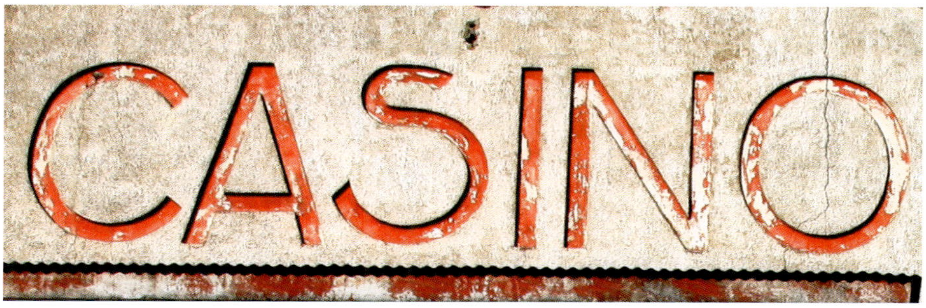
CASINO

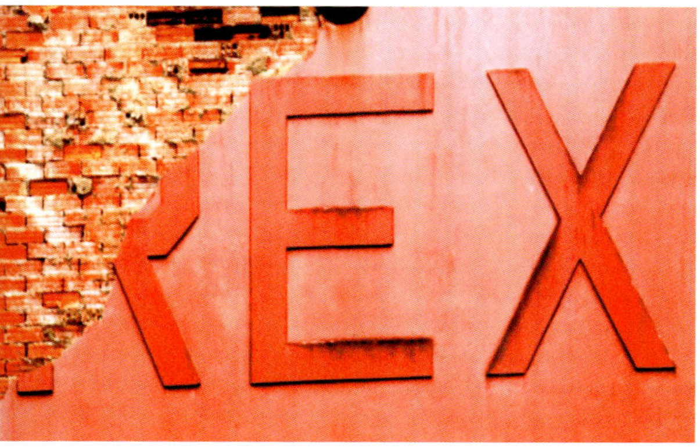
REX

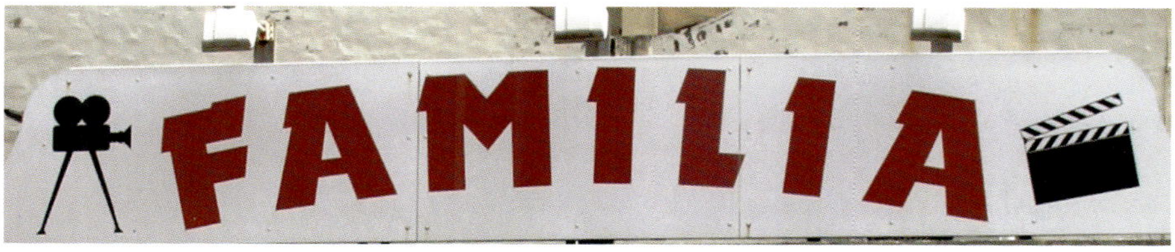
FAMILIA

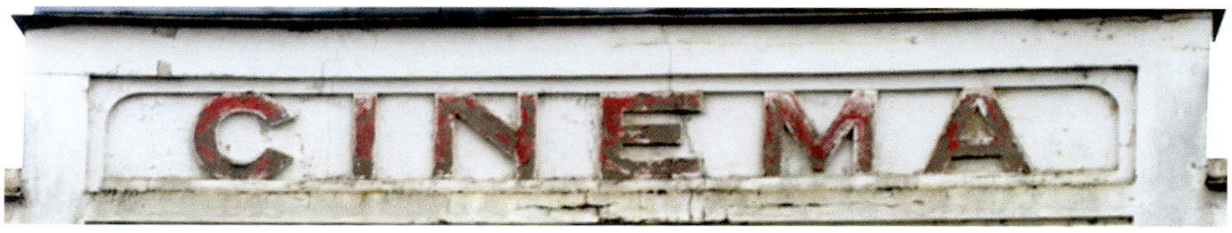
CINEMA

AUVERGNE-RHÔNE-ALPS

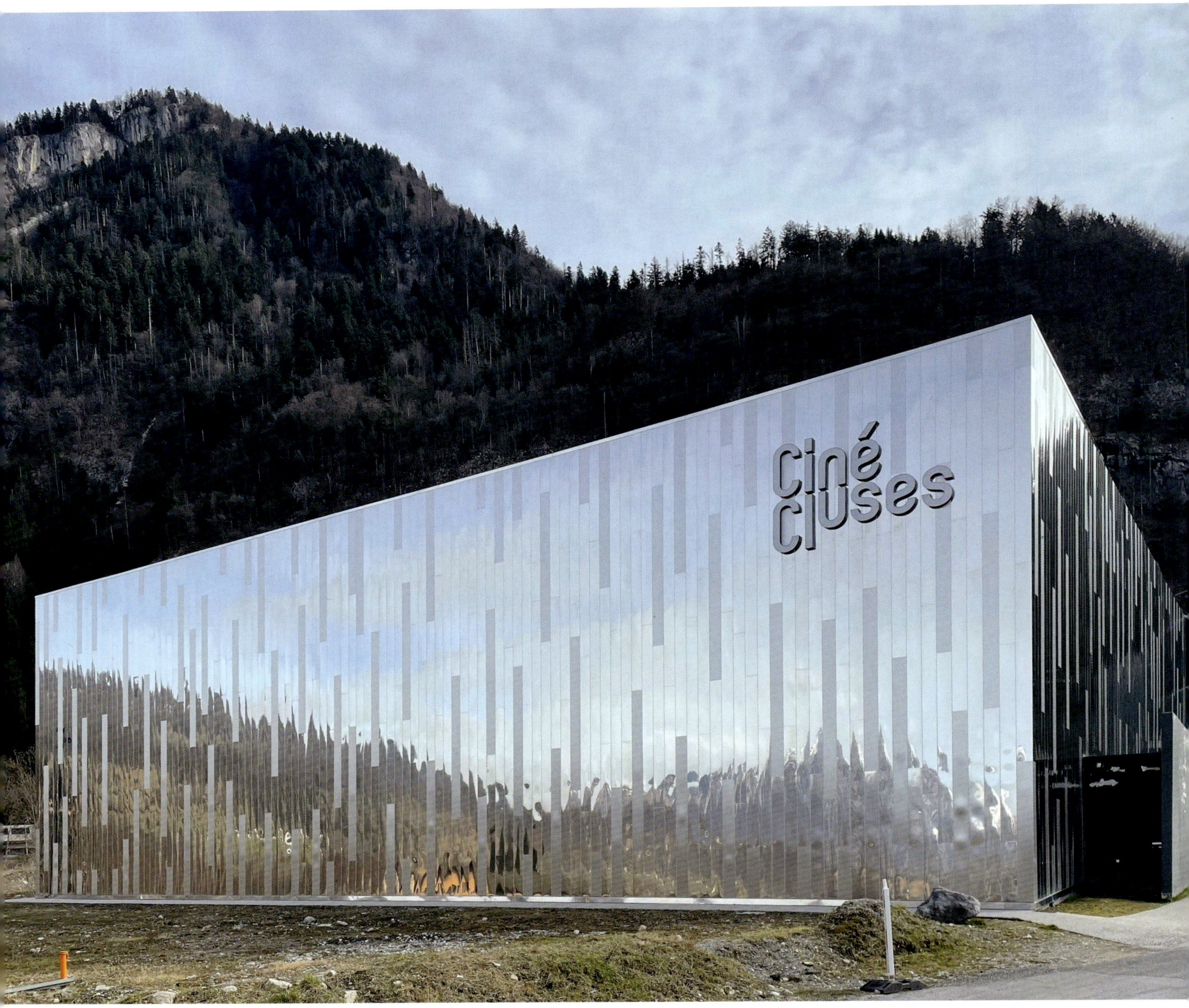

Cluses – Ciné Cluses – 2022

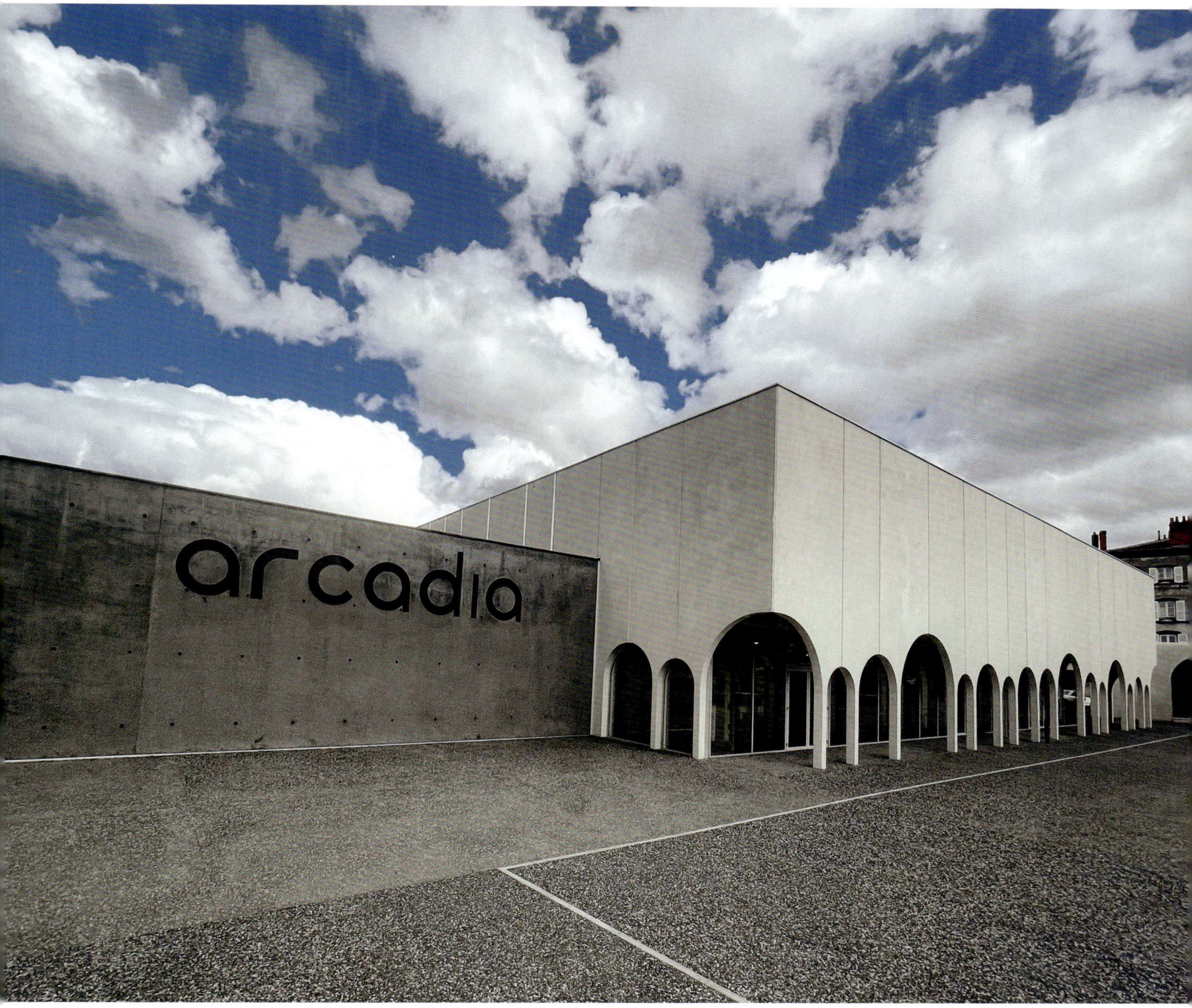

Riom – Arcadia – 2021

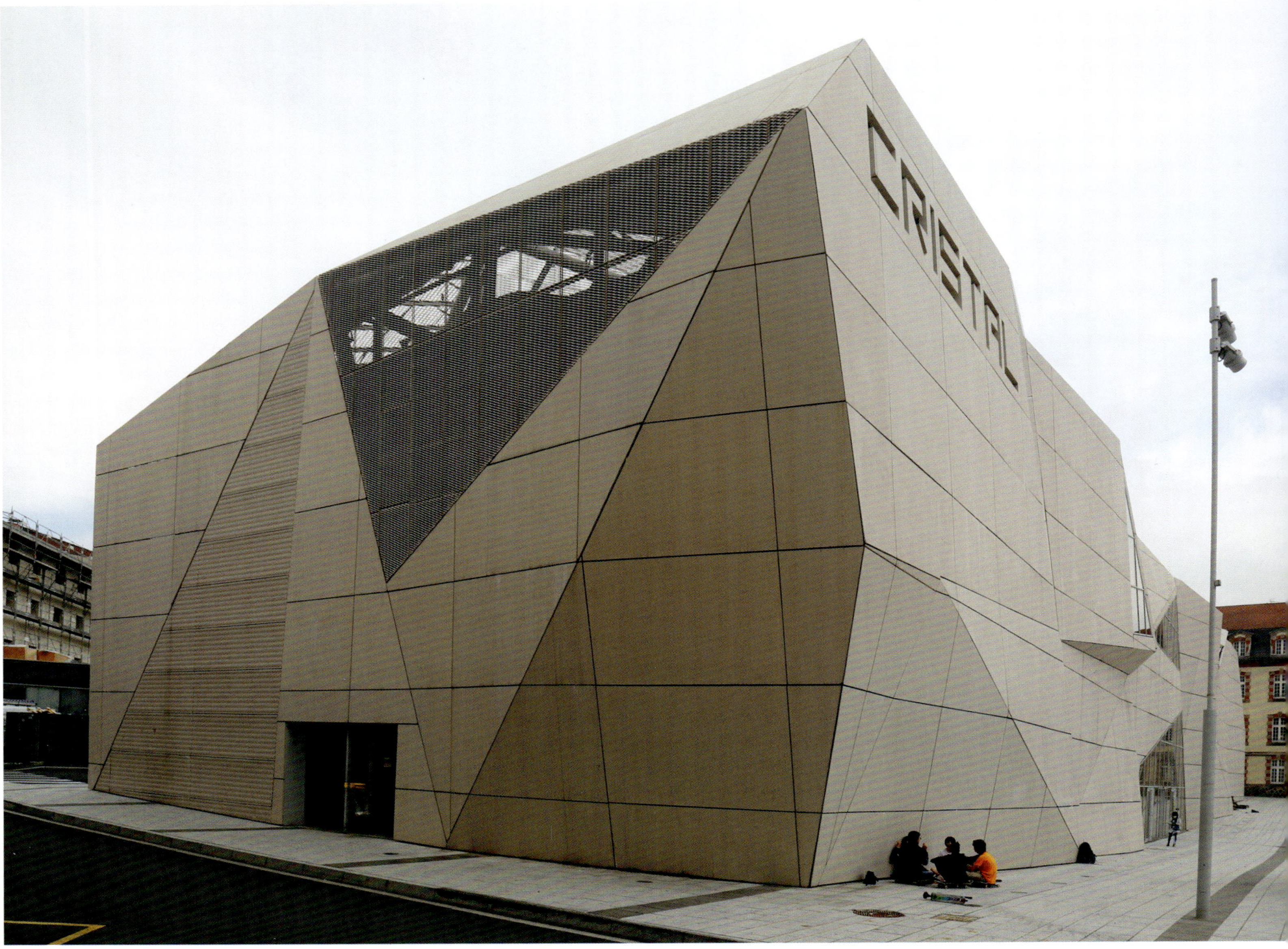

Aurillac – Cristal – 2021

Aurillac, Cristal. A cinema loses its character, slims down, is doomed to disappear even if at a slow pace ... Suddenly, not far away, a giant bubble rises, majestic, rather arrogant, with an astonishing brilliance, overwhelming possible rivals with its sheer size. The heart of the city is changing. However, this new beauty with bold shapes, a little chilling – without sinking into nostalgia – cannot obliterate memories of yesterday's cinemas modelled along more traditionally recognisable lines.

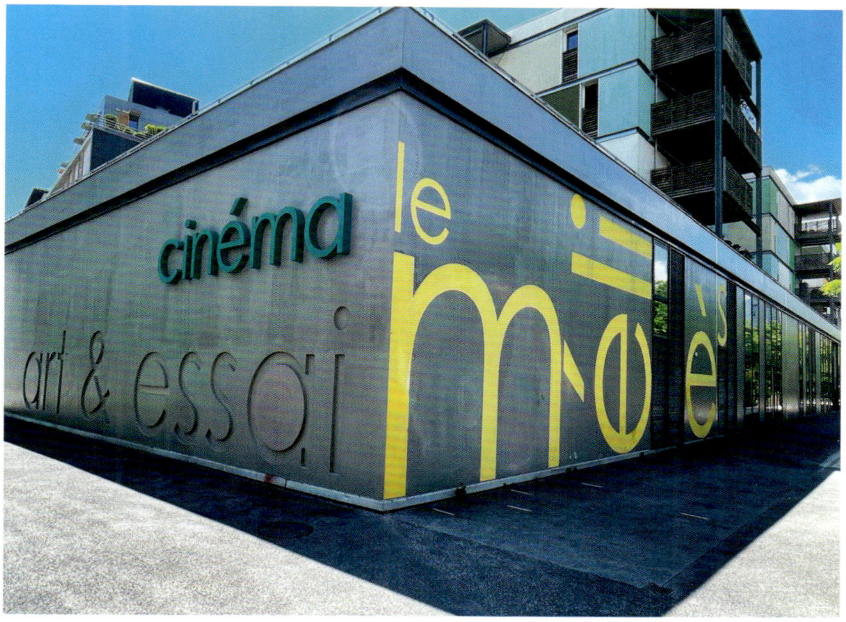

Grenoble – Le Méliès – 2022

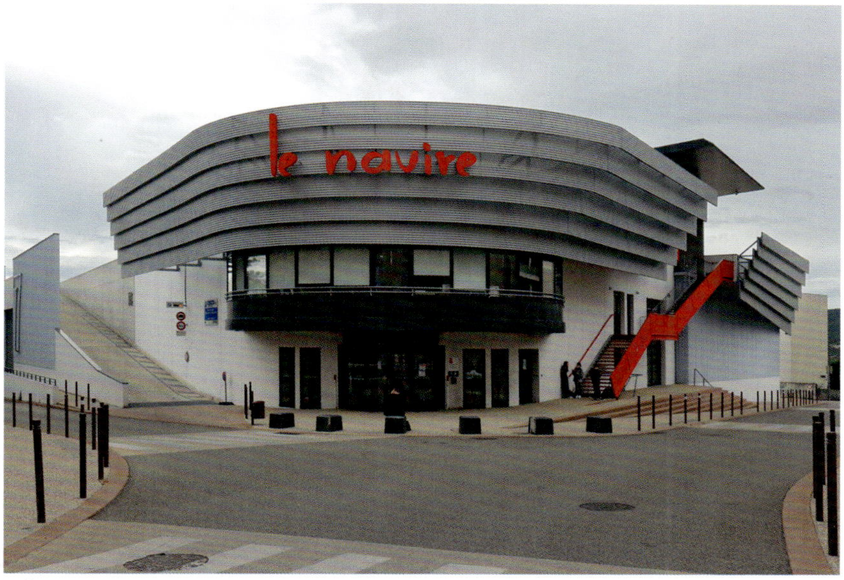

Aubenas – Le Navire – 2021

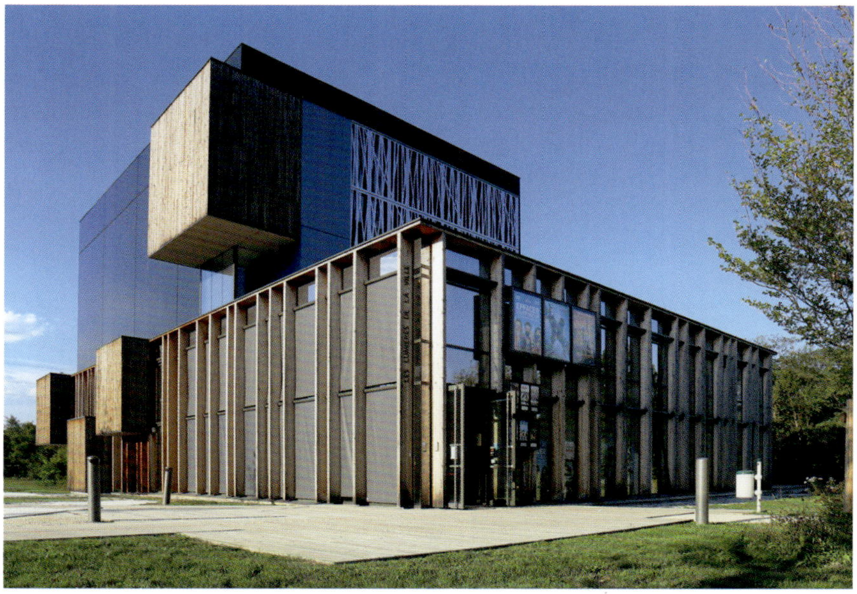

Rumilly – Les Lumières de la ville – 2021

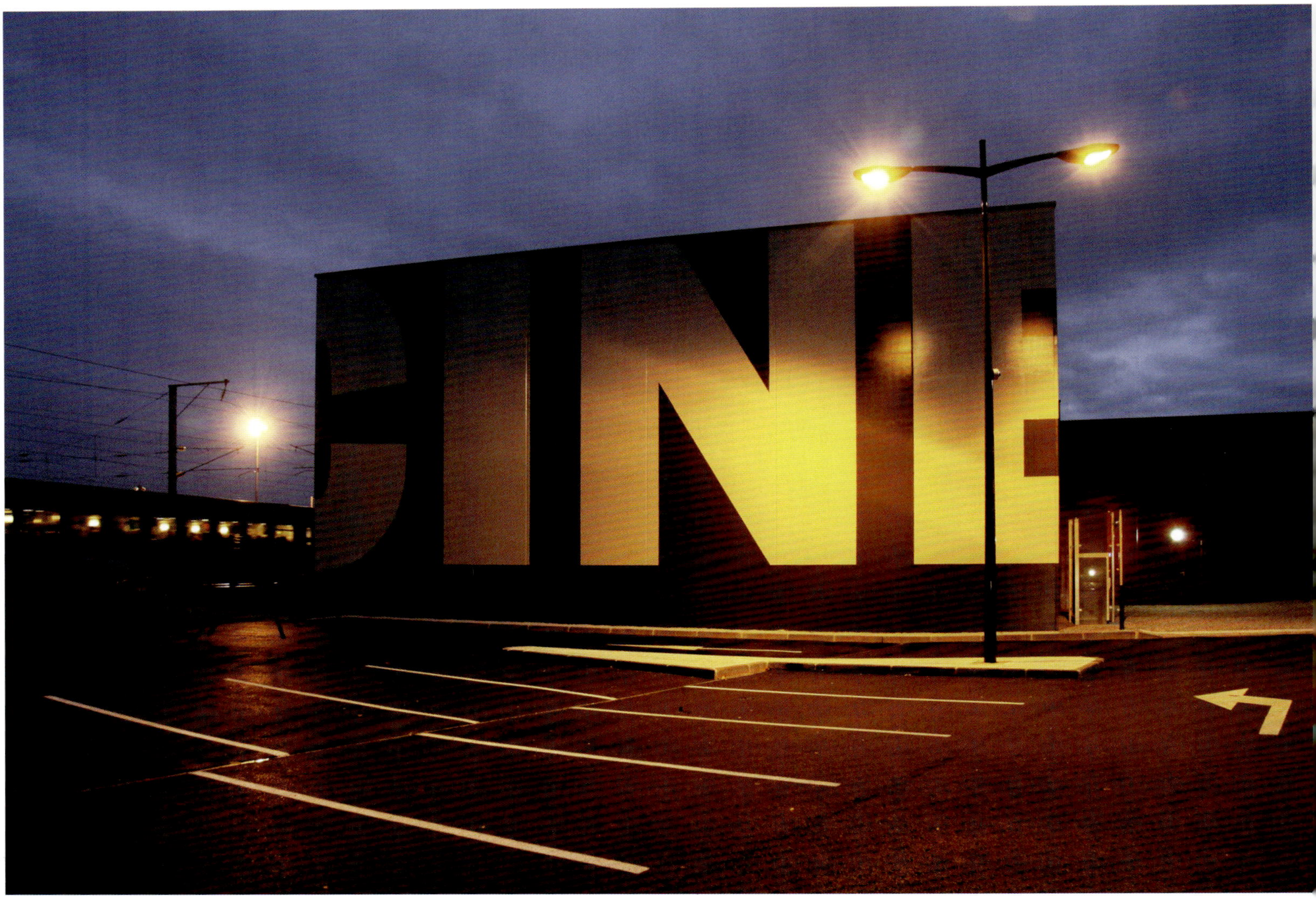

Moulins – Cap Ciné – 2011

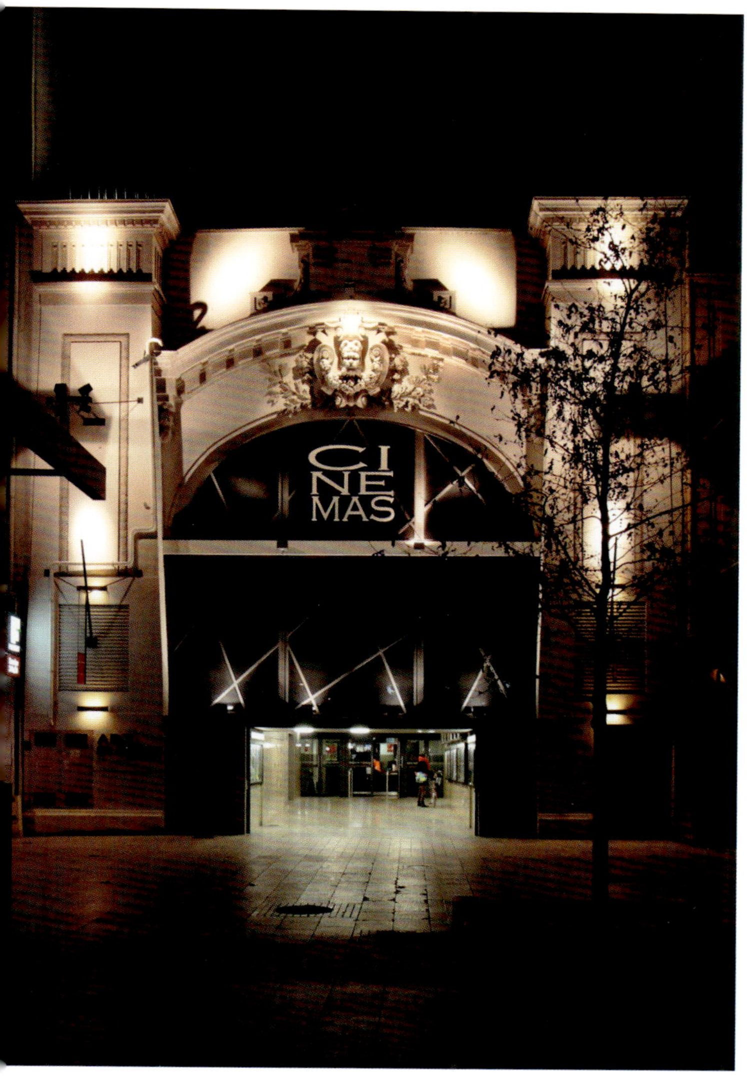

ence – Le Navire – 2012

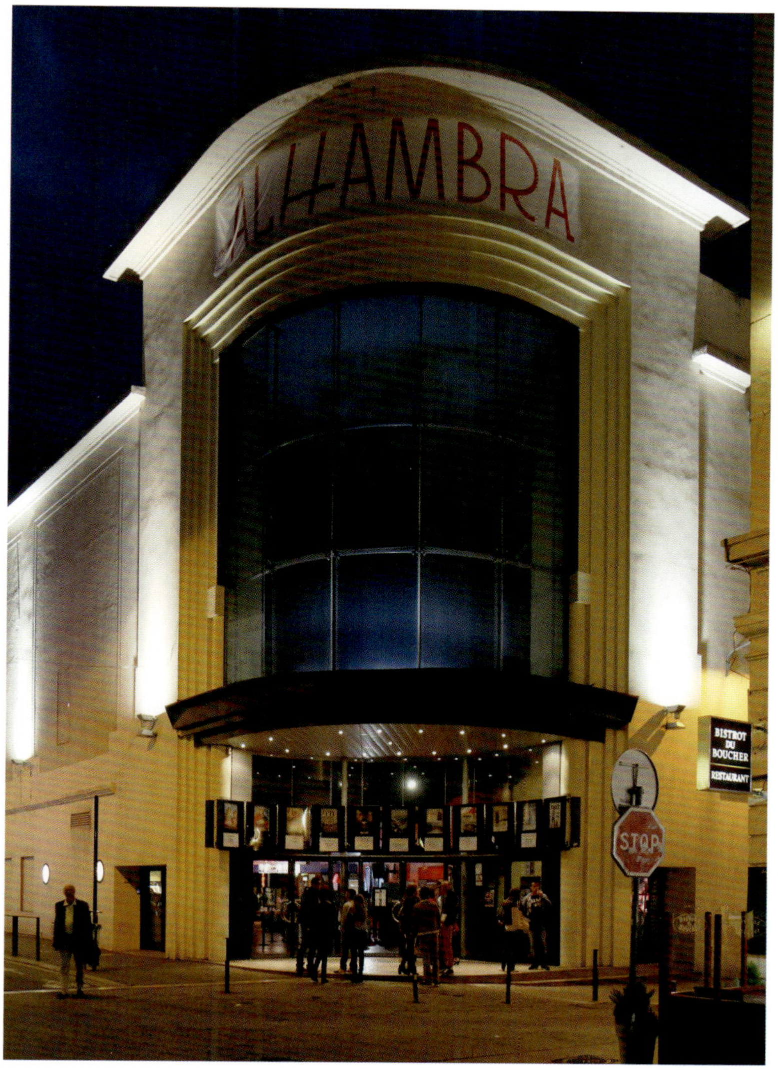

Saint-Étienne – Alhambra – 2016

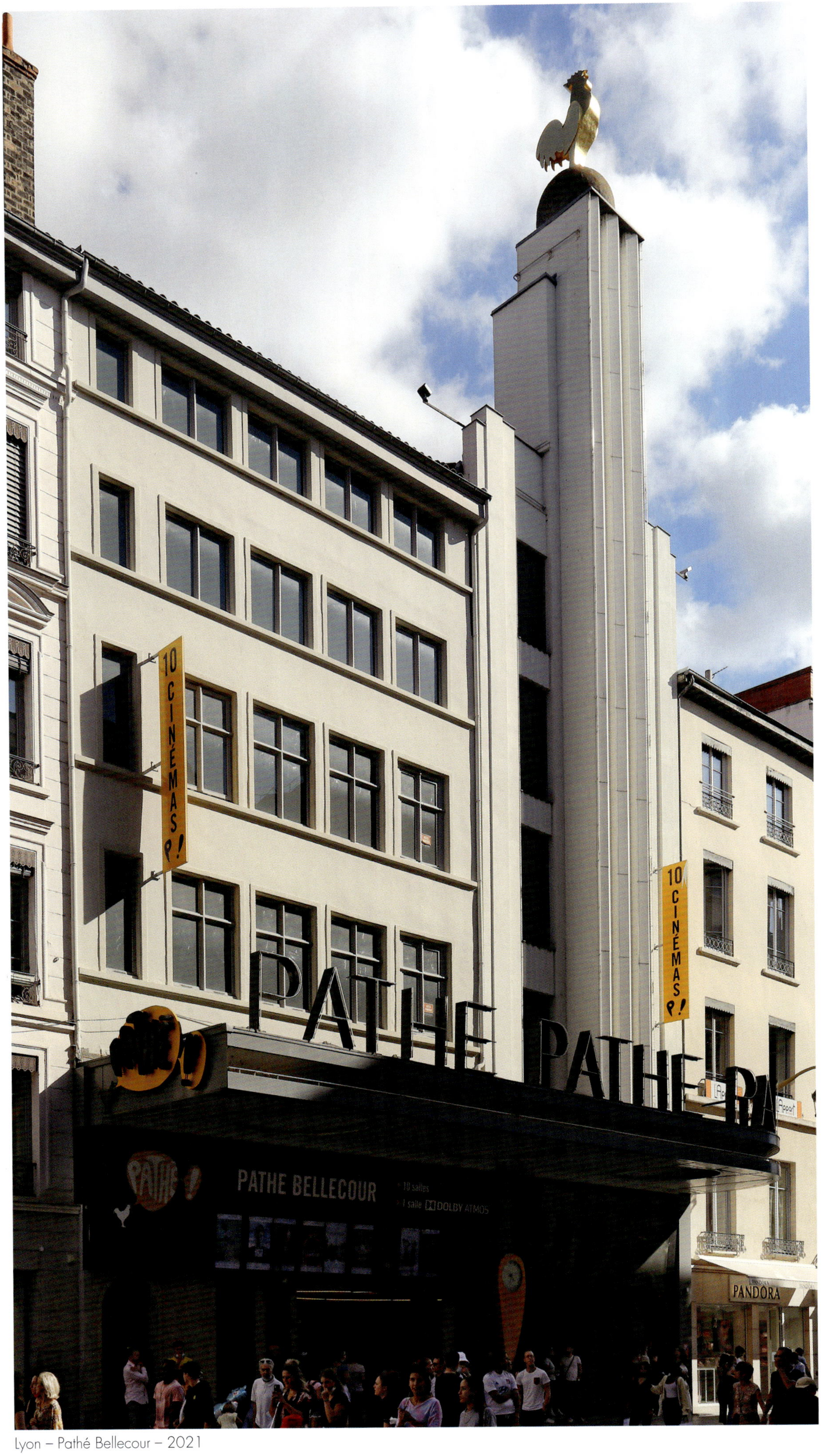

Lyon – Pathé Bellecour – 2021

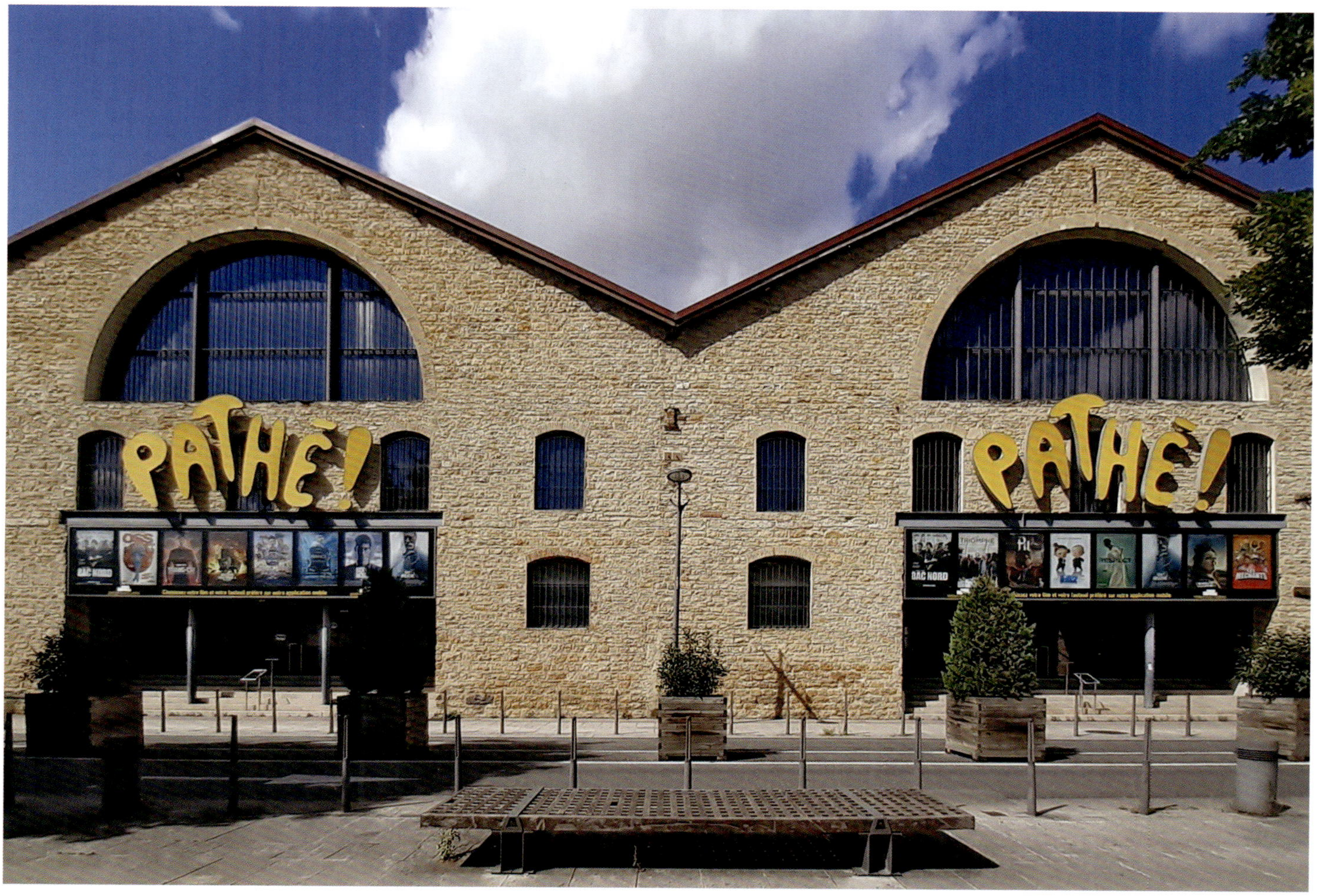

Lyon – Pathé Valse – 2022

Lyon, Pathé Valse. The Pathé Valse cinema is housed in a former measuring instrument factory, one of the region's last relics from the industrial era. The building, dating from the end of the 19th century, is listed in the inventory of historical monuments. In 1934 the factory changed direction to specialise in bottling. This closed in 1992 and the premises were abandoned until a multiplex with 14 screens and 2,800 seats was opened in 2008.

◀ **Lyon, Pathé Bellecour.** Eugène Chirié (1902–1984), born in Marseille, very soon established himself as the indispensable architect of renovation and sound systems in the early days of talkies. New cinemas were being built, larger and more comfortable. Chirié's vision and talent were impressive, despite his youth. First in his own region, but also in Lyon. In 1931 he designed the Pathé-Palace (now Pathé Bellecour) with its 30-metre tower topped by a terrestrial globe and the Pathé rooster visible from afar.

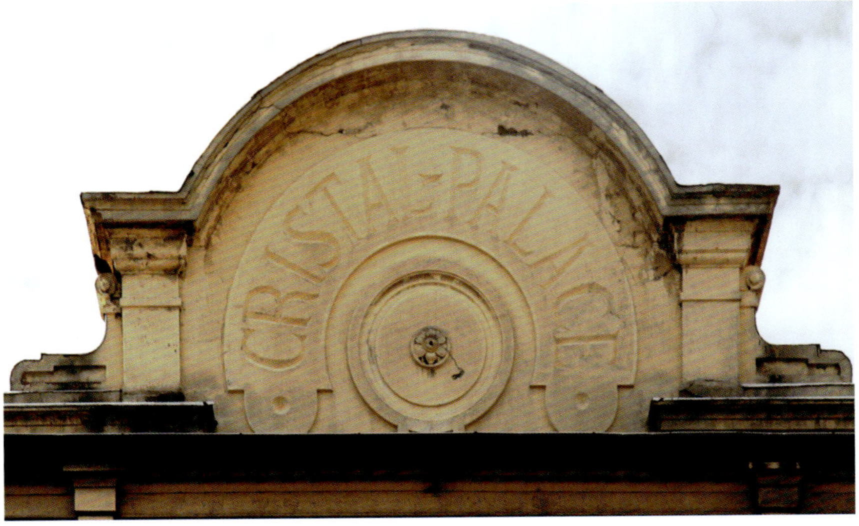

Lyon – Crystal – 2010

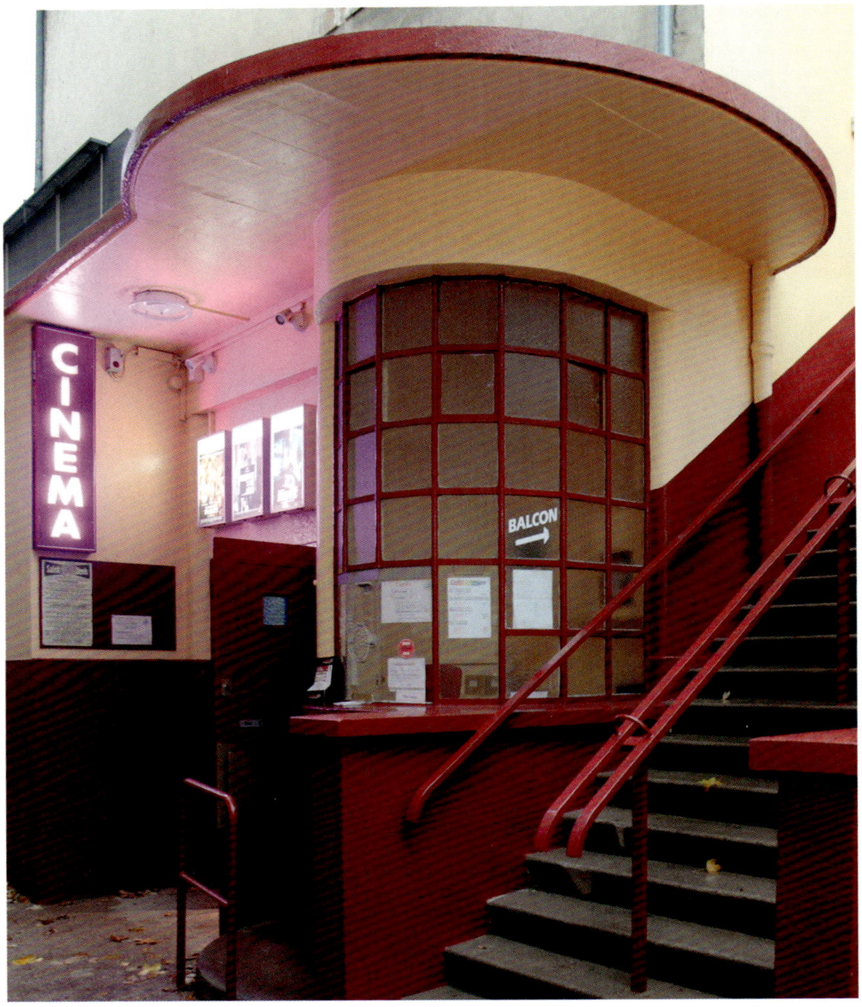

Lyon – Cinéma Saint-Denis – 2011

Lyon, Cinéma Saint-Denis. A lively district away from the centre, a discreet entrance at the end of a narrow passage (you could easily end up in a neighbouring business by mistake) ... The Saint-Denis, a century-old cinema. Has it aged? Apparently not. Always dapper, keeping its original beauty – not even needing a facelift, not a wrinkle. The Saint-Denis is a wonder from a past that's worth reliving.

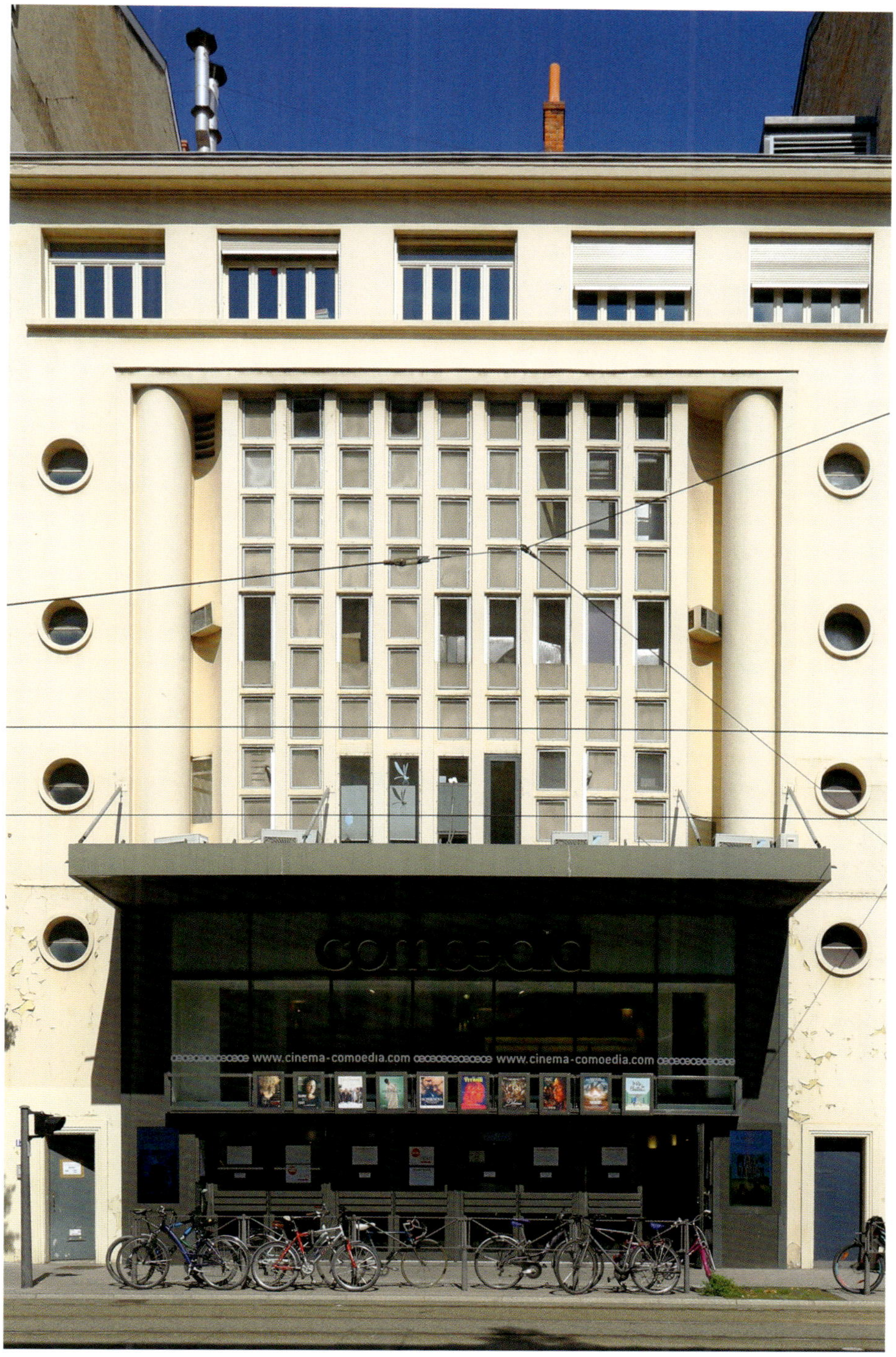

Lyon – Comoedia – 2021

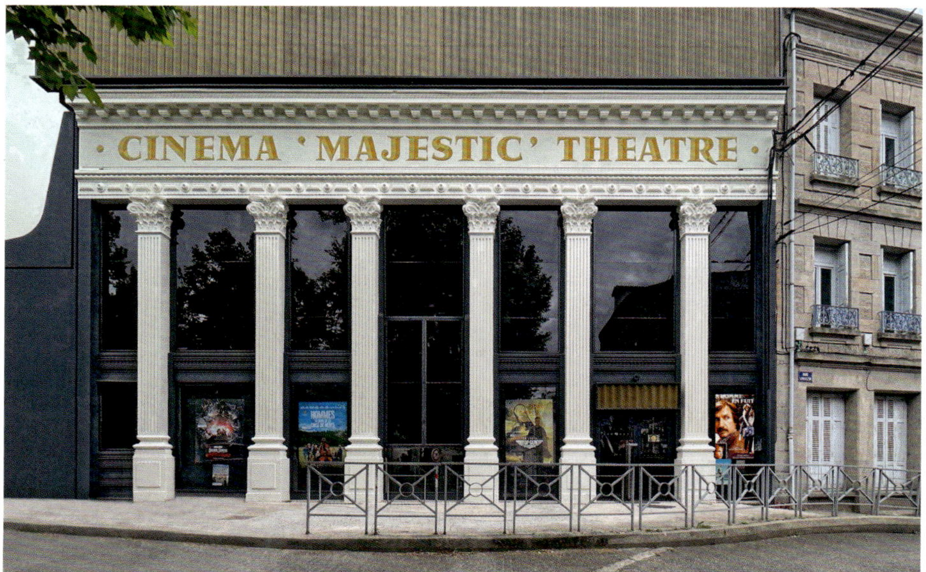

Firminy – Majestic – 2022

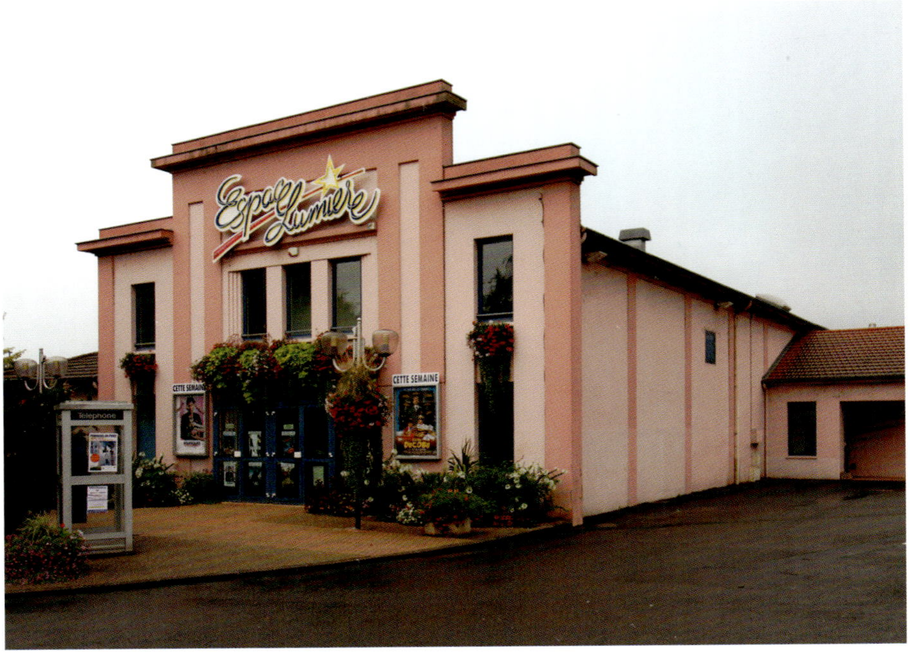

Balbigny – Espace Lumière – 2011

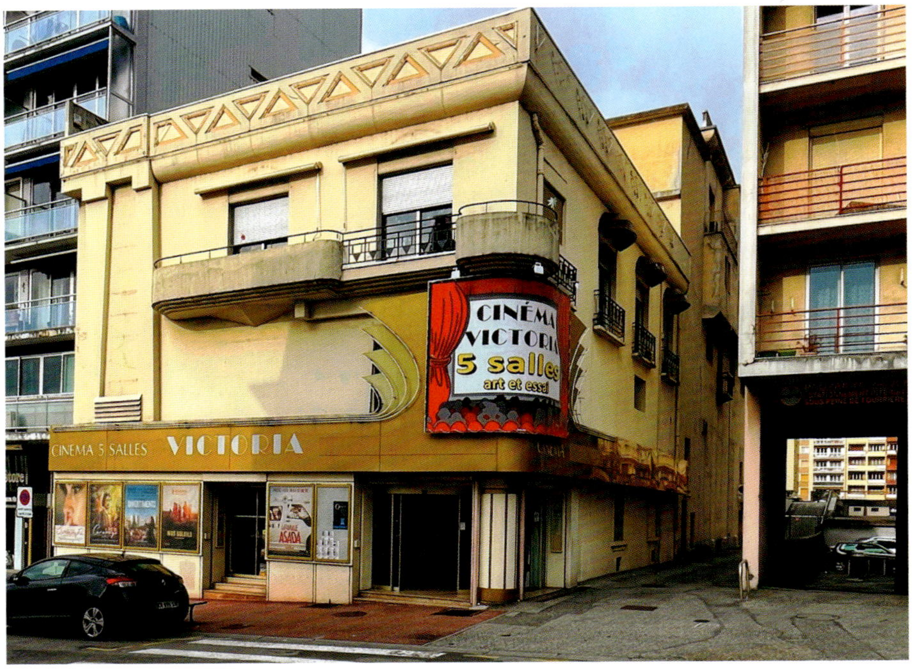

Aix-les-Bains – Victoria – 2023

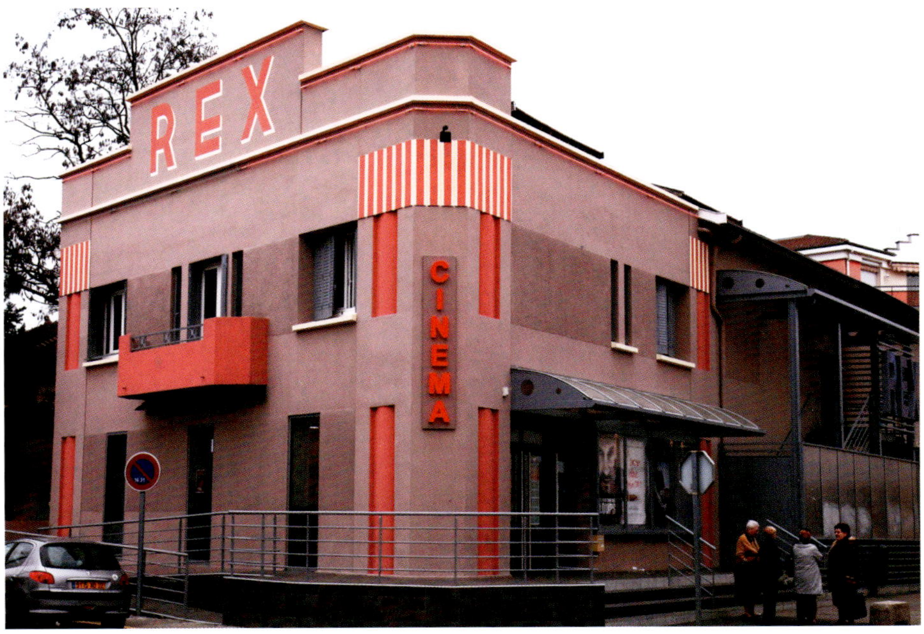

Le Péage-de-Roussillon – Rex – 2012

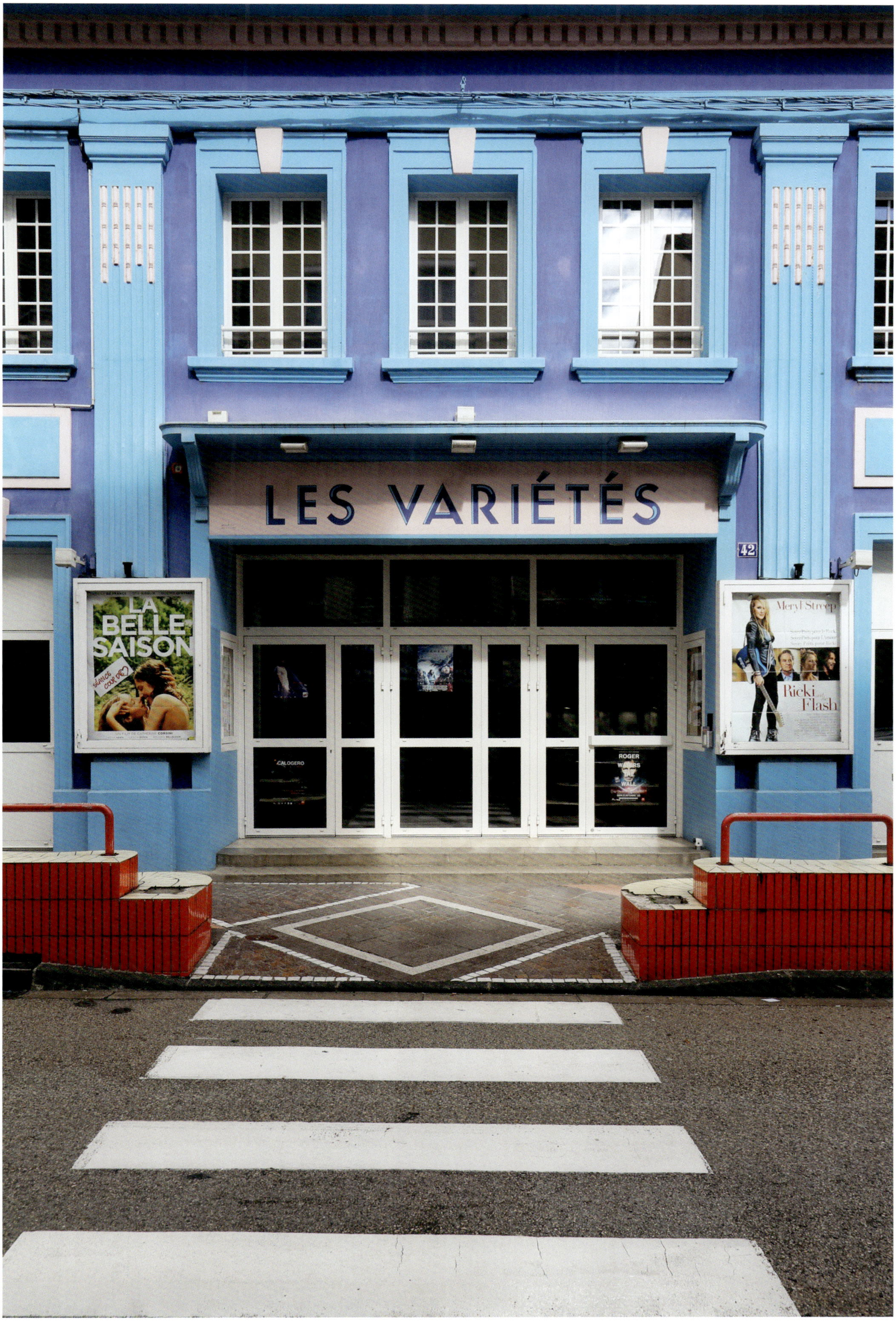

Bellegarde – Les Variétés – 2015

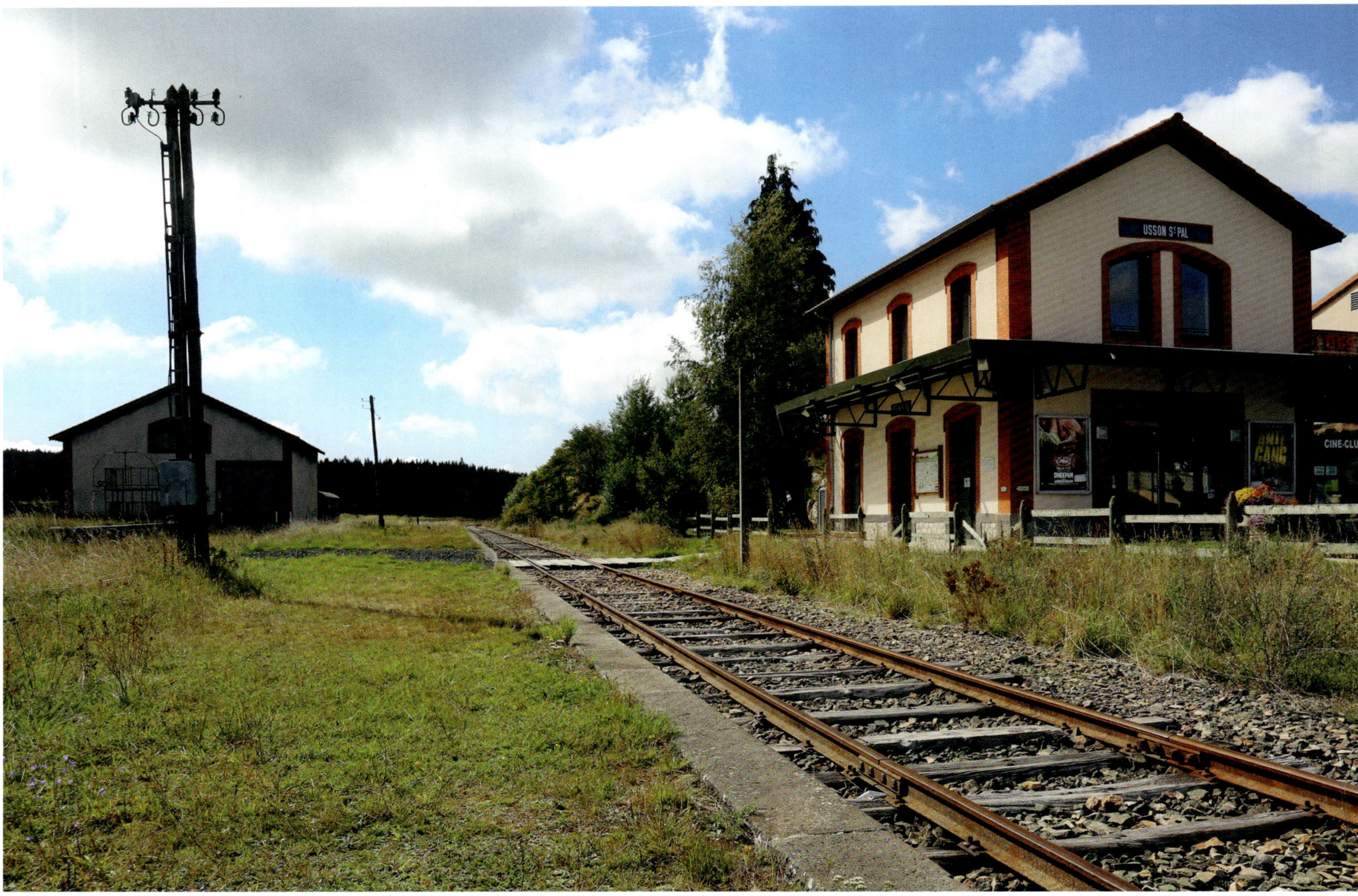

Usson-en-Forez – Le Quai des Arts – 2015

Usson-en-Forez, Le Quai des Arts. The railway lines that meandered through towns and villages have now disappeared from the landscape, while works of art recall their past splendour. High-speed trains (TGV) have taken over, forgetting a good few cities forever. Stations are converted into cinemas as a reminder of the golden age of trains… Like the story of cinemas … Maybe.

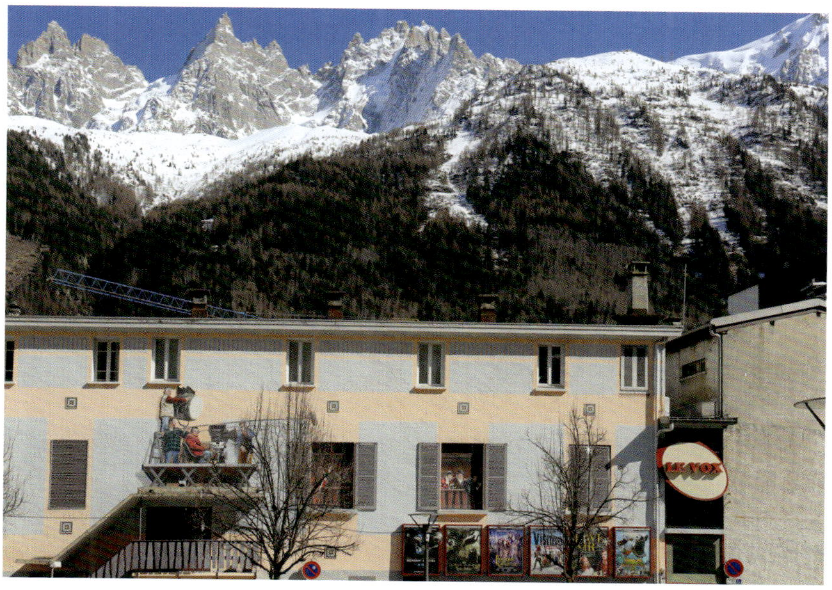

Chamonix – Vox – 2016

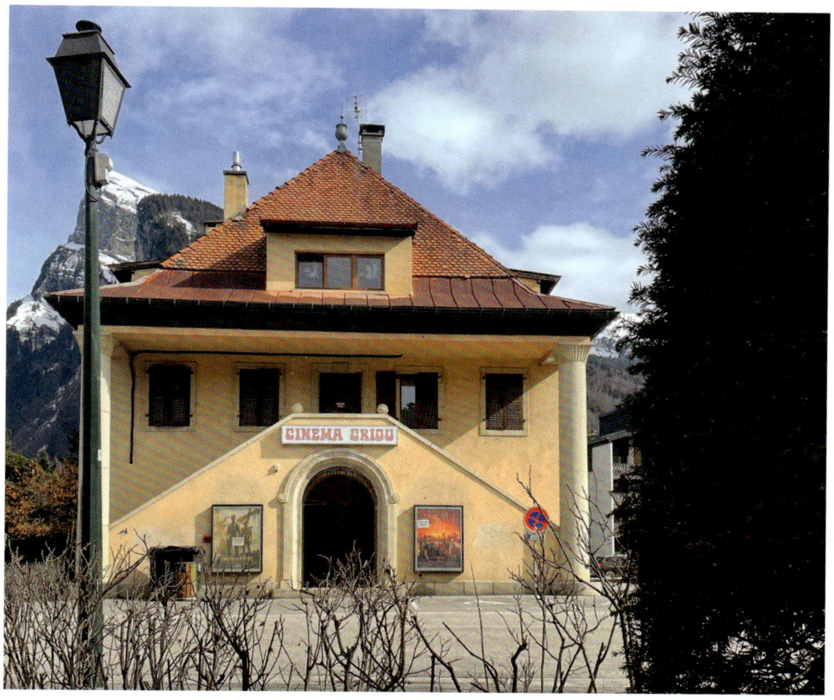

Samoens – Cinéma Griou – 2022

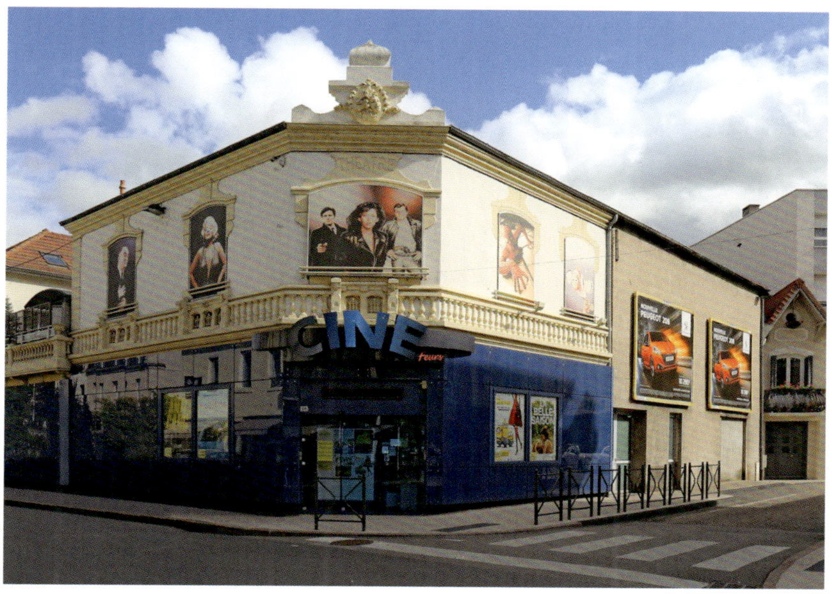

Feurs – Ciné Feurs – 2015

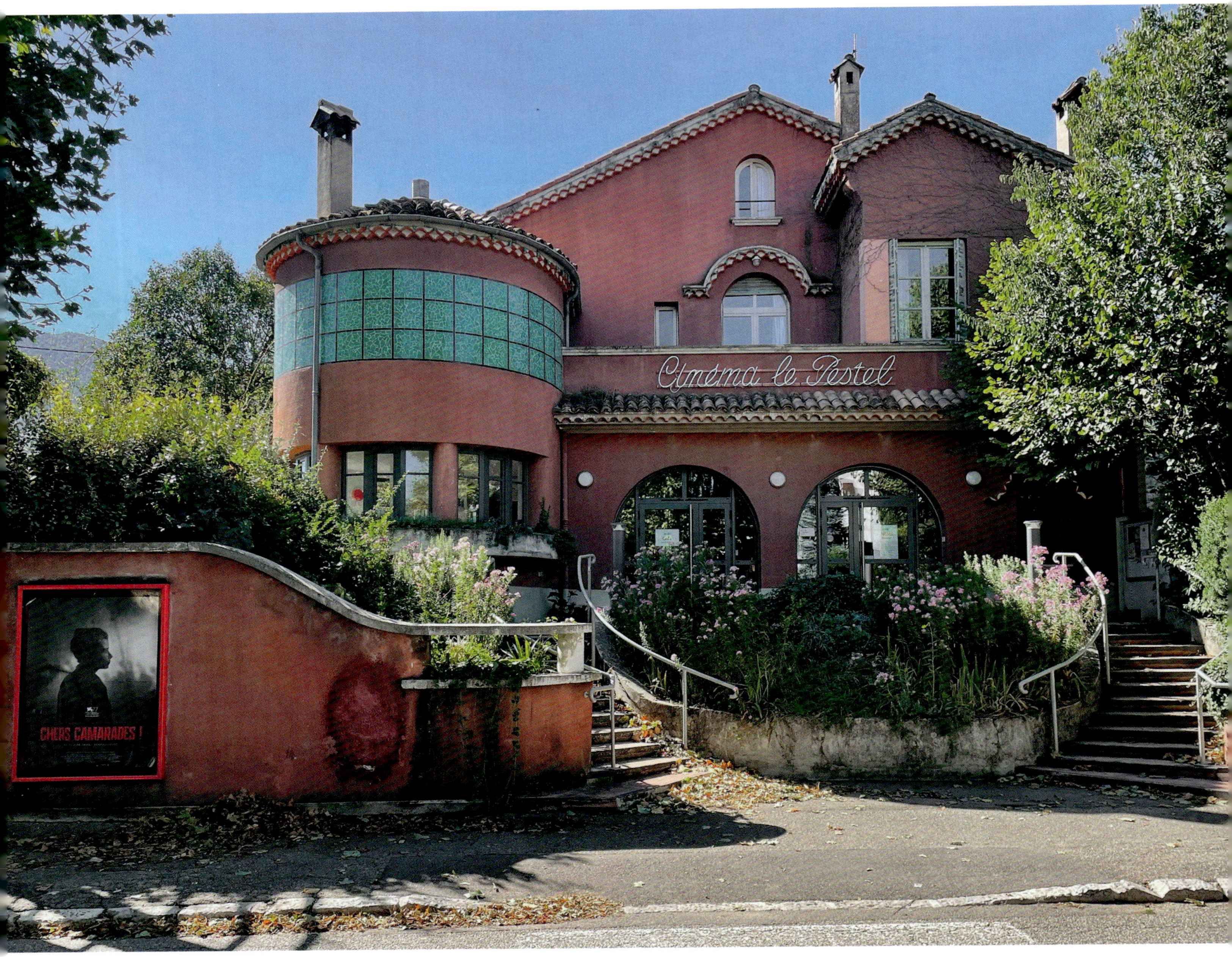

Die – Le Pestel – 2021

Die, Cinéma Le Pestel. My camera observes a small town full of determined walkers streaming past a mansion without stopping. A cinema? Is the theatre in the living room with its bourgeois furnishings? The projection booth in the kitchen? Rolls of film under the marital bed? A dog finally pauses in front of the cinema, looks like it wants to go inside, turns back and ends up pissing against the film poster. Not all creatures love the movies.

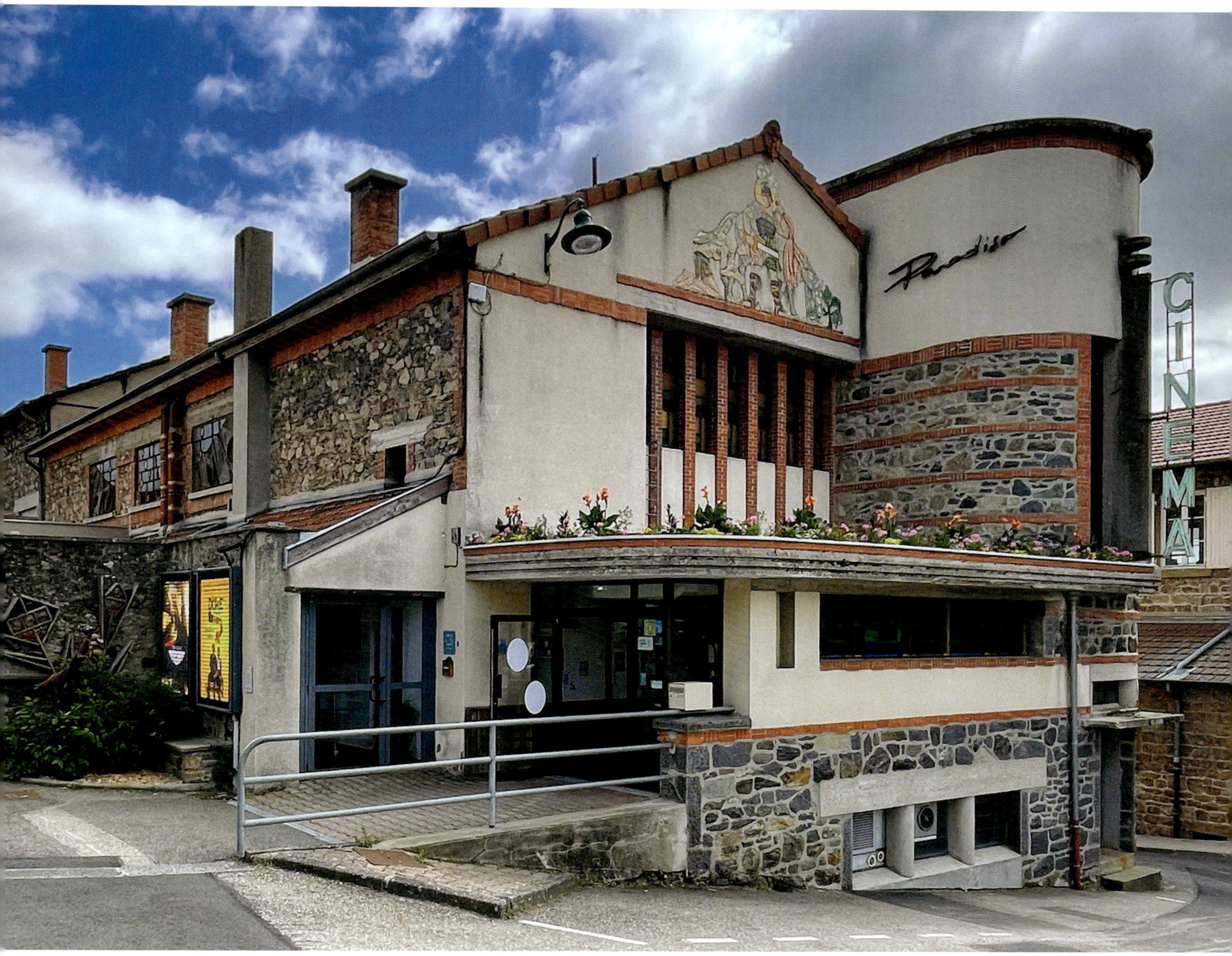

Saint-Martin-en-Haut – Paradis – 2022

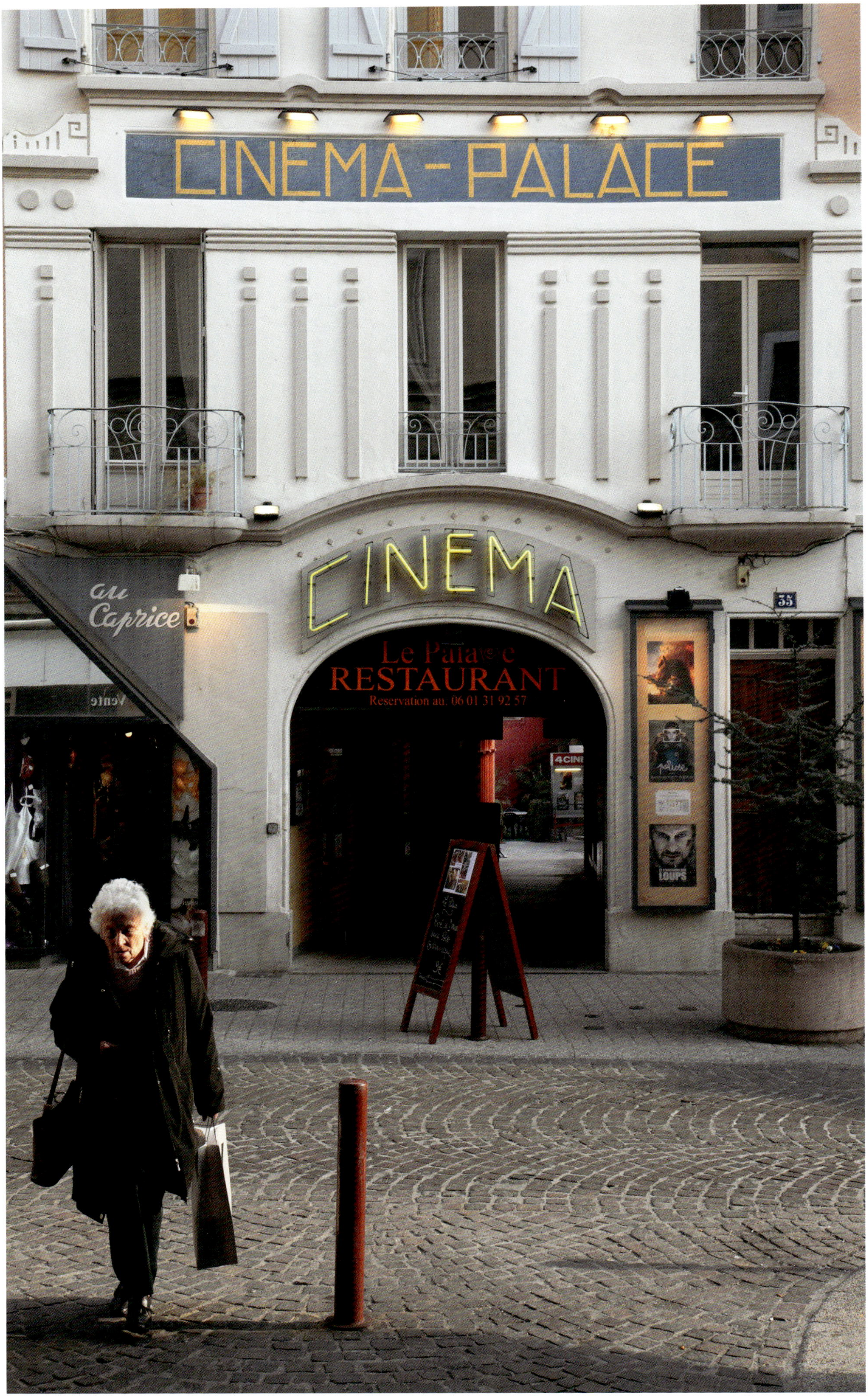

Aubenas – Cinéma Palace – 2012

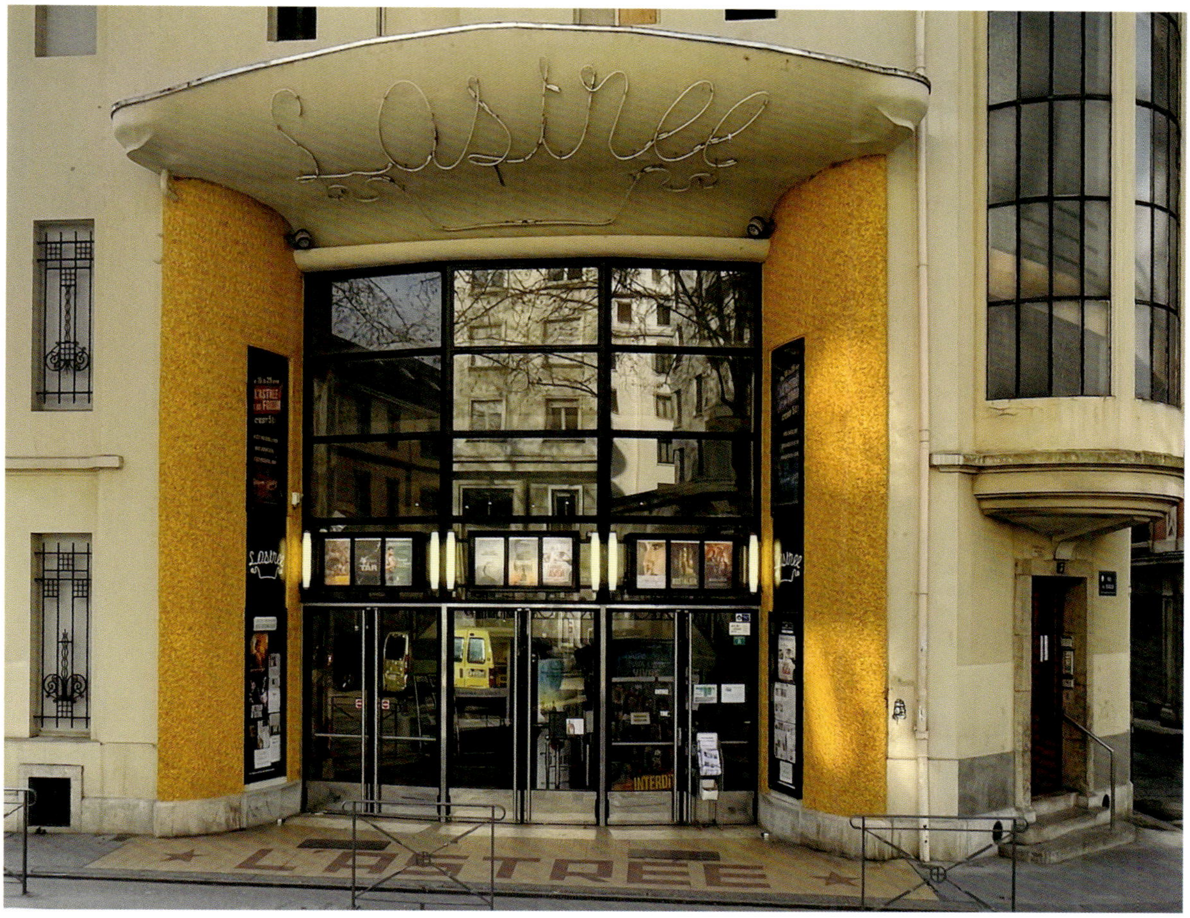

Chambéry – Astrée – 2023

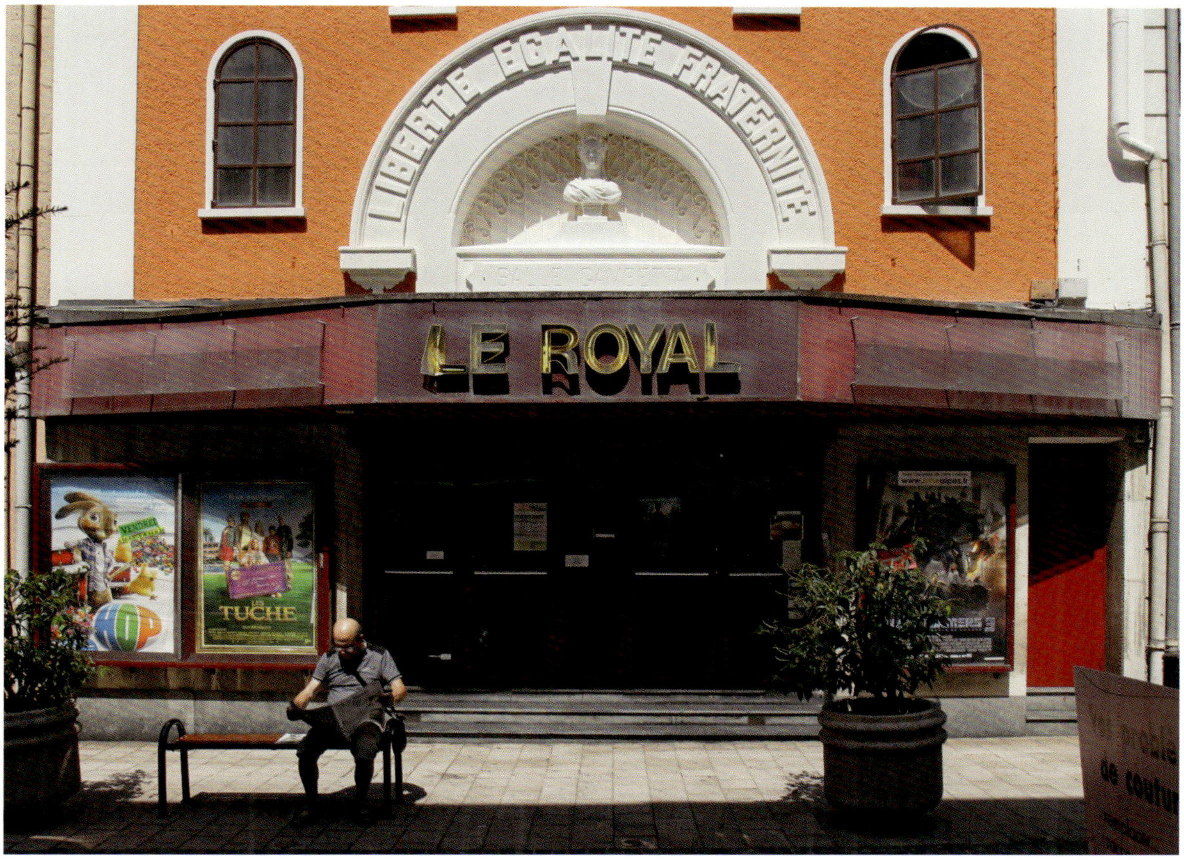

Albertville – Le Royal – 2011

Albertville, Cinéma Le Royal. Ironically, on the façade of The Royal cinema in Albertville, you can read Liberty Equality Fraternity … Only a movie-maker's imagination could reconcile monarchy with democracy.

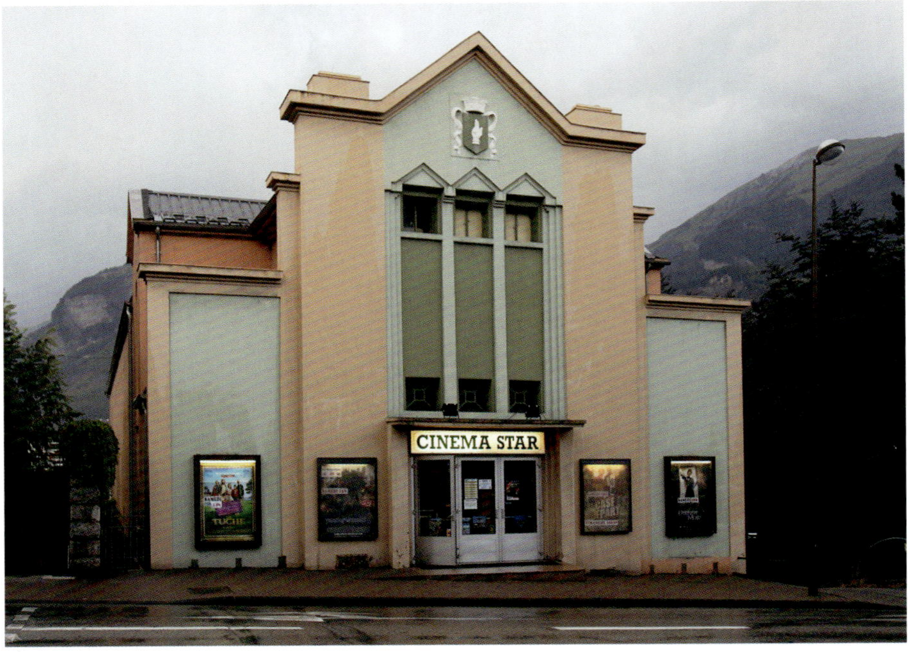

Saint-Jean-de-Maurienne – Cinéma Star – 2011

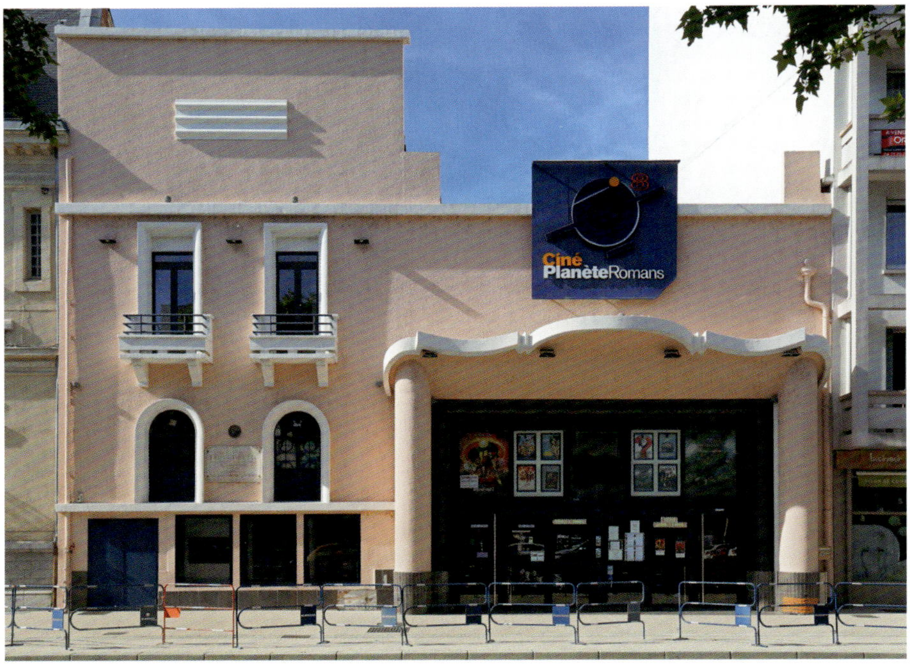

Romans-sur-Isère – Ciné Planète – 2018

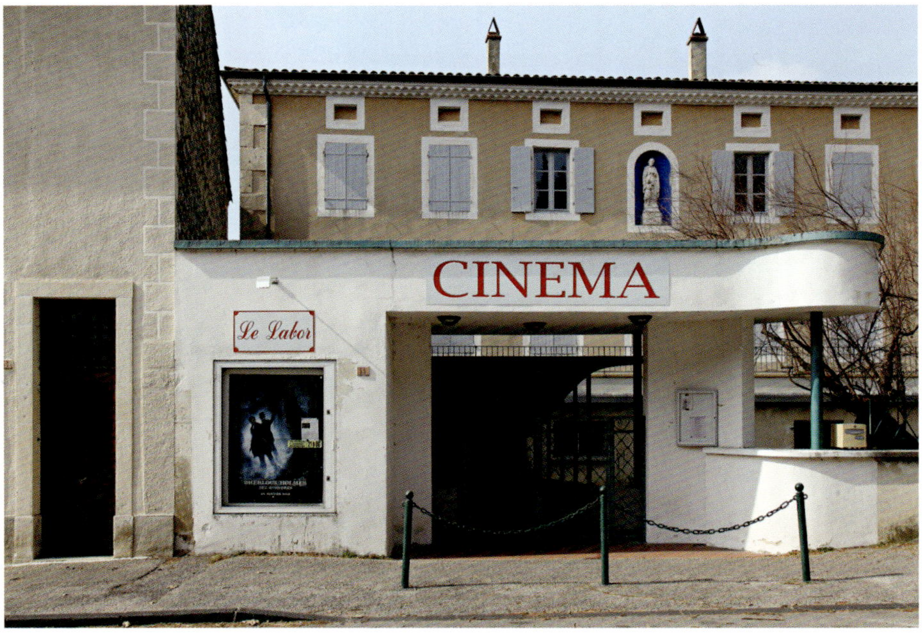

Dieulefit – Le Labor – 2012

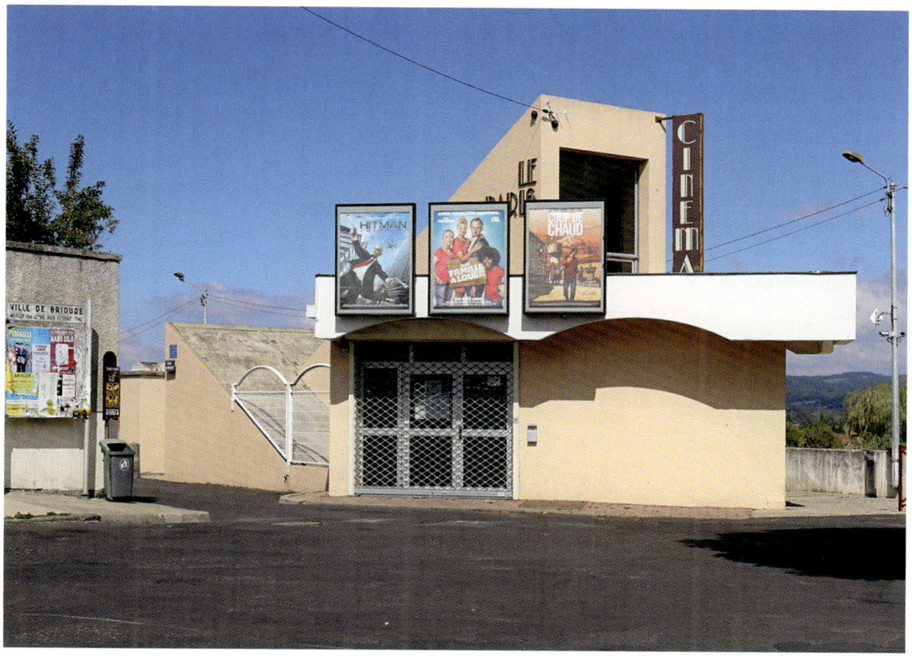

Brioude – Le Paris – 2020

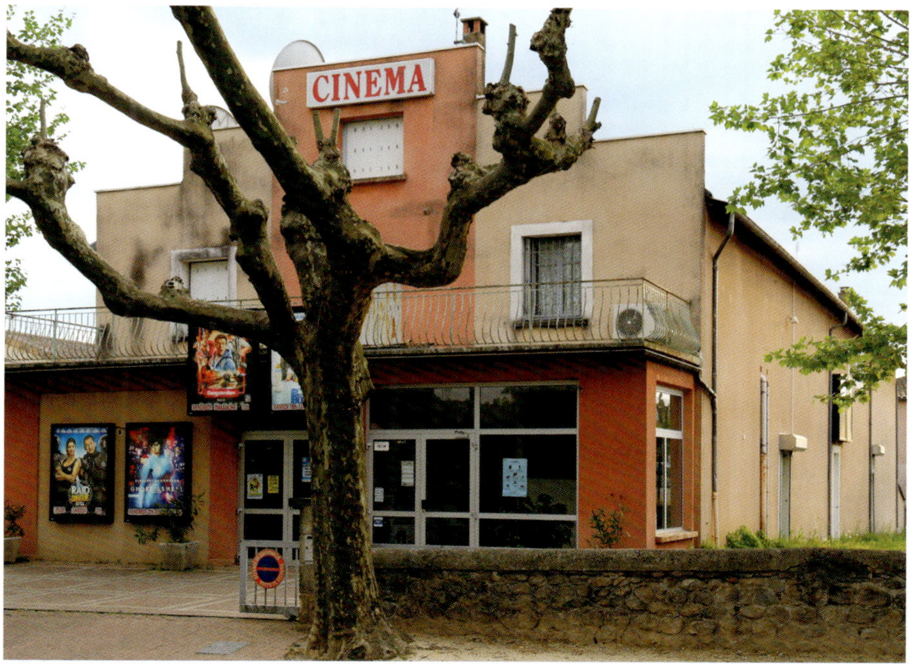

Rosières – Le Foyer – 2015

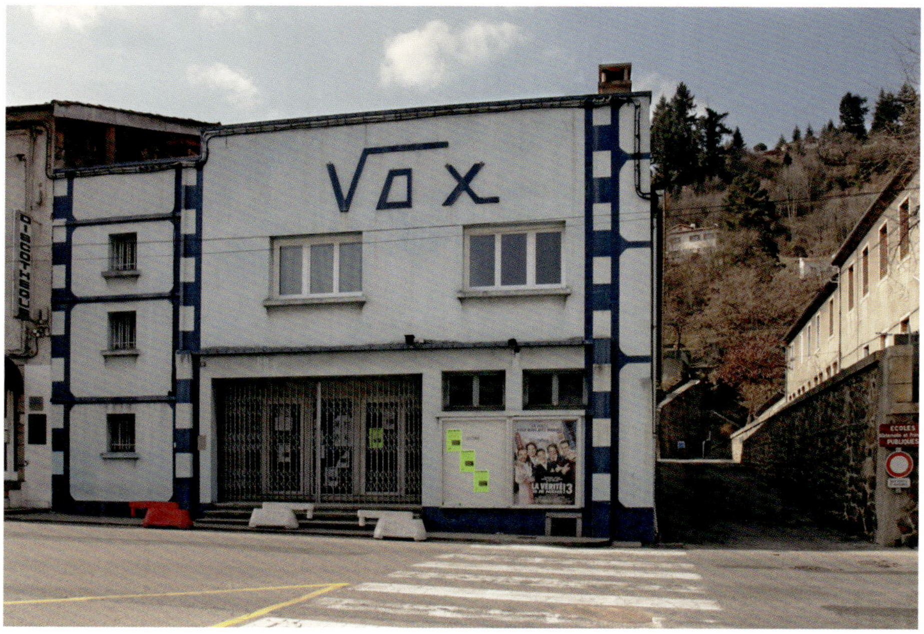

Le Cheylard – Vox – 2018

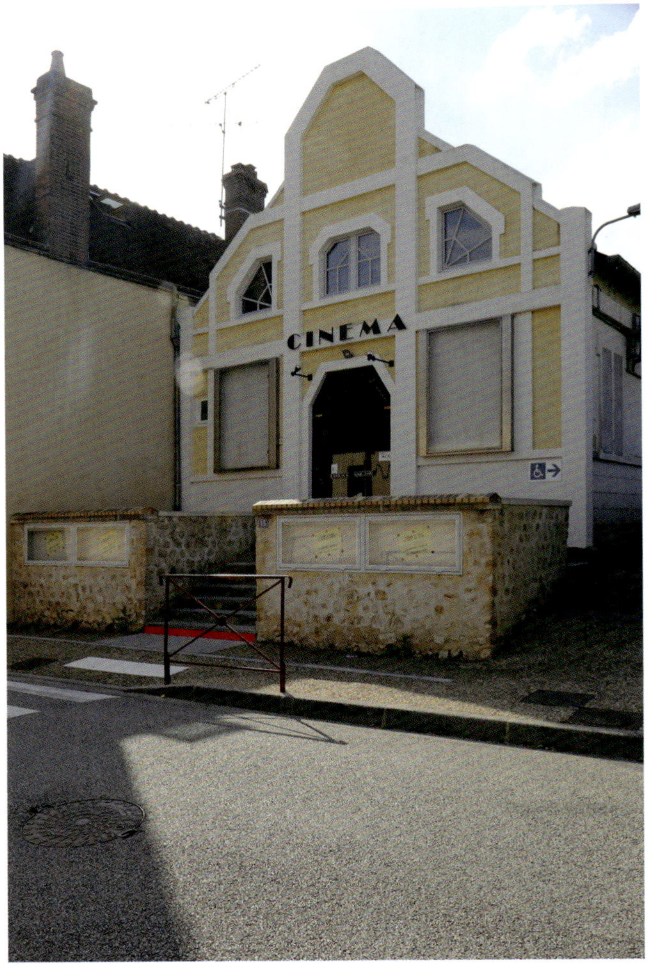

Le Theil – St Louis – 2018

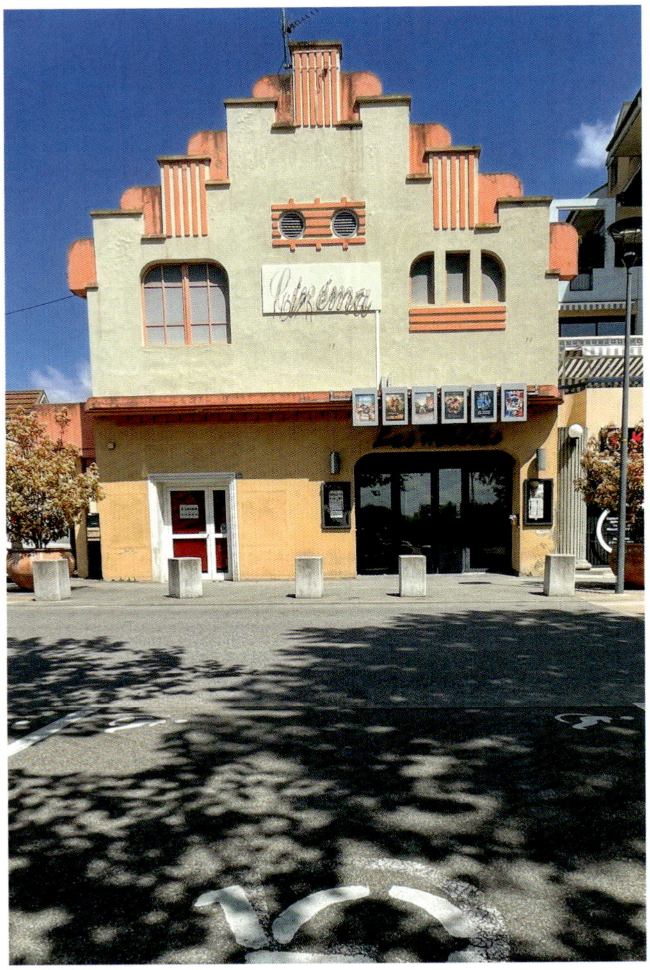

Saint-Marcellin – Les Méliès – 2022

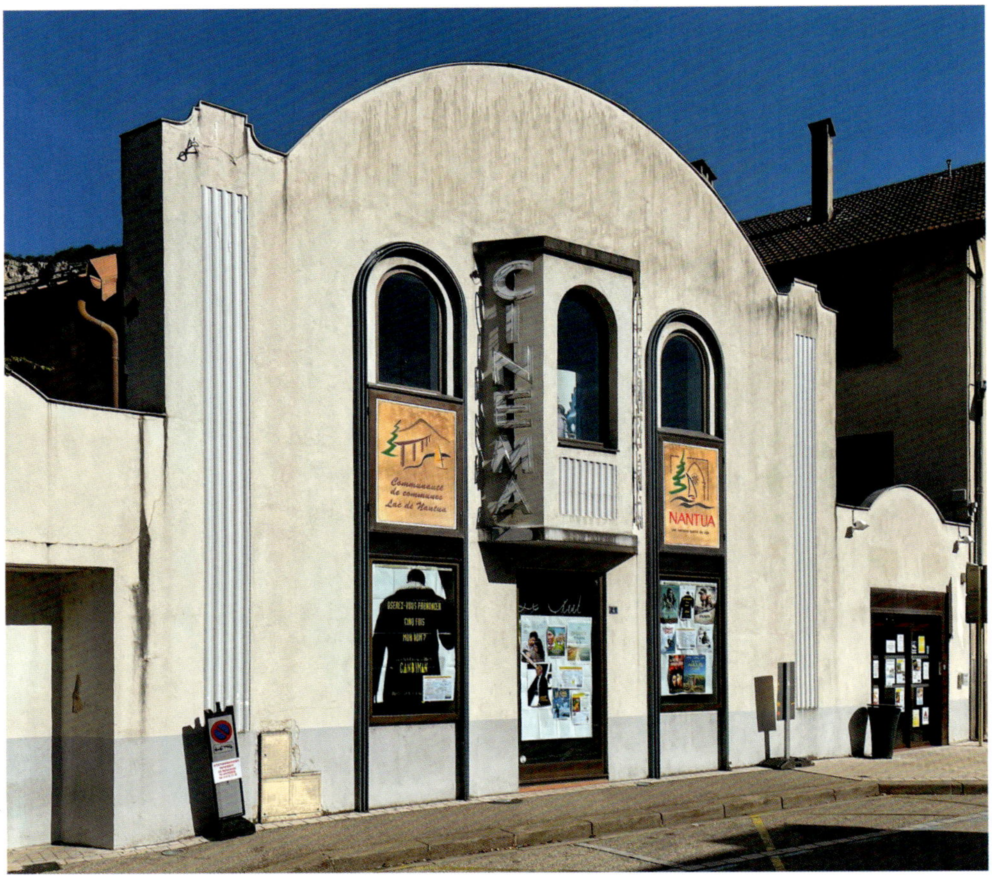

Nantua – Le Club – 2022

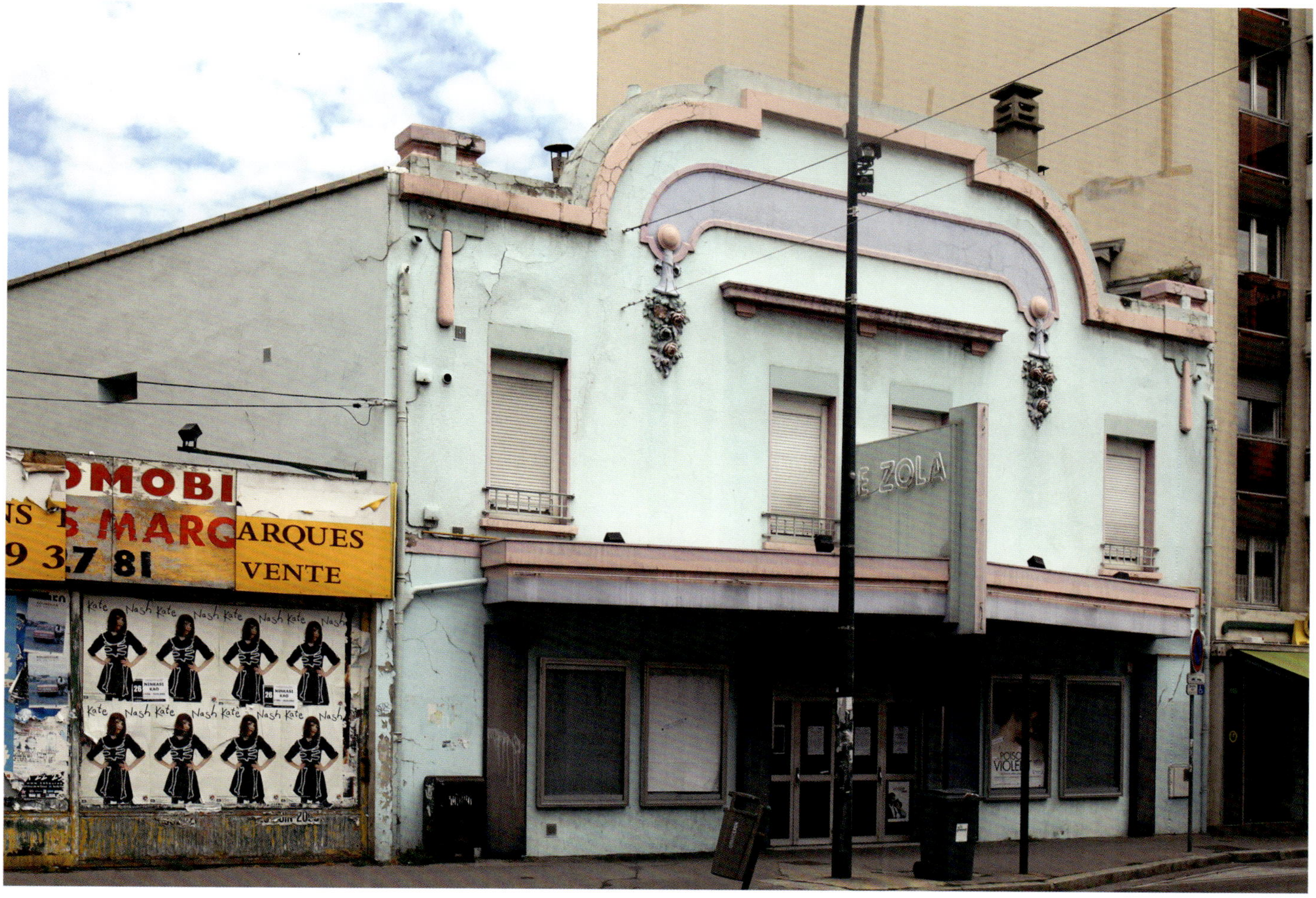

Lyon – Le Zola – 2010

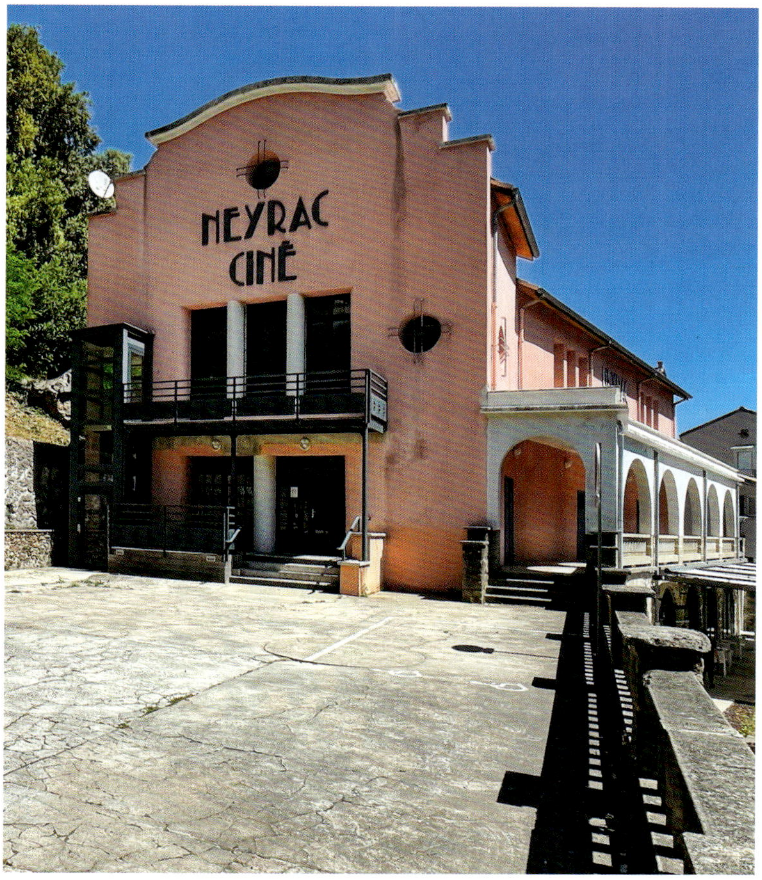

Neyrac-les-Bains – Neyrac Ciné – 2022

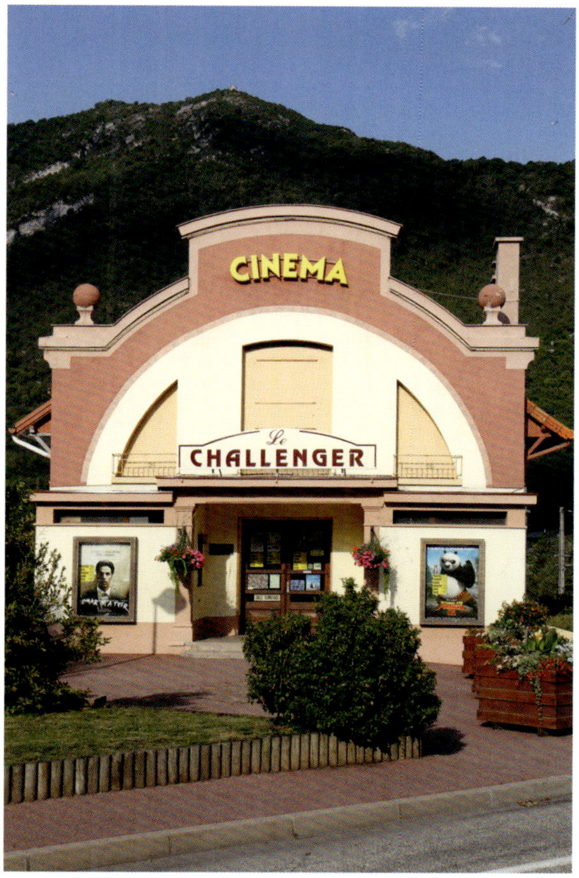

Challes-les-Eaux – Le Challenger – 2011

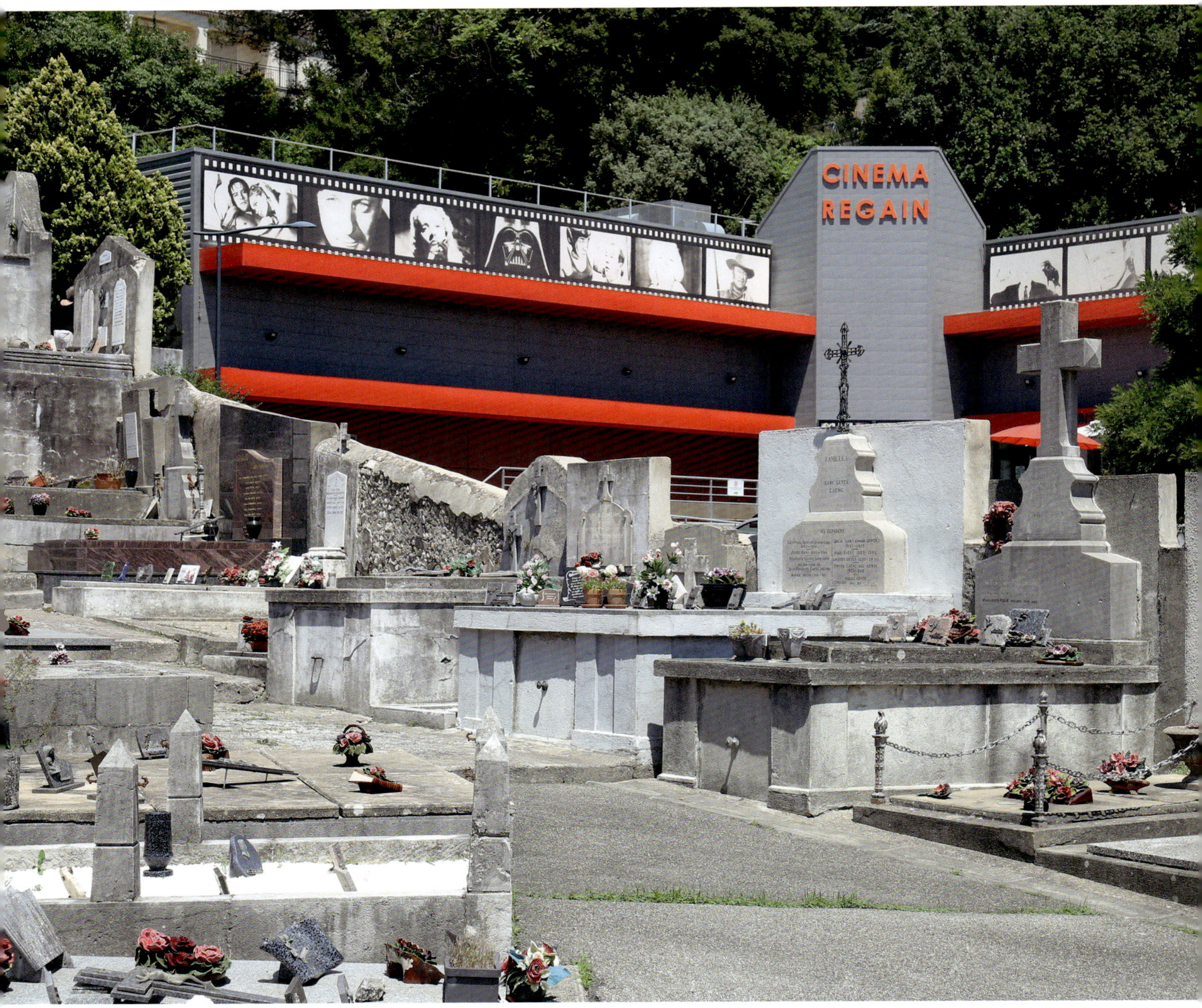

Le Teil – Regain – 2021

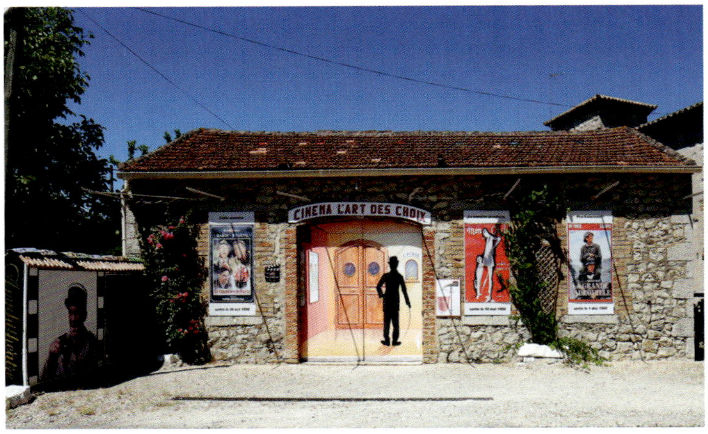

Saint-André-de-Cruzières – Cinéma L'Art des Choix – 2021

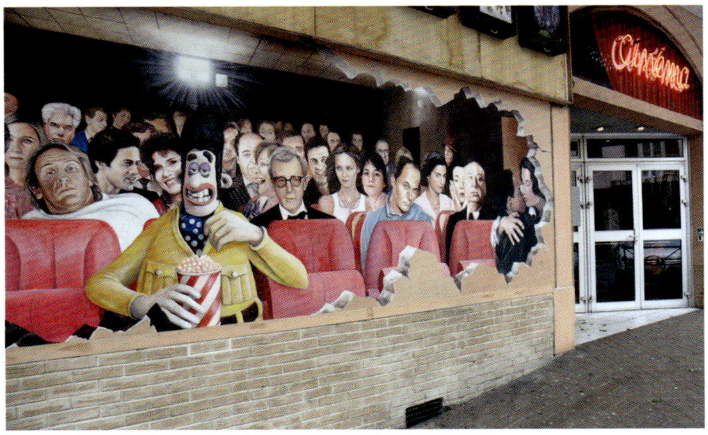

Privas – Vivarais – 2017

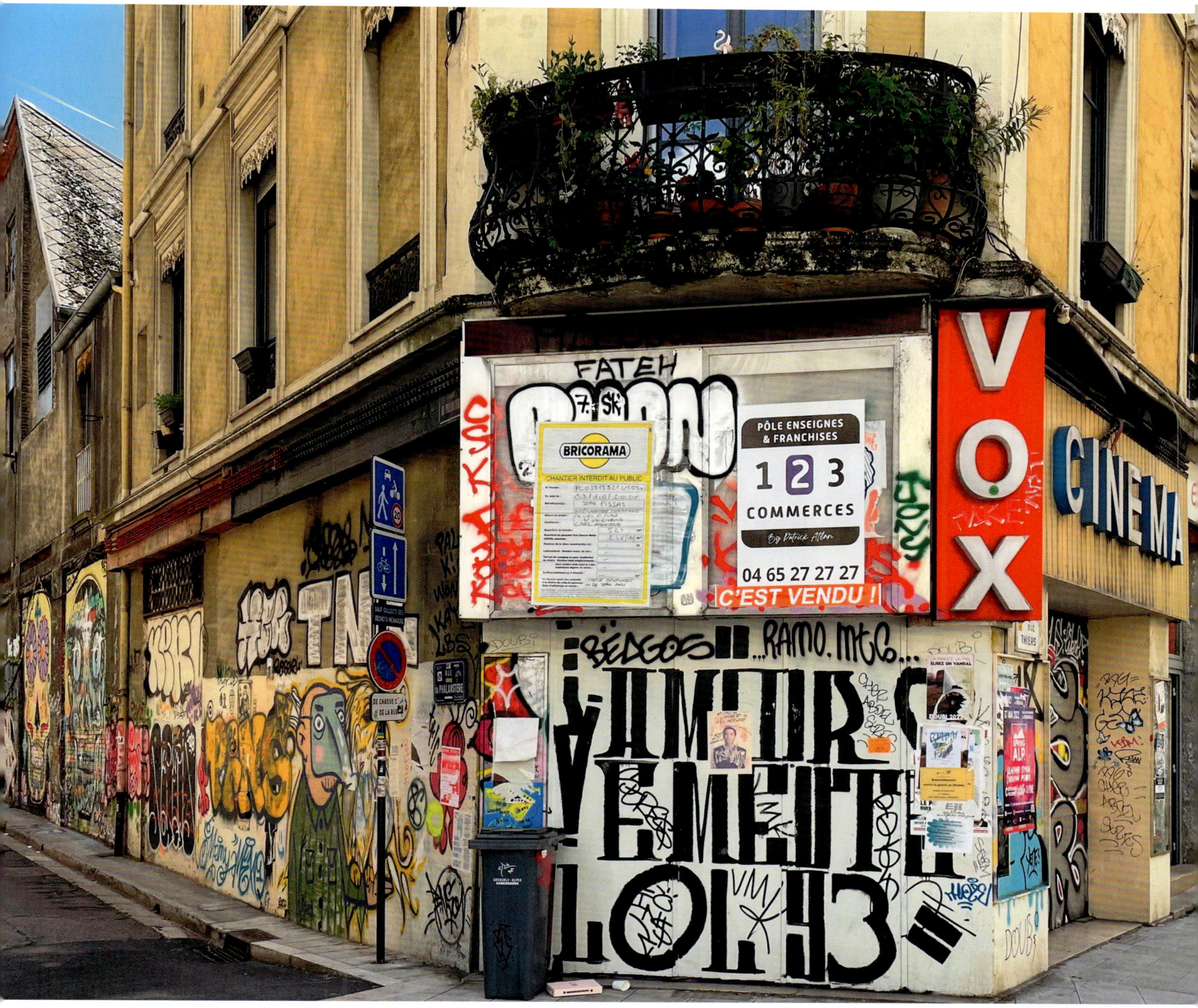

Grenoble – Vox – 2022

Grenoble, Vox. On a street corner a cinema with a boring frontage, long closed down. The degraded walls are becoming almost repulsive. People pass by averting their eyes. Posters stuck on top of each other hide the walls that we no longer want to see, graffiti completes the picture. So we dare to walk past again, opening our eyes to rediscover a cinema with a visual attraction, even a work of art, ready to be sold to a collector ...

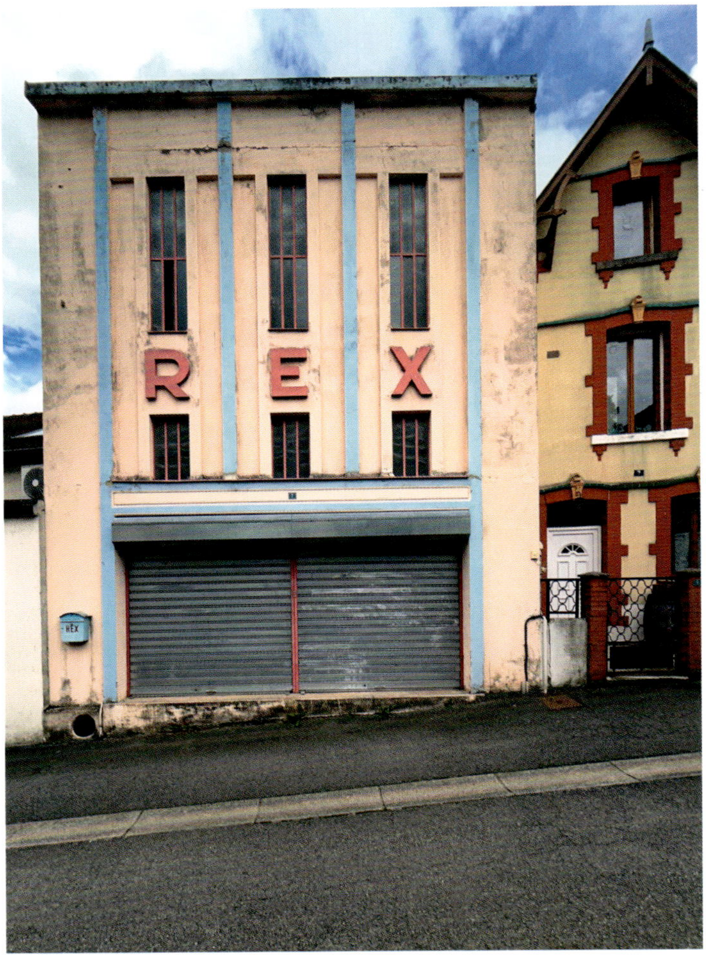

Saint-Éloy-les-Mines – Rex – 2022

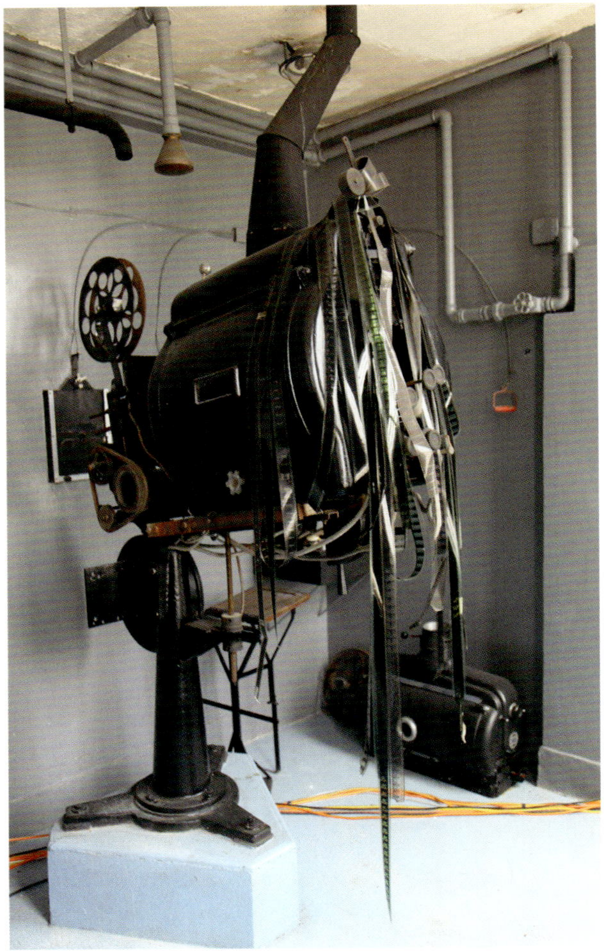

2011

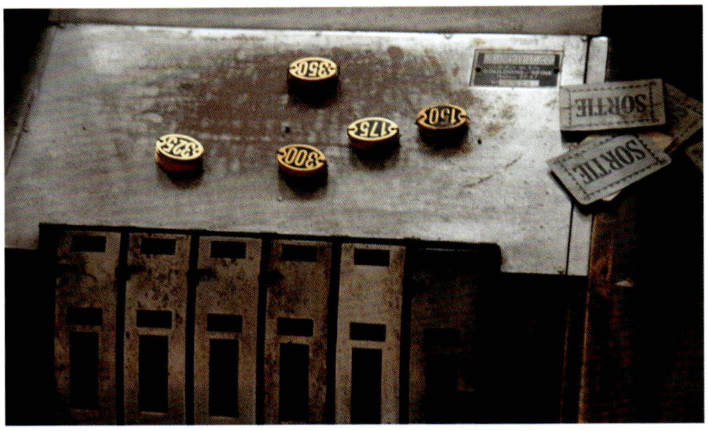

2011

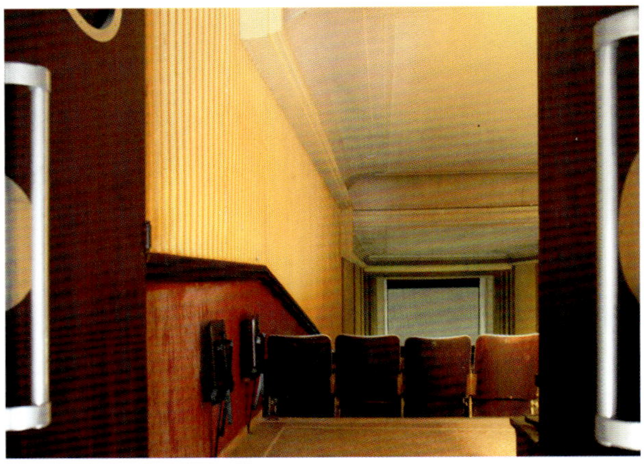

2011

Saint-Éloy-les-Mines, Rex. Saint-Éloy-les-Mines, a name far from the dream world of musicals. A somewhat forgotten town with its storefronts often closed … For good? In a secluded alley, with its dashing façade in flamboyant colours, closed for over fifty years: the Rex. Inside nothing has changed: wooden seats, old-fashioned screen, everything seems as if frozen in time. Audiences can drift back; the Rex is patiently waiting for them. Snuggled up against the cinema, a bijou little house dreams of once again hearing the gentle hum of the projector.

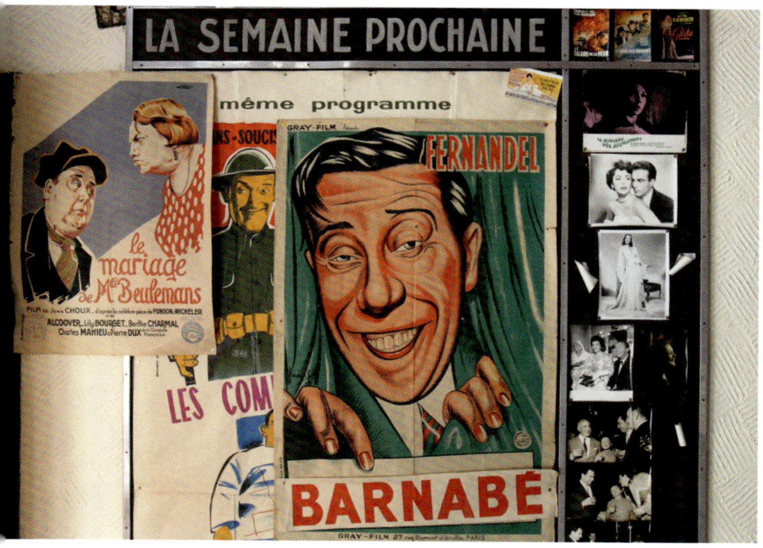

11

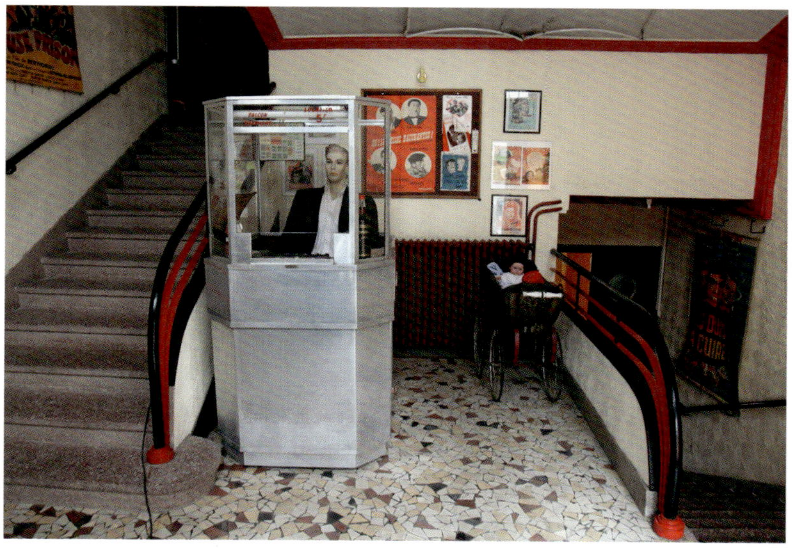

2011

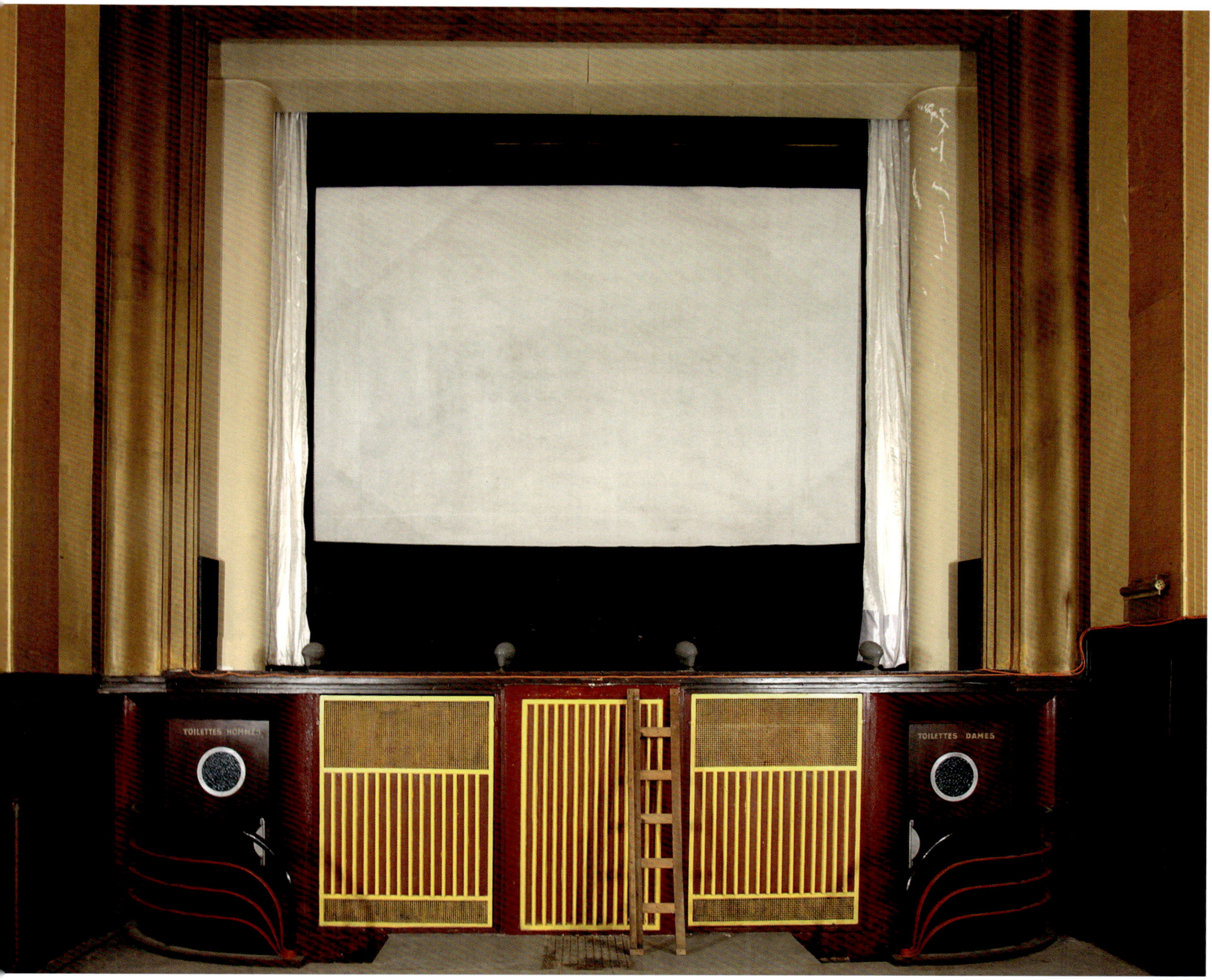

t-Éloy-les-Mines – Rex – 2011

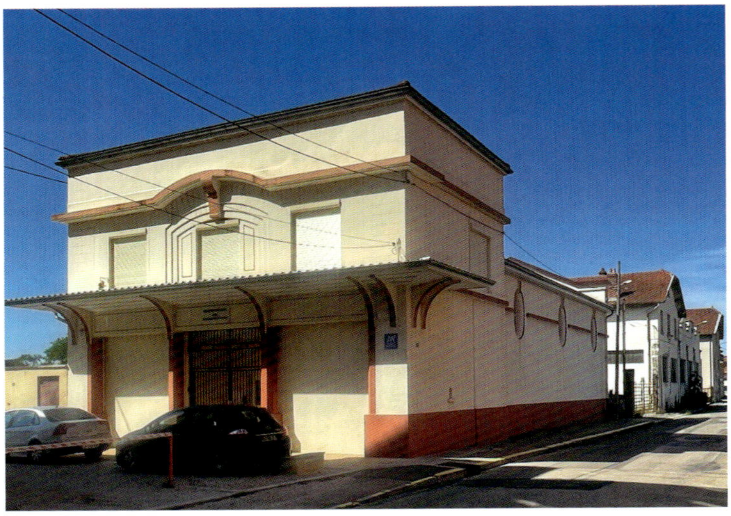

Amberieu – Rex – 2022

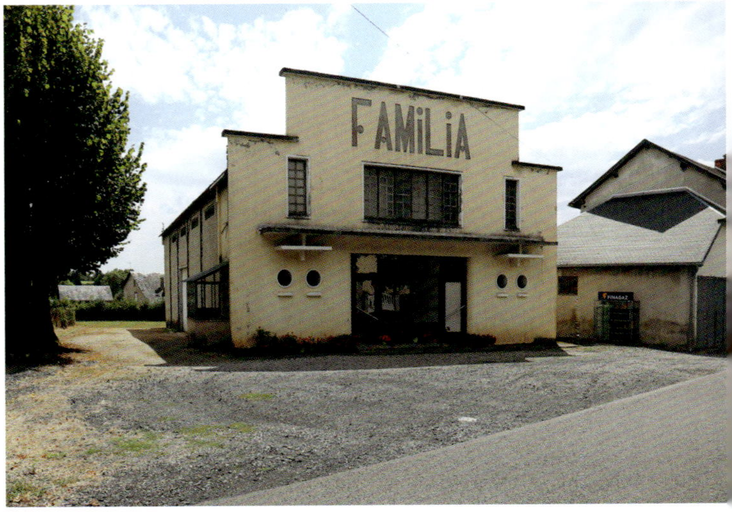

Messeix – Familia – 2020

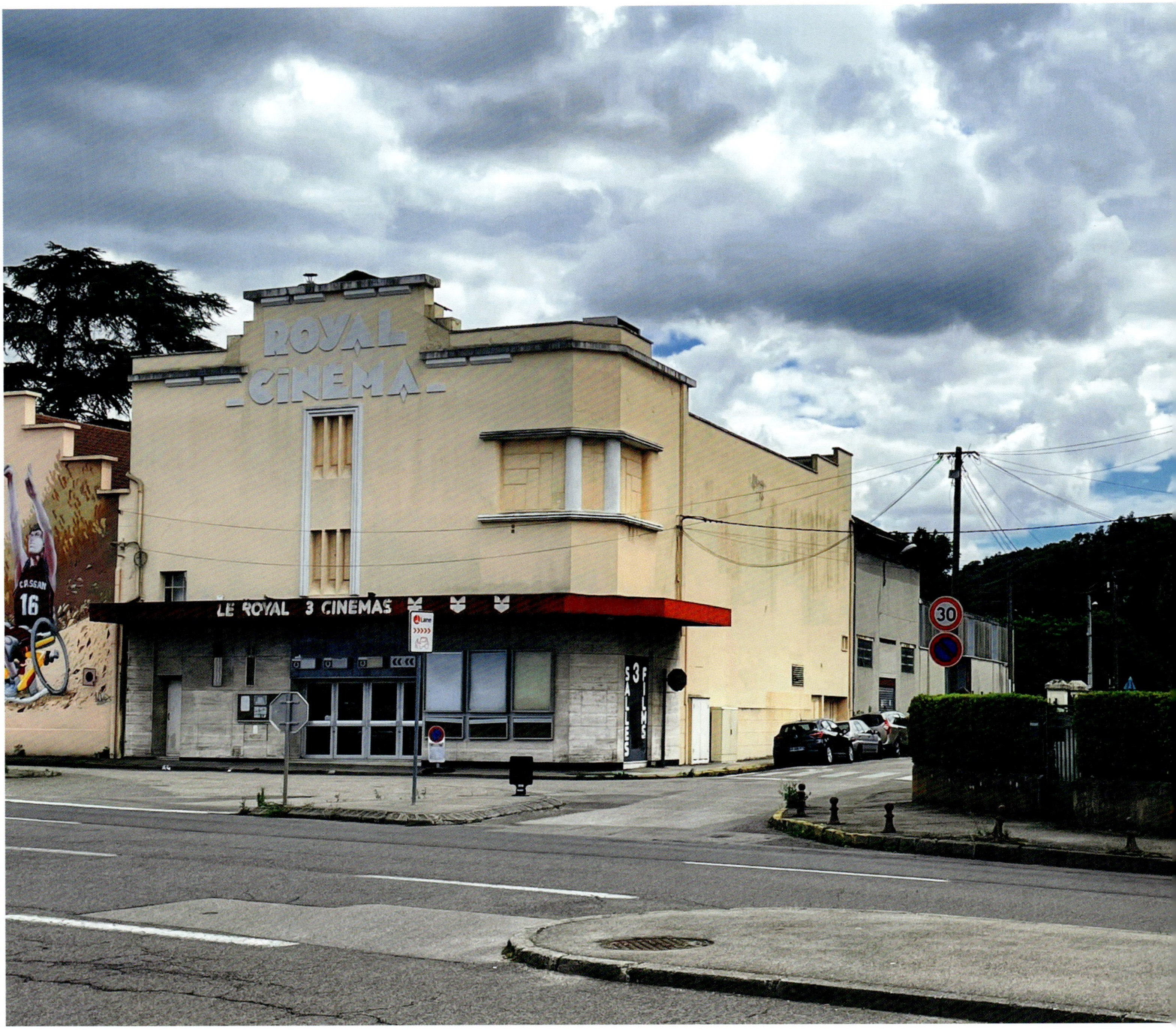

Bourgoin-Jallieu – Royal Cinéma – 2022

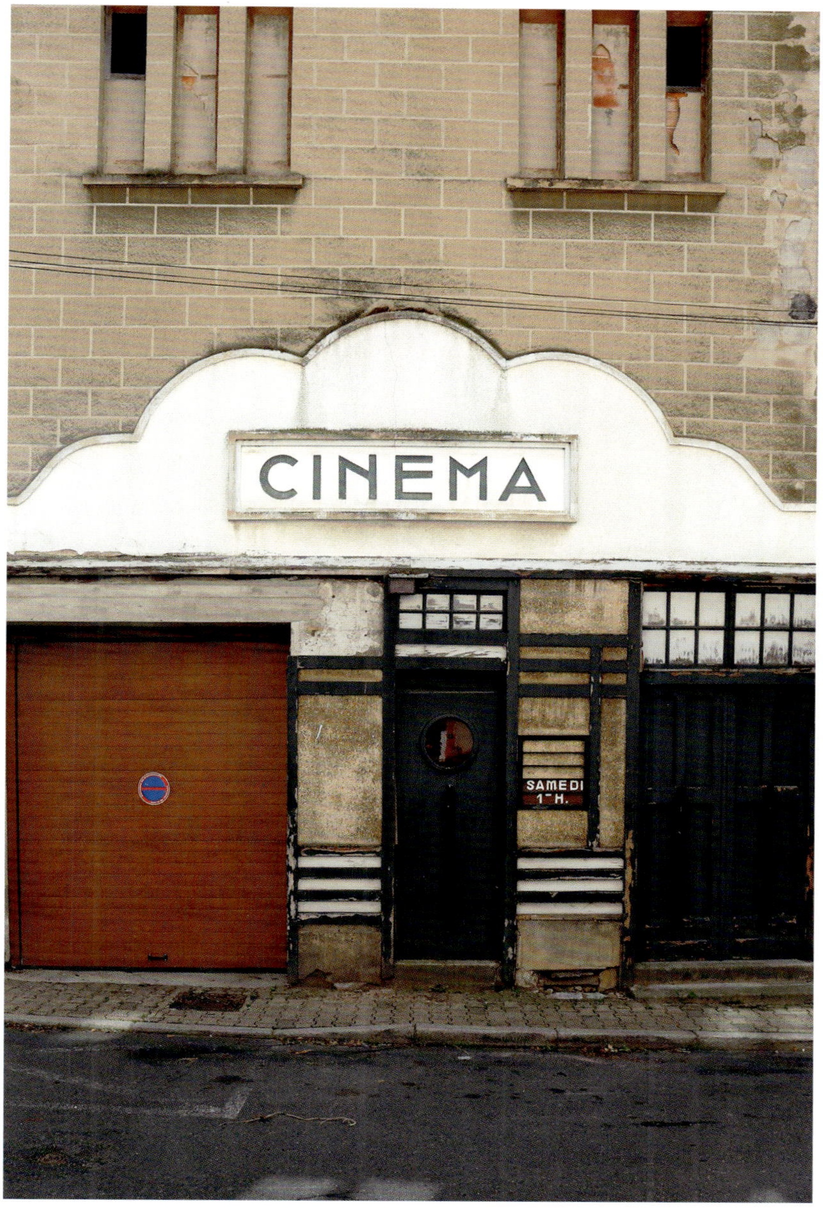

Usson-en-Forez – cinéma – 2015

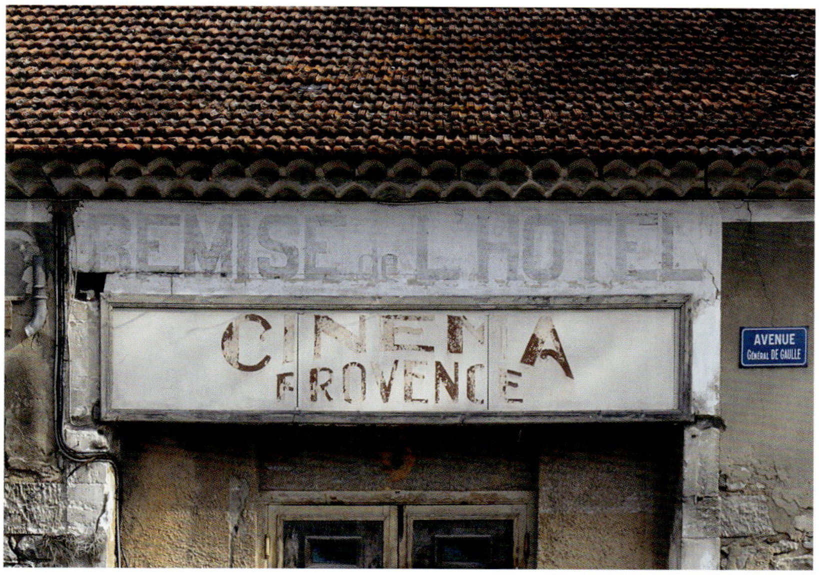

Saint-Paul-Trois-Châteaux – Cinéma Provence – 2013

Saint-Paul-Trois-Châteaux, Cinéma Provence. Cinema at the weekend, cut-price hotel during the week, or the opposite? How does the story begin? We don't know. But, obviously, it ends sadly. No more cinema, no more discount. Just a forgotten place.

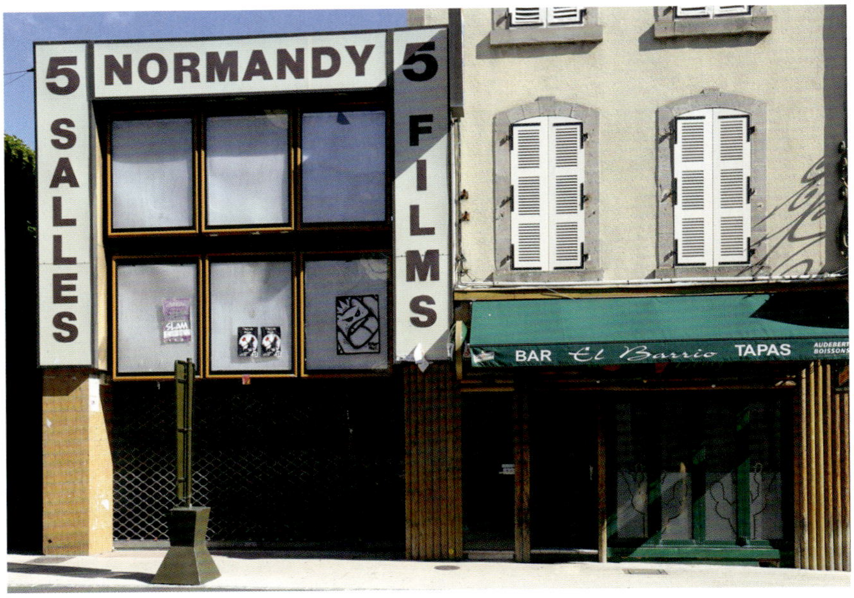

Aurillac – Normandy – 2015

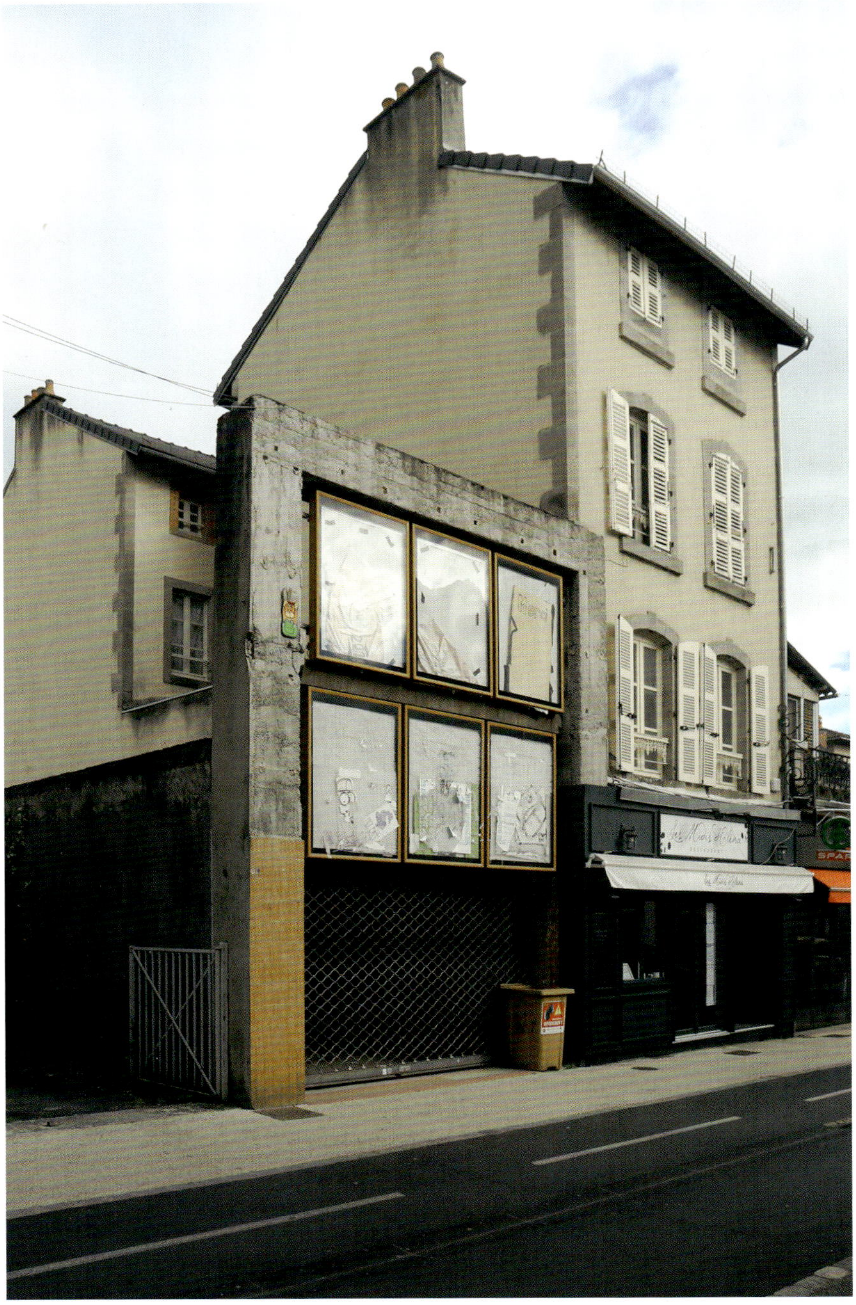

2021

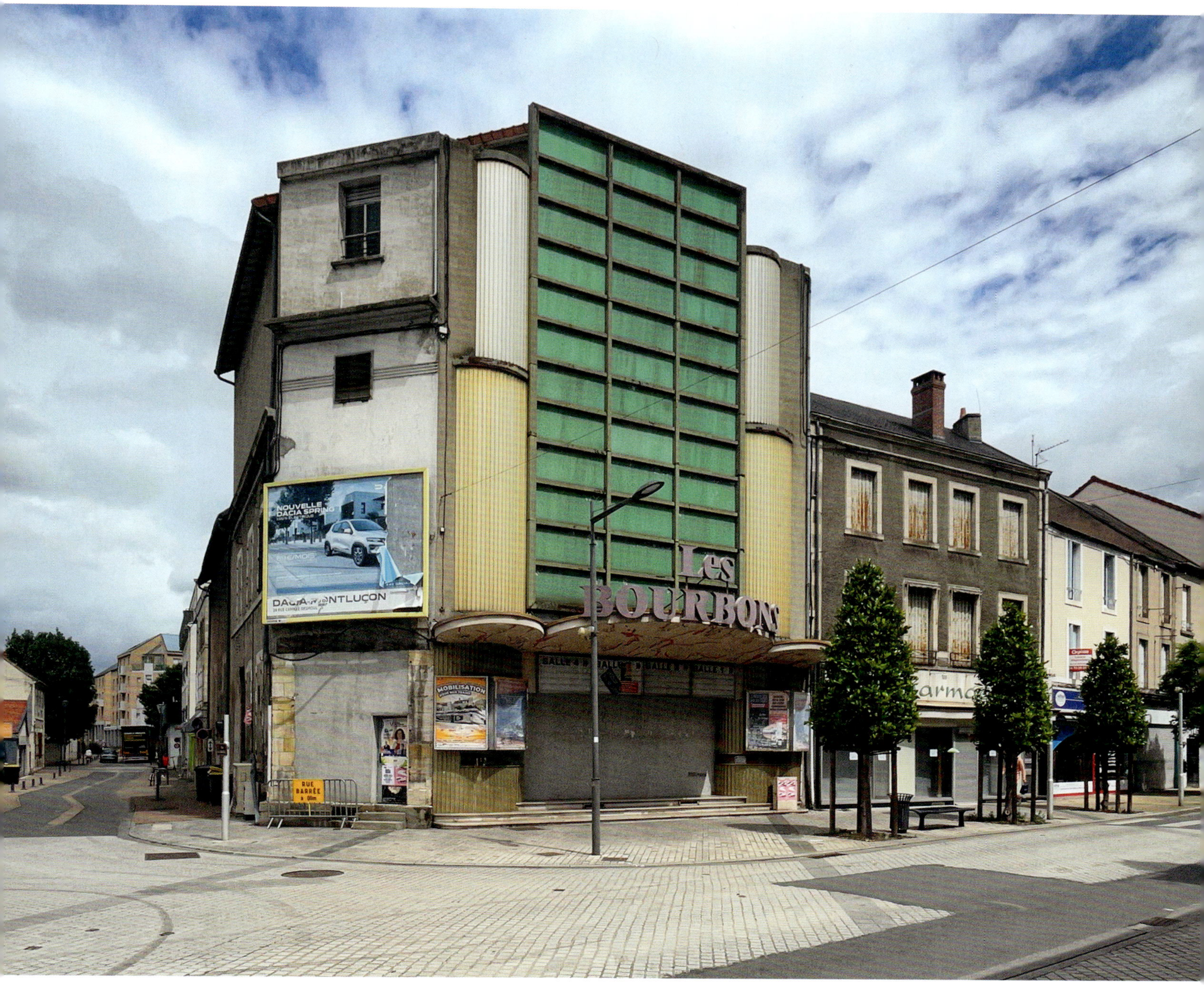

Montluçon – Les Bourbons – 2021

Montluçon, Cinéma Les Bourbons. Can life go on without cinemas in the city centre? The authorities sometimes think so, for sure ... Yet some cinemas, even dead, abandoned, decrepit, oozing misery through their entrails, don't want to be buried. Don't want to be reborn in suburbs haunted by gas stations, a few restaurants with dubious names and shopping malls visited by a population gradually forgetting the existence of the cinema.

BURGUNDY-FRANCHE-COMTÉ

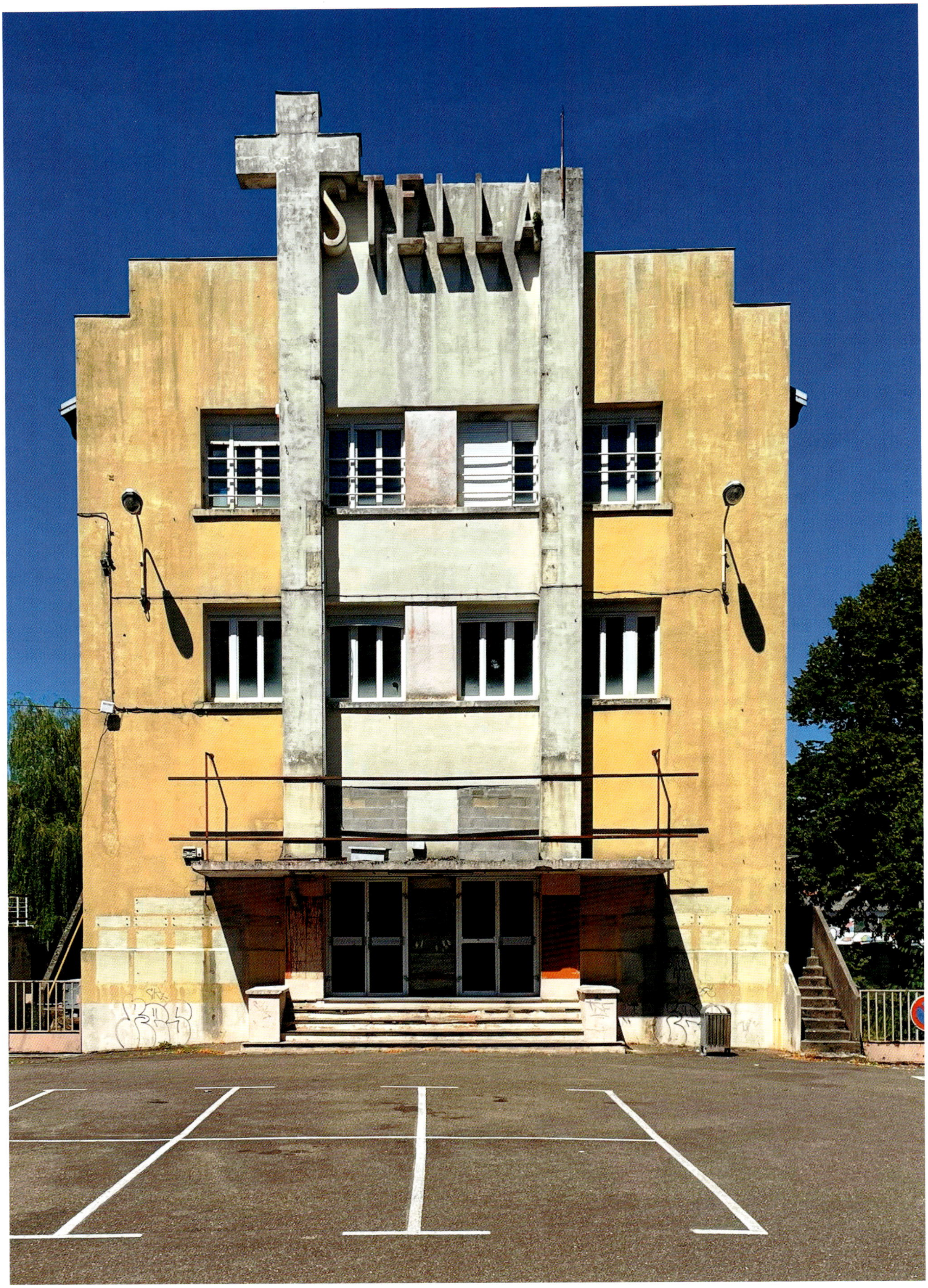

Vesoul – Stella – 2022

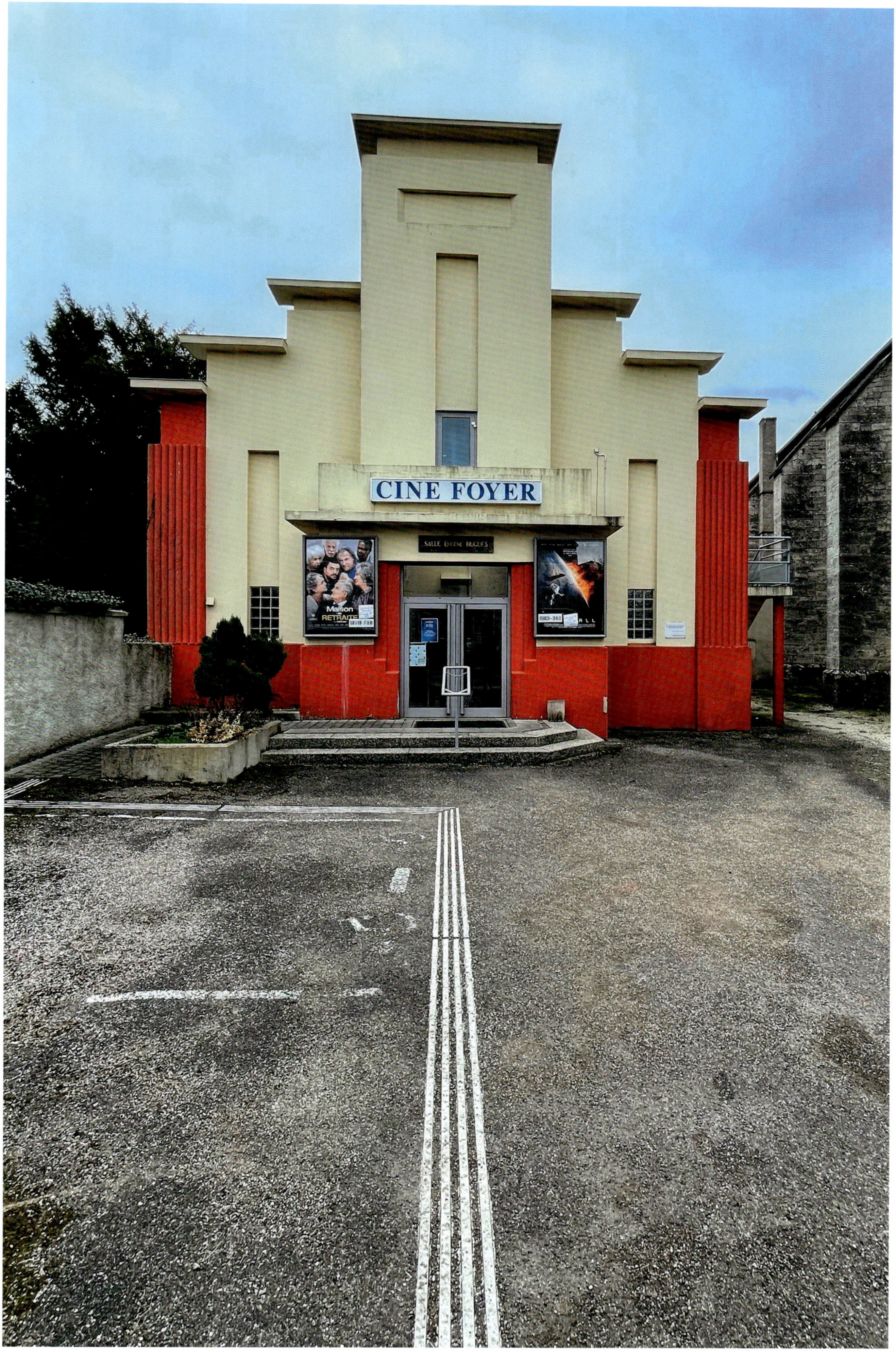

Dampierre-sur-Salon – Ciné Foyer – 2021

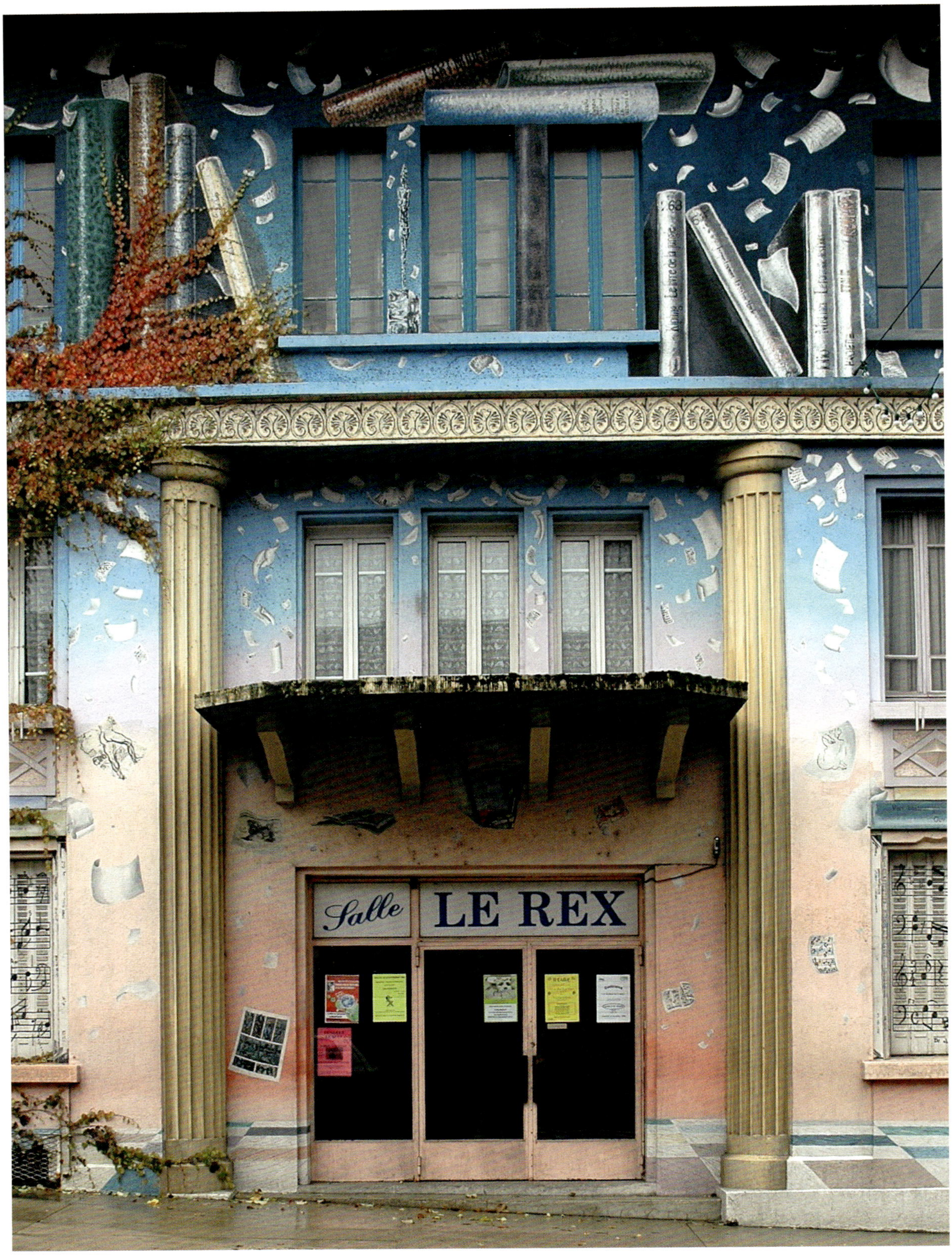

Champagnole – Le Rex – 2006

Champagnole, Rex. A cinema nestled in a building with no particular sign. The Rex seemed to slumber for eternity, despite the incessant stream of cars unwilling to slow down. Suddenly, one day, the Rex wakes up sparkling, illuminated with a thousand colours. But, alas, too late, it's no longer a cinema.

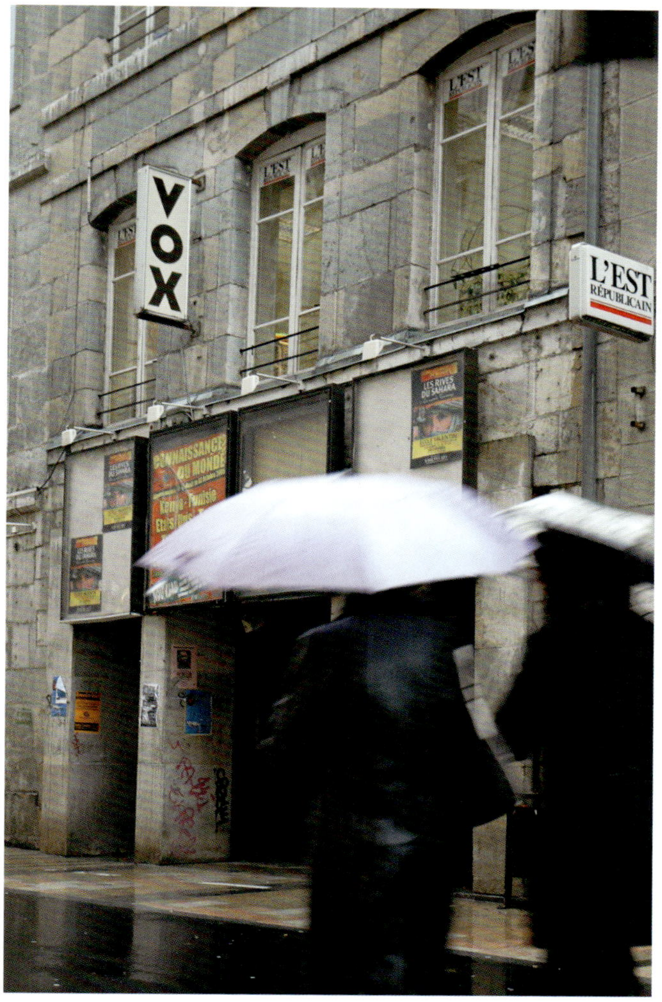

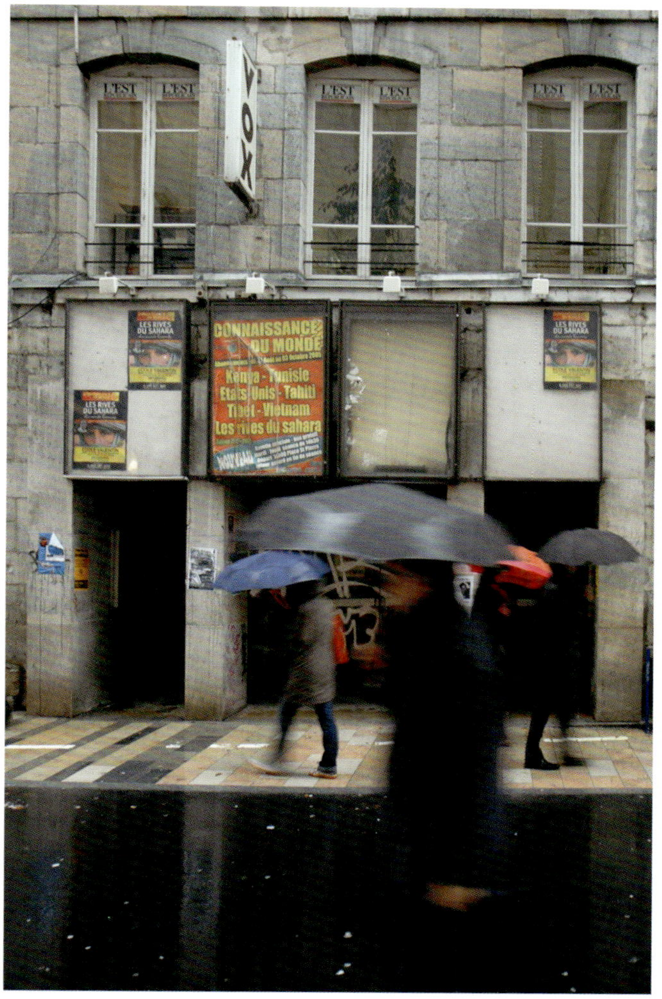

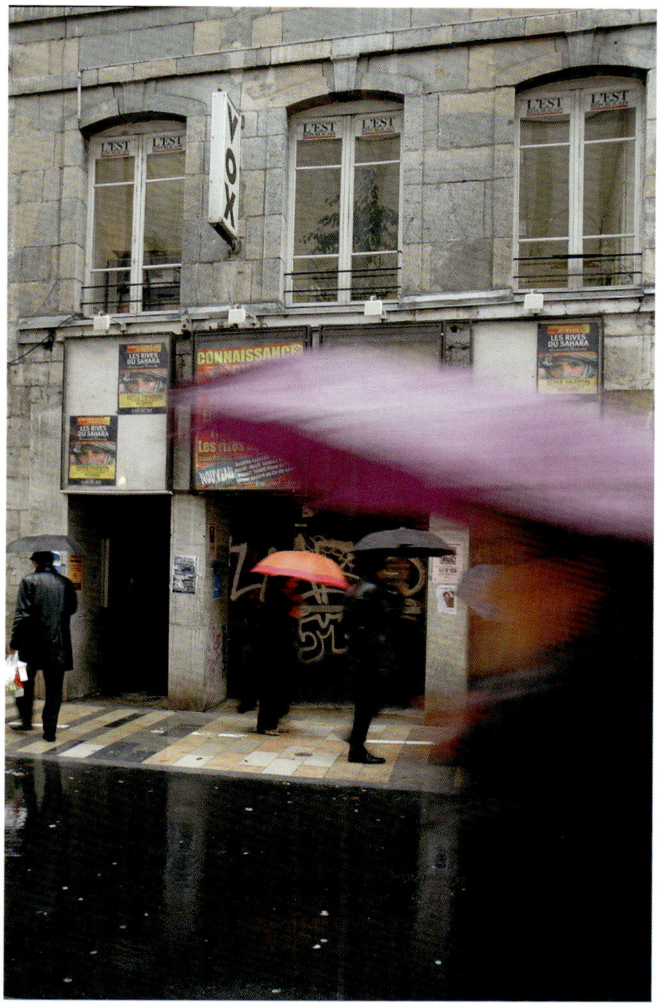

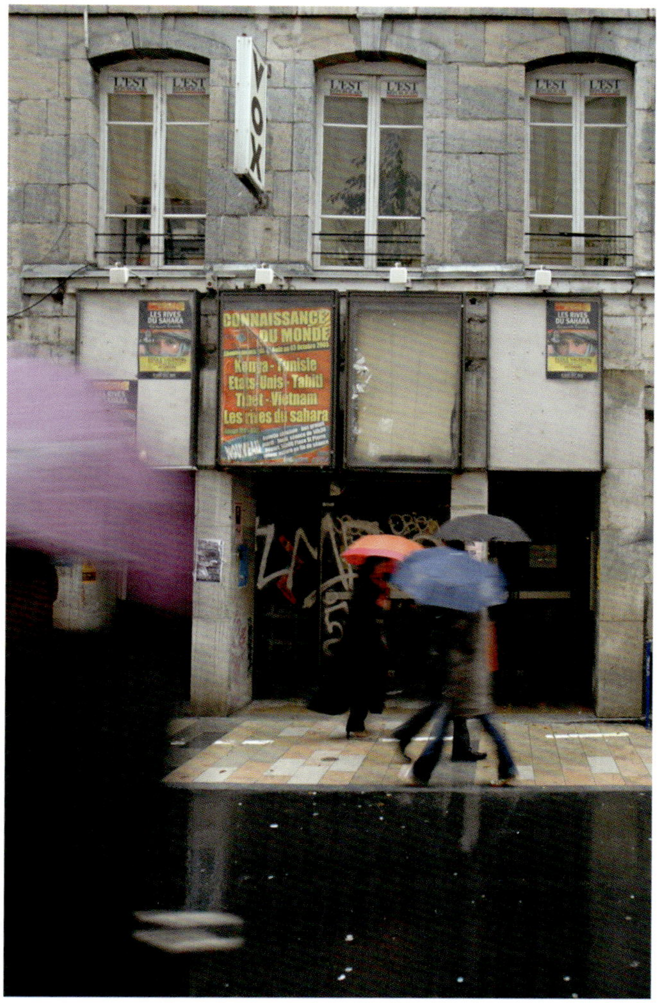

Besançon – Vox – 2006

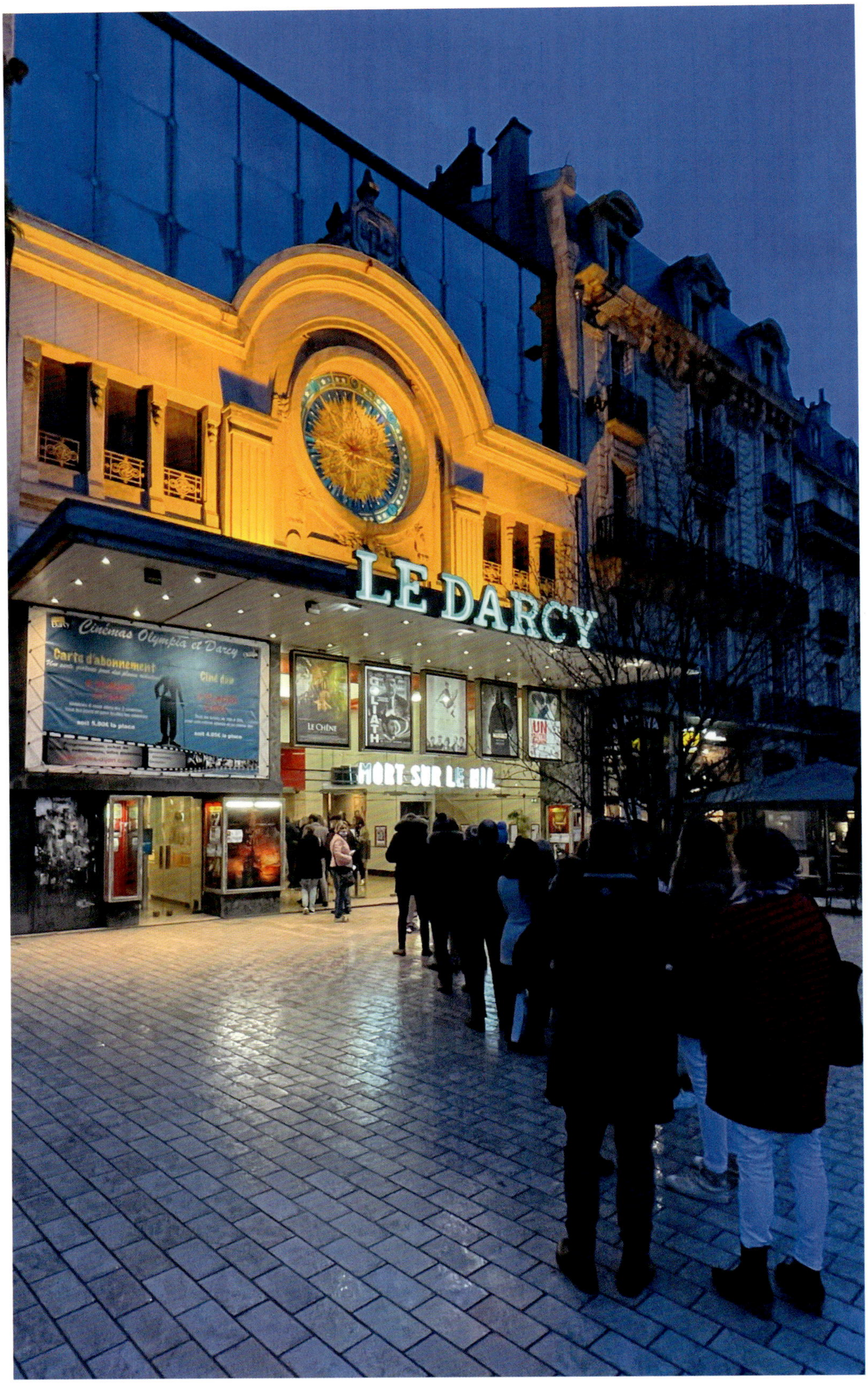

 Dijon – Le Darcy – 2022

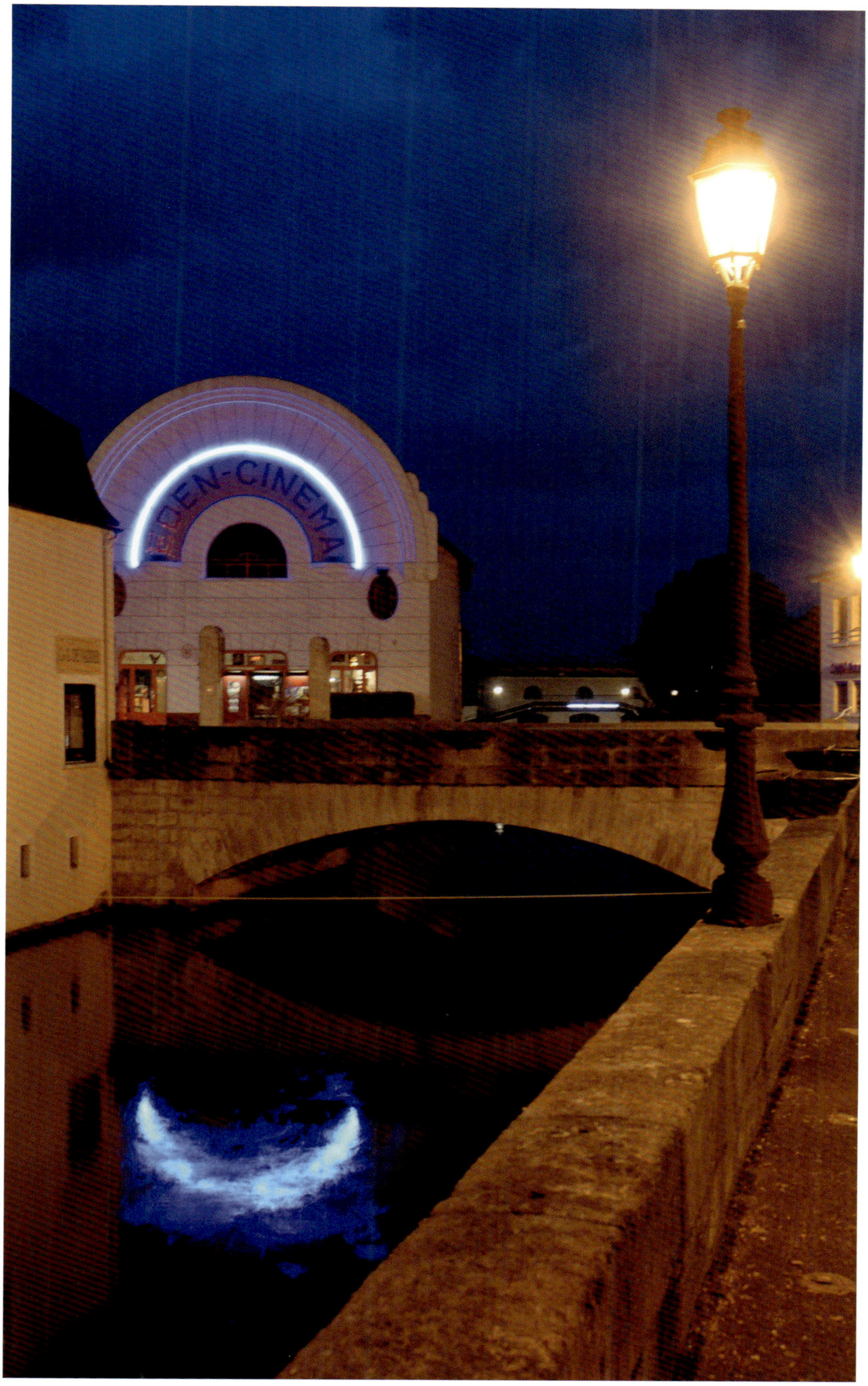

Cosne-Cours-sur-Loire – Éden – 2008

Cosne-Cours-sur-Loire, Éden. The Éden, with its Art Deco façade (1935) and Briare enamel sign, is listed as a historical monument. The beauty of the cinema immersed us in dreams even before taking a seat. Even before seeing the stars taking shape on the screen. Finally seated, elegantly dressed – the show could begin, our daily troubles flew far away. A new life, very brief, was beginning.

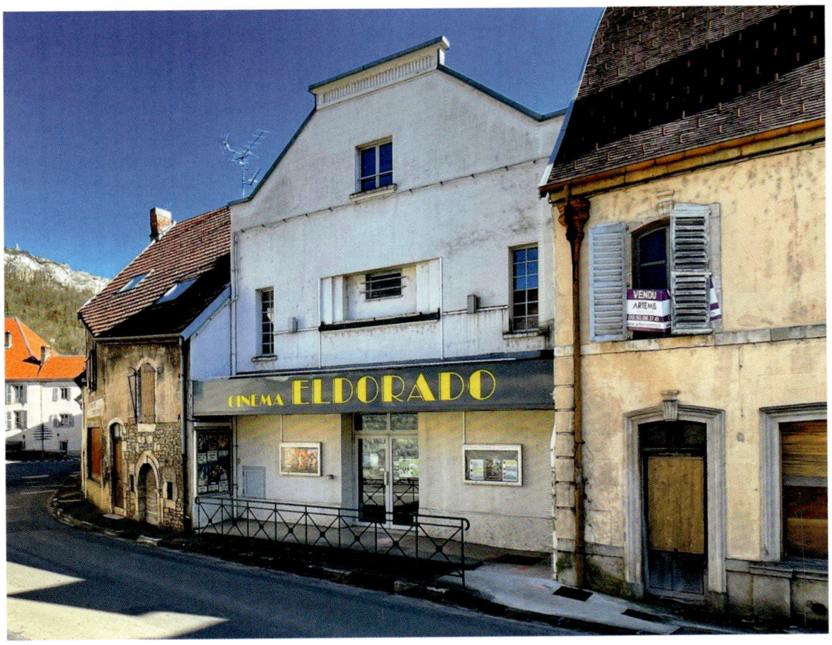

Ornans – Eldorado – 2022

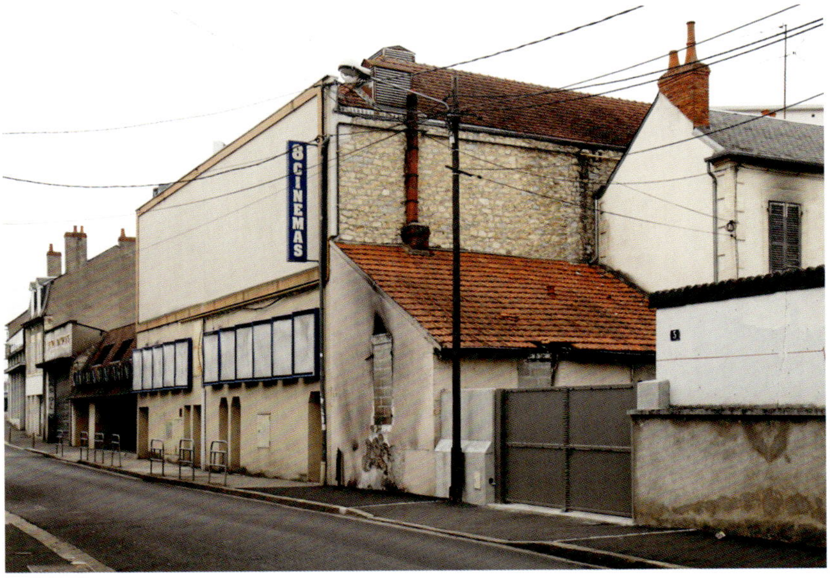

Nevers – Mazarin – 2014

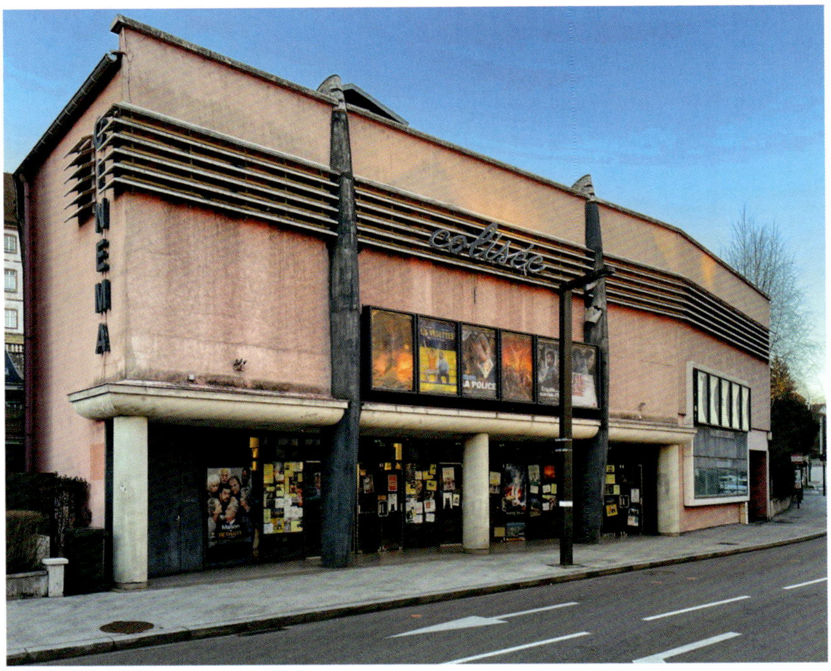

Montbéliard – Colisée – 2022

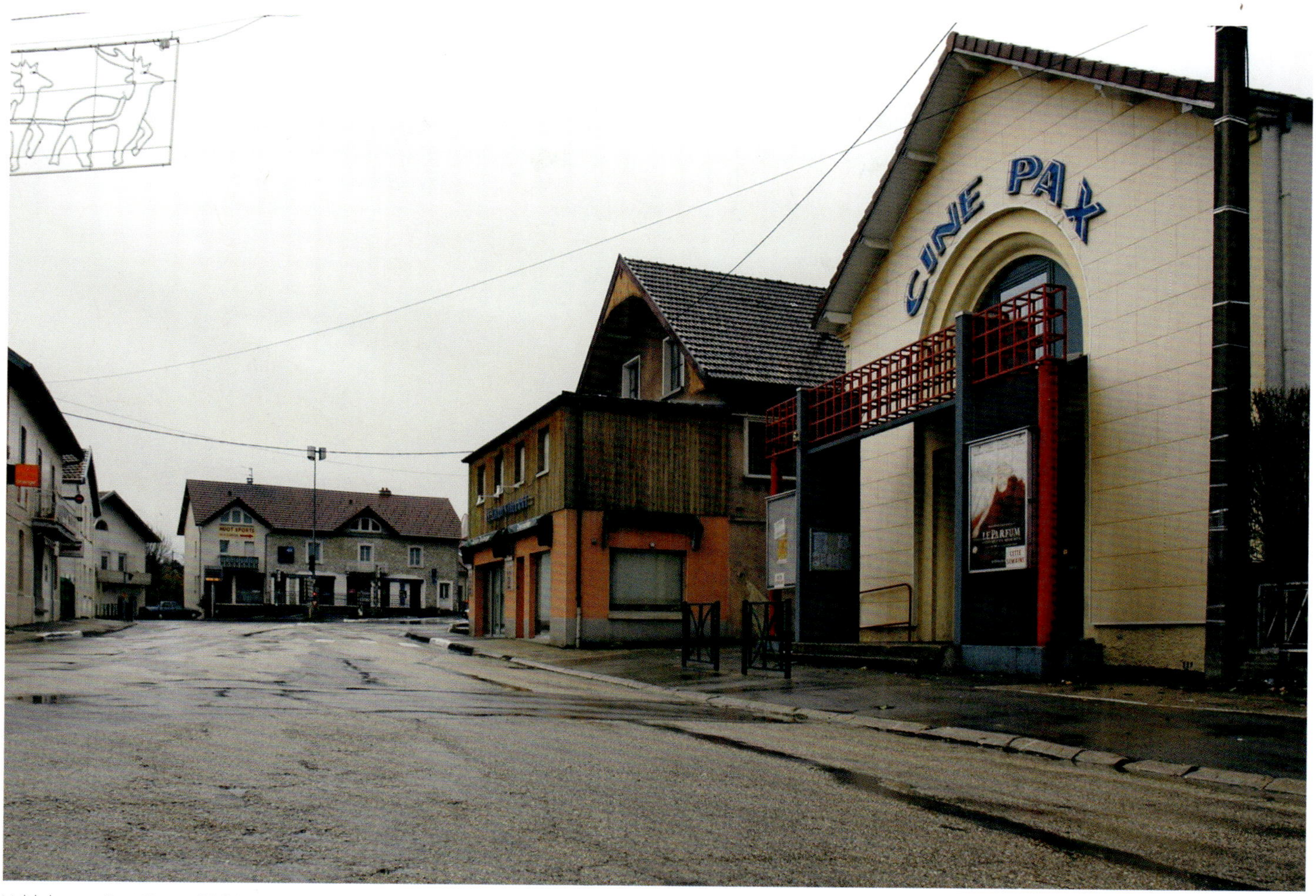

Valdahon – Ciné Pax – 2006

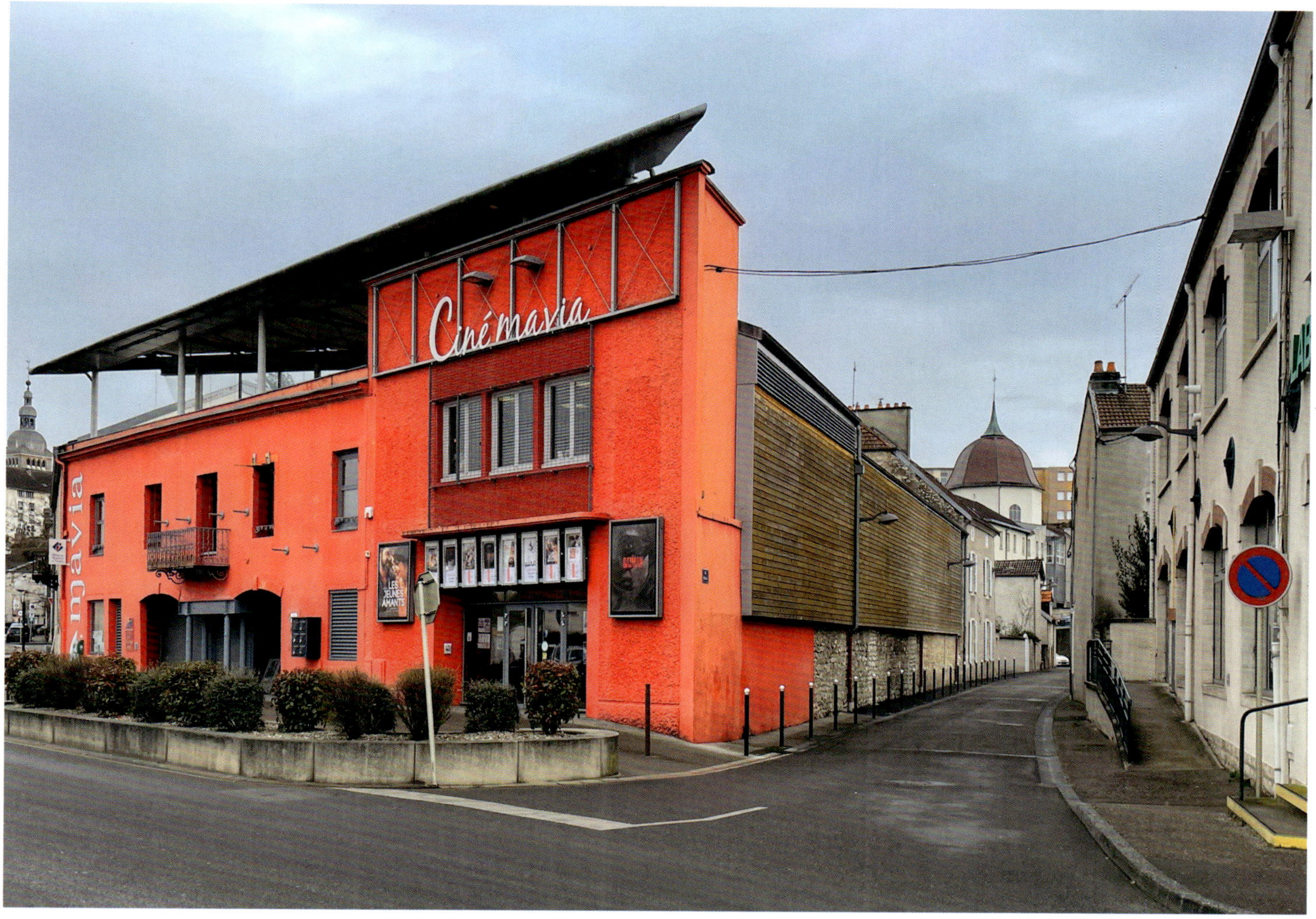

Gray – Ciné Mavia – 2022

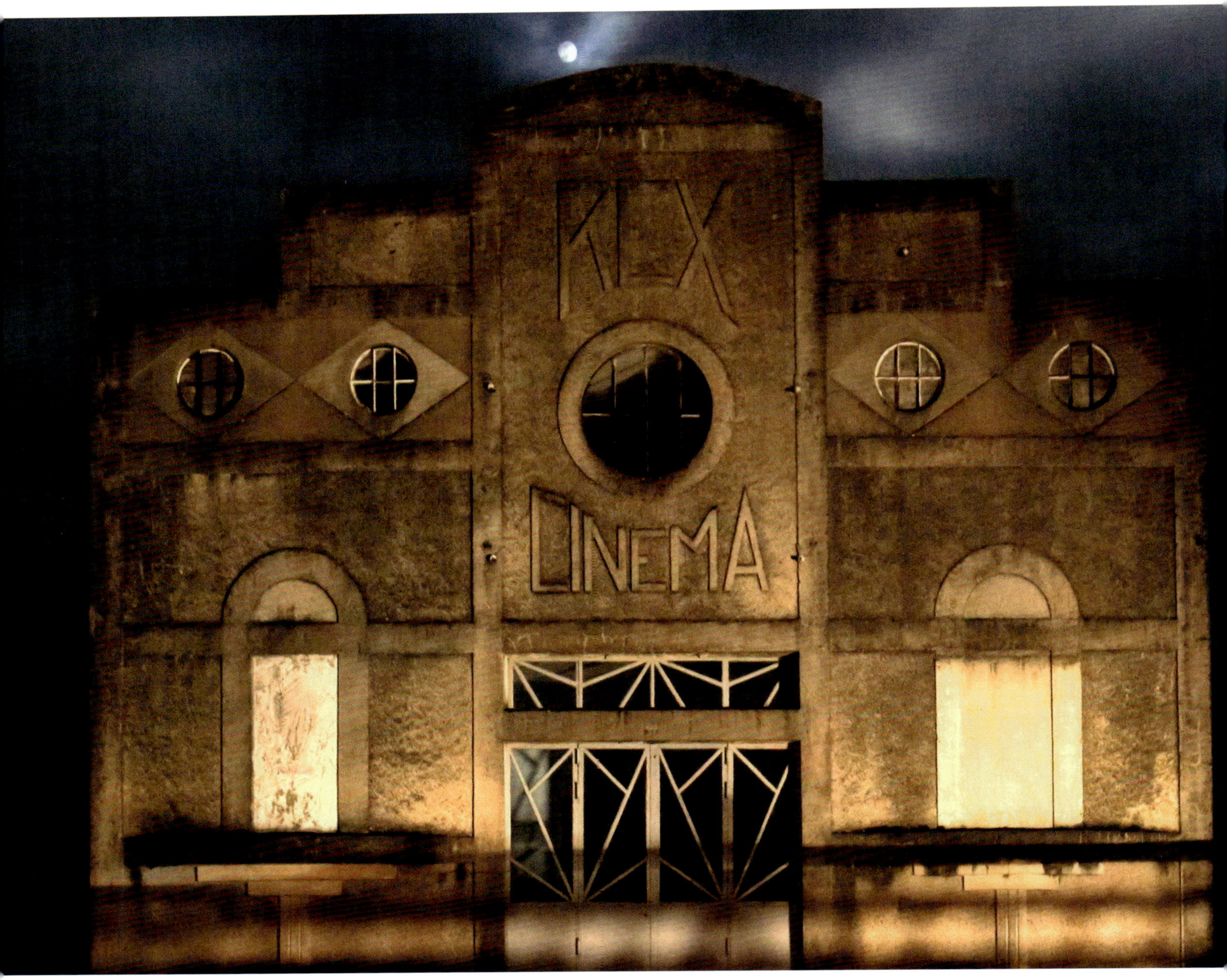

Guérigny, Rex. The life of a cinema is sometimes short, with the occasional dream of rebirth. The Rex at Guérigny began to show movies in 1950 and stopped in 1968. With its creaking seats the cinema replaced the church, which was being renovated at the end of the 1970s, allowing the faithful to meditate … Close to God, to Marilyn or Fred Astaire, depending on their beliefs. This place is now part of our heritage. With the asbestos removed, it sometimes becomes a cinema again.

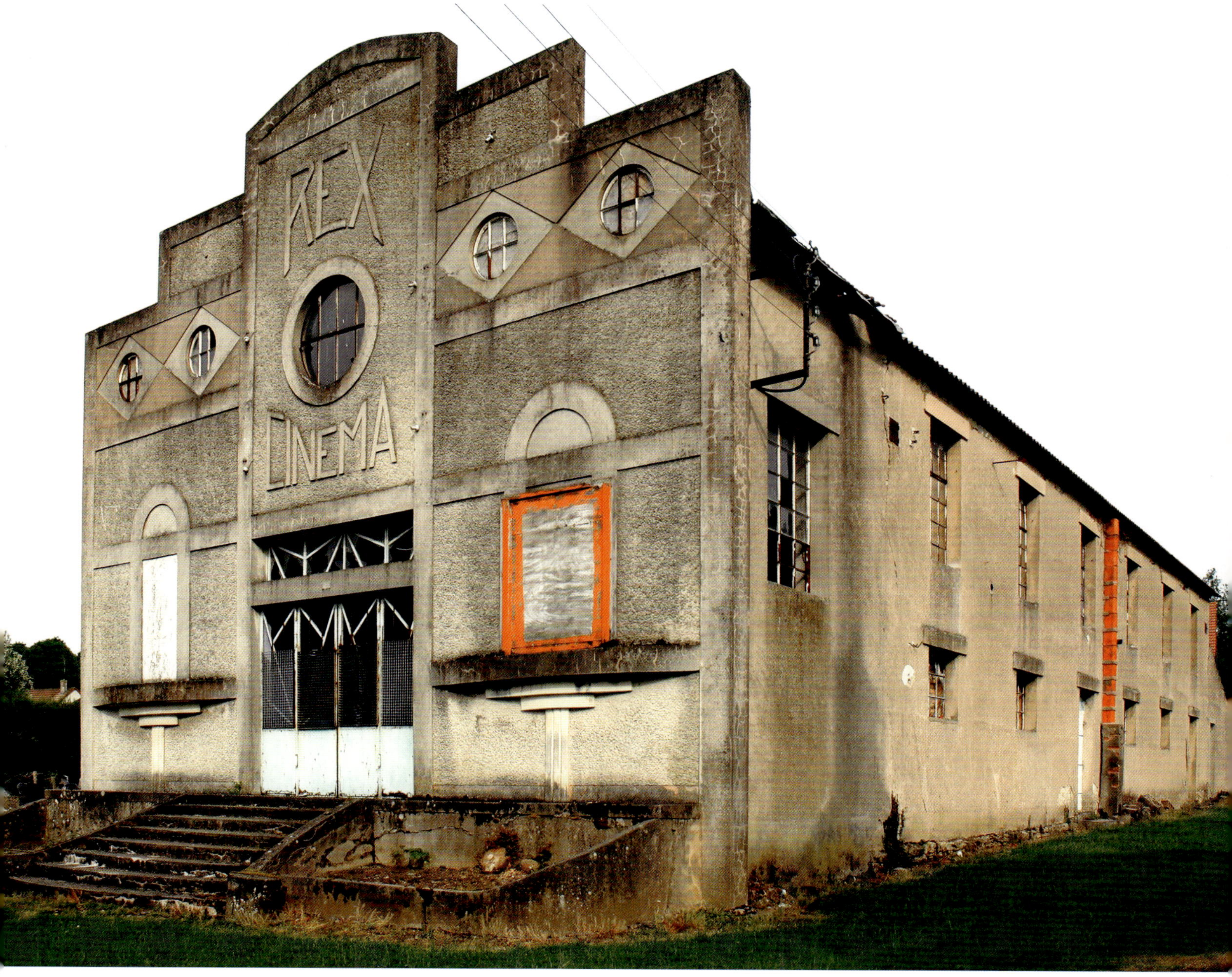

Guérigny – Rex – 2018

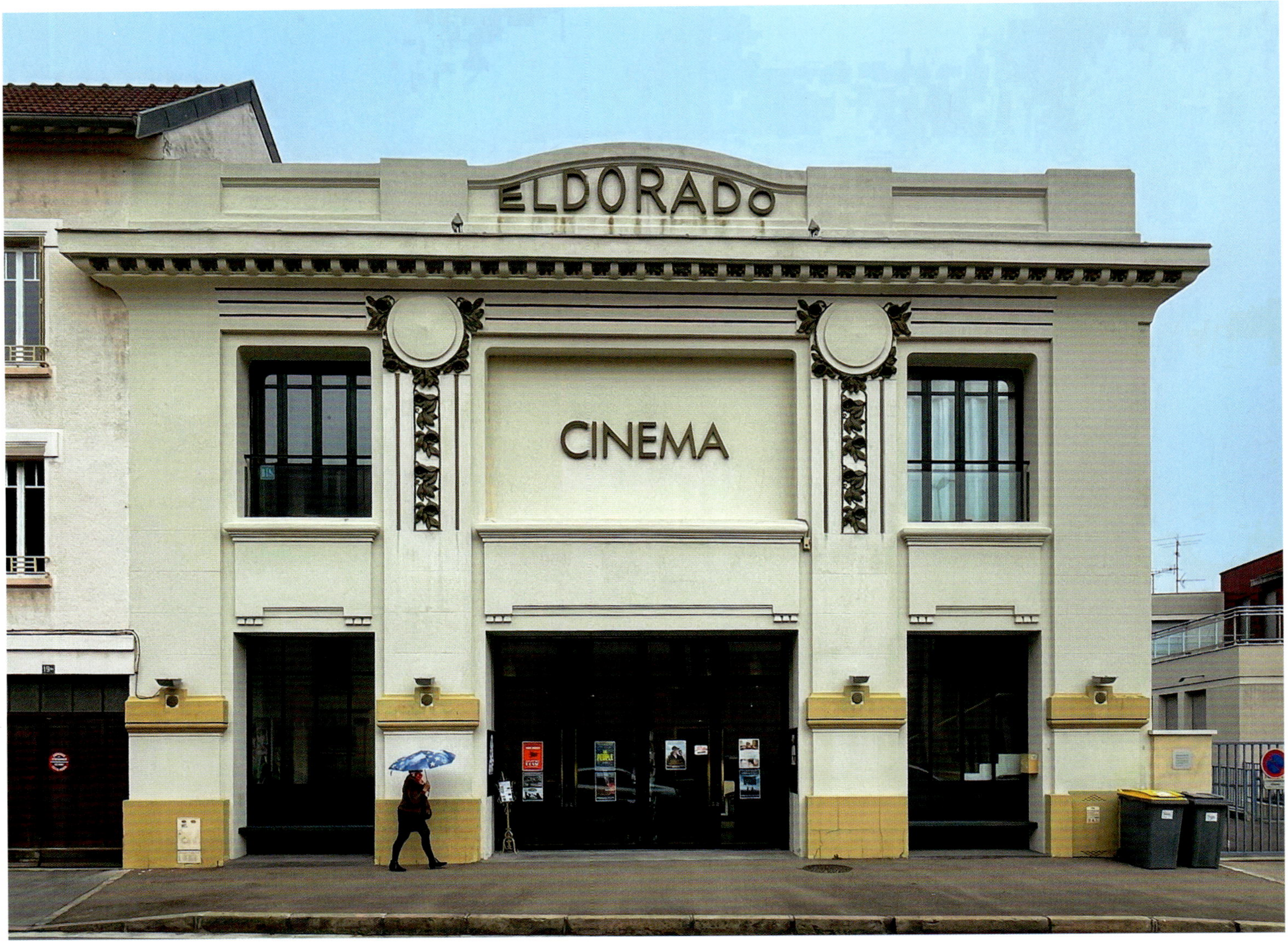

Dijon – Eldorado – 2022

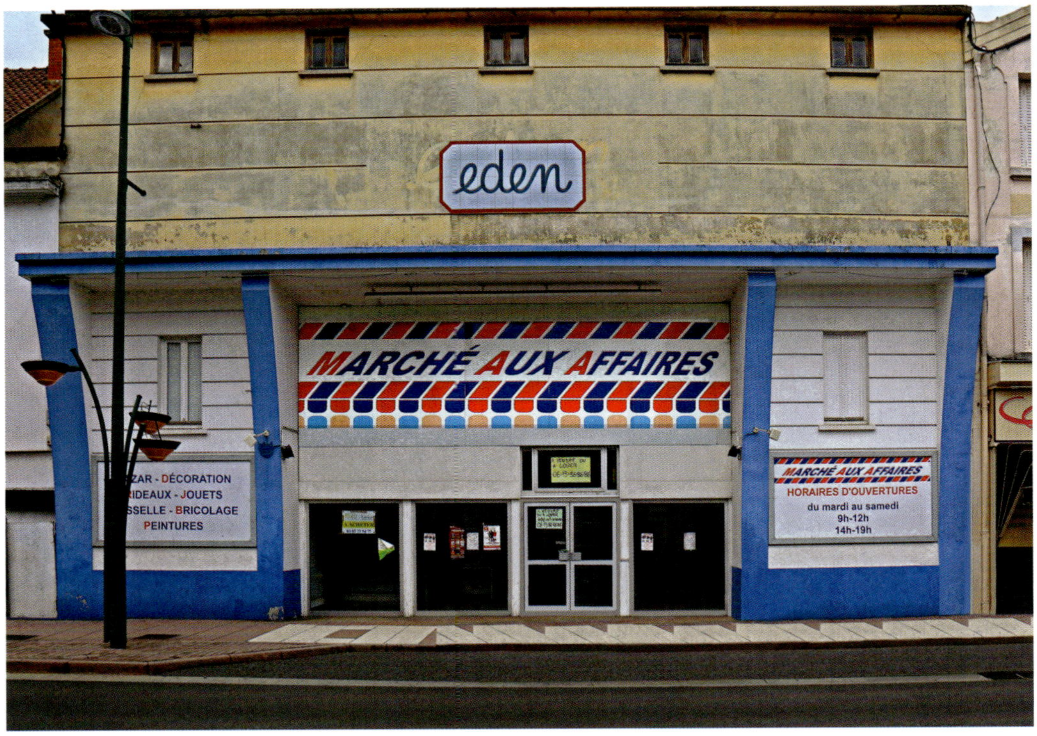

Le Creusot – Eden – 2015

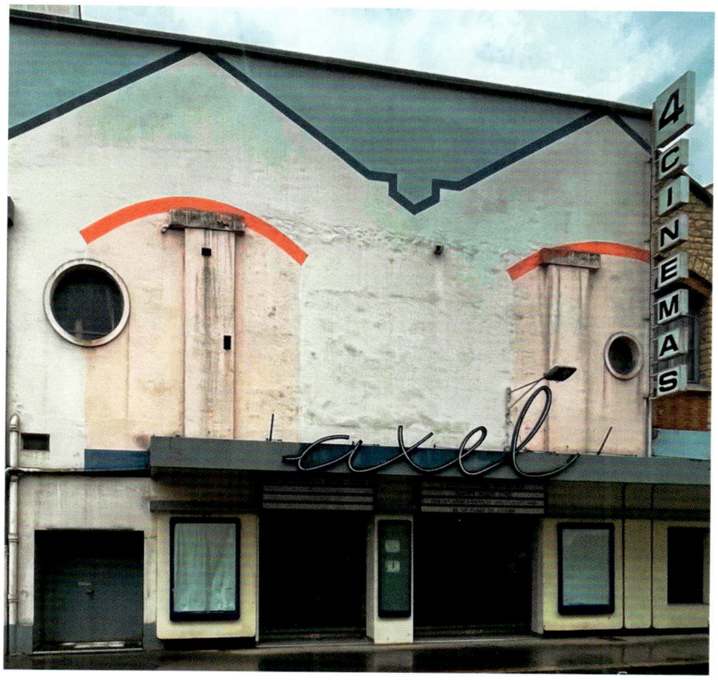

Chalon-sur-Saône – Axel – 2021

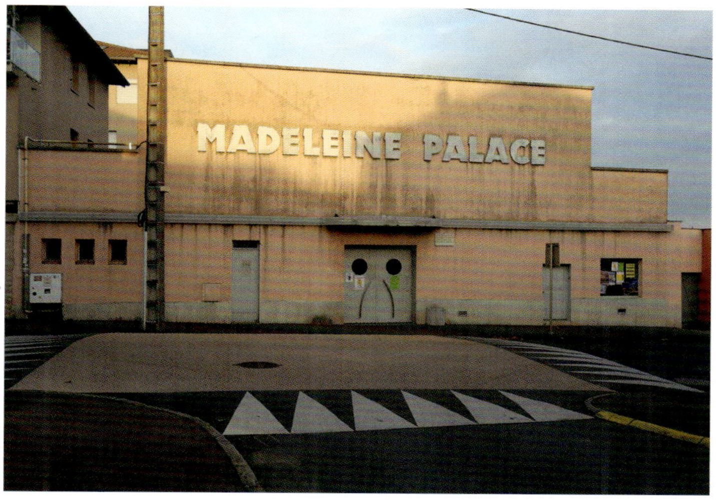

Tournus – Madeleine Palace – 2015

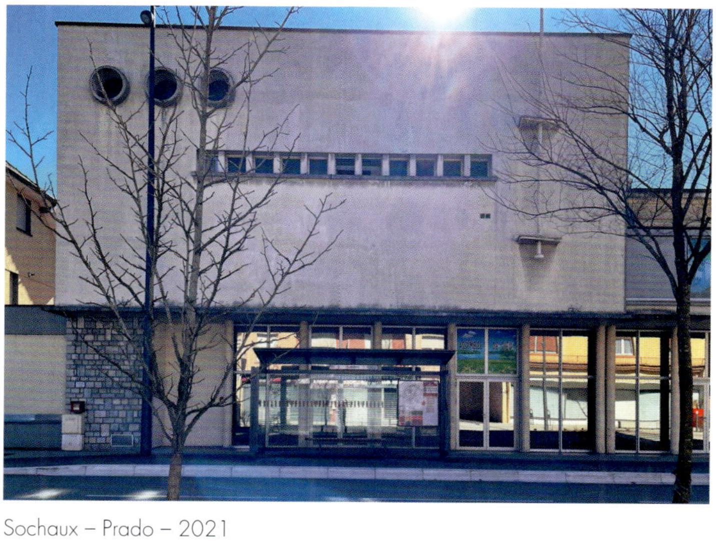

Sochaux – Prado – 2021

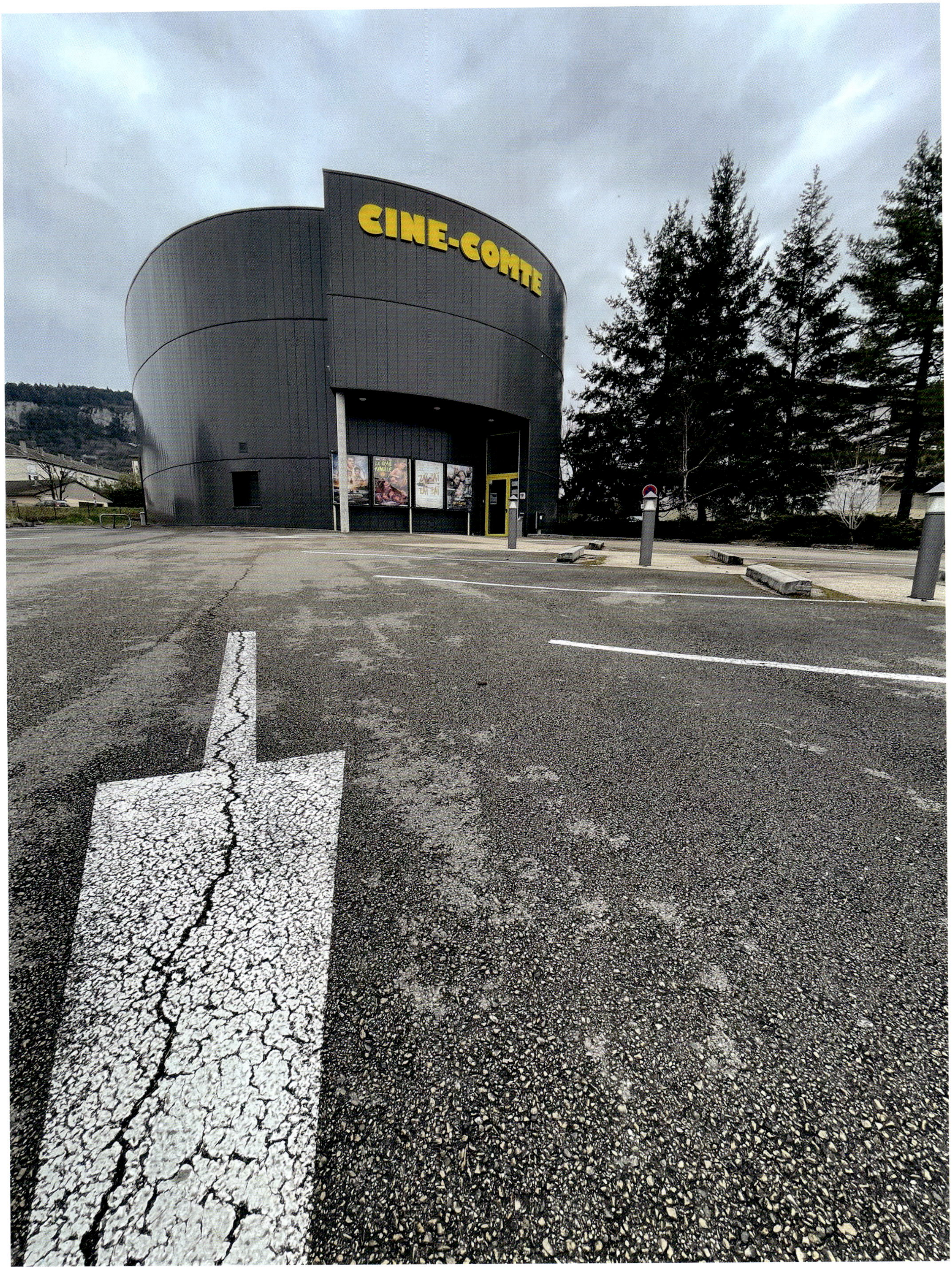

Poligny – Ciné-Comté – 2021

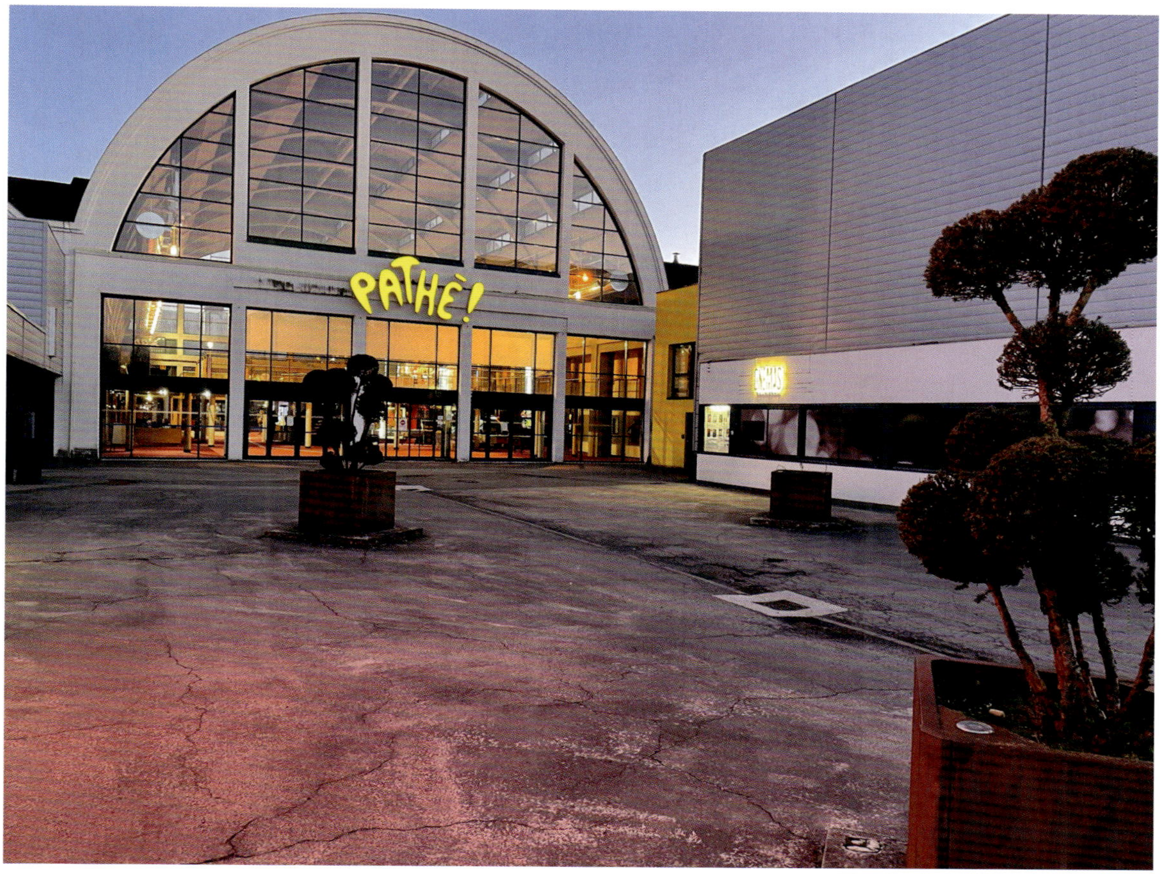

Belfort – Pathé – 2021

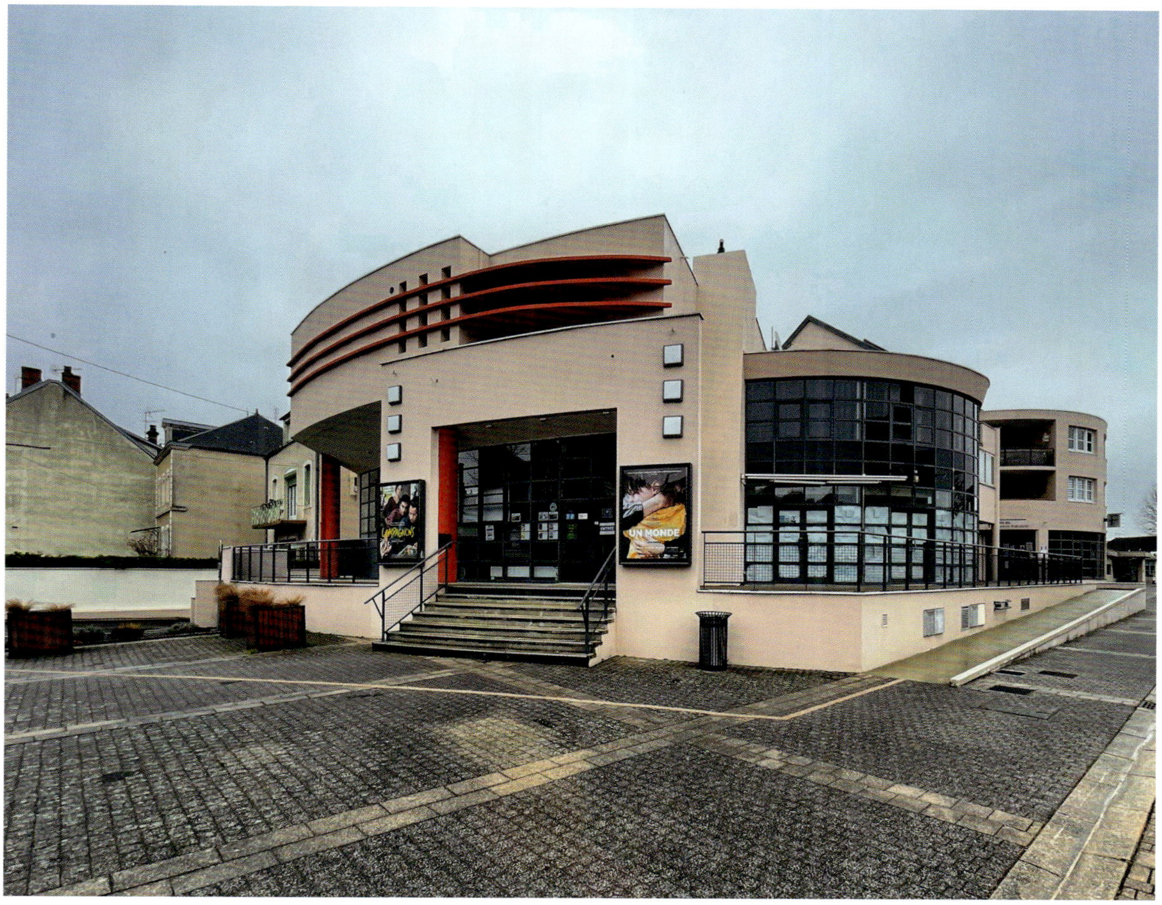

Montbard – Le Phénix – 2021

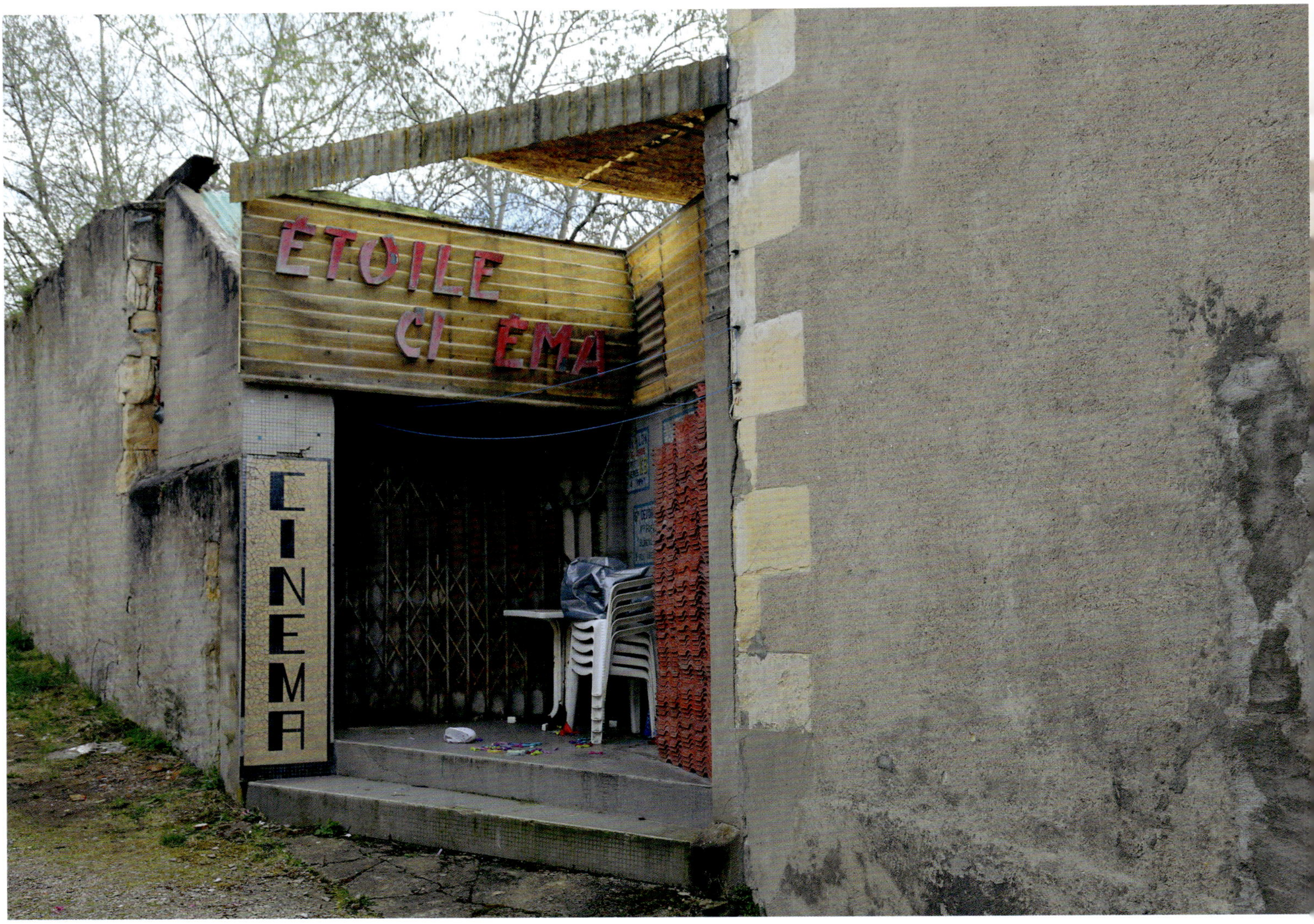

Imphy – Cinéma Étoile – 2018

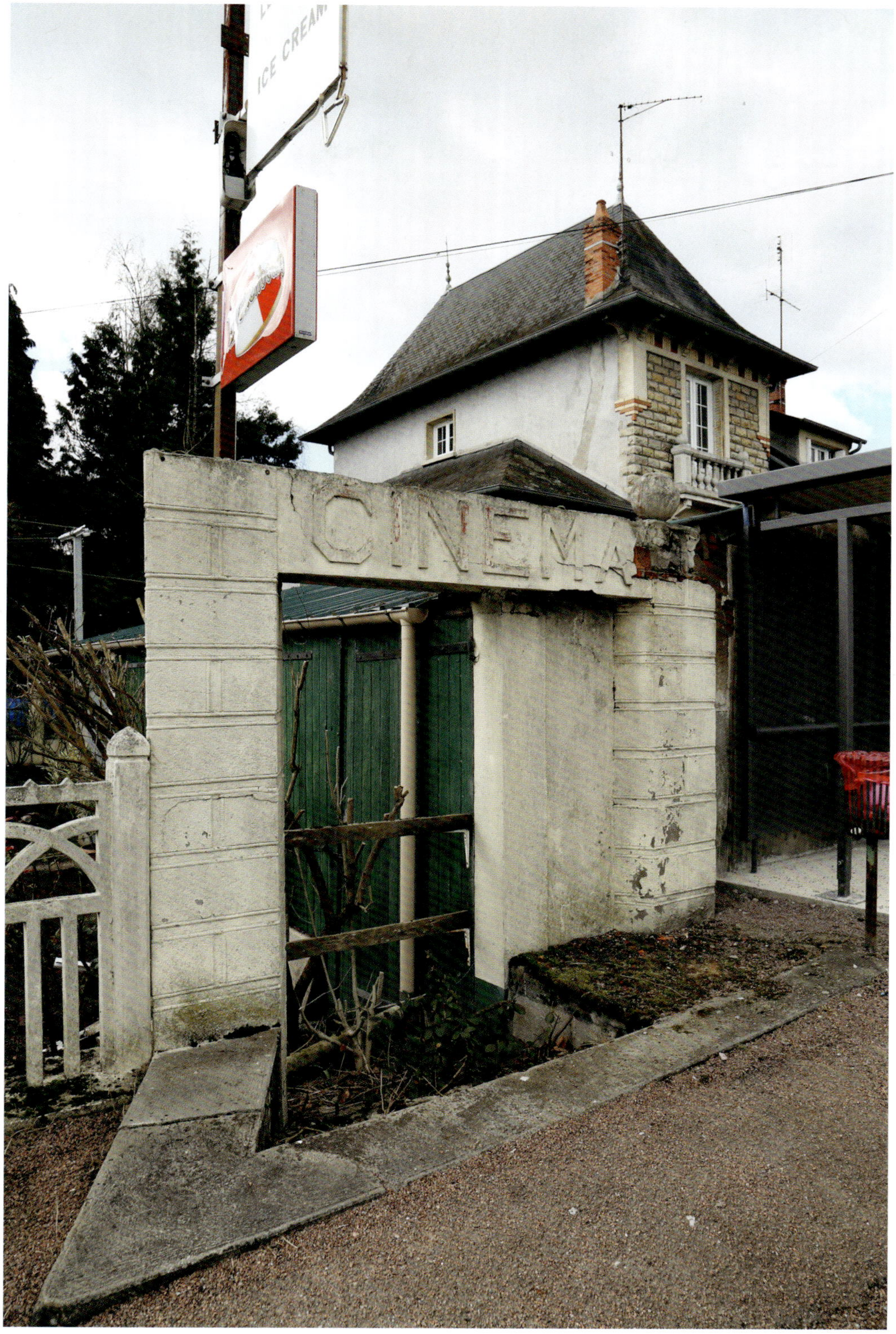

Prémery – Cinéma – 2018

Prémery, Cinéma. Only the word 'cinema' remains, engraved in stone on a section of the wall, miraculously preserved like a final trace of an unknown civilisation now given over to residential buildings. Only our imagination can reconstruct its façade, a hall, wooden seats that have grown creaky over the years, a charming usher, a vigilant cashier and films with titles such as *Nous irons à Paris* (*We will go to Paris*), with Françoise Arnoul, whose silhouette used to send shivers down the spine of those taking their first taste of love.

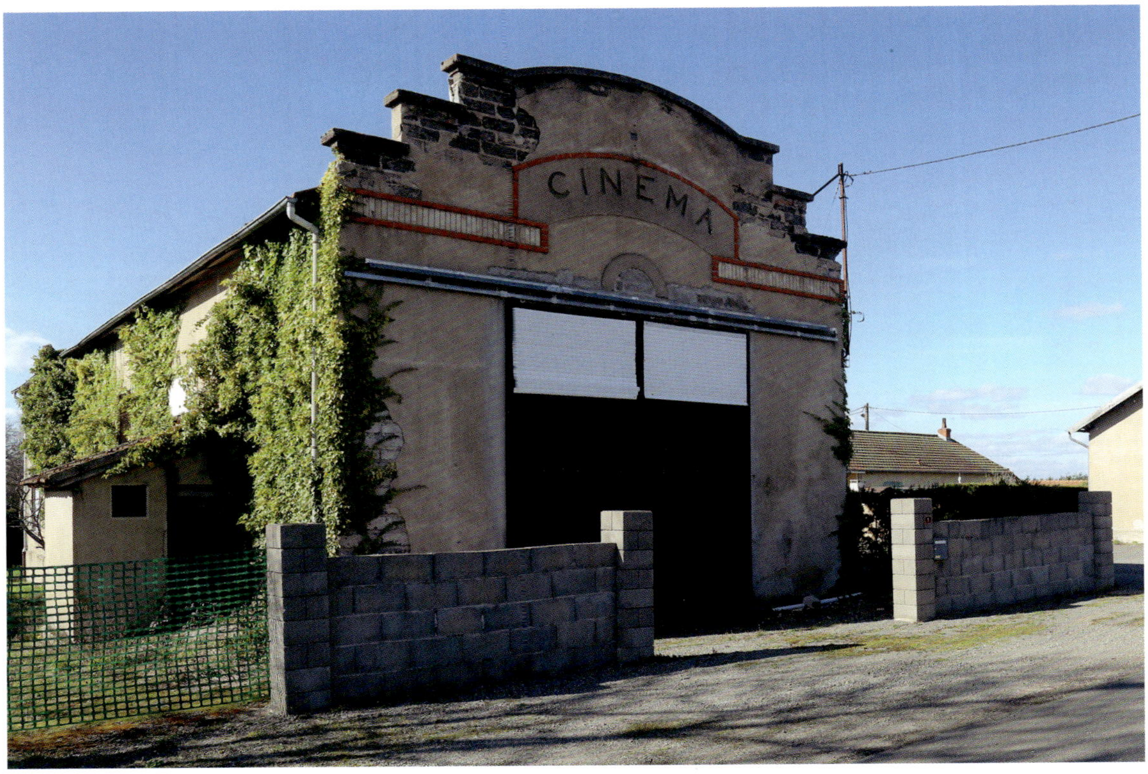

Chalmoux – Cinéma – 2018

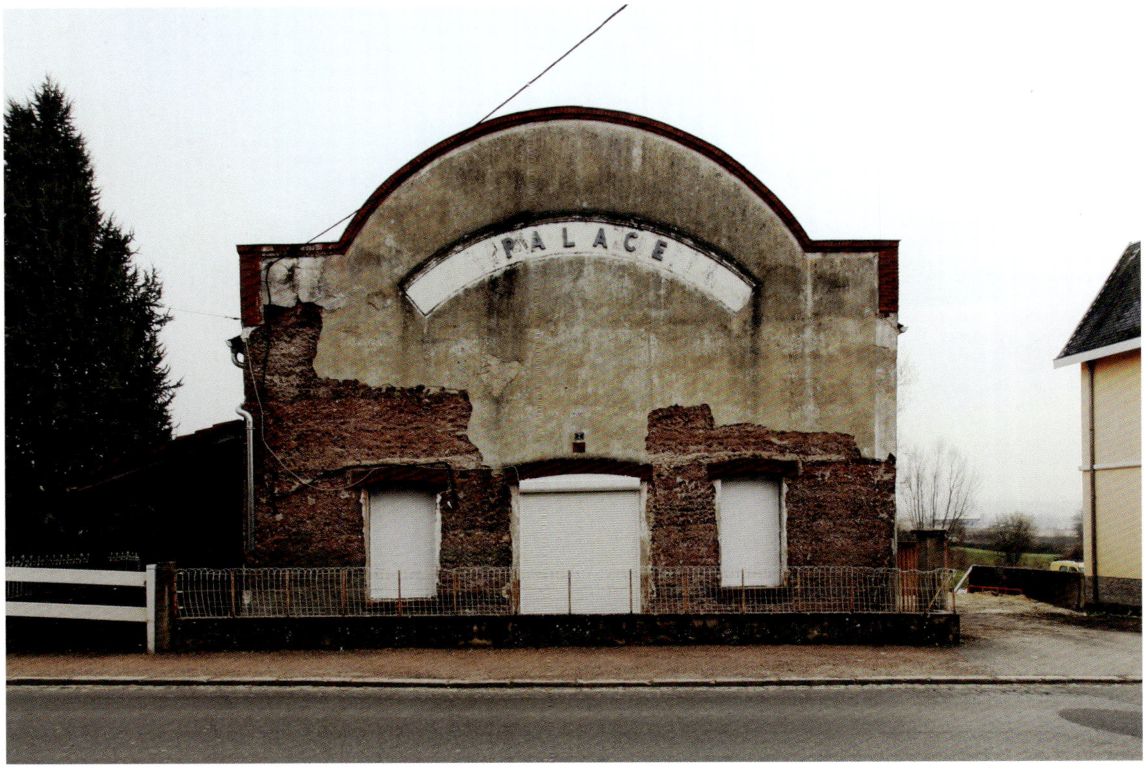

Montceau-les-Mines – Palace – 2014

Montceau-les-Mines, Palace. What remains of a cinema converted into a residence? A balcony? Posters? A projector? A few seats? Usually nothing. A story erased, wiped from the memory of movie-lovers ... Sometimes, all the same, the name of the cinema. Fortunately.

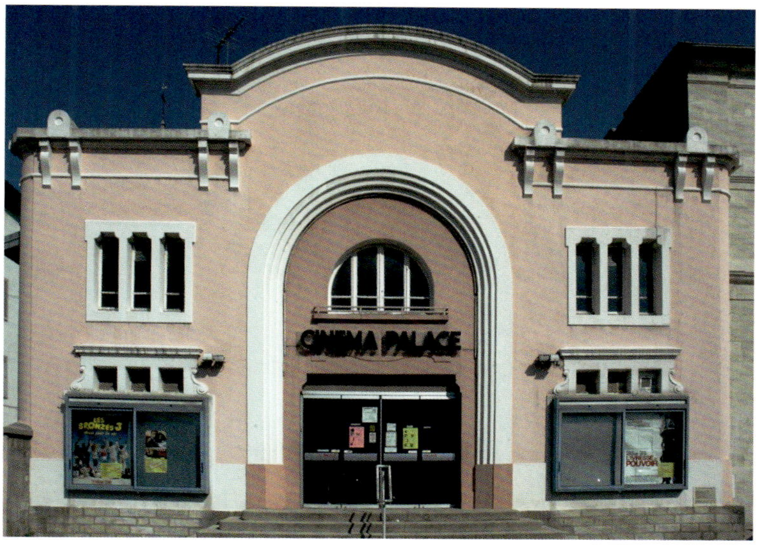

Lons-le-Saunier – Cinéma Palace – 2006

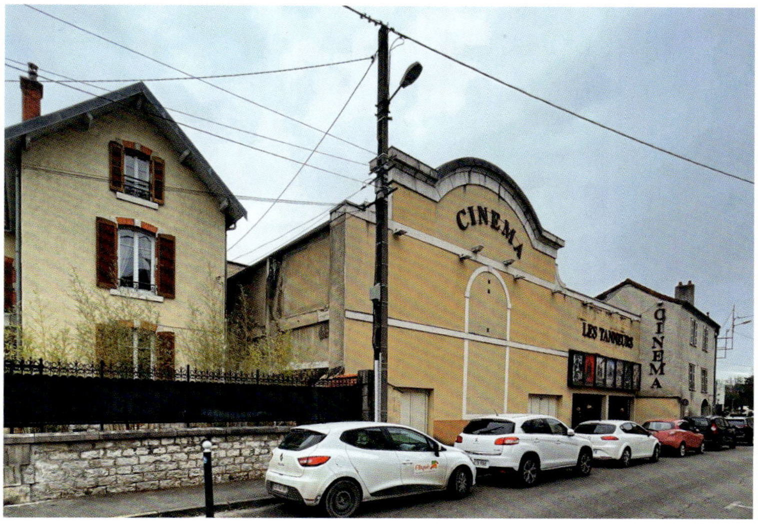

Dôle – Les Tanneurs – 2022

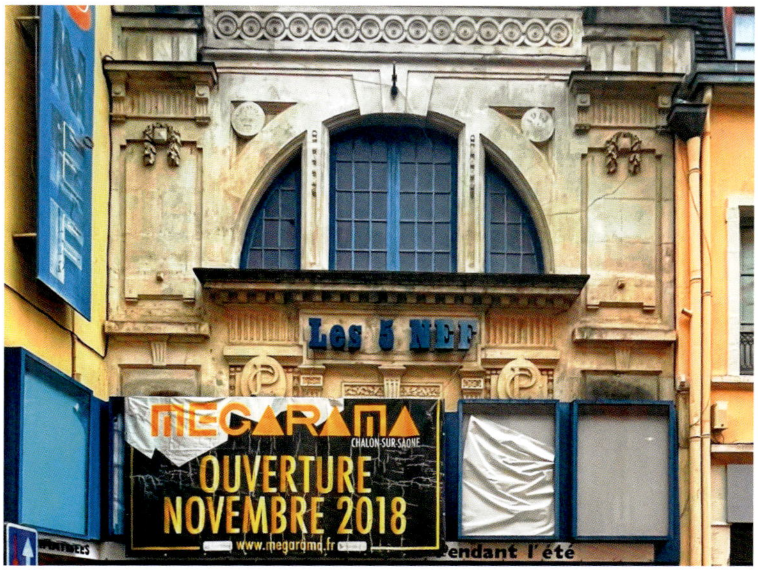

Chalon-sur-Saône – Les 5 Nef – 2022

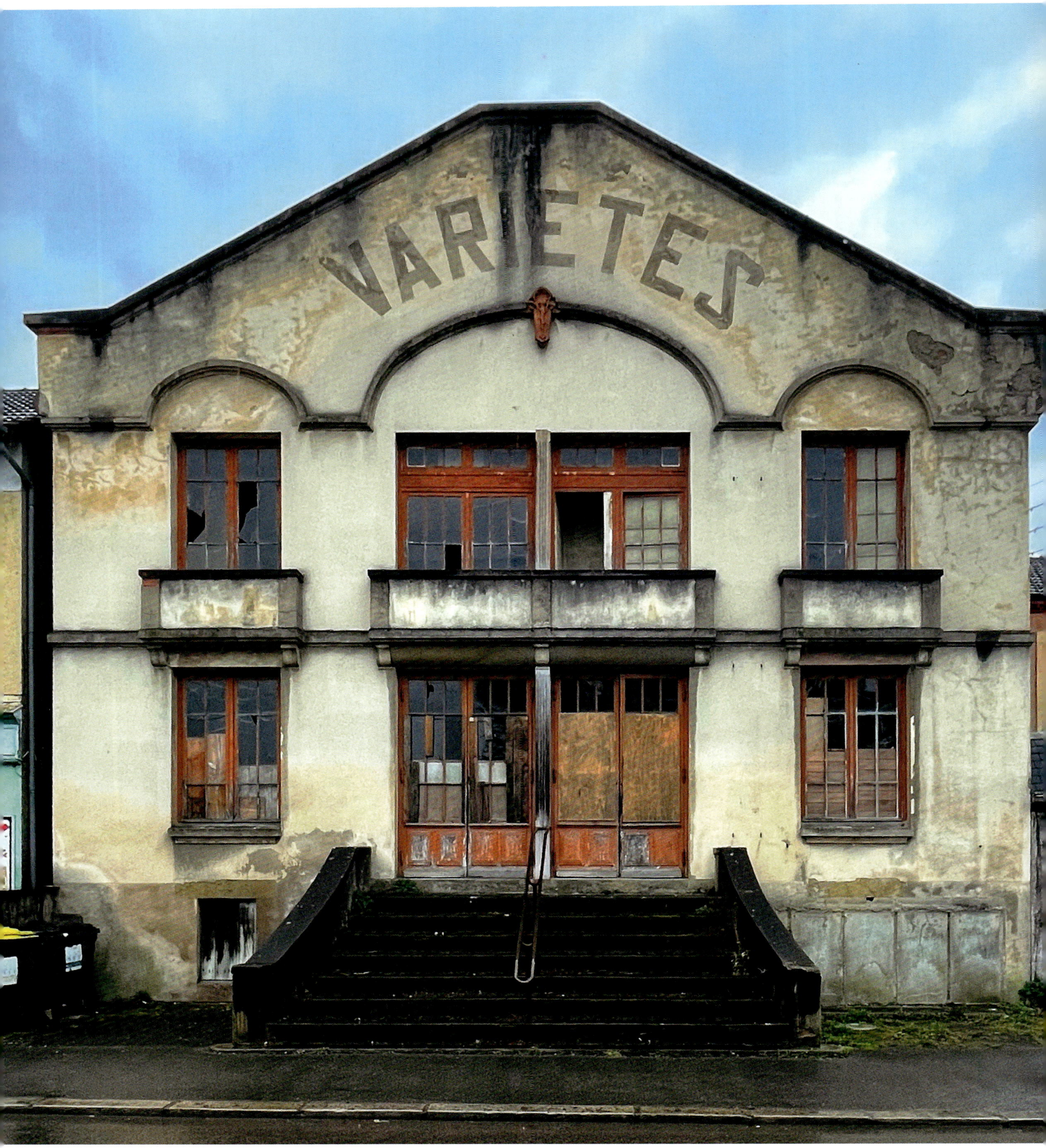

Montchanin – Variétés – 2021

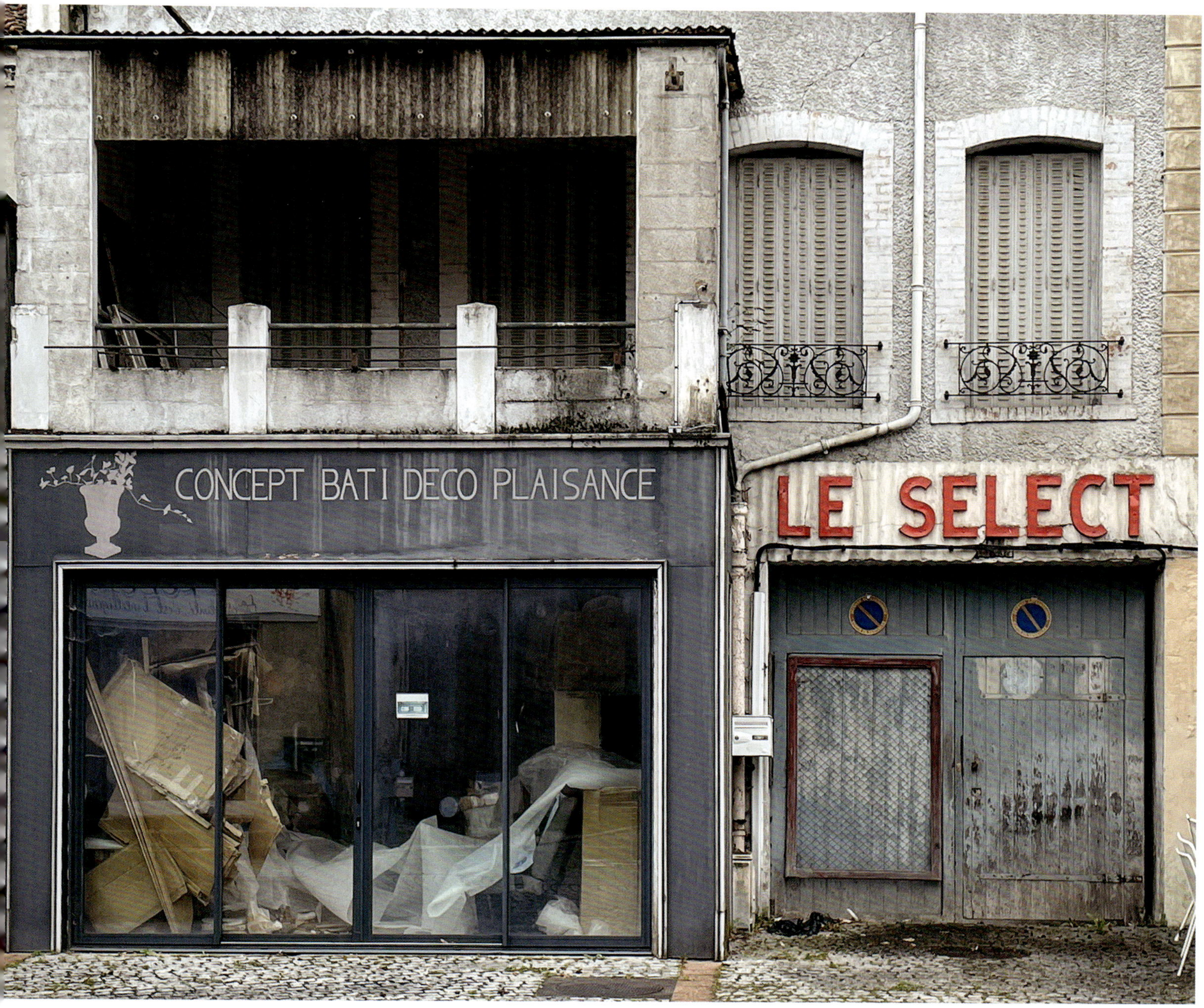

narey-les-Laumes – Le Select – 2022

Venarey-les-Laumes, Le Select. I stroll around Venarey-les-Laumes, guided by vague details on finding a trace of the Select. A difficult mission. Nobody seems to remember it. Doubt sets in … what if this cinema had never existed? Demolished, maybe. Obstinately I walk up and down each street. Suddenly an apparition appears before me, almost religious, admittedly a bit modest, a somewhat vague sketch depending on how hard I look. A sign degraded by the passage of time, the indifference of the few passers-by, but for me of an almost mystical beauty.

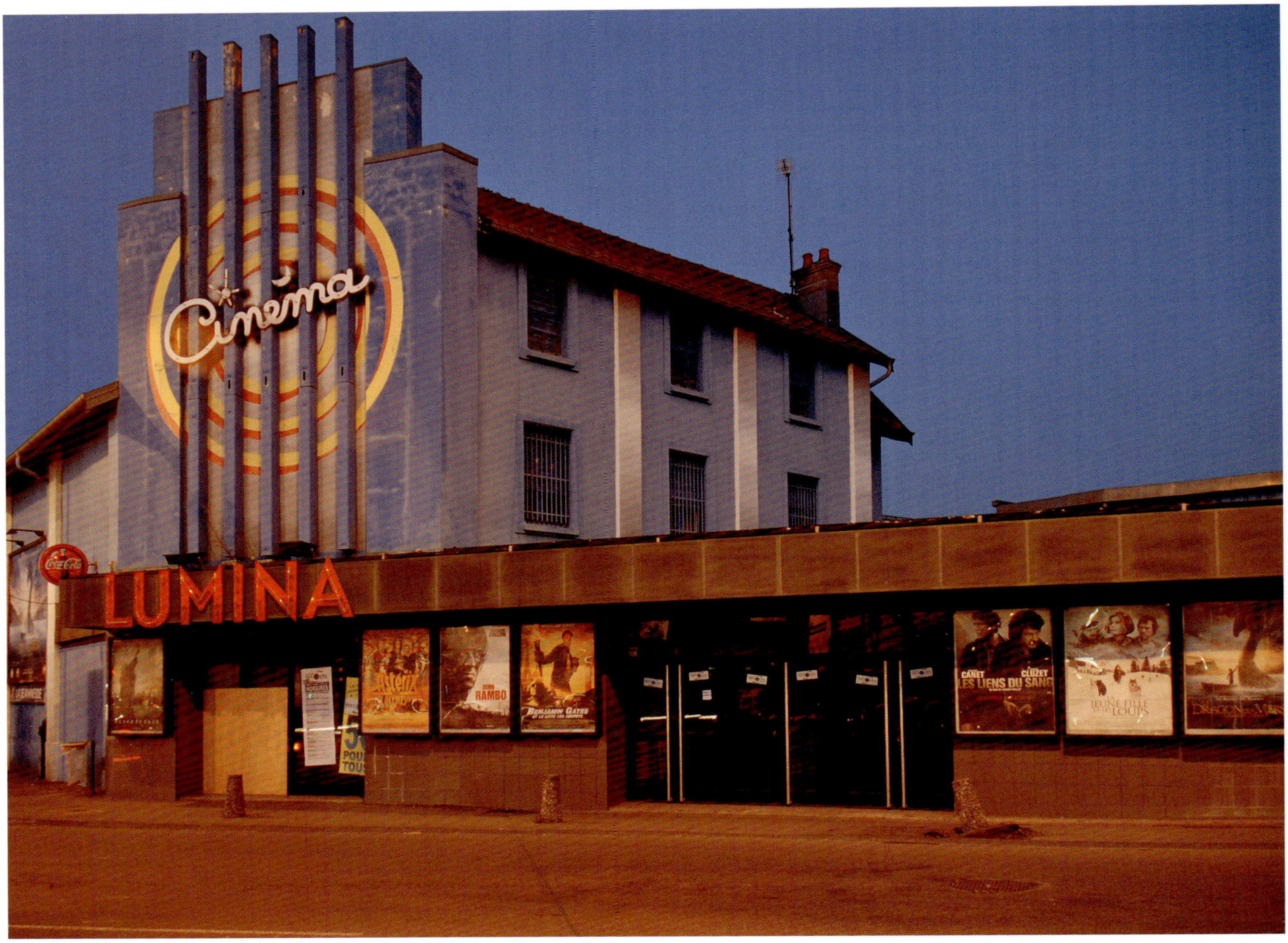

Audincourt – Cinéma Lumina – 2008 (destroyed)

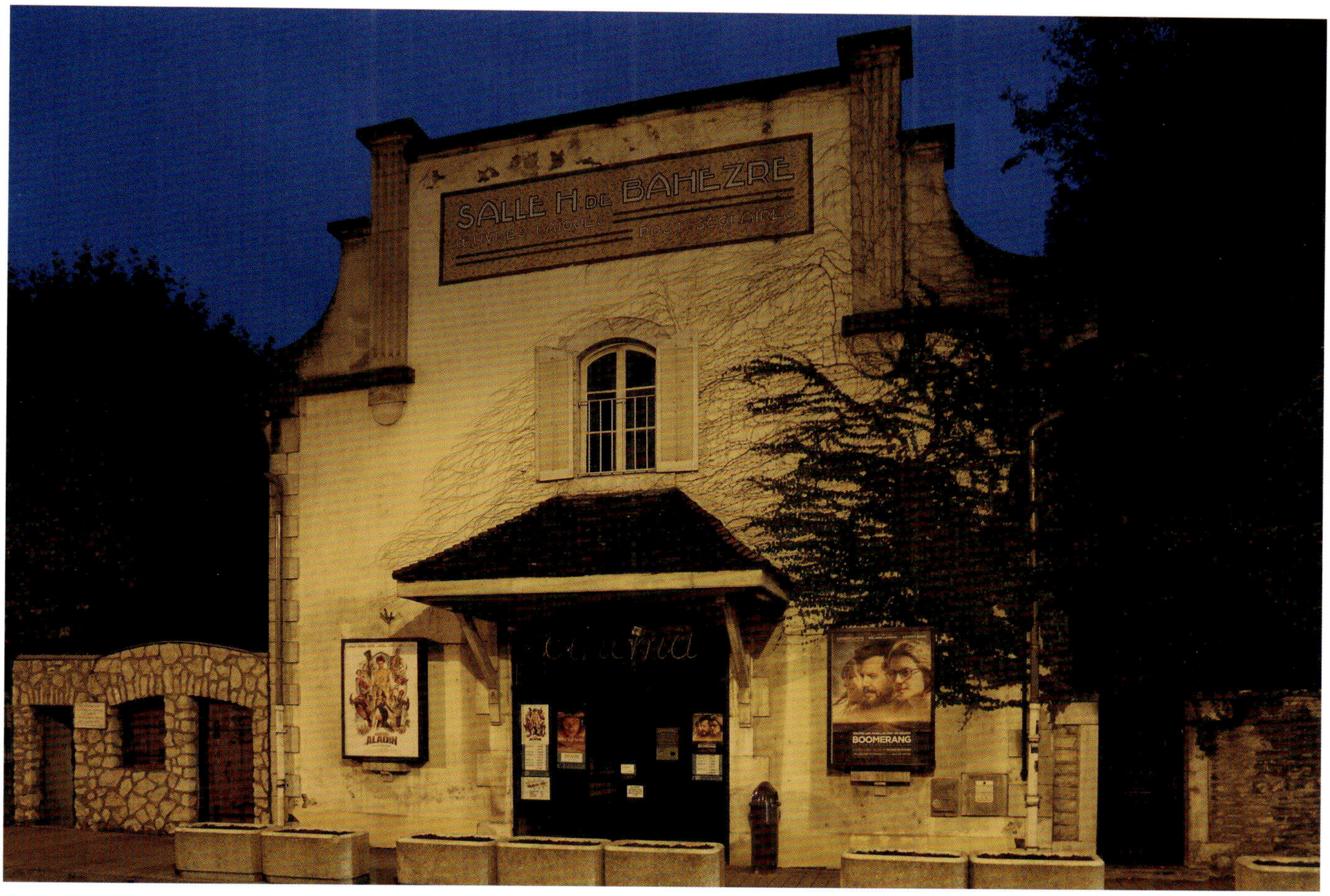

Nuits-Saint-Georges – Nuiton – 2015

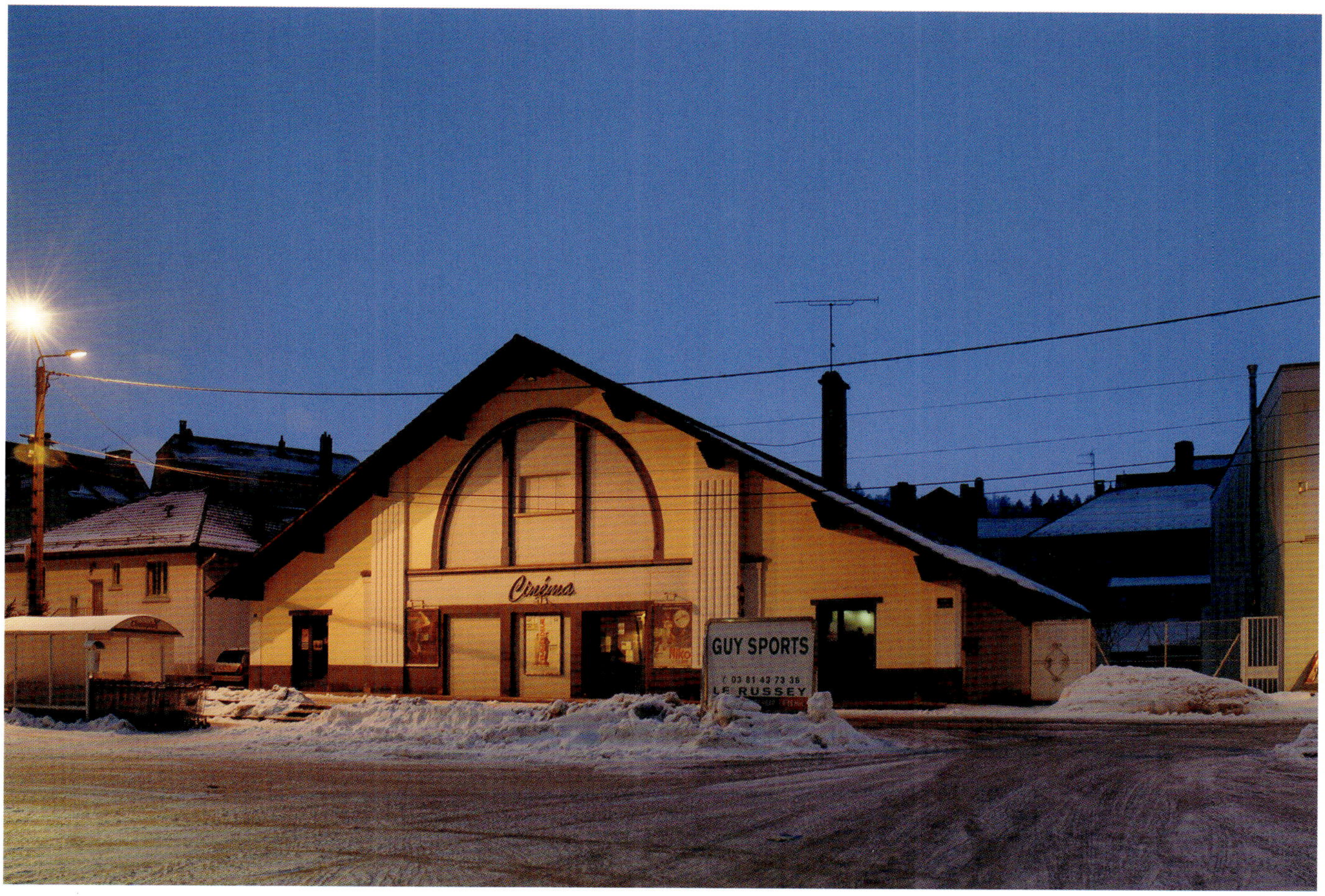

Maiche – Cinéma Saint Michel – 2009

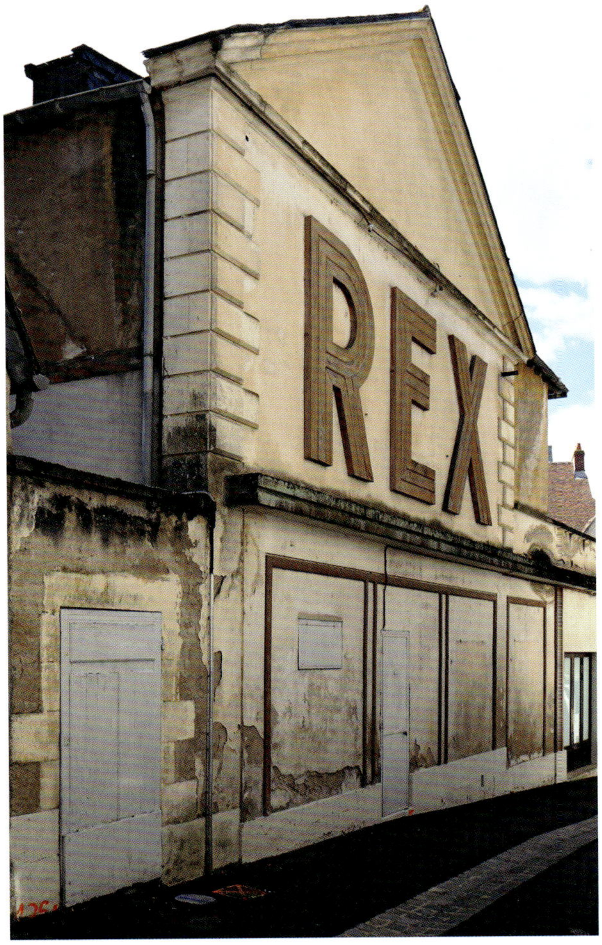

La-Charité-sur-Loire – Rex – 2018

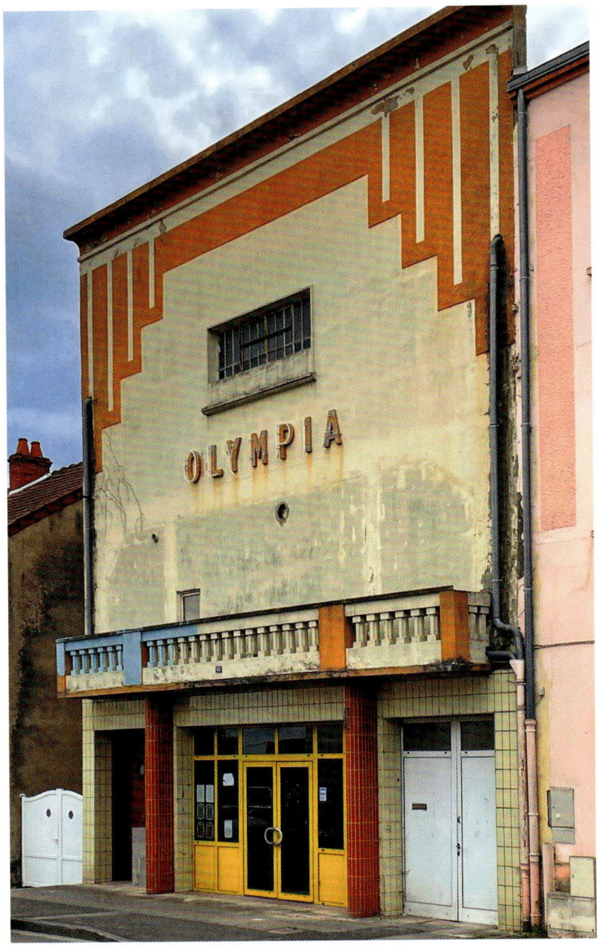

Saint–Vallier – Olympia – 2022

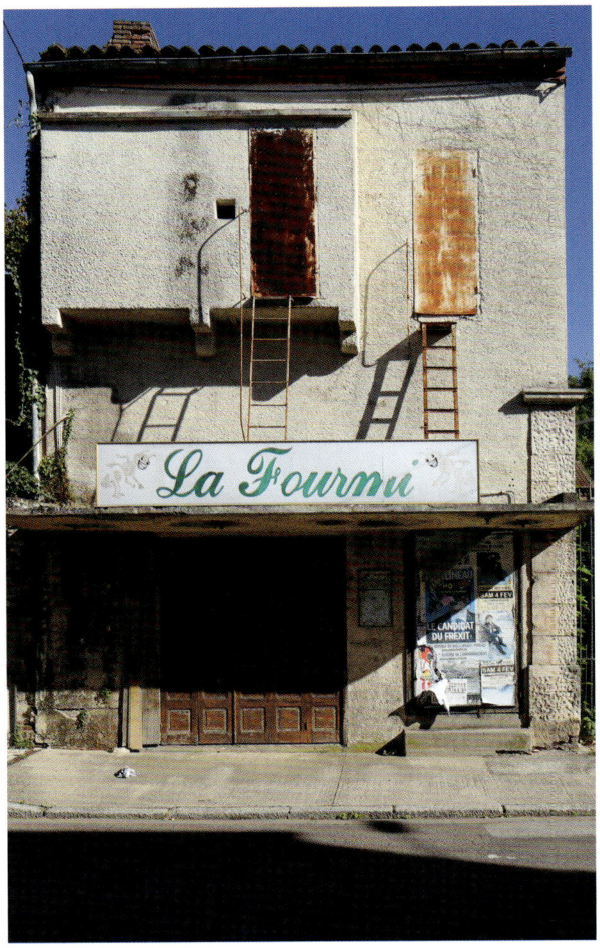

Seurre – La Fourmi – 2018

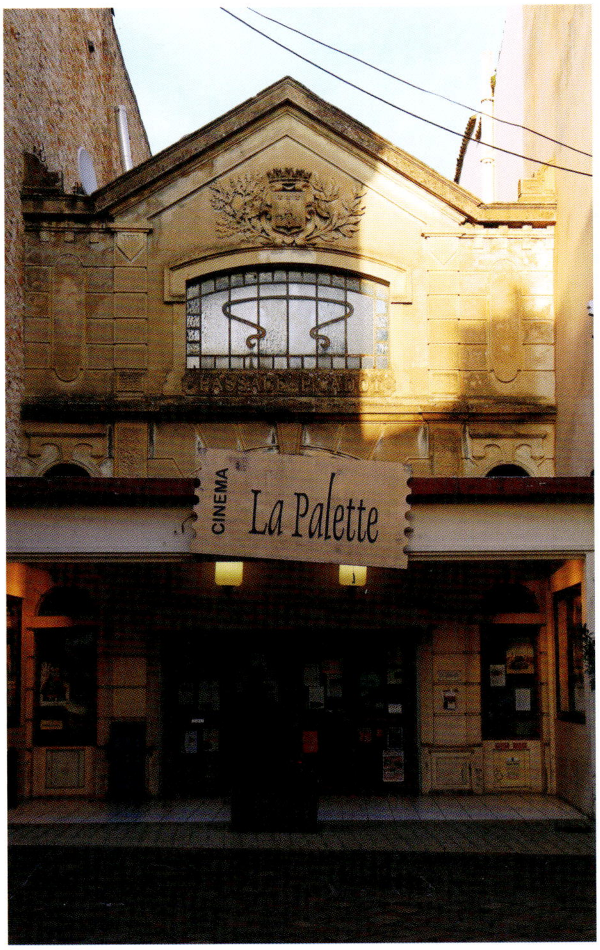

Tournus – La Palette – 2015

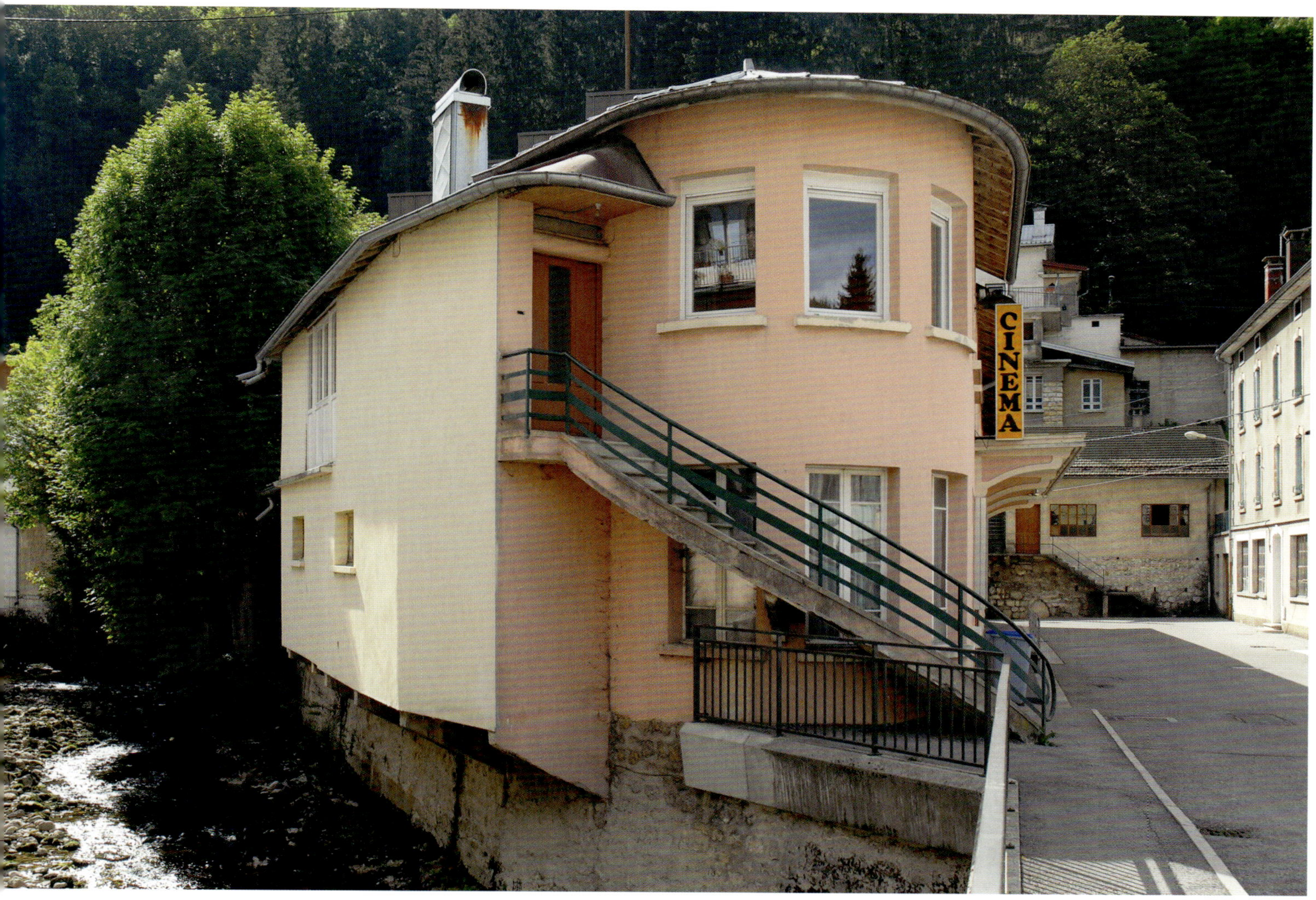

Morez – Cinéma Casino – 2007

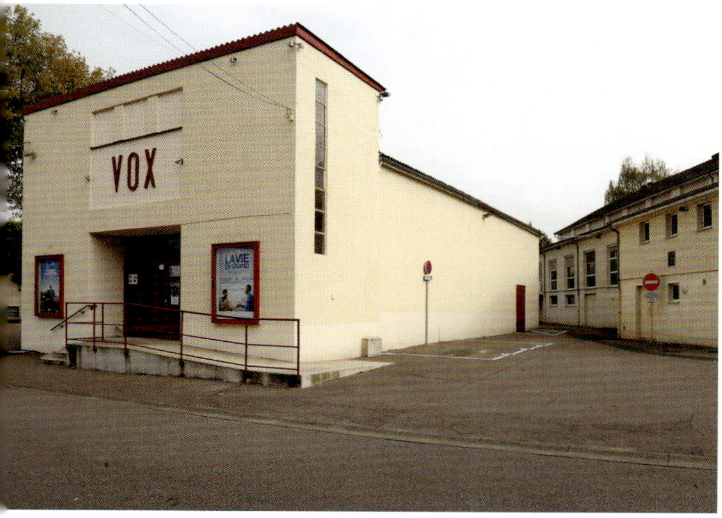

uzy – Vox – 2015

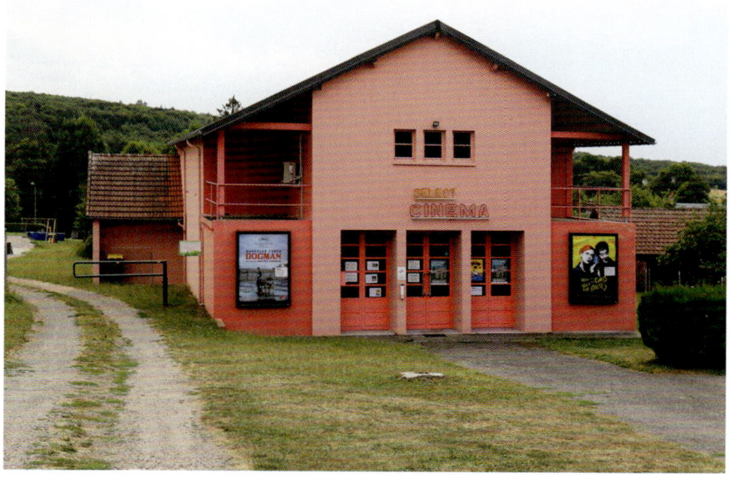

Saint-Honoré-les-Bains – Select Cinéma – 2018

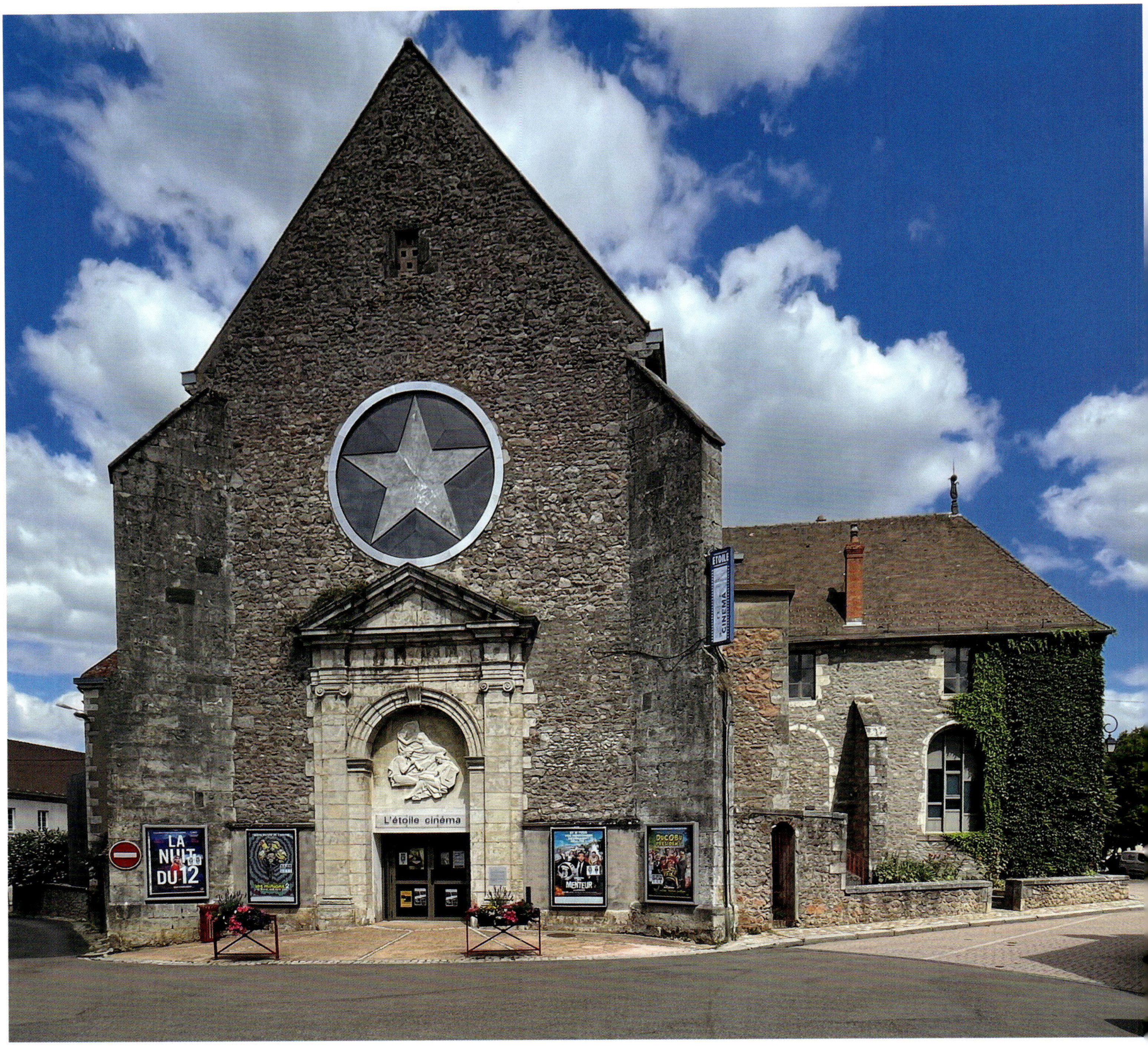

Saulieu – L'Étoile – 2022

Saulieu, L'Étoile. The Étoile cinema is located in what used to be the Ursulines convent chapel (1624). Being a movie-lover is a religion like anything you can practise in a church, all the more easily since the worshippers have left. Perhaps tired of the clergy's message, which they find as boring as a bad movie.

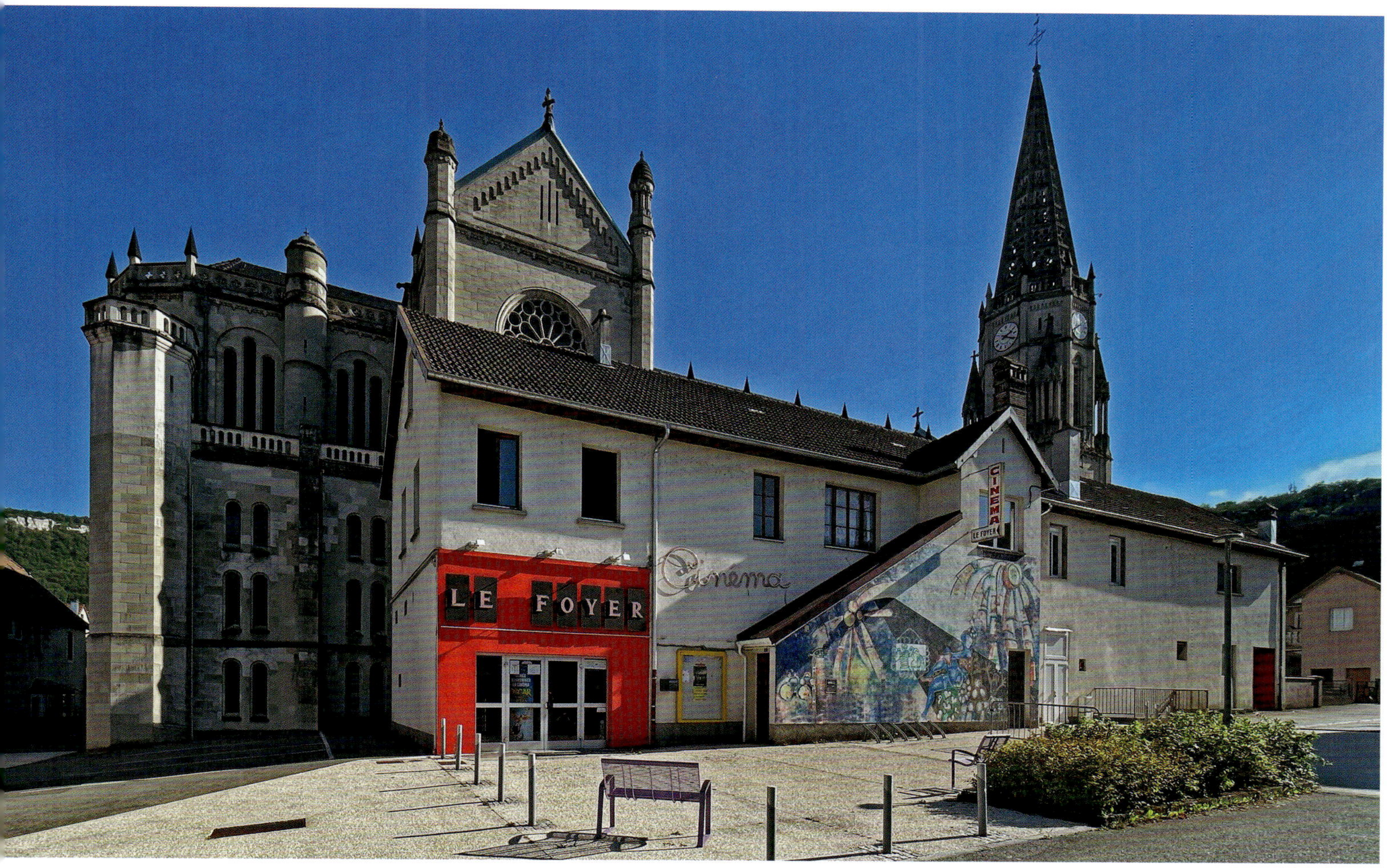

ont-de-Roide – Le Foyer – 2022

BRITTANY

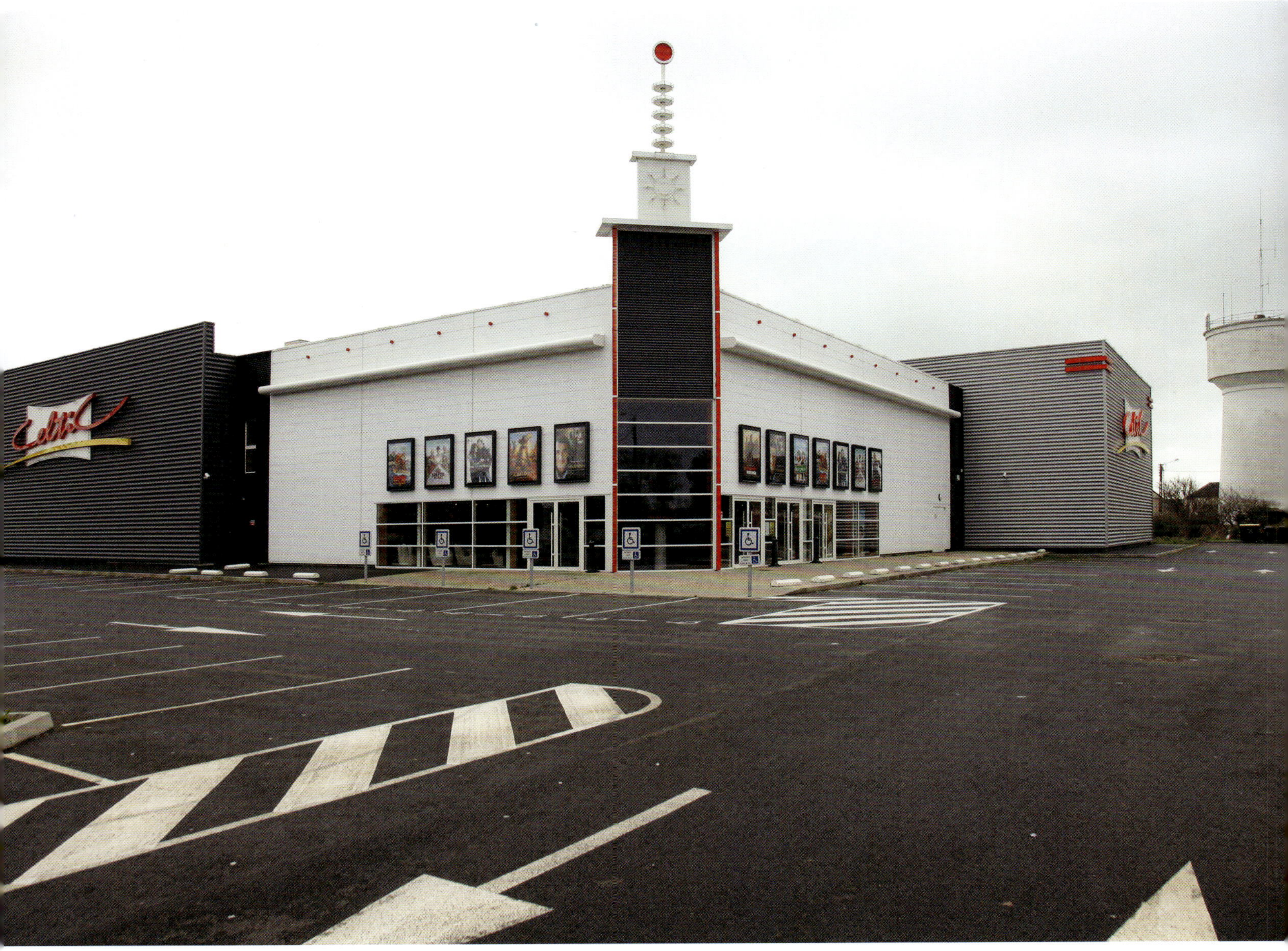

Concarneau – Celtic Cinéville – 2012

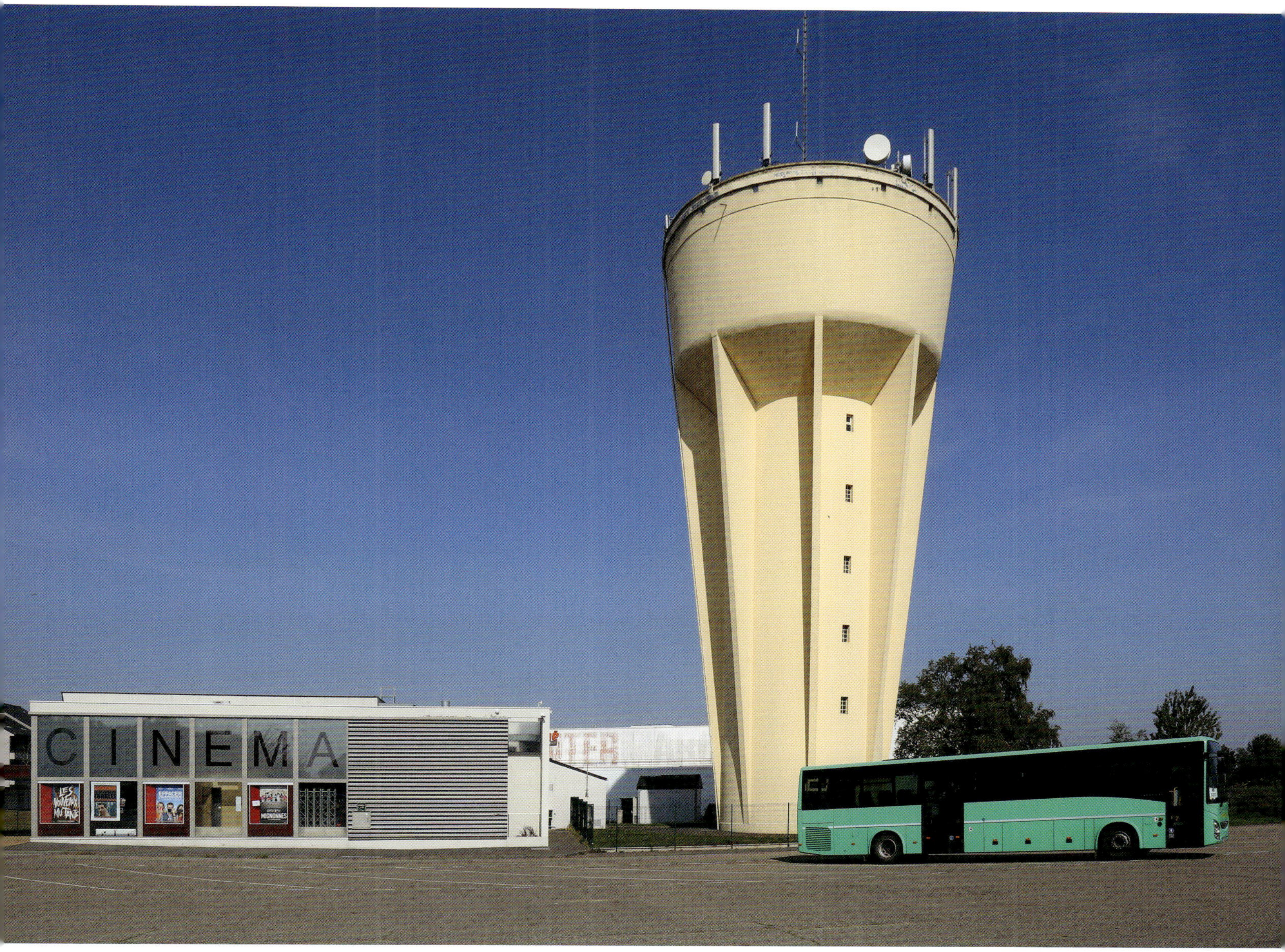

Bain-de-Bretagne – Le Scénario – 2021

Bain-de-Bretagne, Le Scénario. A conventional cinema, with the addition of a creatively-shaped water tower and an acid-green bus. A sense of spaciousness. The decor becomes cinematic. Filming can begin, especially since the screenplay is on the front of the building where everyone can see it.

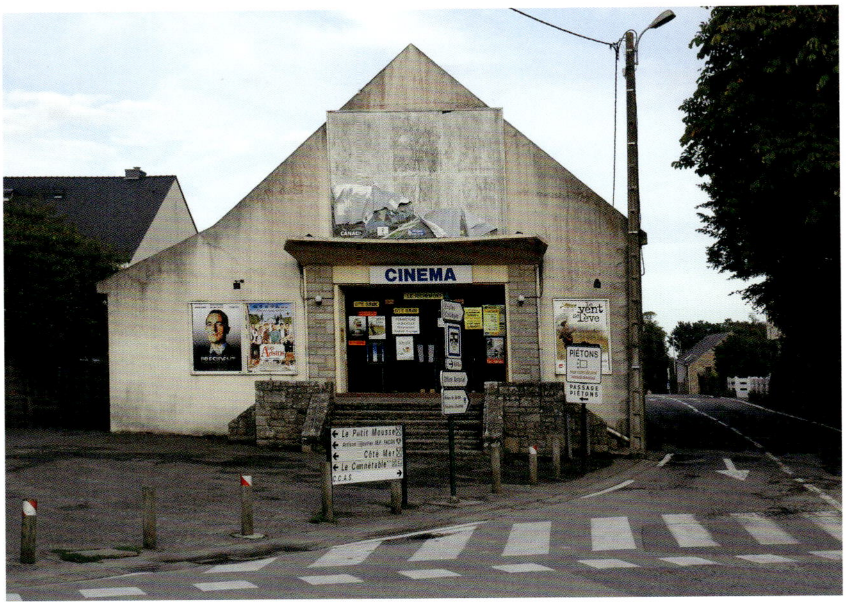

Sarzeau – Le Richemont – 2006

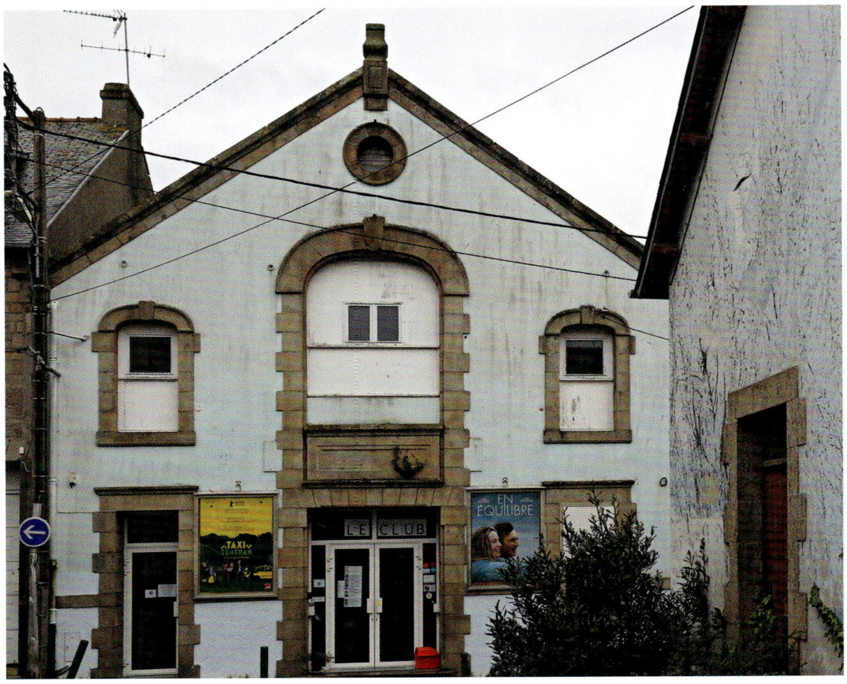

Douarnenez – Le Club – 2015

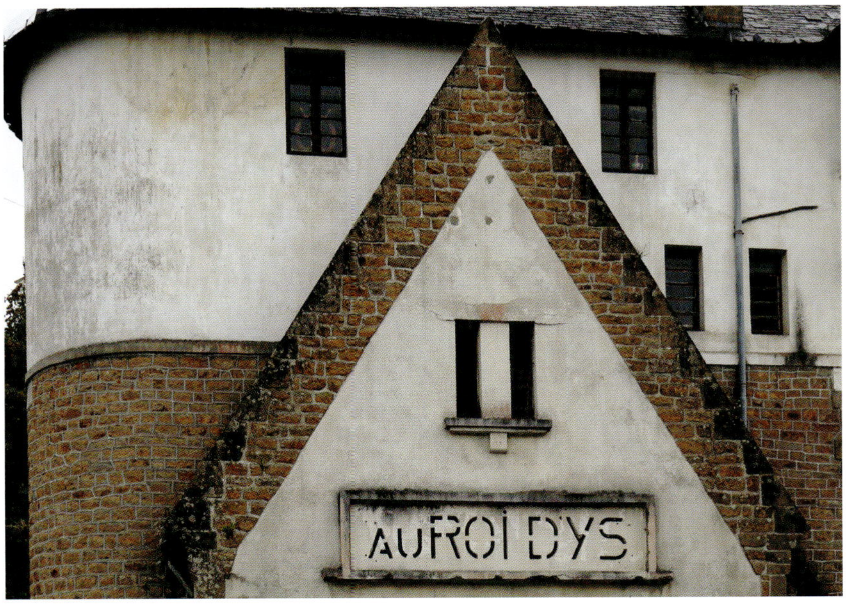

Audierne – Au Roi Dys – 2015

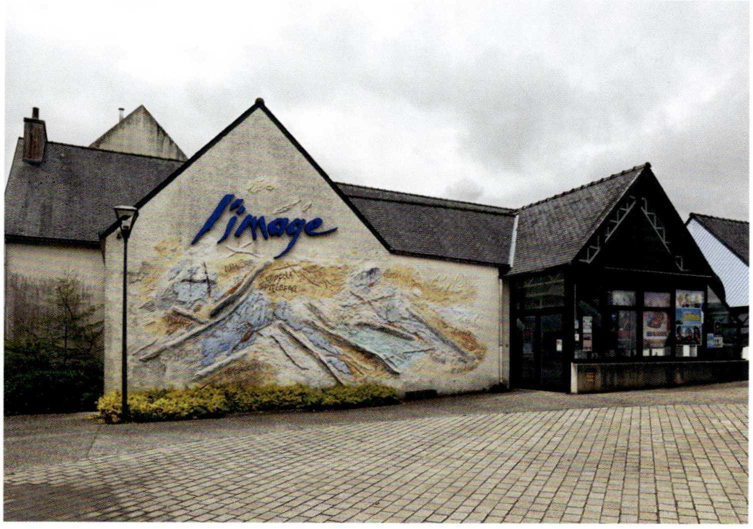

Plougastel – L'Image – 2015

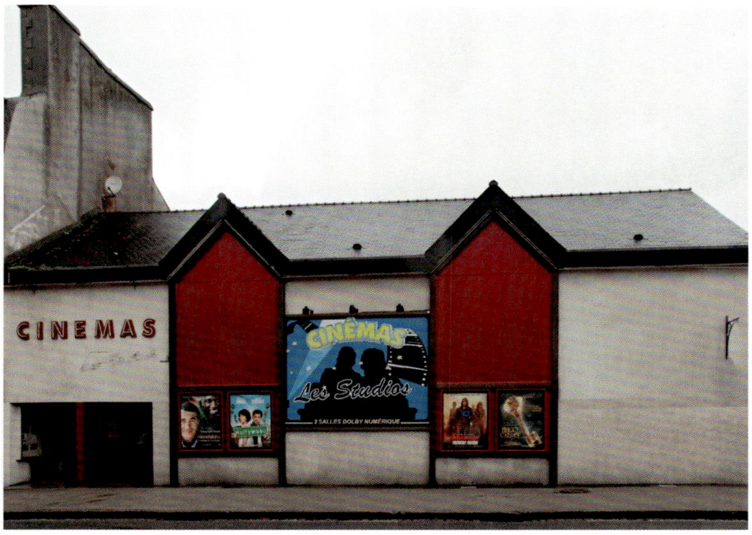

Landivisau – Les Studios – 2012

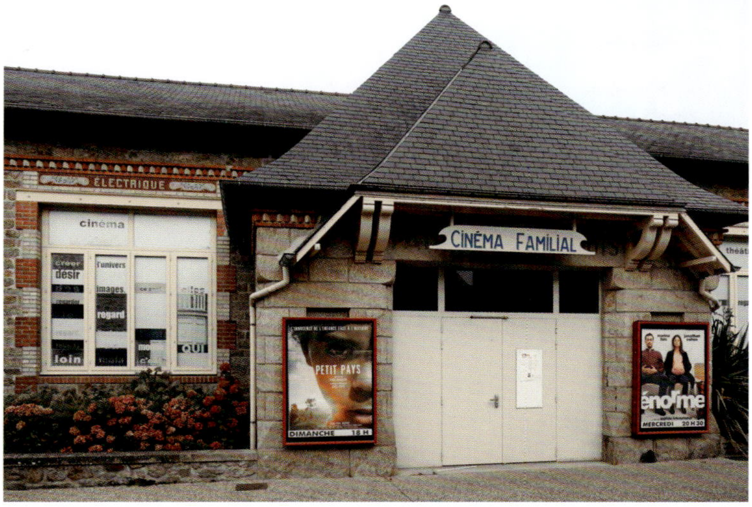

Saint-Lunaire – Cinéma Familial – 2020

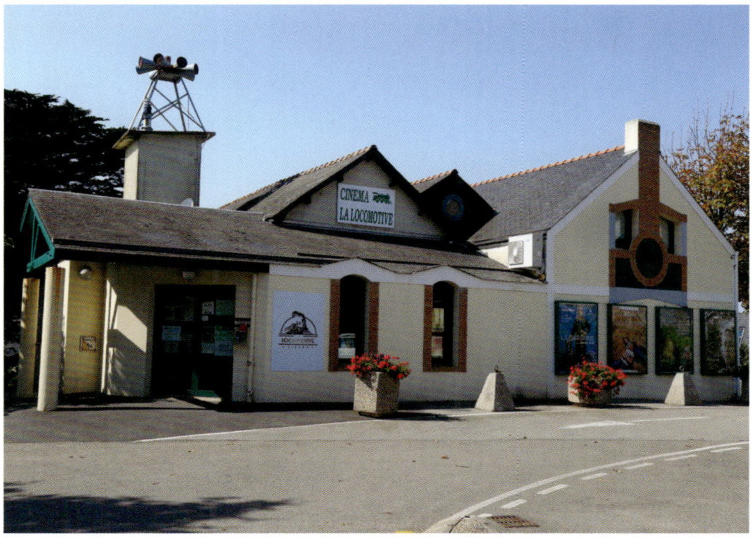

Arzon – La Locomotive – 2020

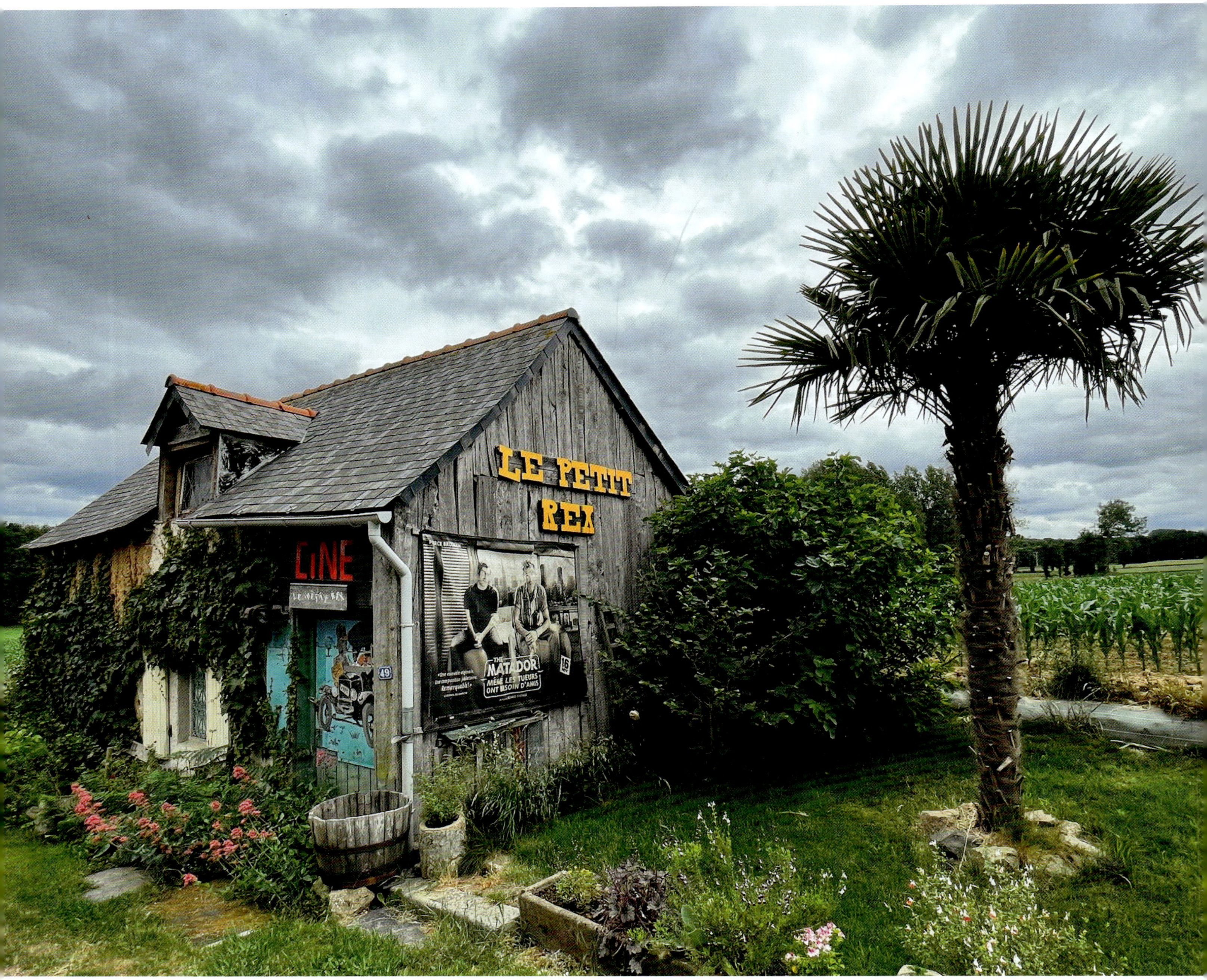

Saint-Judoce – Le Petit Rex – 2022

Saint-Judoce, Le Petit Rex. Jean-Jacques Boinet, with many past ventures to his name, settled in Saint-Judoce, a Breton village of 560 residents, in 2007. He fulfilled his dream of opening a 15-seat cinema in an old forge: Le Petit Rex, in memory of the Parisian Rex he knew as a kid. The sessions often came as a surprise. Neither day nor time was fixed in advance: everything was done by word of mouth in this museum-like place. A long illness carried him off in 2019. But this little corner of paradise still exists.

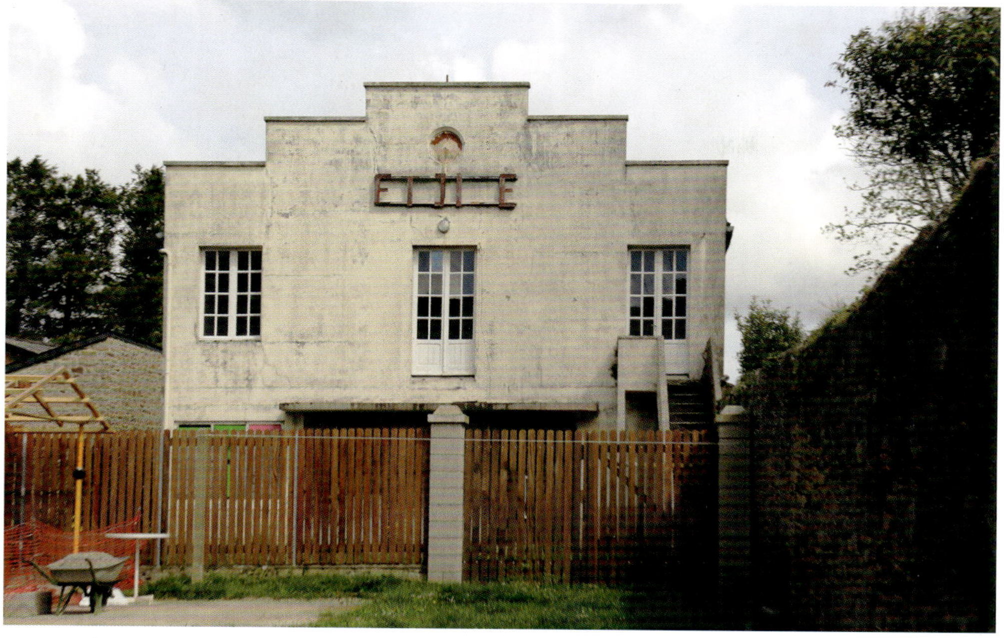

Lannilis – Étoile – 2015

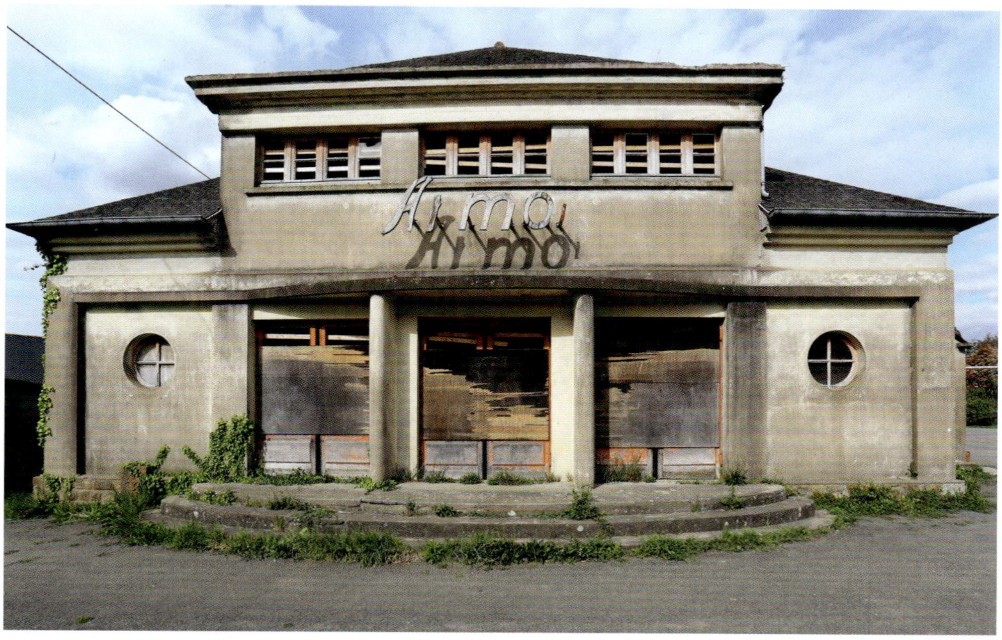

Montreuil-sur-Ille – Armor – 2015

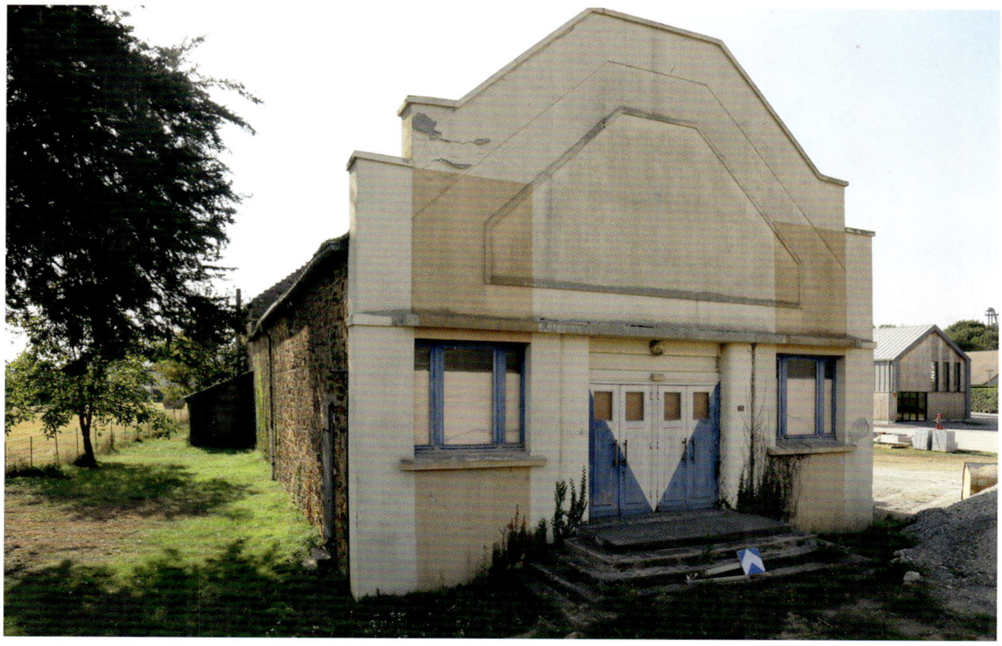

Bais – Le Foyer – 2019

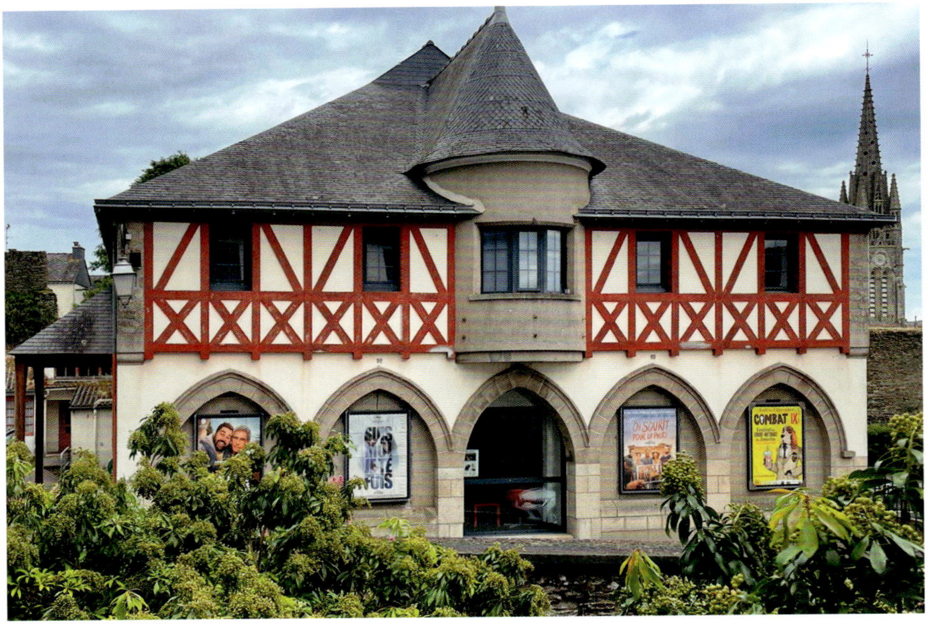

Josselin – Le Beaumanoir – 2022

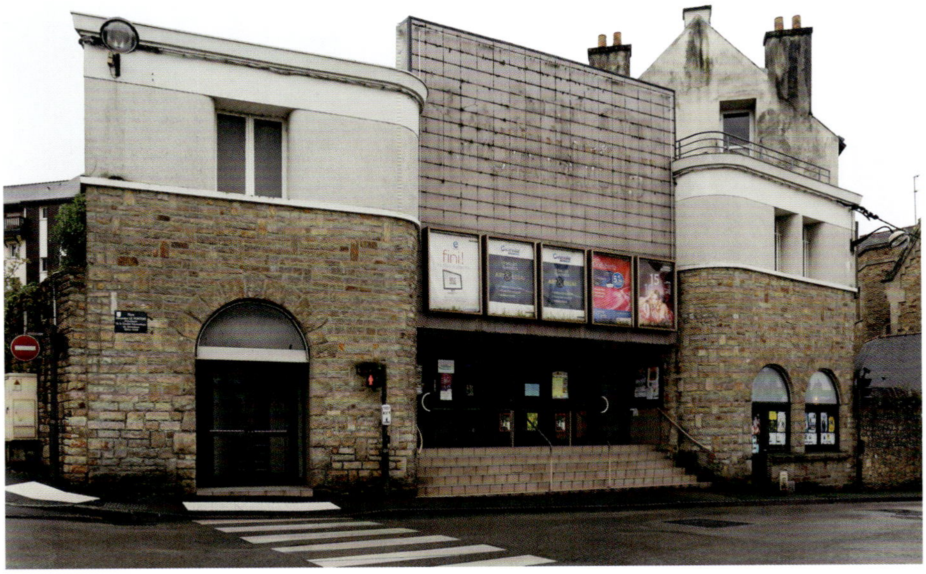

Vannes – Garenne – 2017

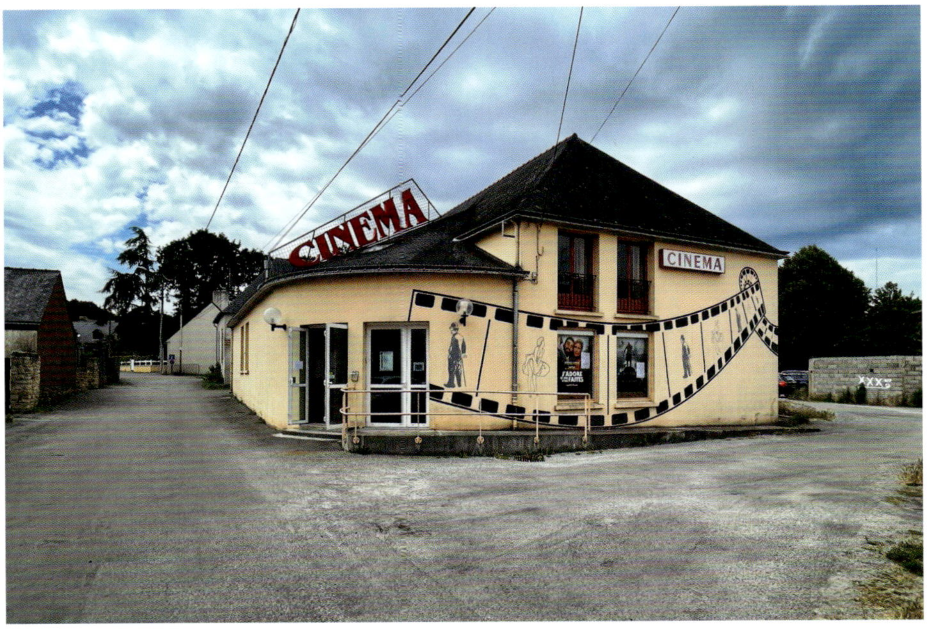

Malestroit – Armoric – 2022

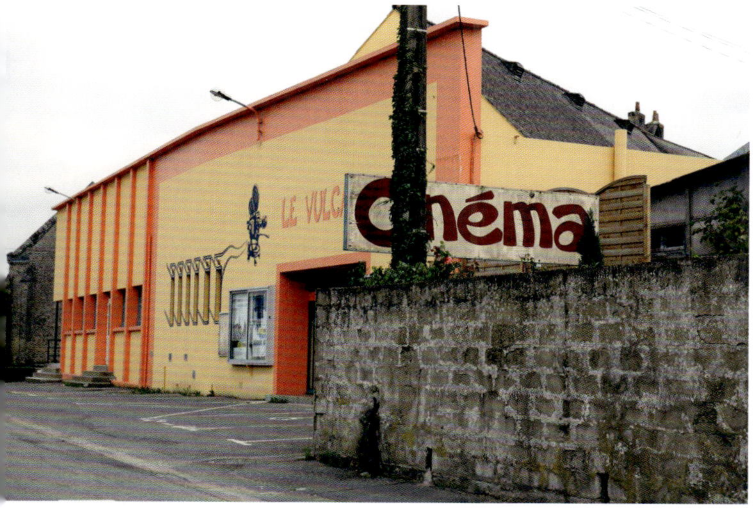

nzinzac-Lochrist – Le Vulcain – 2006

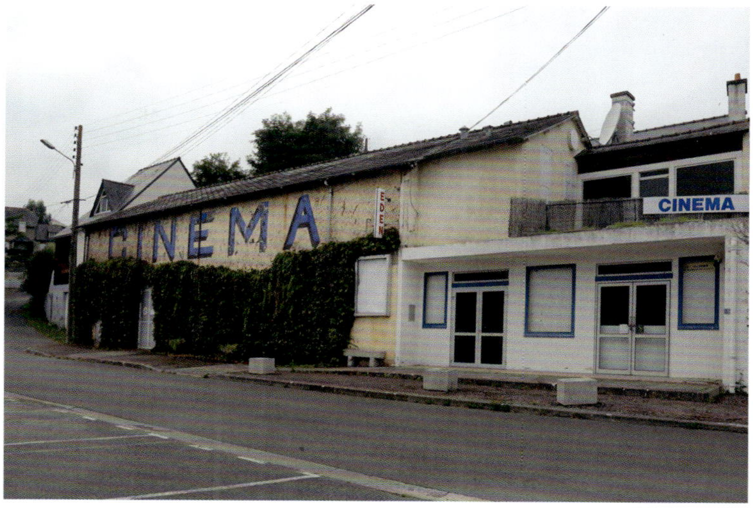

Saint-Cast – Le Guildo – 2020

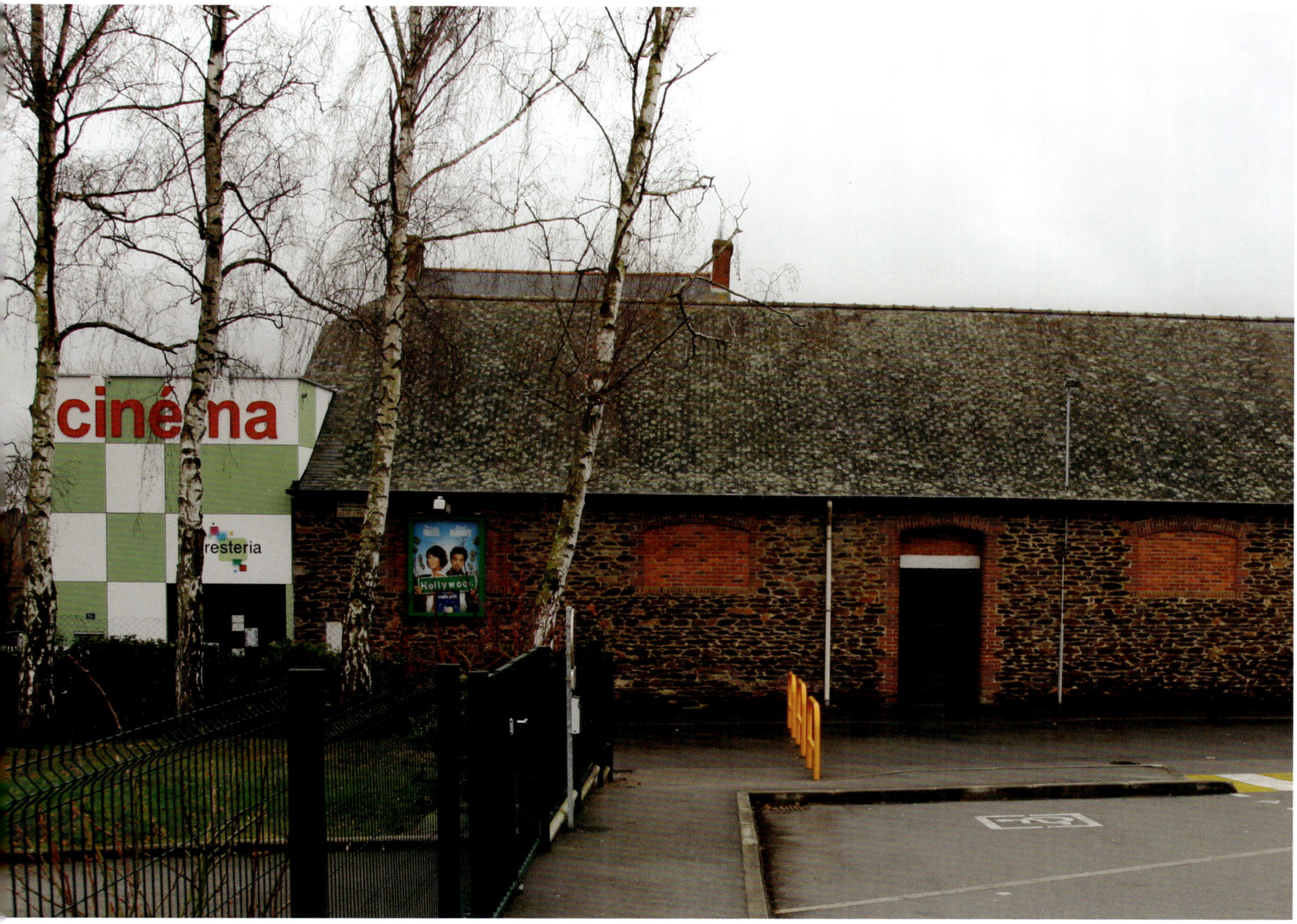

etiers – Resteria – 2011

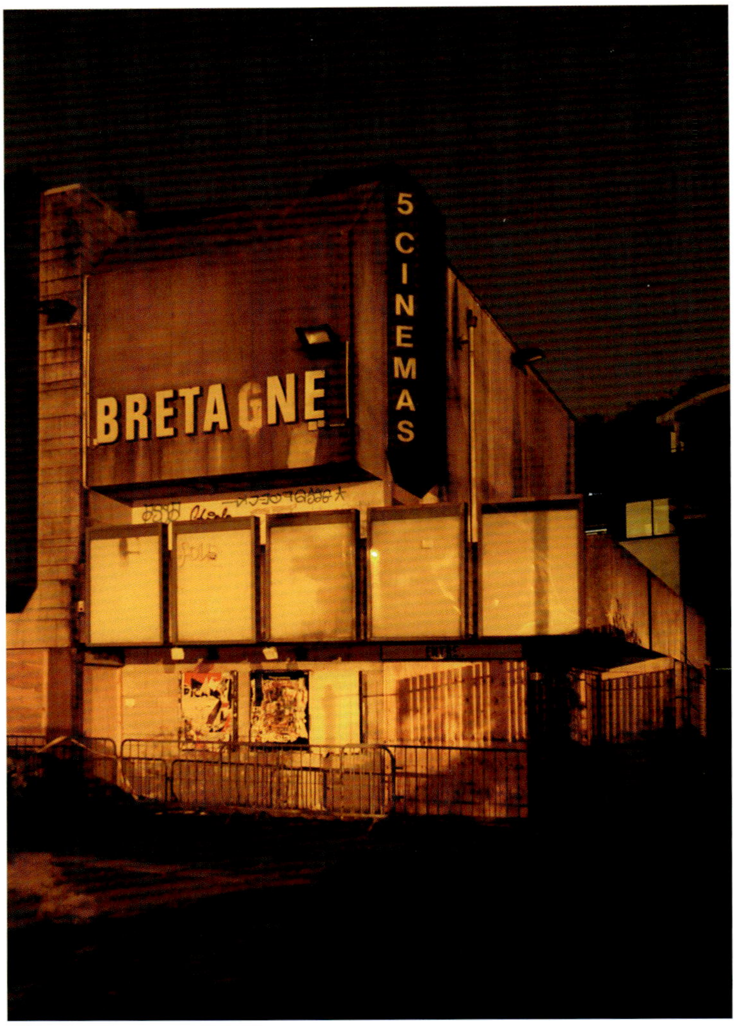

Quimper – Bretagne – 2020 (détruit)

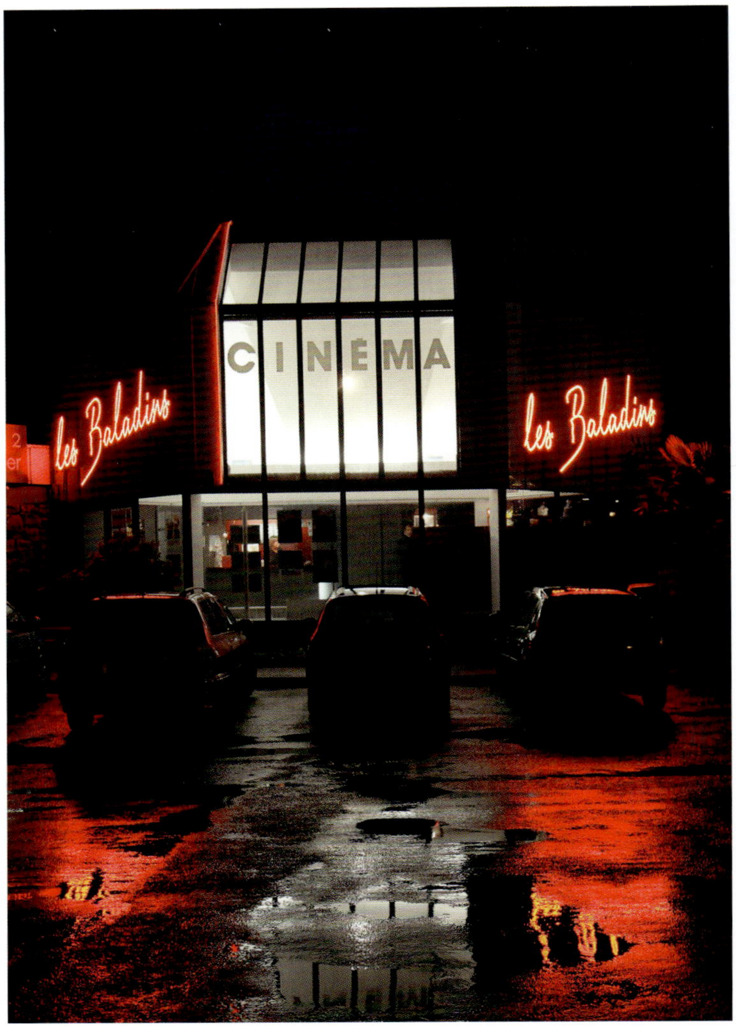

Perros-Guirec – Les Baladins – 2012

Quimper, Bretagne. Sometimes (often?) cinemas catch fire. Tired and neglected by ever more fickle audiences, their seats worn out by thousands of bums of all shapes and sizes, fading carpets and constantly fickle lighting. Insurance companies, often suspicious, don't know if the fire is part of a whodunit or just a stroke of bad luck.

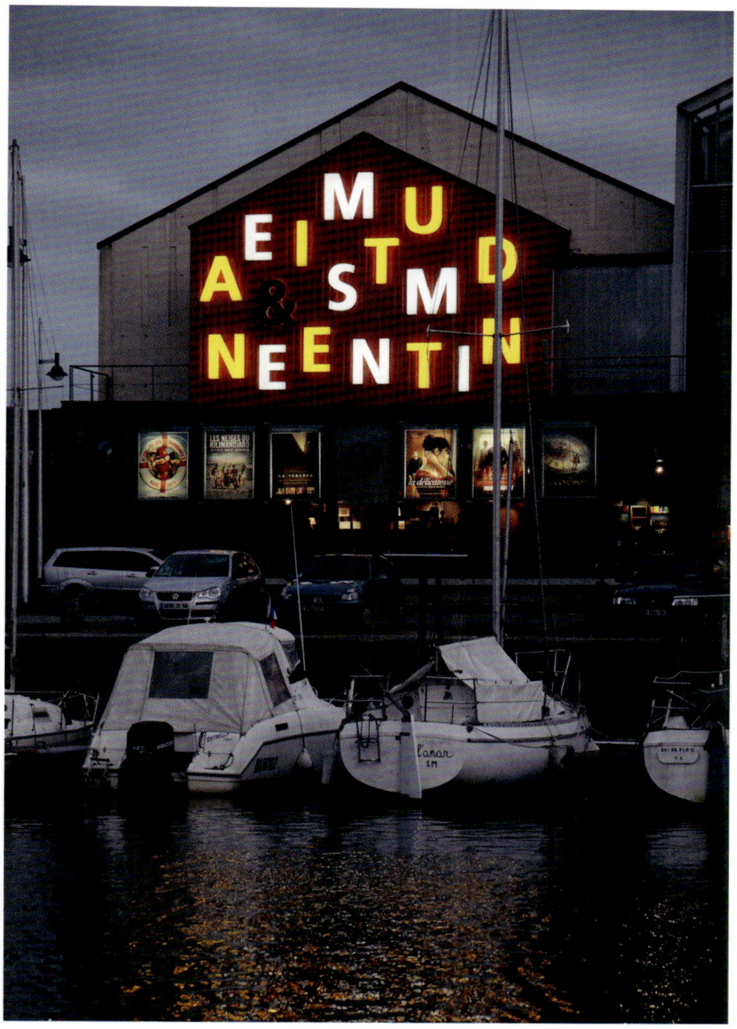

Redon – Manivel – 2012

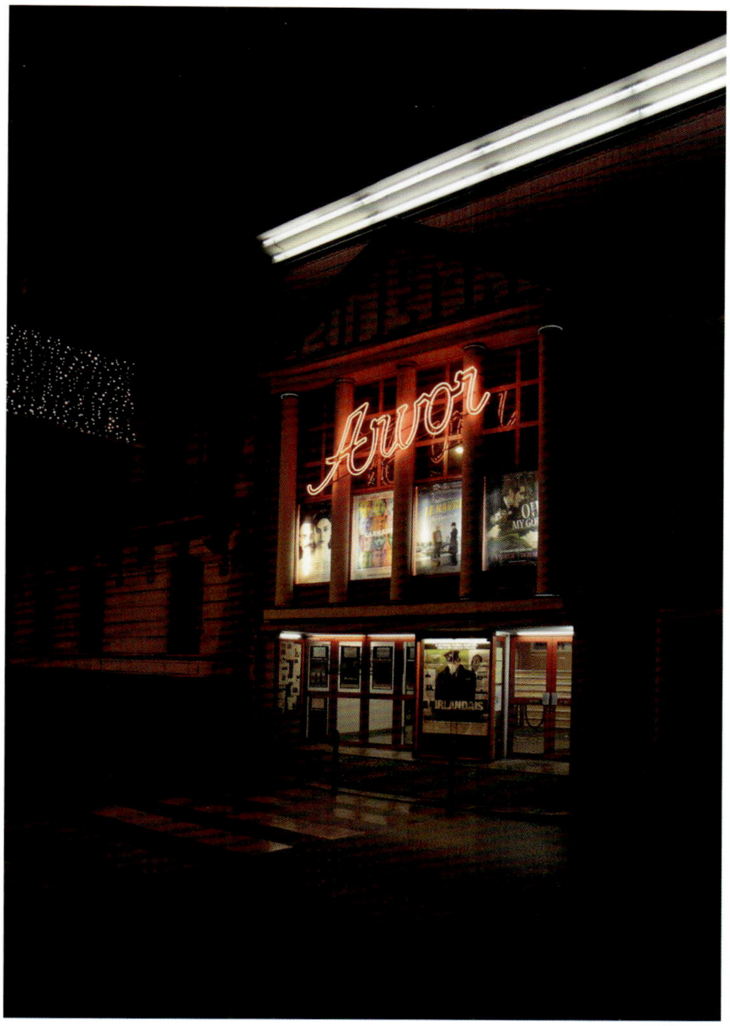

Rennes – Arvor – 2011

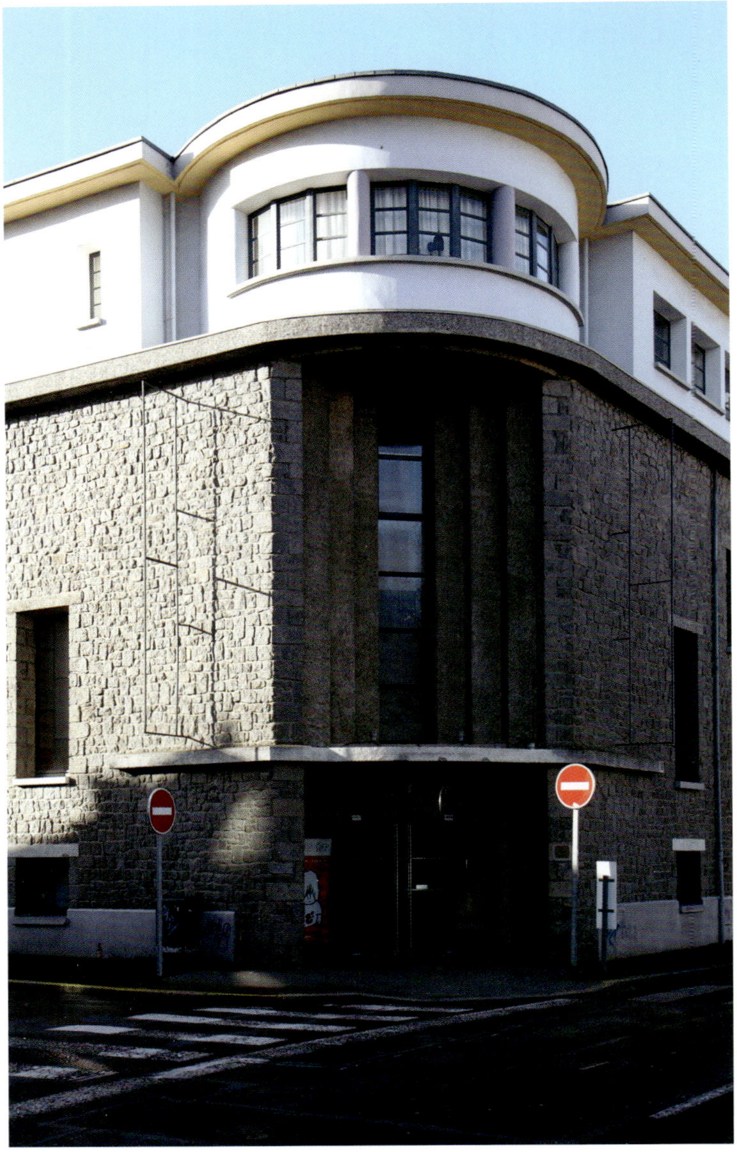

Saint-Brieuc – Ancien Royal – 2014

Saint-Brieuc, Le Royal. Built by Jean Fauny (1895–1973), also architect of the Arletty in Saint-Quay-Portrieux, the Saint-Brieuc Royal, with a capacity of 1,072, opened in 1934. Yves Bruyant, who used to work there as a projectionist, remembers being struck by the beauty of the interior. We can well believe it. In 1975, another vision, the cinema ran *Les Baiseuses* (*That Girl is a Tramp*) for thirty weeks. Audiences converged on it in buses from all around the region …

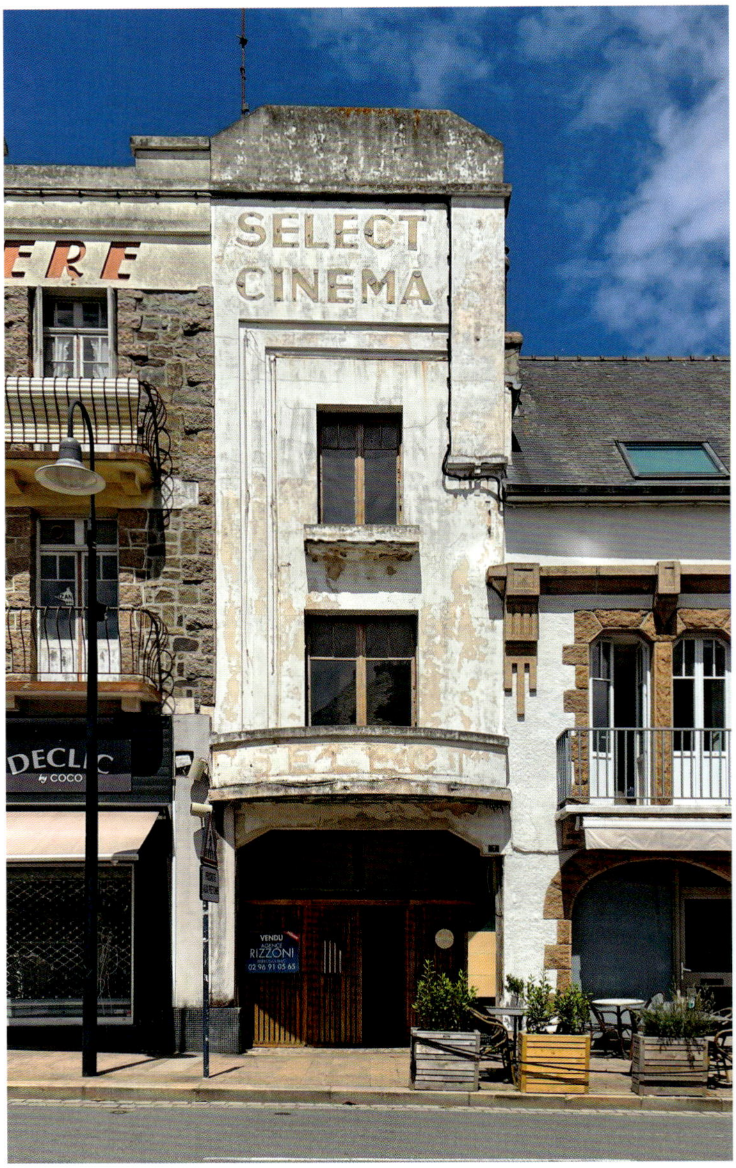

Perros-Guirec – Select – 2022

Perros-Guirec, Select. When this cinema opened in 1932, the locals were full of pride for its modernity, comparable to the finest Parisian cinemas. Since 1981 the building has been for sale. Conversion enthusiasts, supermarket specialists respectful of the Select logo, seem to hesitate to erase this prestigious name … For how long?

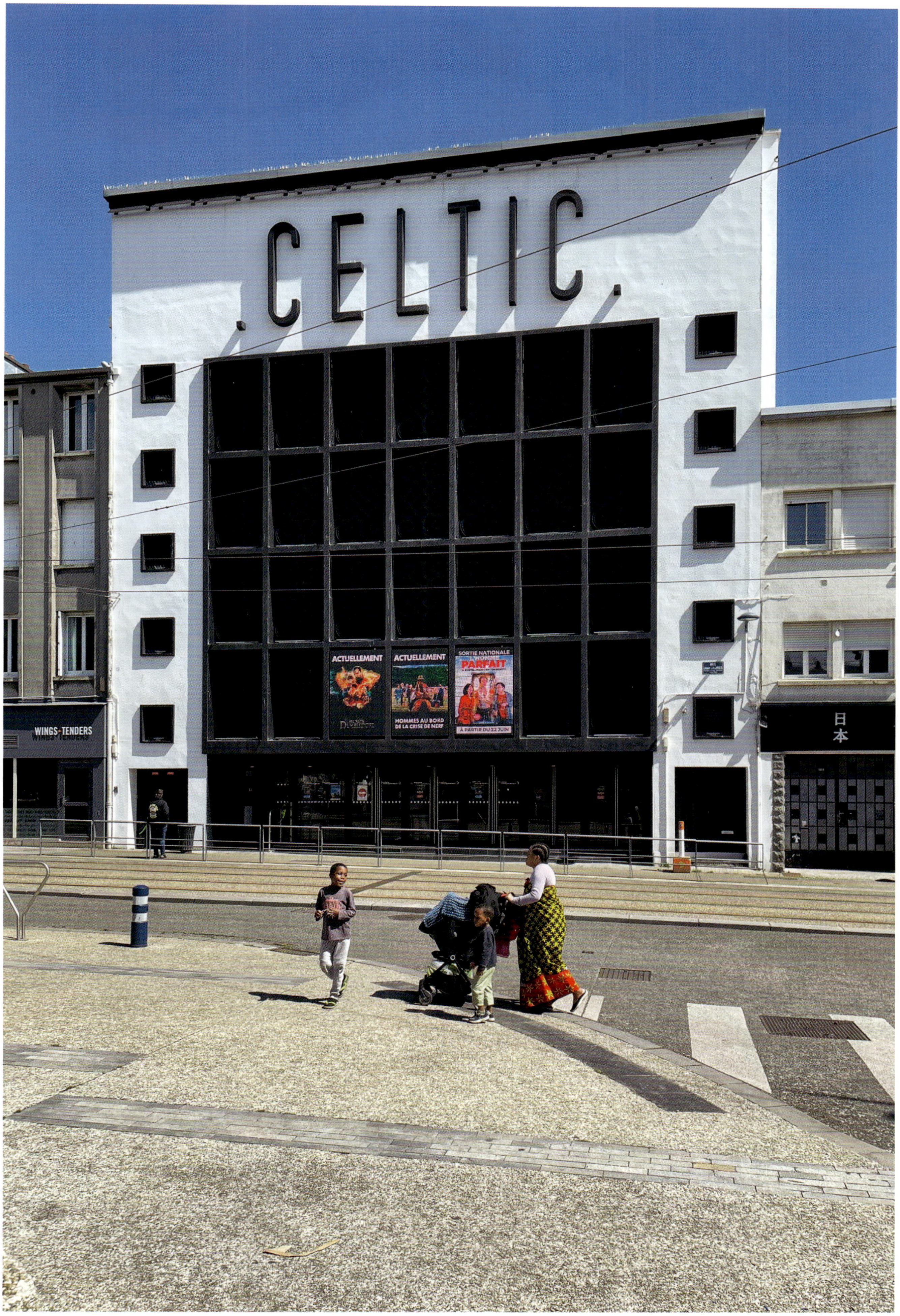

Brest – Celtic – 2022

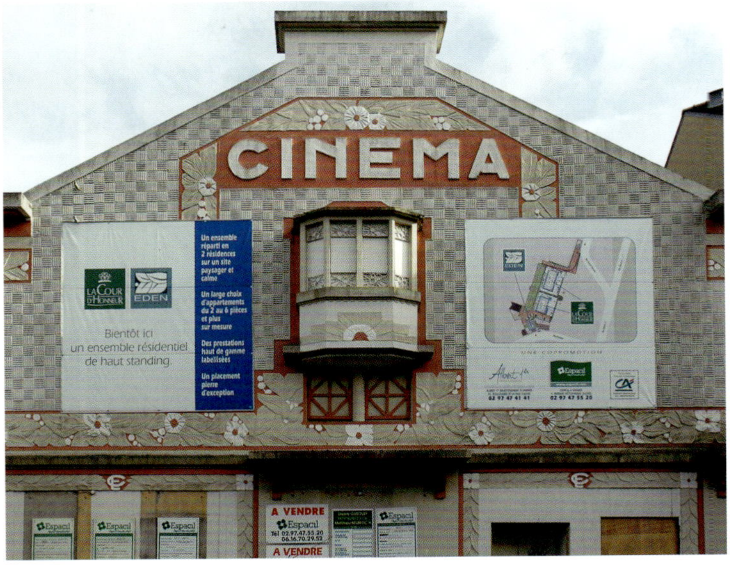

Vannes – Eden – 2006

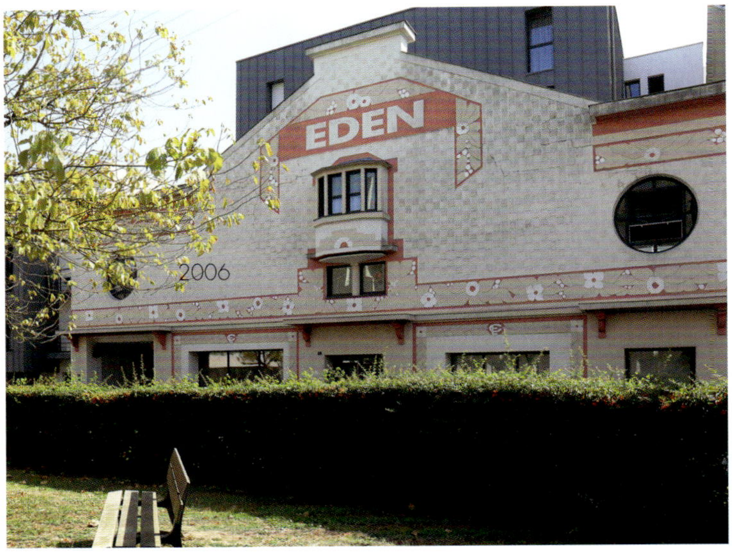

2020

Vannes, Eden. The cinema becomes a set. A preserved, even renovated, façade conceals a group of anonymous buildings behind the wall, daily obliging the occupants to remember that a cinema with the splendour worthy of a work of art used to occupy this place. The age of beautiful buildings is over.

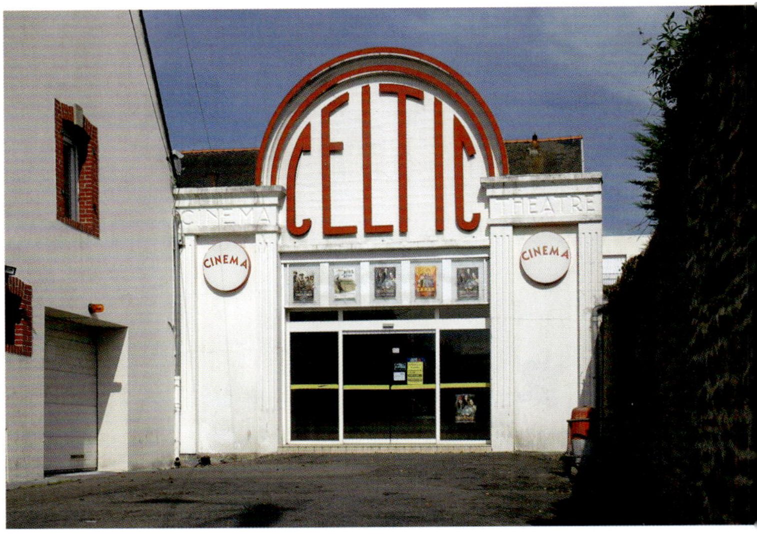

Concarneau – Celtic – 2006

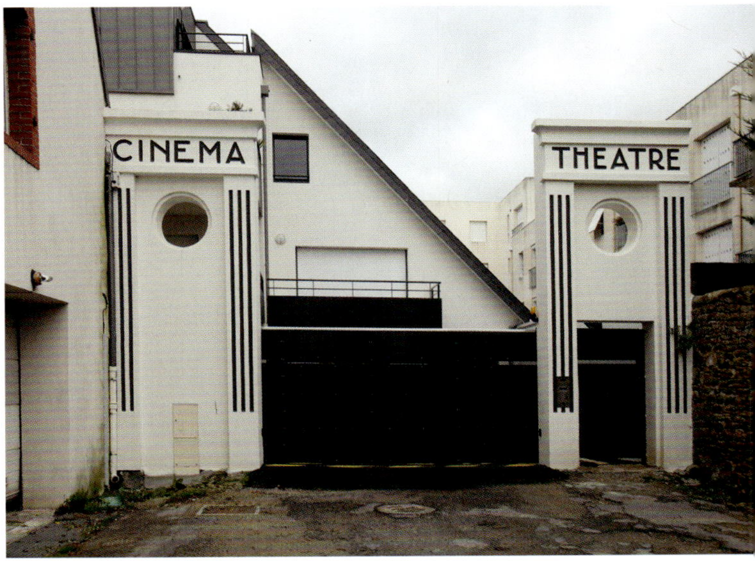

2012

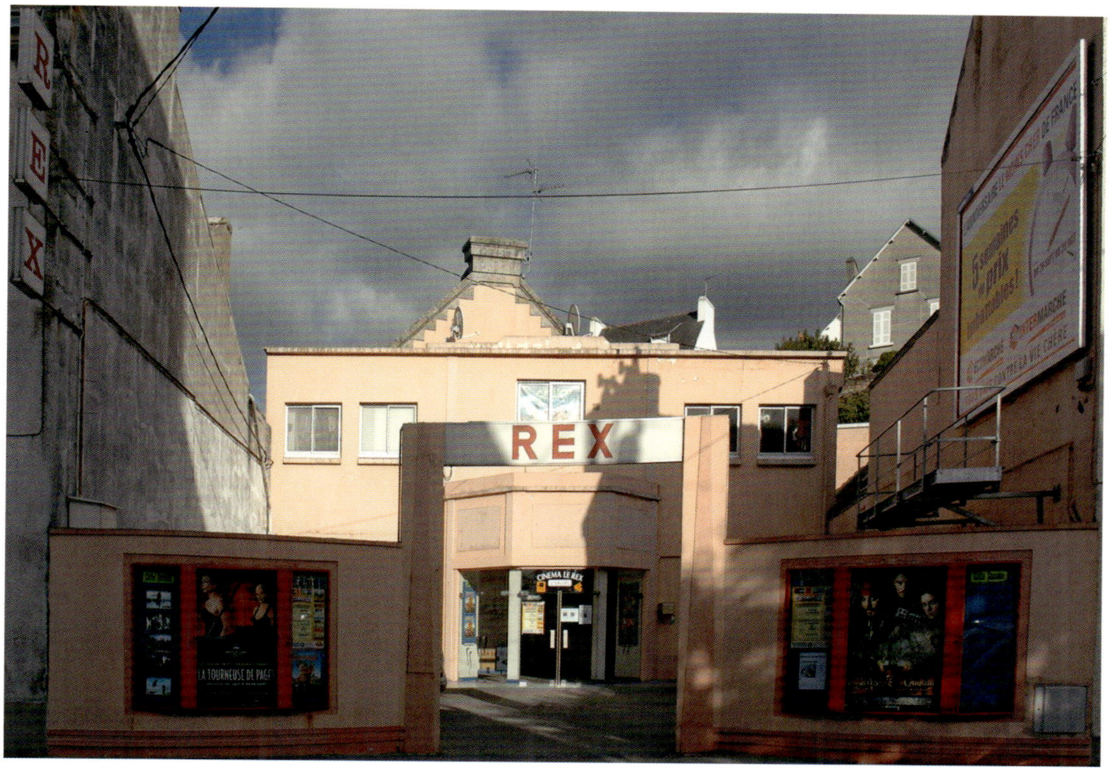

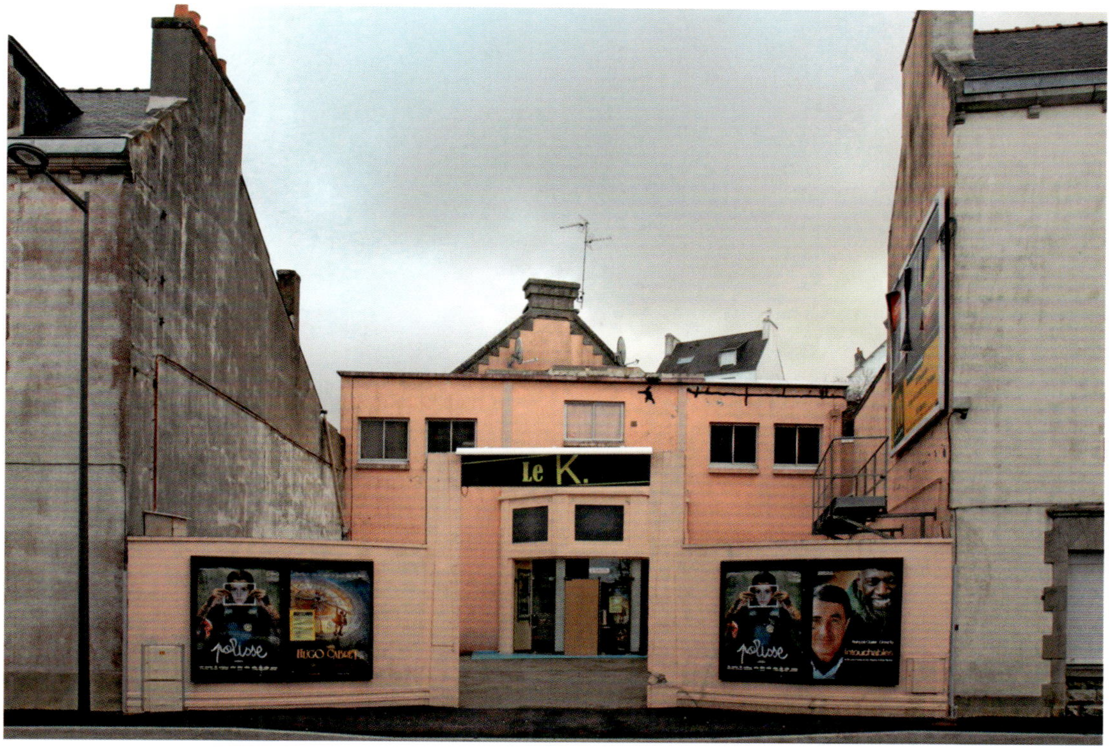

Douarnenez – Le K, ex Rex – 2012

Douarnenez, Rex and Le K. Not all cinemas are called Rex, but all Rexes are cinemas. The Rex at Douarnenez, with its rather chaotically charming façade and foyer worthy of a dilapidated palace, changed its name in 2012: it became Le K. with a full stop. One letter. Why? What is this stop hiding? Kamikaze? Maybe, because this cinema will finally close its doors, killed off by the neighbouring multiplex.

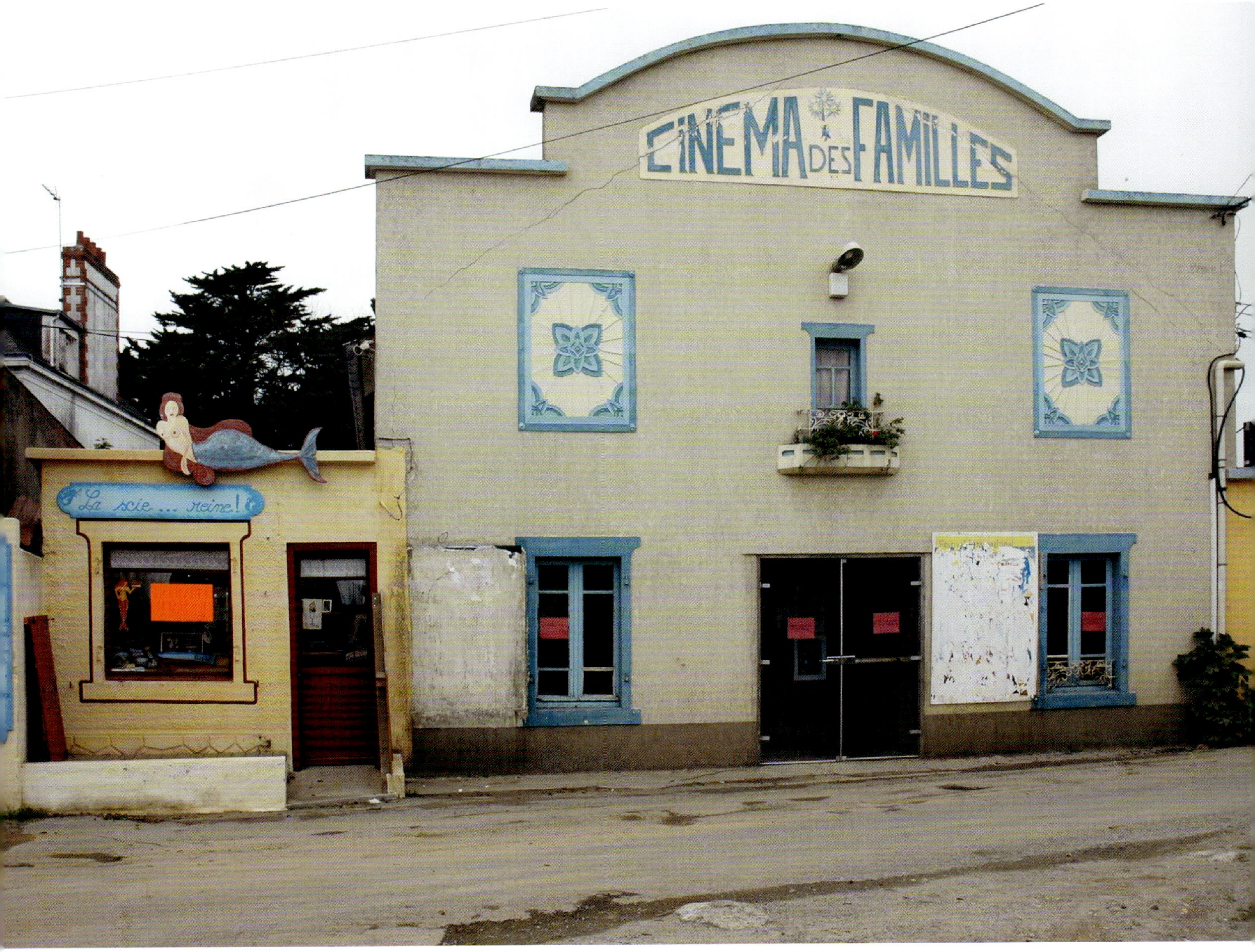

Île de Groix – Cinéma des Familles – 2006

Crozon, Rex. Did this house come along to cling to the side of the Rex cinema? Do its occupants have their ears glued to the wall trying to pick up a few snippets of dialogue? Have they drilled a hole in order to see the shadow of a gun or a swaggering gait, suggesting some torrid moments they could share if they enlarged this opening in their home? A complex plot. The mystery will never be solved.

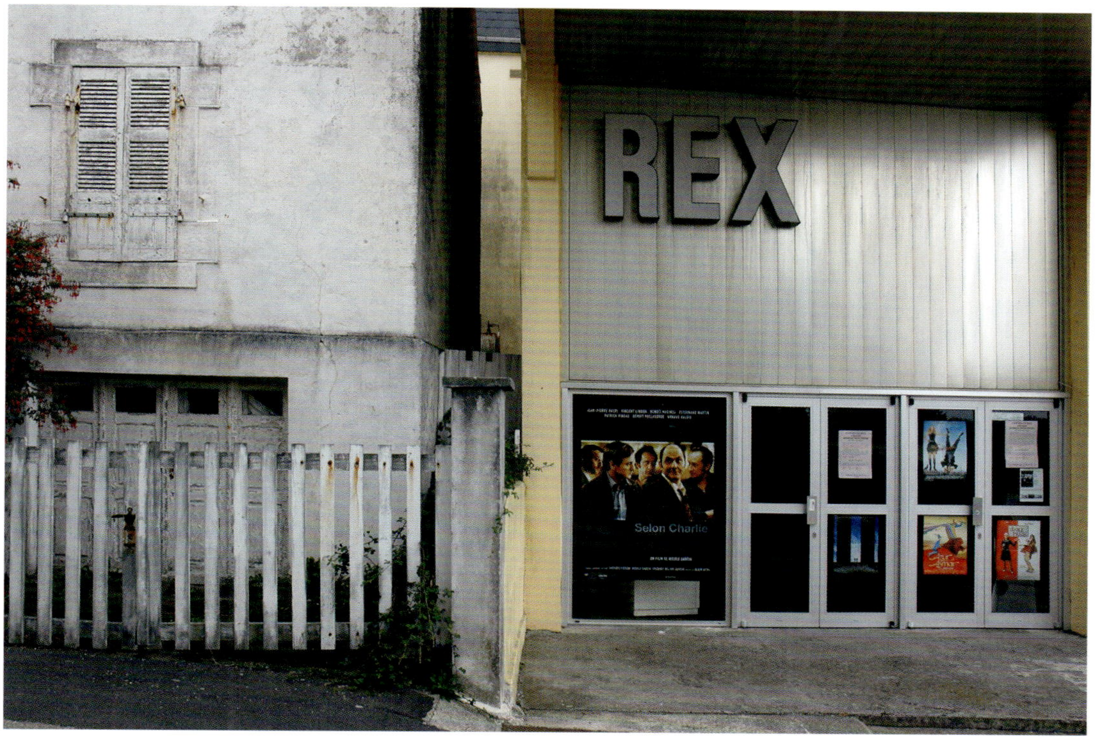

Crozon – Rex – 2006

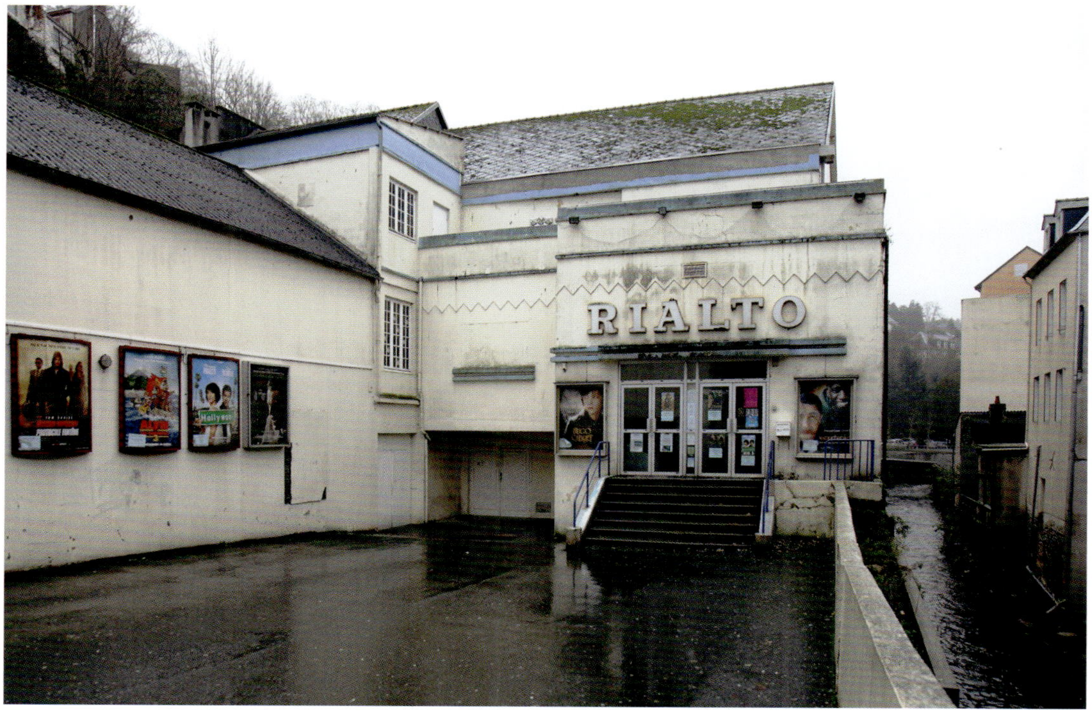

Morlaix – Rialto – 2012

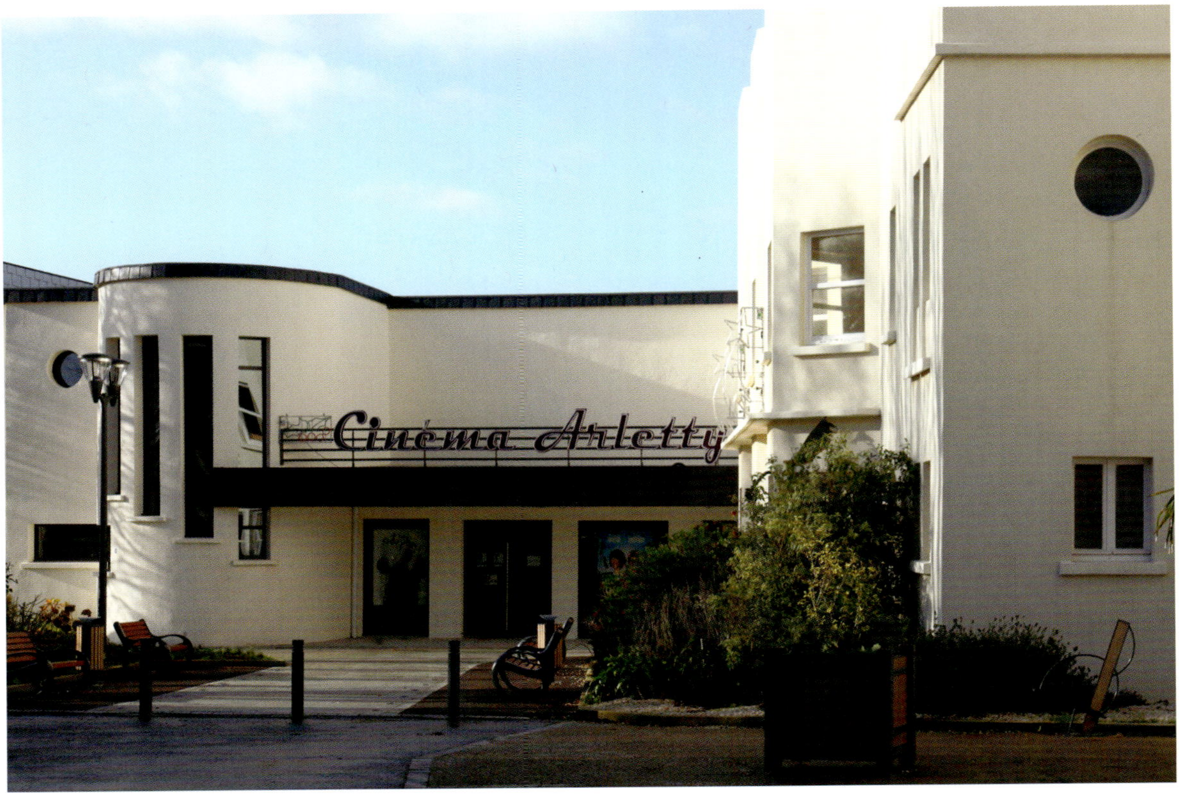

Saint-Quay-Portrieux – Arletty – 2020

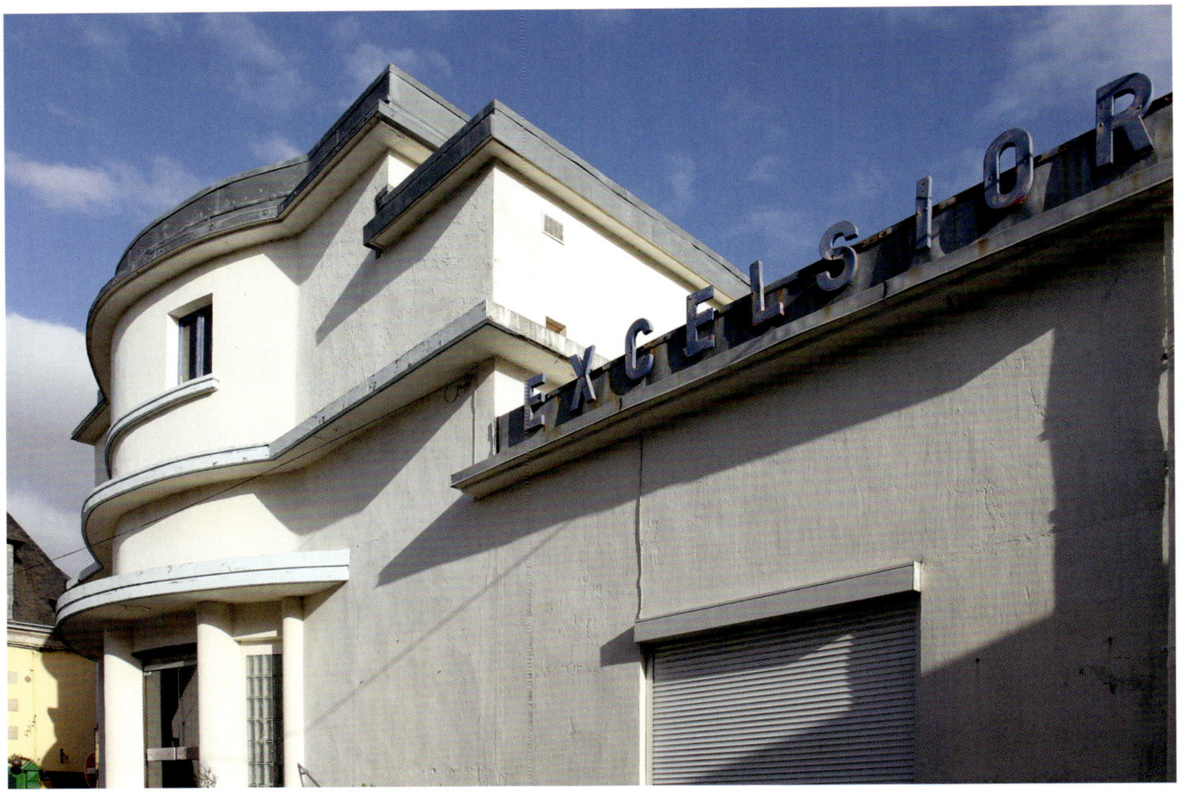

Pont-l'Abbé – Excelsior – 2012 (destroyed)

Pont-l'Abbé, Excelsior. Ravaged by fire in 2013, the Excelsior cinema with its Art Deco façade was slowly dying. After being bought by the town in 2018 it was frantically tagged. The diggers, parked in waiting for the appeals of local residents to be rejected without any consideration, went into action on 23 March 2022. Today only the metal letters of the cinema remain. They'll be used as part of the decoration of the planned square. Memories of a poor screenplay …

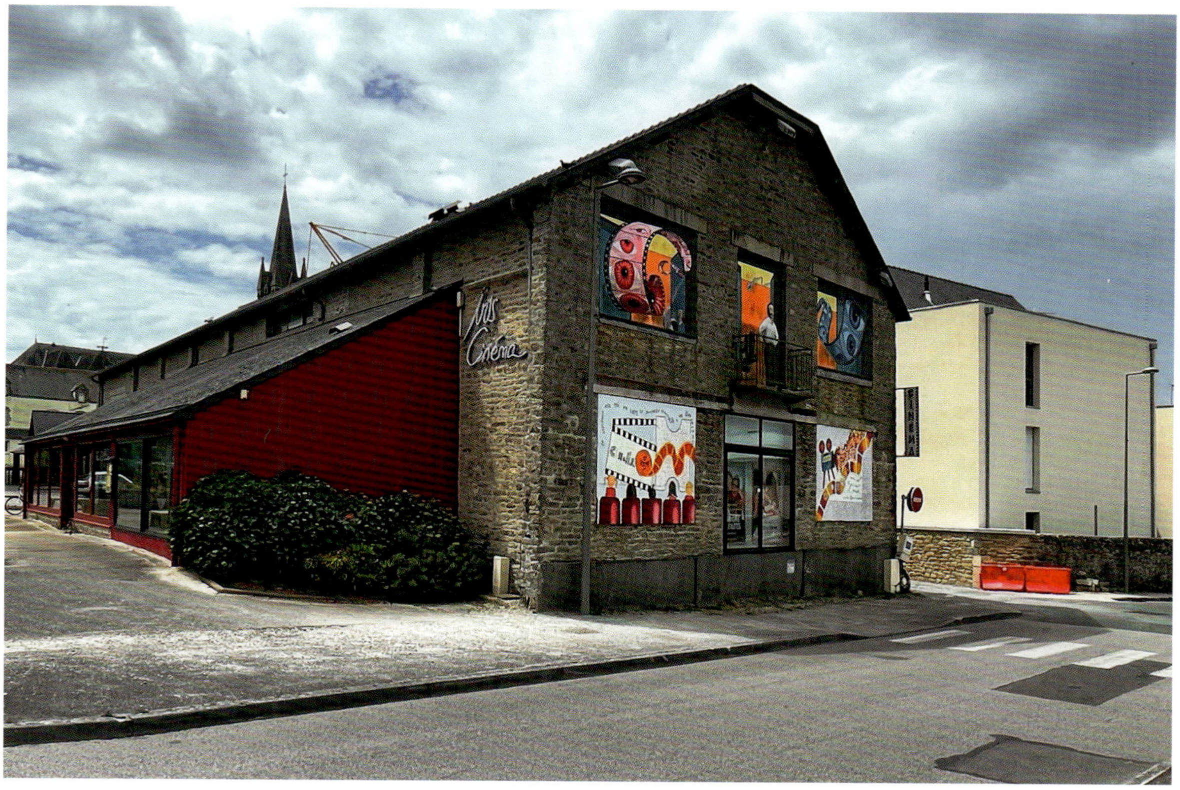

Questembert – Iris Cinéma – 2022

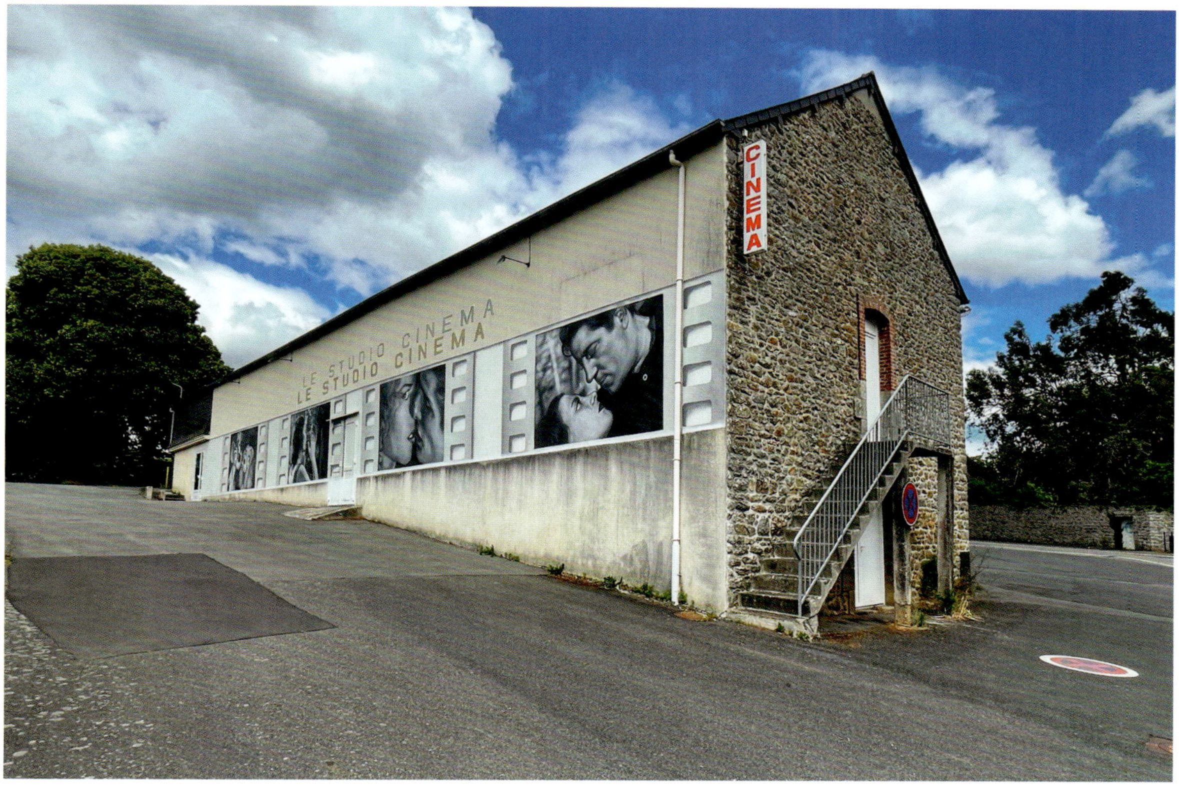

Merdrignac – Le Studio – 2022

Merdrignac, Le Studio. A cinema that looks like an affluent farmhouse? A peasant farmer who's abandoned her barn? Dream of movie kisses with Jean Gabin or Tom Cruise. They're ready to leap from the screen to hug her. While waiting for this delicious moment, a new cinema was born.

CENTRE-VAL DE LOIRE

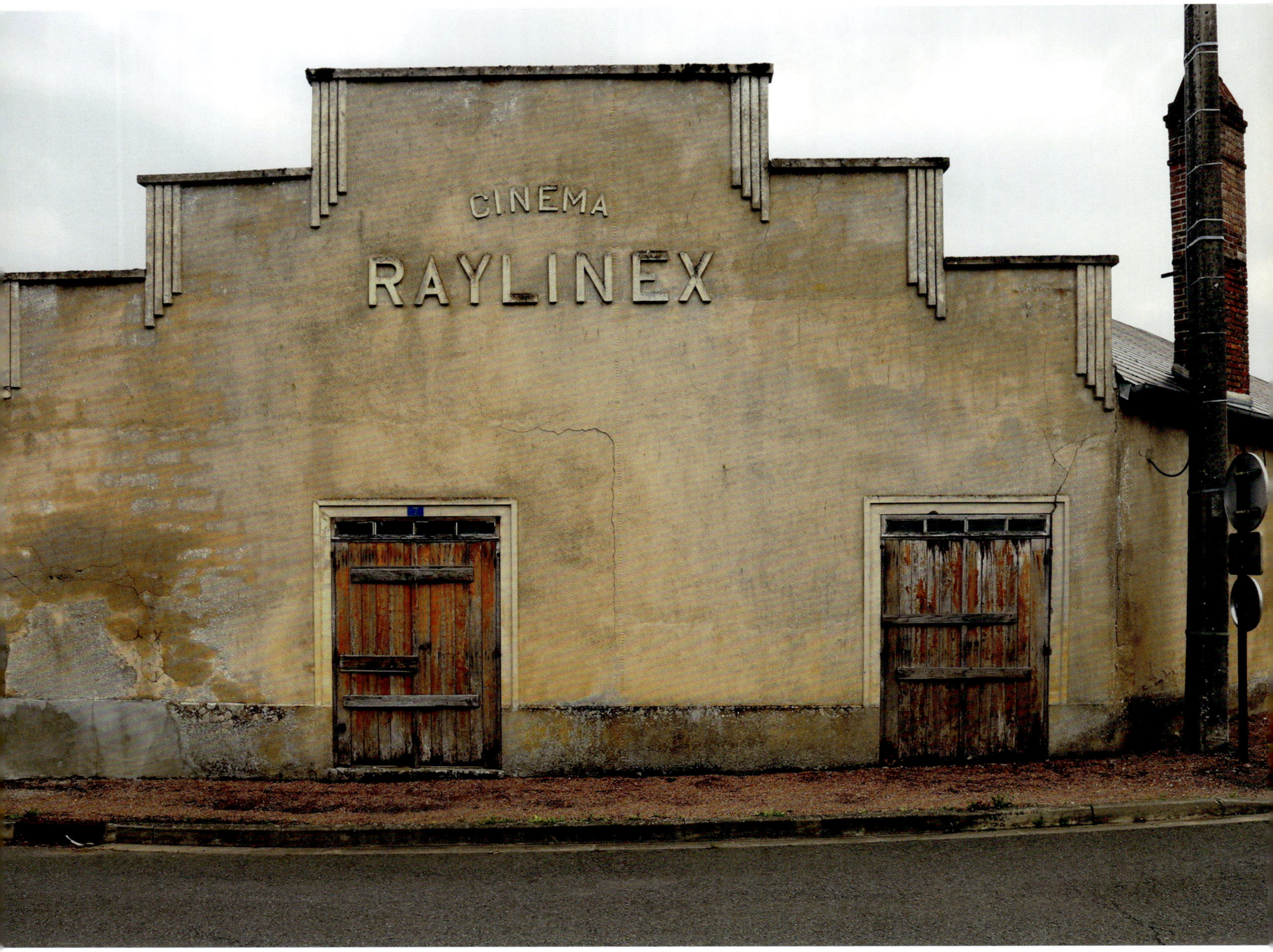

Menetou-Salon – Raylinex – 2020

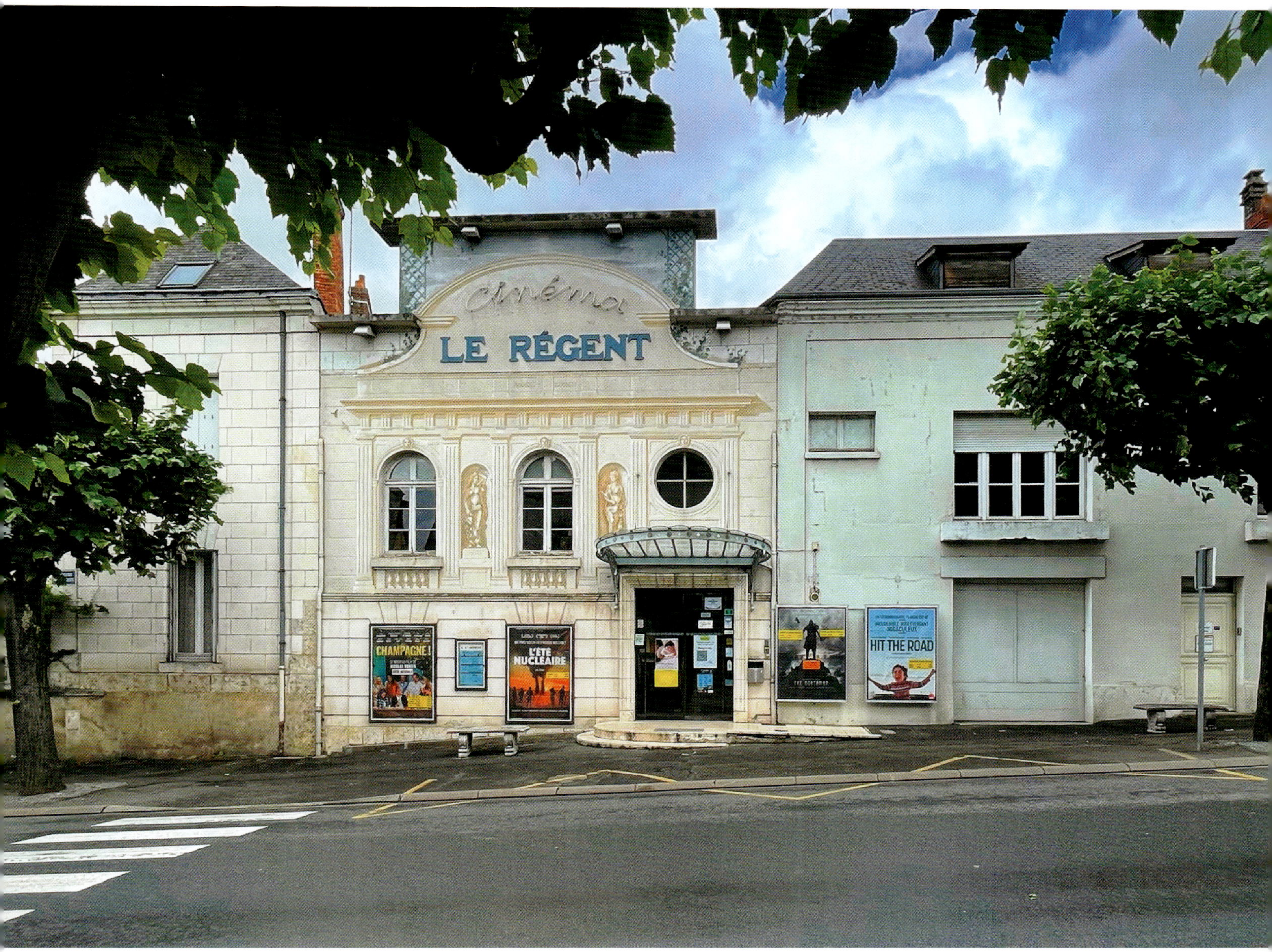

Montrichard – Le Régent – 2021

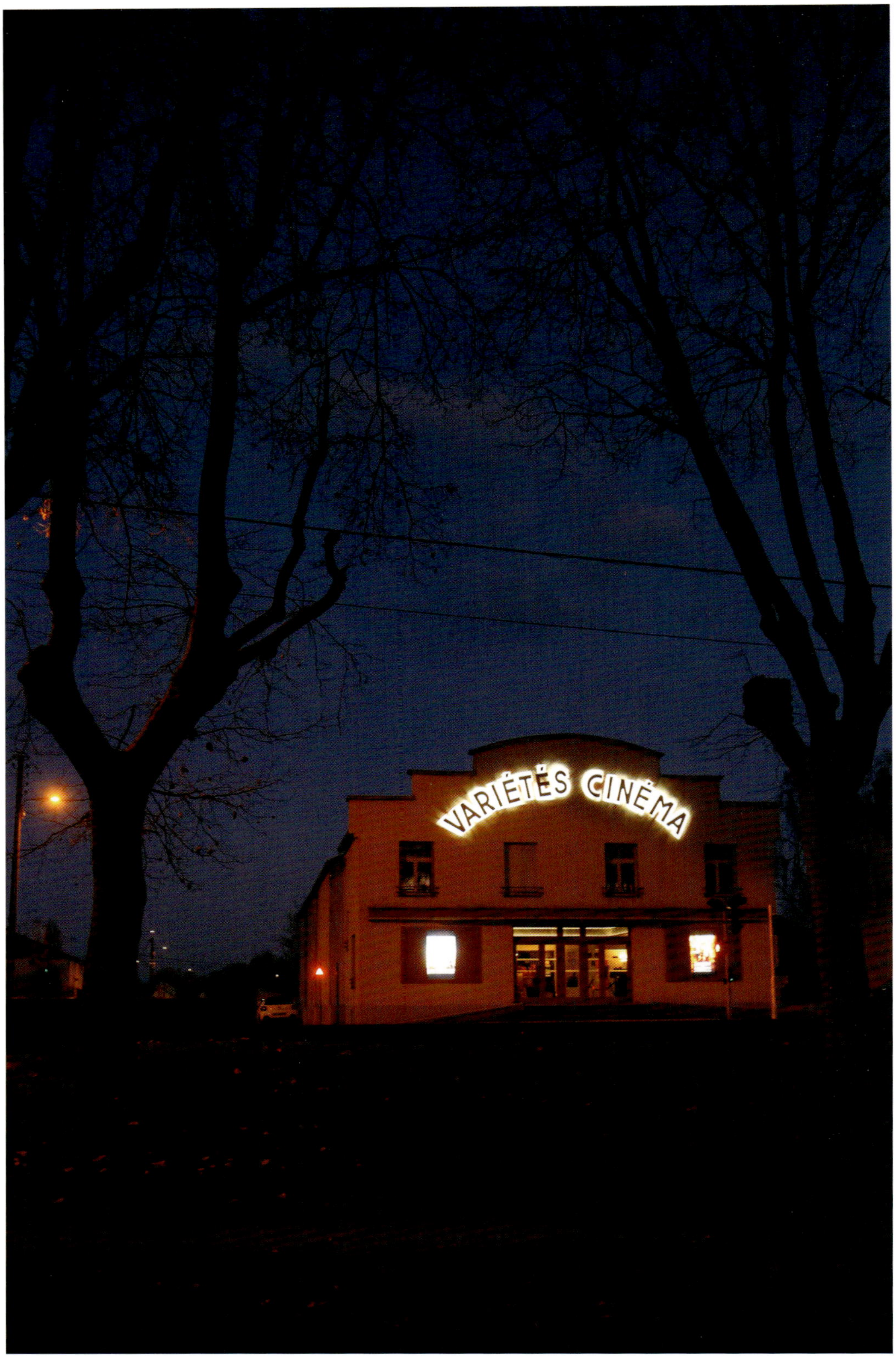

La Ferté-Saint-Aubin – Variétés Cinéma – 2023

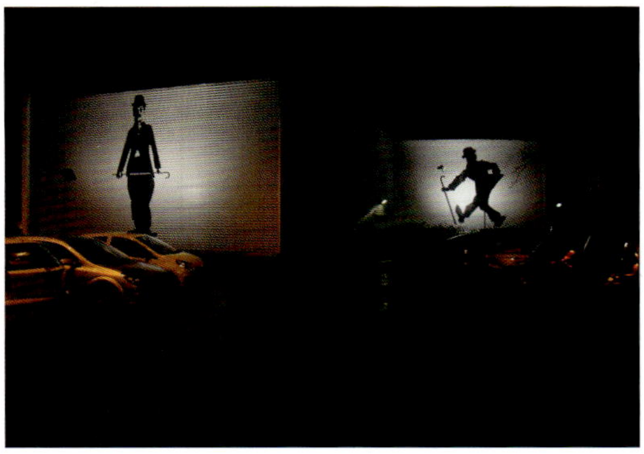

Tours – CGR – 2011

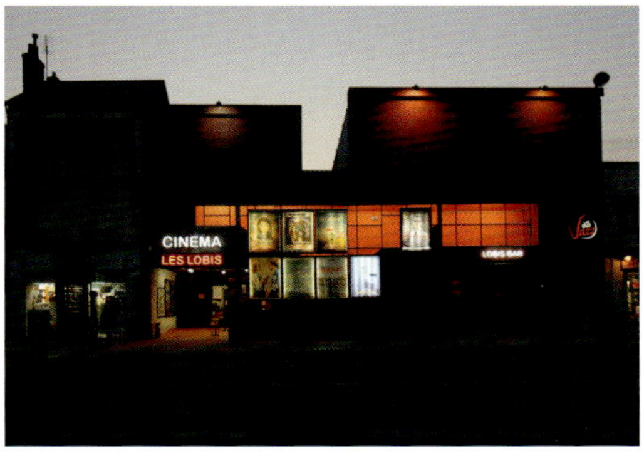

Blois – Les Lobis – 2018

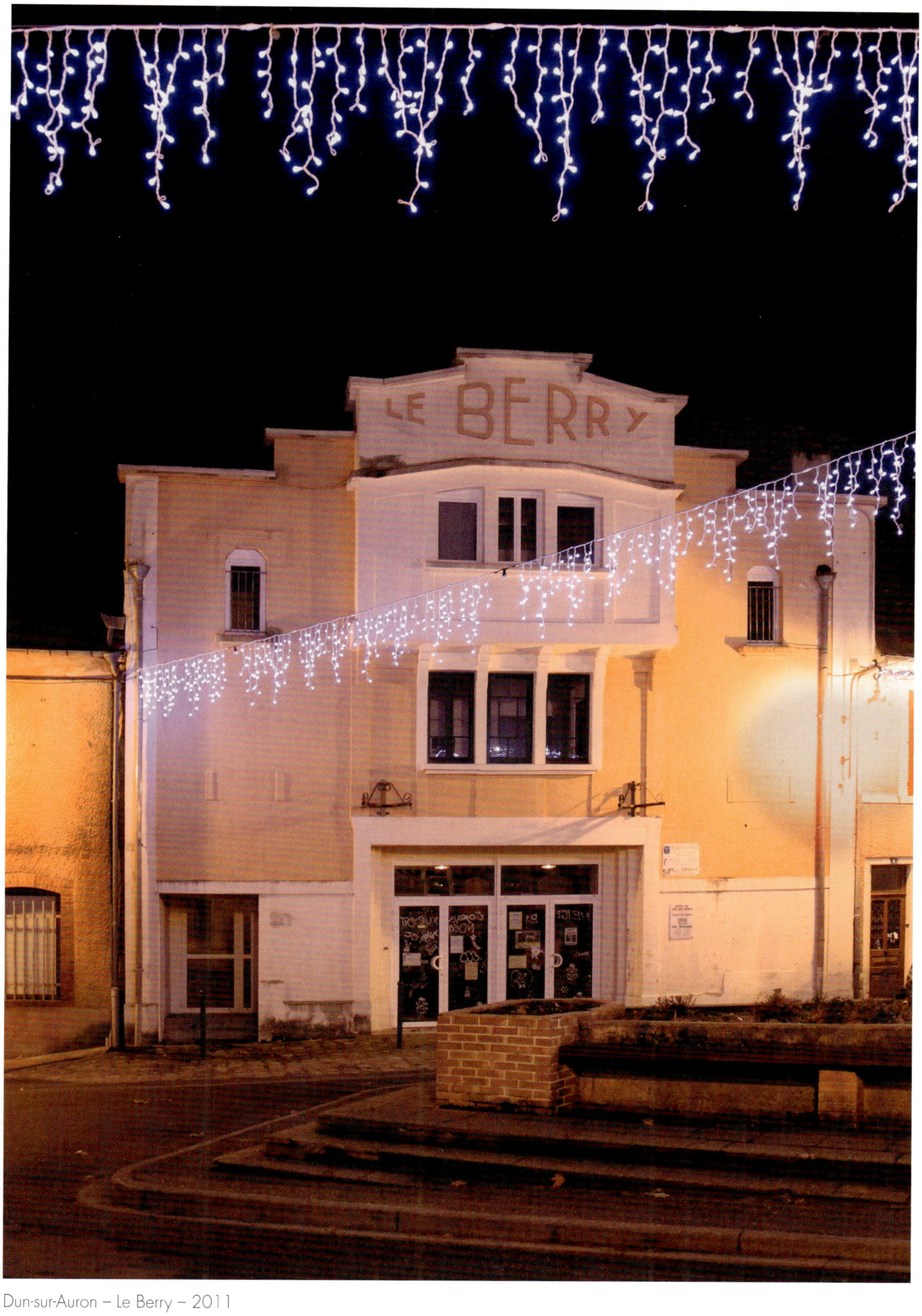

Dun-sur-Auron – Le Berry – 2011

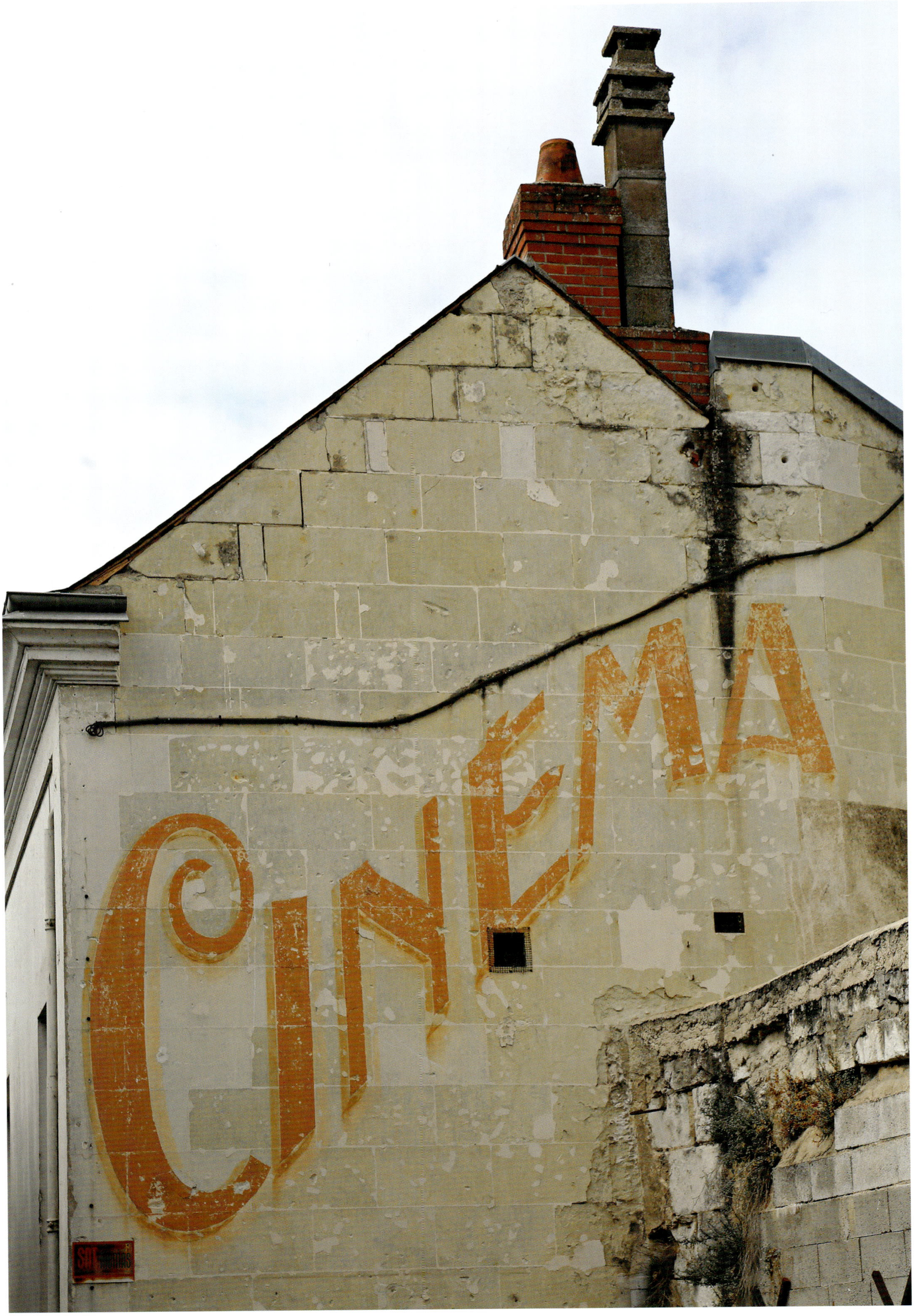

Montrichard – Le Régent – 2017

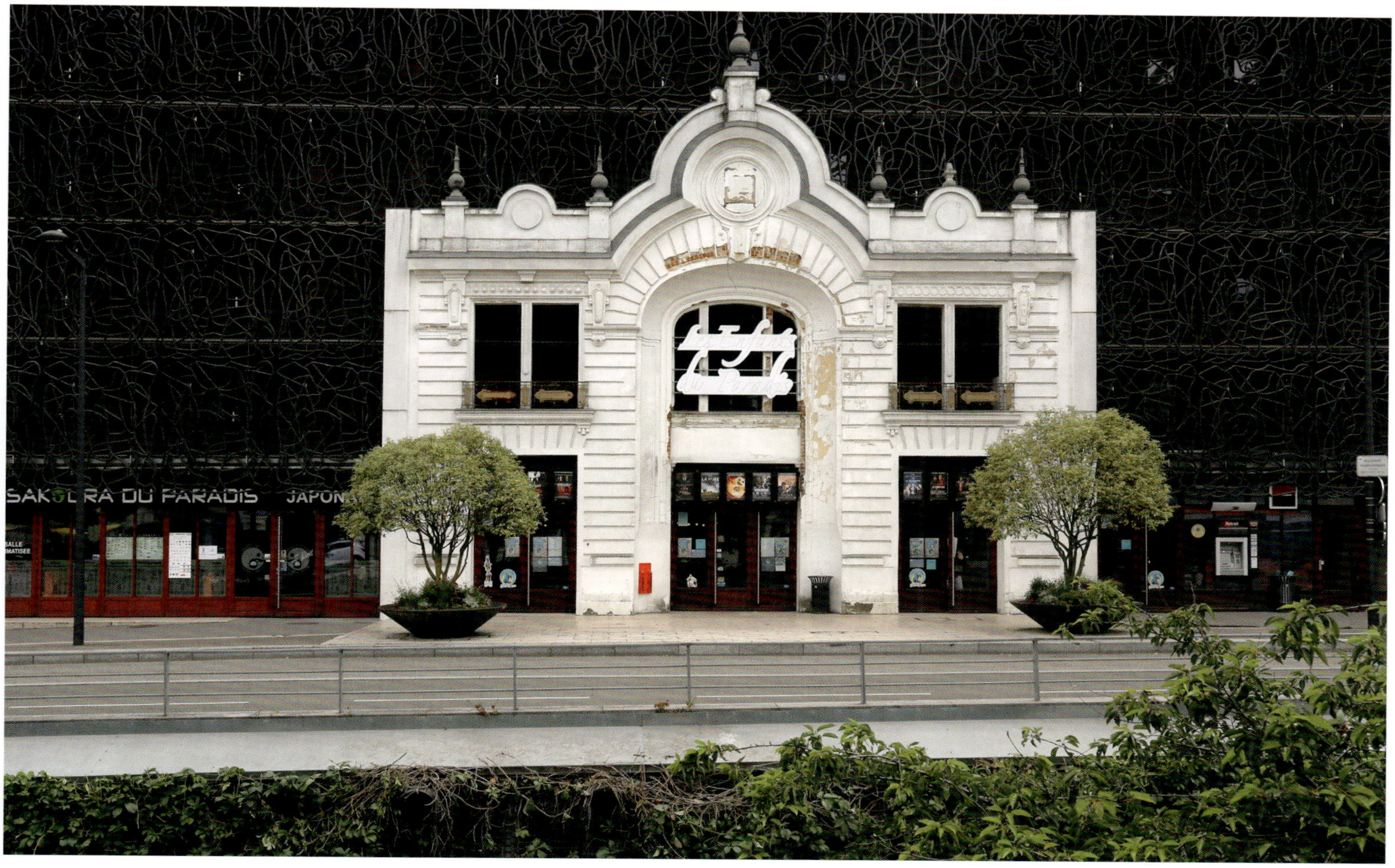

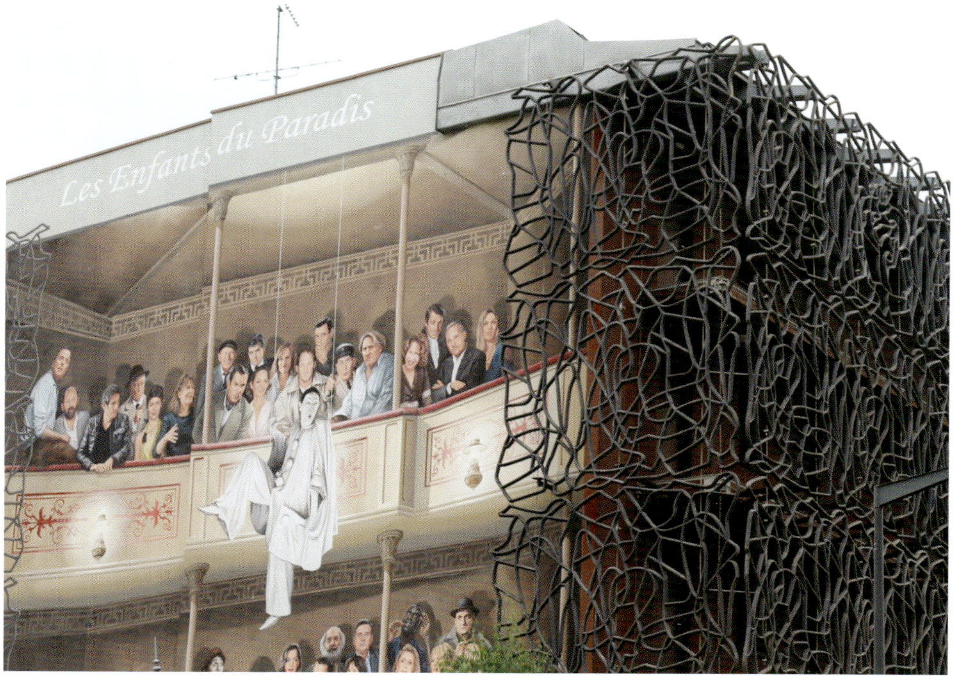

Chartres – Les Enfants du paradis – 2021

Chartres, Les Enfants du paradis. In France more than anywhere else beautiful films never leave the screen or our memory. They parade through our brains like the chorus of a song. Certain sequences become embedded in our heads. For eternity, maybe. Marcel Carné's *Les Enfants du paradis* (Children of Paradise) in Chartres. Charlie Chaplin's *Les Lumières de la ville* (City Lights) in Rumilly.

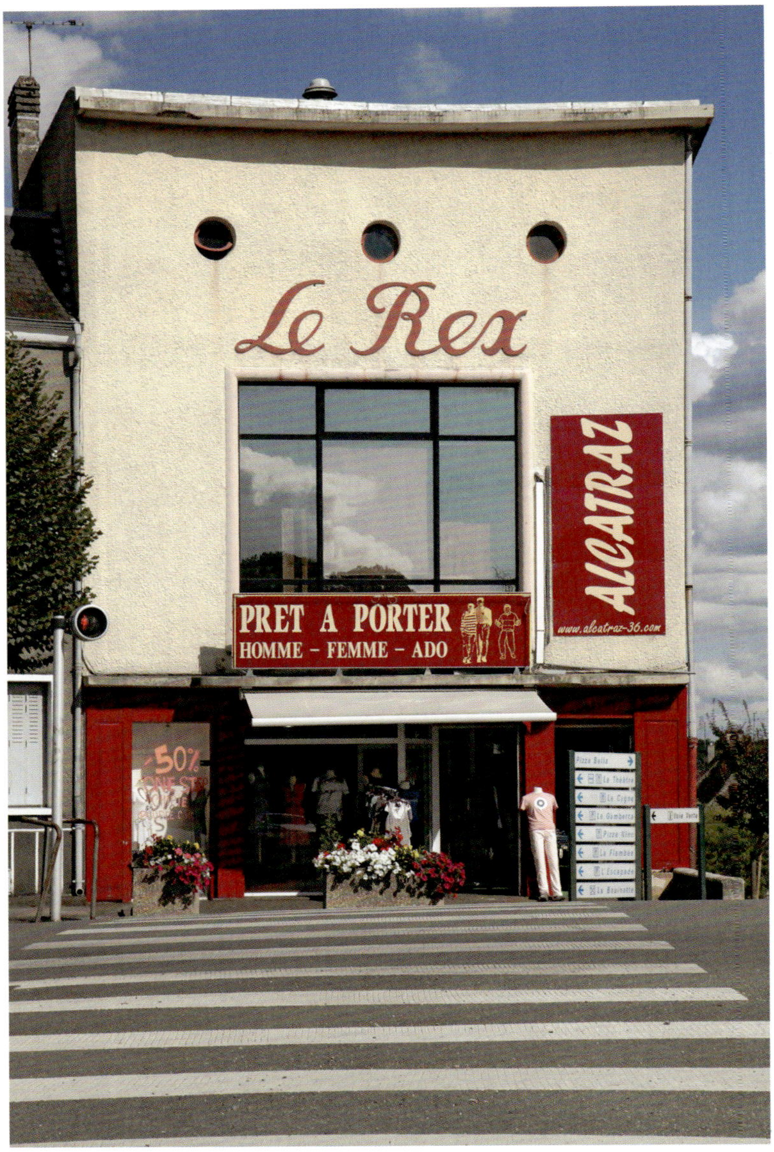

Le Blanc – Le Rex – 2012

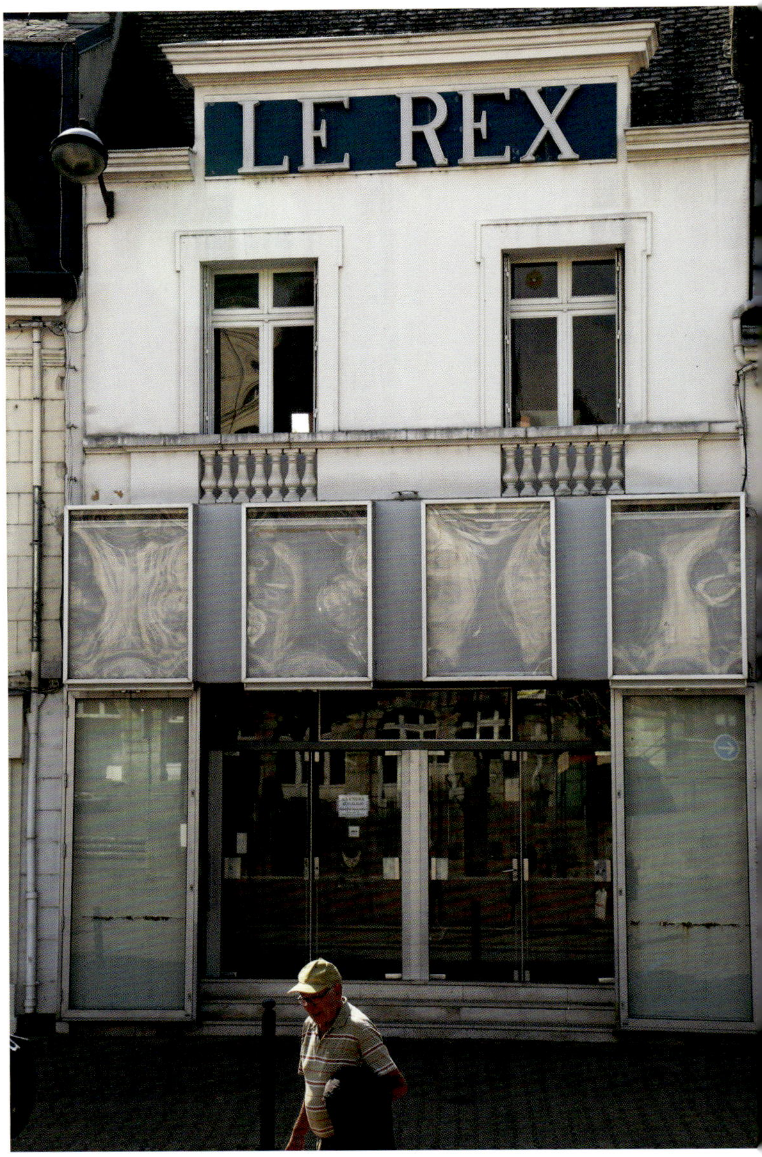

Nogent-le-Rotrou – ancien Rex – 2018

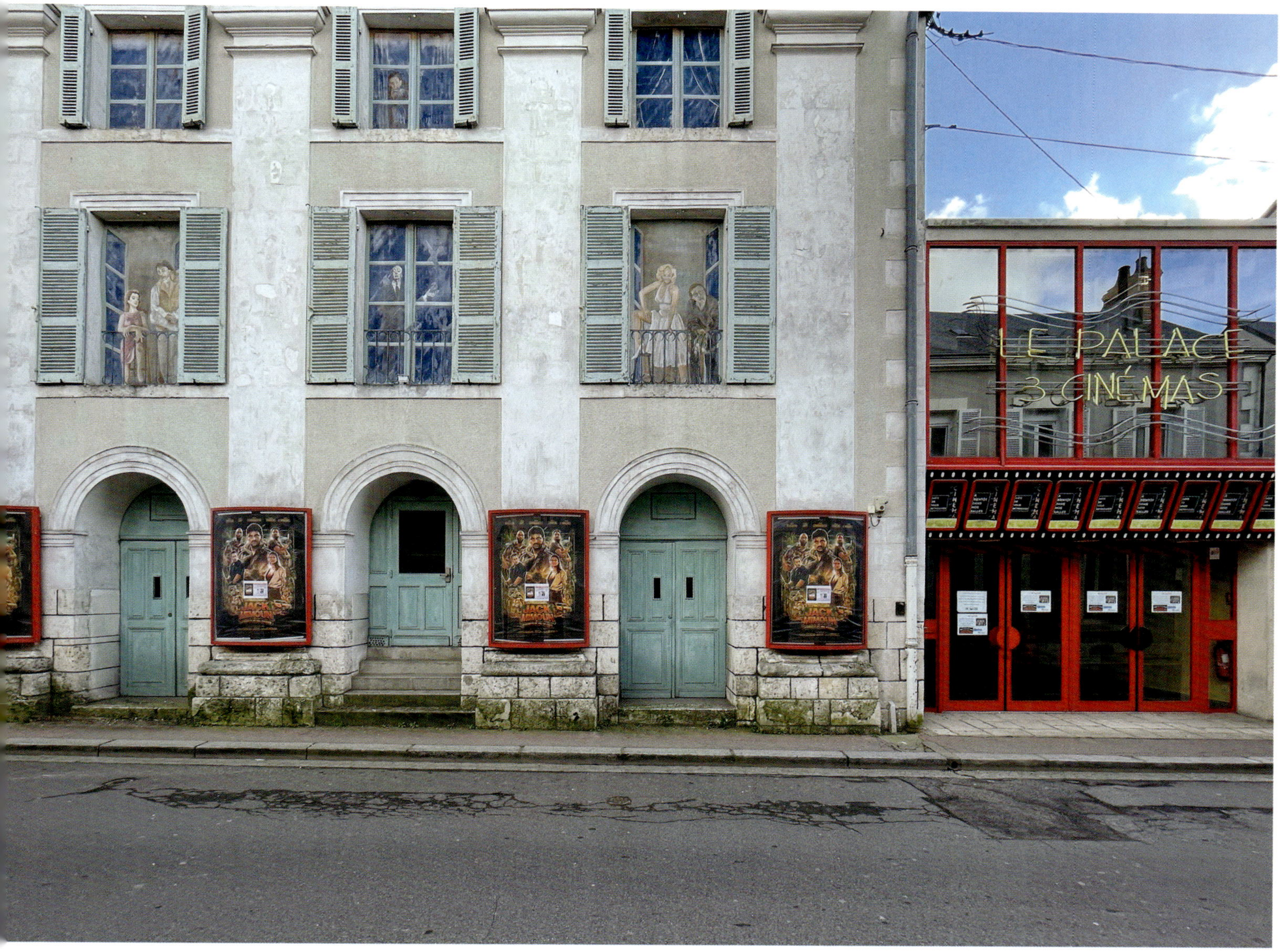

omorantin-Lanthenay – Le Palace – 2023

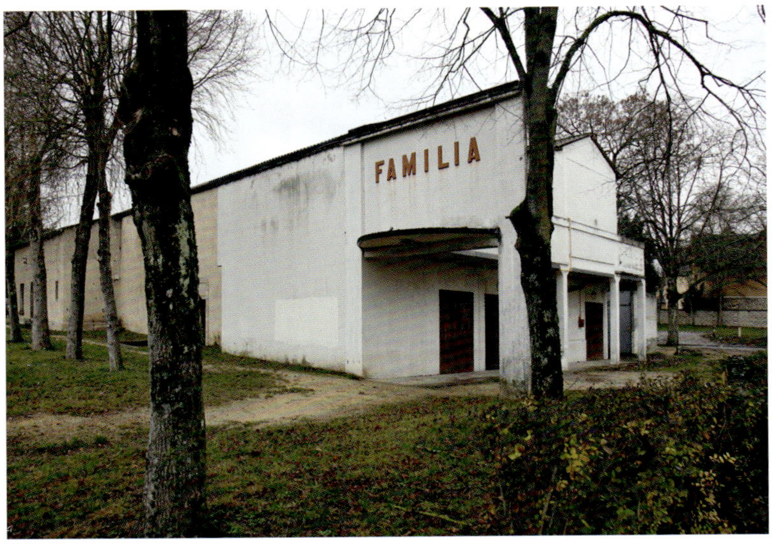

Bourges – Familia – 2011

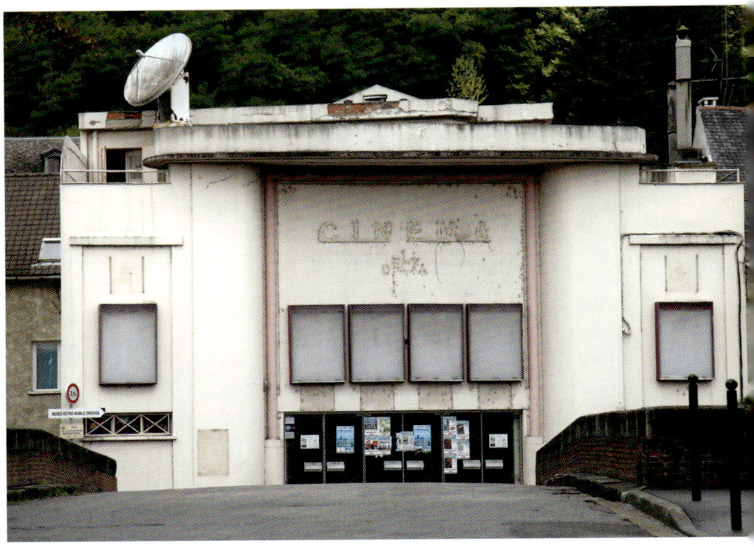

Dreux – Delta – 2013

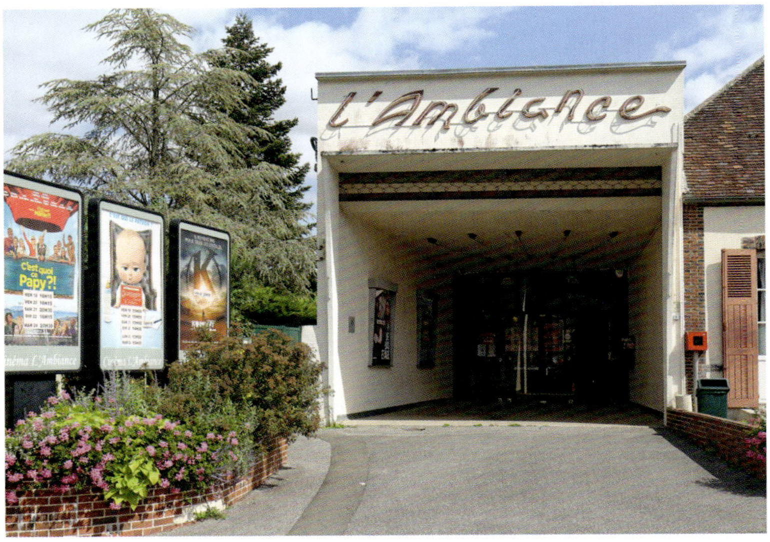

Senonches – L'Ambiance – 2021

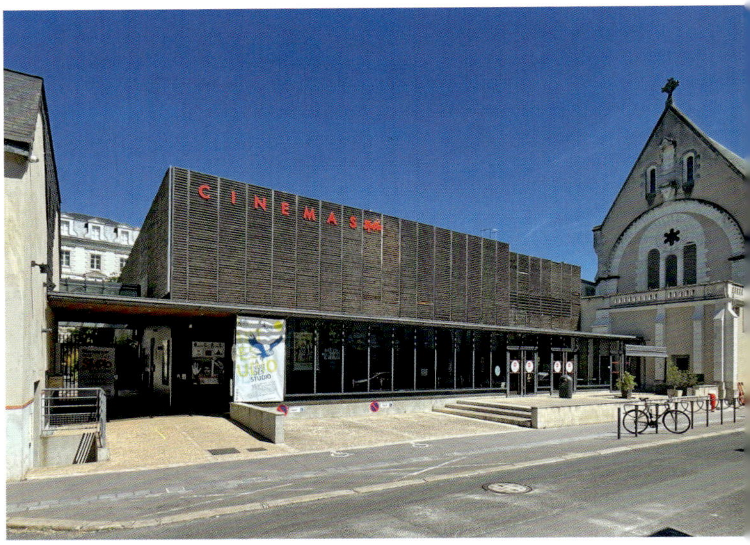

Tours – Studio – 2021

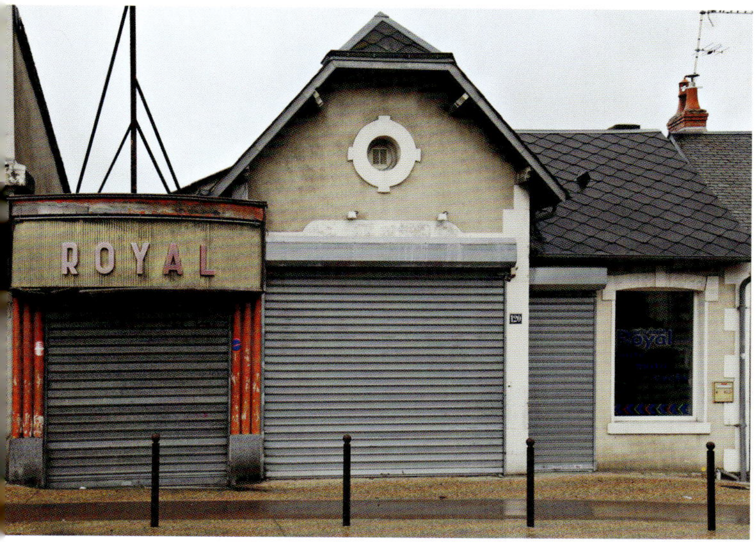

ourges – Royal – 2011

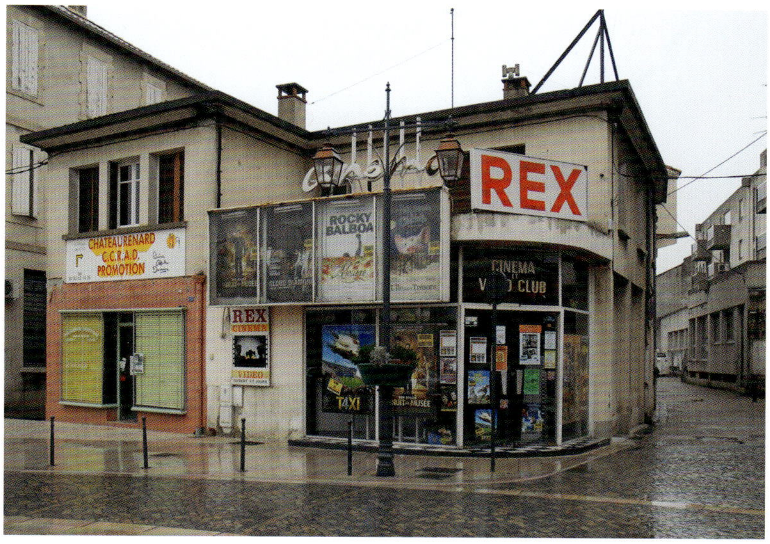

Château-Renard – Rex – 2006

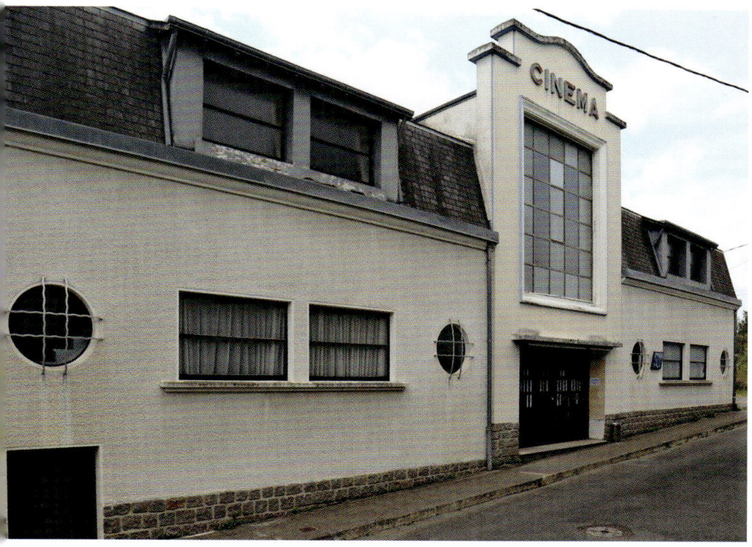

guerande – Moderne – 2017

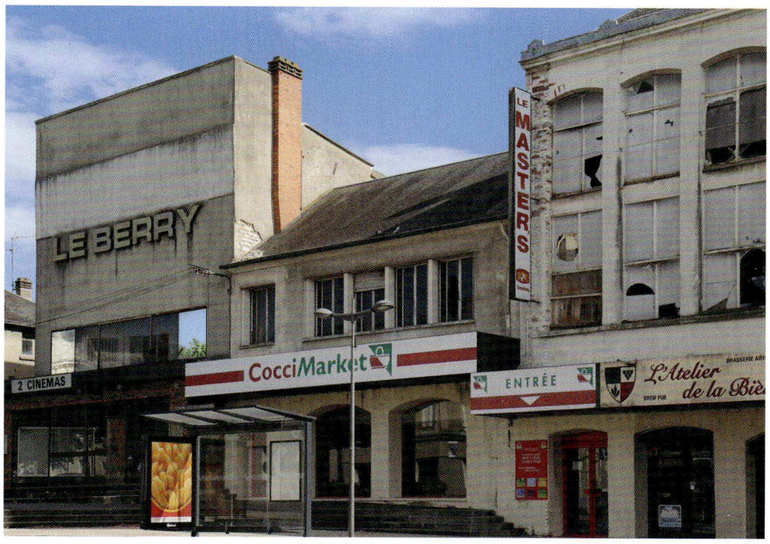

Issoudun – Le Berry – 2020

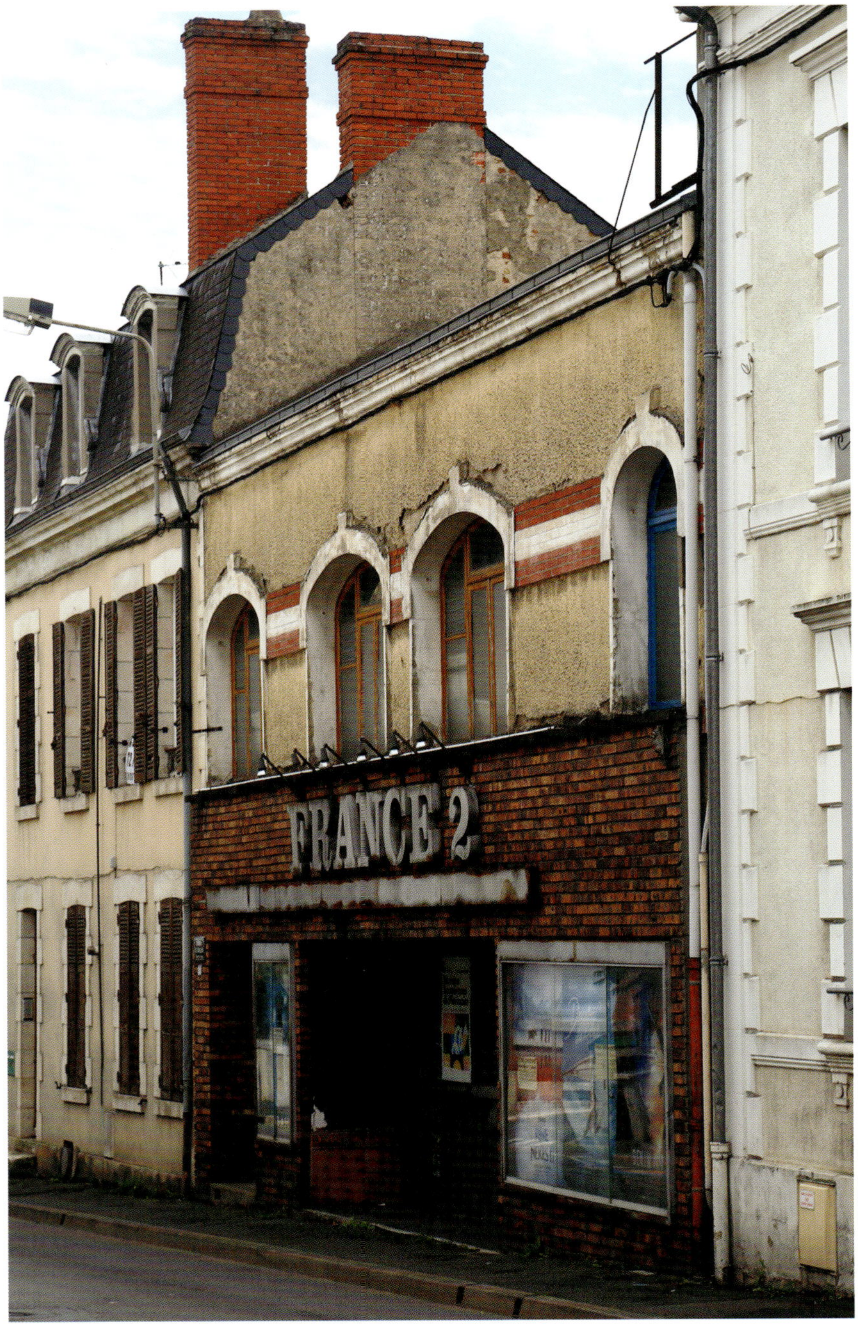

Vierzon – France 2 – 2020

Vierzon, France 2. Not a very cinematographic town, a sad and endless street with noisy cars that never stop and even seem to want to avoid this corner where the long-forgotten France 2 cinema survives its conversion. It was bought by Jack Pascaux to turn into an Aladdin's cave of a thousand treasures. Inside, an apocalyptic vision meets the visitor's gaze – projectors sitting on the armchairs and just about anywhere else. Visually a lovely film sequence. Difficult to walk through this overcrowded labyrinth, to squeeze in perhaps, and how. A life for a passion. Posters and assorted objects offer a succession of flashbacks to the amazed visitor. Without the stubbornness of Pascaux, these religiously preserved marvels would have fallen into the jaws of a few hungry skips ... But what will become of them one day anyway?

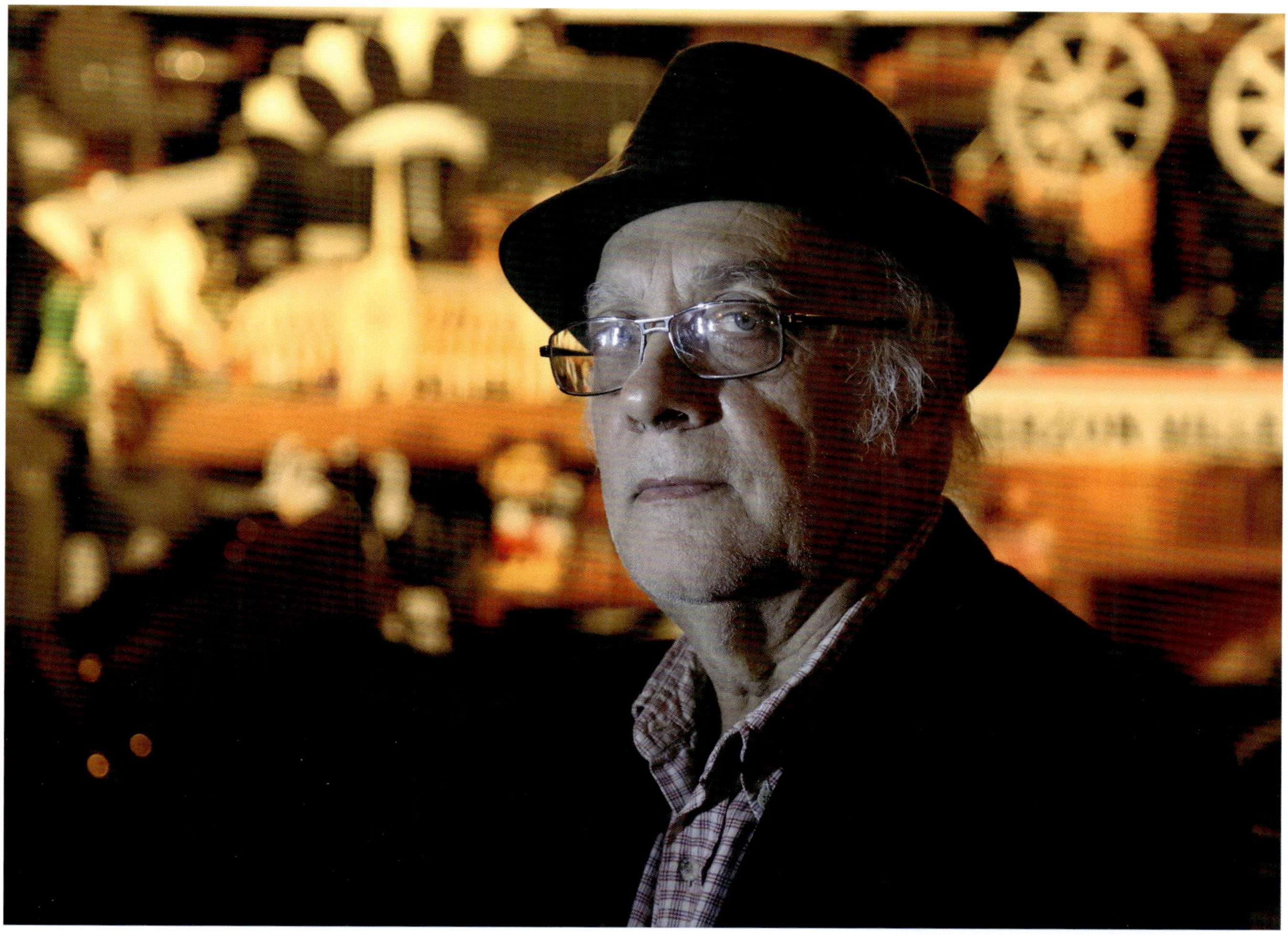

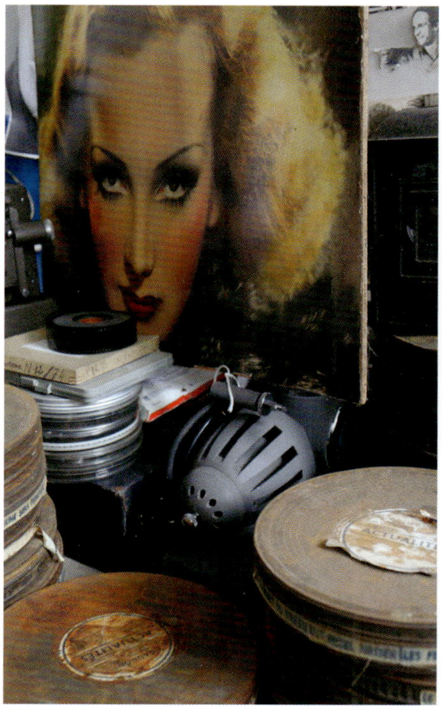

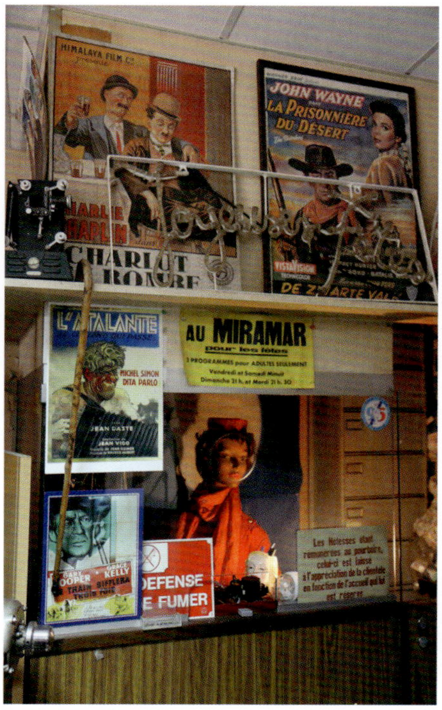
HIMALAYA FILM
JOHN WAYNE
LA PRISONNIÈRE DU DÉSERT
CHARLOT
L'ATALANTE
MICHEL SIMON
DITA PARLO
JEAN DASTÉ
AU MIRAMAR
pour les fêtes
KELLY
DÉFENSE
FUMER

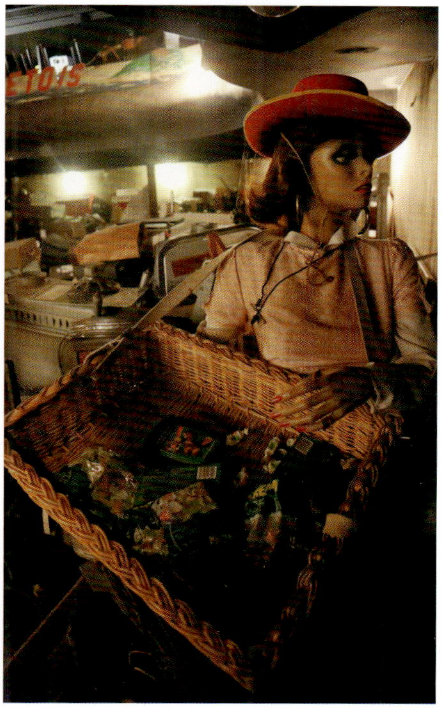

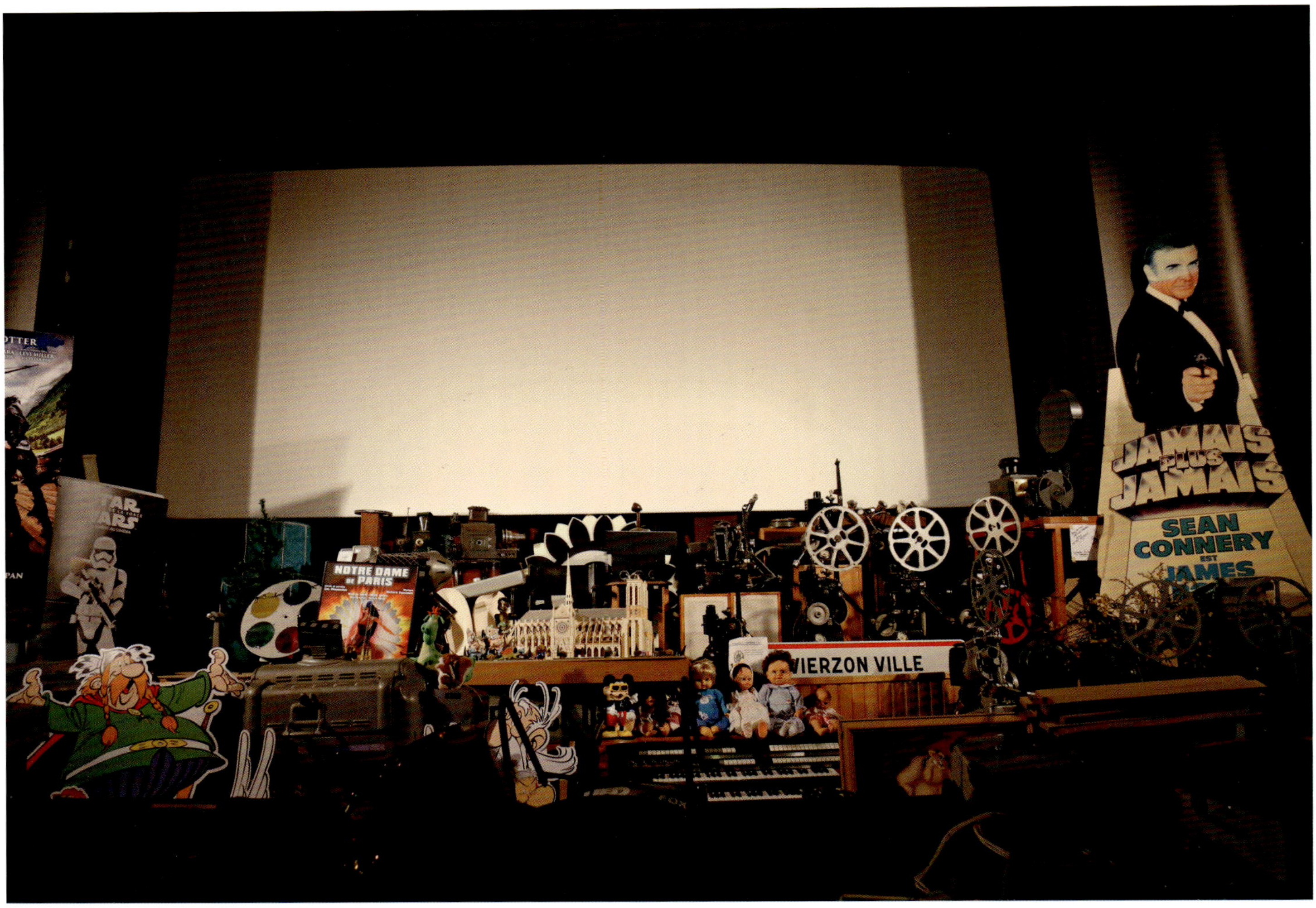

Vierzon – France 2

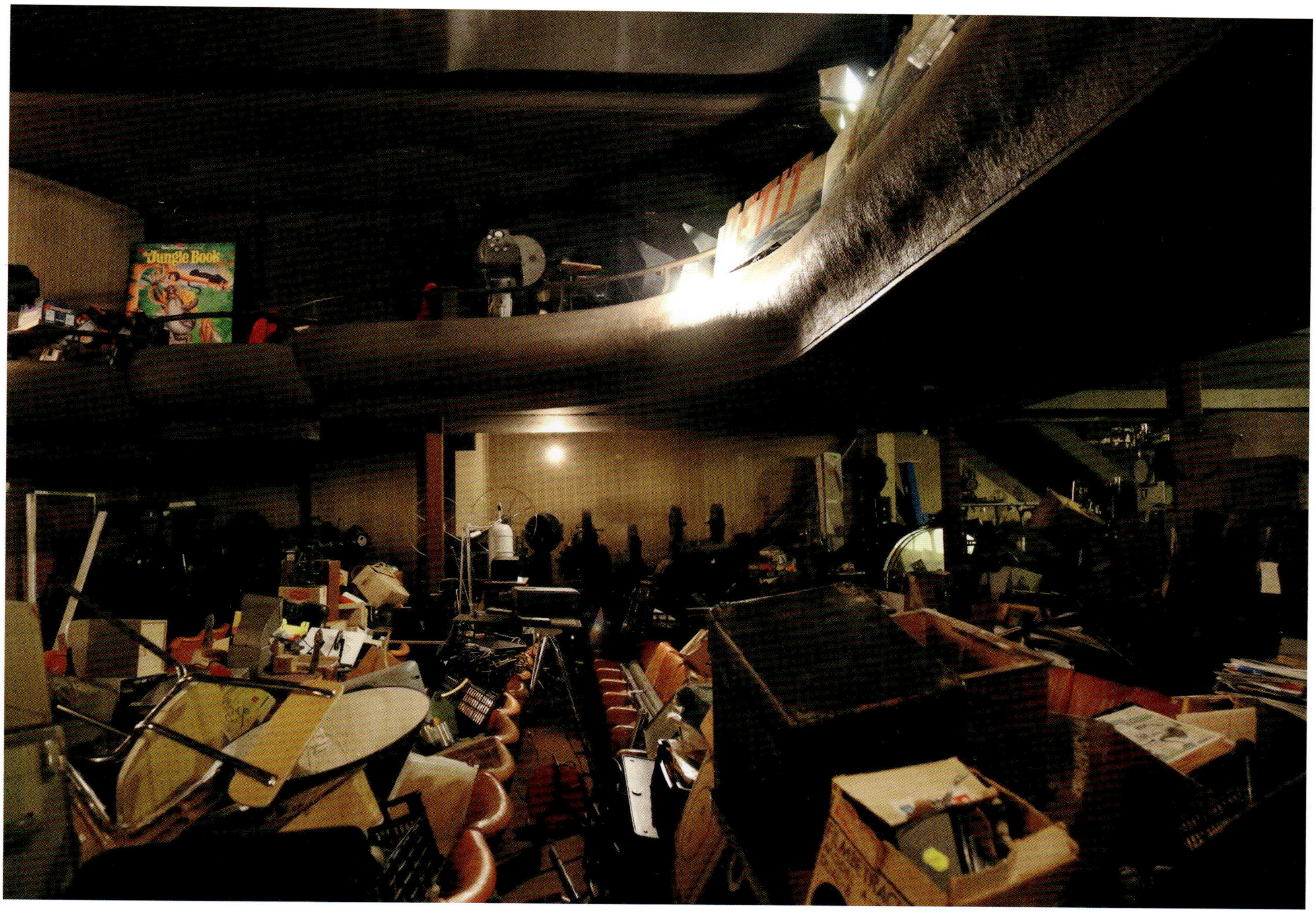

Vierzon – France 2

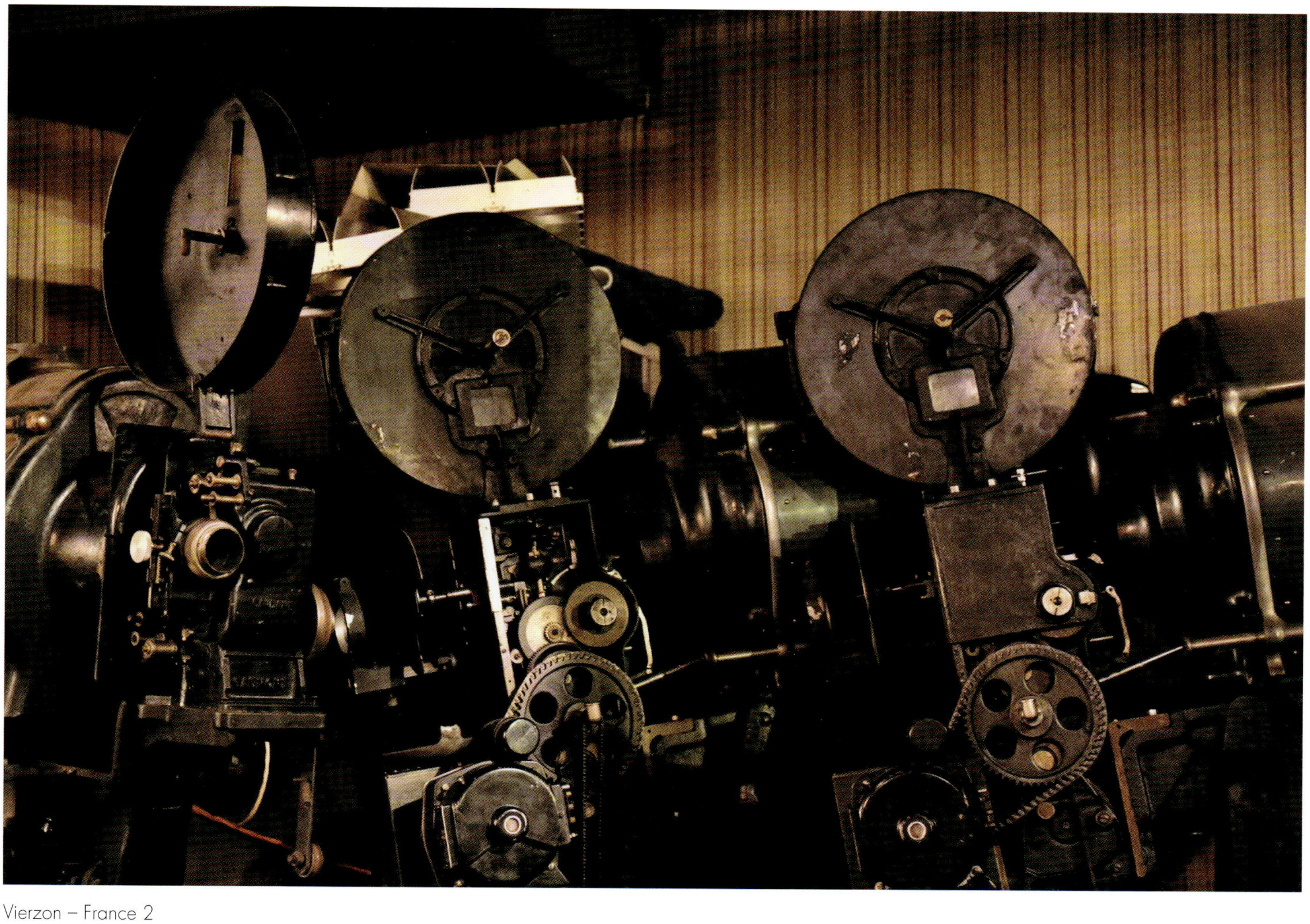

Vierzon – France 2

GRAND EST

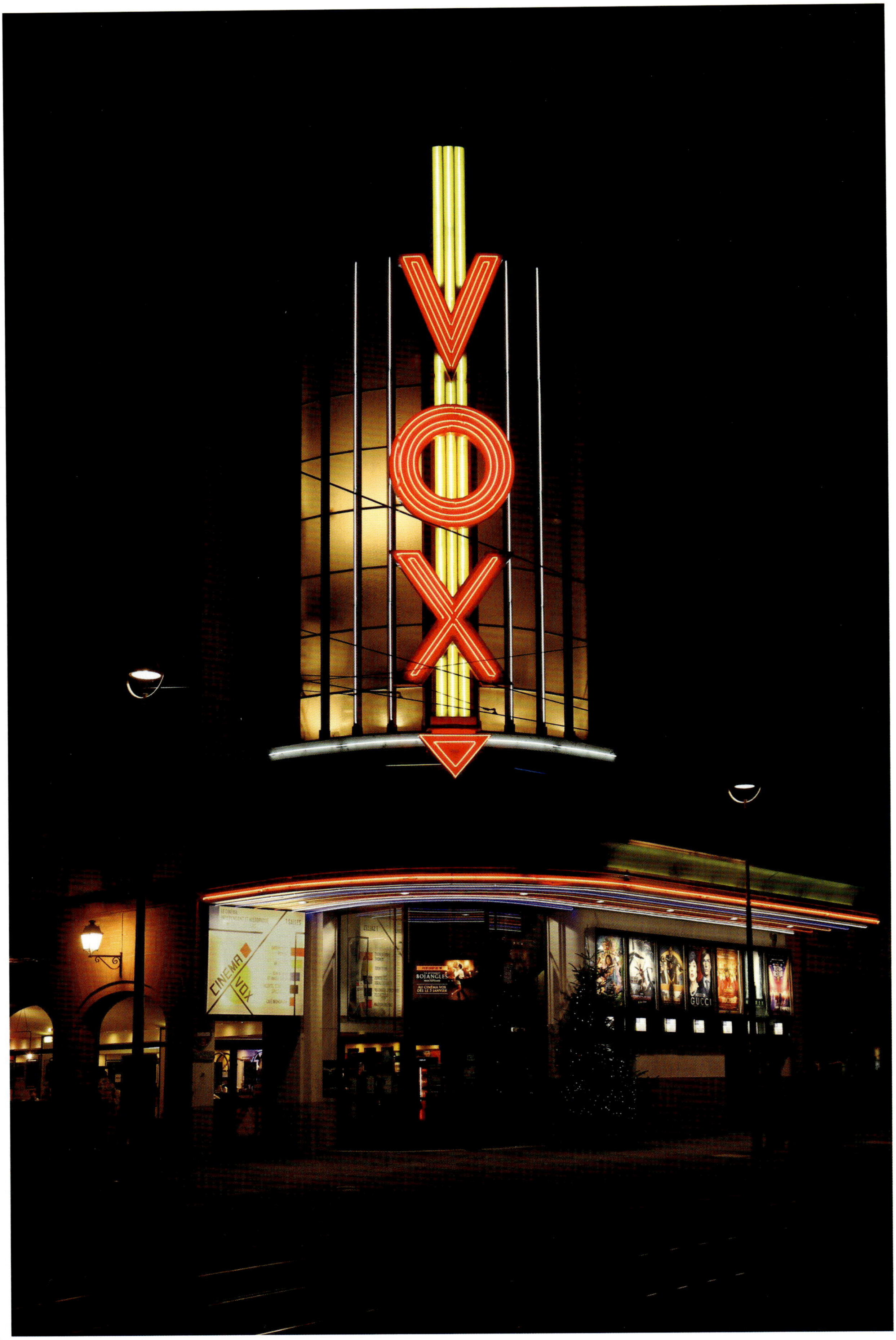

Strasbourg – Vox – 2022

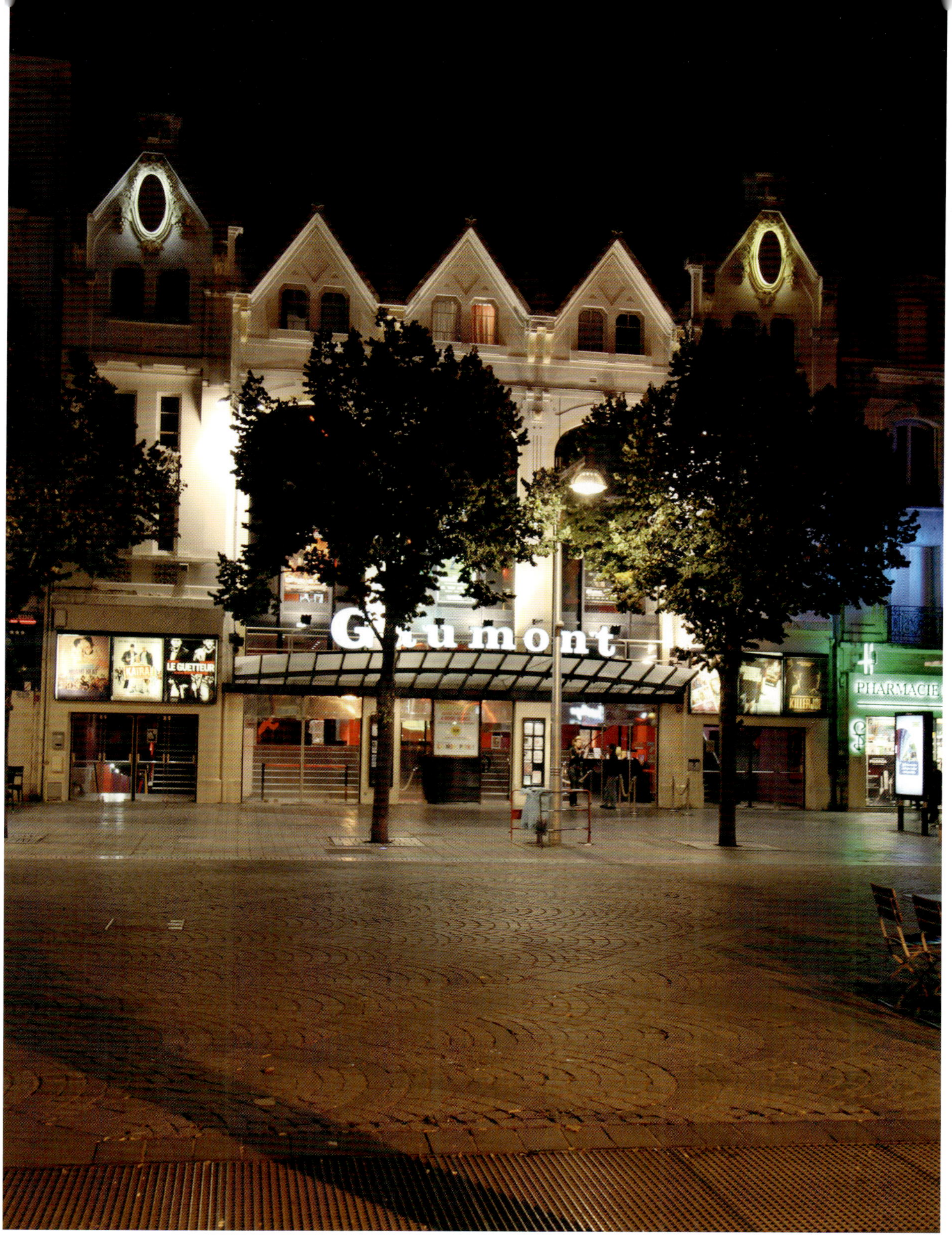

Reims – Gaumont – 2012

Strasbourg, Vox. The Hollywood-style Vox is impressive with its sparkling neon lights and concrete façade. Designed before the war, it didn't open until 1946. In the French movie landscape the architecture of this cinema is exceptional. Stare at it for a long time at sunset, then close your eyes, open your ears. The traffic noise fades, the cars and the tram disappear. Your head becomes a giant screen on which John Ford's westerns and Vincente Minnelli's musicals scroll past. Life becomes possible again.

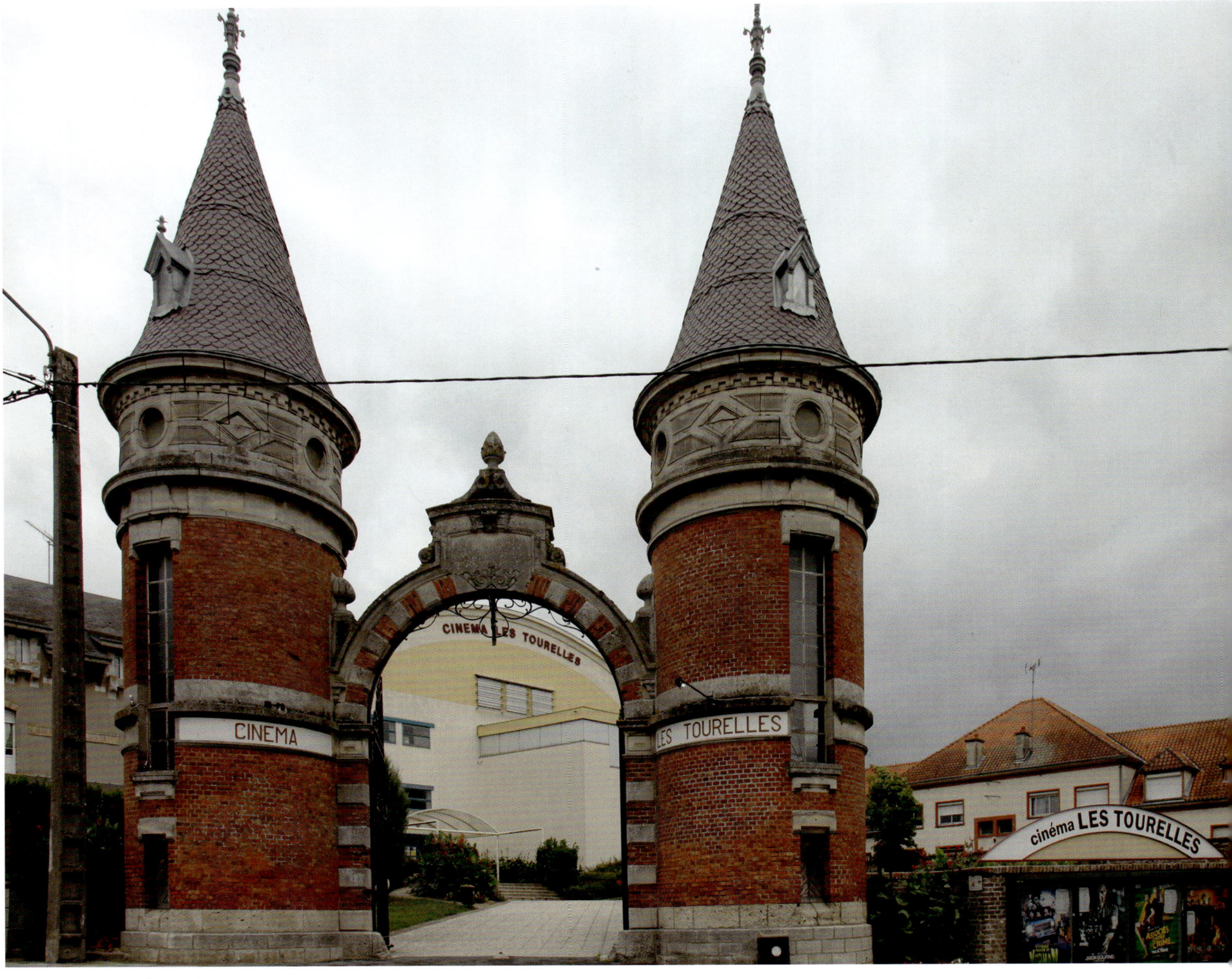

Vouziers – Les Tourelles – 2012

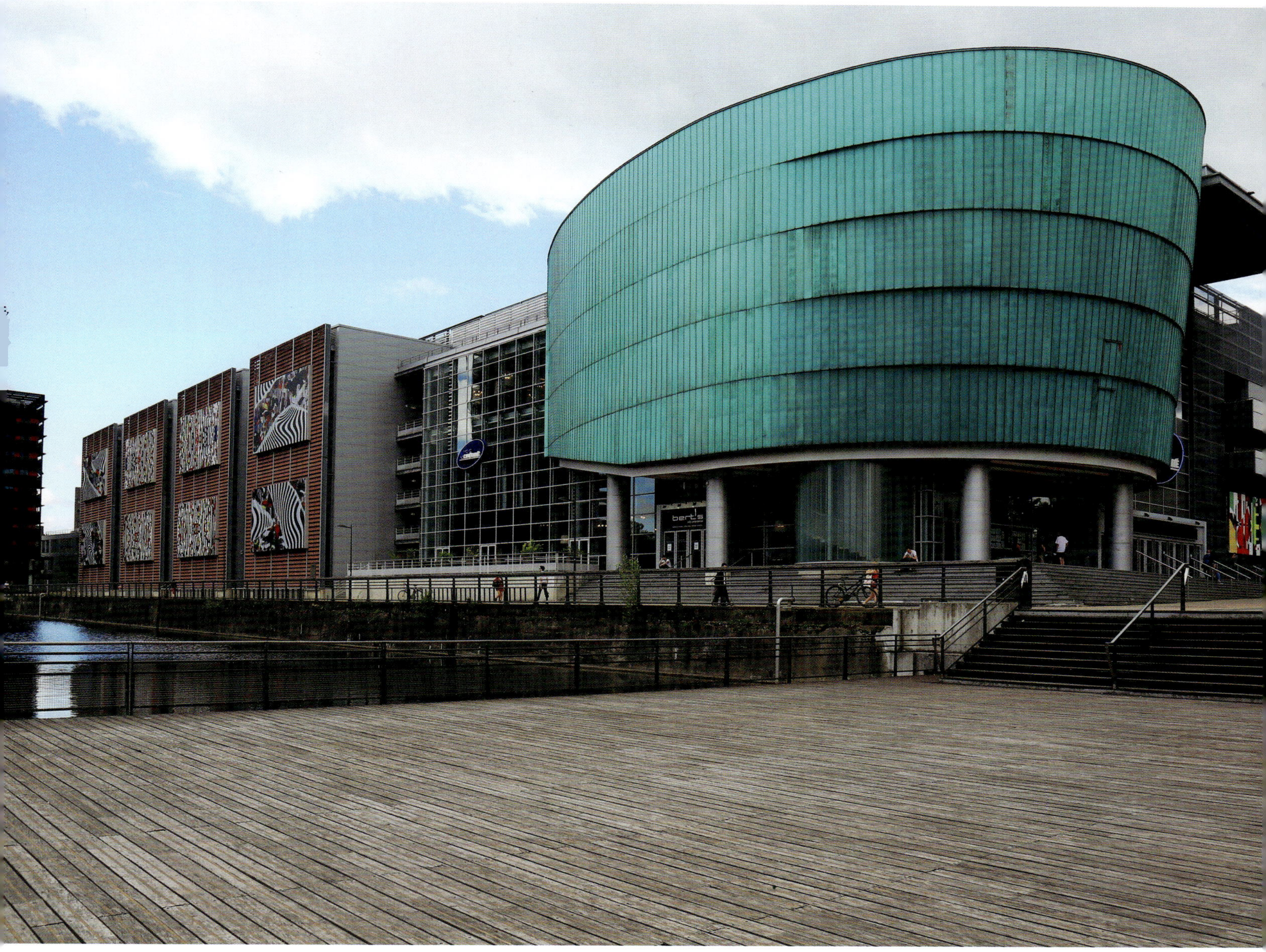

Strasbourg – Ciné Cité – 2020

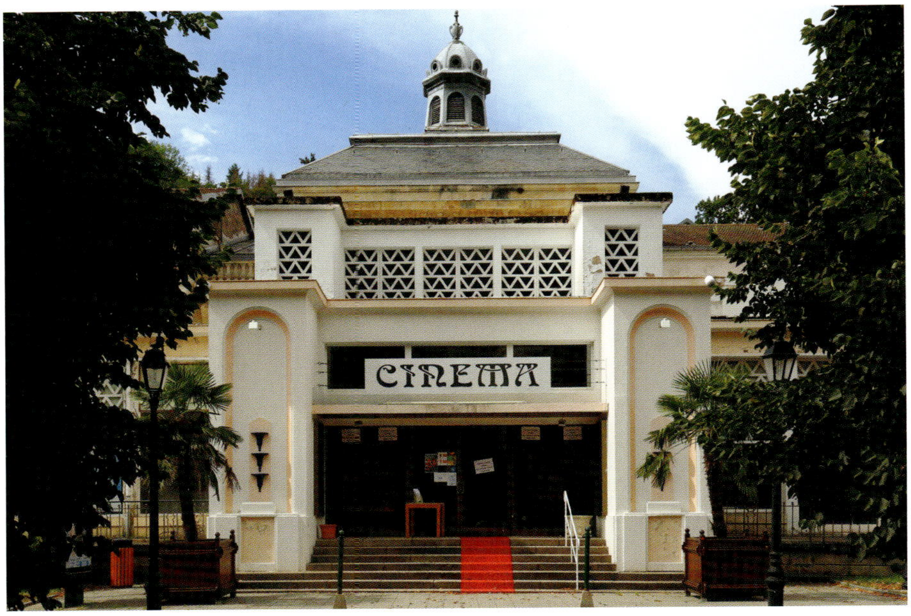

Plombières-les-Bains – Cinéma – 2020

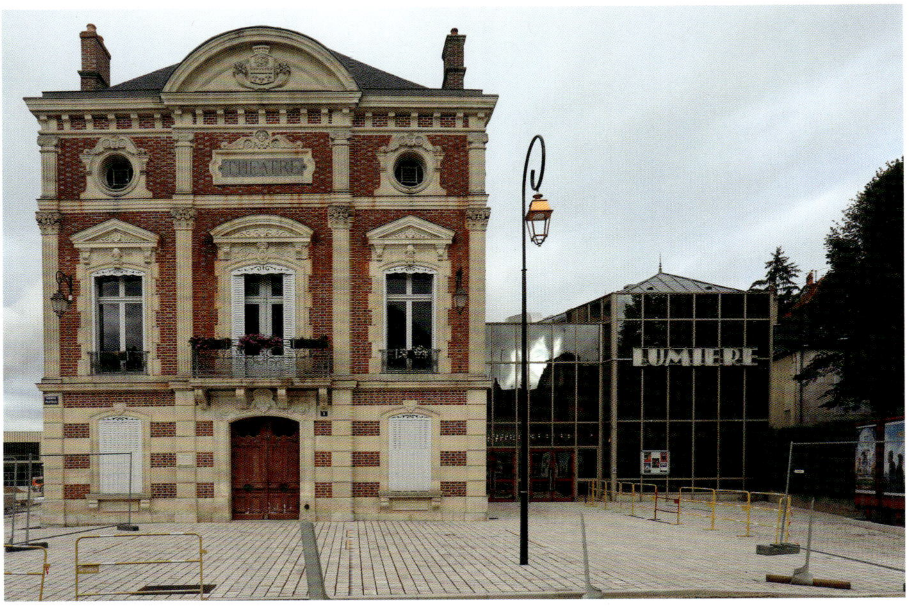

Nogent-sur-Seine – Lumière – 2019

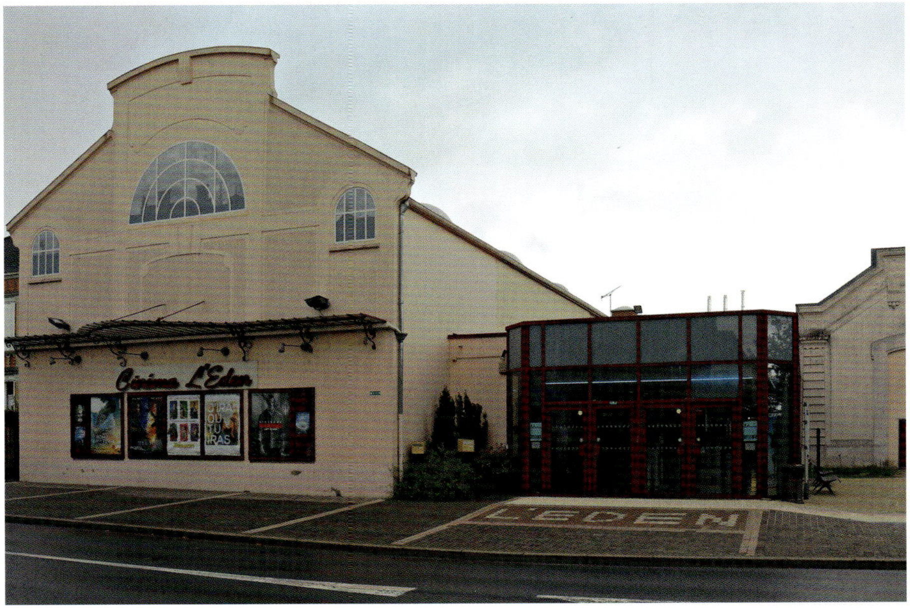

Romilly – L'Eden – 2019

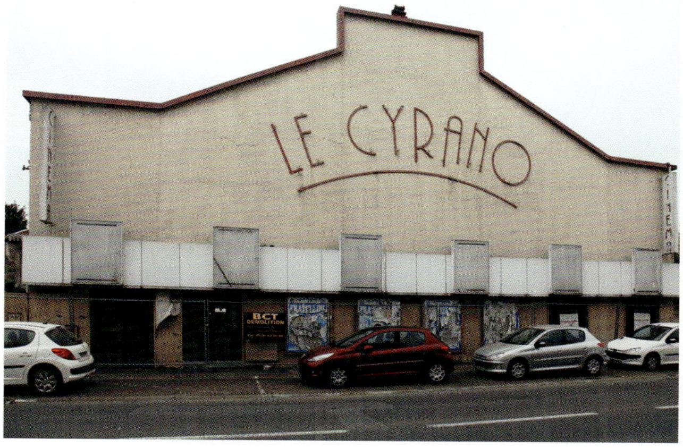

Saint-Dizier – Le Cyrano – 2014

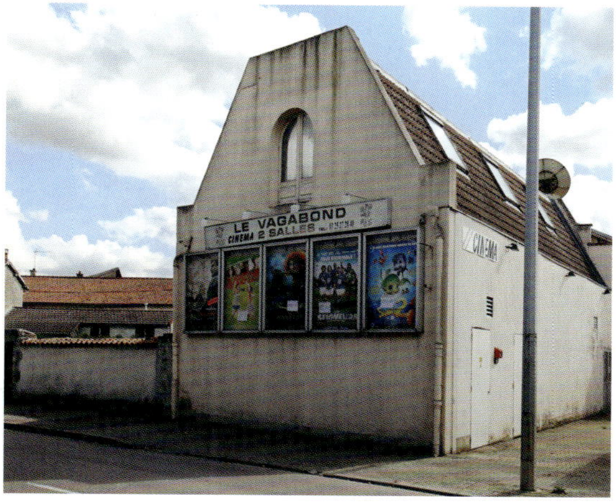

Bar-sur-Aube – Le Vagabond – 2012

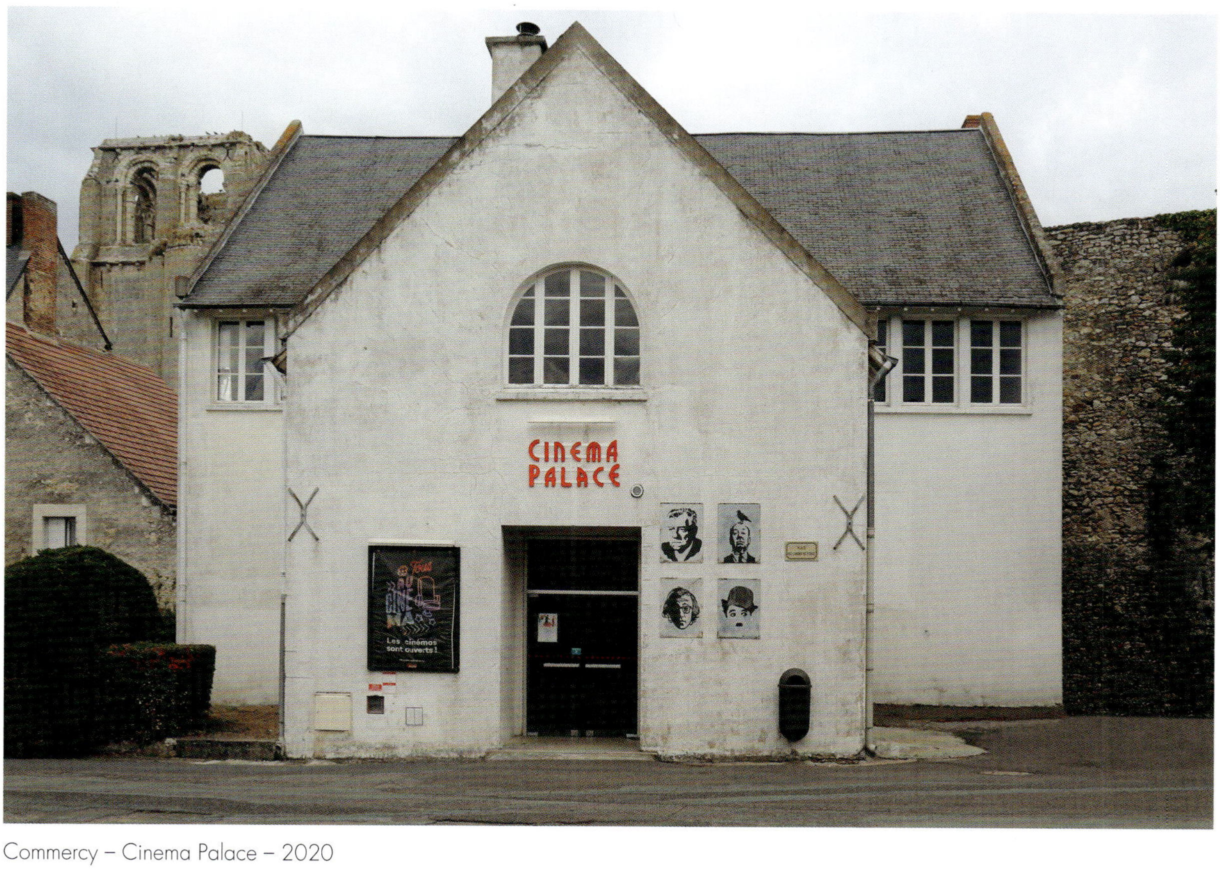

Commercy – Cinema Palace – 2020

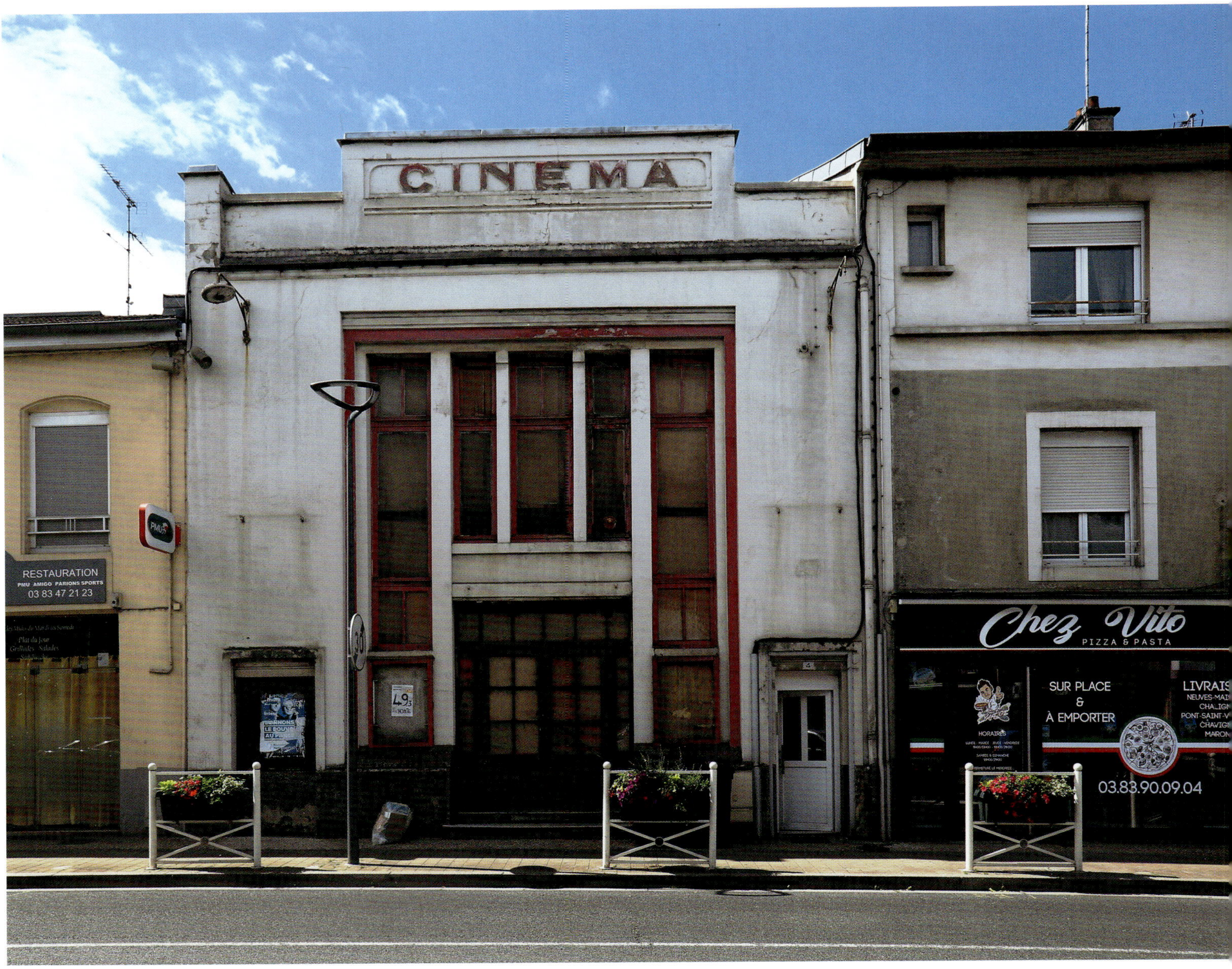

Neuves-Maison – Gérard – 2020

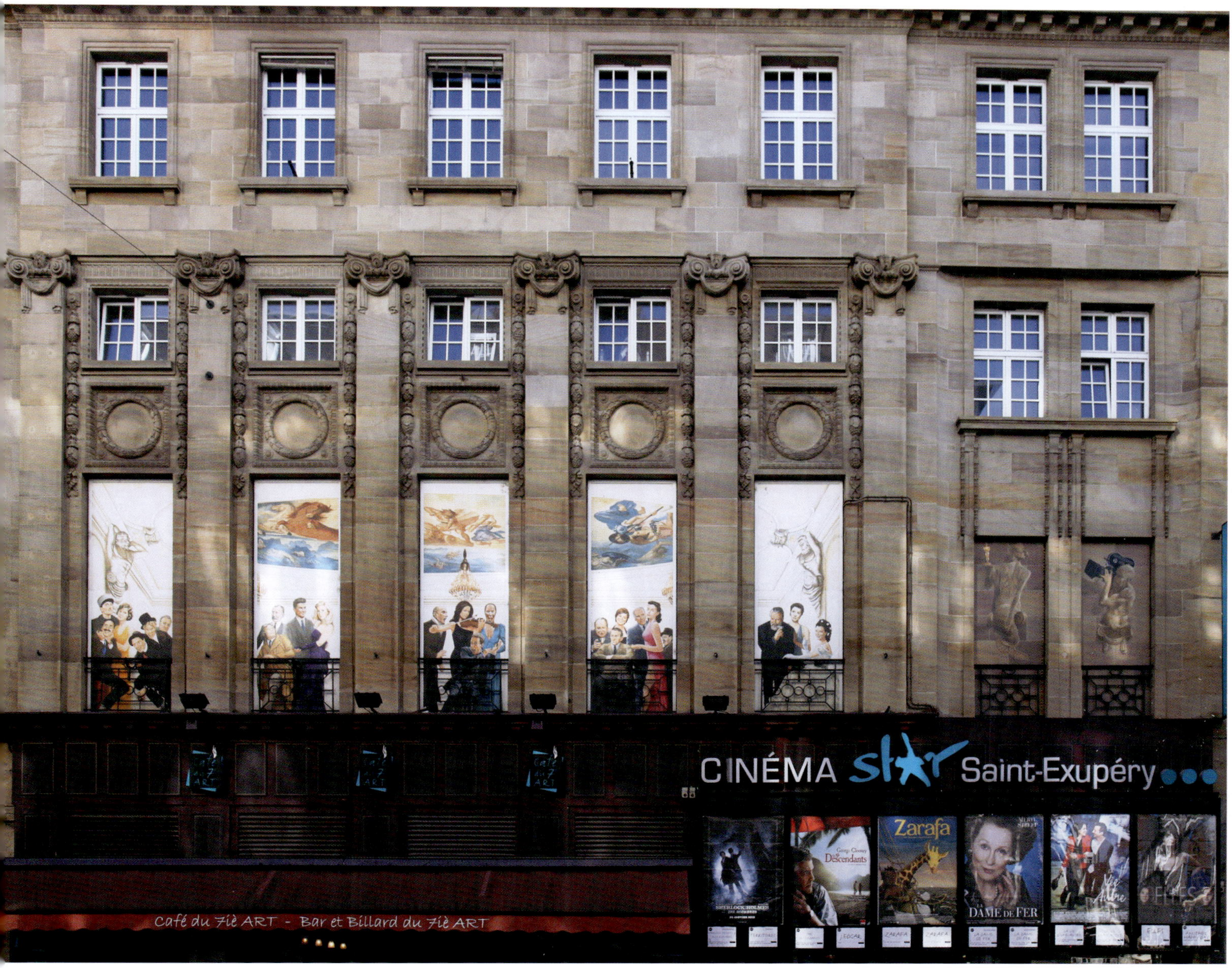

Strasbourg – Star Saint–Exupéry – 2012

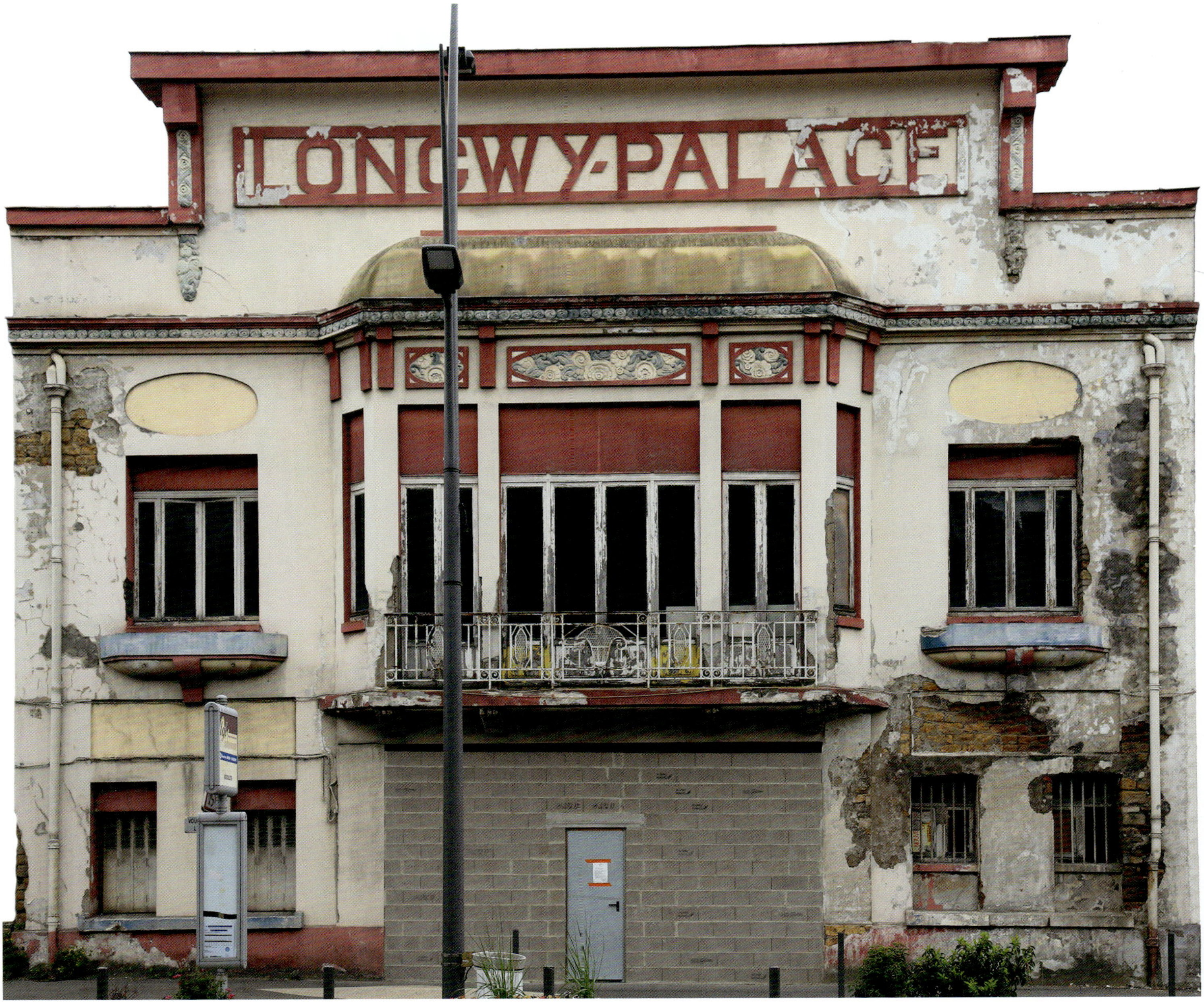

Longwy – Palace – 2020

Longwy, Palais du cinéma – Cinéma des familles – Longwy-Palace. The Palais du Cinéma, Cinéma des Familles and Longwy-Palace, with their sweet-sounding names, are no more than tottering shadows almost erased from the landscape of Longwy. This place is in search of a new identity to forget that it's a dormitory town reigned over by a Kinepolis as ugly as an airport reception hall.

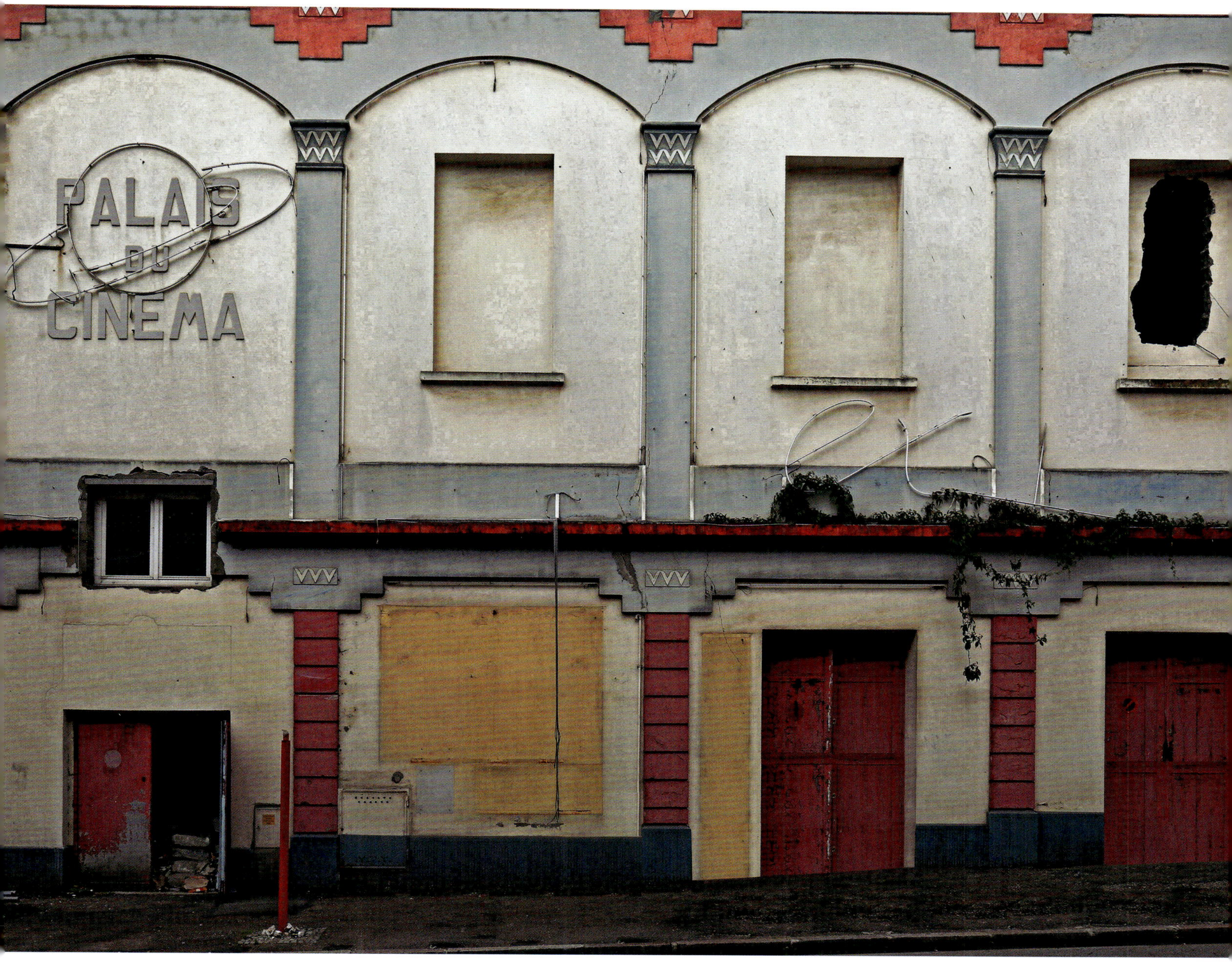

Longwy – Palais du Cinéma – 2020

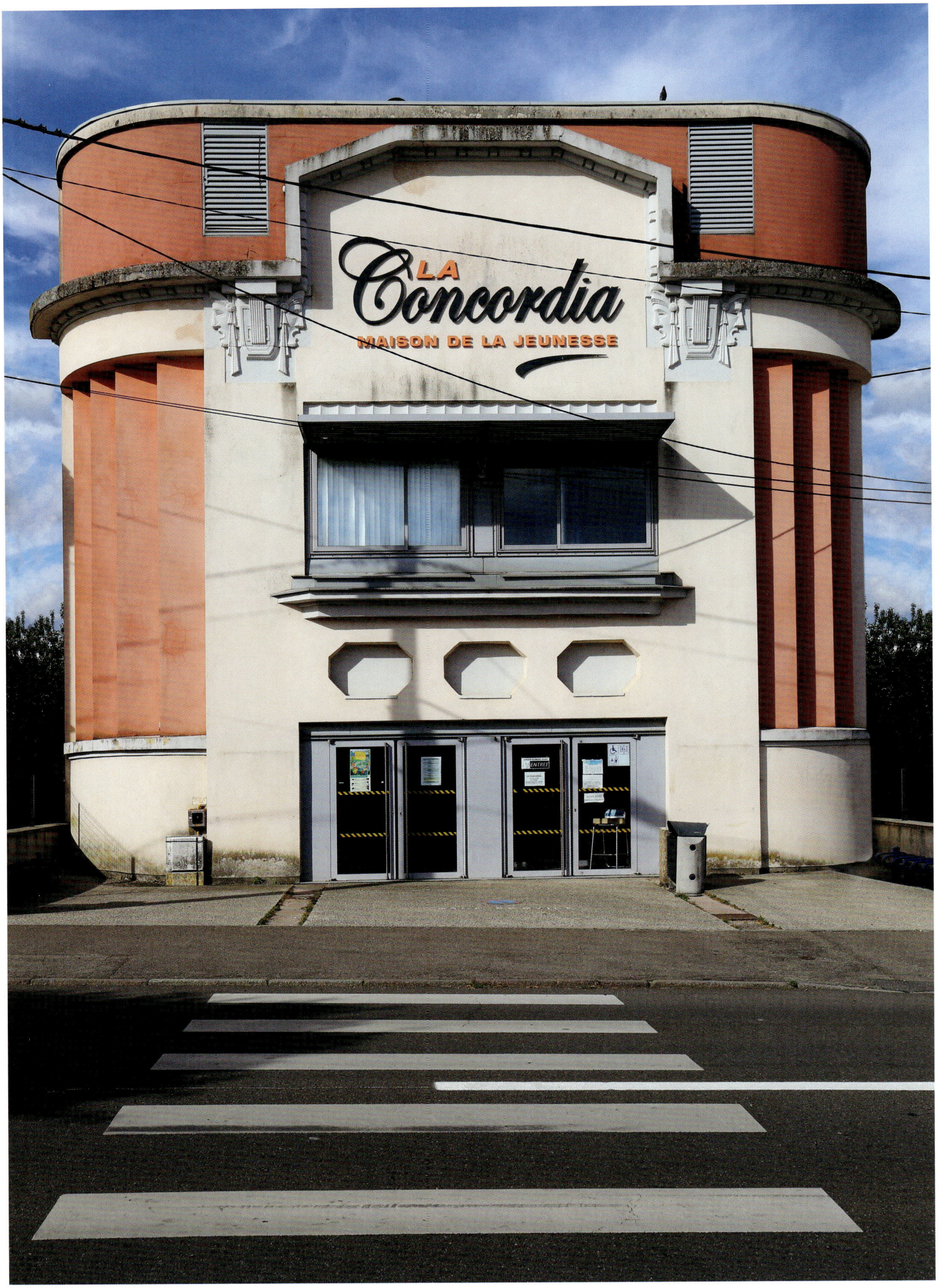

Jarny – Concordia – 2020

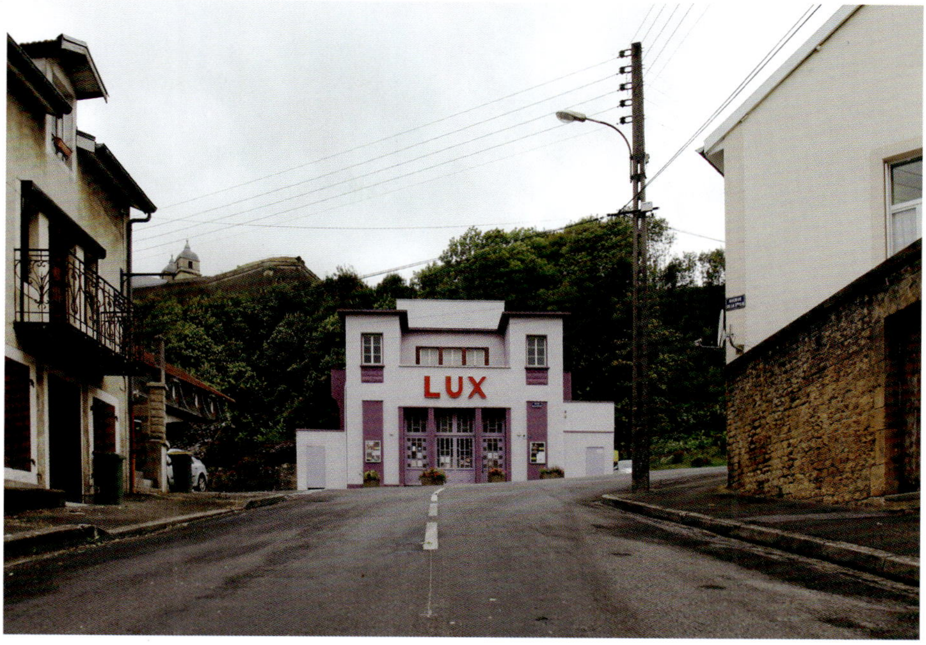

Montmédy – Lux – 2012

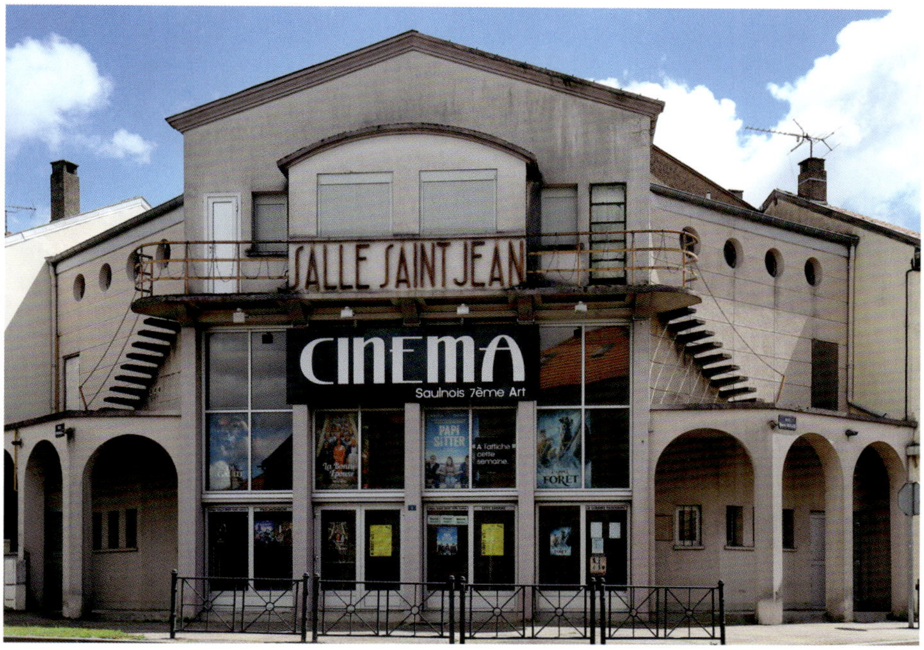

Château-Salins – Le Saulnois – 2020

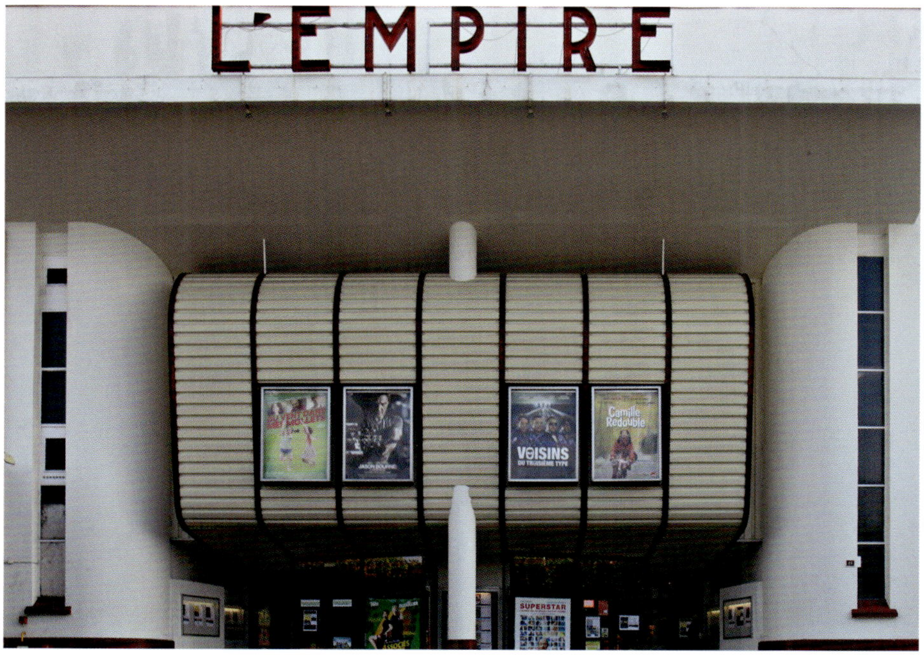

Saint-Dié-des-Vosges – L'Empire – 2012

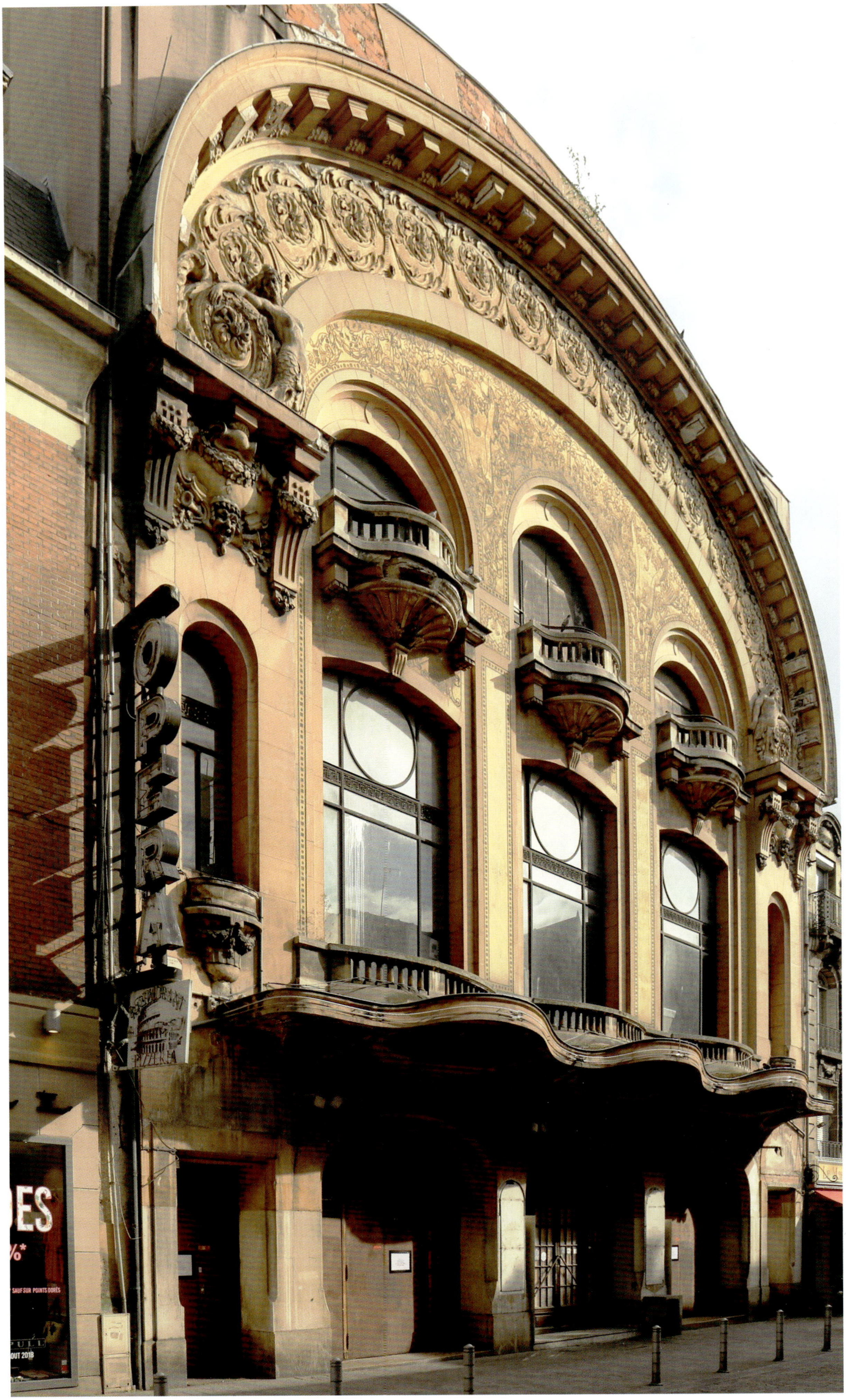

Reims – Opéra – 2018

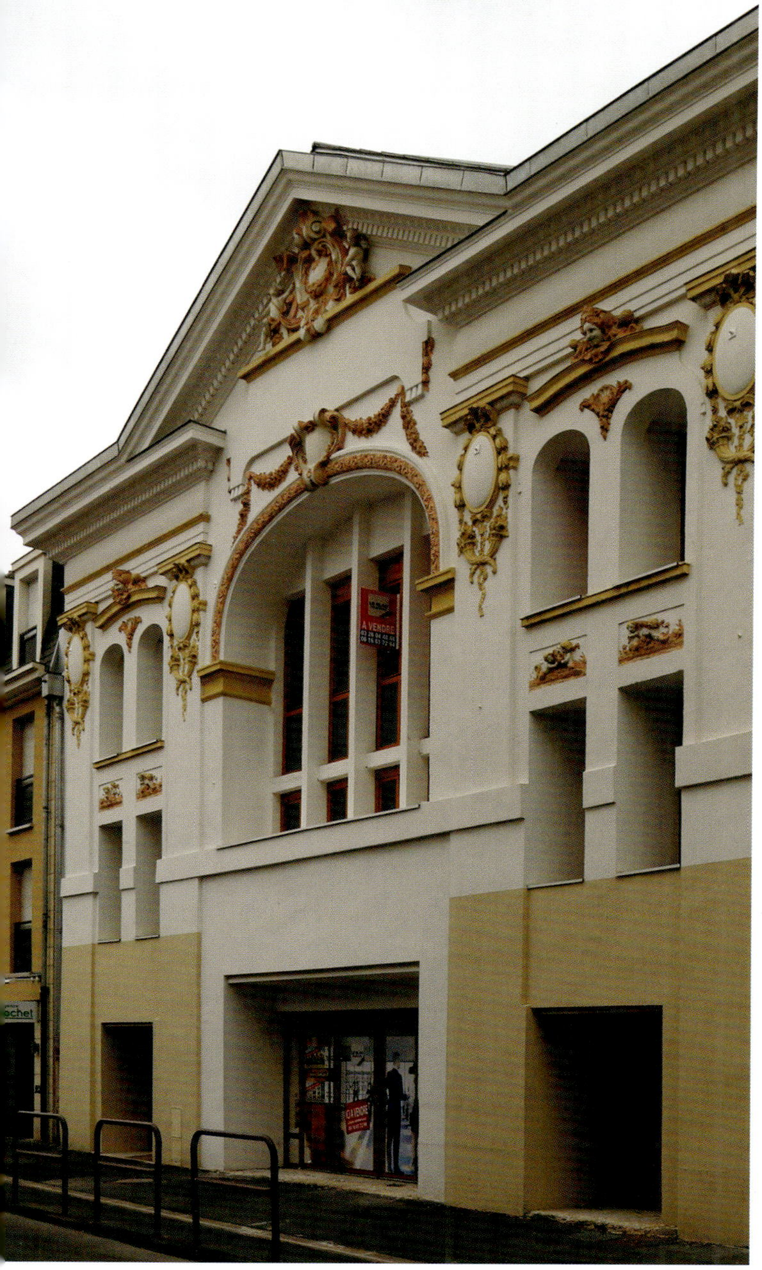

âlon-en-Champagne – Bernard Blier – 2018

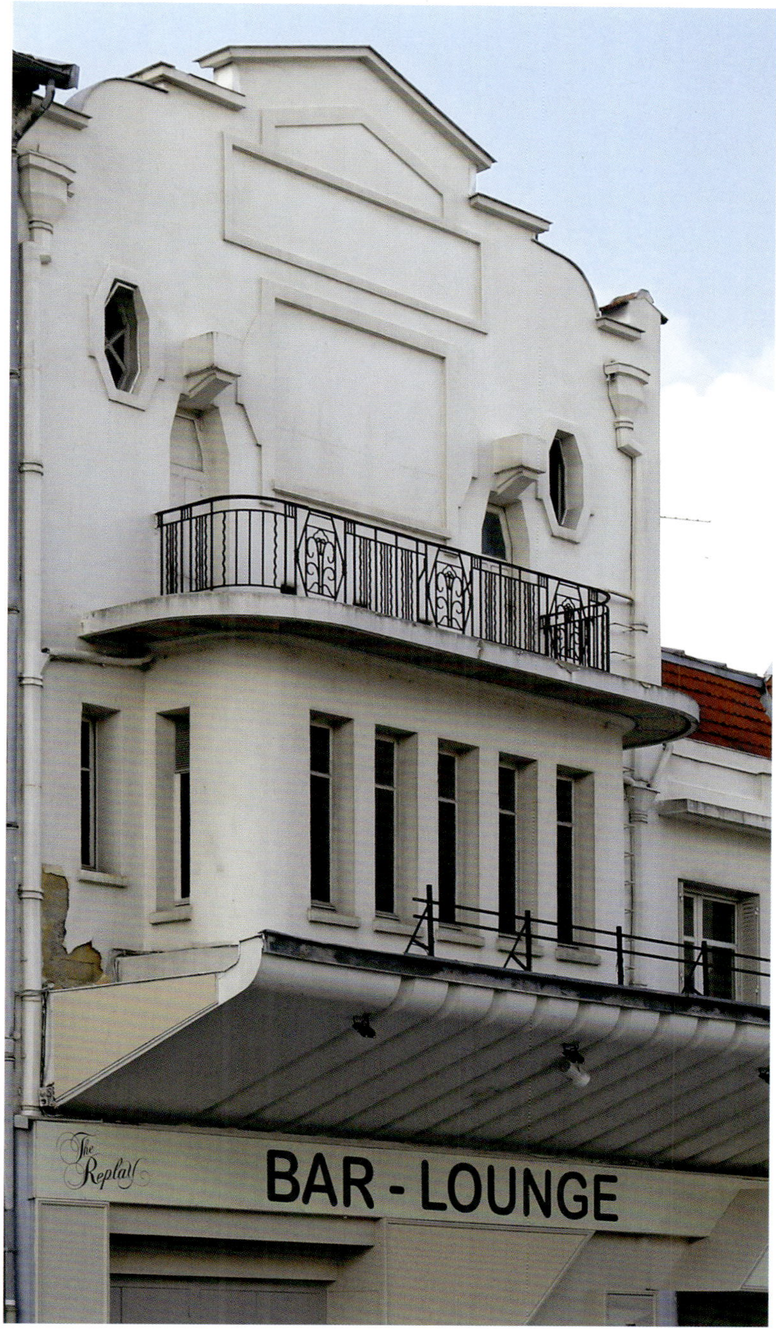

Reims – Eden – 2018

◀ **Reims, Opéra.** Opened in 1923, the sumptuous Opéra cinema with the stained-glass windows, friezes, mosaics and sculptures of its Art Deco façade, will blow away anyone who cares to looks up. It has been closed for a long time and even became a pizzeria. But … business is picking up. Much is destroyed, much less is renewed. The old Opéra, by a mysterious wave of the magic wand, has been converted into a luxury residence. Its listed façade has been renovated. As for the rest, memories, memories …

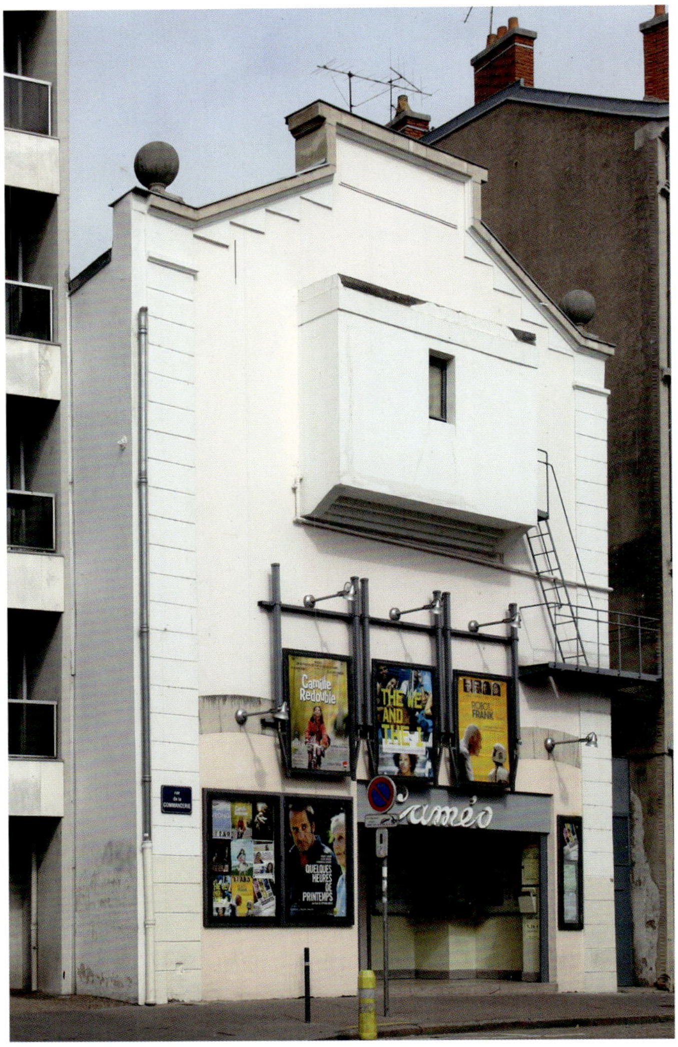

Nancy – Caméo – 2012

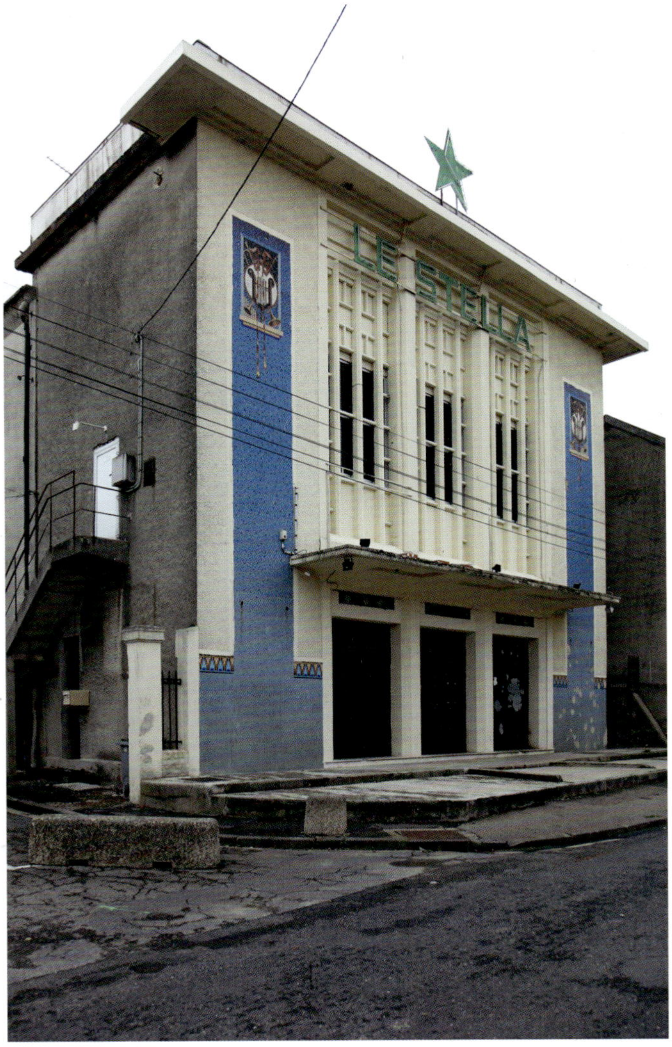

Vouziers – Stella – 2012

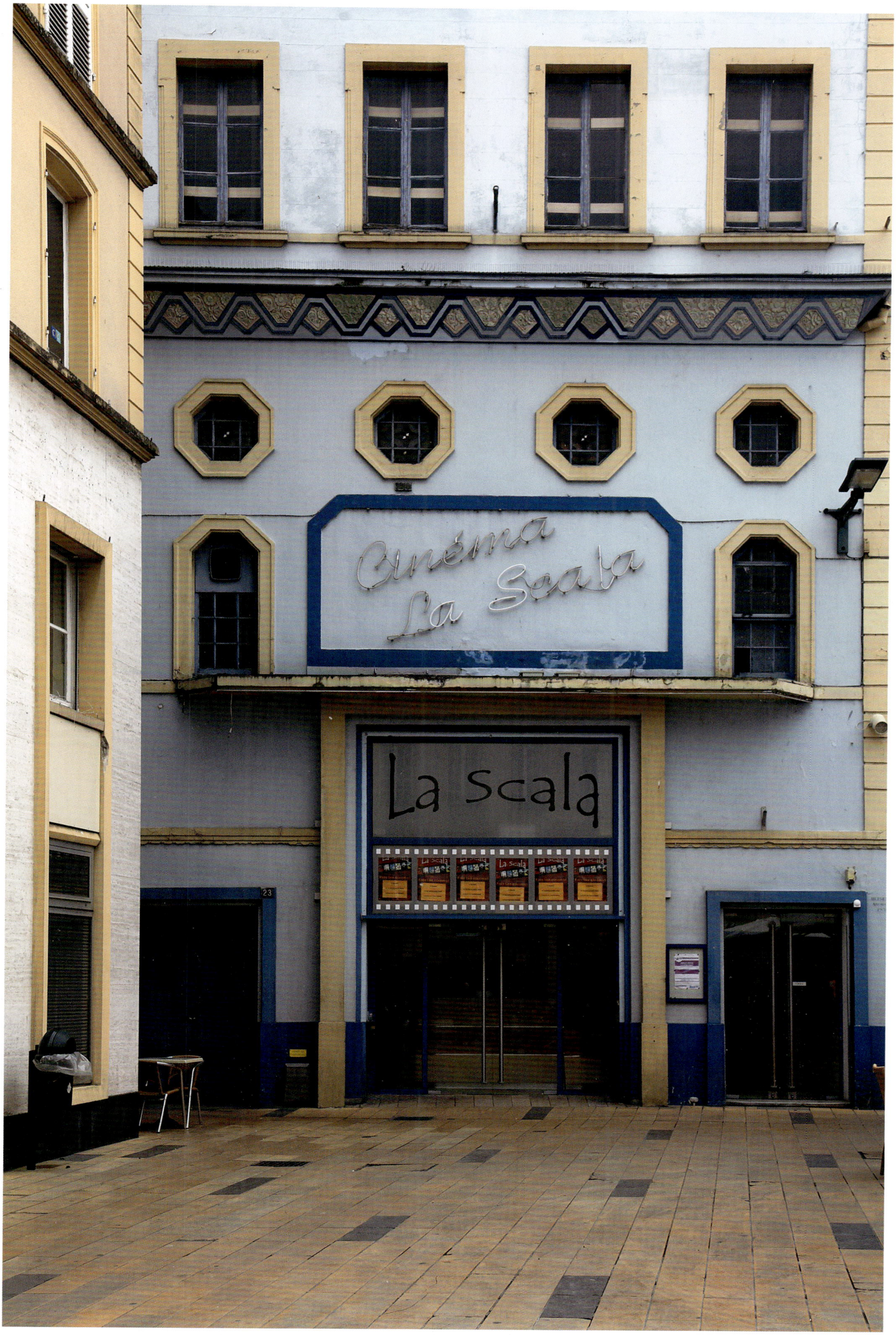

Thionville – La Scala – 2014

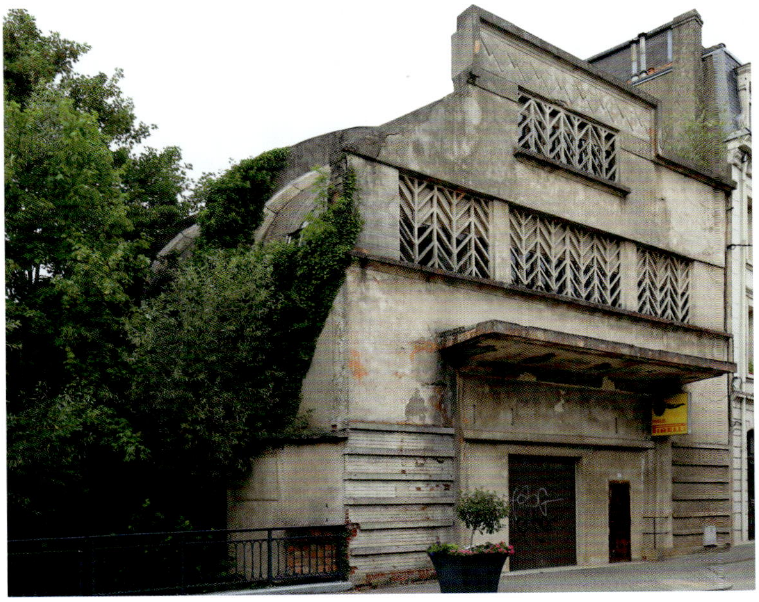

Algrange – Odéon – 2020

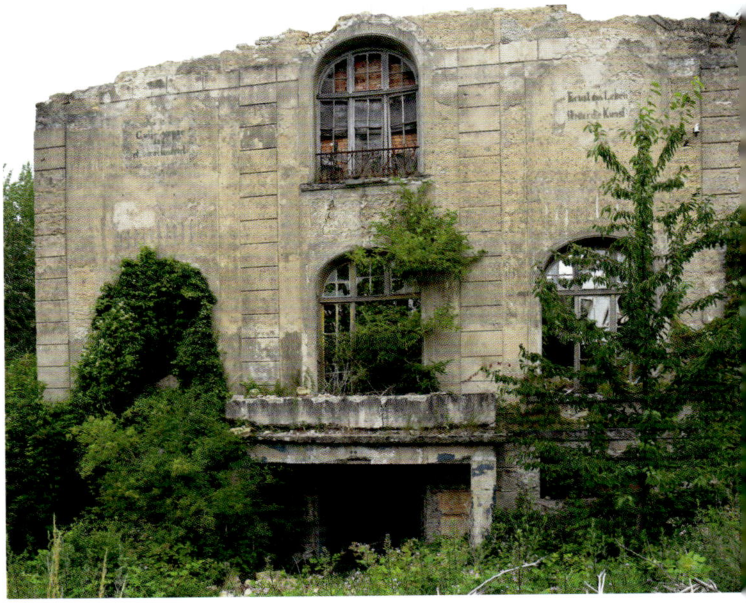

Auboué – Trianon – 2020

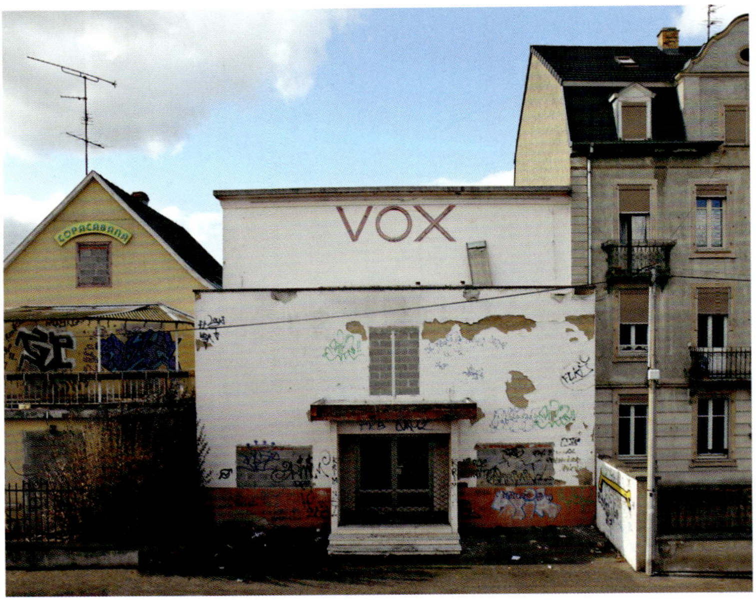

Colmar – Vox – 2012 (destroyed)

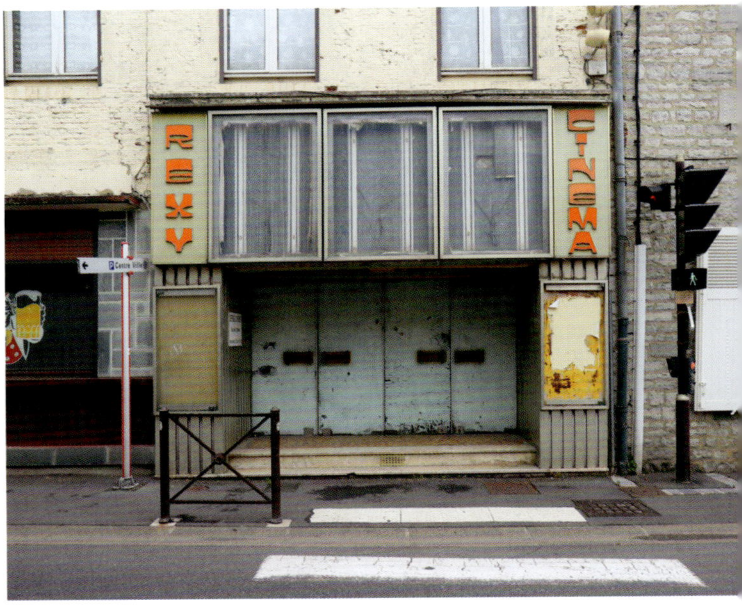

Givet – Rexy – 2020

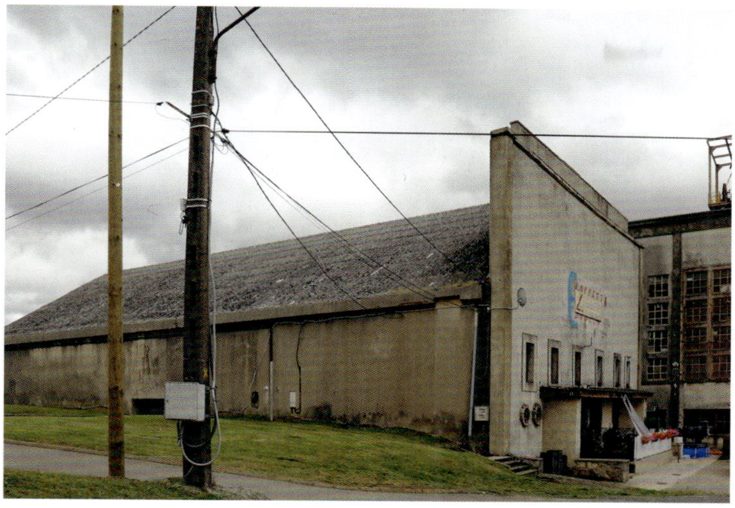

Aumetz – cinéma – 2020

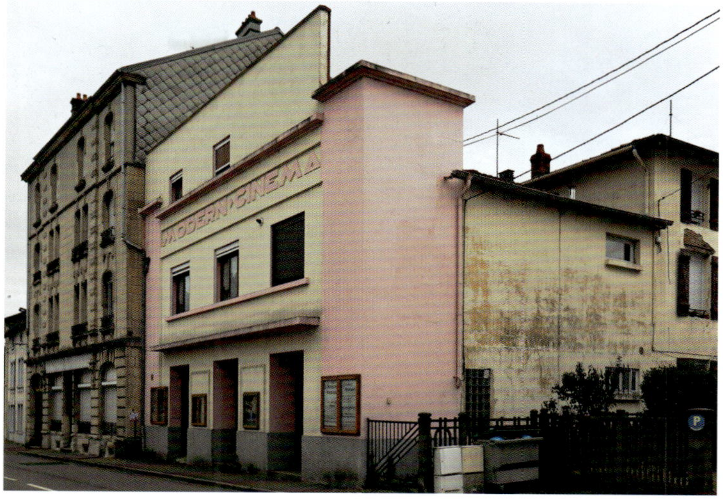

Thaon – Modern – 2020

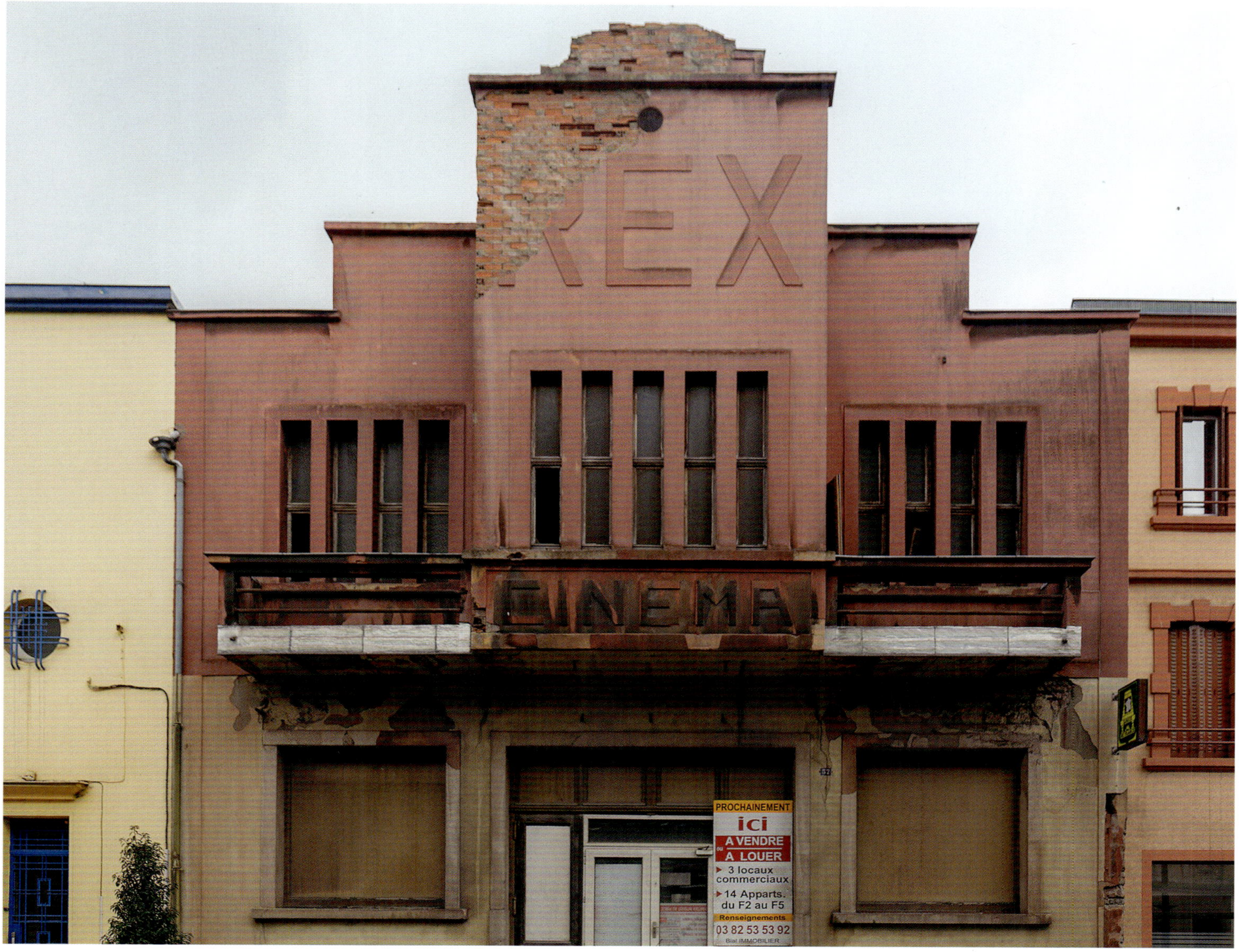

Audun-le-Tiche – Rex – 2014 (destroyed)

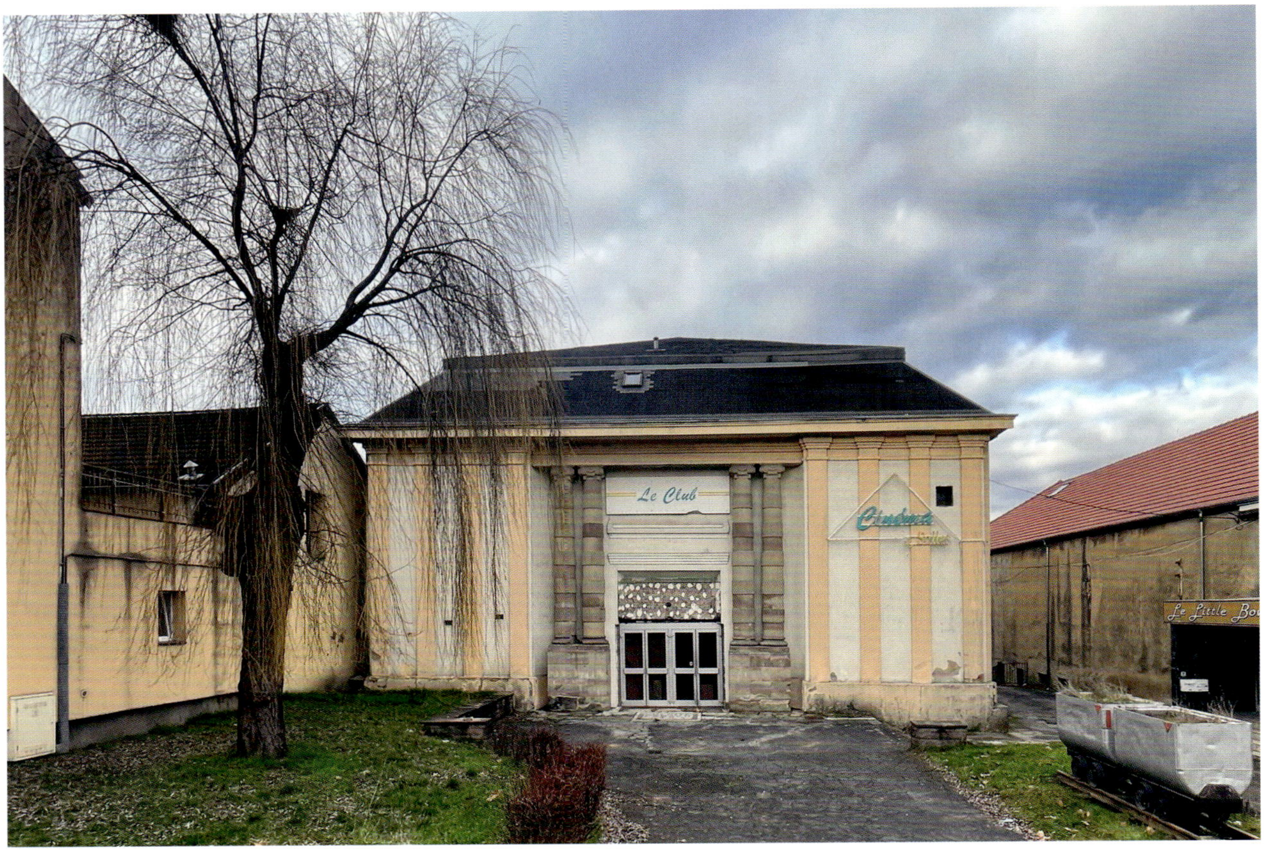

Freyming – Le Club – 2021

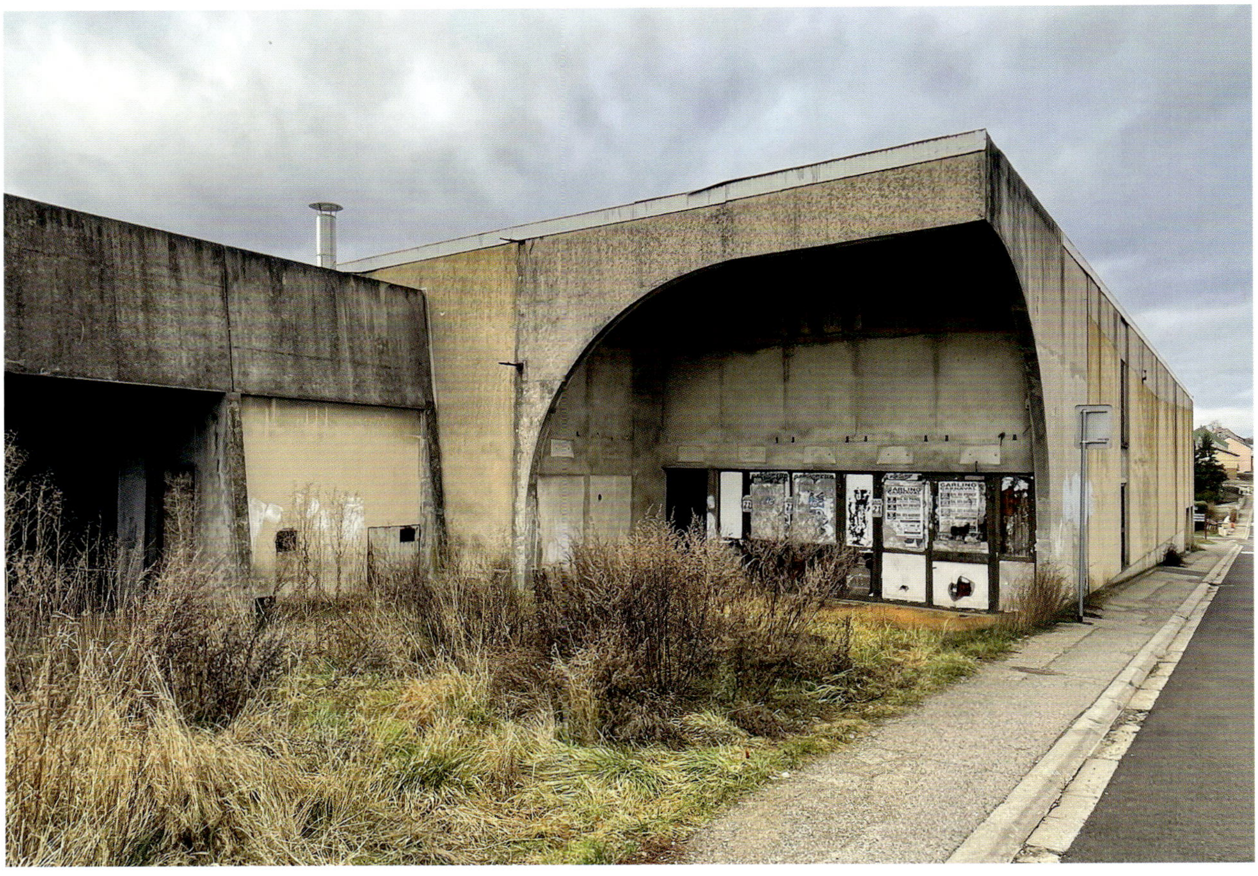

L'Hôpital – Star – 2021

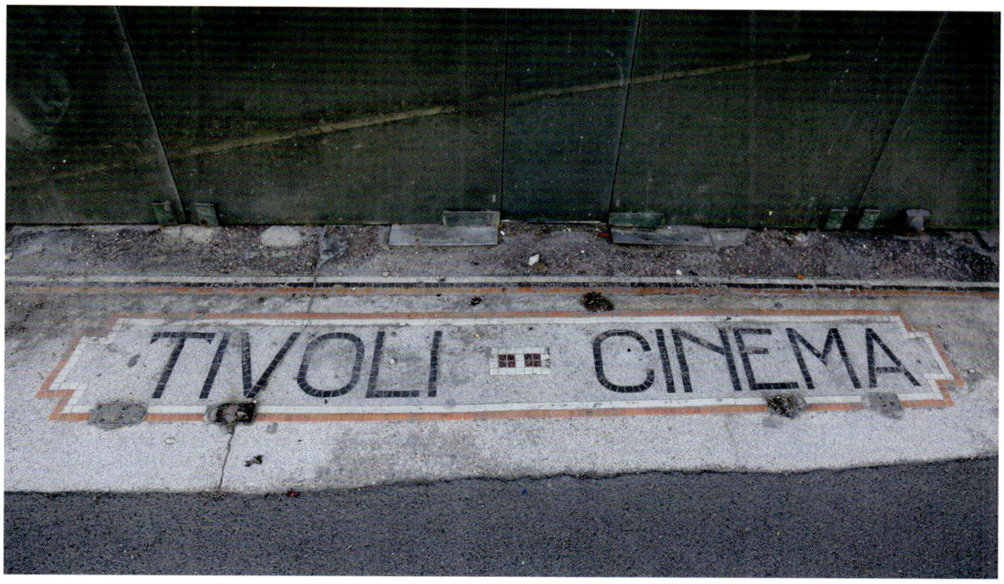

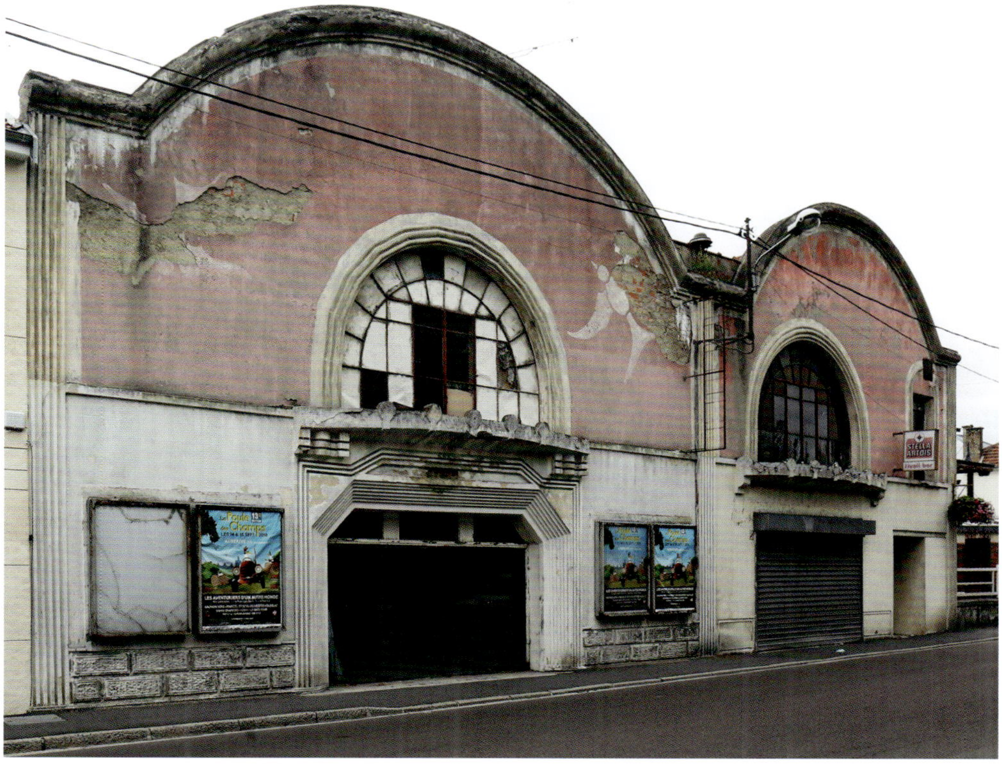

Mourmelon-le-Grand – Tivoli – 2018

Mourmelon-le-Grand, Tivoli. The Tivoli cinema, a minor splendour from the 1930s, now abandoned, decrepit façade, looking a little devastated, wonders if it will end up destroyed by evil forces or saved by an association of militant movie-lovers. It tries desperately to seduce anyone strolling past, telling of past glories, packed halls, daft comedies that the public loved, ice creams greedily swallowed at the interval. It would like to relive those moments once more. Let it be heard.

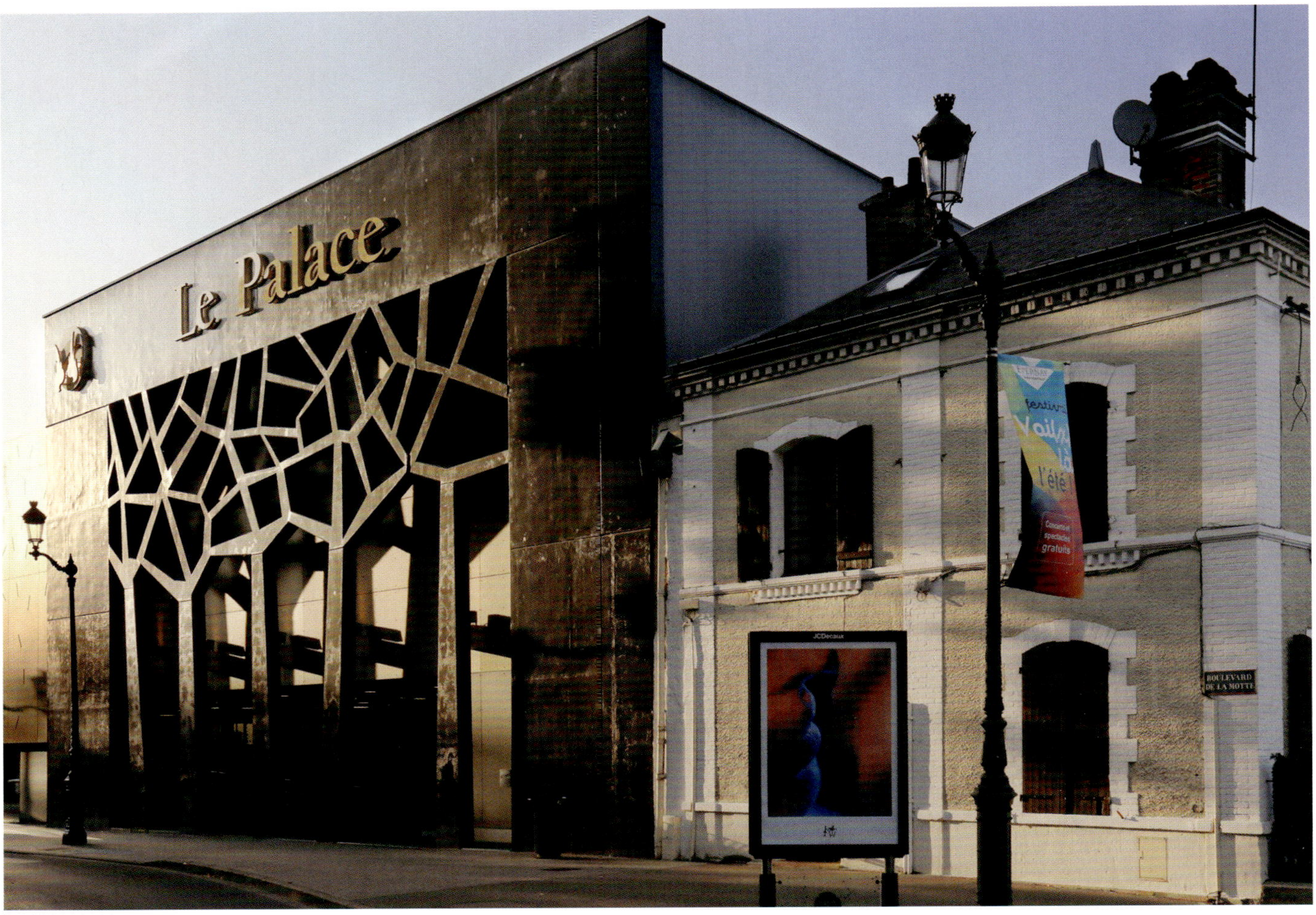

Epernay – Le Palace – 2021

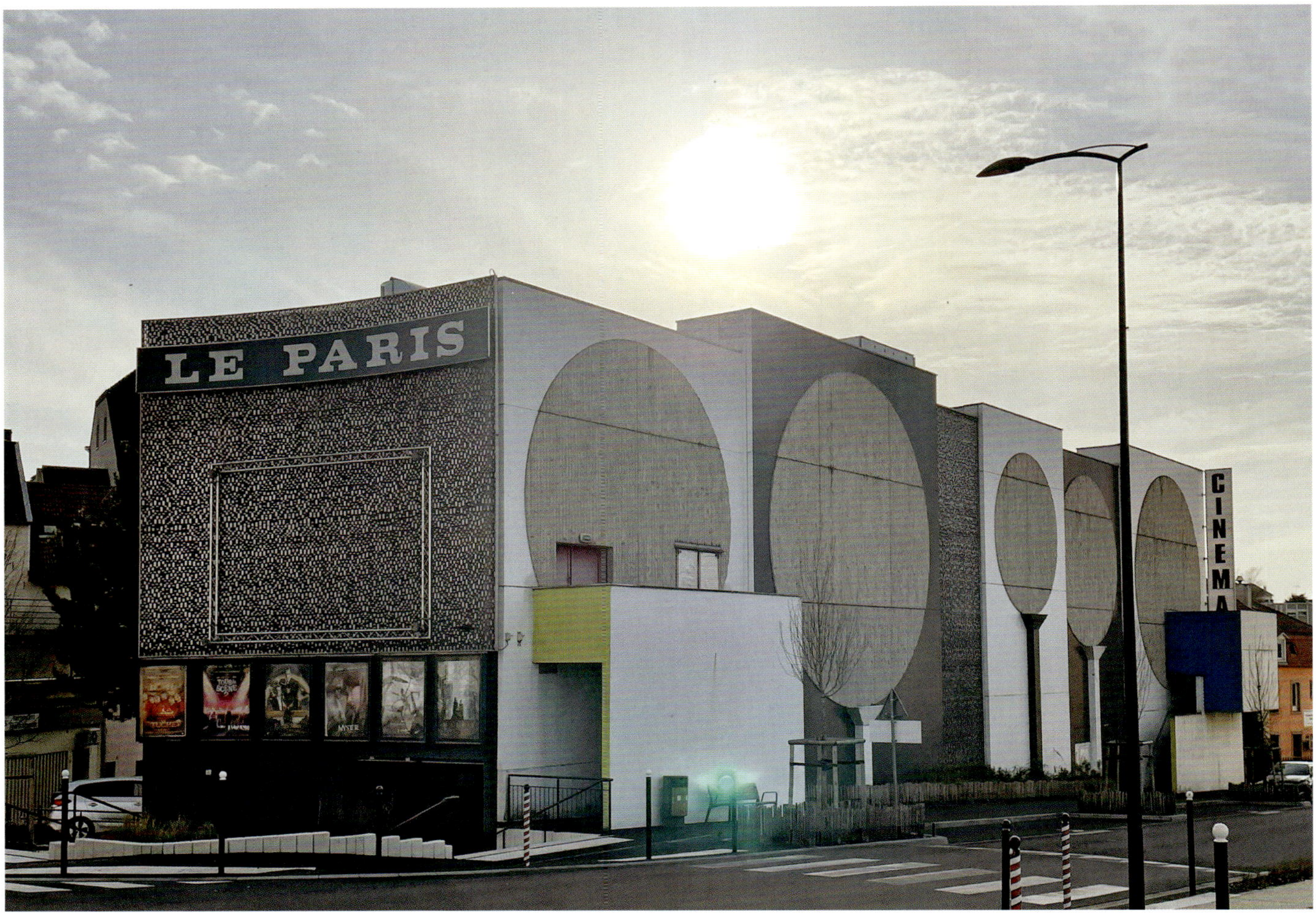

Forbach – Le Paris – 2021

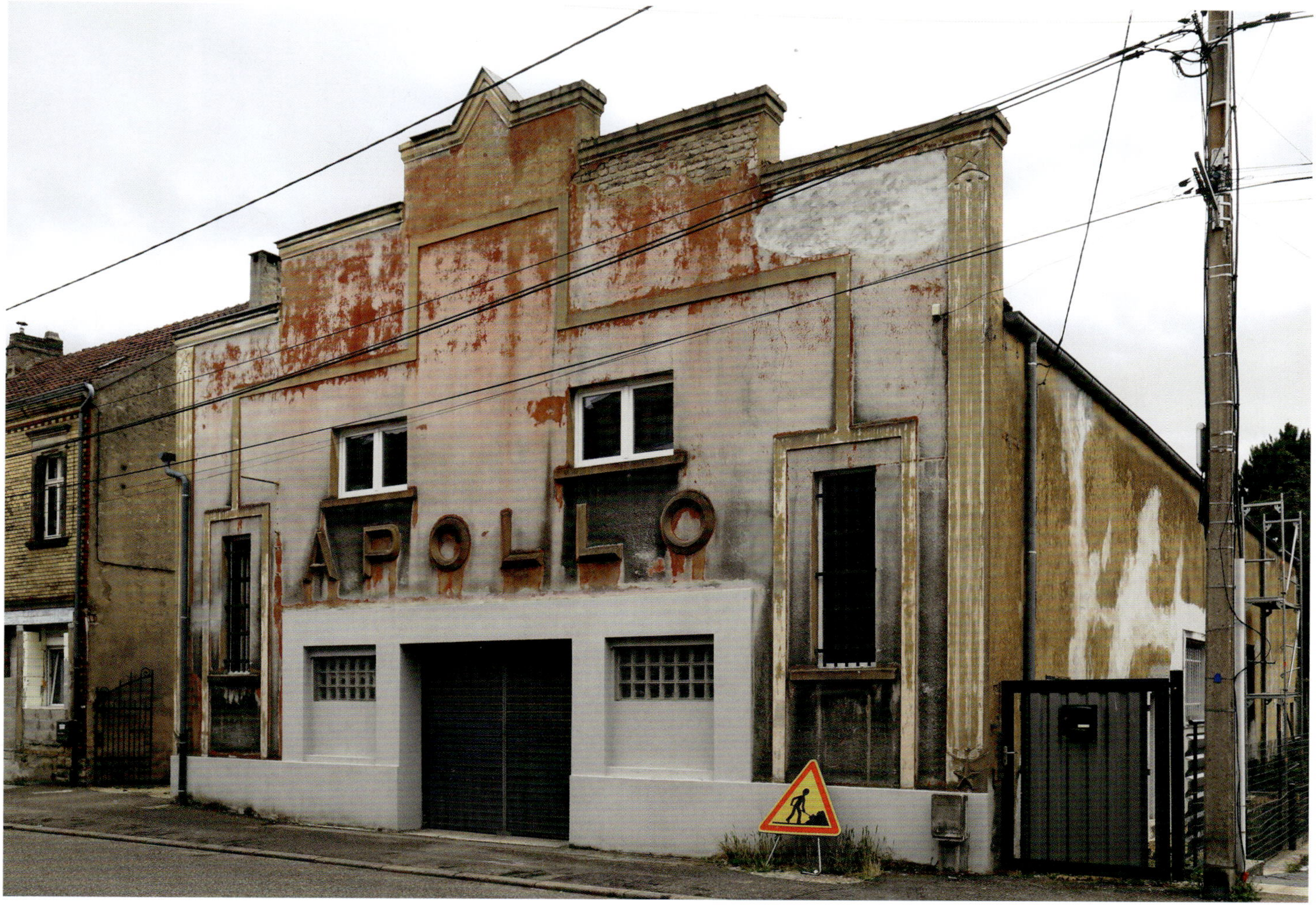

Stiring-Wendel – Apollo – 2020

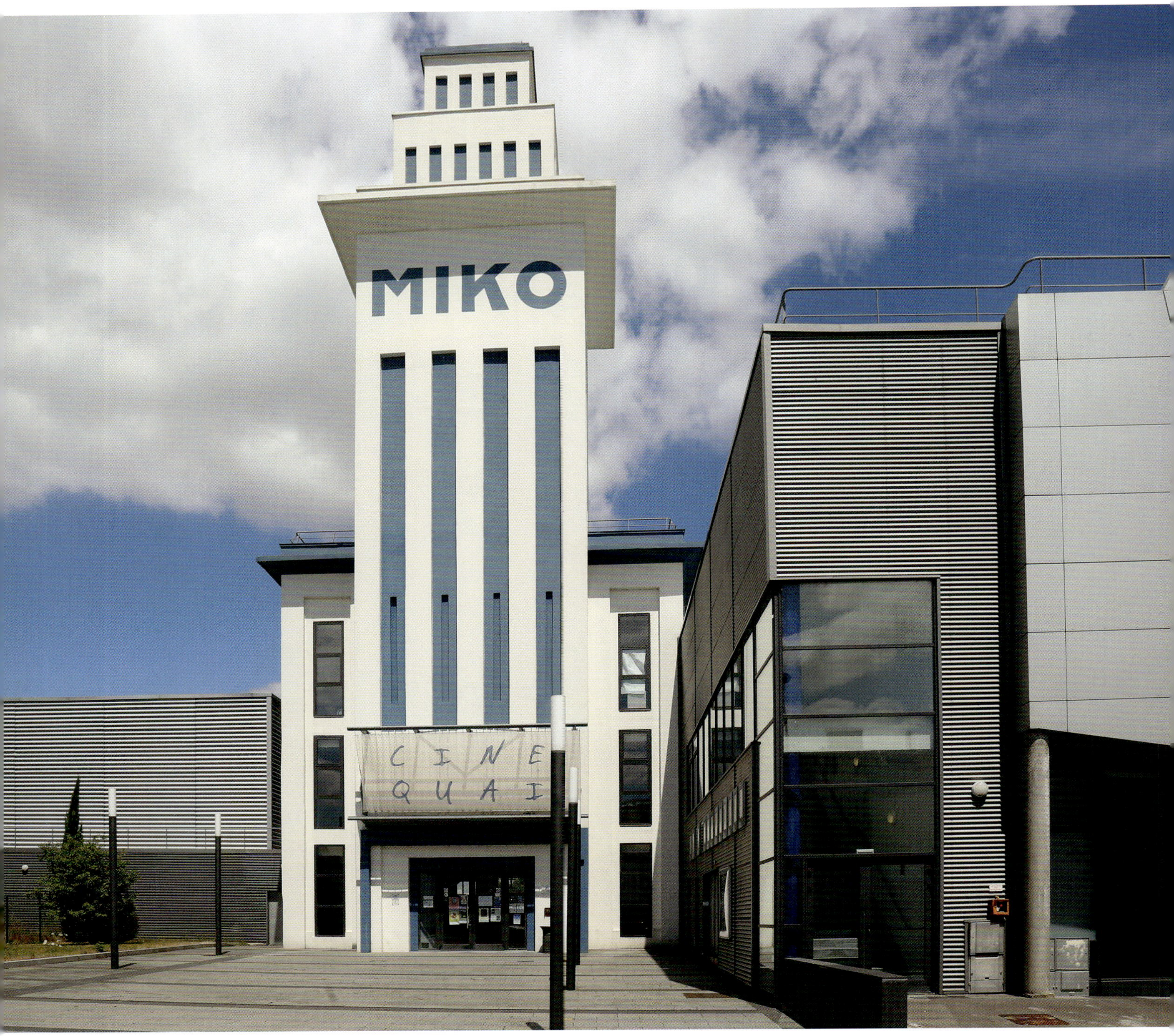

Saint-Dizier – Ciné Quai – 2018

Saint-Dizier, Ciné Quai. Ciné Quai opened in 2006 in the former Miko factory, which also houses a museum dedicated to that brand of frozen chocolates. 'Miko, the best way to spend the interval!' At that time the first session consisted of a short film and newsreels then a break during which the usher, wicker basket straps hugging her neck, sold the famous Miko ice creams, tirelessly repeating in a monotone: 'Candy! caramels! eskimos! chocolates!'

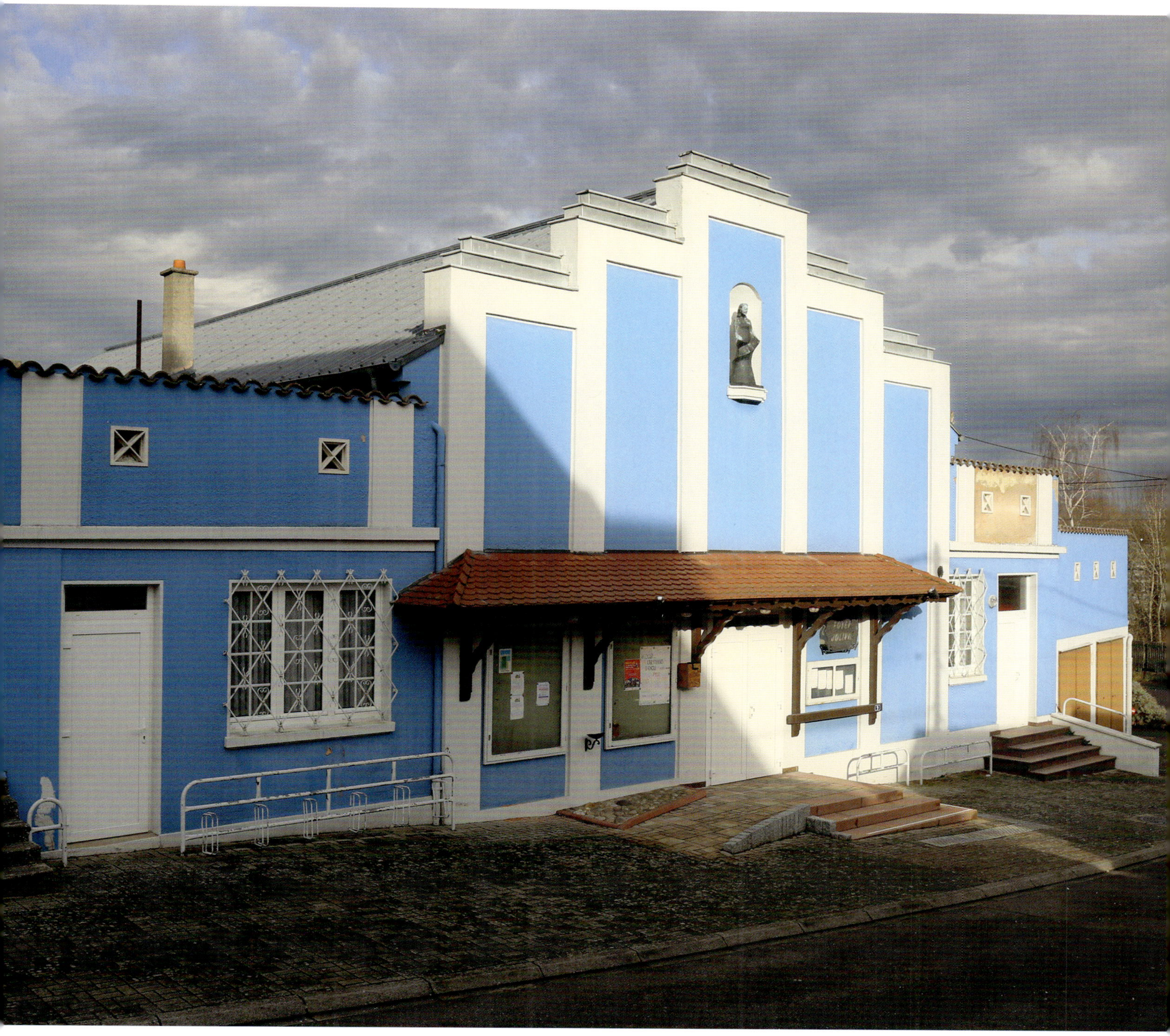

Le Val-de-Guéblange – Foyer Jolival – 2021

HAUTS-DE-FRANCE

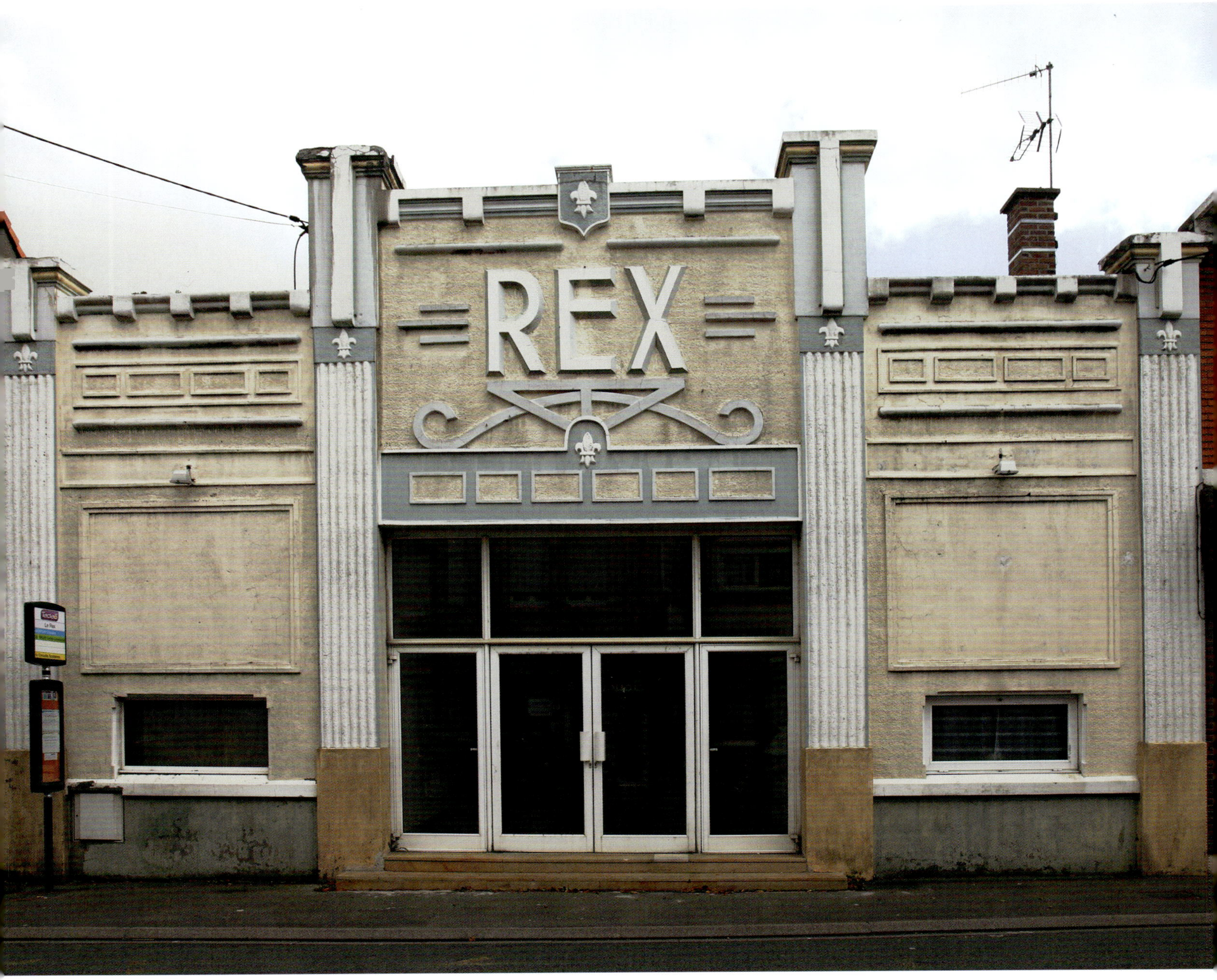

Haillicourt – Rex – 2012

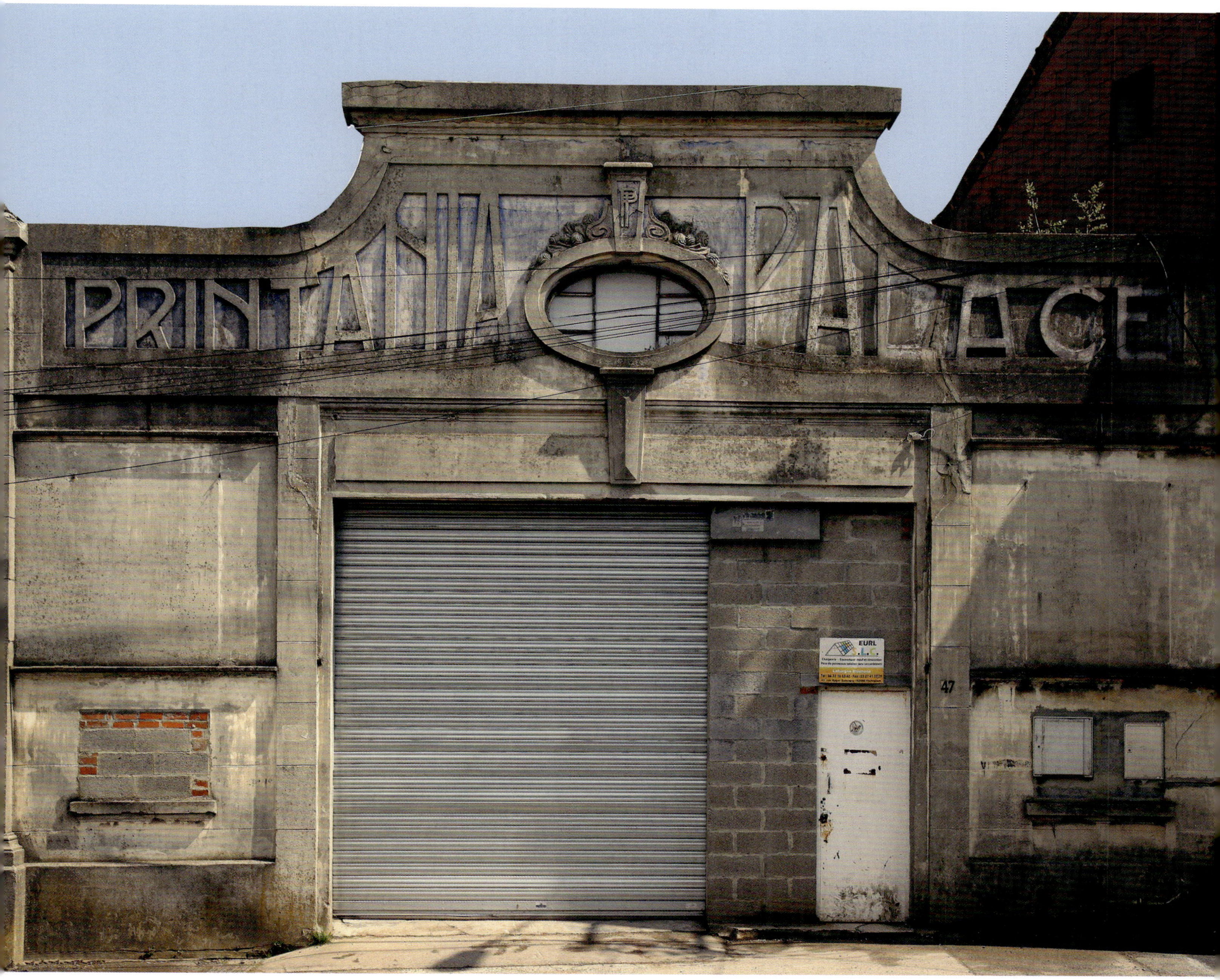

Auchel – Printania Palace – 2022

Auchel, Printania Palace. Your gaze is drawn to a nebulous wall inscription. Something of an archaeologist, with sharp eyes, you try to decipher it. Guided by an infallible instinct, you sense something essential. So, equipped with a brush, trowel or whatever, you scrub and rinse down the wall and a miracle happens. The Printania Palace sign is revealed before your amazed eyes.

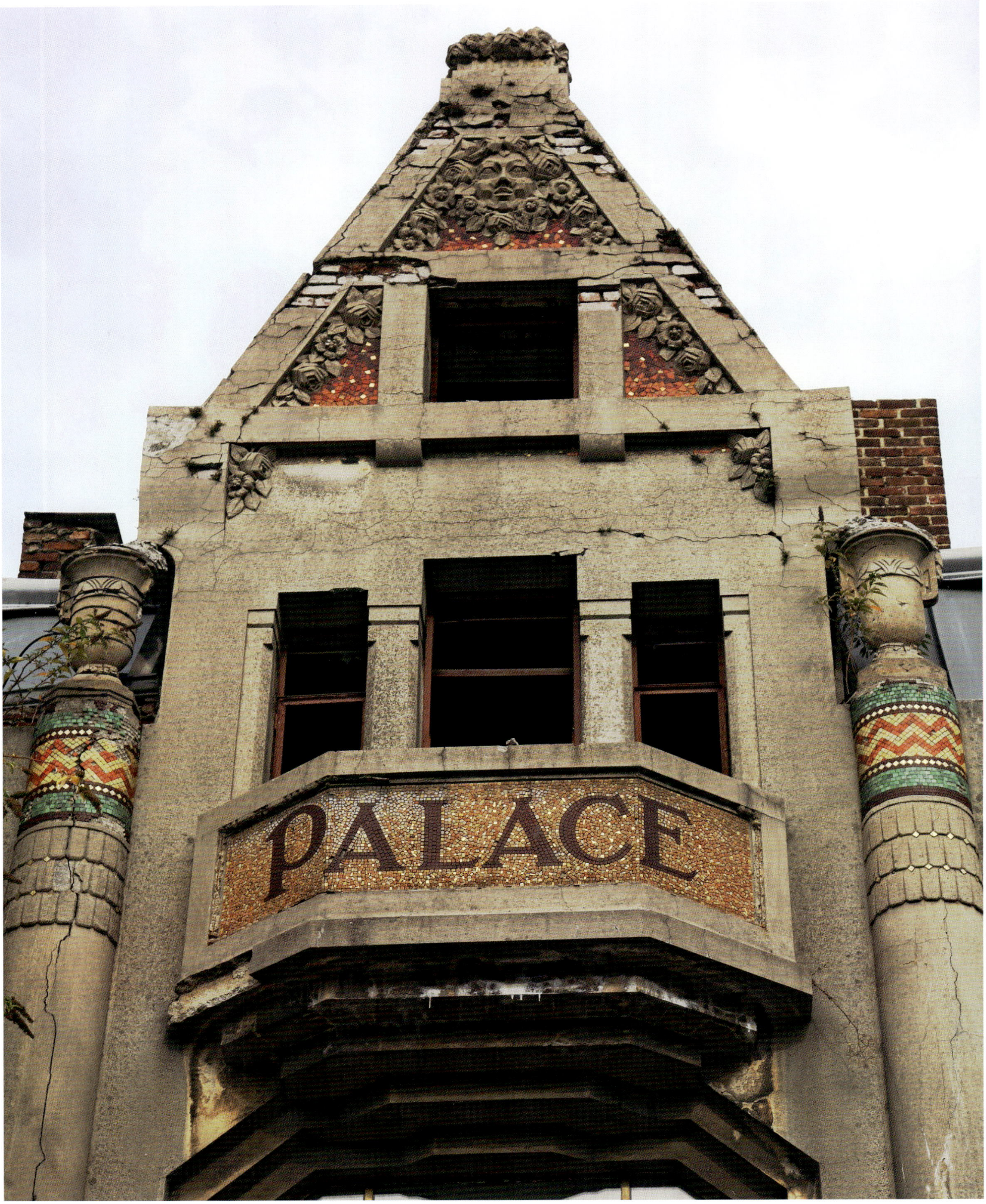

Valenciennes – Palace – 2012

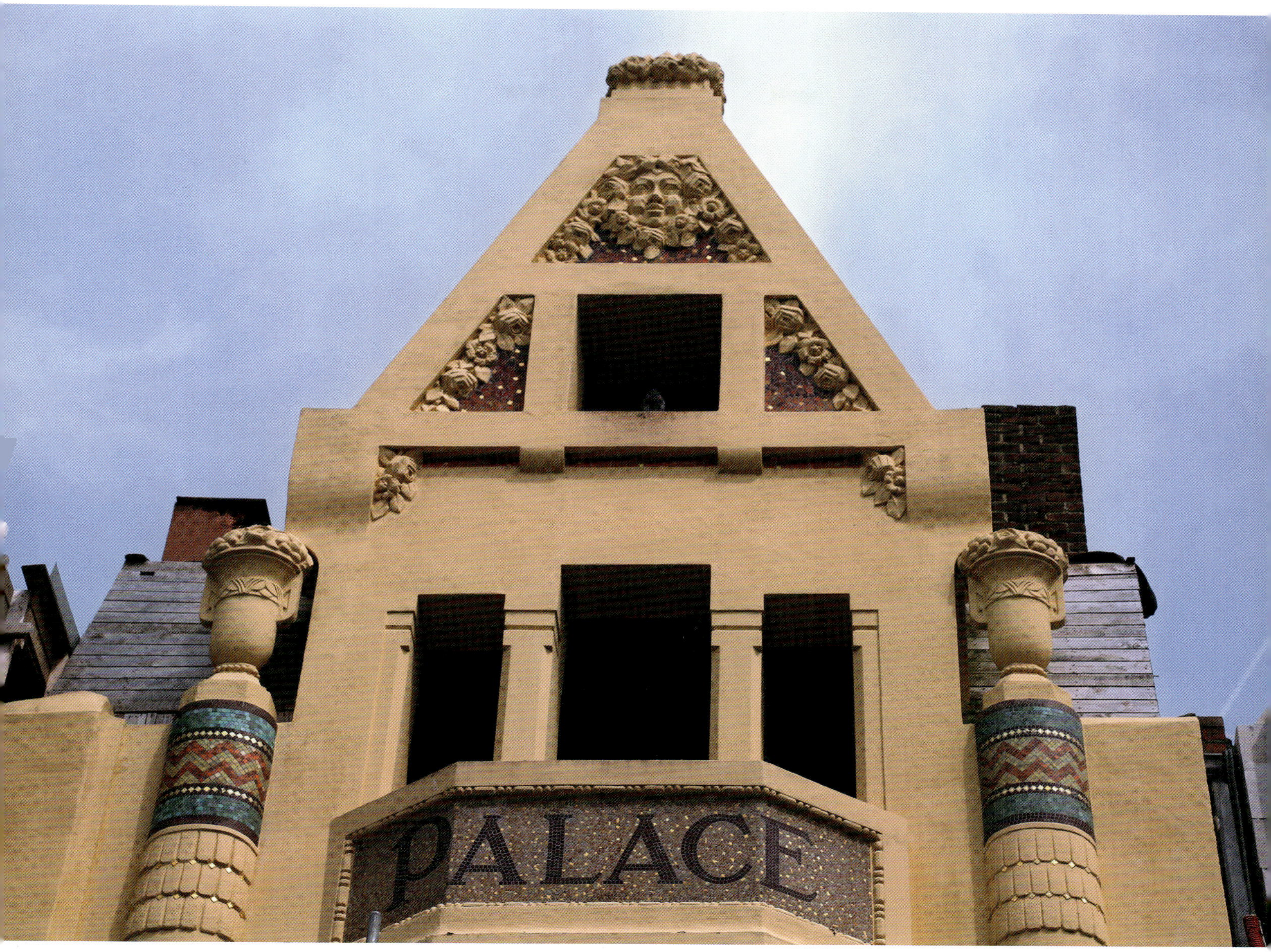

Valenciennes – Palace – 2021

Valenciennes, Palace. Built in 1927 in Art Deco style with shades of Egyptian motives mixed in, this cinema was operated by the Bartolotti family for three generations. It closed in 1981, the hall deteriorated. There was a plan to demolish it in 2010, but in 2019 the façade with its well-preserved mosaics and sculptures was listed and has been undergoing renovation ever since ... slowly.

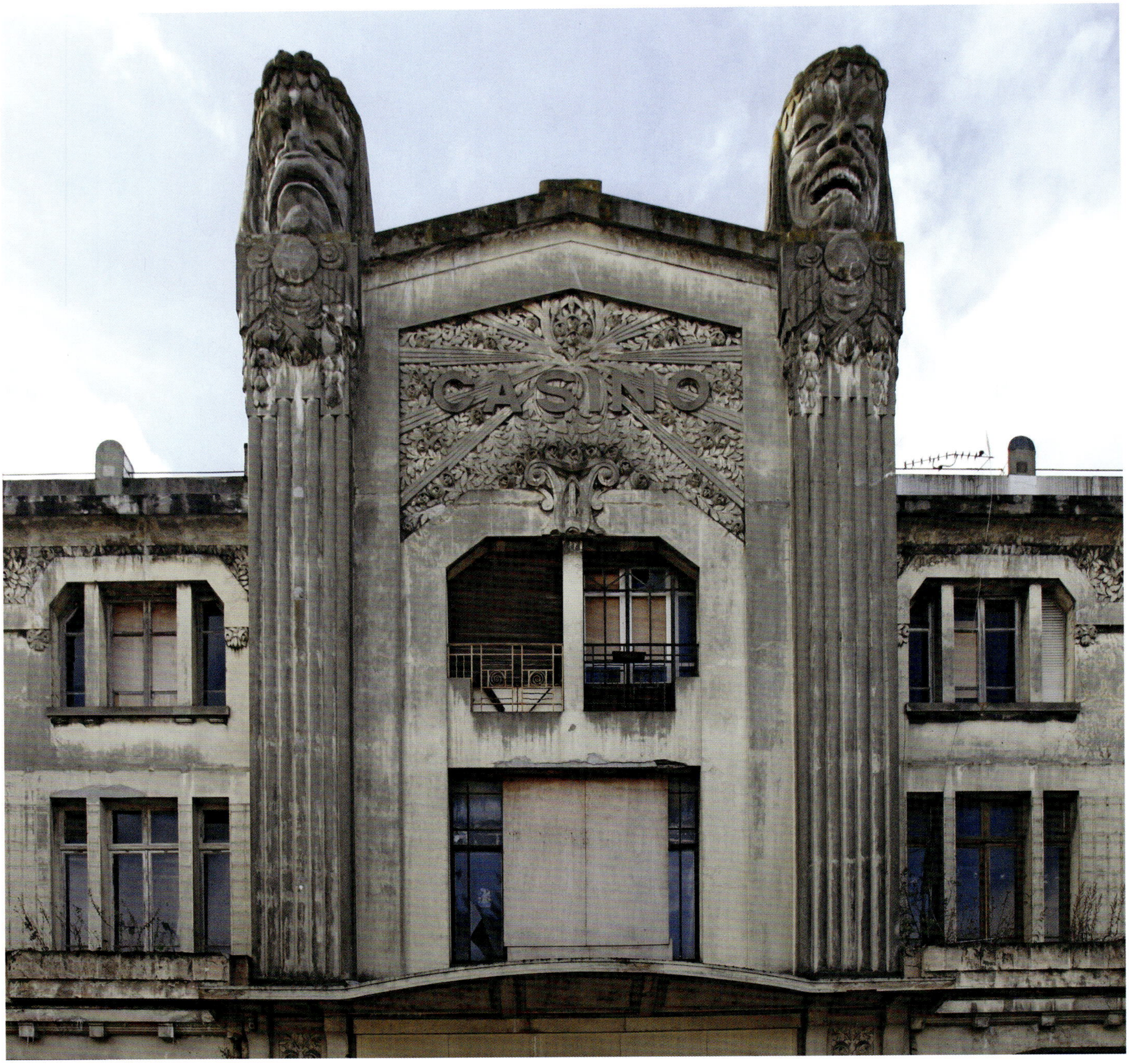

Saint-Quentin – Casino – 2012

Saint-Quentin, Casino. Majestic, flamboyant, sparkling, the Casino at Saint-Quentin, built in 1929, has 1,300 seats. Audiences flocked to this Art Deco jewel. Then came the same refrain you'd never want to hear: the public evaporated like the ebb tide and got bogged down in other pleasures. Closure, disco, furniture store, always the same route, excavated until the final explosion ... destruction. Happily this place will be saved. Two and a half years of work, a proper renovation budget. This cinema, which has become an association meeting hall, is once again majestic, flamboyant and sparkling.

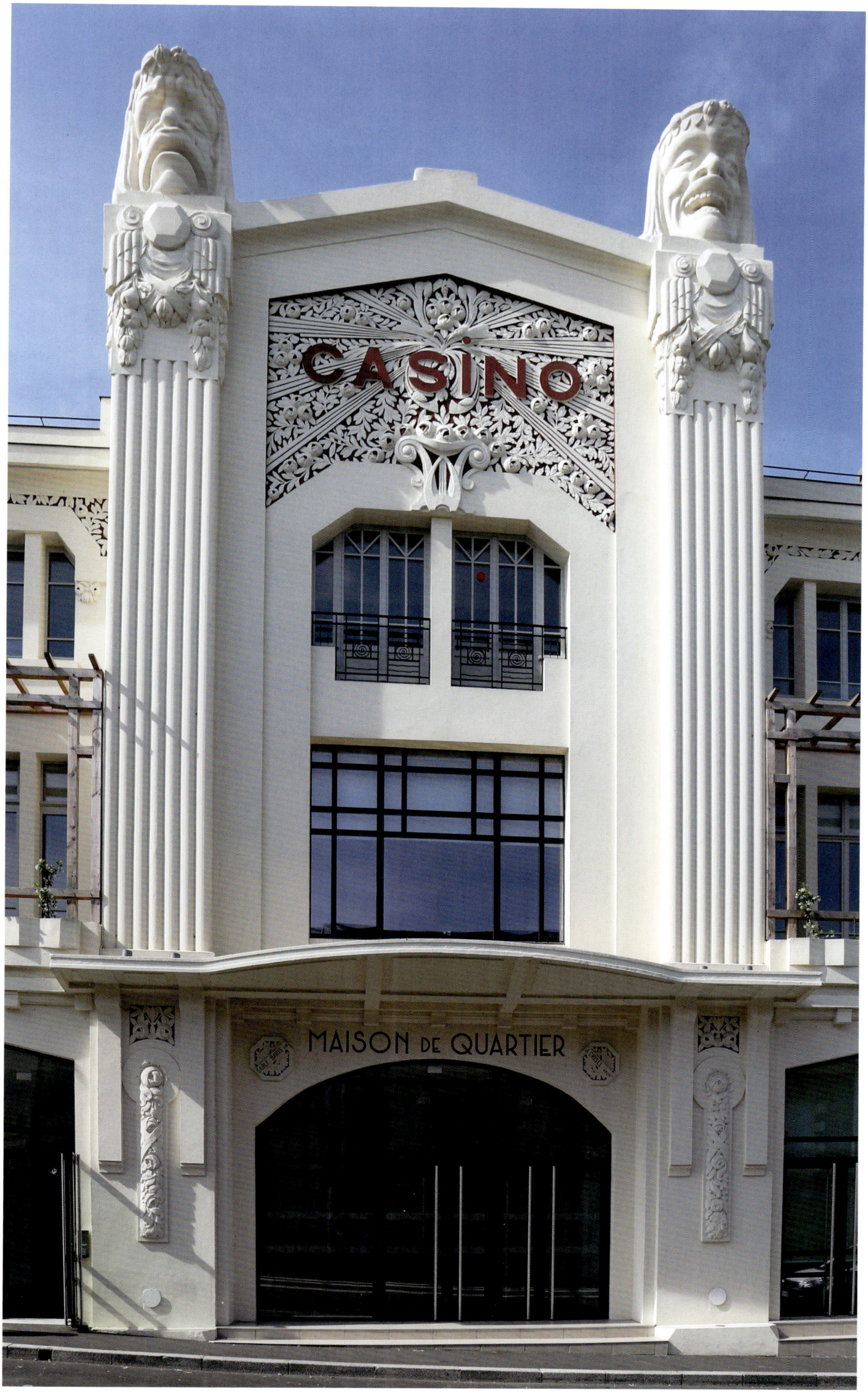
CASINO
MAISON DE QUARTIER

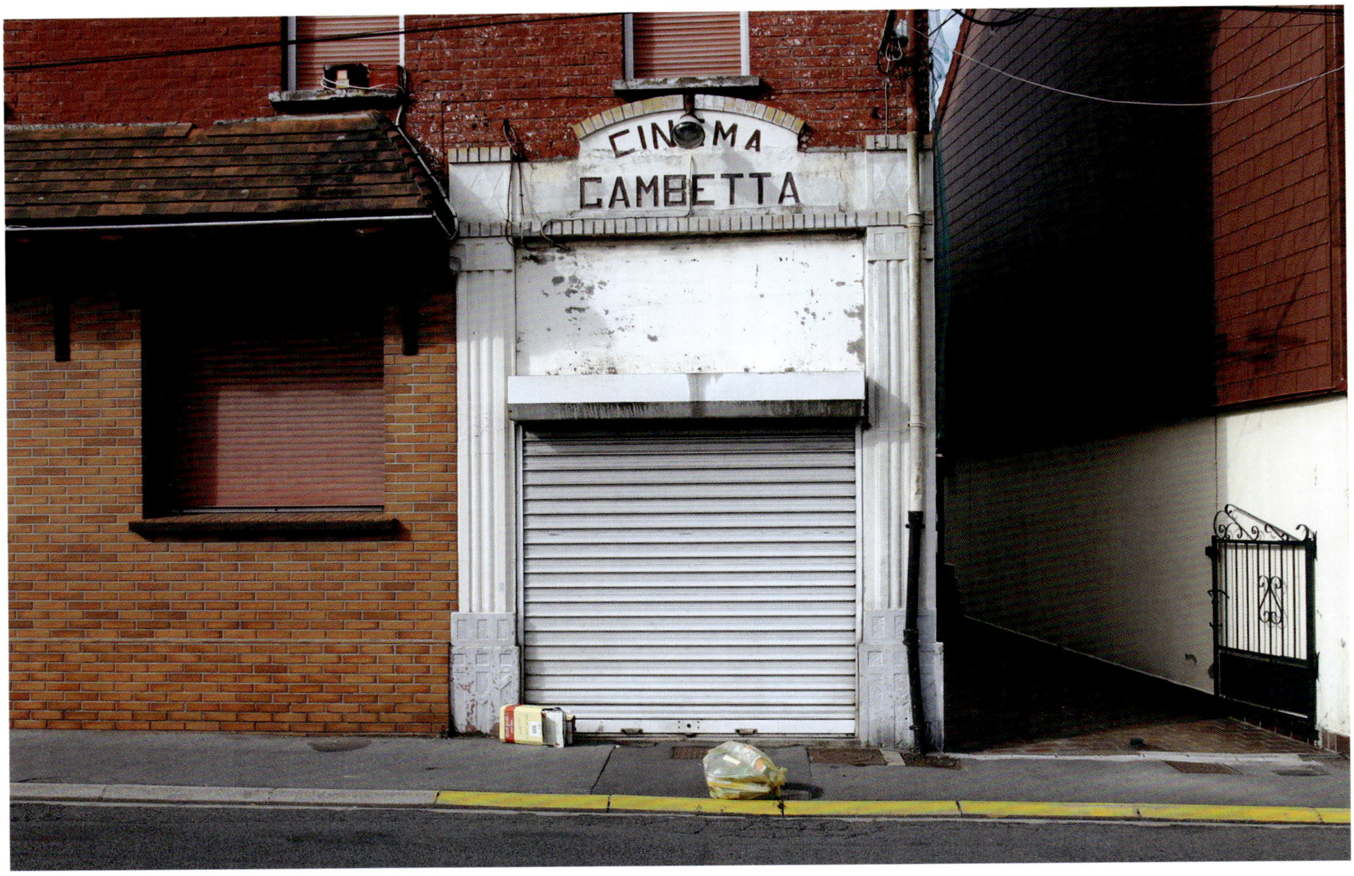

Marles-les-Mines – Cinéma Gambetta – 2012

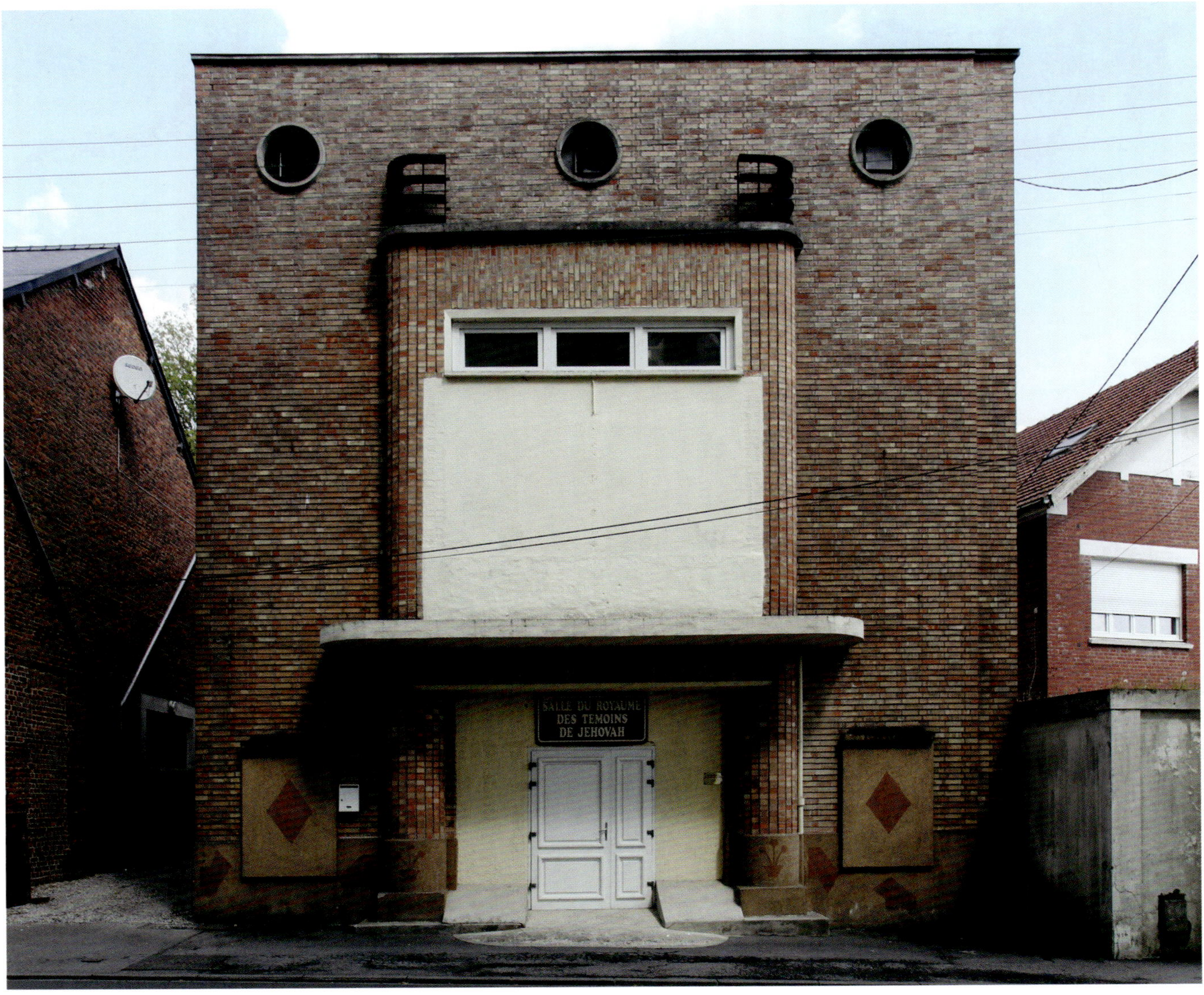

Avesnes-sur-Helpe – Impérial – 2014

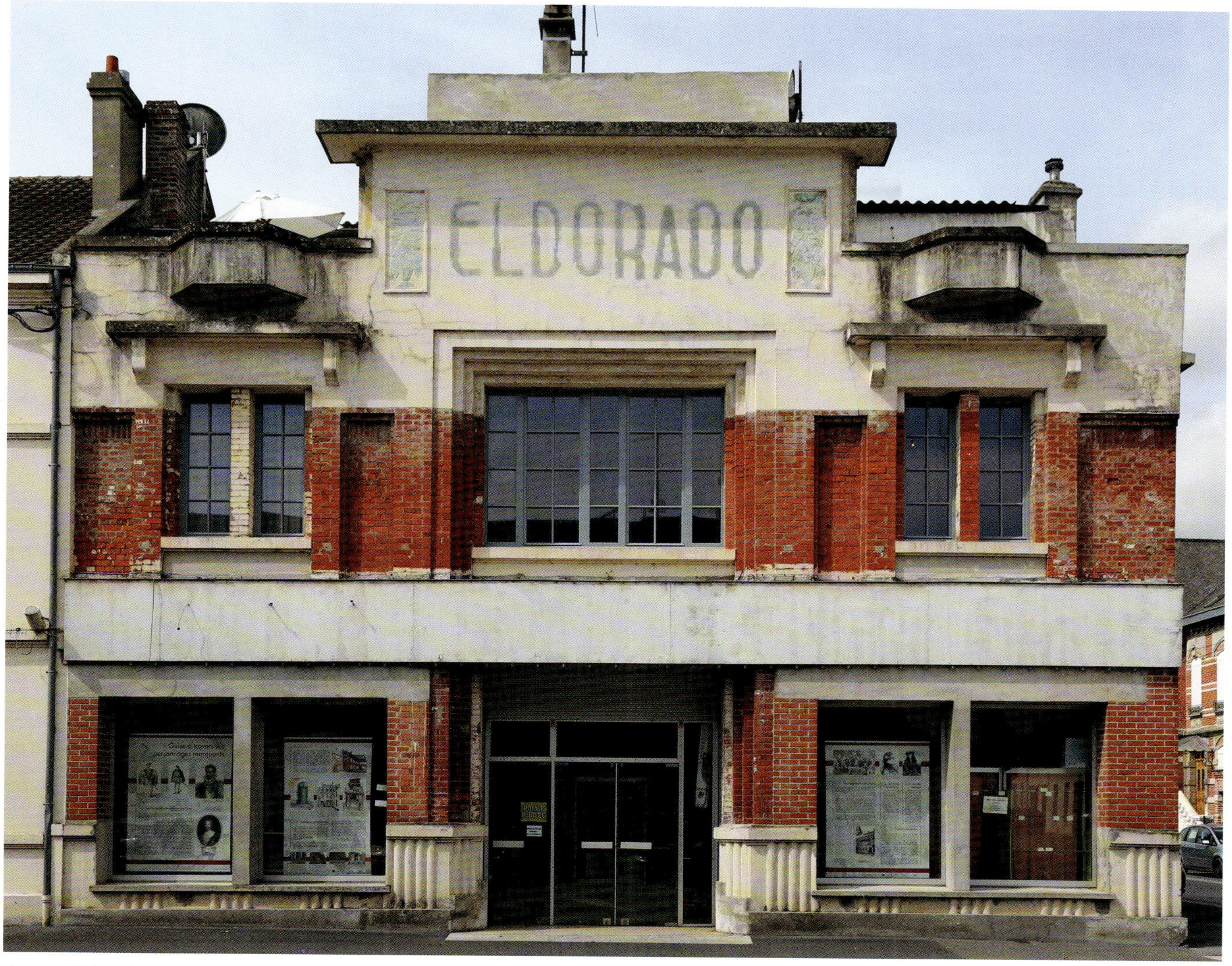

Guise – Eldorado – 2021

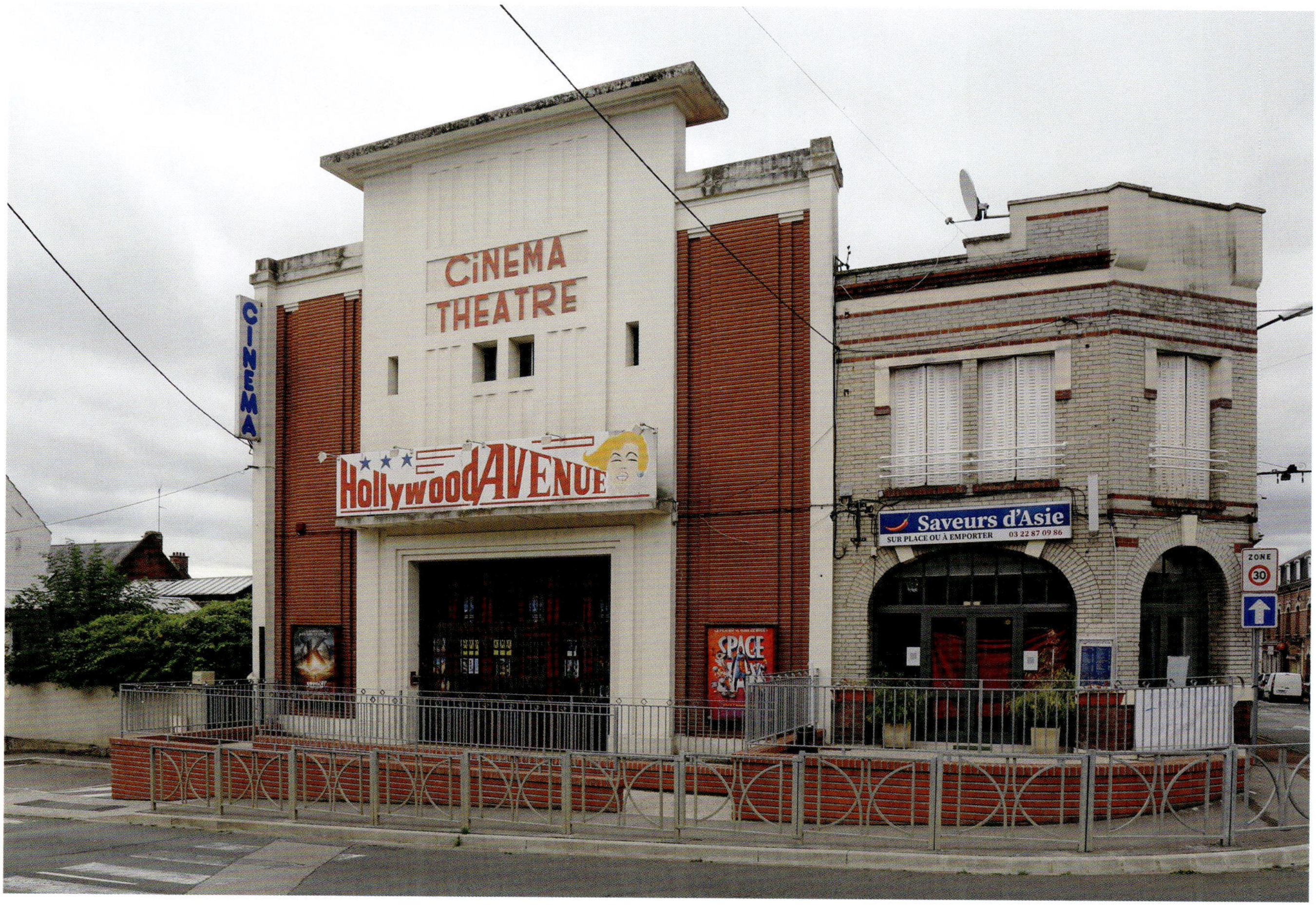

Montdidier – Hollywood Avenue – 2021

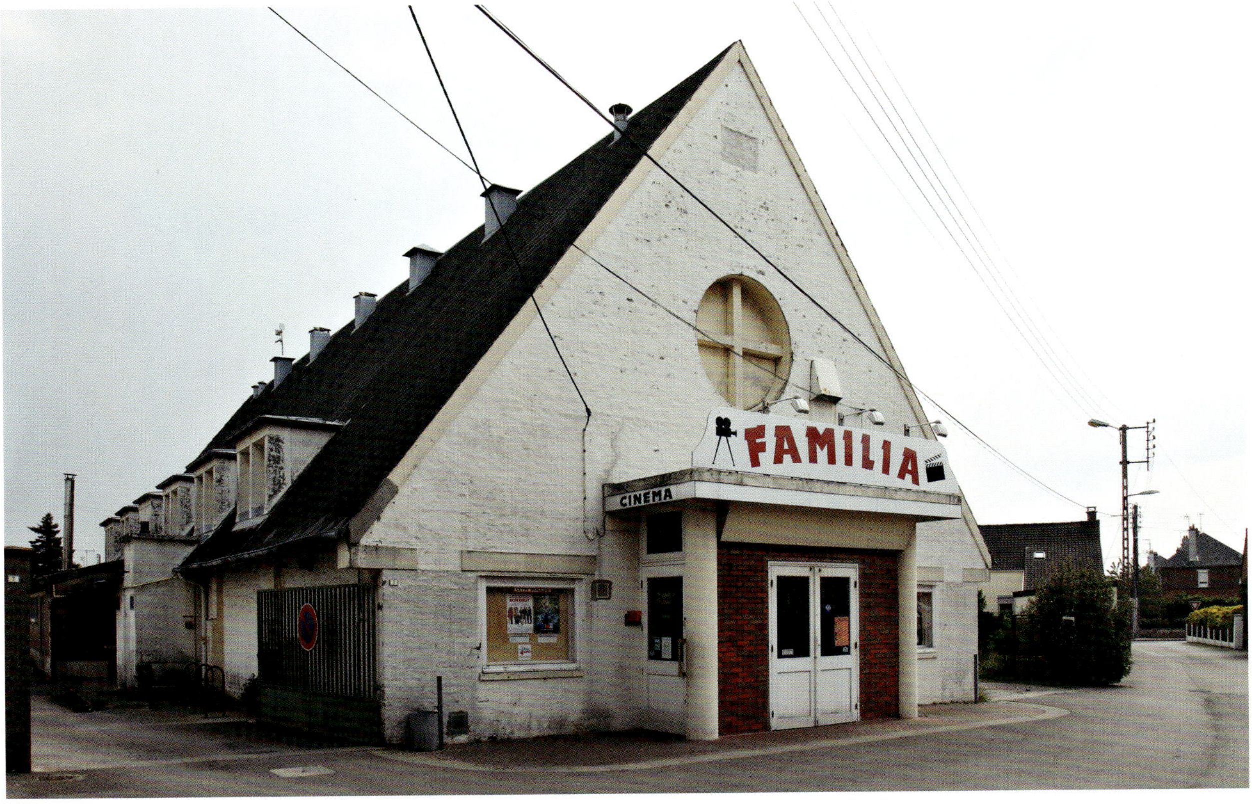

Berck – Familia – 2014

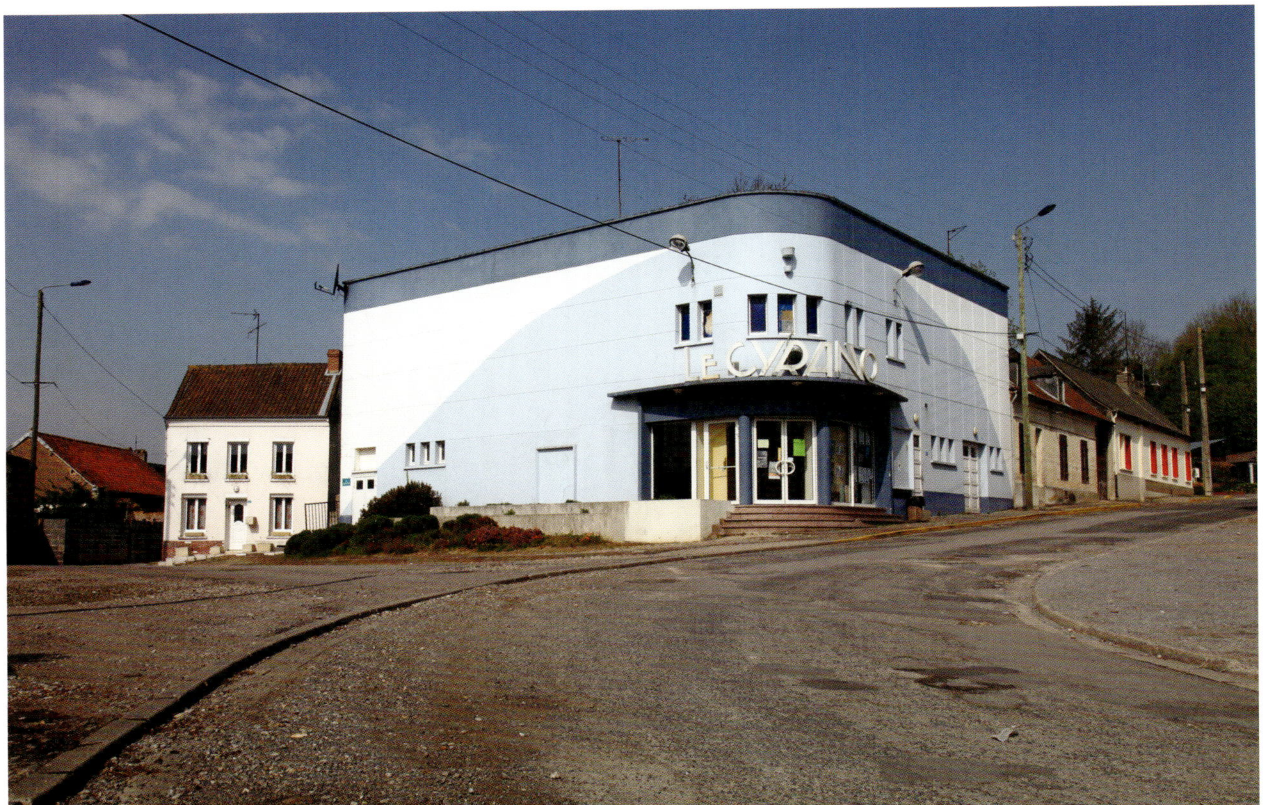

Crécy-en-Ponthieu – Le Cyrano – 2014

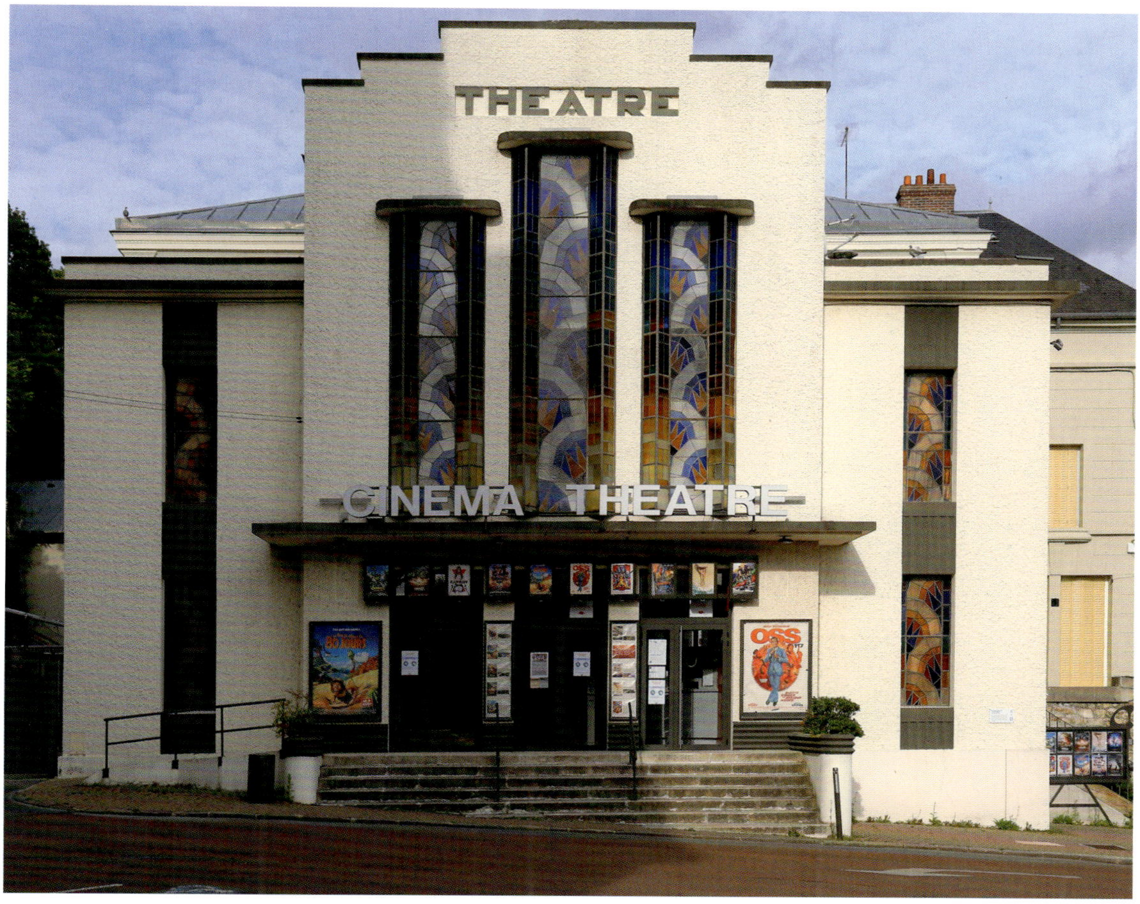

Château-Thierry – Cinéma Théâtre – 2021

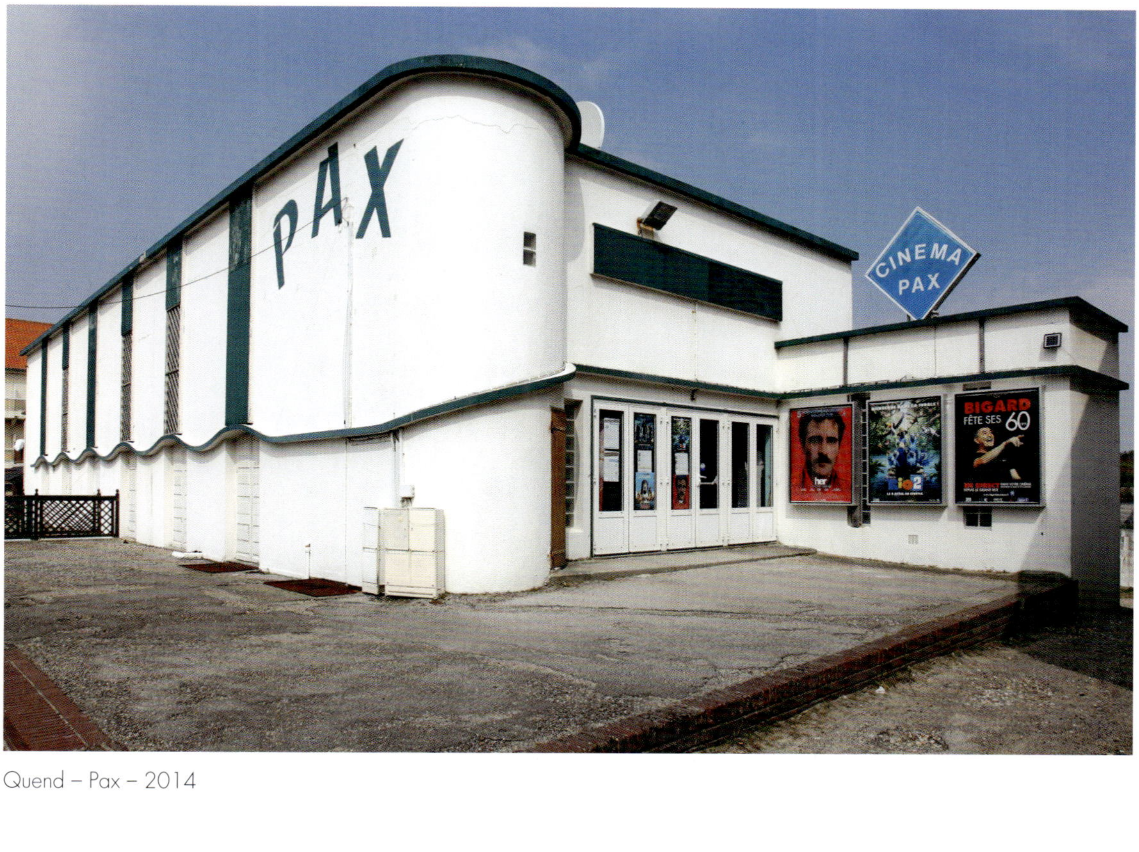

Quend – Pax – 2014

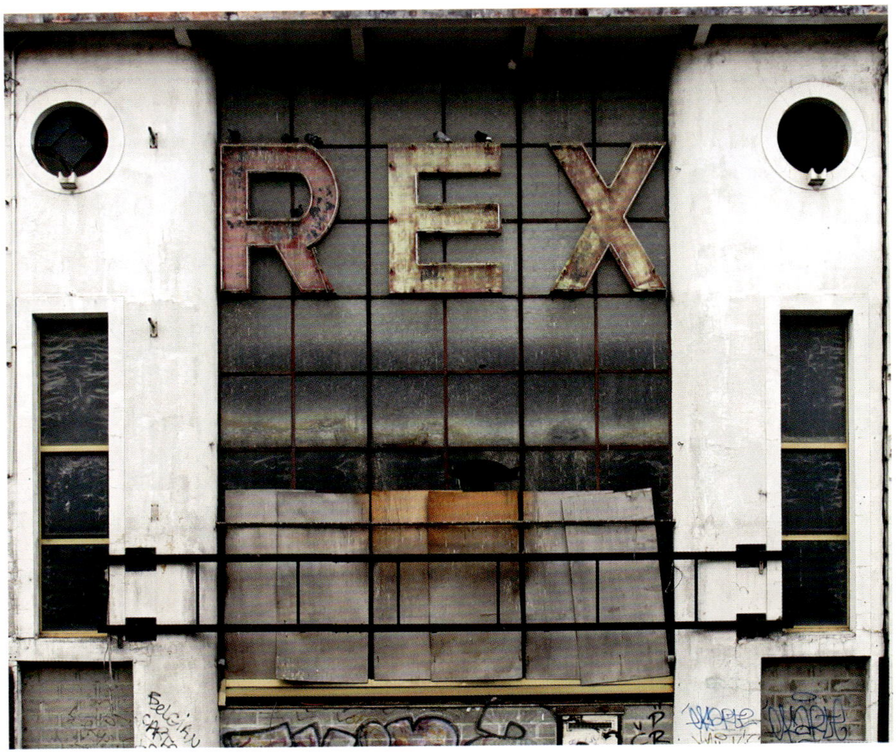

Armentières – Rex – 2012

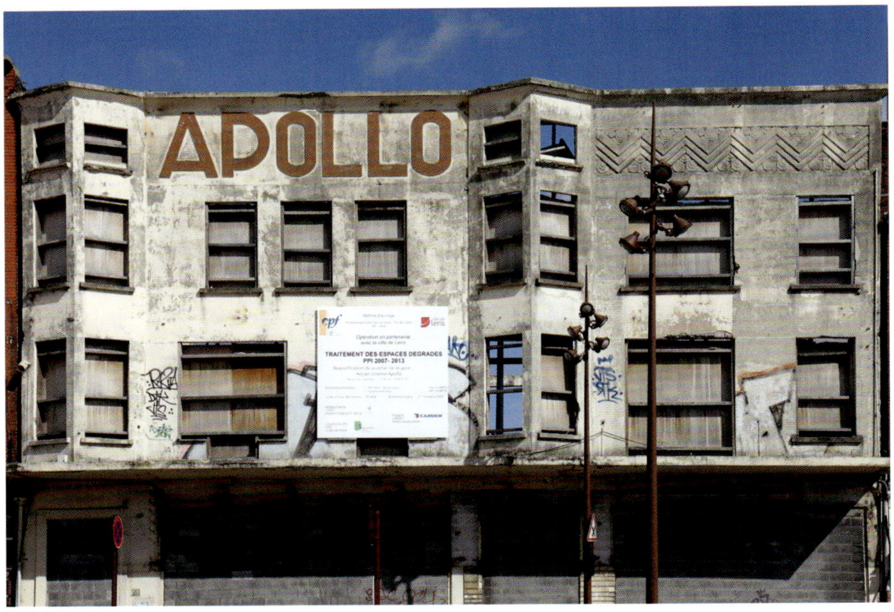

Lens – Apollo – 2012 (destroyed)

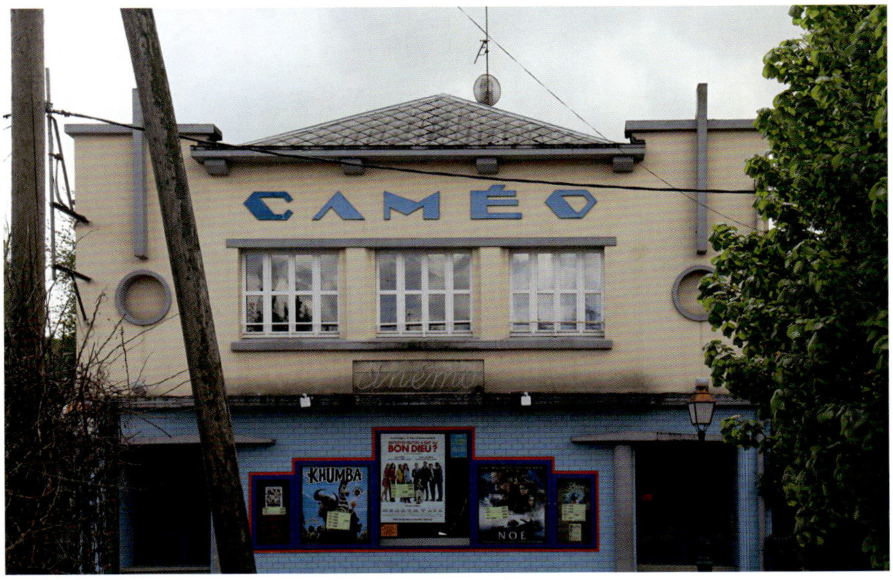

Avesne-sur-Helpe – Caméo – 2014

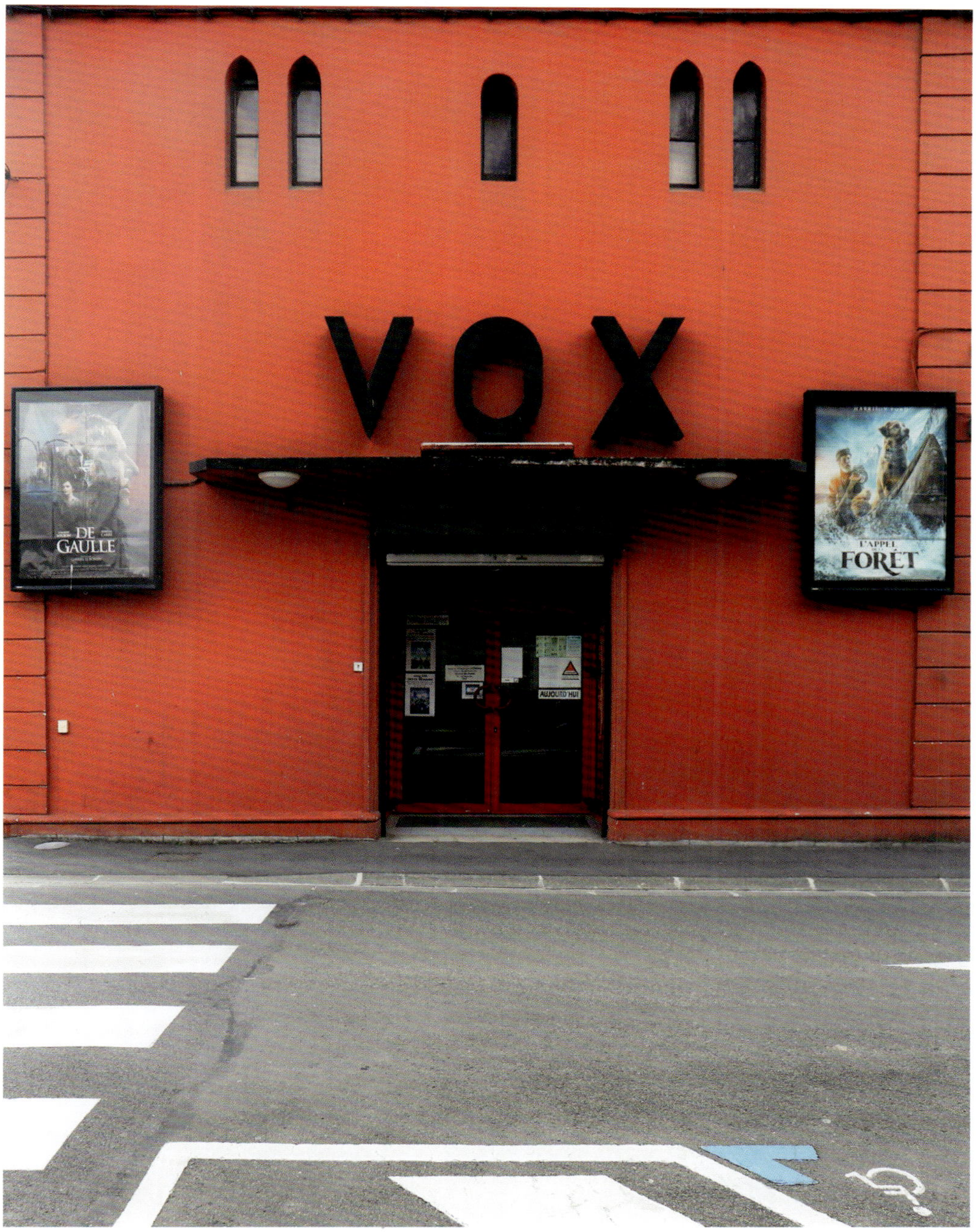

Guise – Vox – 2020

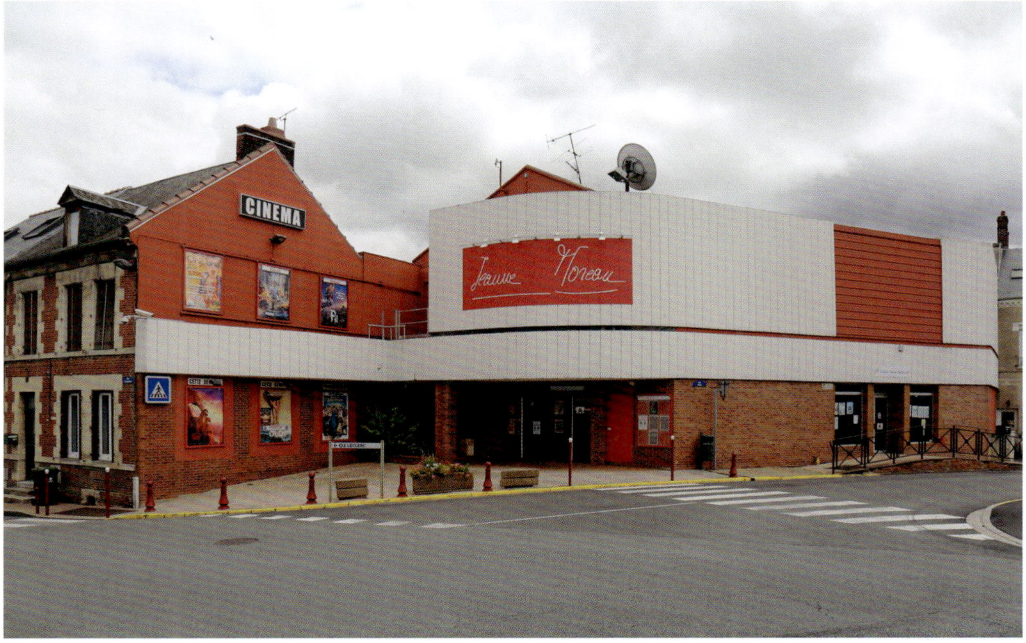

Saint-Just-en-Chaussée – Jeanne Moreau – 2021

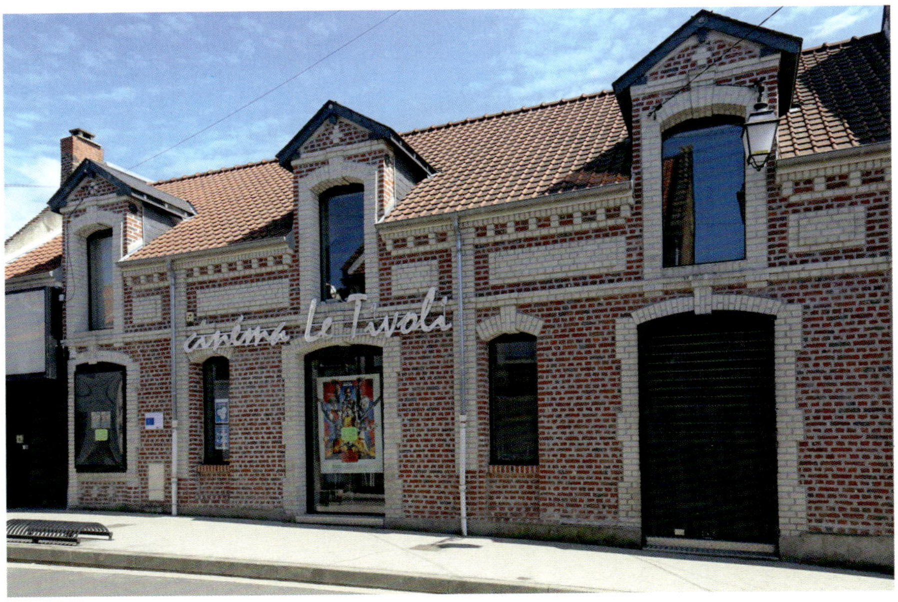

Doullens – Cinéma Le Tivoli – 2021

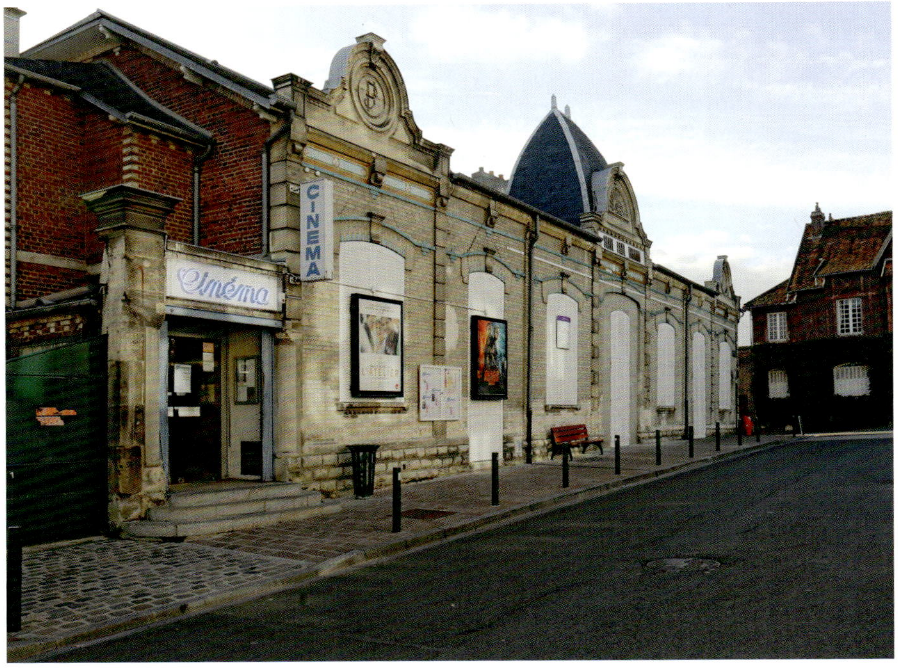

Clermont – Paul Lebrun – 2017

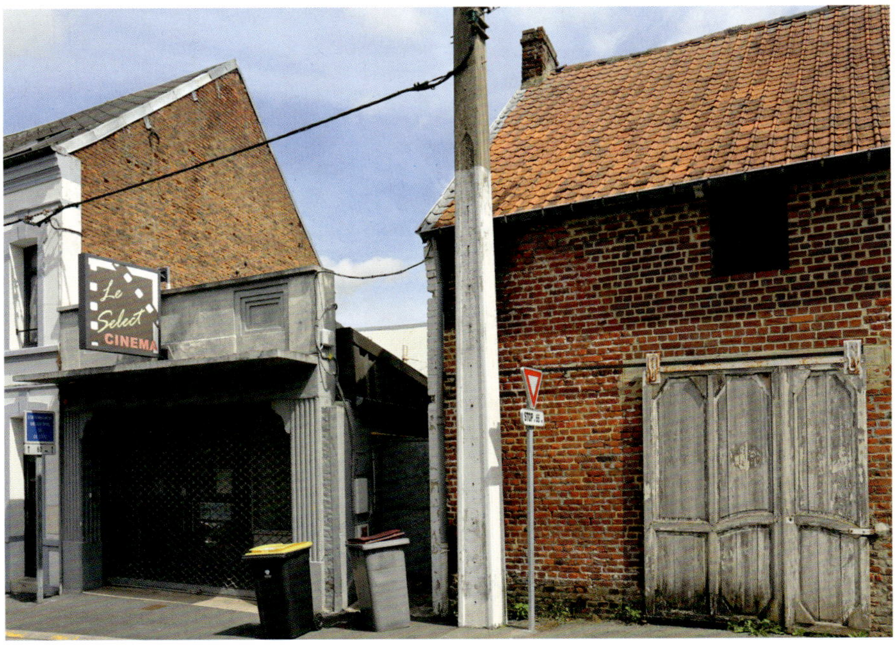

Le Cateau-Cambrésis – Le Select – 2021

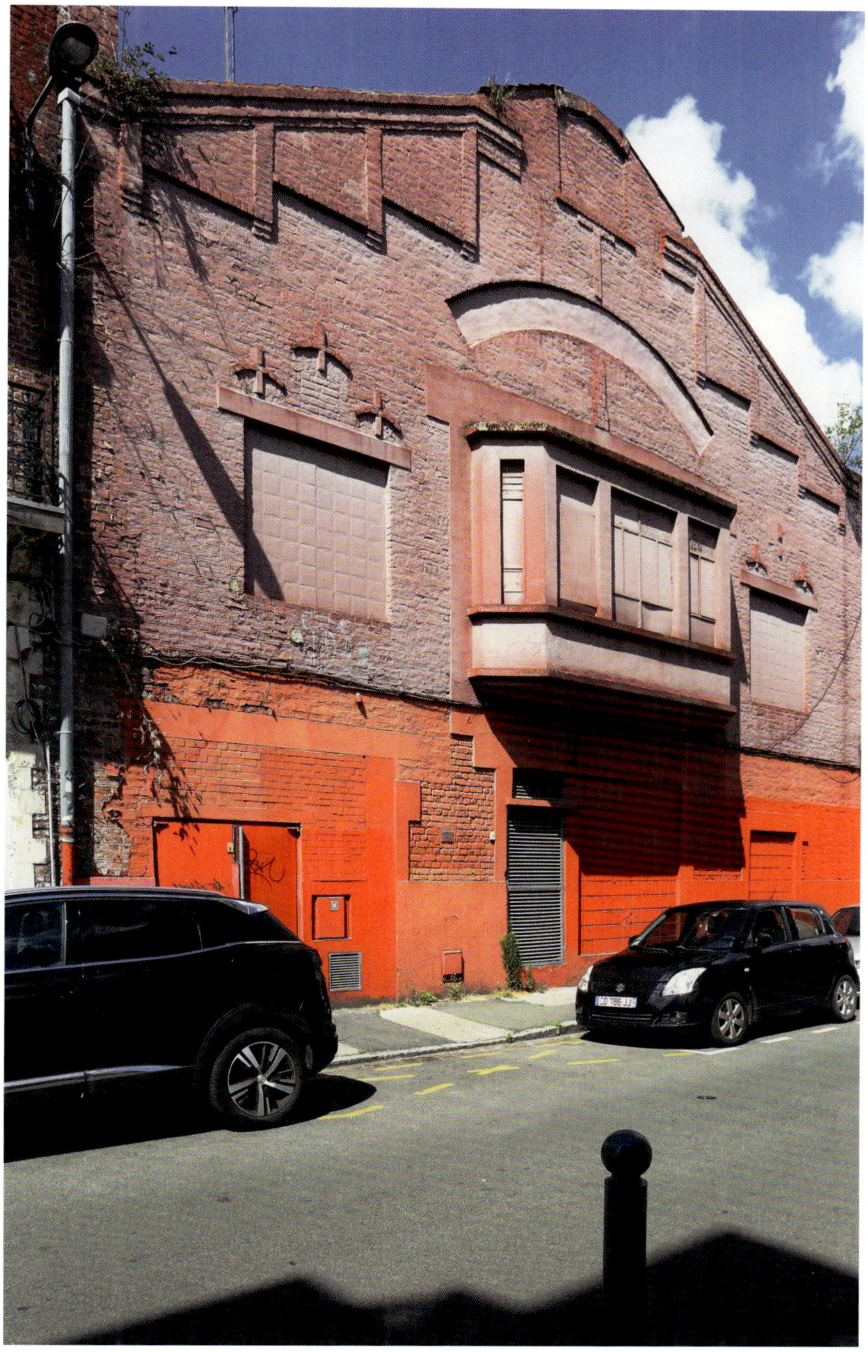

Lille – Vog – 2020

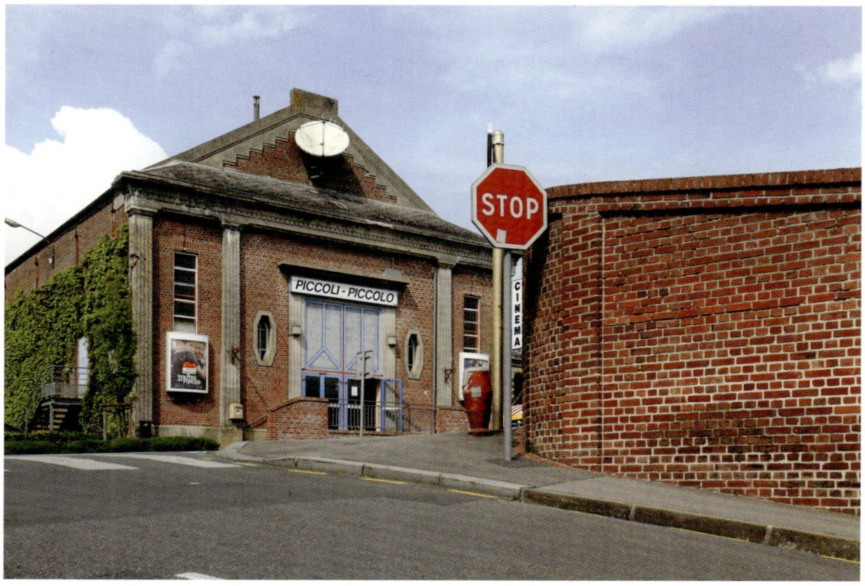

Vervins – Piccoli - Piccolo – 2014

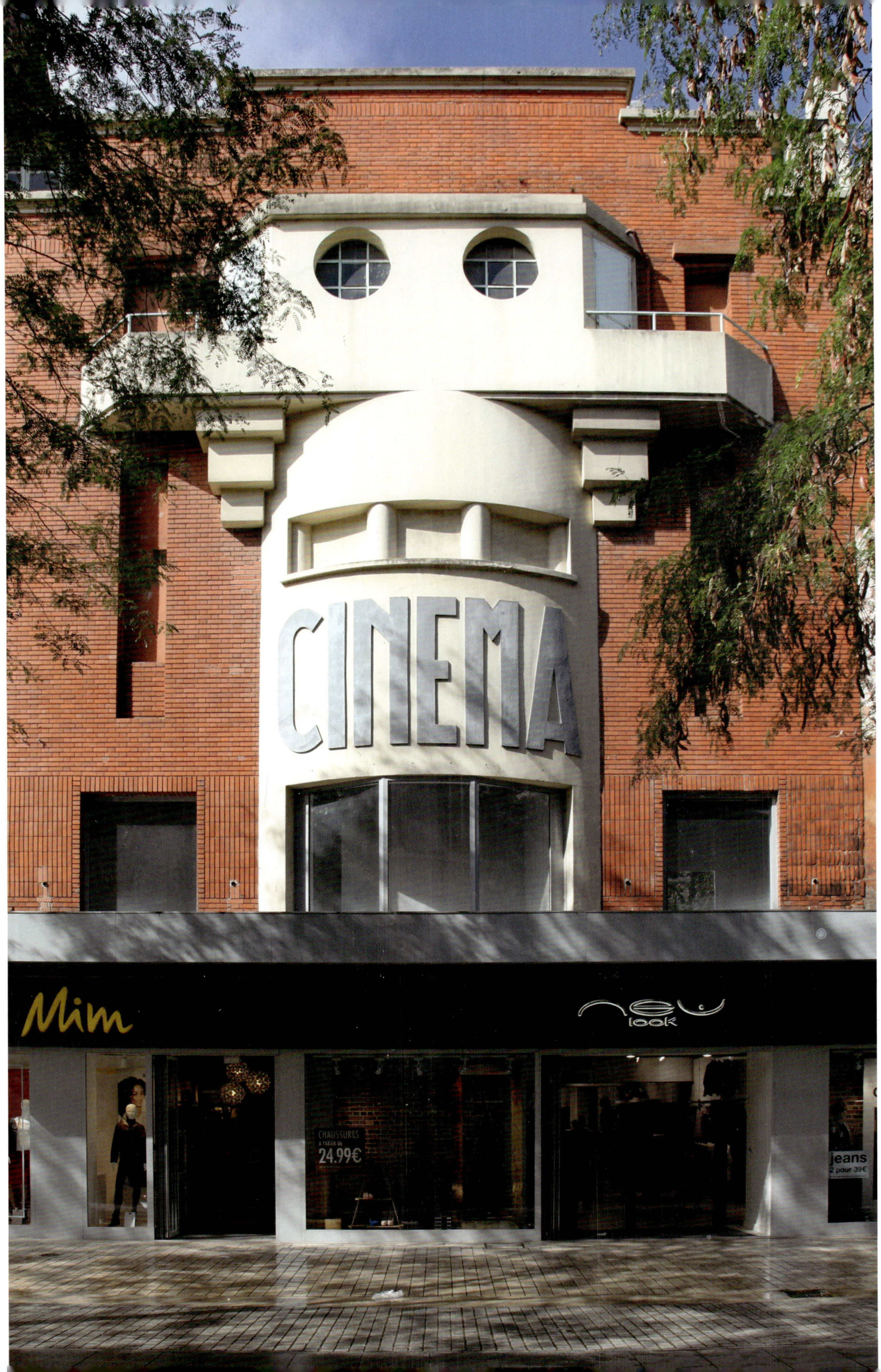
CINEMA
Mim
new look
CHAUSSURES
24.99€
jeans

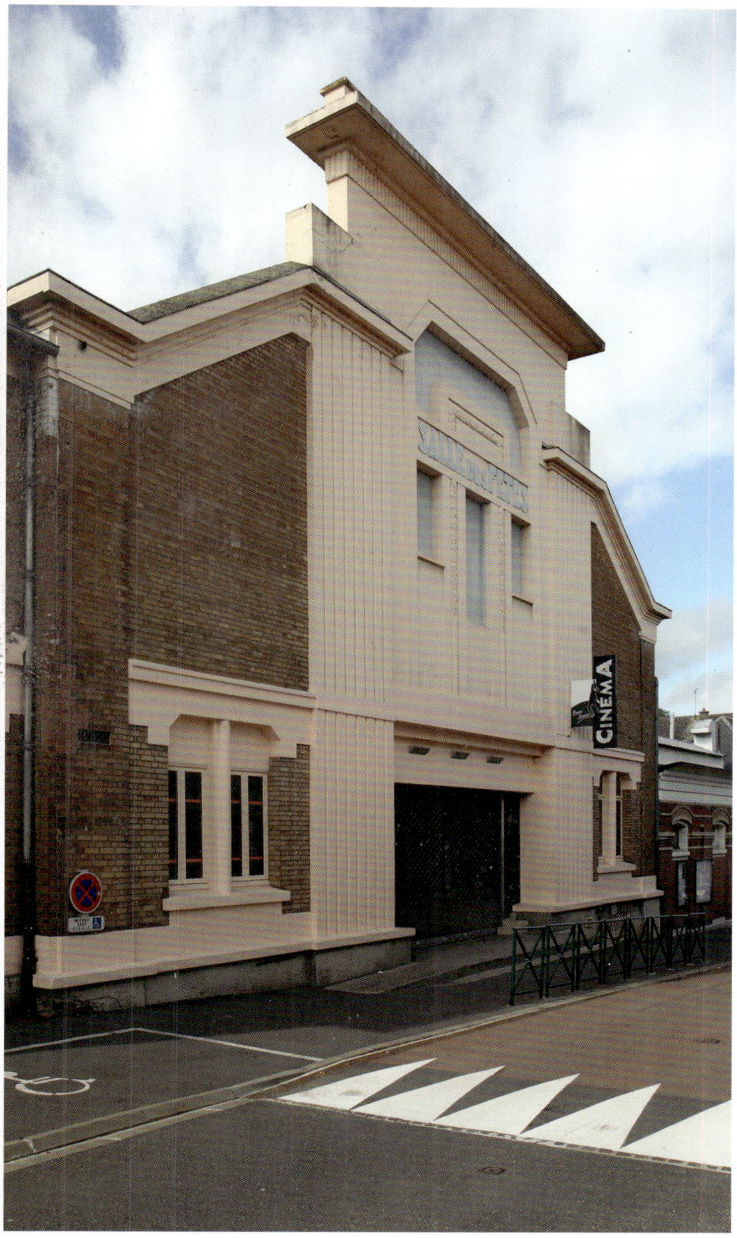

Bohain-en-Vermandois – Cinéma Louis Jouvet – 2012

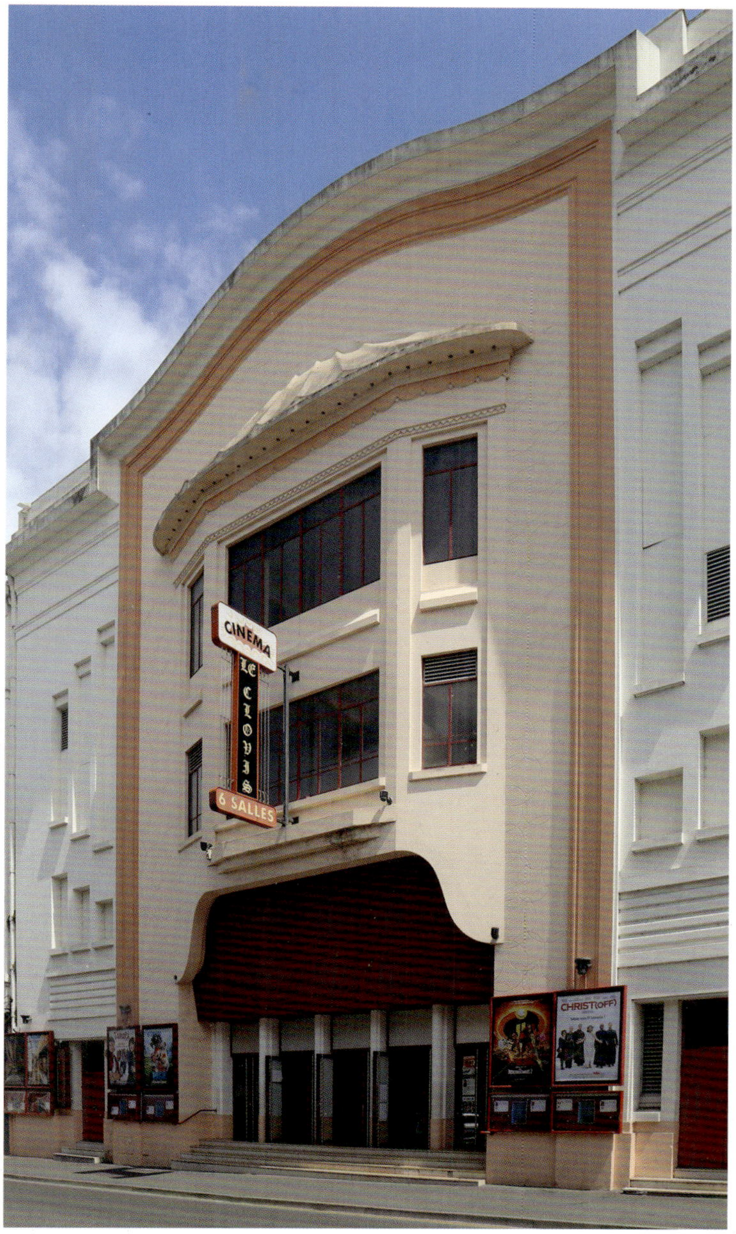

Soissons – Le Clovis – 2018

Left:
Amiens – Gaumont – 2012

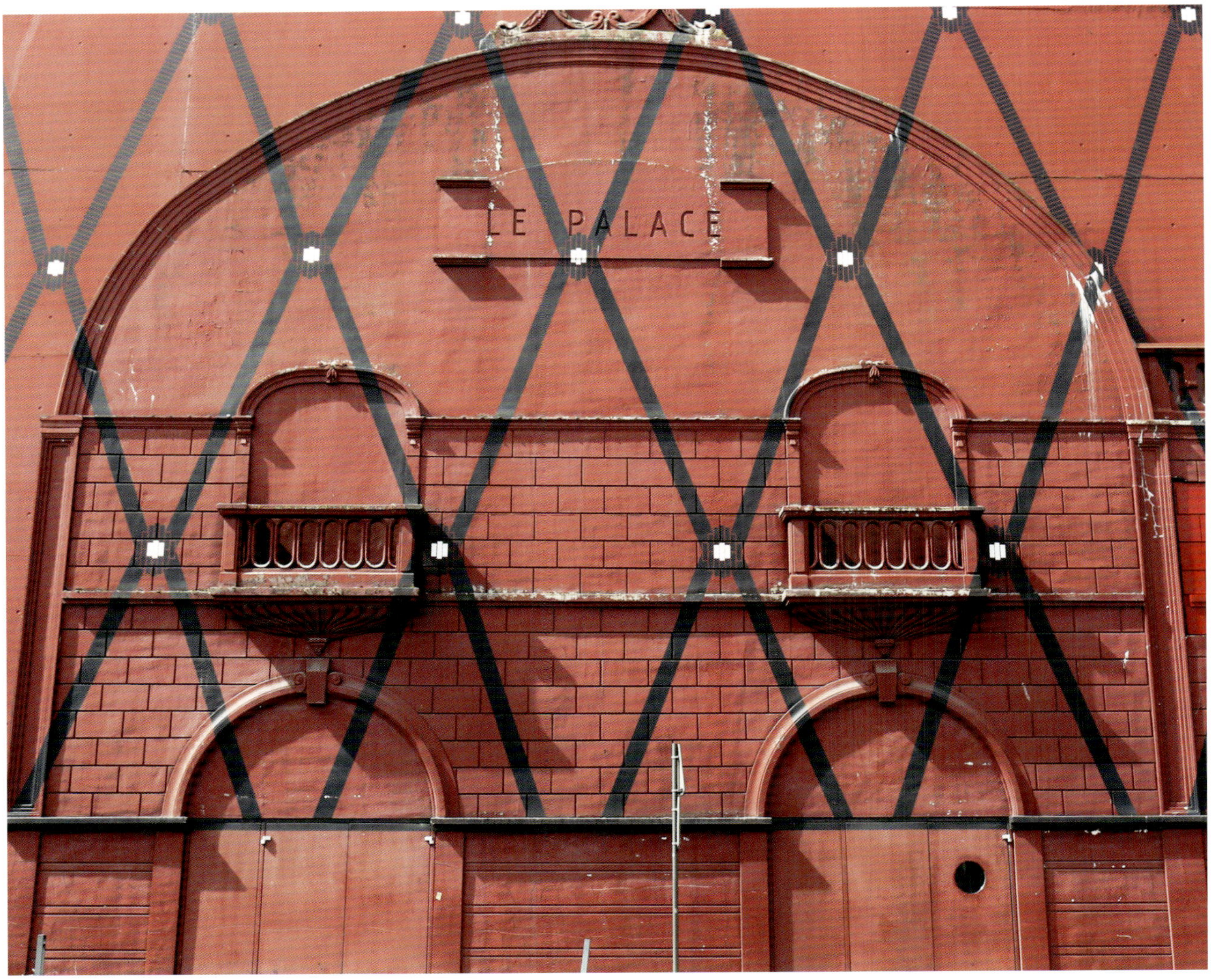

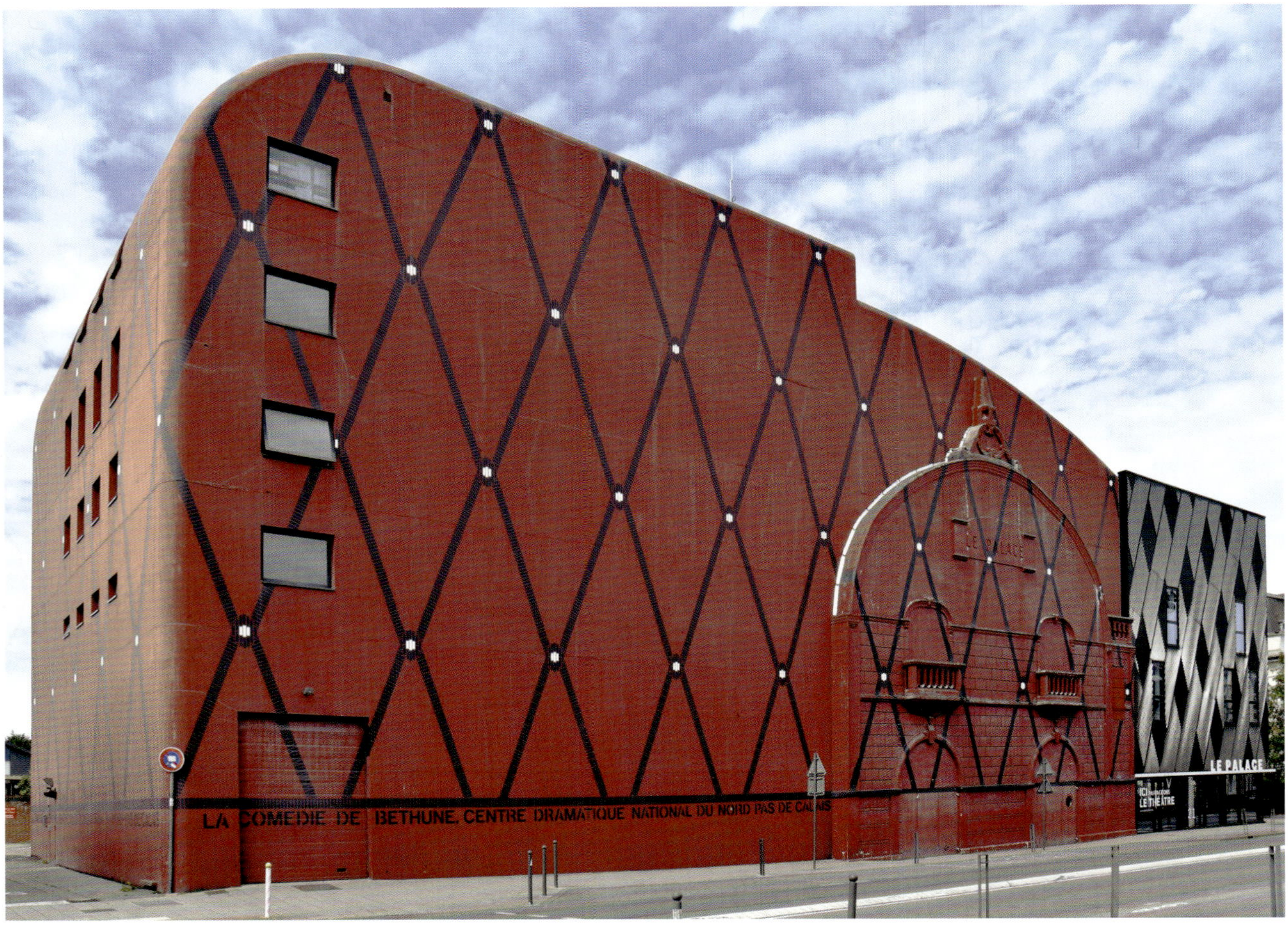

Béthune – Le Palace – 2021

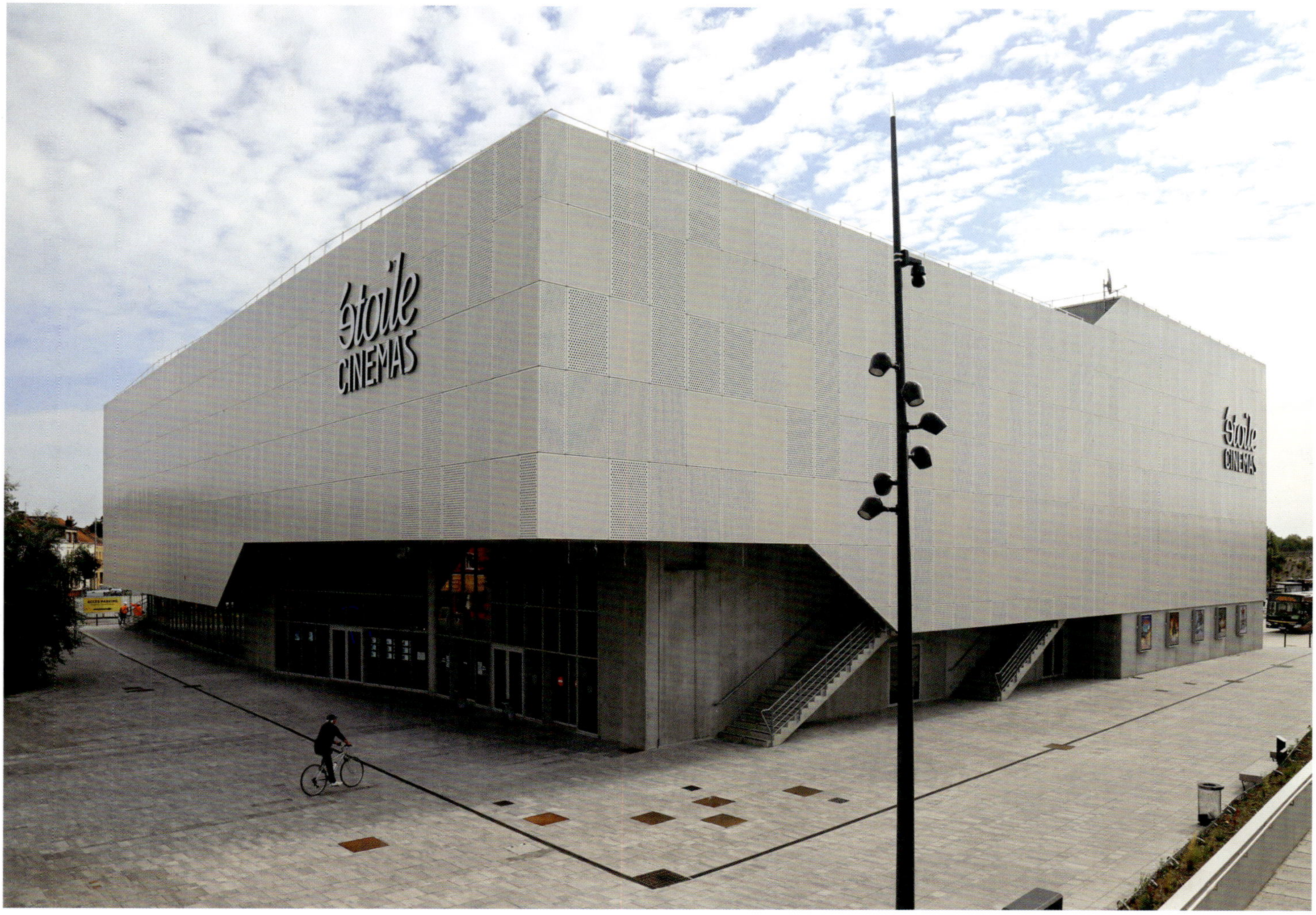

Béthune – Étoile – 2021

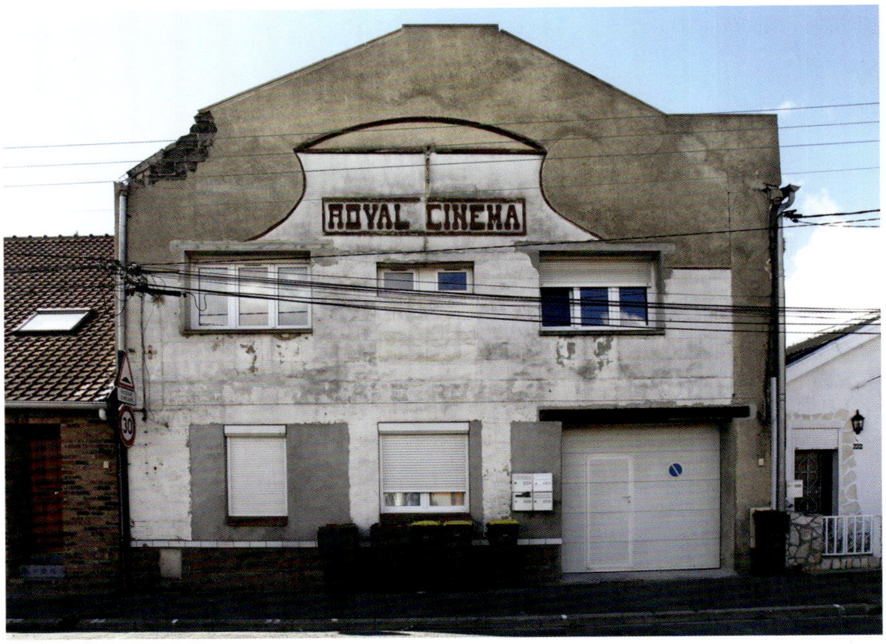

Lievain – Royal Cinéma – 2012

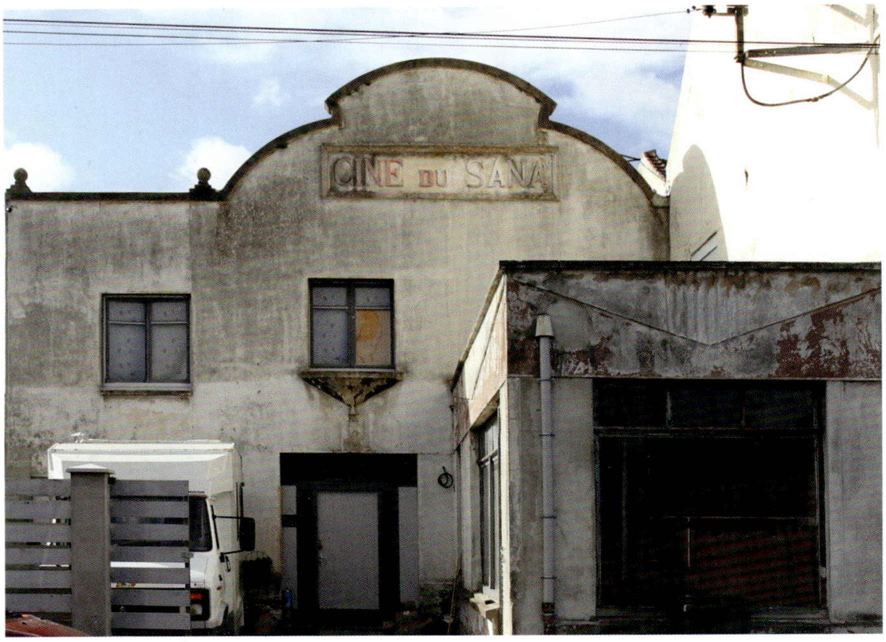

Montigny-en-Ostrevent – Ciné du Sana – 2012

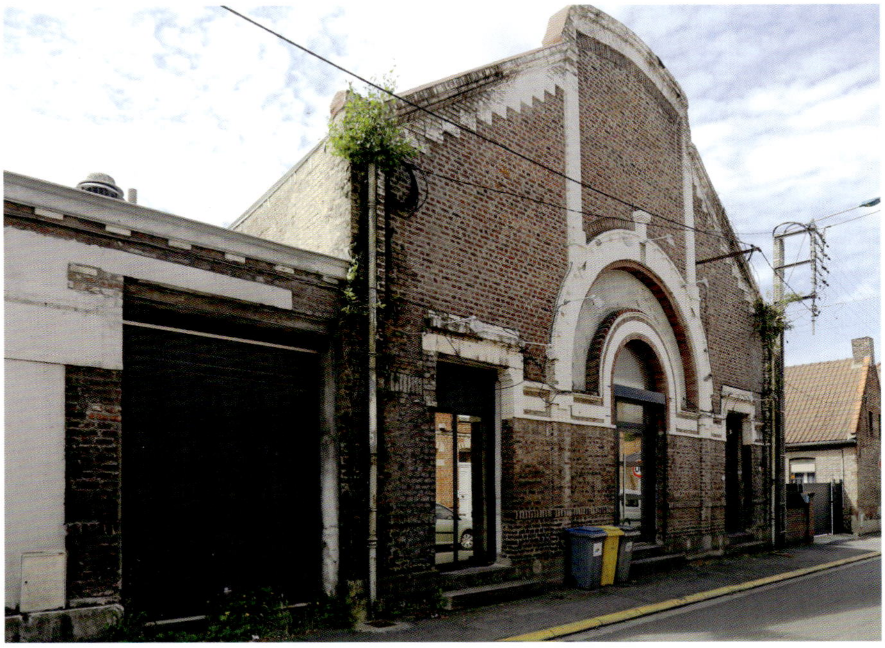
Waziers – Omnia – 2021

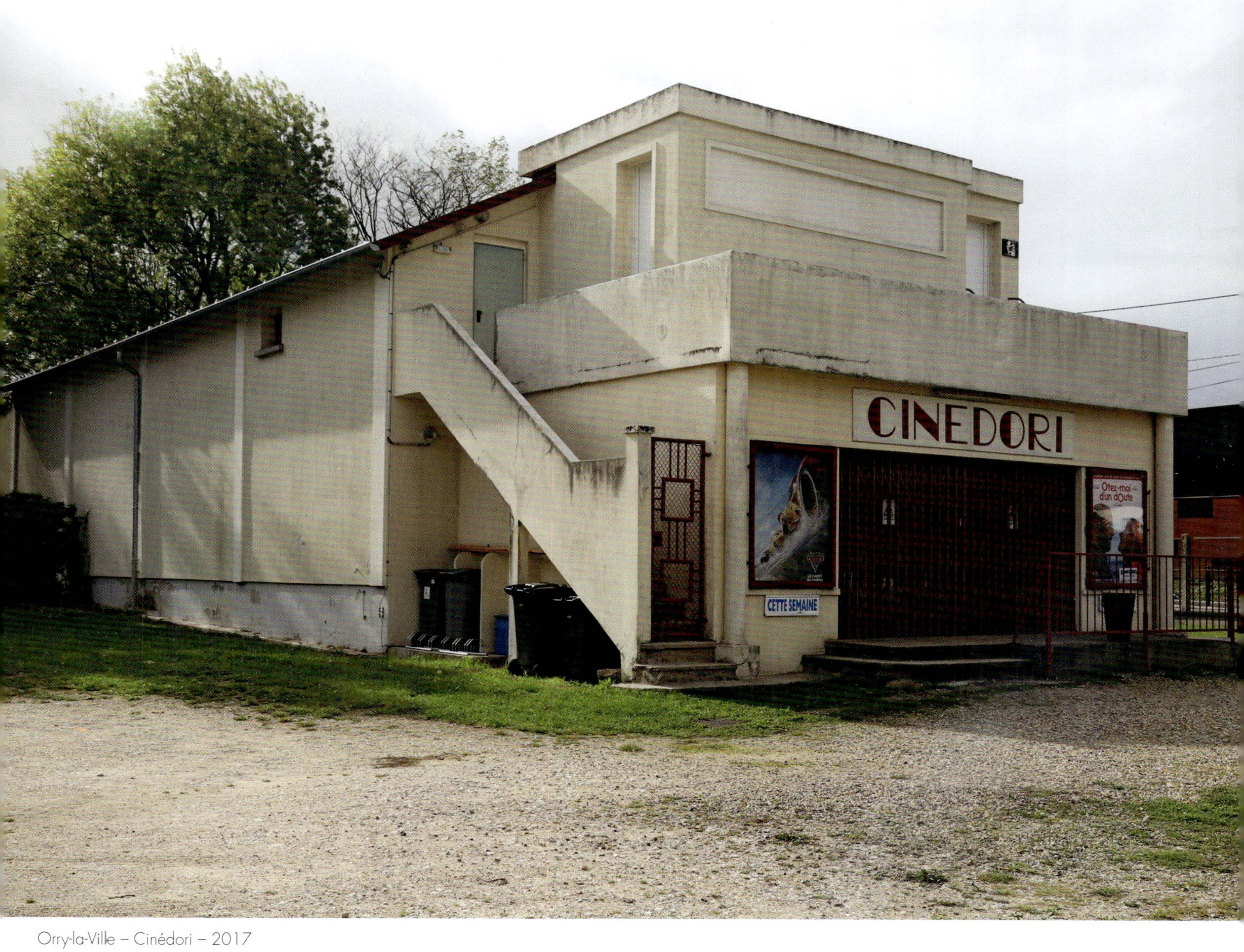

Orry-la-Ville – Cinédori – 2017

ÎLE-DE-FRANCE

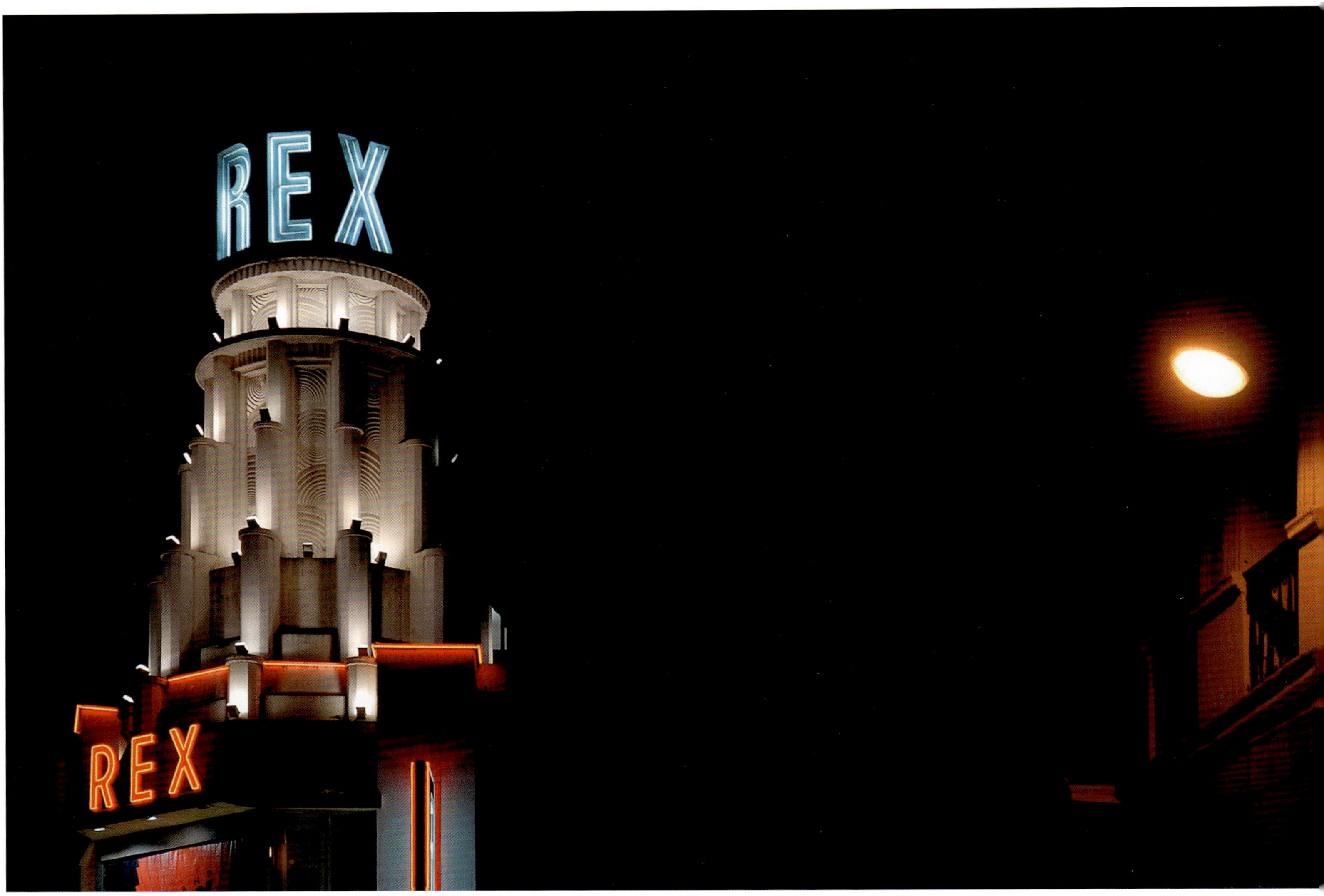

Paris – Le Grand Rex – 2008

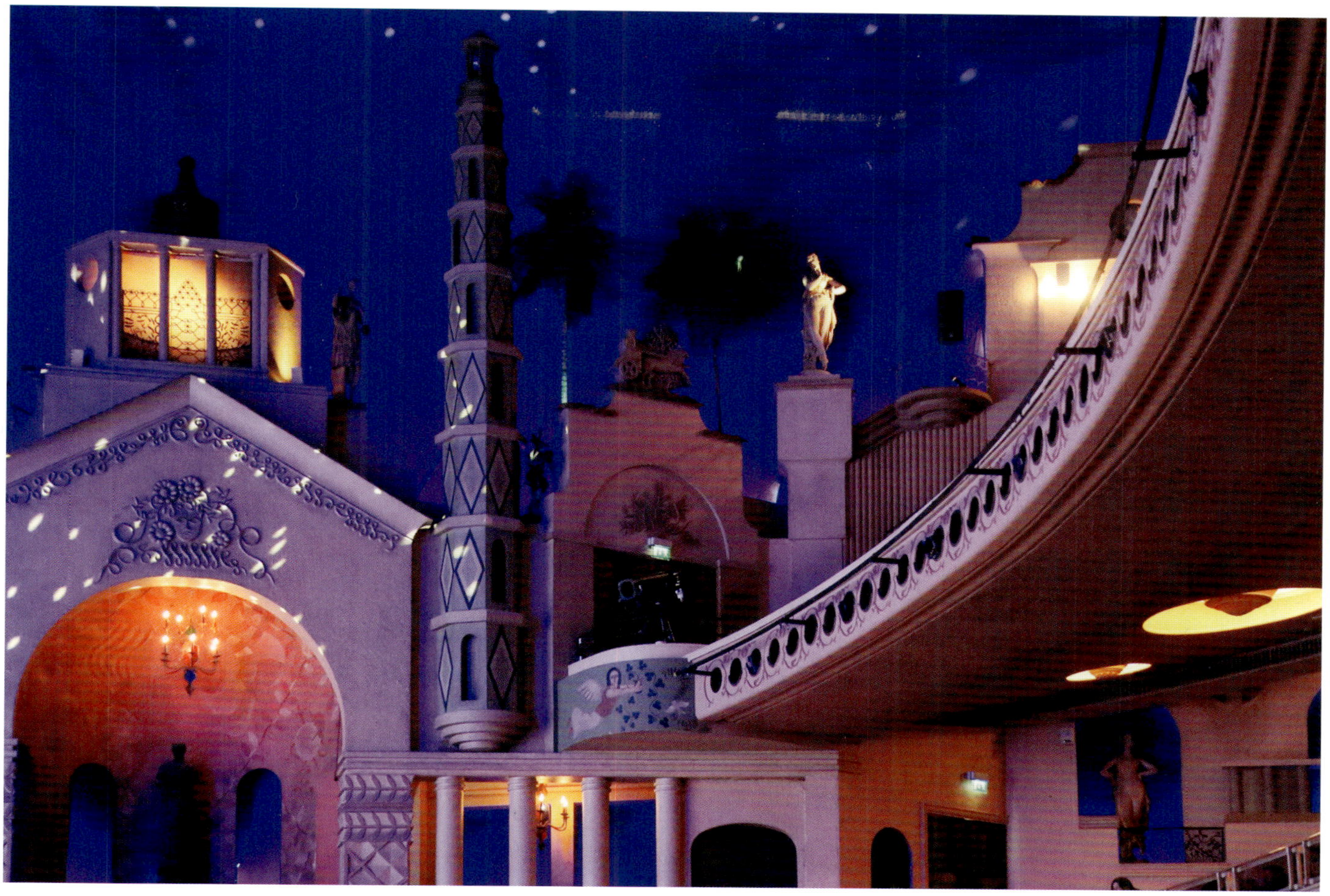

2022

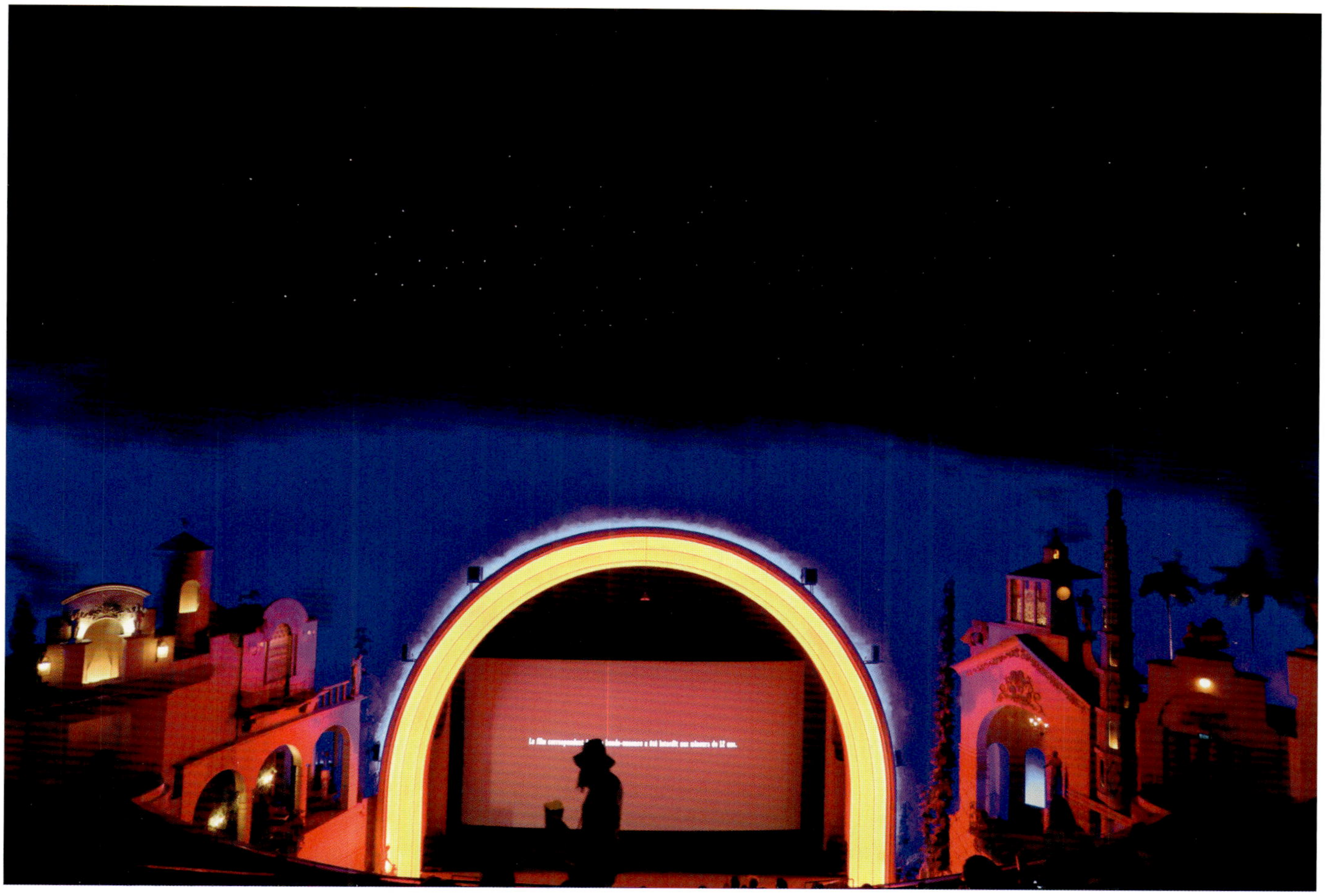

2022

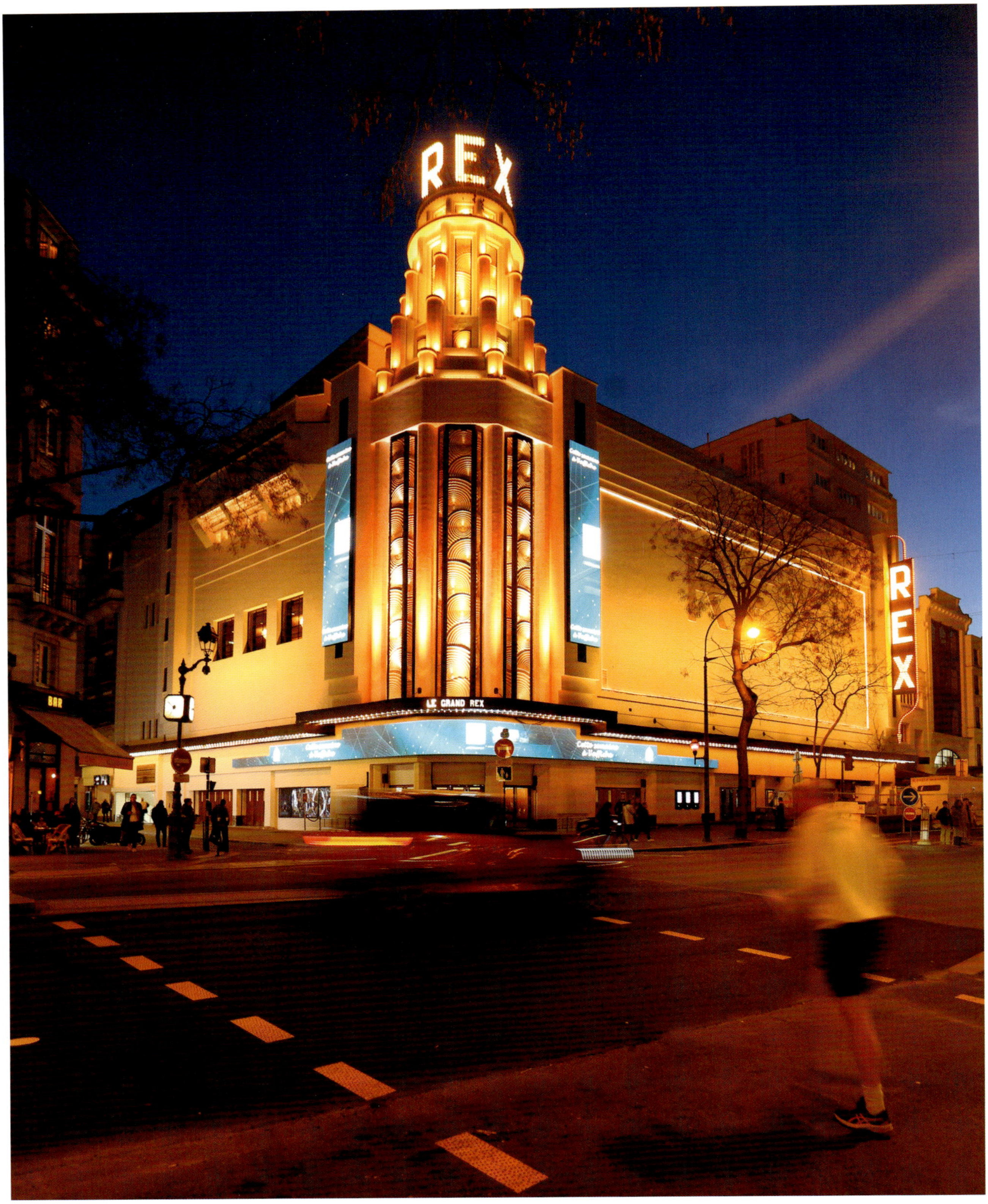

Paris – Le Grand Rex – 2023

Paris, Le Grand Rex. On 8 December 1932, 3,300 guests in tuxedos and sequined frocks crowded in front of the cinema's huge Art Deco façade. Le Tout-Paris celebrates the birth of the largest cinema in Europe. Welcomed by 80 ushers in livery and white gloves, the guests discovered a room filled with palm trees swaying limply in front of minarets, ancient colonnades, Venetian palaces and a sky sparkling with stars. In 2022, the starry sky is still there. The Rex hasn't changed.

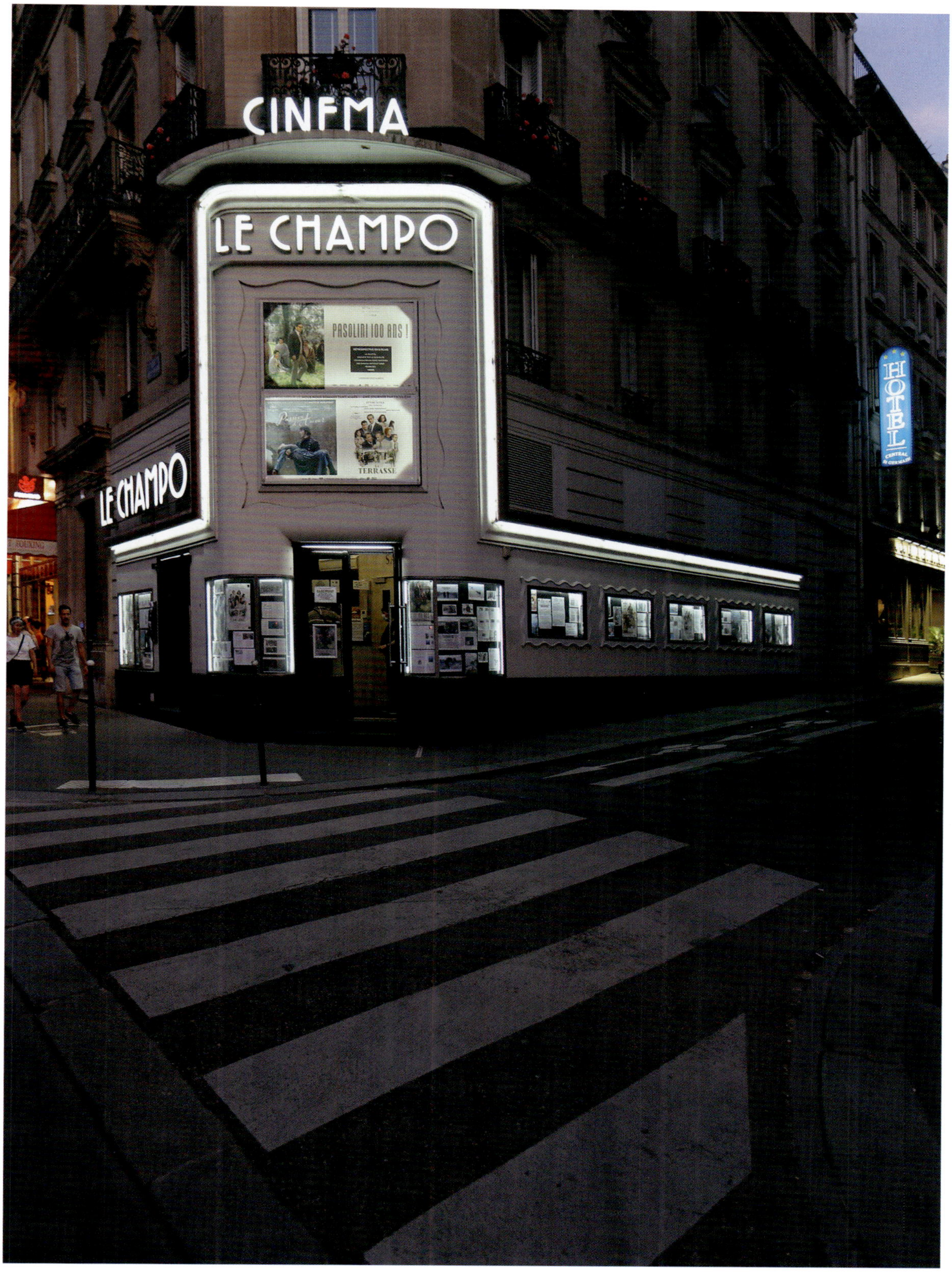

Paris – Le Champo – Espace Jacques-Tati – 2022

Paris, Le Champo – Espace Jacques-Tati. The Champo shelters a universe from another age. Discreet by day and sparkling when night falls. The Reflet Médicis cinema and La Filmothèque in the Latin Quarter cling close to it. They personify a disappearing world. Love of cinema, an active passion in this corner of Paris, has already faded from many cities and countries.

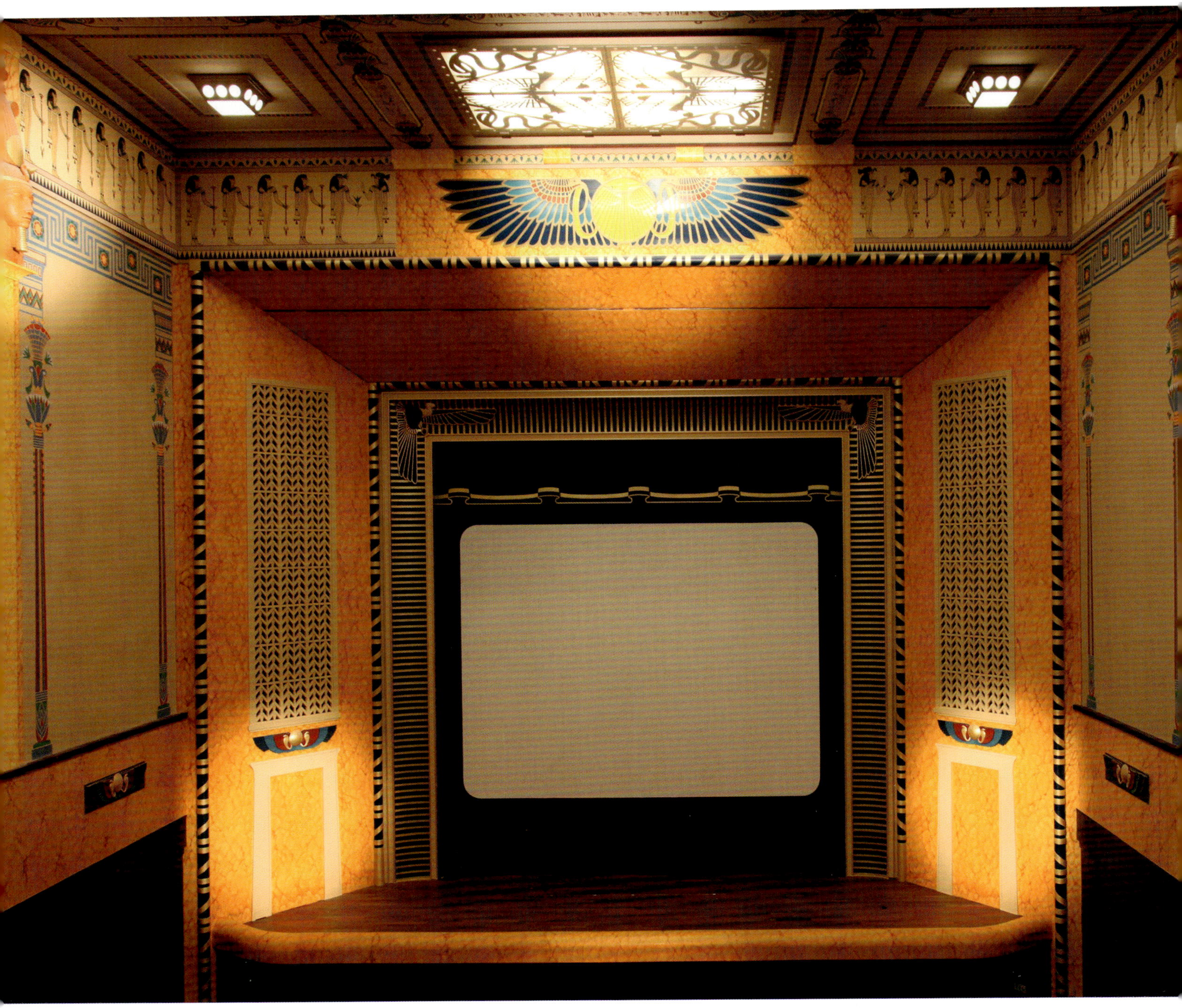

Paris – Louxor – 2013

Paris, Louxor. The Louxor opened in 1921. It closed its doors in 1987. According to tradition, its descent into hell was harsh. Storage depot, a series of nightclubs, decay, vandalism. And yet the Louxor is still a unique example in France of the Egyptian architecture of the 1920s, very fashionable in the USA at that time. Often threatened with destruction, as the saying goes, the building was first saved by residents' associations, then supported by various wealthy individuals and finally bought by the City of Paris in 2003. Renovated, it was reborn on 17 April 2013.

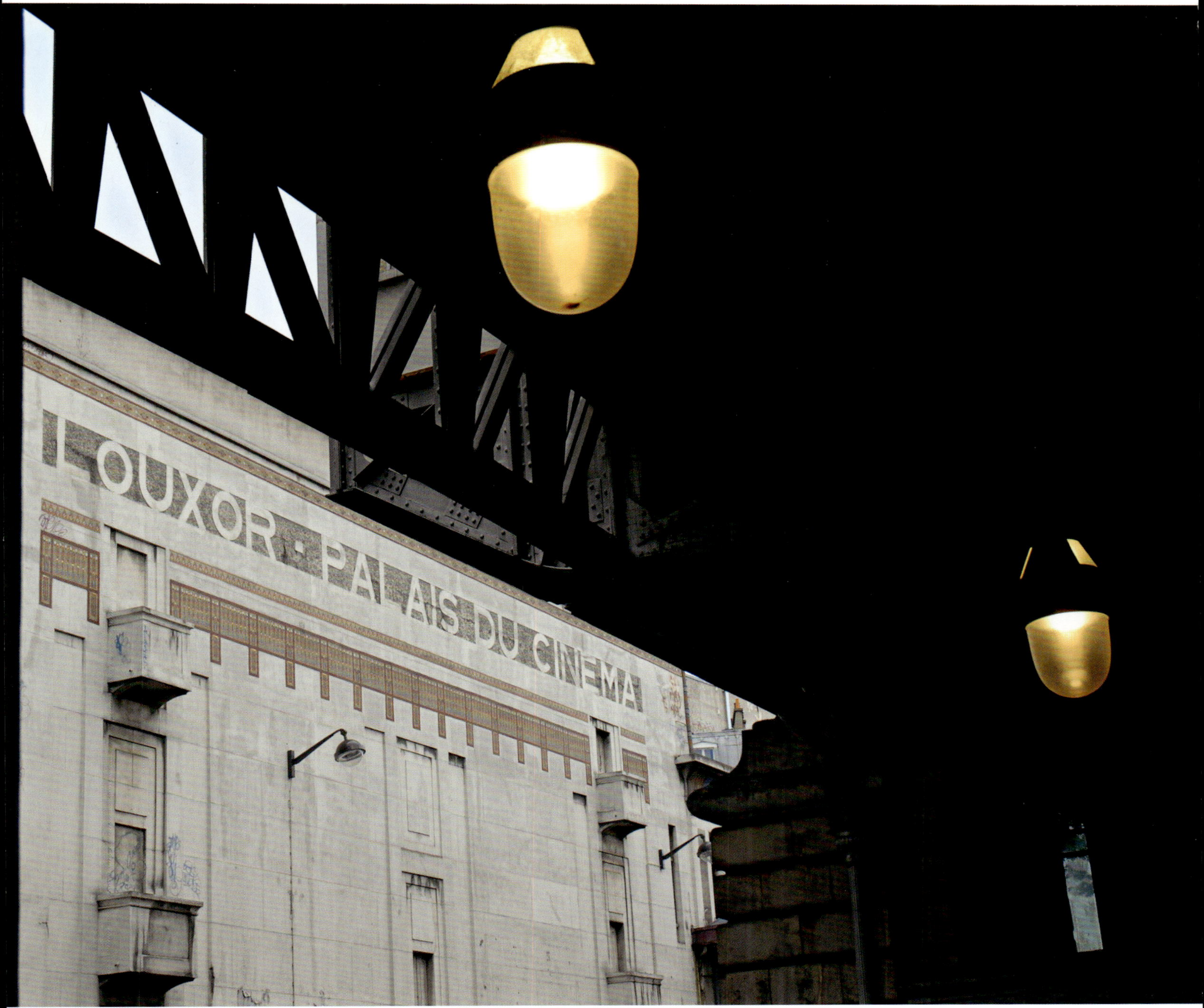

Paris – Louxor – 2008

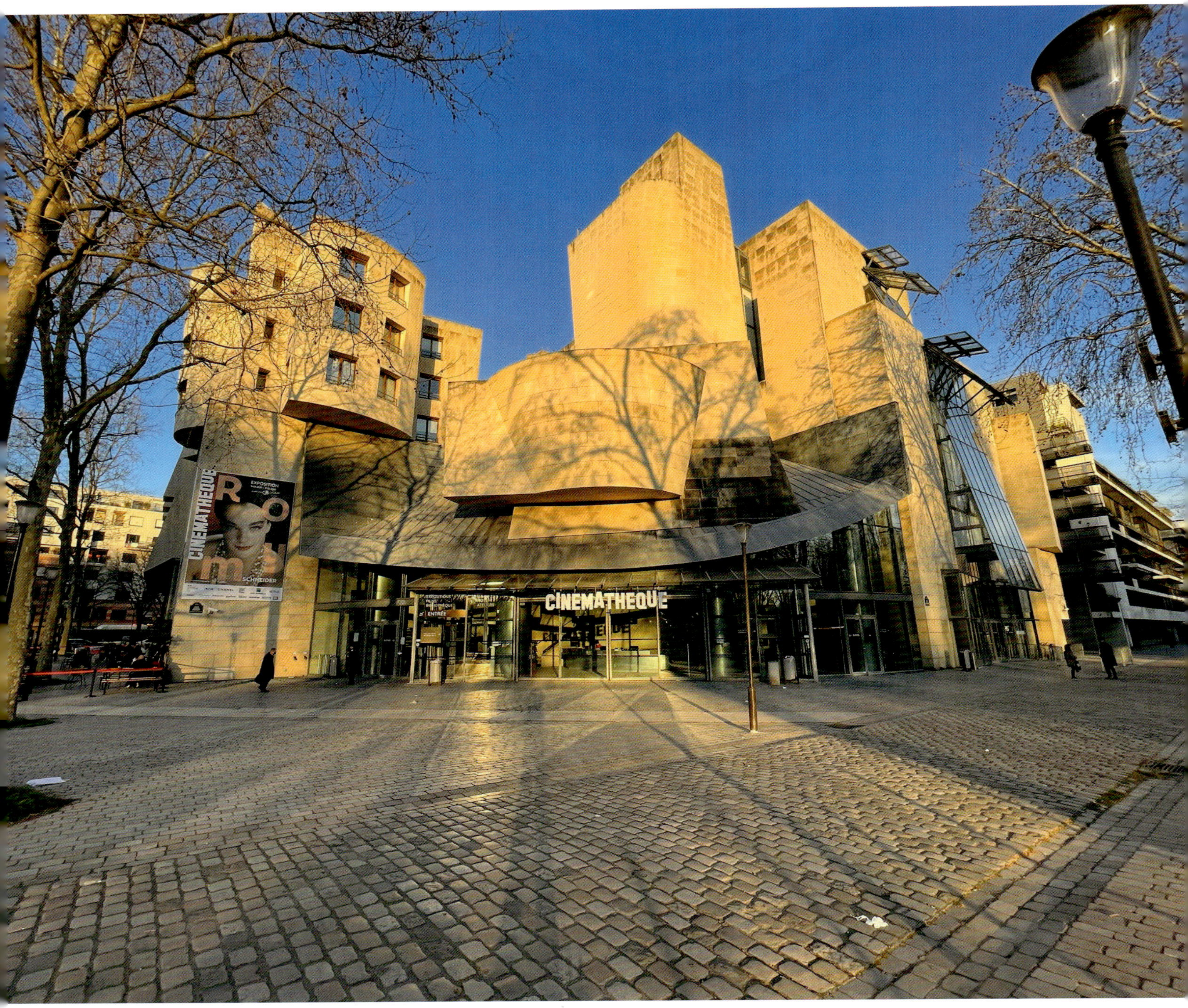

Paris – La Cinémathèque française – 2022

Paris, La Cinémathèque française. The only project carried out in France by architect Frank Gehry (designer of the Guggenheim Museum Bilbao, Spain). It was built in 1993 for the American Center. The Cinémathèque française took over the premises in 2005. This change of use required major work and movie buffs used to frequenting the former Cinémathèque had to change their habits. Not easy.

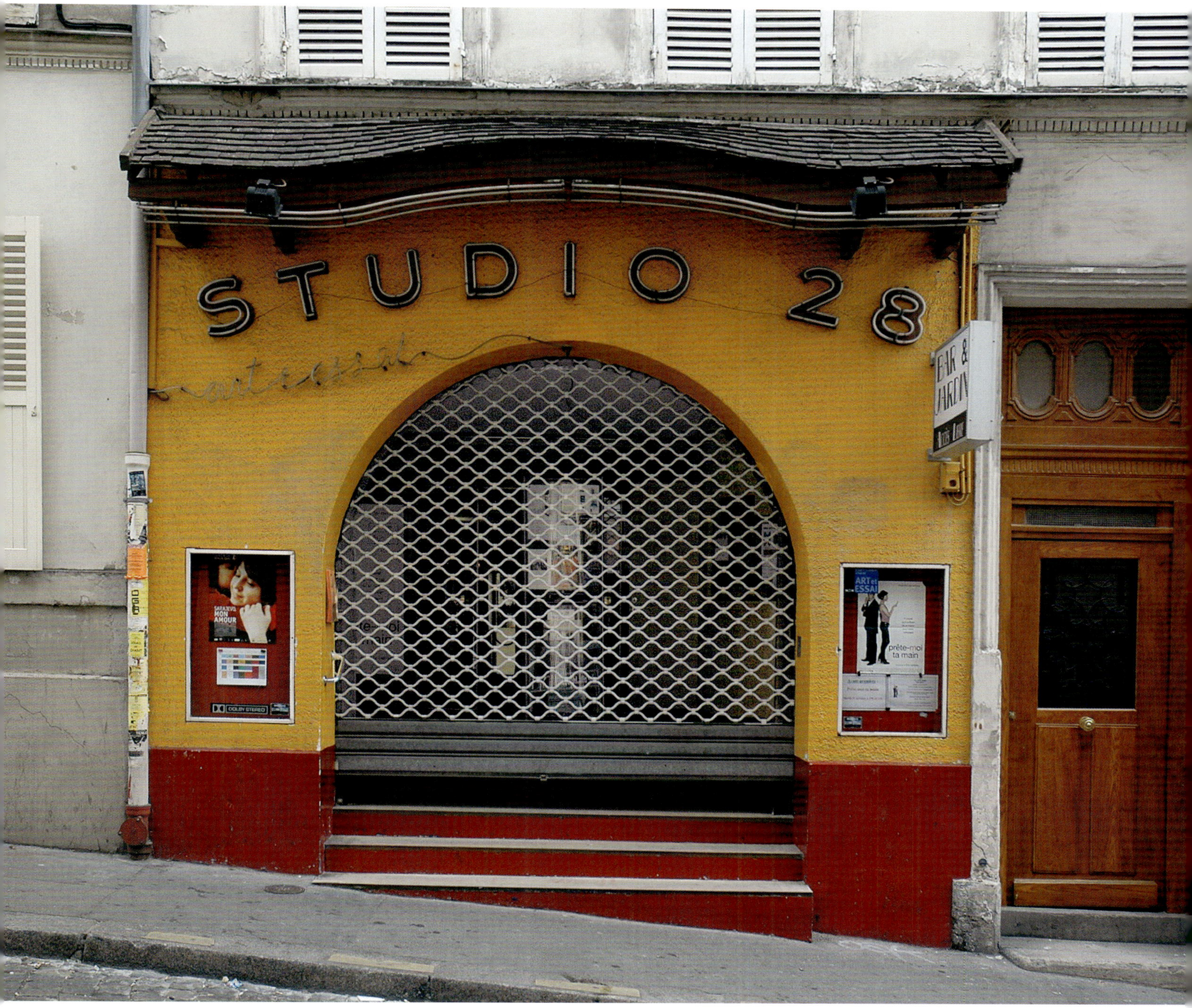

Paris – Studio 28 – 2006

Paris, Studio 28. Studio 28 opened in … 1928. The undulating shapes of its unusual façade are unchanged. As Jean Cocteau said: '*the room of masterpieces, the masterpiece of rooms*', recalling that he designed the magical lights – and Alexandre Trauner the main hall. This place soon became legendary, with a bold programme that stood out from other cinemas. The cinema was soon frequented by innovative directors. Luis Buñuel presented *L'Âge d'or* (*The Golden Age*) there. This film provoked violent reactions from far-right activists who ransacked the venue, and it was censored. But the long story of this cinema continues.

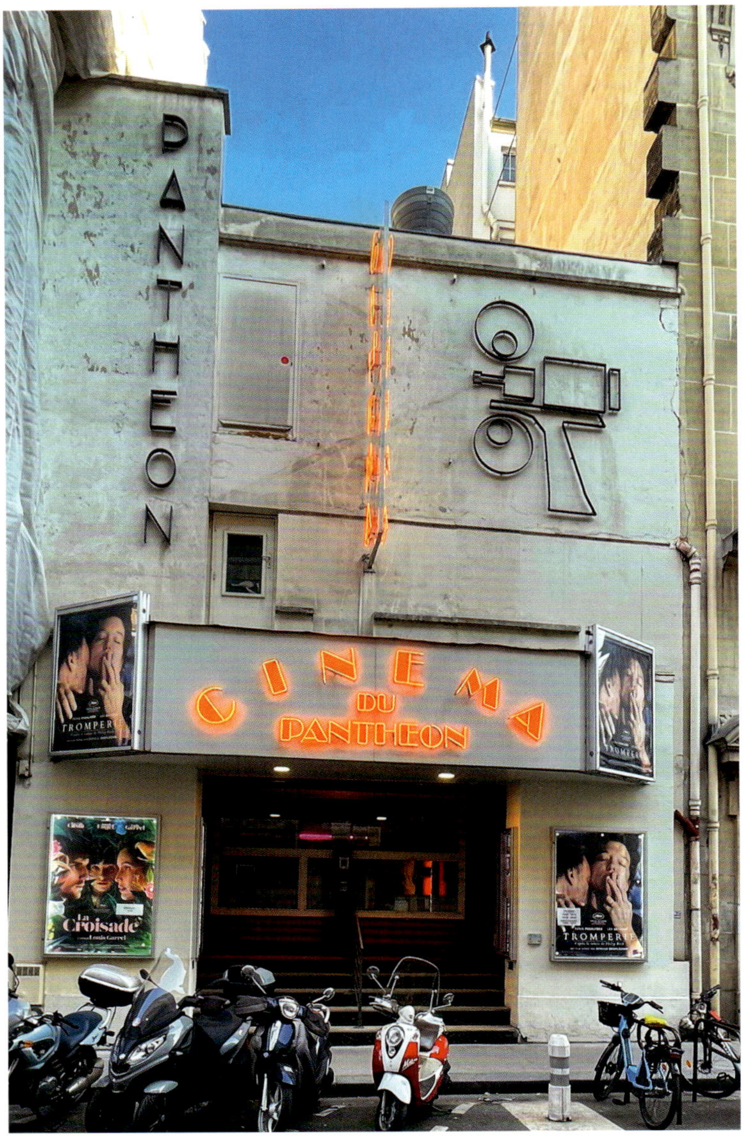

Paris – Cinéma du Panthéon – 2022

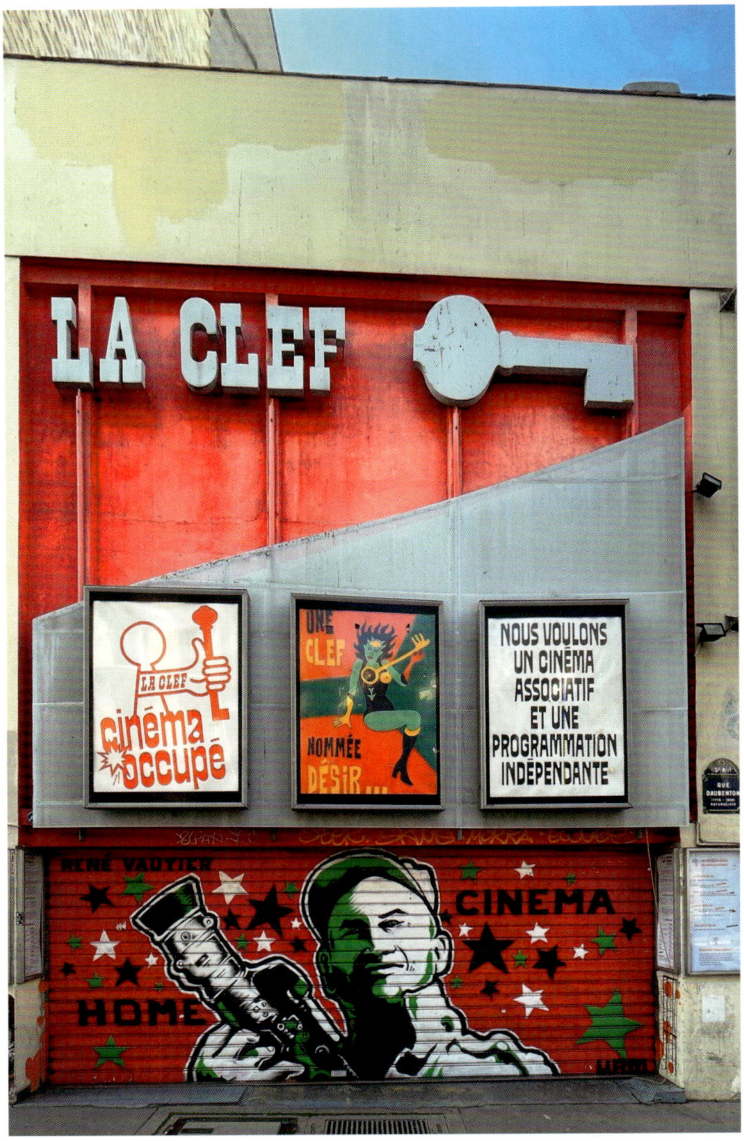

Paris – La Clef – 2021

Paris, La Clef. In 2018 the cinema handed over the keys. It took them back in September 2019, occupied by committed movie-lovers. Since then there have been screenings of rare films, successive debates, animated by large and militant audiences. But the eternal screenplay will relaunch or follow on ... On the one hand, a place of culture, which has become the symbol of a certain resistance; on the other, the threat of armed force and eviction by the police for illegal occupation. Alas, alas. Usually, sweet dreams end in nightmares.

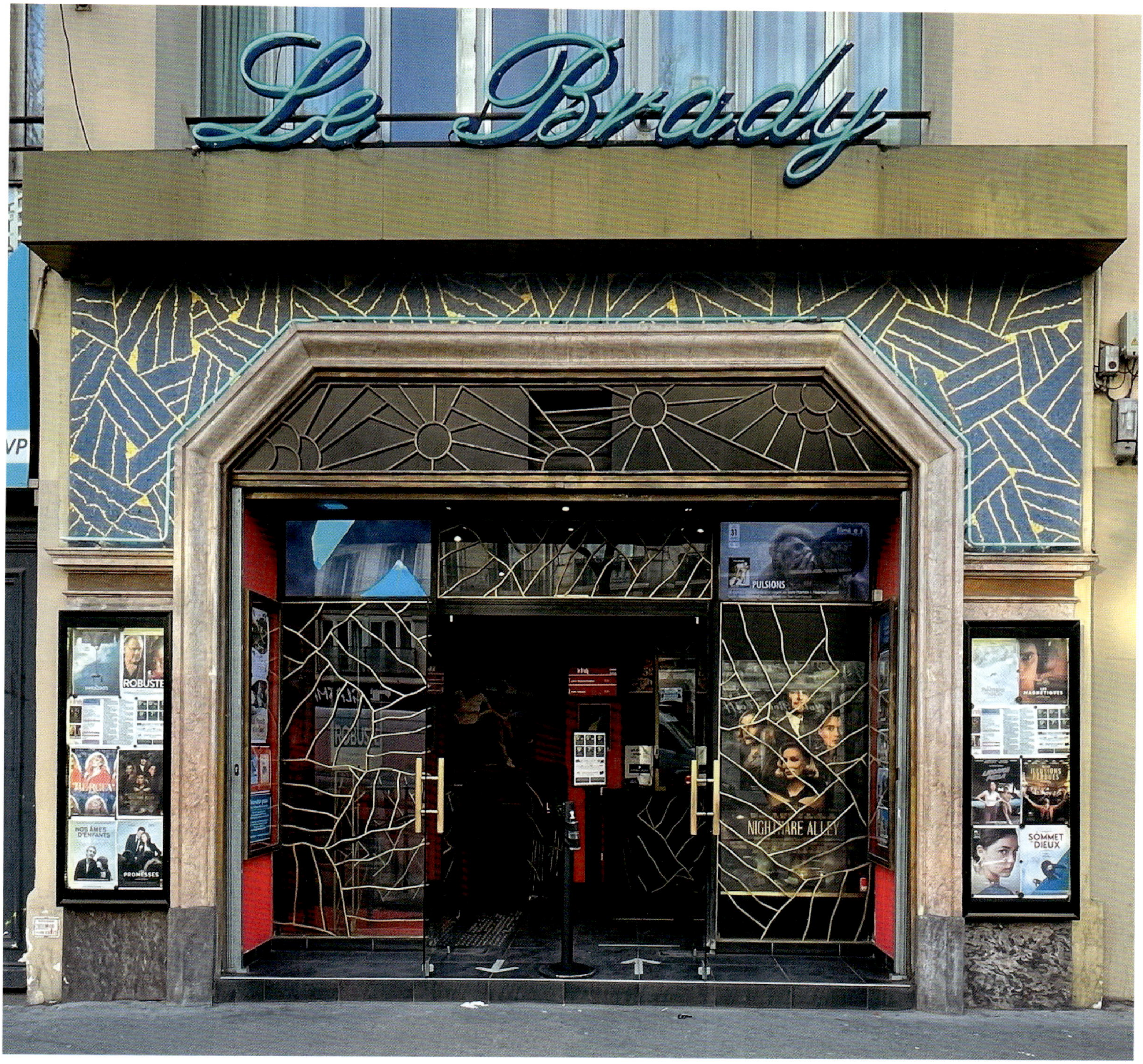

Paris – Le Brady – 2022

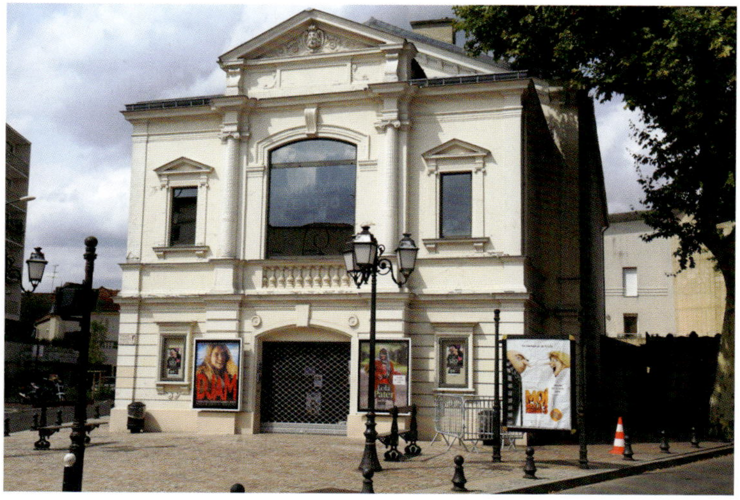

St-Maur – Lido – 2017

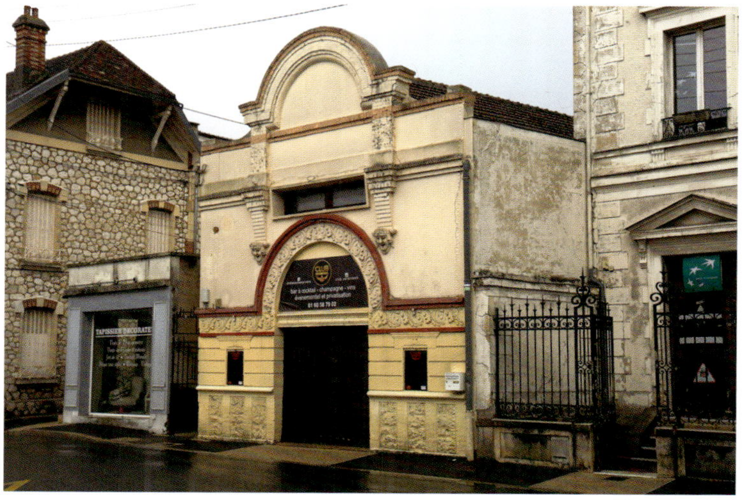

Provins – former Cinéma des Familles – 2019

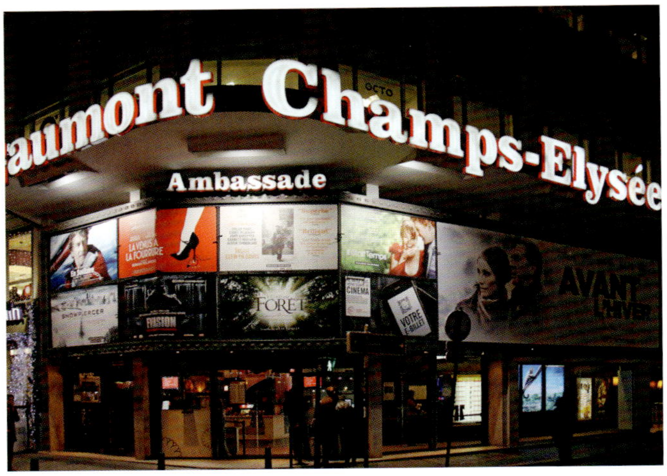

Paris – Gaumont Champs-Élysées Ambassade – 2014

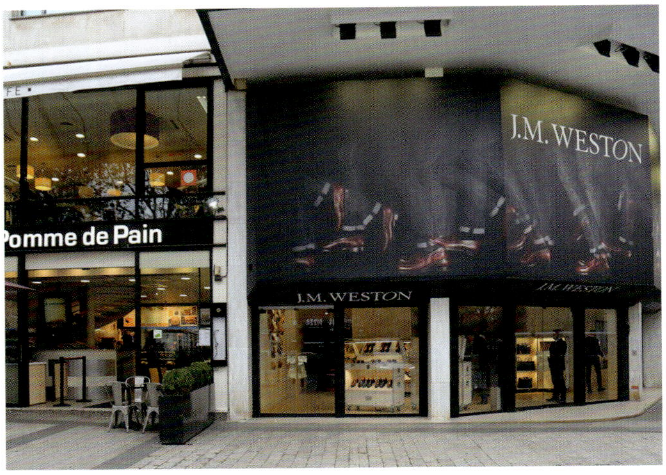

2016

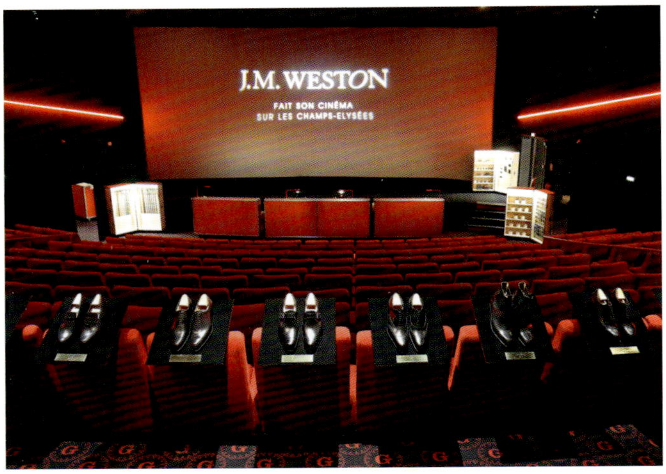

2016

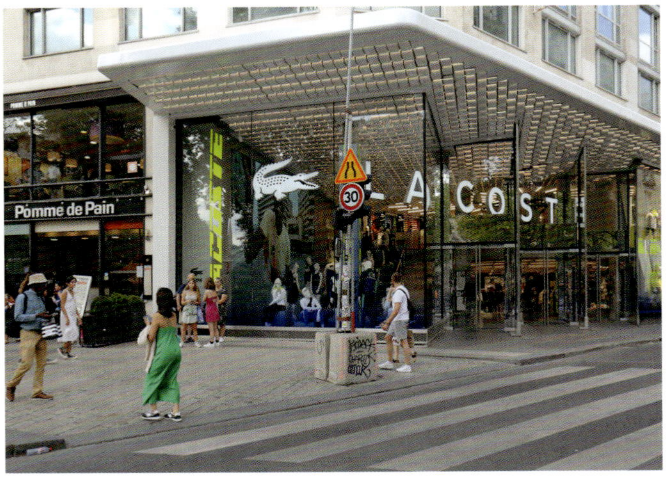

Paris – Gaumont Champs-Élysées – 2022

At the Champs-Élysées fantasy factory, that dream location, the Coliseum cinema opened in 1913. A sumptuous hall, padded seats ideal for a nap, spiralling cigar smoke enveloping the audience if the film grew boring. Other venues followed in rapid succession. The golden age culminated in the 1960s. Producers set up their offices with a view down the most beautiful avenue in the world. The stars wandered, dined, filmed there, the world of cinema came alive along the Champs-Élysées.

Discreetly, since the 80s, the cinemas would disappear, skyrocketing real-estate prices, alteration of the social fabric, fewer residents, more tourists. Habits change, as always, chain stores with brassy names arrive. The page has turned. The Gaumont Champs-Élysées Ambassade, opened in 1959, closed in 2016. Initially a demonstration facility for Weston shoes, it's now a Lacoste boutique. The film no longer scrolls across a screen, replaced by a clay court. Another kind of entertainment begins.

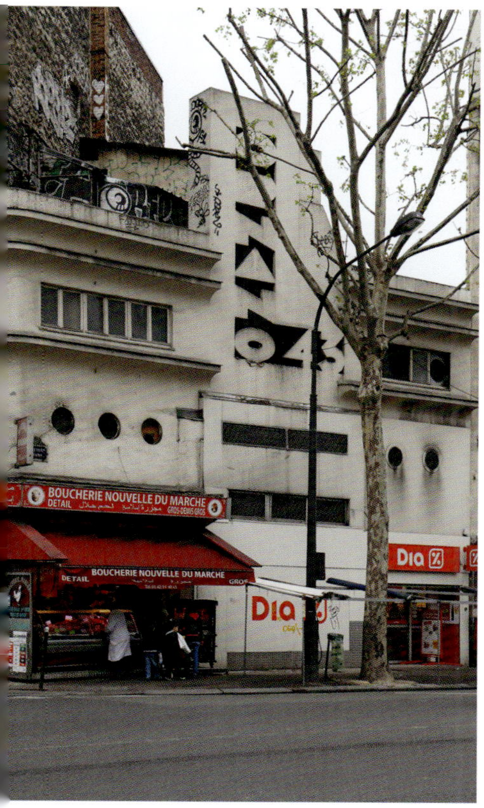

– Ornano 43 – 2015

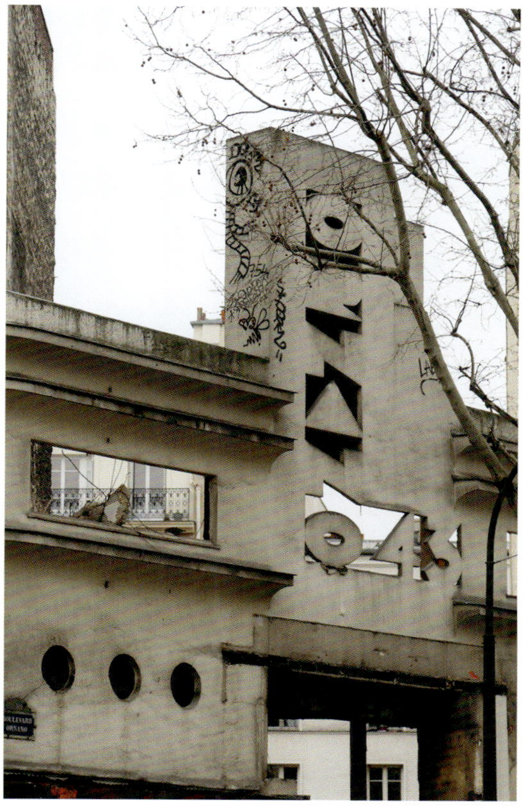

2021

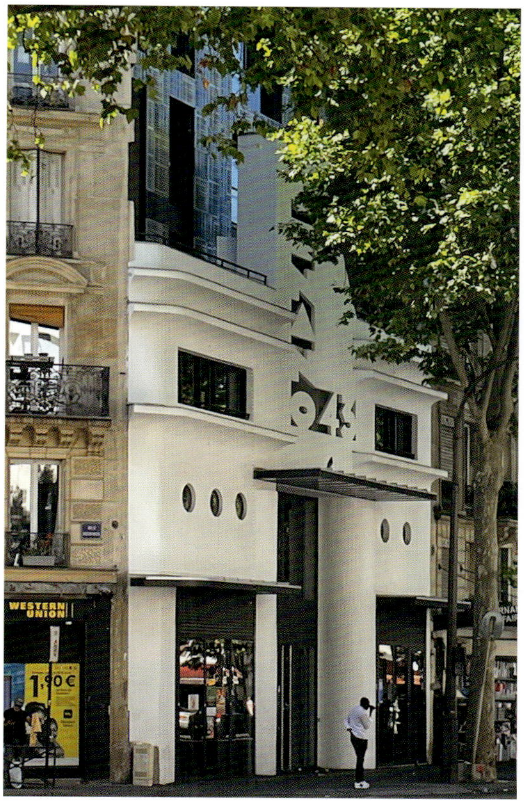

2022

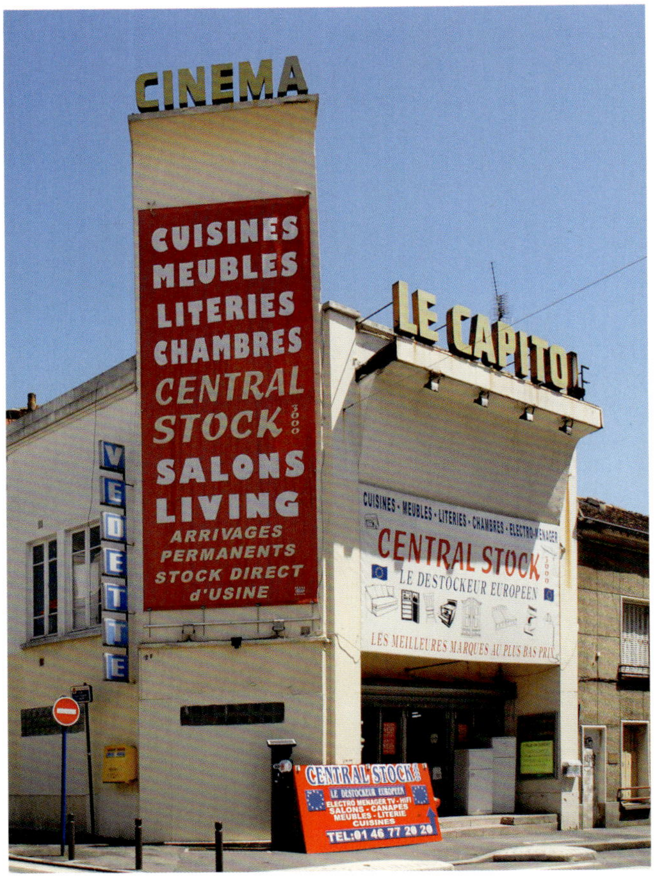

Villejuif – Le Capitole – 2007 (destroyed)

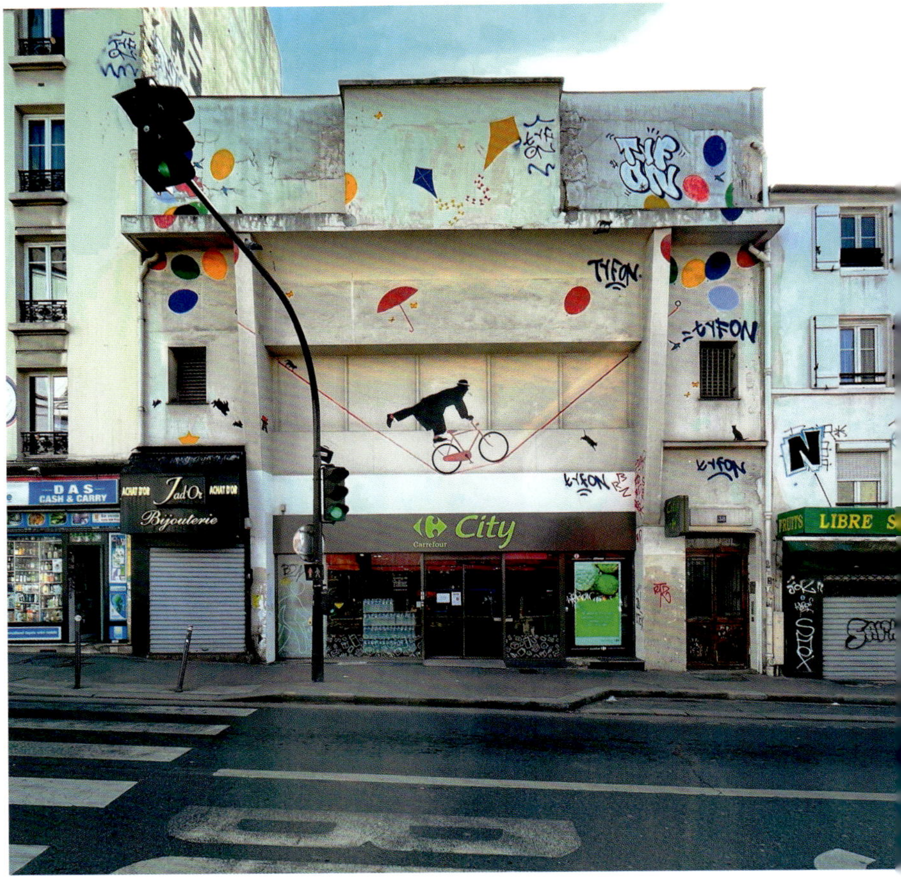

Paris – Ménil-Palace – 2021

Paris, Ménil-Palace. Many cinemas, once their first life is over, find themselves converted into supermarkets. Let's run through the script: the cinema closes, slowly but surely deteriorates, and not being of earth-shattering beauty sinks into oblivion. One day, a food chain sets its sights on this space, of which it only sees the advantages. The projection booth is reserved for fruit and veg. The foyer becomes the checkout area. The screen, perfect for projecting promotions, except the new managers never thought of that, too bad. The gallery – great for a café, and the theatre a dream space to line up merchandise on the shelves, with a few film magazines in full view anyway. What if we tried the opposite?

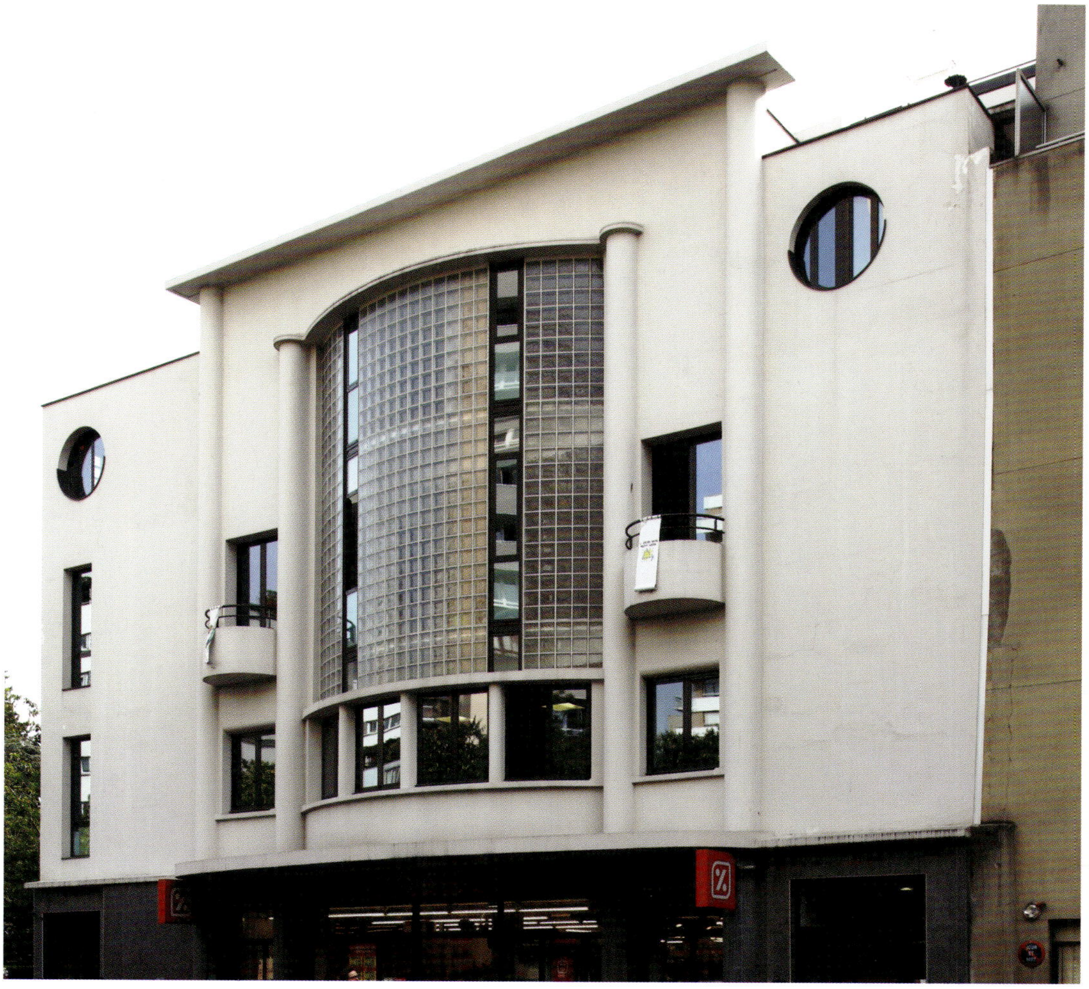

Paris – Météore – 2013

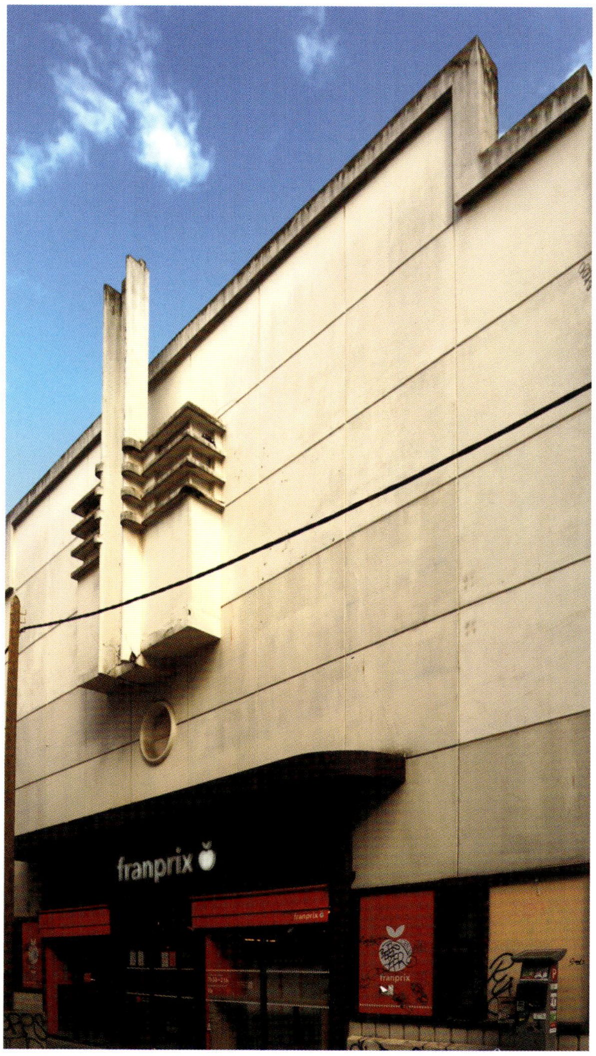

Colombes – Les Vallées – 2020

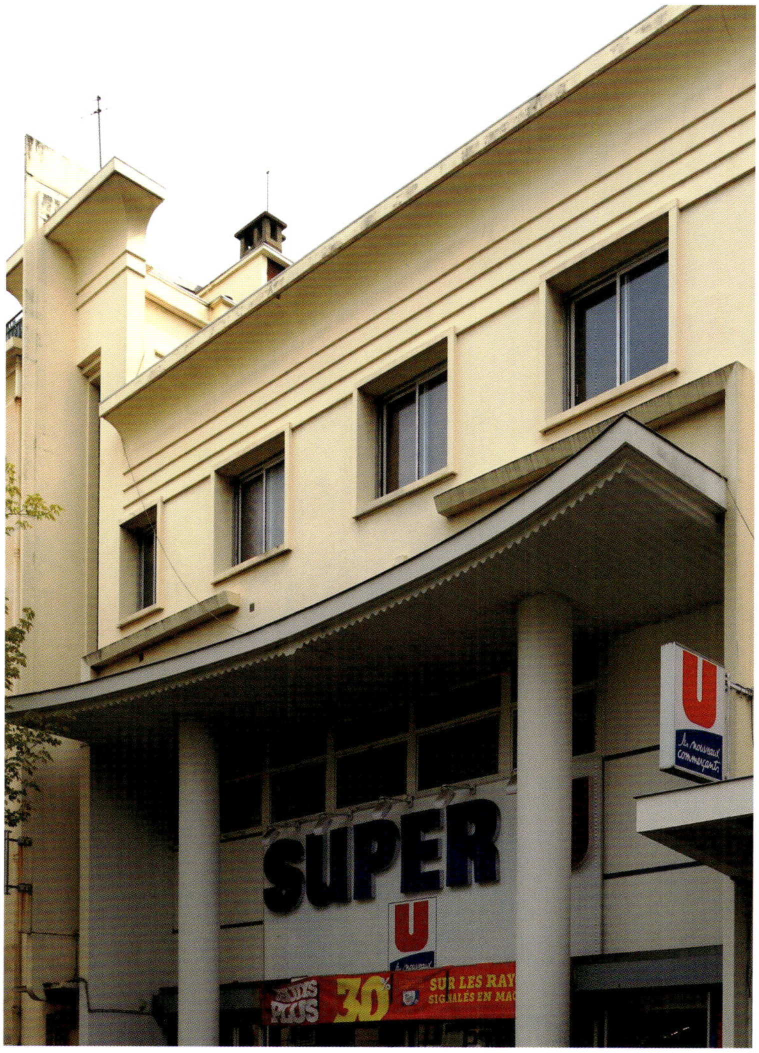

Clamart – Le Paris – 2021

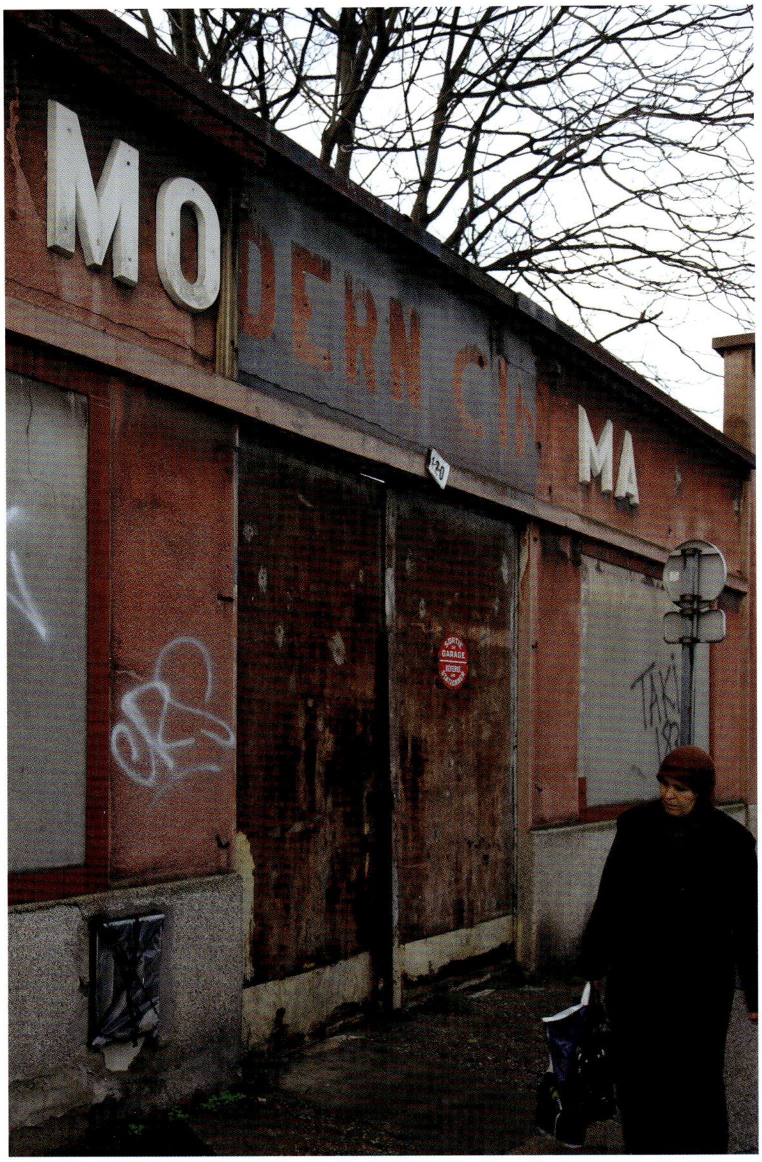

Argenteuil – Modern Cinéma – 2009 (destroyed)

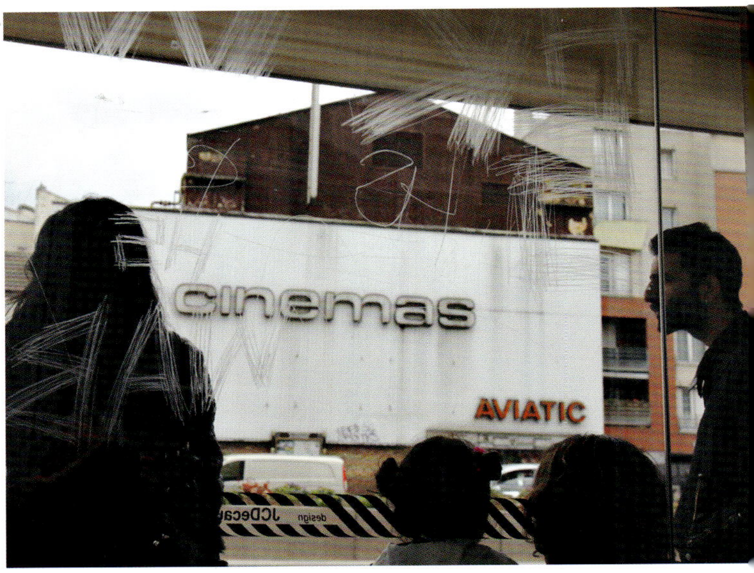

Le Bourget – Aviatic – 2014

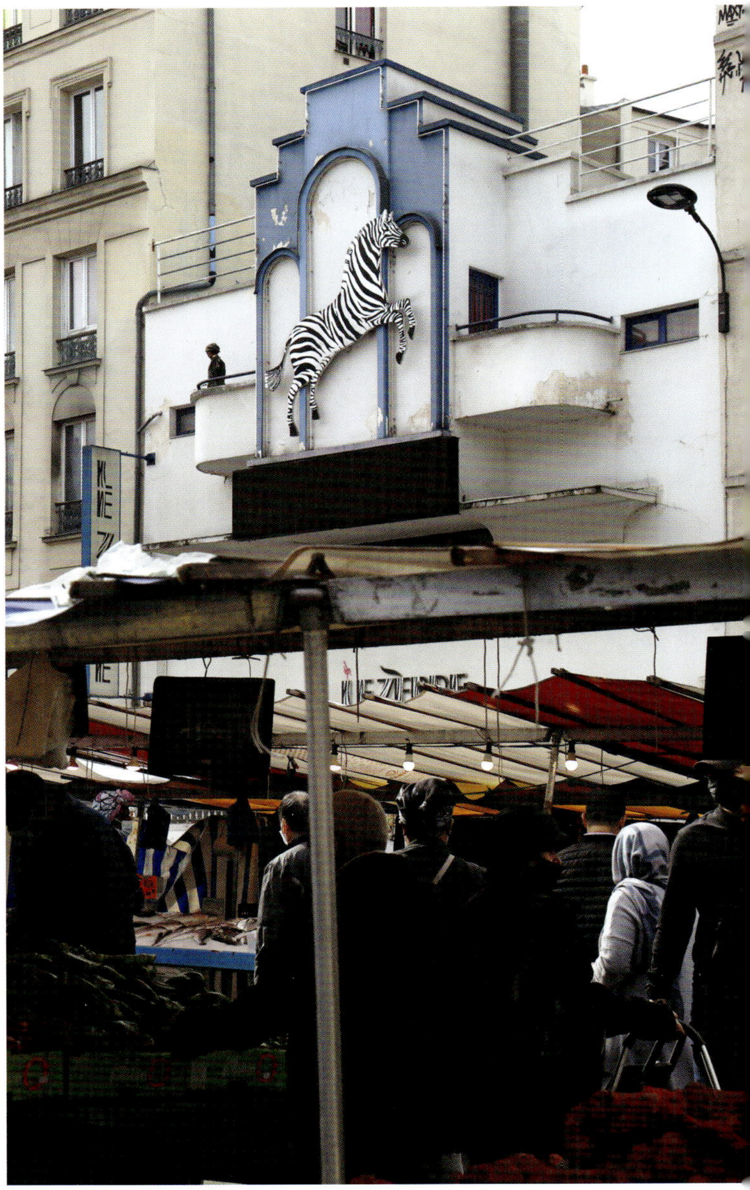

Paris – Le Zèbre – 2021

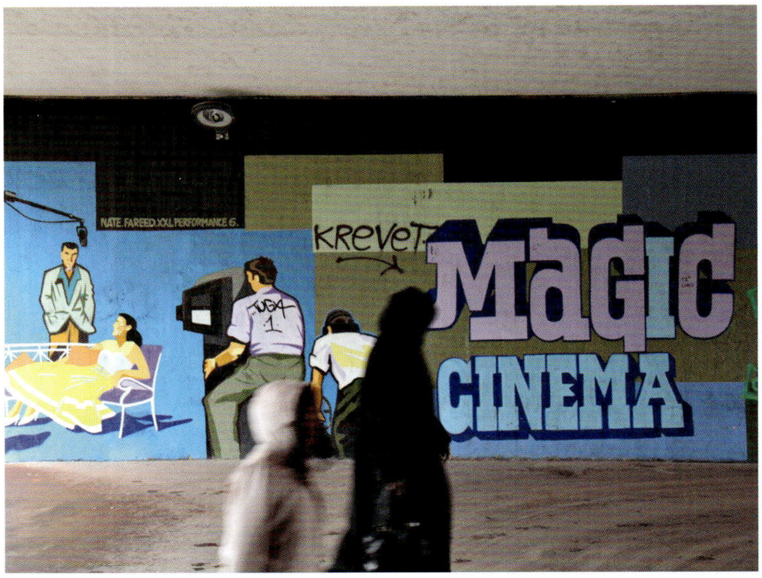

Bobigny – Magic Cinéma – 2009

Paris, MK2 Bastille. This embattled cinema in the heart of the Bastille would gladly take to the streets to demand … a drop in ticket prices? Greater patience on the part of operators to let rare films live longer? Or simply to settle in a neighbourhood deprived of cinemas for a long time?

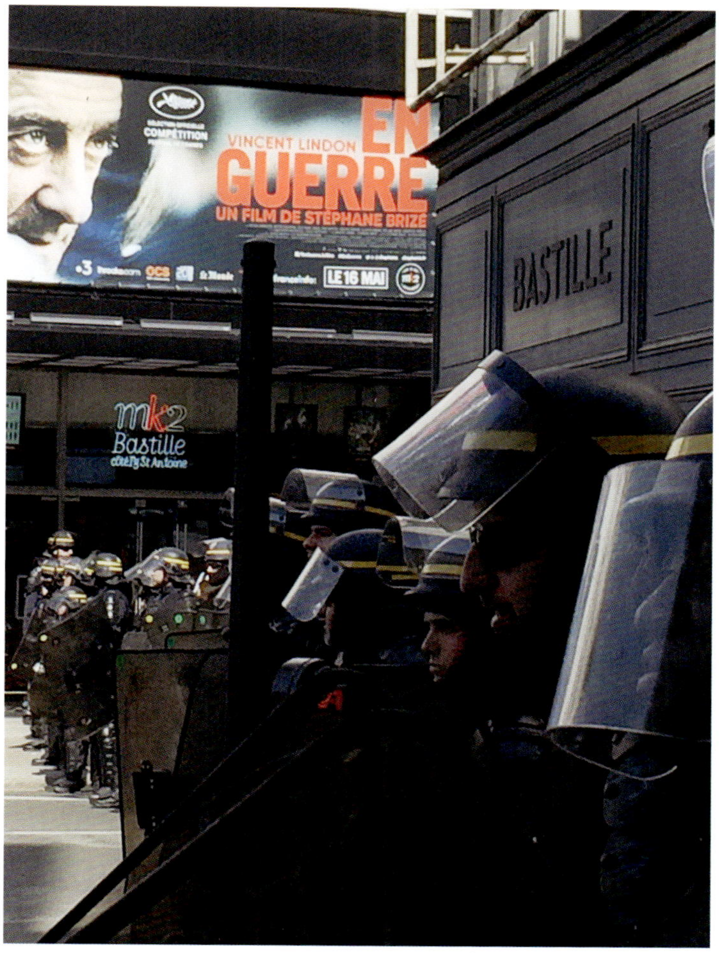

Paris – MK2 Bastille – 2018

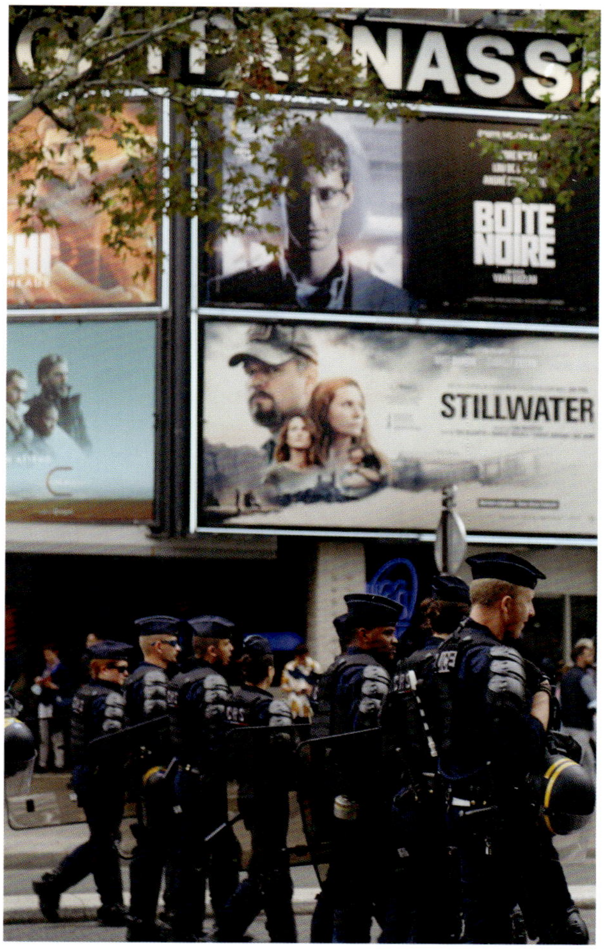

Paris – UGC Montparnasse – 2021

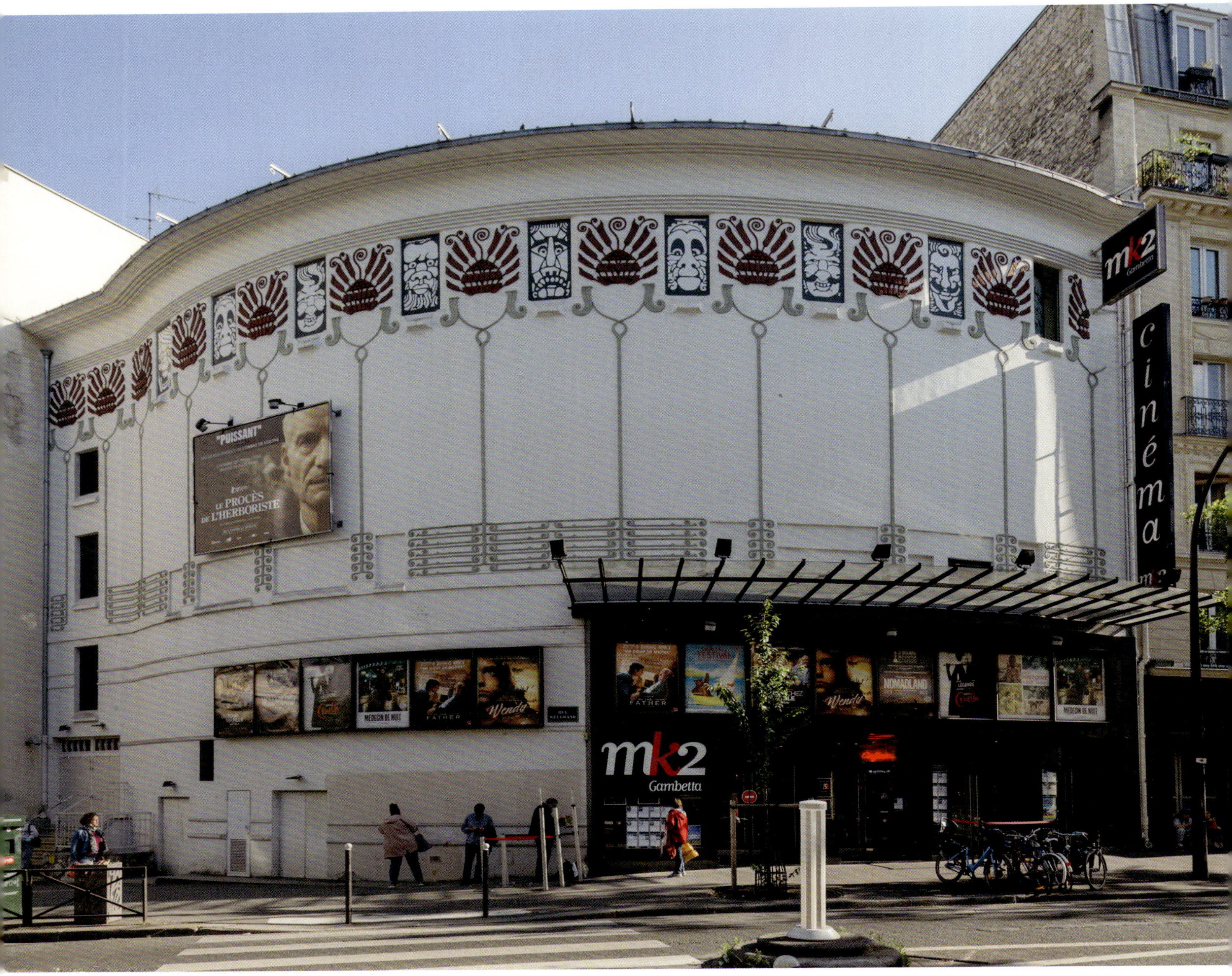

Paris – MK2 Gambetta – 2021

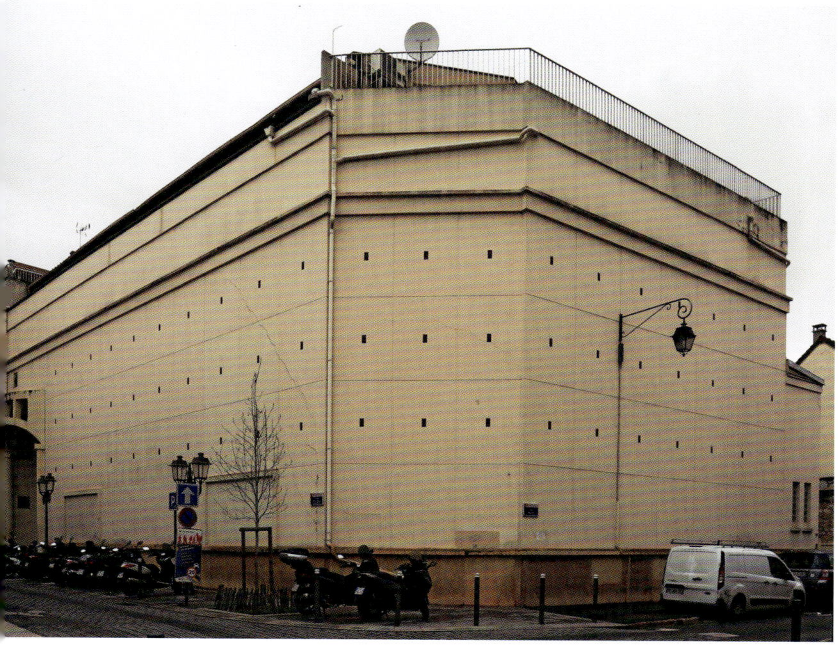

resnes – Capitole – 2020

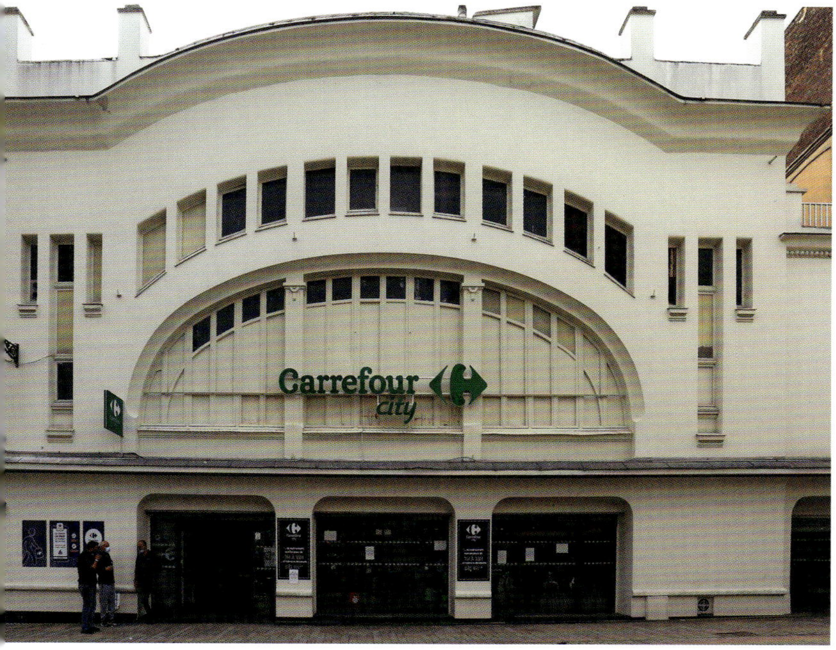

olombes – Palace – 2021

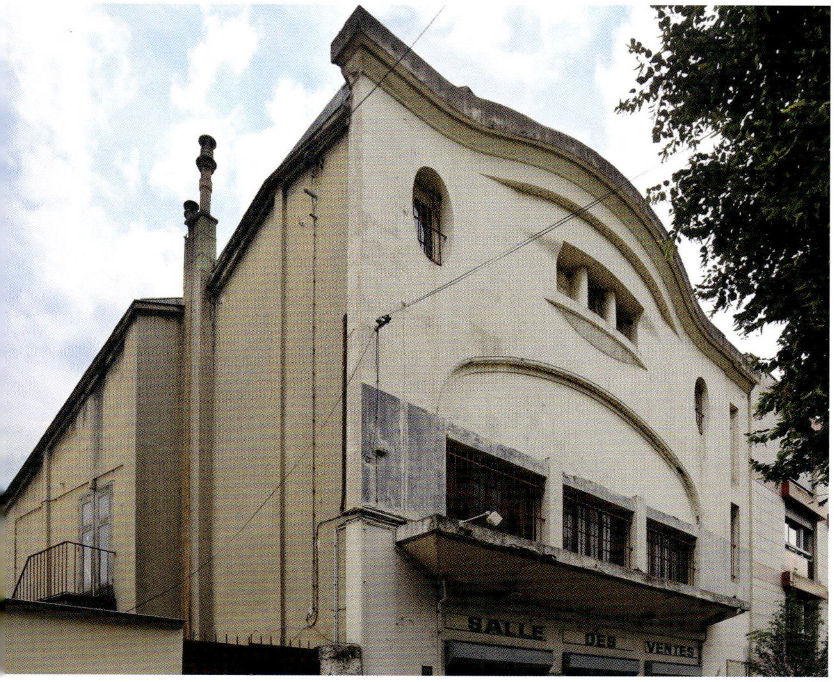

atou – Olympia – 2014

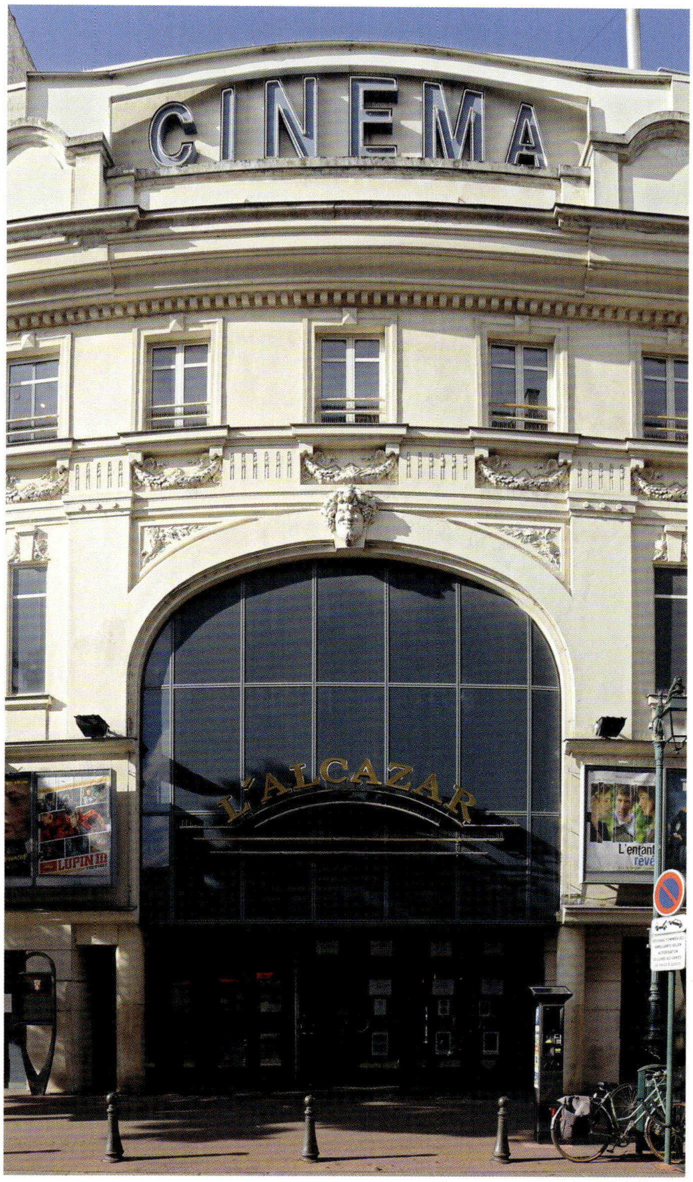

Asnières-sur-Seine – L'Alcazar – 2020

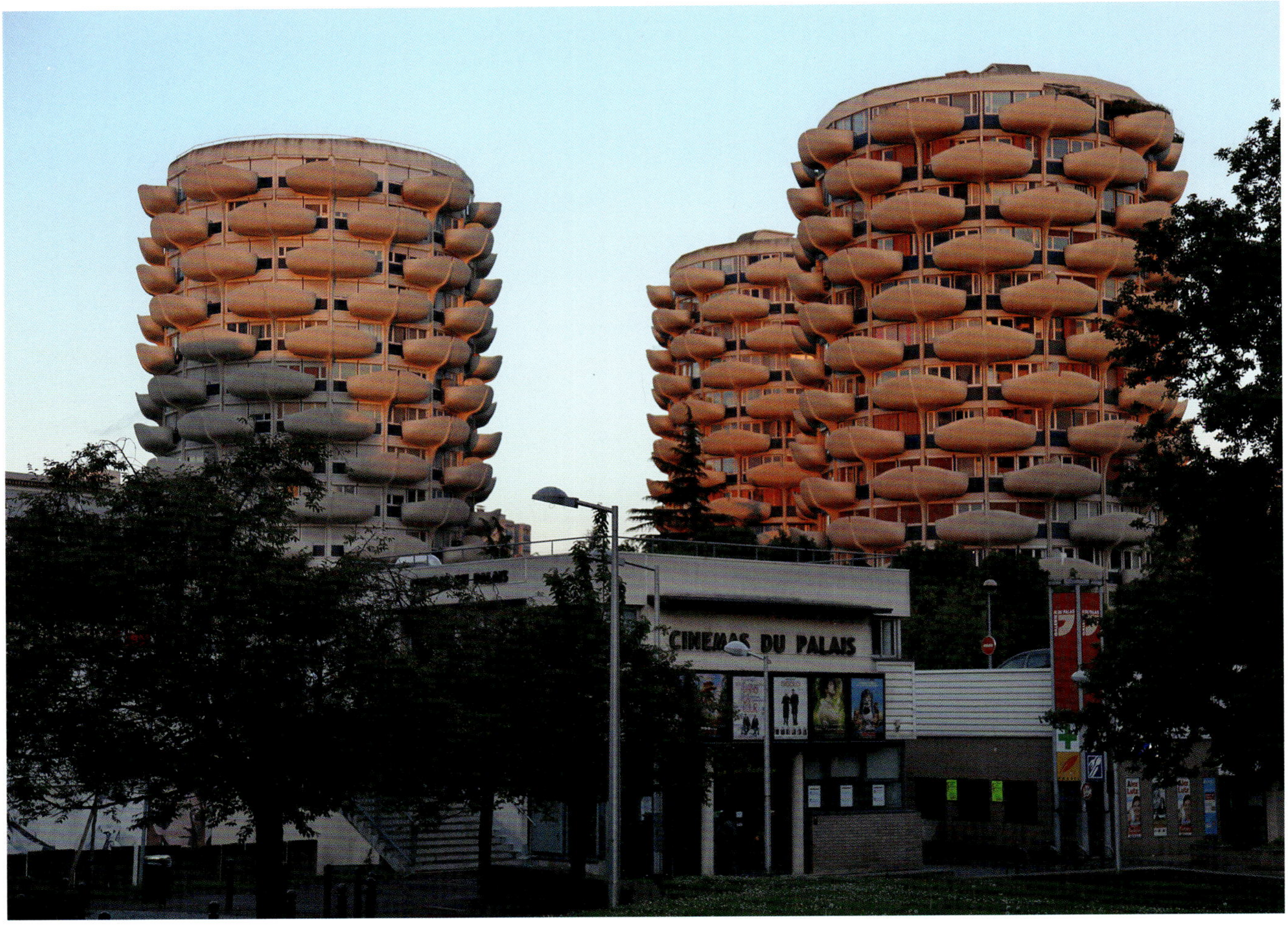

Créteil – Cinéma du Palais – 2014

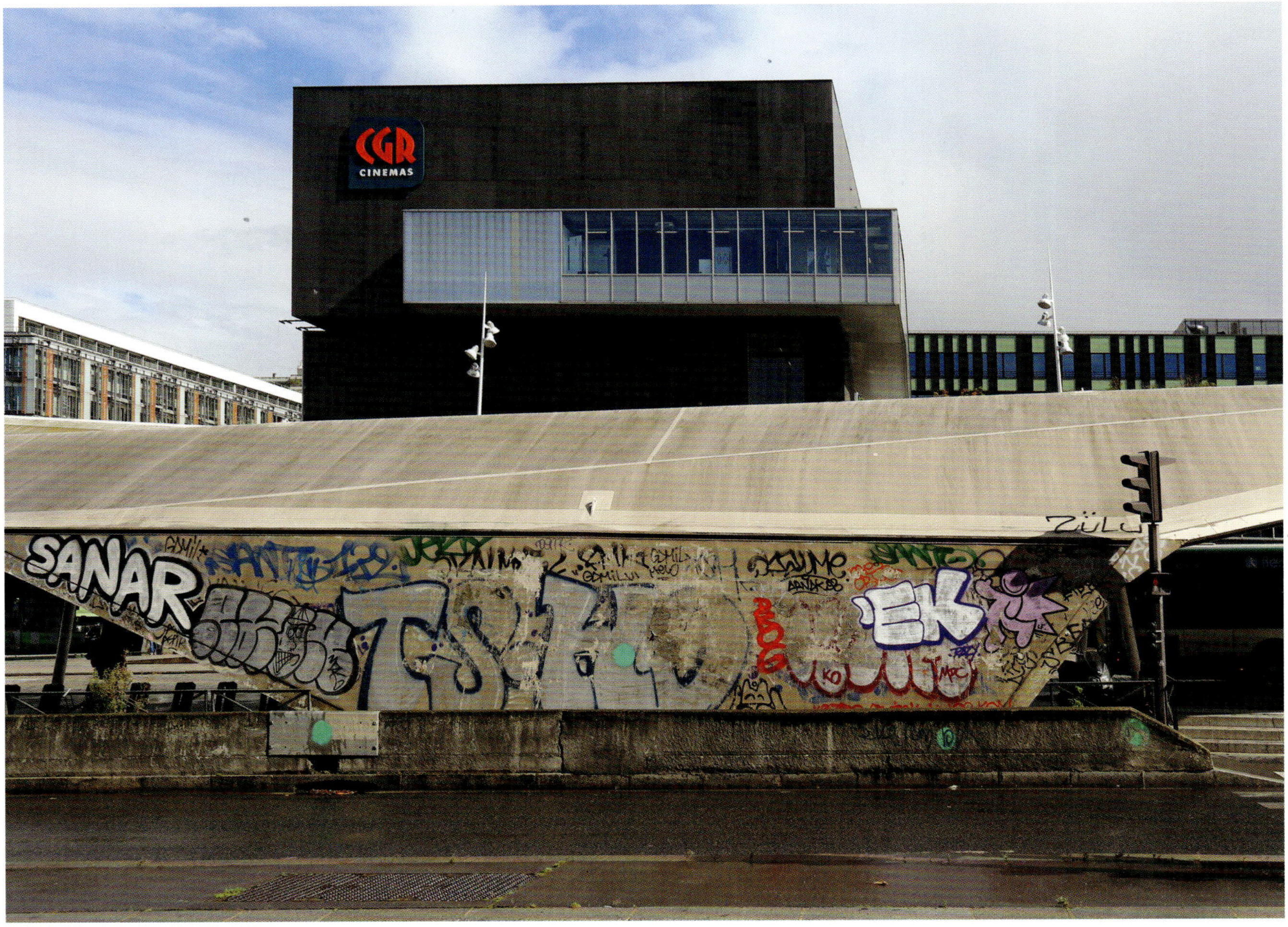

Paris – CGR – 2021

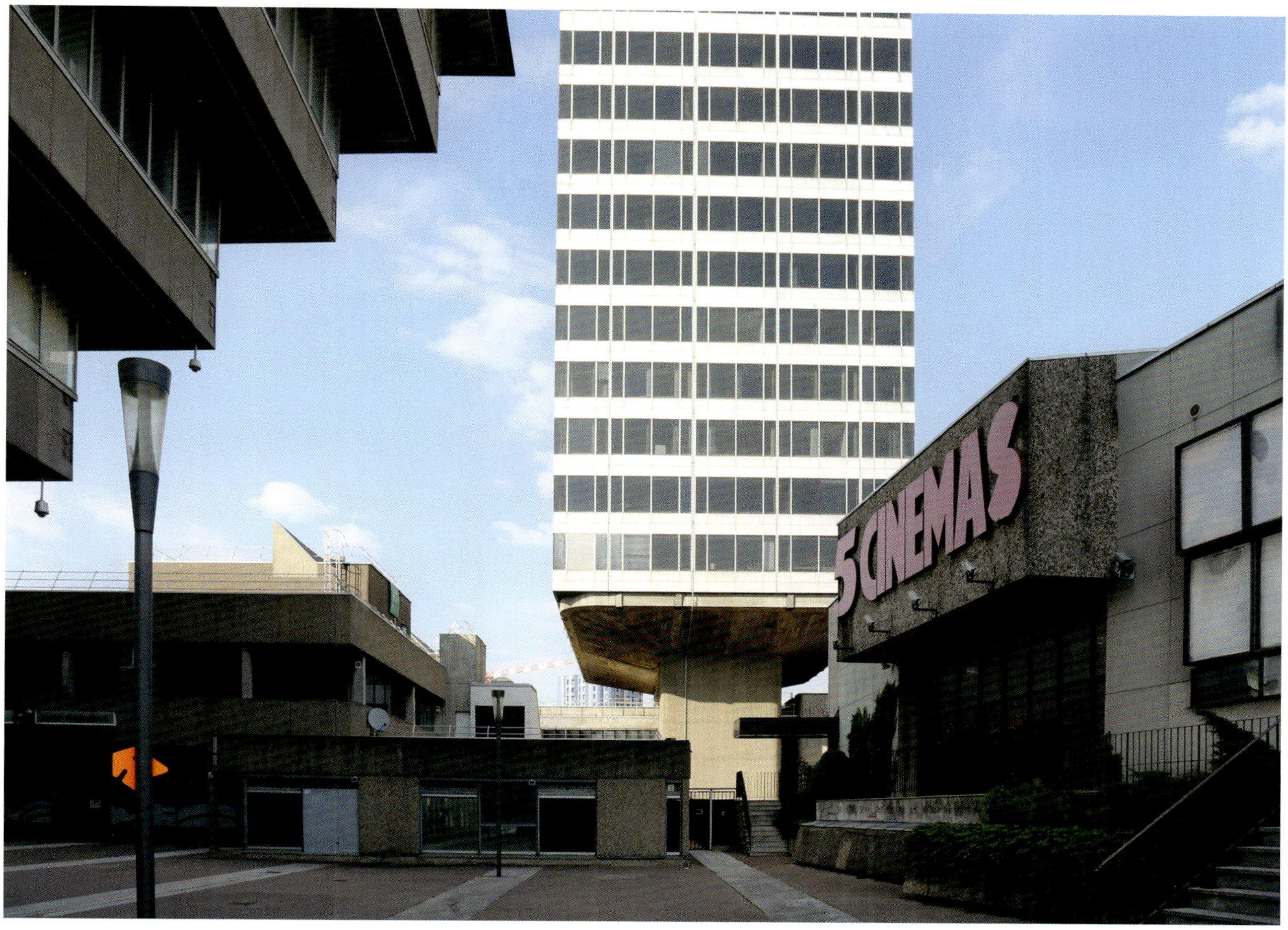

Cergy – UGC Grand Centre – 2018

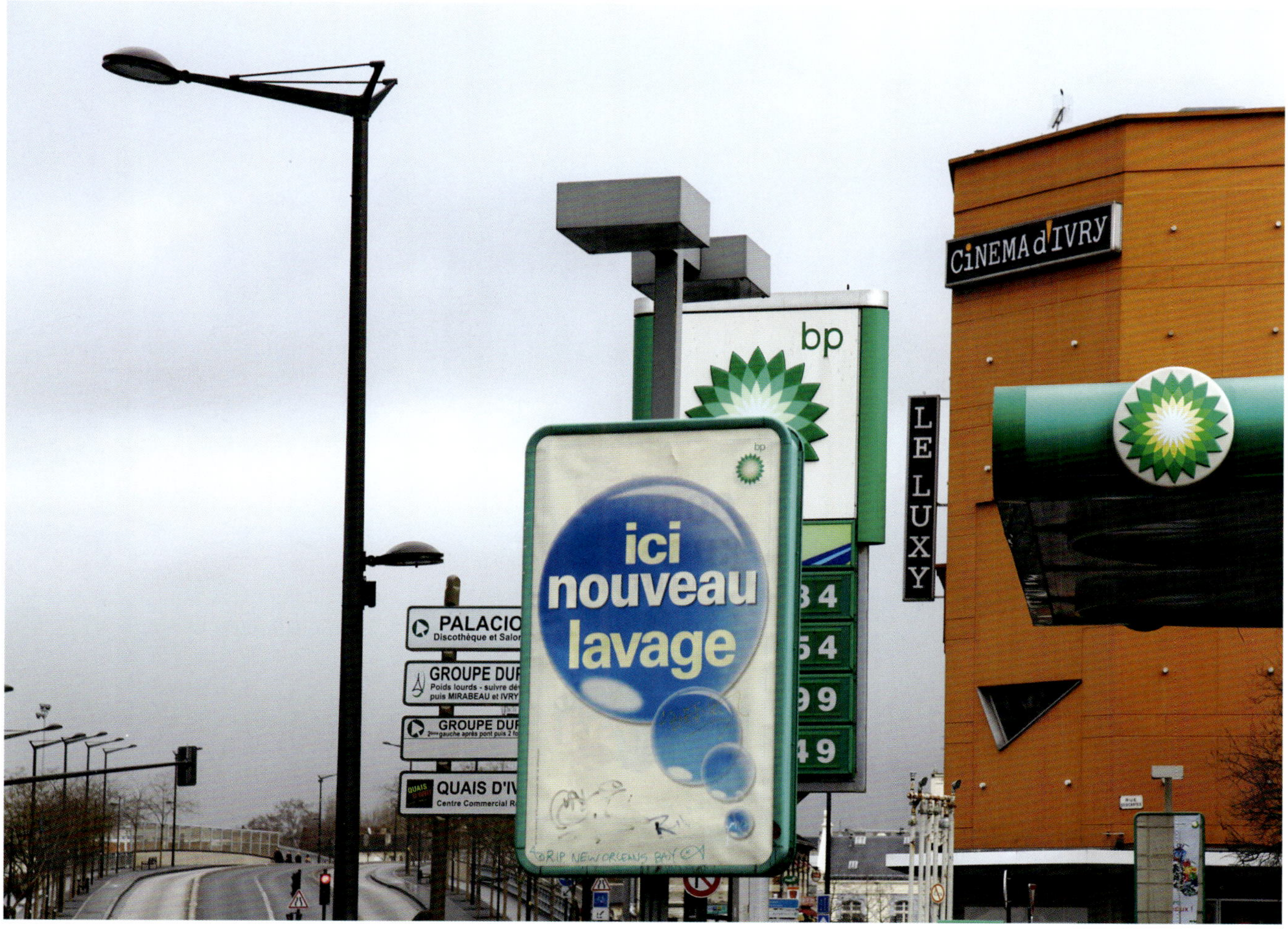

Ivry – Le Luxy – 2012

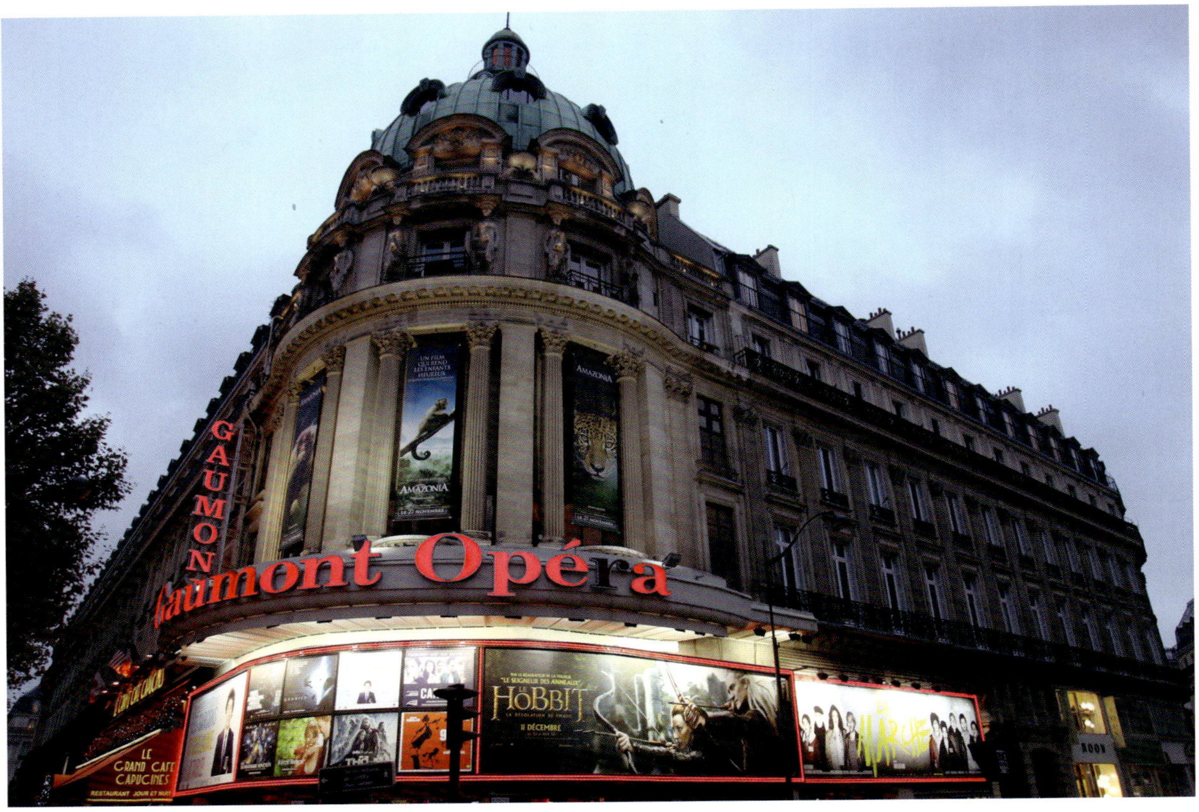

Paris – Gaumont Opéra – 2013

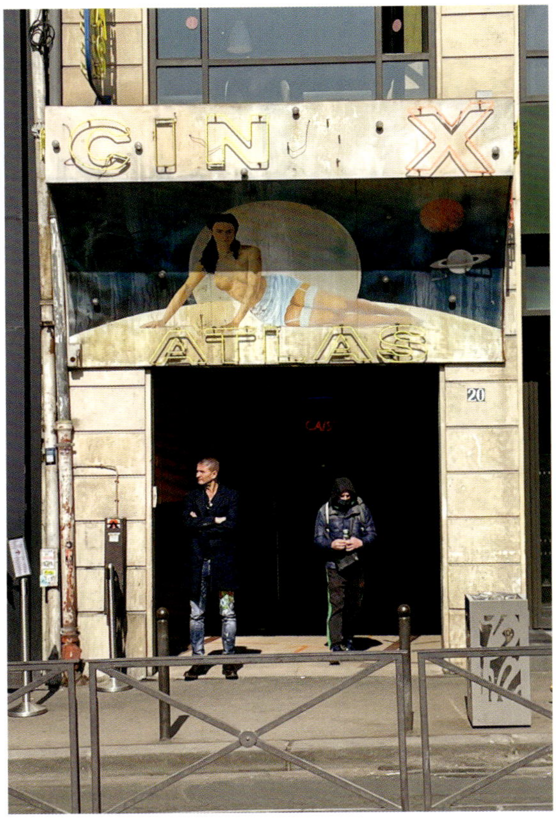

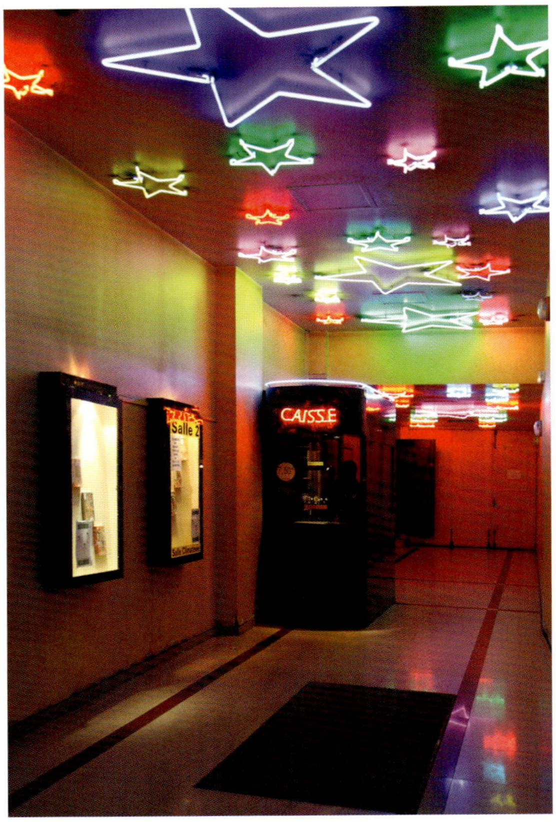

Paris – Atlas – 2021

Paris, Atlas. Porn cinema, temple of licentiousness? Spectators ogled more often, pants down, their only focus on the heroine bottom-flashing on the screen. But times are changing and porn sites are proliferating, changing the habits of some regulars. Could the Atlas be the last witness of a bygone era?

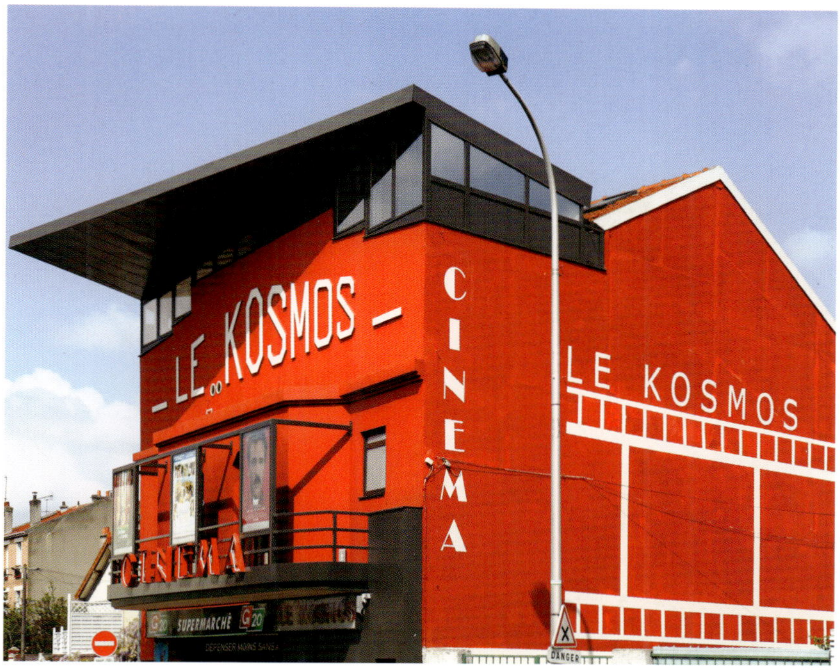

Fontenay-sous-Bois – Kosmos – 2014

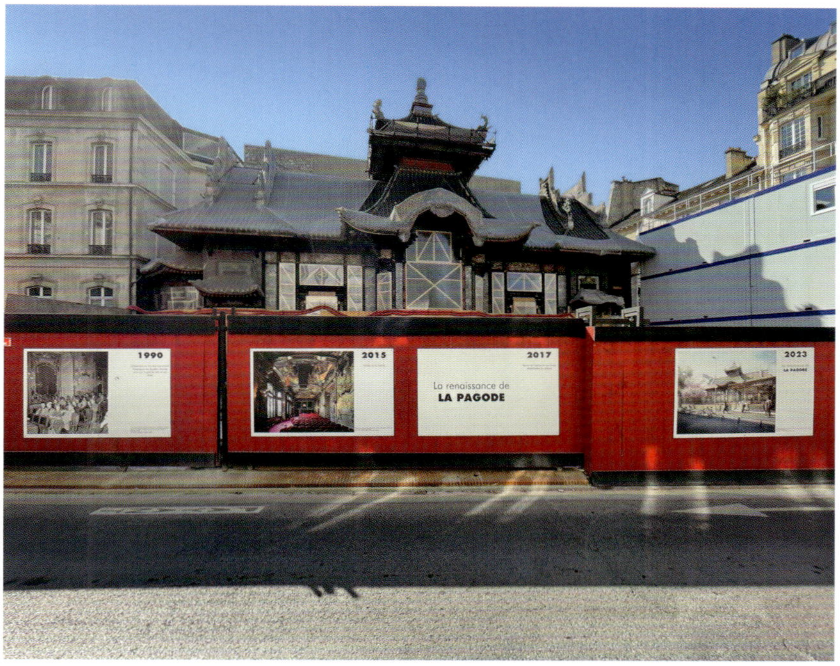

Paris – La Pagode – 2022

Paris, La Pagode. A cruel love story is that of La Pagode. At the end of the 19th century, Mr Morin (director of the Bon Marché), passionately in love with his wife (herself in love with Japanese art), had a palace built inspired by a 17th-century sanctuary. Unfortunately for him, a few months after it opened his wife left him. He sank into despondency, the palace into oblivion. In 1931 it became a cinema. The involvement of great directors soon created a myth around this splendid place. But by 2015 the cinema had become dilapidated and closed its doors. A few years of uncertainty and depredation followed, before it was bought in 2017 by the American movie buff and producer Charles S. Cohen. The completely renovated building was due to reopen in late 2022.

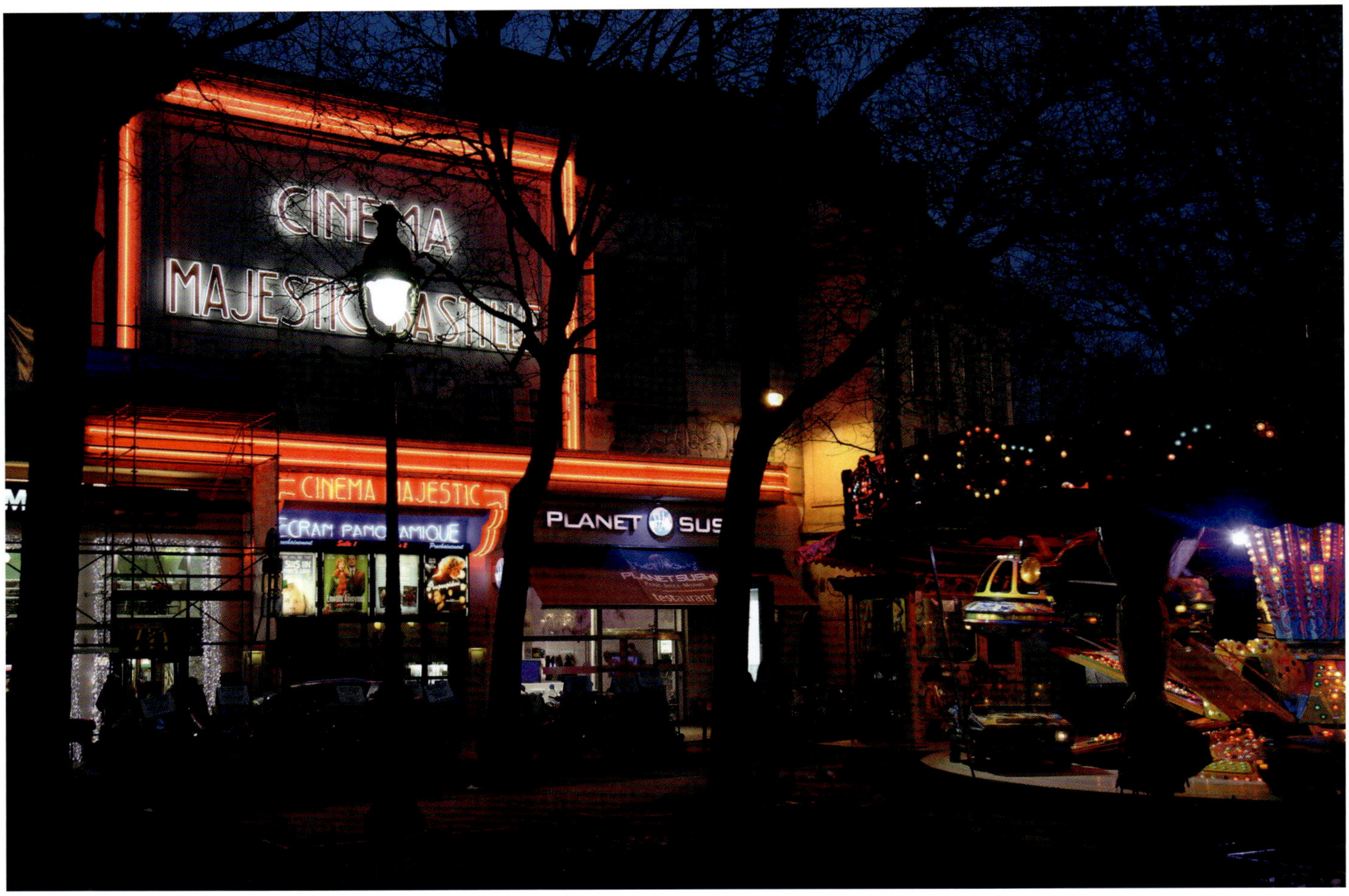

Paris – Majestic Bastille – 2010

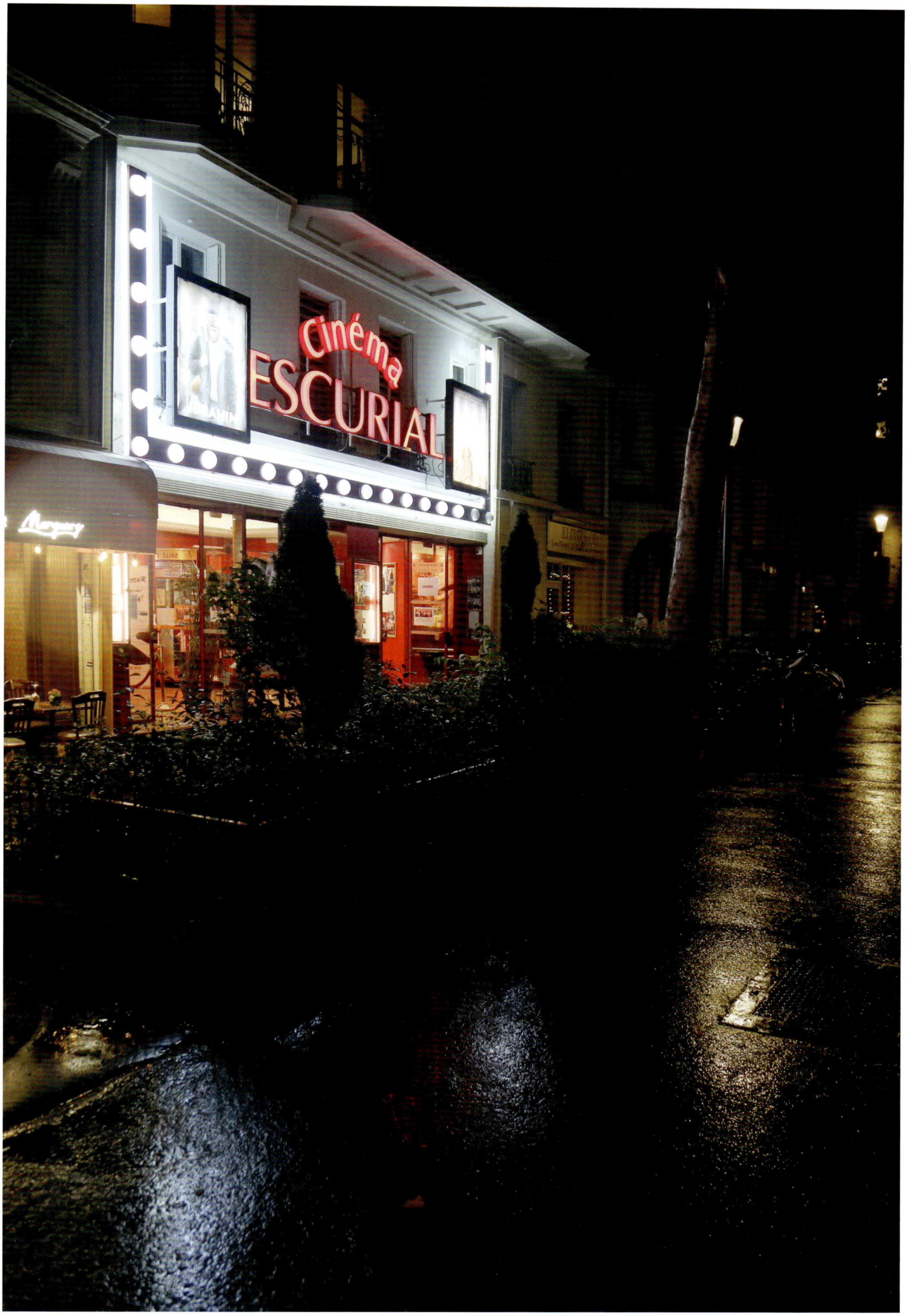

Paris – Escurial – 2021

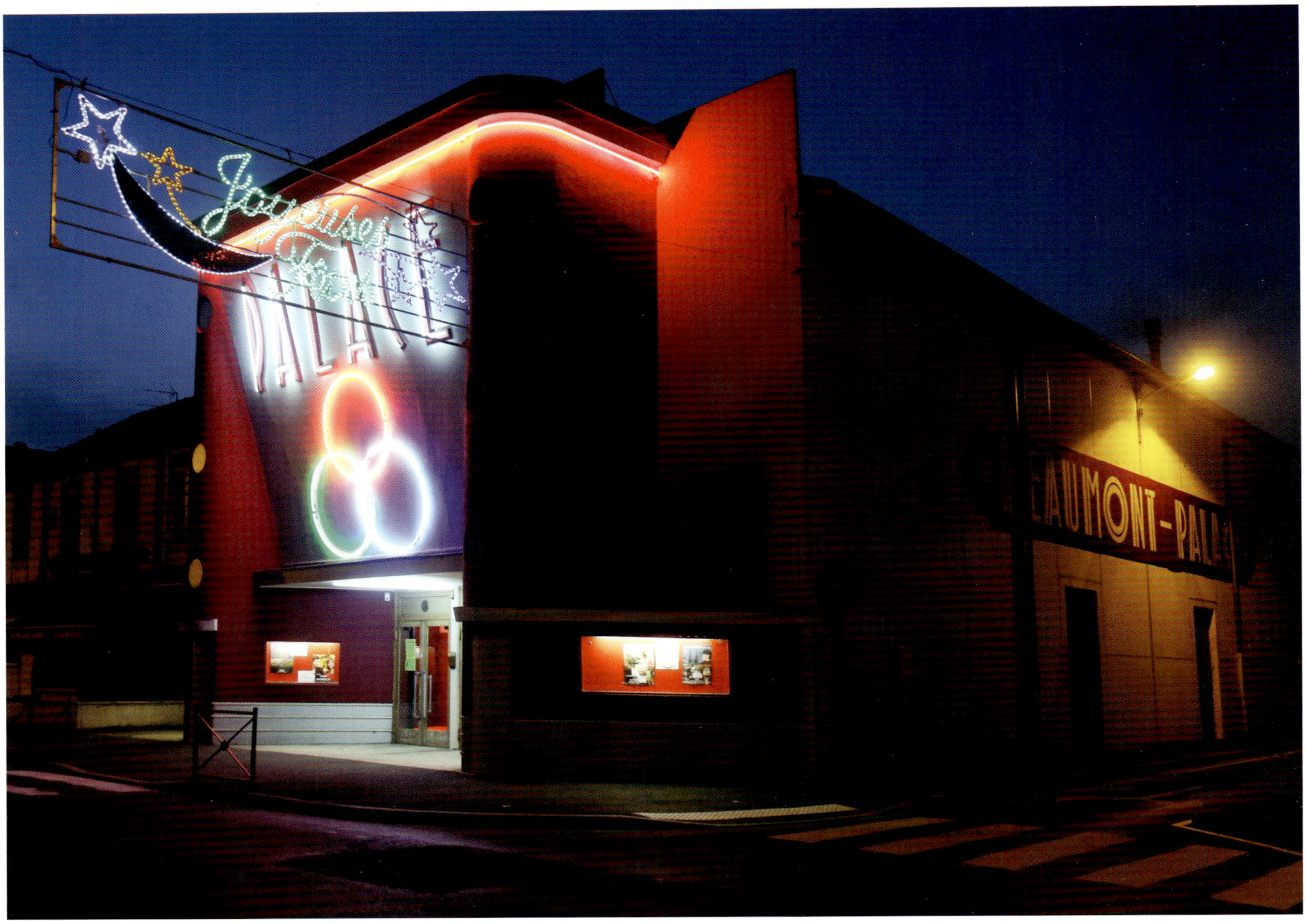

Beaumont-sur-Oise – Beaumont-Palace – 2015

Beaumont-sur-Oise, Beaumont-Palace. Opened to the public in 1928, the Beaumont-Palace is an Art Deco cinema, its luminous hoops and porthole-shaped openings influenced by the ocean liner style. It became a multi-purpose venue with dancing, a roller-skating track and then a music hall. Charles Aznavour gave his first concert there and Eddy Mitchell's *La Dernière Séance* (*The Last Session*) made the exterior famous. The interior scenes for that film were mainly shot at the Trianon in Romainville.

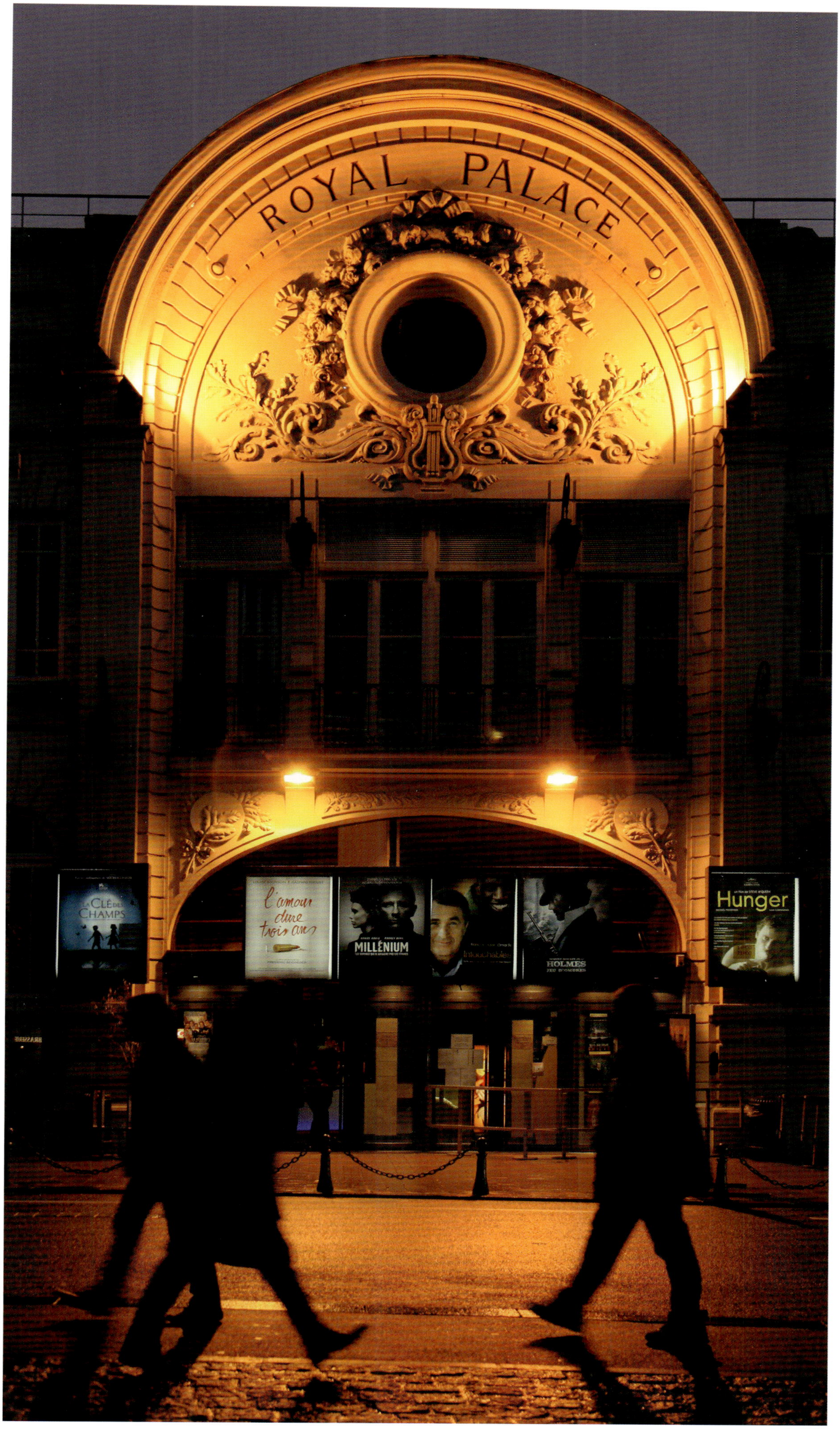

Nogent-sur-Marne – Royal Palace – 2012

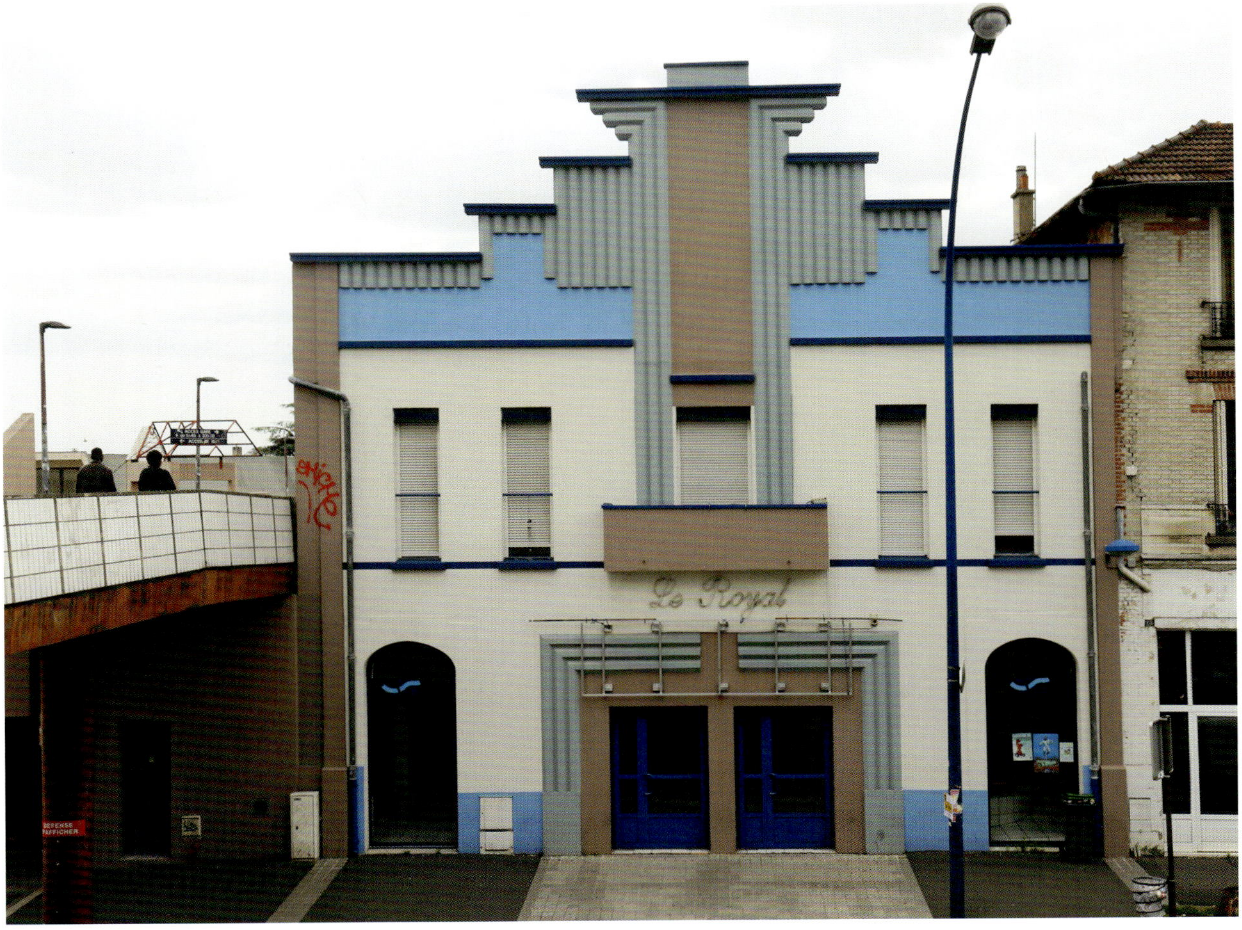

Choisy-le-Roi – Le Royal – 2016

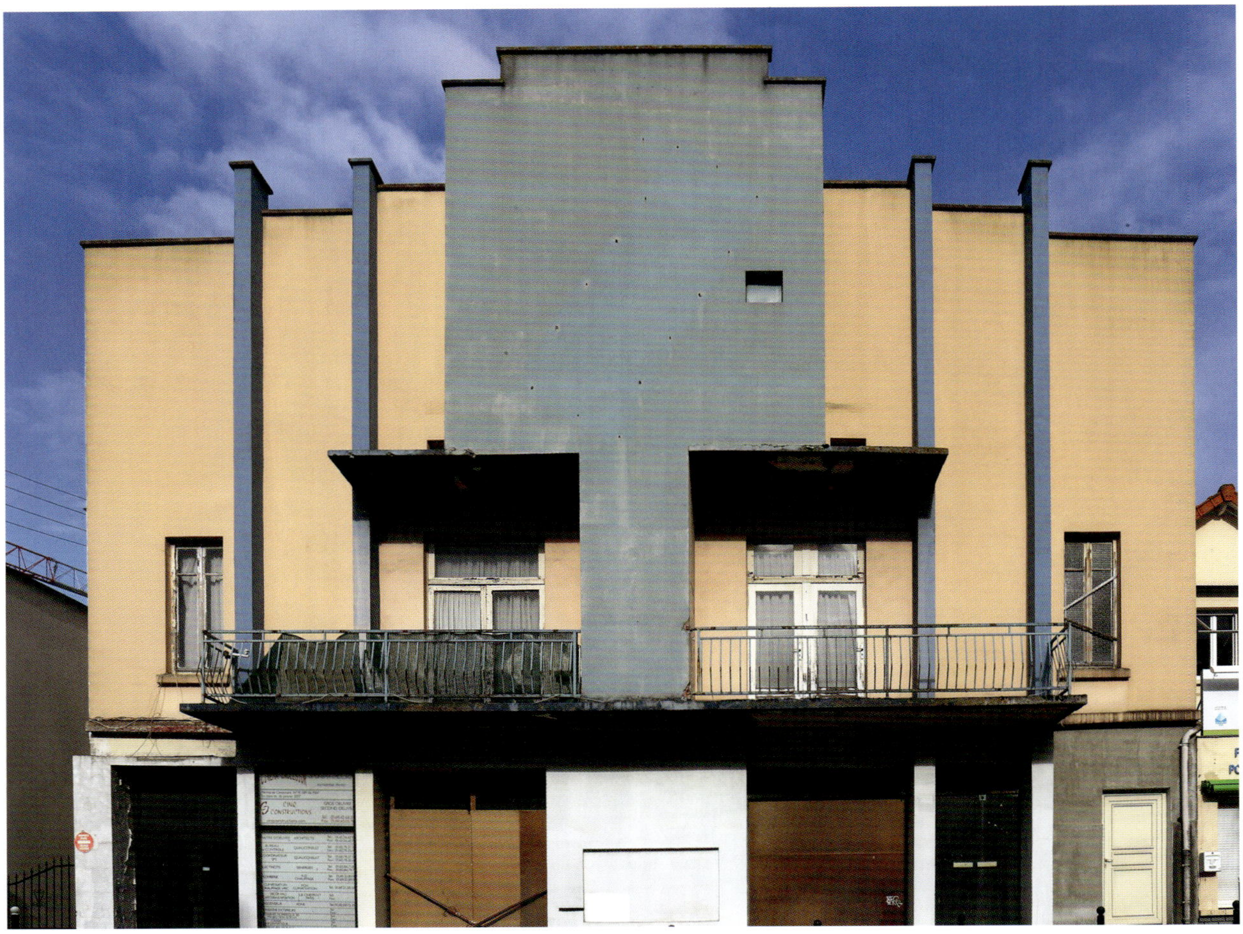

Savigny-sur-Orge – Excelsior – 2020

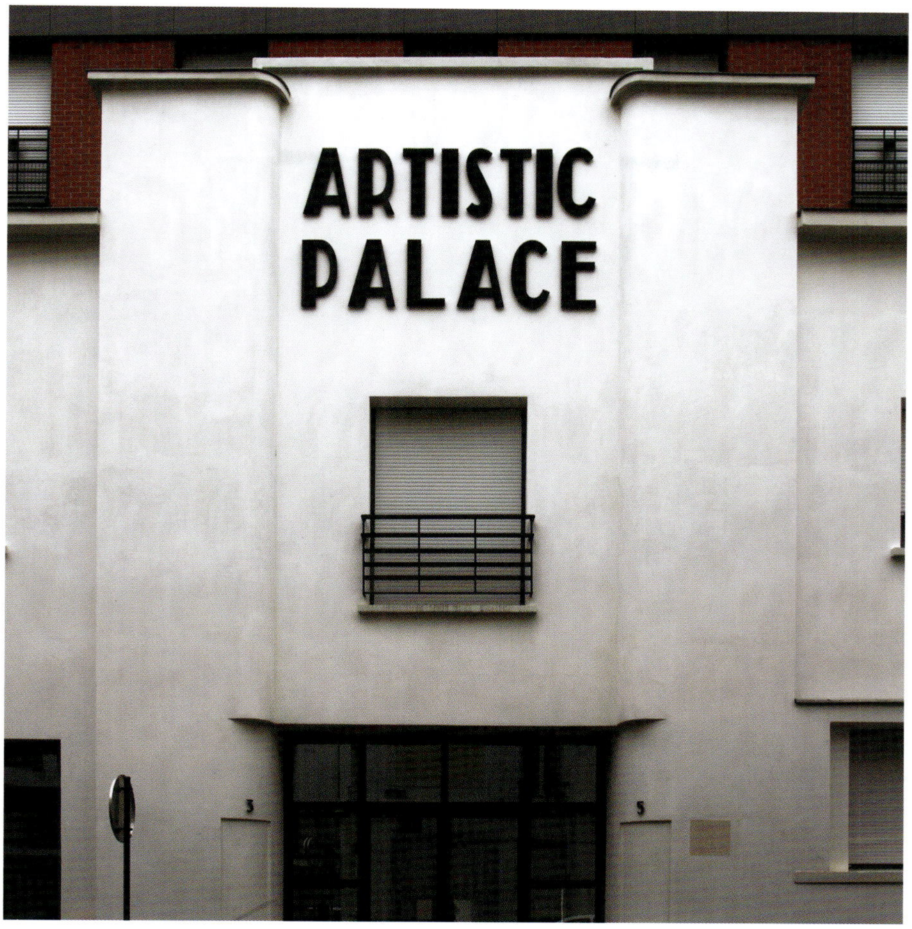

Boulogne-Billancourt – Artistic Palace – 2011

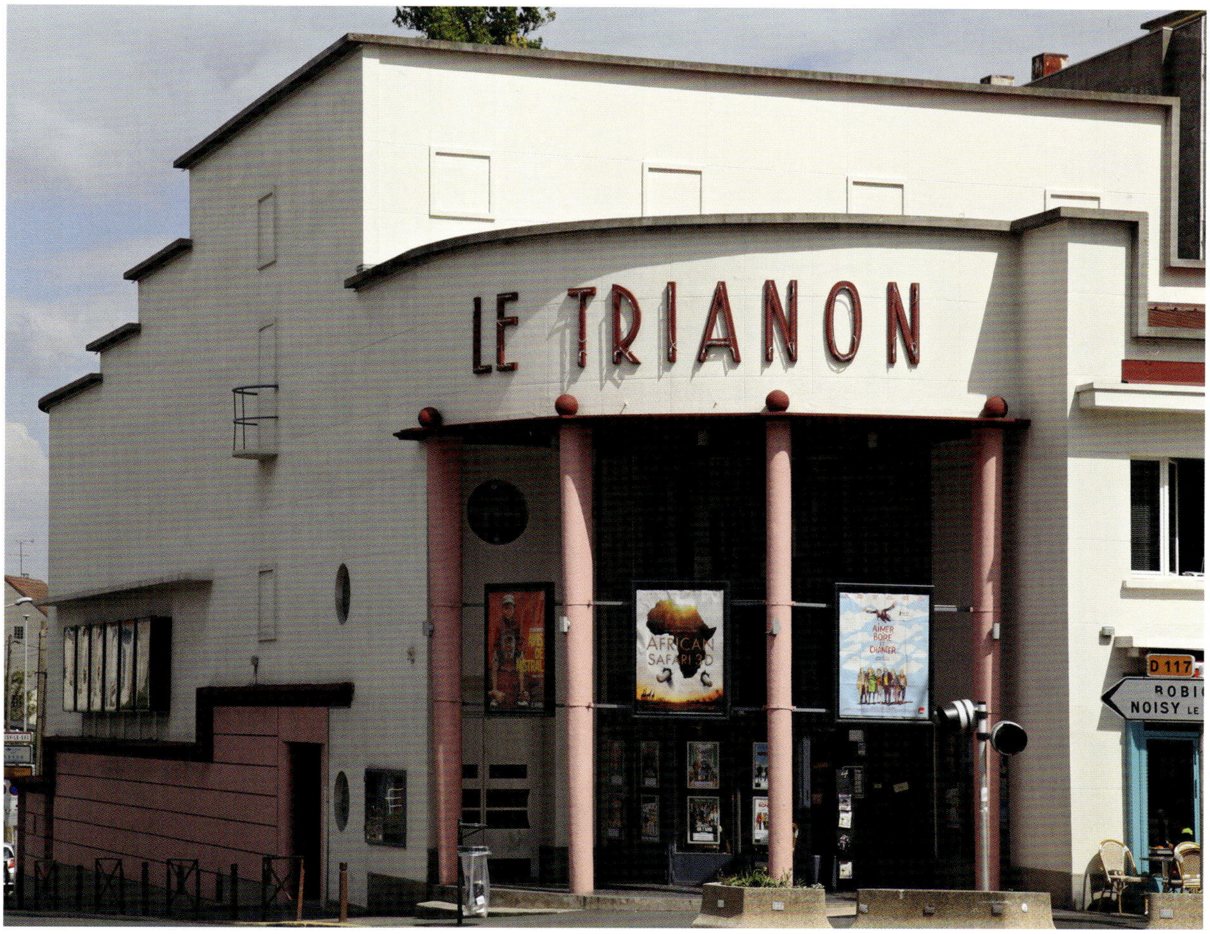

Romainville – Le Trianon – 2014

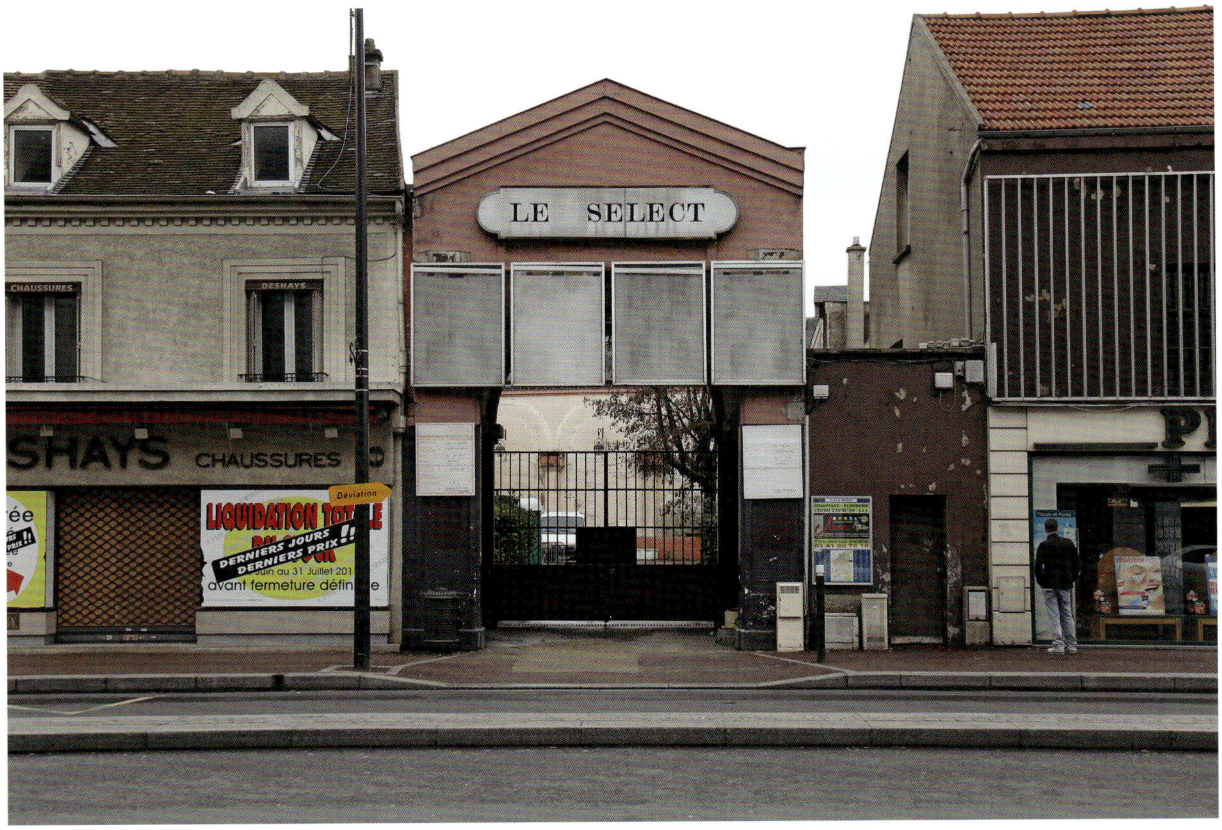

Antony – Le Sélect – 2008

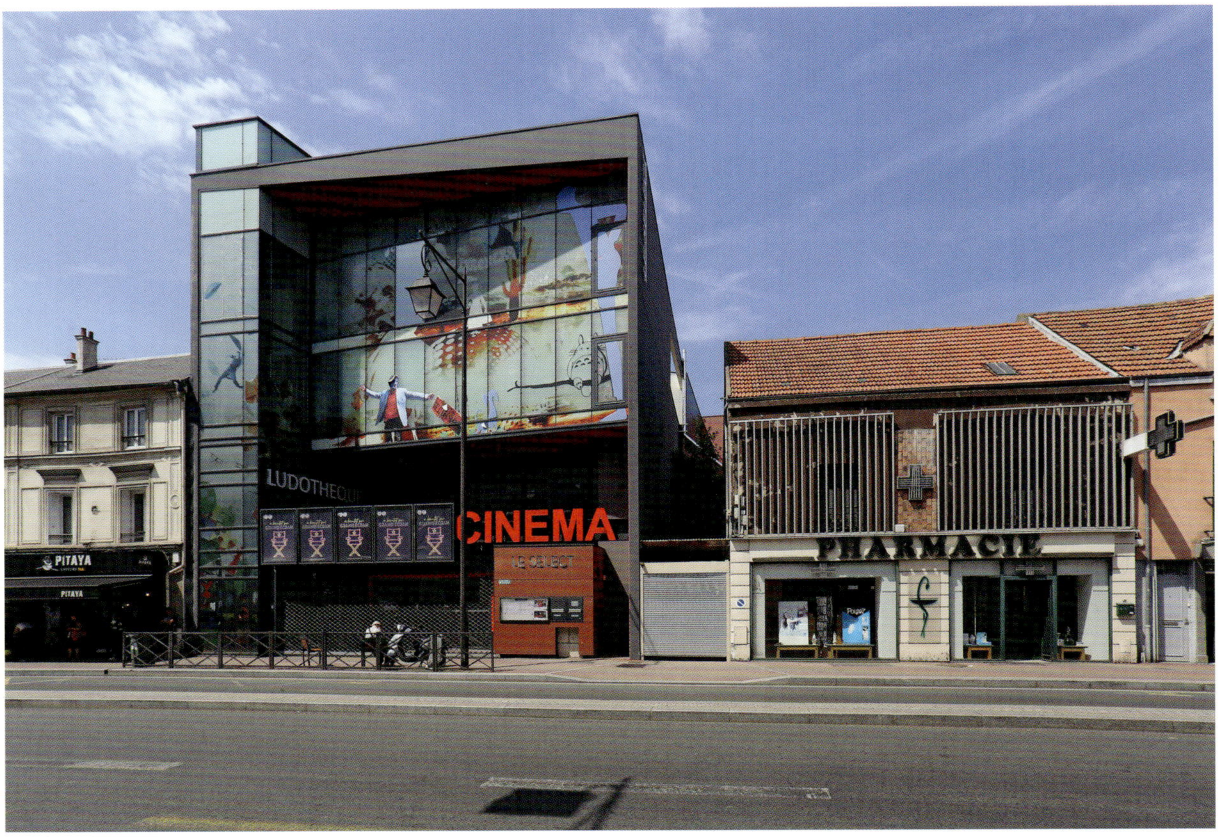

Antony – Le Sélect – 2022

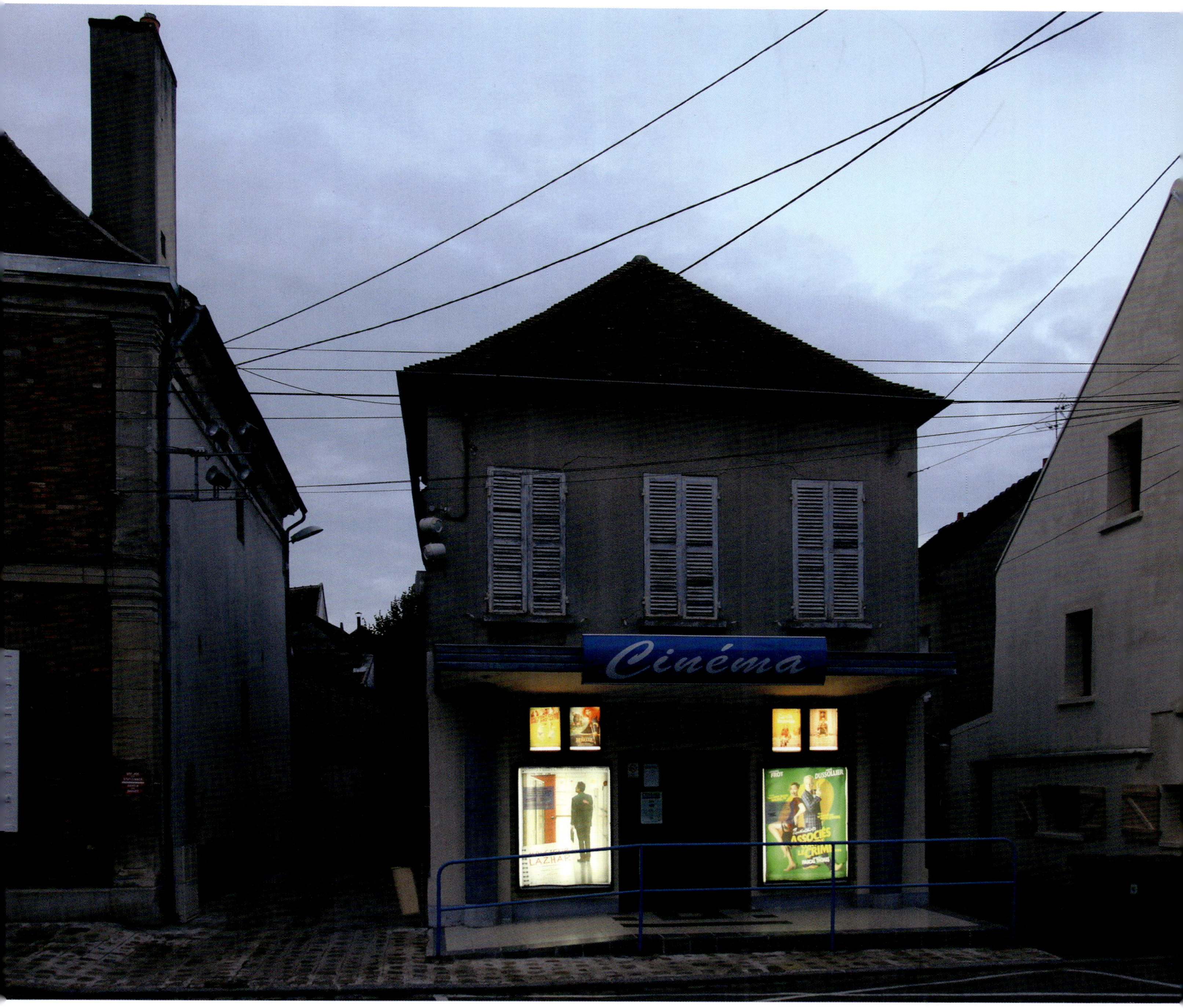

y-sur-Seine – Le Renaissance – 2012

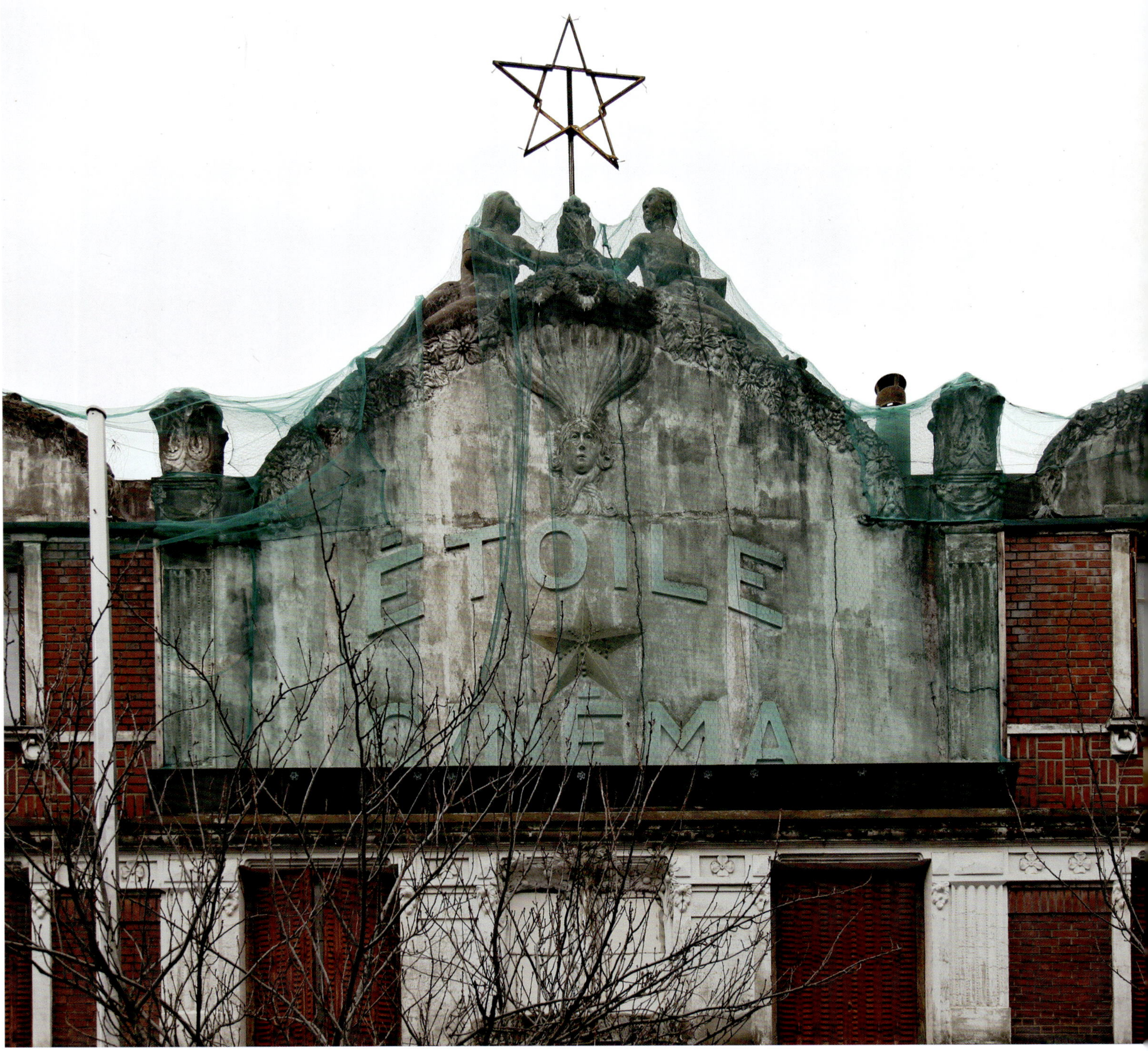

La Courneuve – L'Étoile Cinéma – 2012

La Courneuve, L'Étoile. This cinema was built by Italian brothers Martin-Perolino in 1934. The façade, decorated with a few sculptures of indeterminate style but genuine charm, is protected by a green net to prevent debris falling. Now owned by the city, it has long deserved a proper renovation.

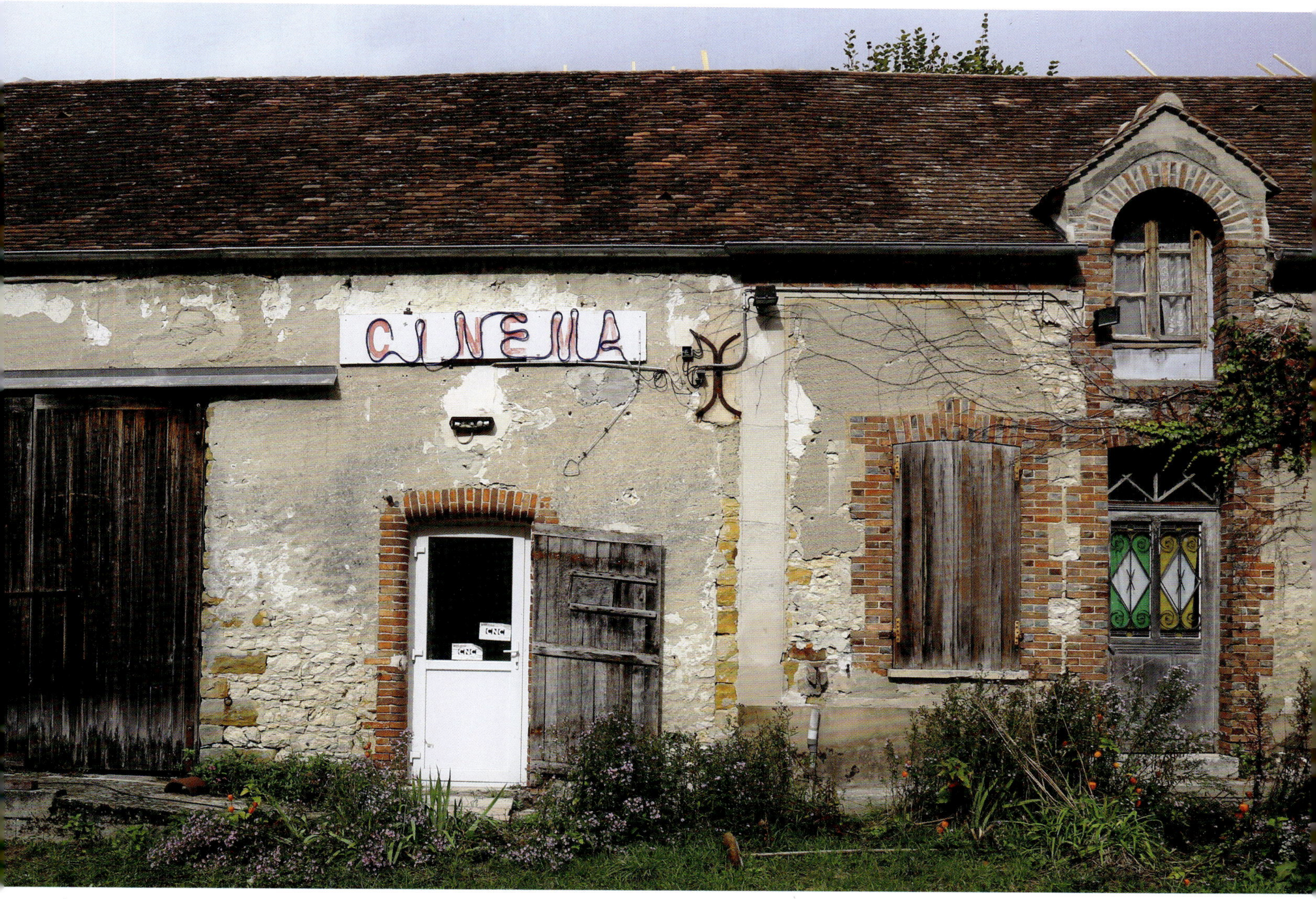

Mons-en-Montois – Cinéma 11 x 20 + 14 – 2019

Mons-en-Montois, Cinéma 11 × 20 + 14. You first have to find Mons-en-Montois, a name that sounds like a pseudonym, then its cinema: the 11 × 20 + 14. This enigmatic and original name comes from a historical episode. In 1430 the 234 residents (11 × 20 + 14) of Mons-en-Montois were massacred by Anglo-Burgundians 'for having defended their freedom, their family and their property'. At the bend of a path, rather than a road, through a renovated farm, the 50-seat cinema is in a village that now has a population of 471. A story of passion and survival – its owner is around the same age as the cinema and fights with a teenager's ardour to see his venue not die, despite poor attendance. A true arthouse cinema. 'No ads, no popcorn, movies, real ones, in the country,' as their website puts it.

NORMANDY

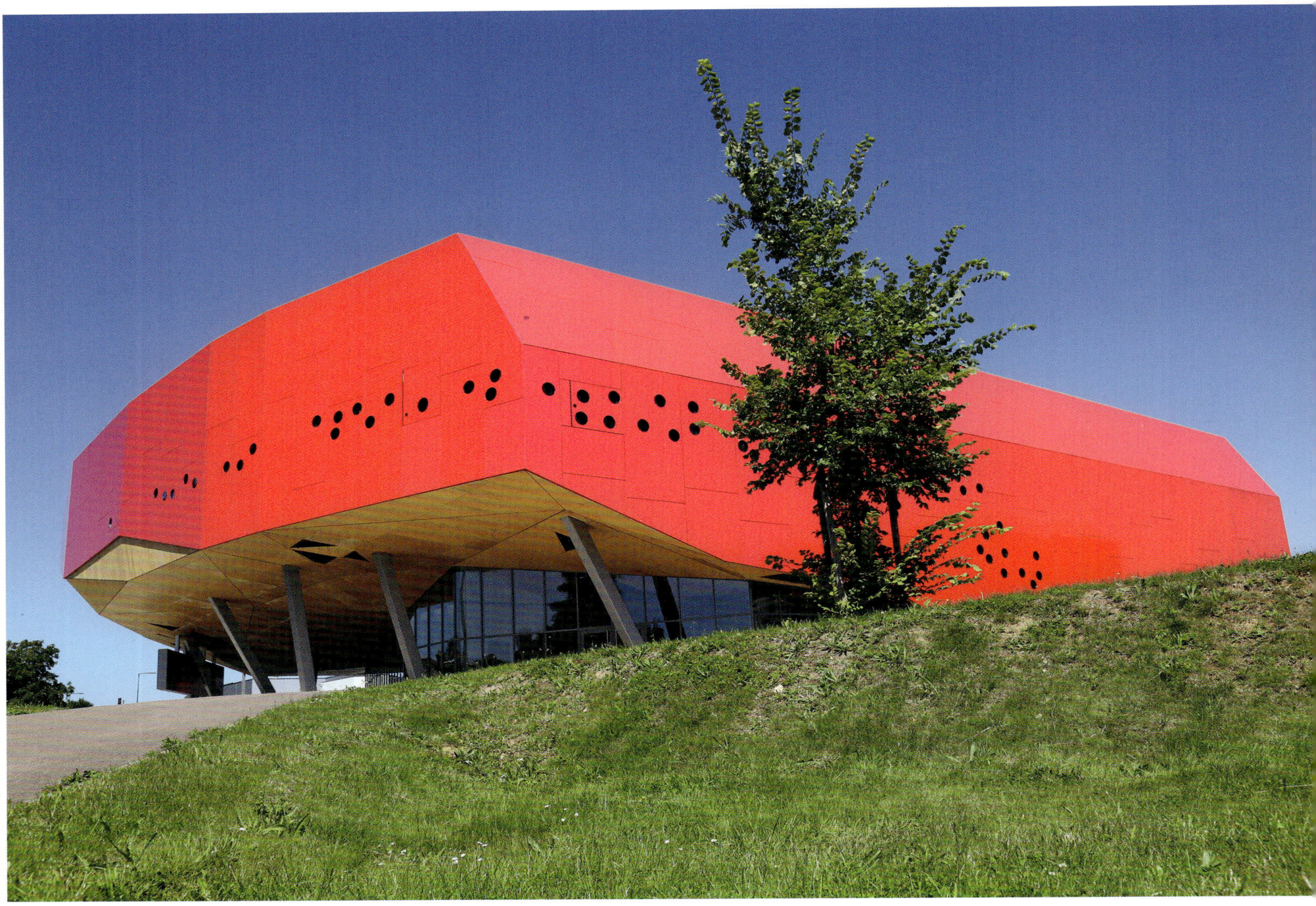

Pont-Audemer – Le Ciné – 2021

Pont-Audemer, Le Ciné. The flamboyant and very daring Ciné in fuchsia pink has aroused some controversy: 'It's a big mass', 'We no longer have the view we had before of the woods', 'Me, I don't like pink', exclaims a worthy citizen. The city says it will try to win over the nay-sayers. Fortunately, 90 per cent of Pont-Audemer residents support this magnificent building.

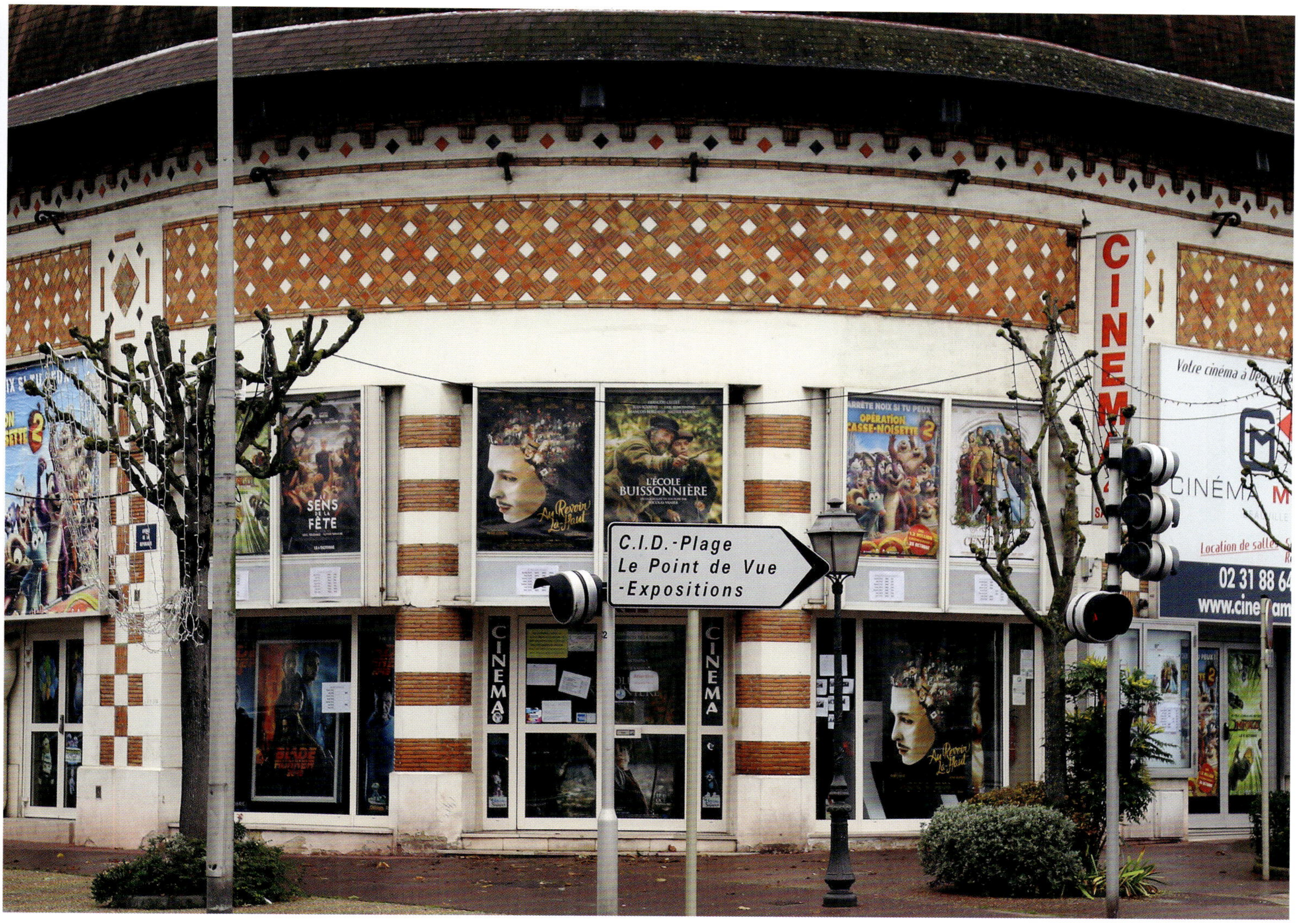

Deauville – Morny Club – 2017

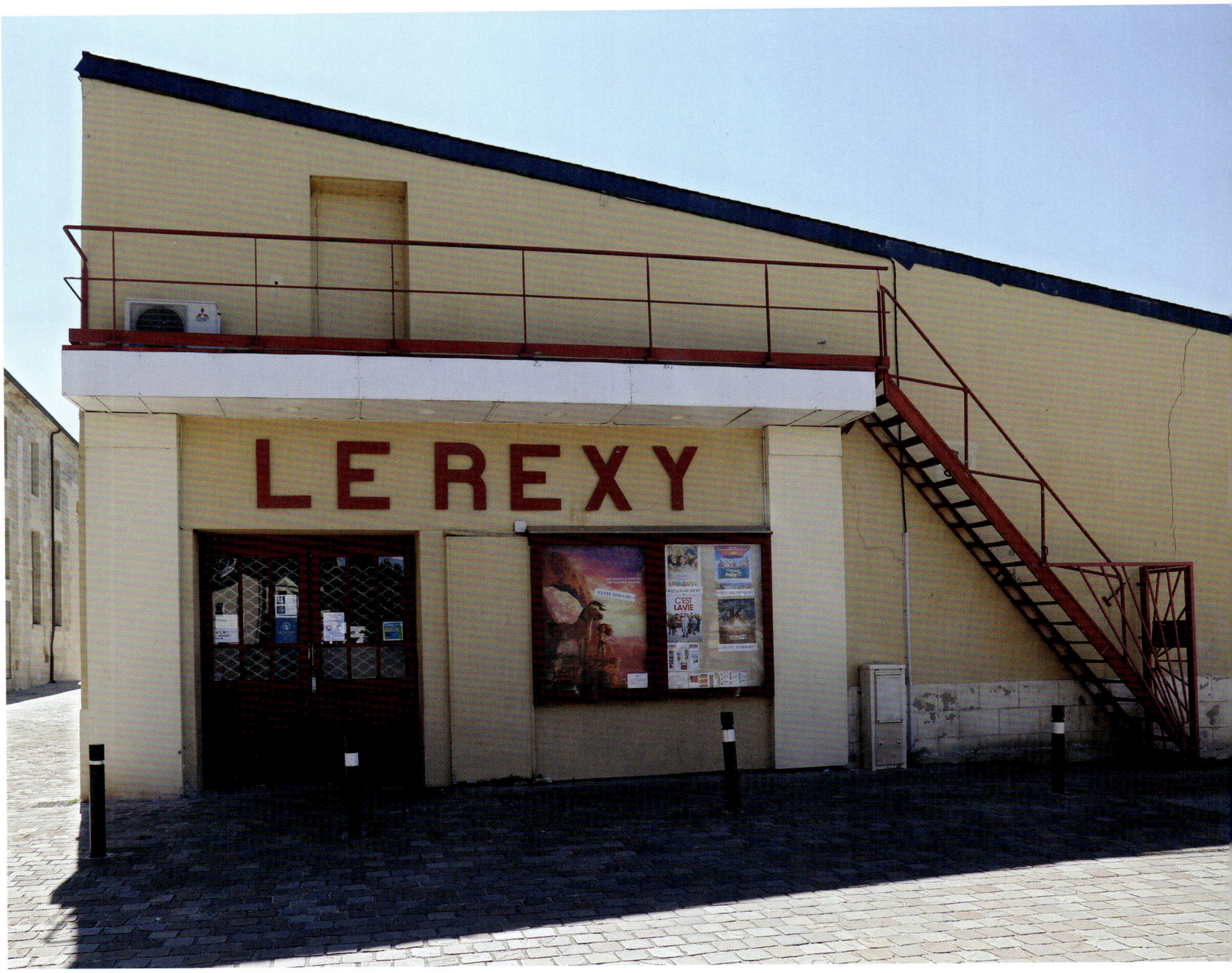

St Pierre-sur-Dives – Le Rexy – 2013

St-Pierre-sur-Dives, Le Rexy. Haunted by the spectre of the empty cinema, the cashier's mind gradually slips into melancholy mode, even disturbing her sleep. She fantasises about an endless line of movie-goers jostling to get in, some desperately even sitting in the front row, eyes glued to the screen. Others almost fighting for the last available, though clearly sagging, seat. And the boldest resigning themselves to sitting behind hulking bodies, twisting their necks trying to watch Bergman's last post-mortem film.

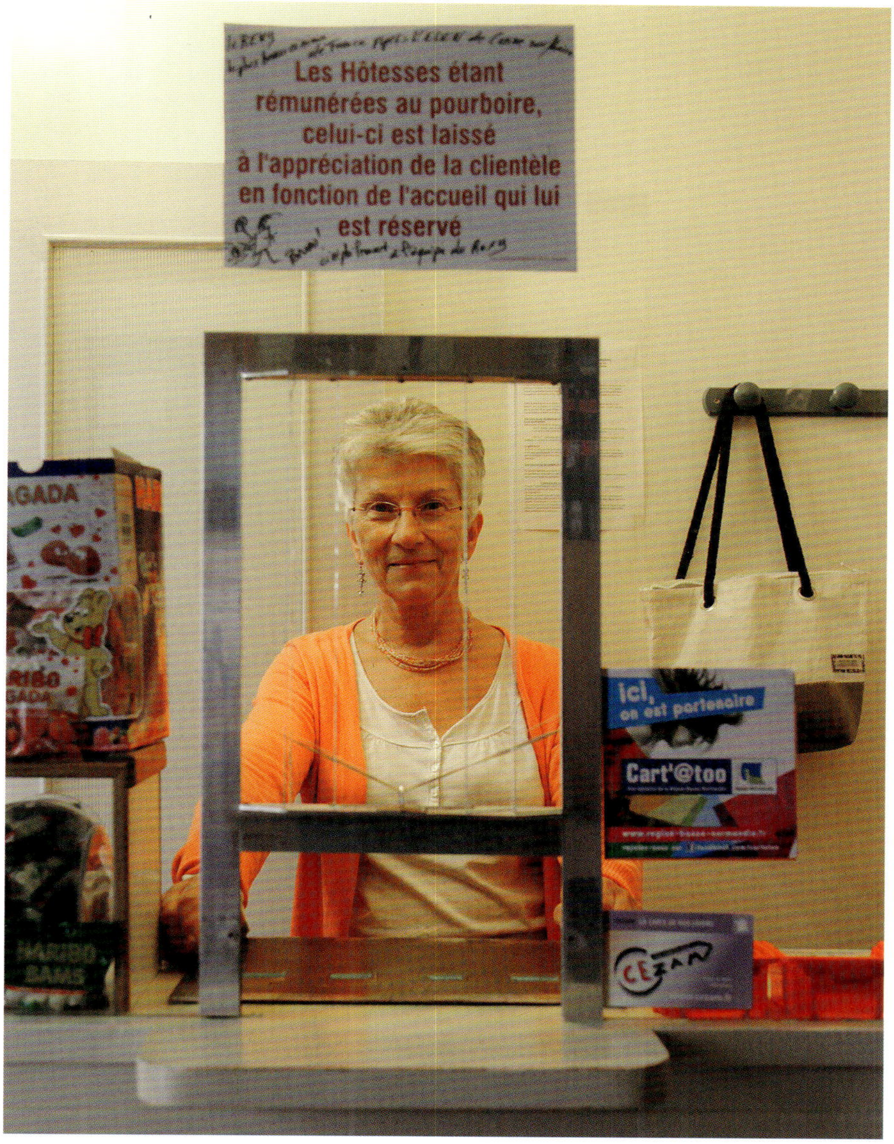
Les Hôtesses étant
rémunérées au pourboire,
celui-ci est laissé
à l'appréciation de la clientèle
en fonction de l'accueil qui lui
est réservé
ici,
on est partenaire
Cart'@too

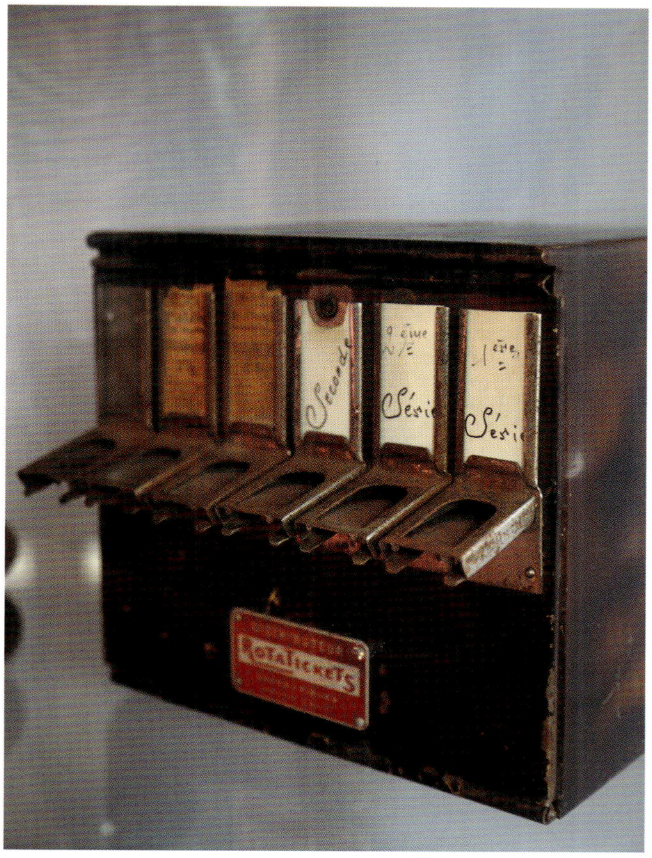
ROTATICKETS

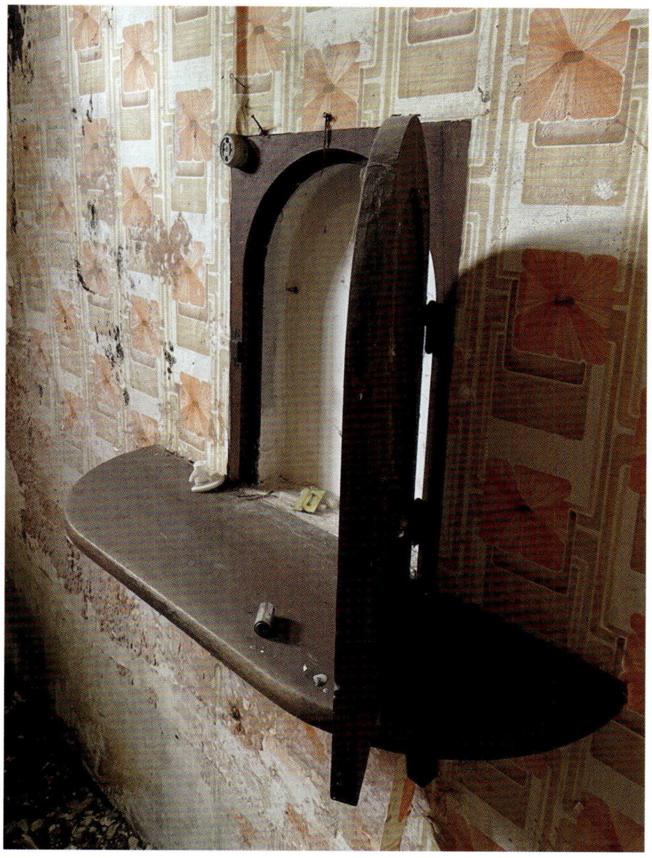

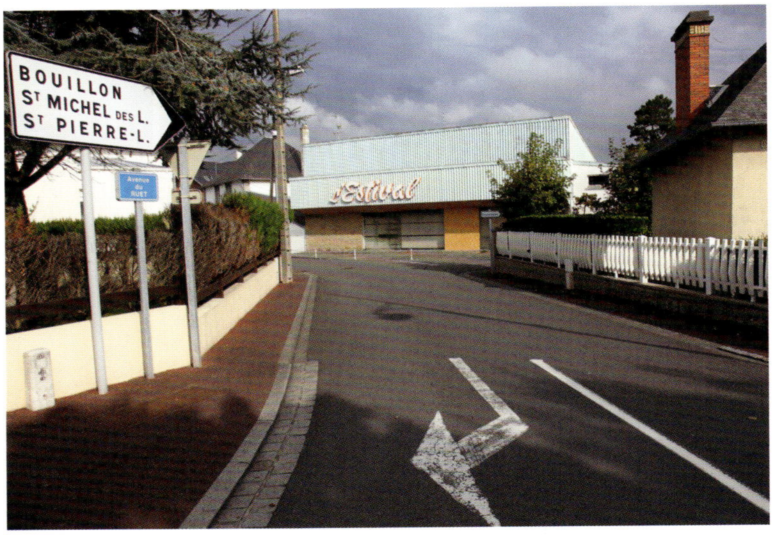

Jullouville – L'Estival – 2013

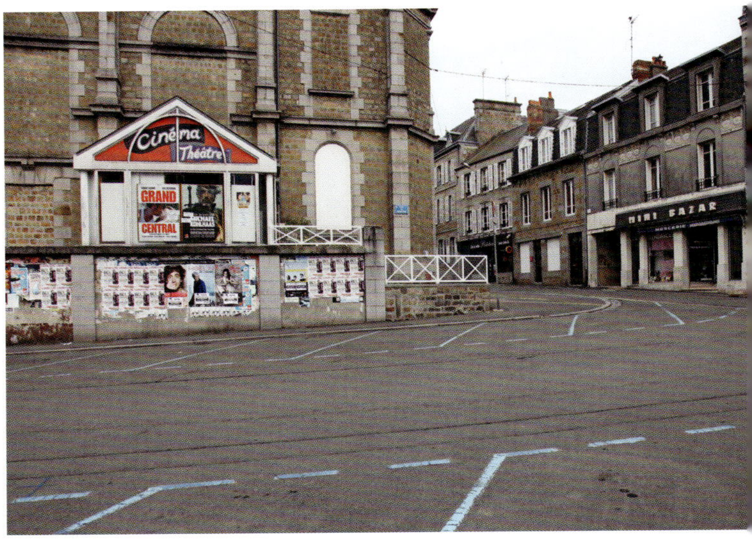

Villedieu-les-Poêles – cinéma – 2013

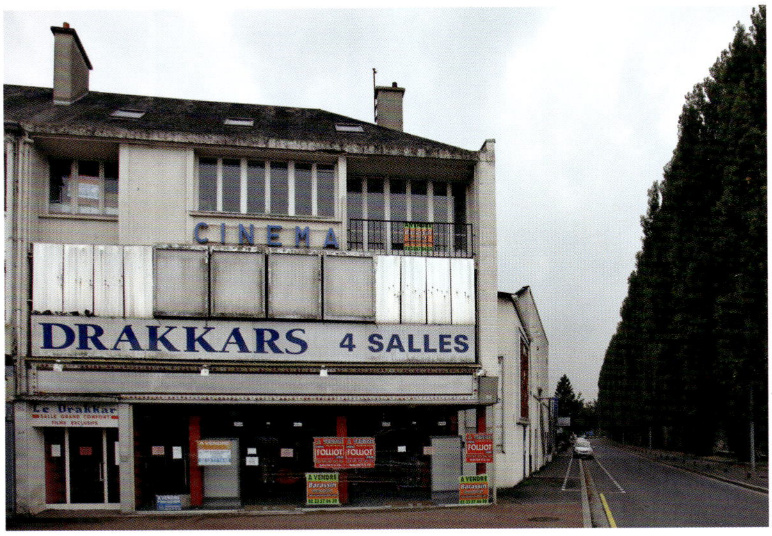

Saint-Lô – Drakkars – 2013

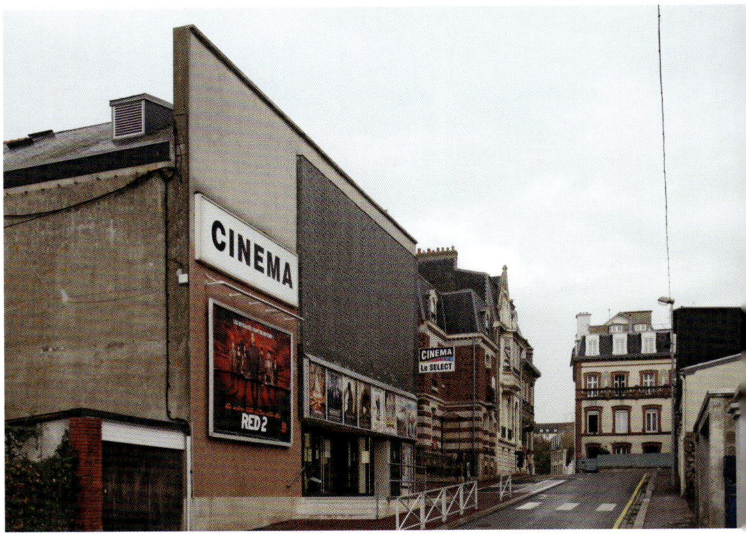

Granville – Le Select – 2013

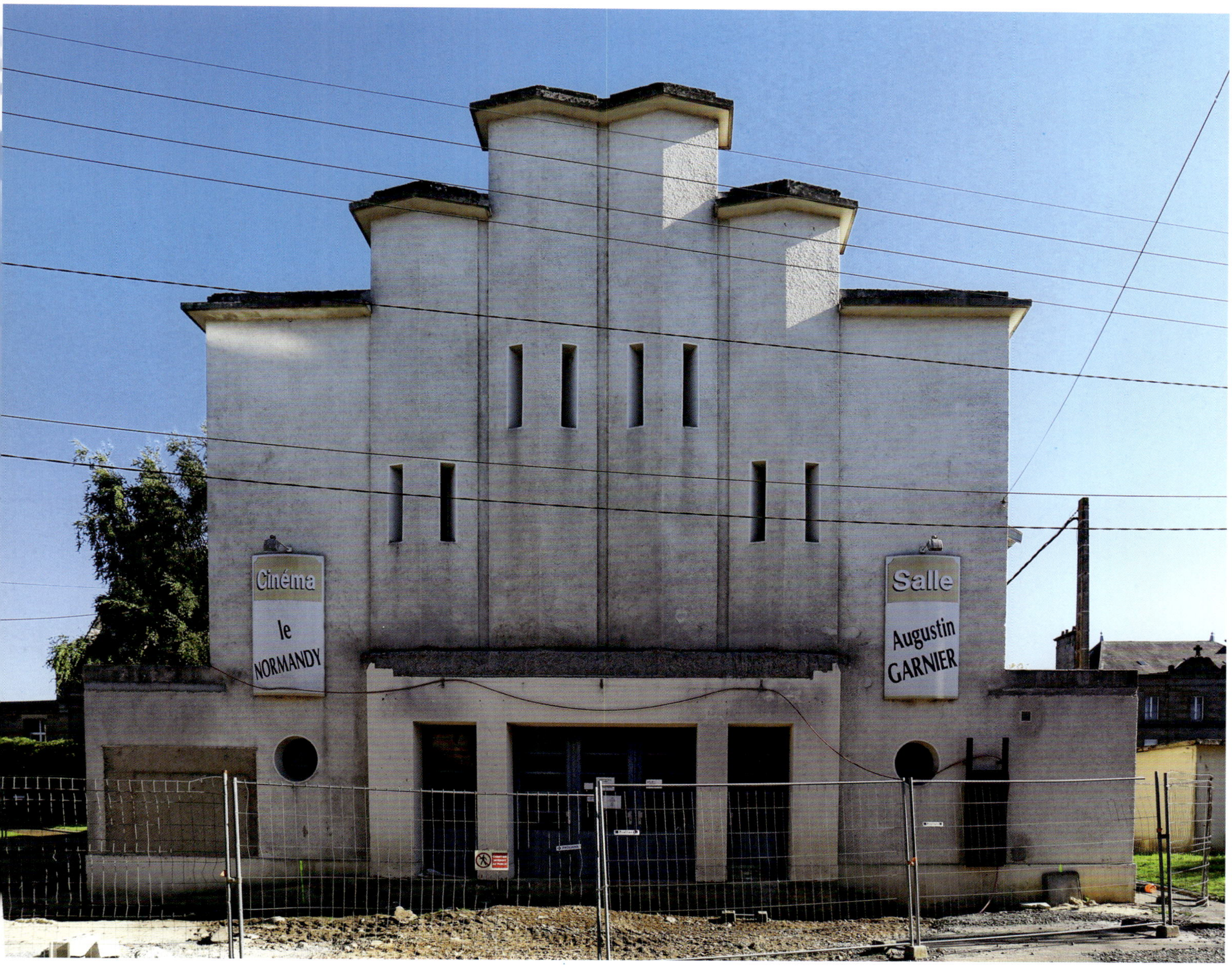

Tinchebray-Bocage – Le Normandy – 2021

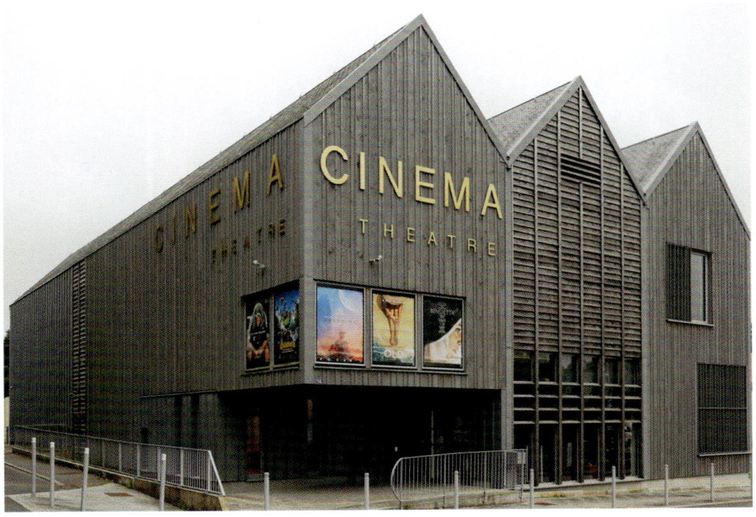

Villedieu-les-Poêles – cinéma – 2021

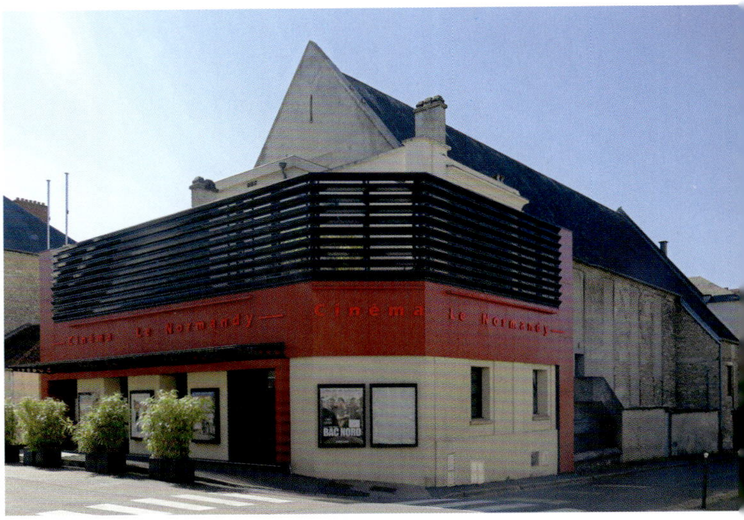

Argentan – Le Normandy – 2021

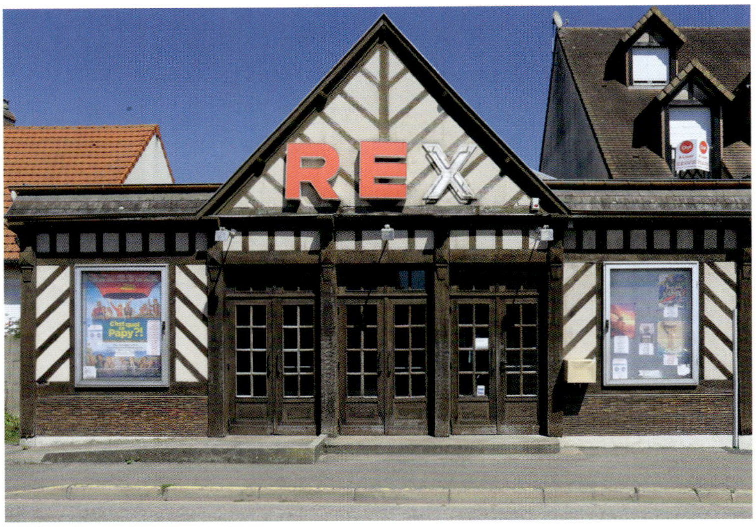

Bernay – Rex – 2021

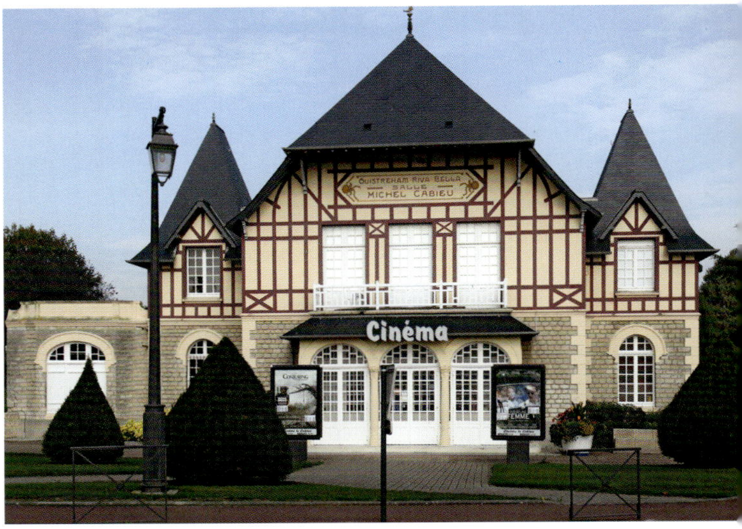

Ouistreham – Le Cabieu – 2013

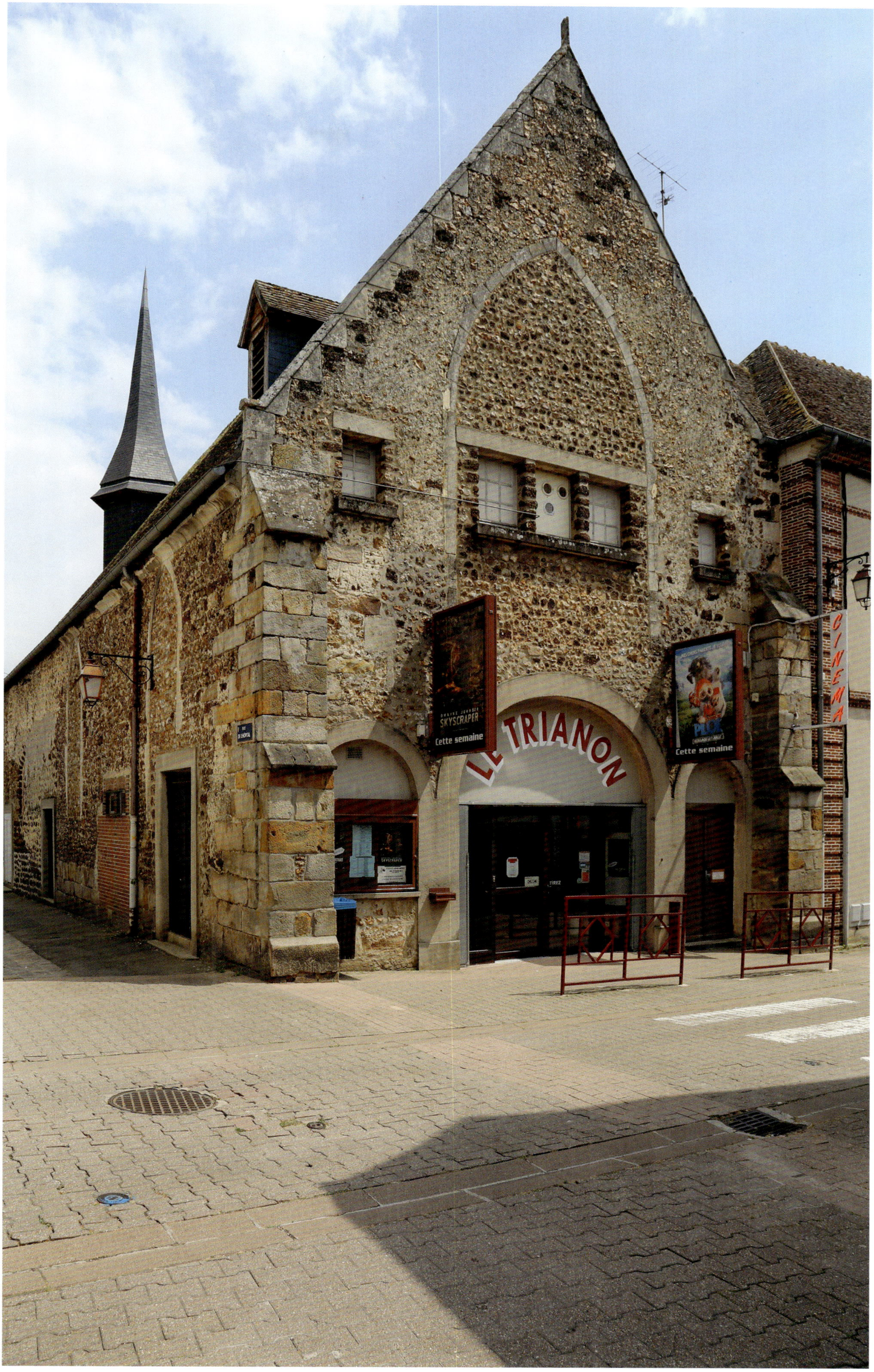

Verneuil-sur-Avre – Le Trianon – 2018

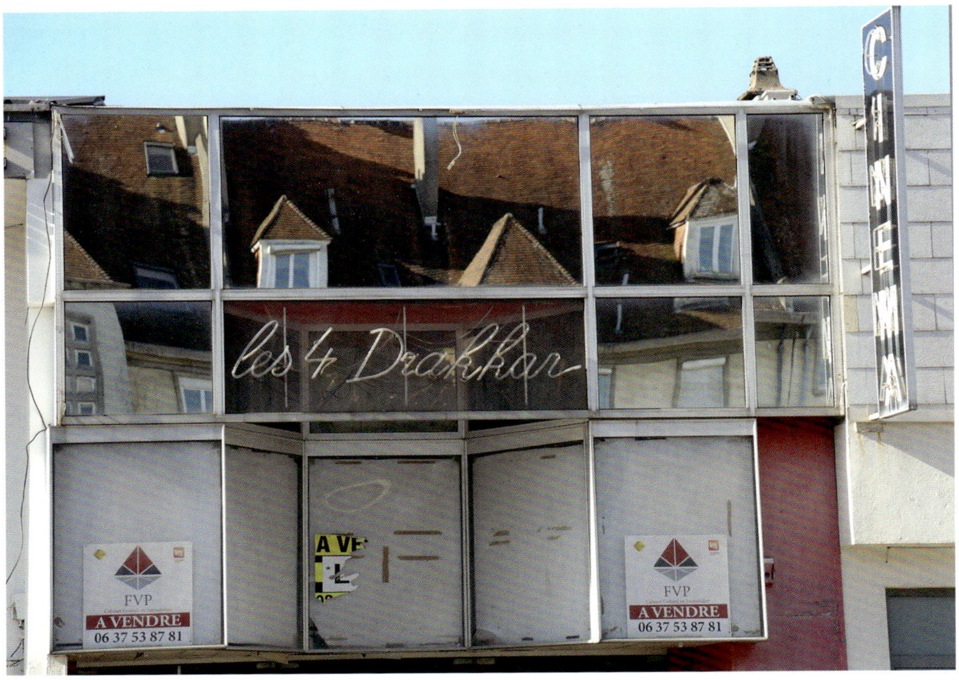

Yvetot – Les 4 Drakkar – 2021

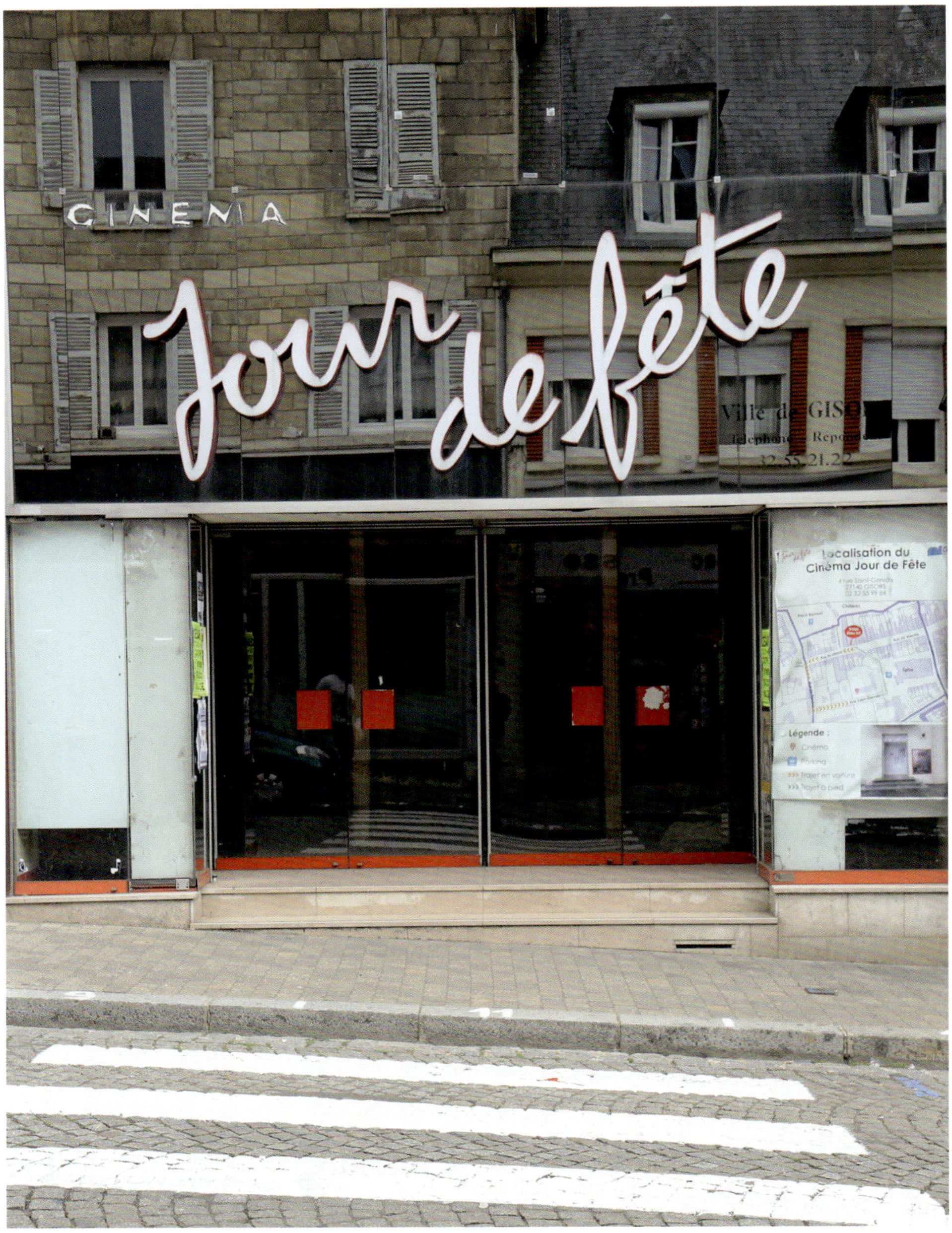

Gisors – Jour de Fête – 2018

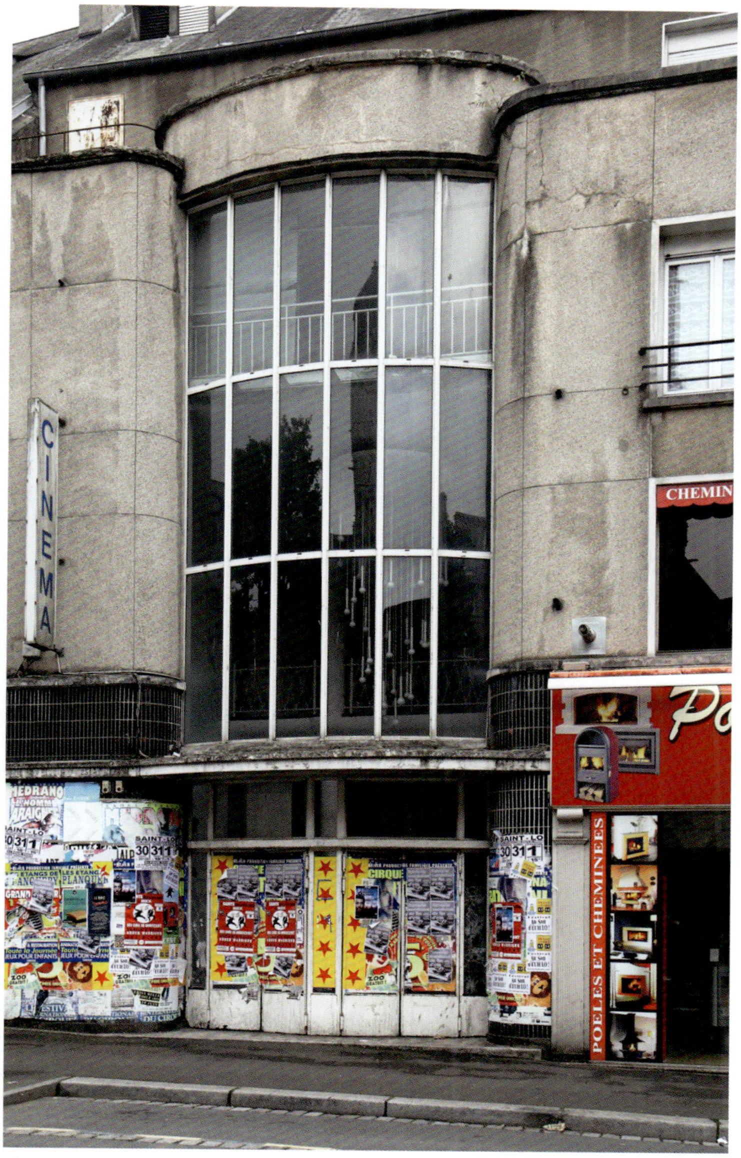

Saint-Lô – Majestic – 2013

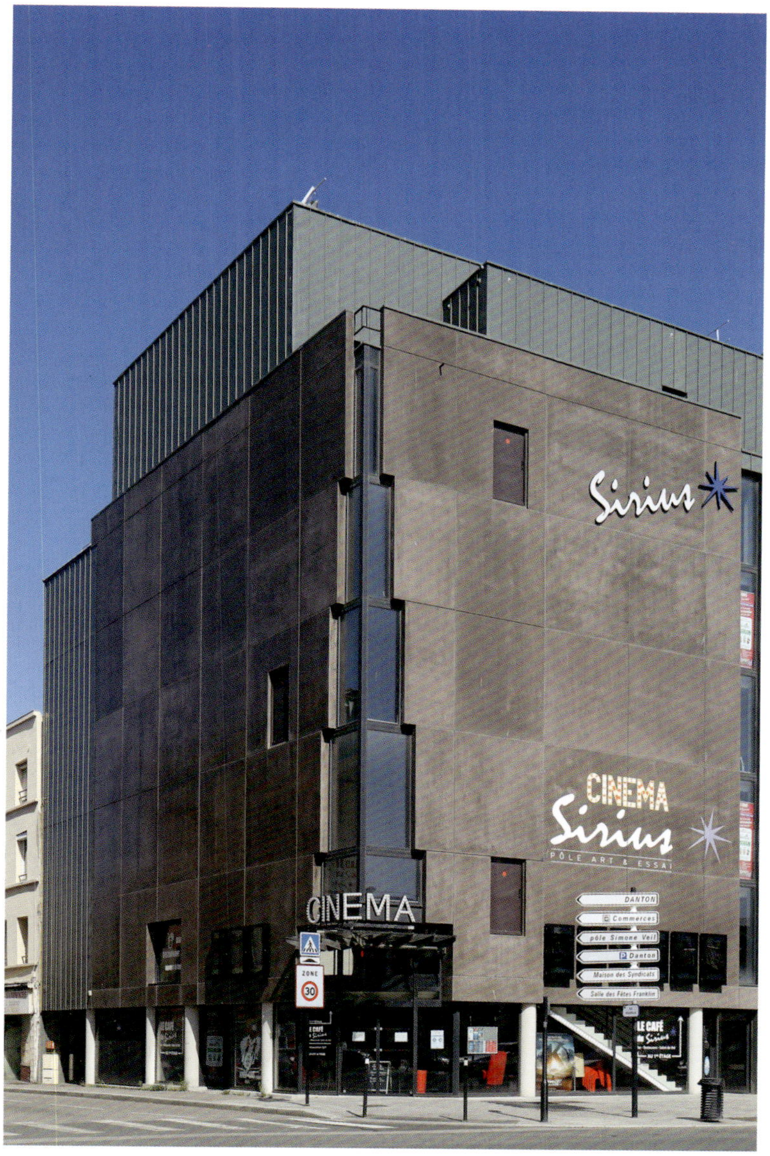

Le Havre – Sirius – 2021

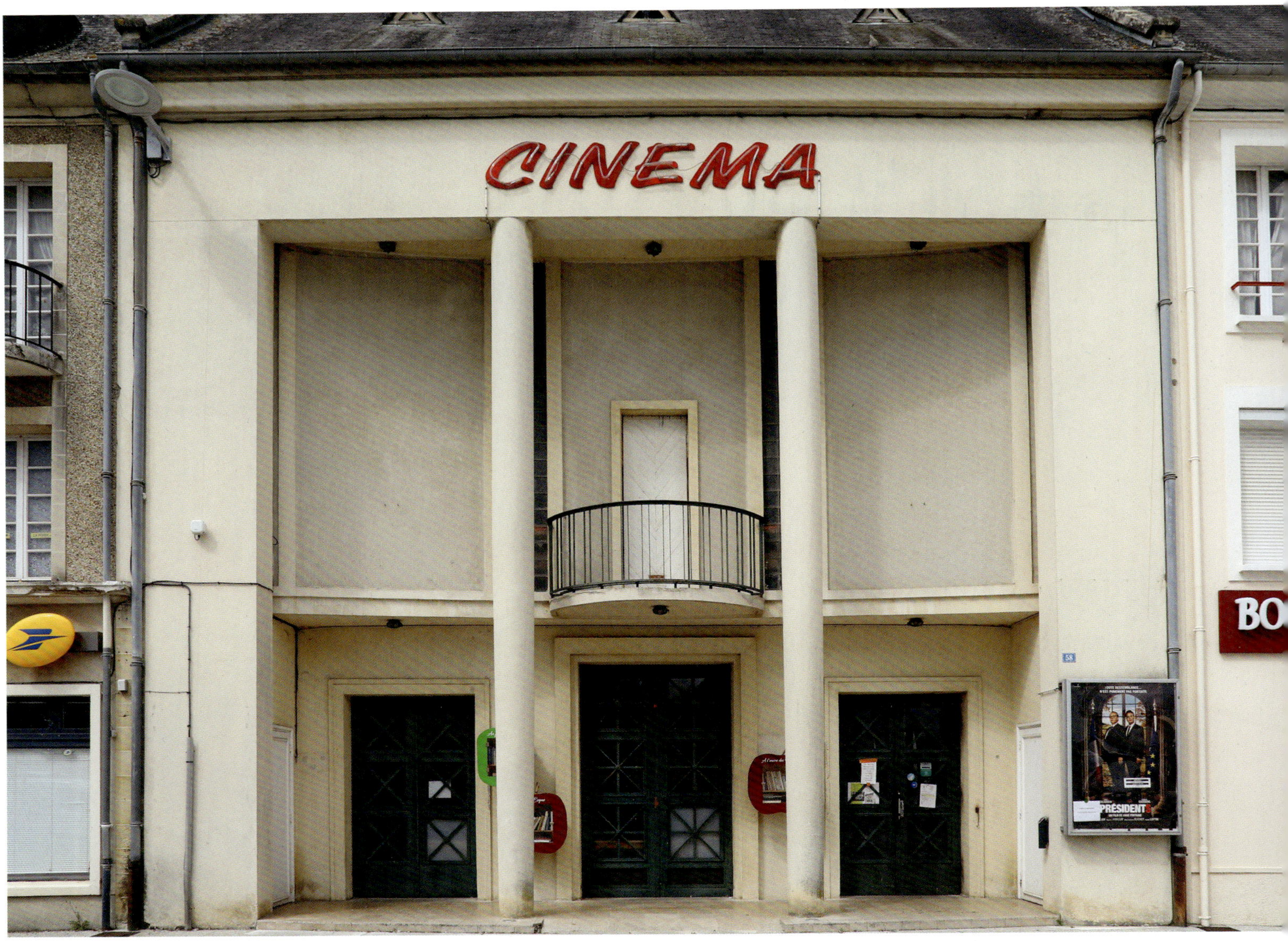

Trévières – Normandy – 2021

Trévières, Normandy. At the front of the Normandy cinema, an intriguing balcony projects onto the square. Perhaps built to allow immortal stars to greet a patient audience, still dreaming of seeing Greta Garbo, Cary Grant or a few others? They won't be disappointed ...

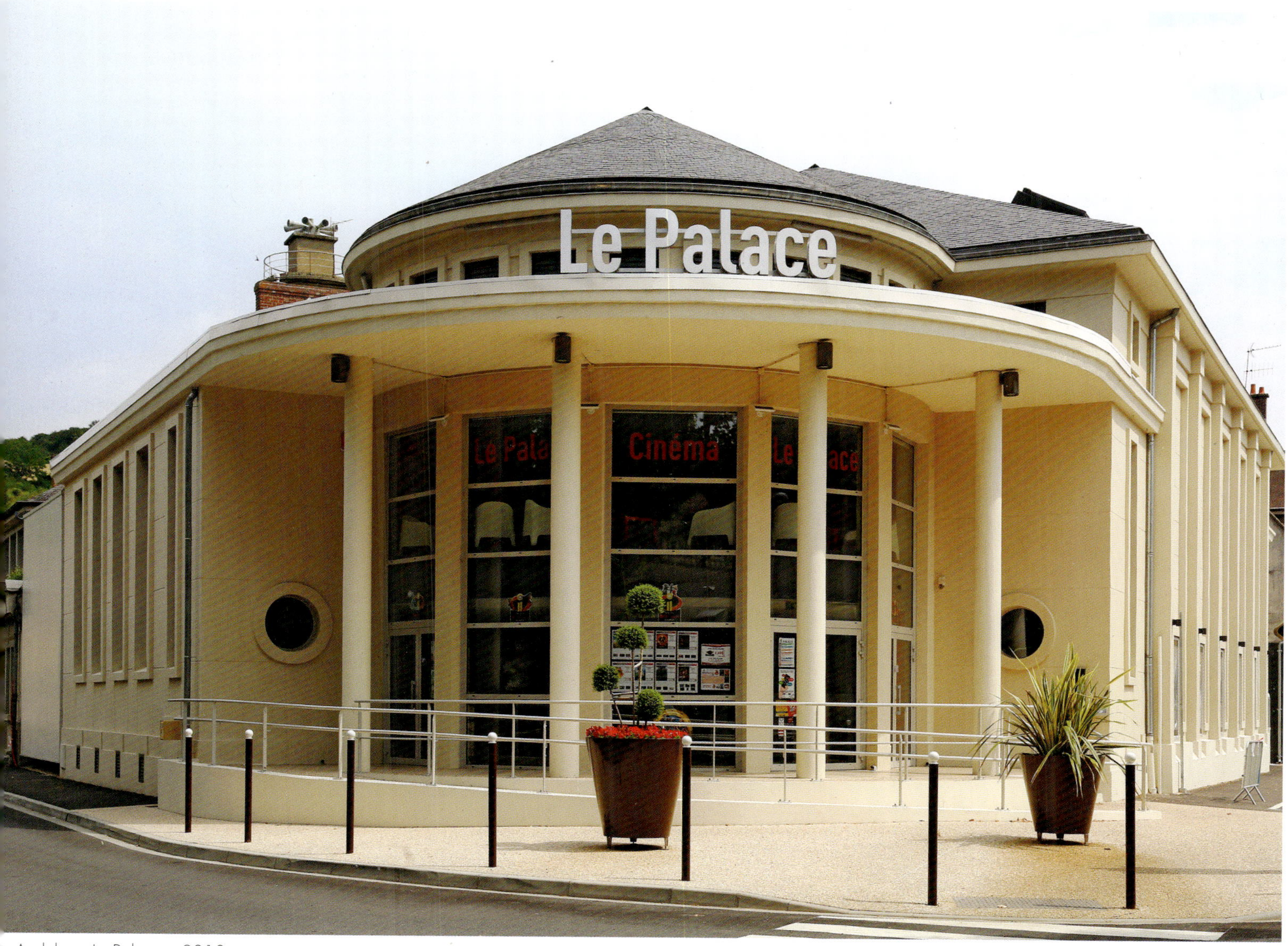

s Andelys – Le Palace – 2018

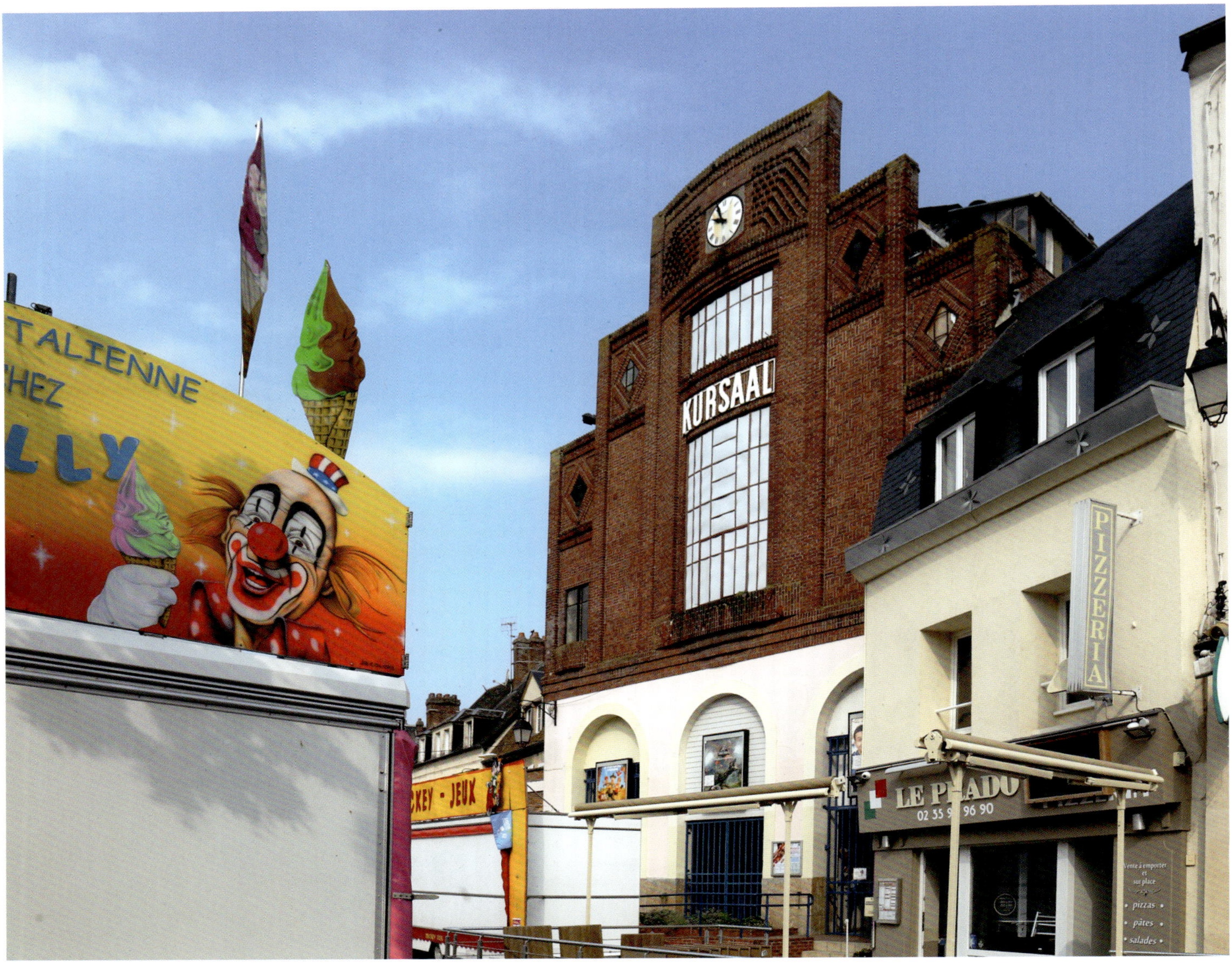

Gournay-en-Bray – Kursaal – 2018

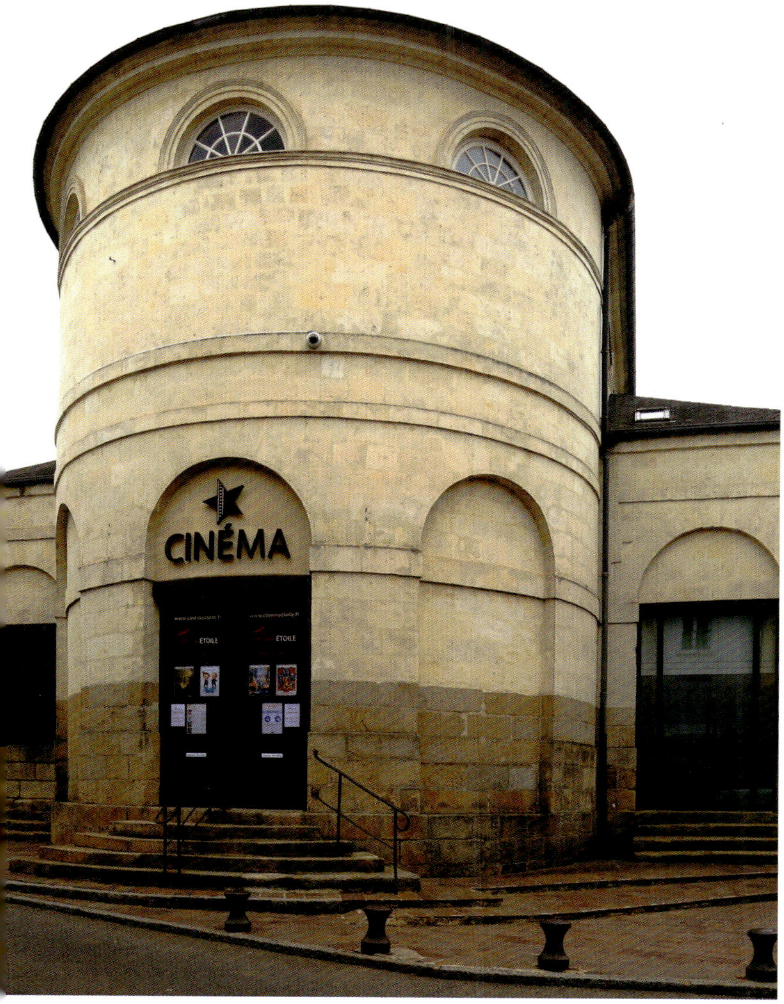

ortagne-au-Perche – Étoile –2021

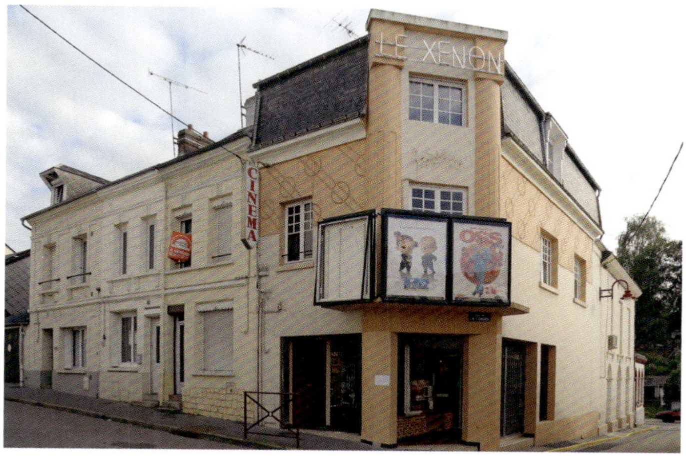

Bolbec – Le Xenon – 2021

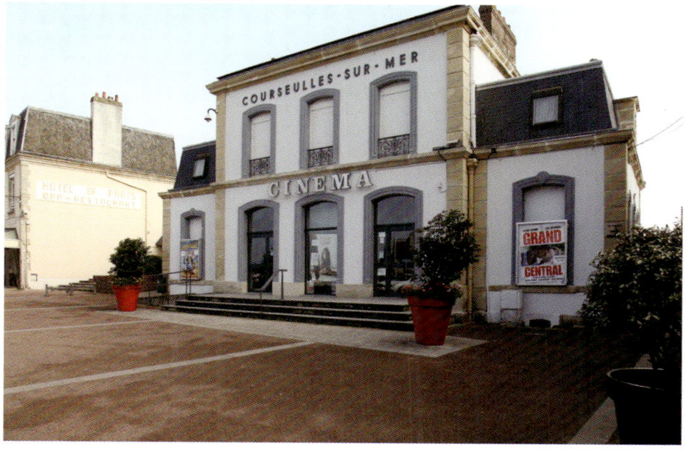

Courseulles-sur-Mer – Cinéma de la Gare – 2013

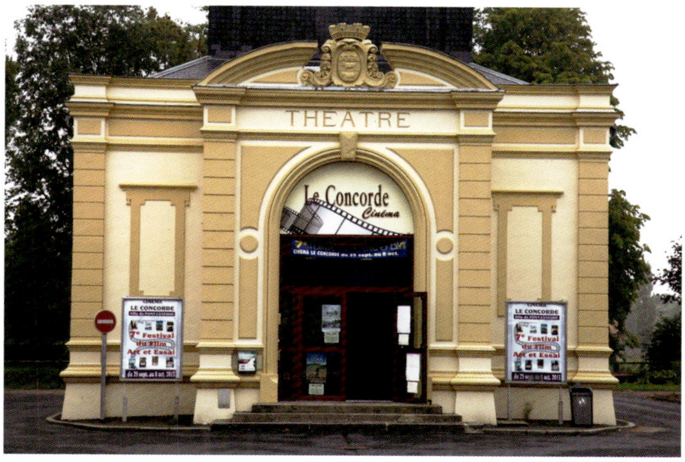

Pont-l'Évêque – Le Concorde – 2013

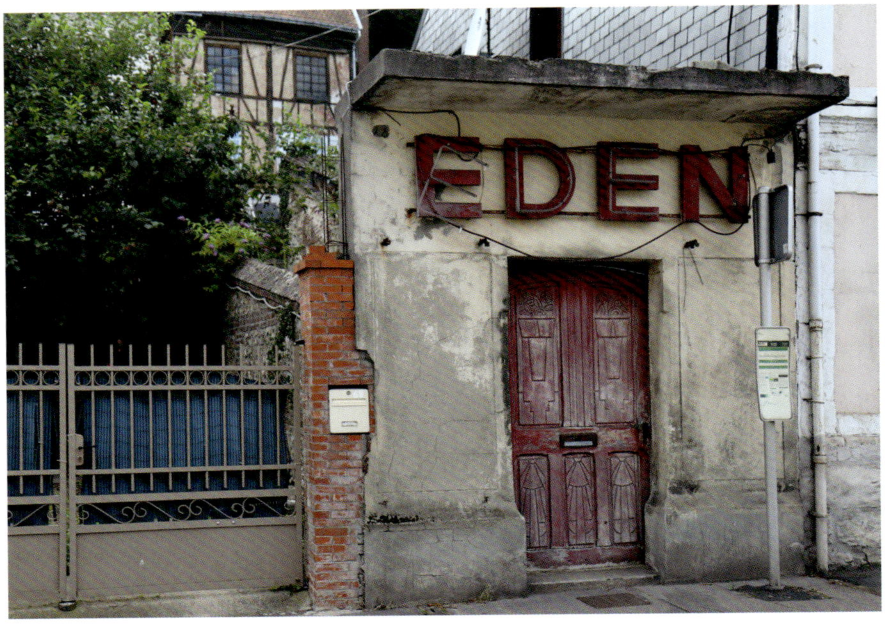

Bolbec – Eden – 2021

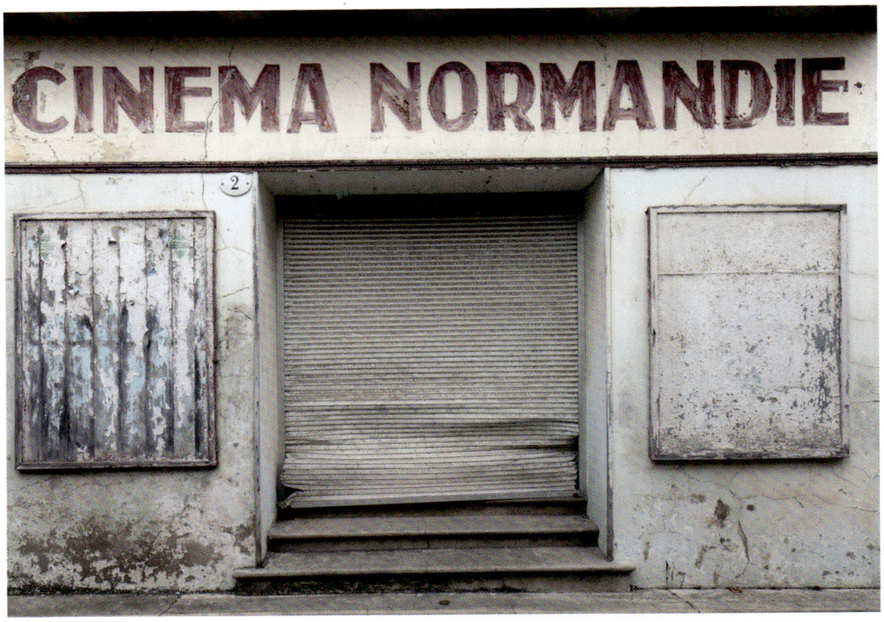

Bayeux – Cinéma Normandie – 2013

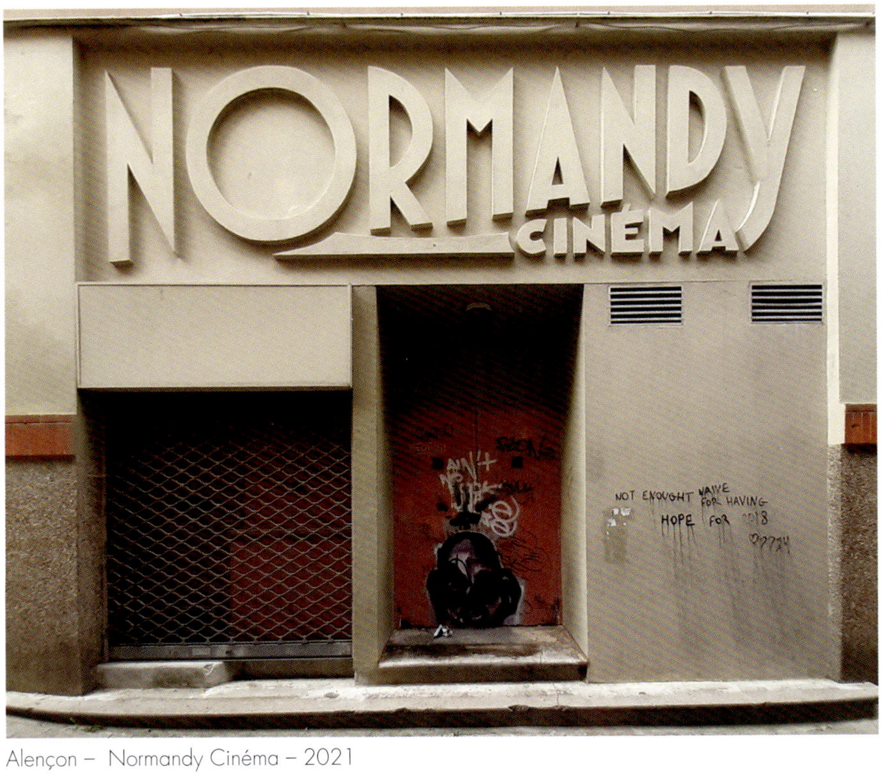

Alençon – Normandy Cinéma – 2021

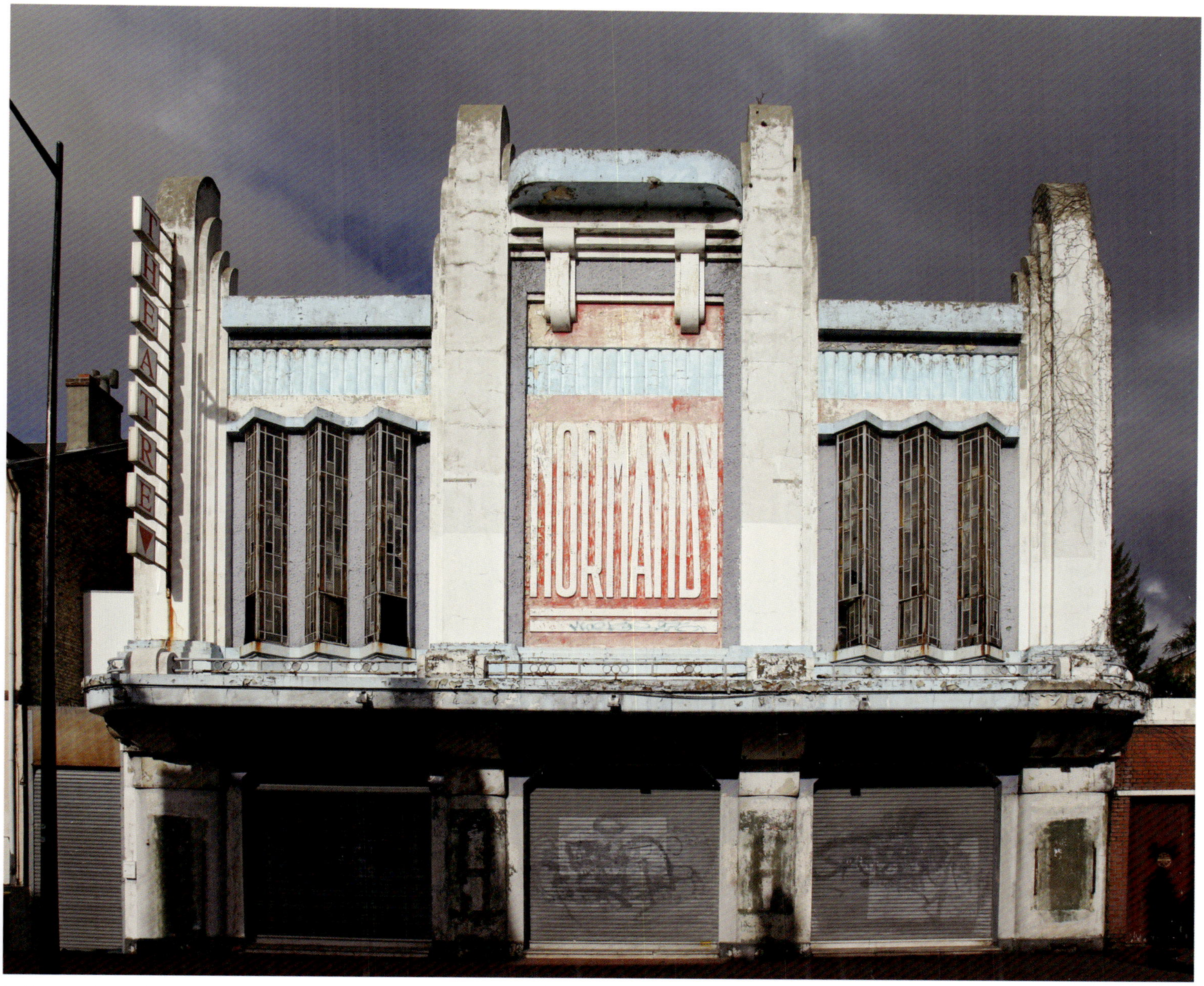

Le Havre – Normandy – 2012

Le Havre, Normandy. The story begins like a fairytale: a woman sleeping in the back of a convertible wakes up as her car drives past the Normandy, an abandoned cinema adrift, opened in 1934, closed in 1991. Love at first sight. The Spahija family bought it. That was in 1999. Faced with a number of difficulties, including lack of knowledge of what to do with the place, their dream evaporated and became a nightmare. The ghost ship was about to sink. They tried to resell with a guarantee that the façade would be preserved, but the promoters dreamed of demolishing this Art Deco jewel to set up some sinister dwellings – a common field of expertise. Undeterred and full of energy, the Spahija family started all over again and had the façade renovated with the support of companies sensitive to its beauty. Miraculously, the Le Havre Heritage Rescue Association, local elected officials and mayor Édouard Philippe are now very aware of the situation. Yet they bear a heavy responsibility for this mess. The identically renovated façade was inaugurated in September 2021.

NOUVELLE-AQUITAINE

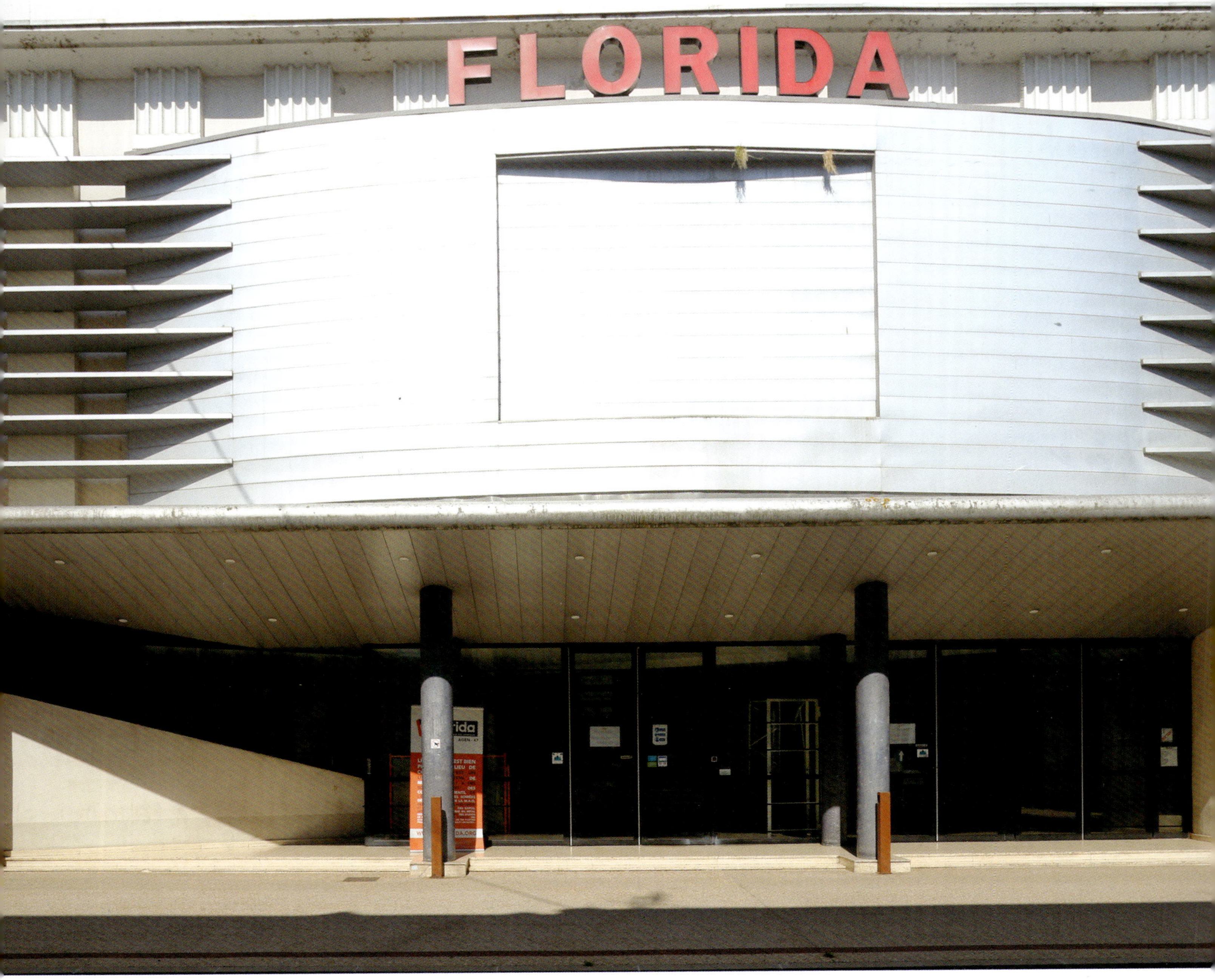

Agen – Florida – 2021

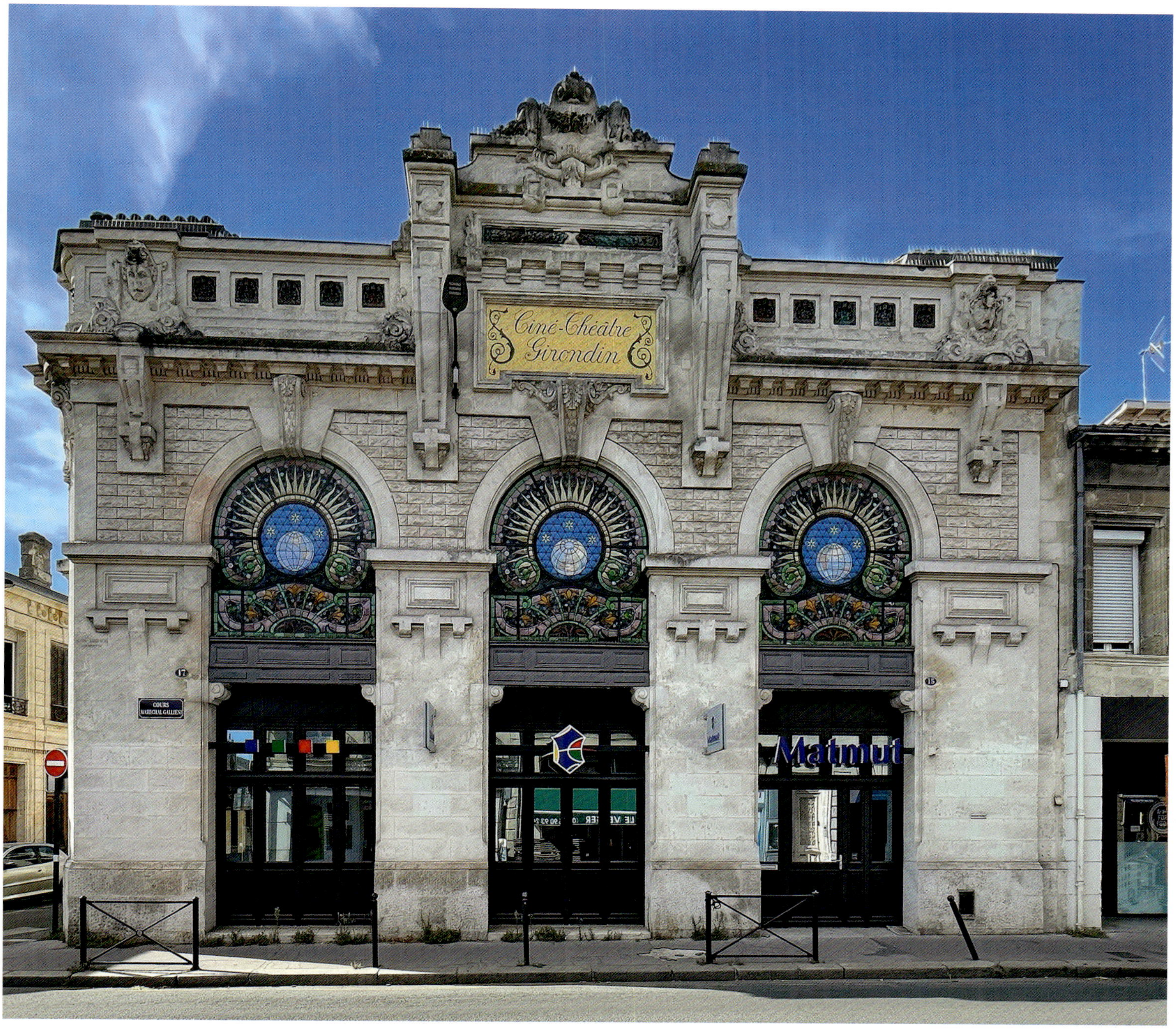

Bordeaux – Ciné-Théâtre Girondin – 2022

Bordeaux, Ciné-Théâtre Girondin. The architecture of Ciné-Théâtre Girondin, opened in 1916 as a neighbourhood cinema, is inspired by the plans of an Argentine theatre. Its name is engraved in mosaic above the entrance. The three entrances to the building are decorated with beautiful stained glass, representing three sides of the terrestrial globe, each surmounted by a star and floral motifs. The cinema closed in 1980, first converted into a market then decommissioned, and in 2013 became an apartment block.

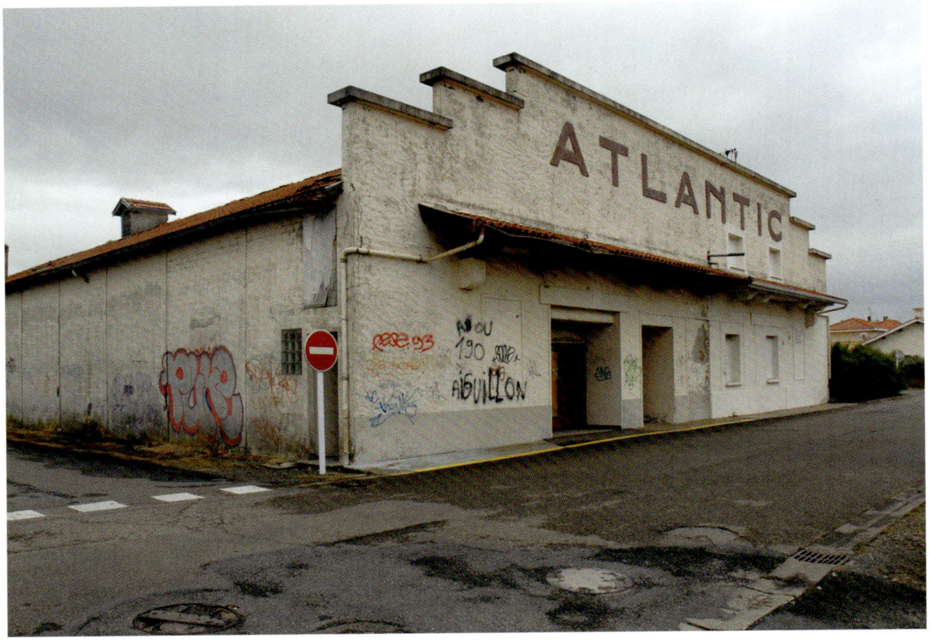

Biscarosse – Atlantic – 2008 (destroyed)

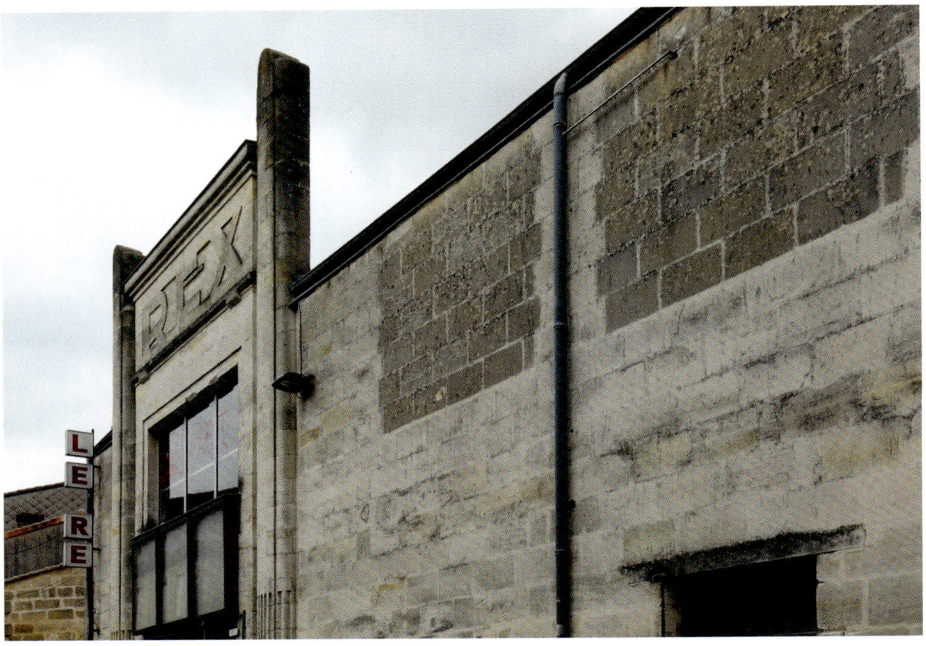

Libourne – Rex – 2018

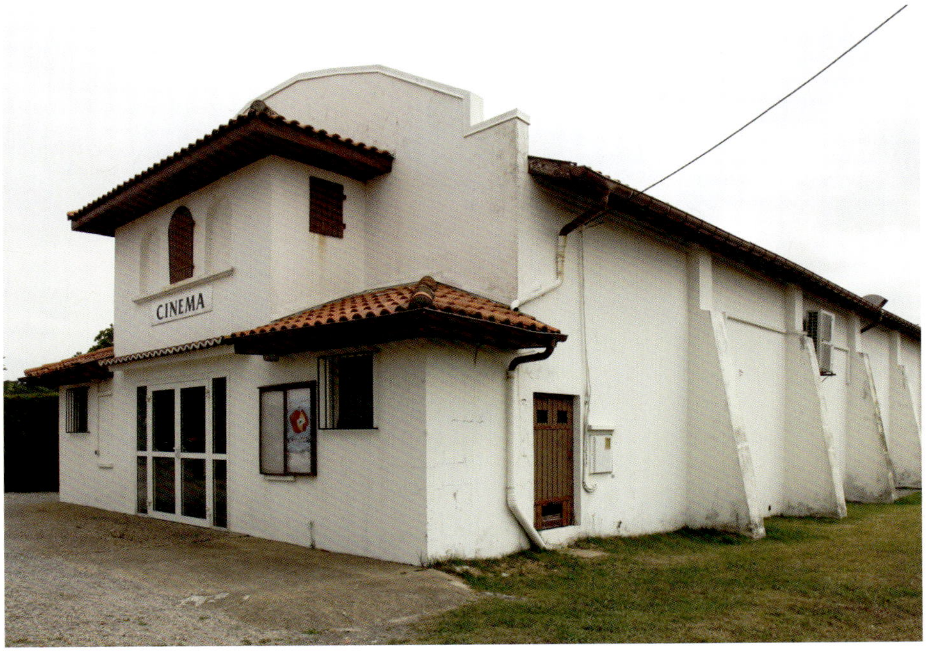

Bidart – Family – 2012

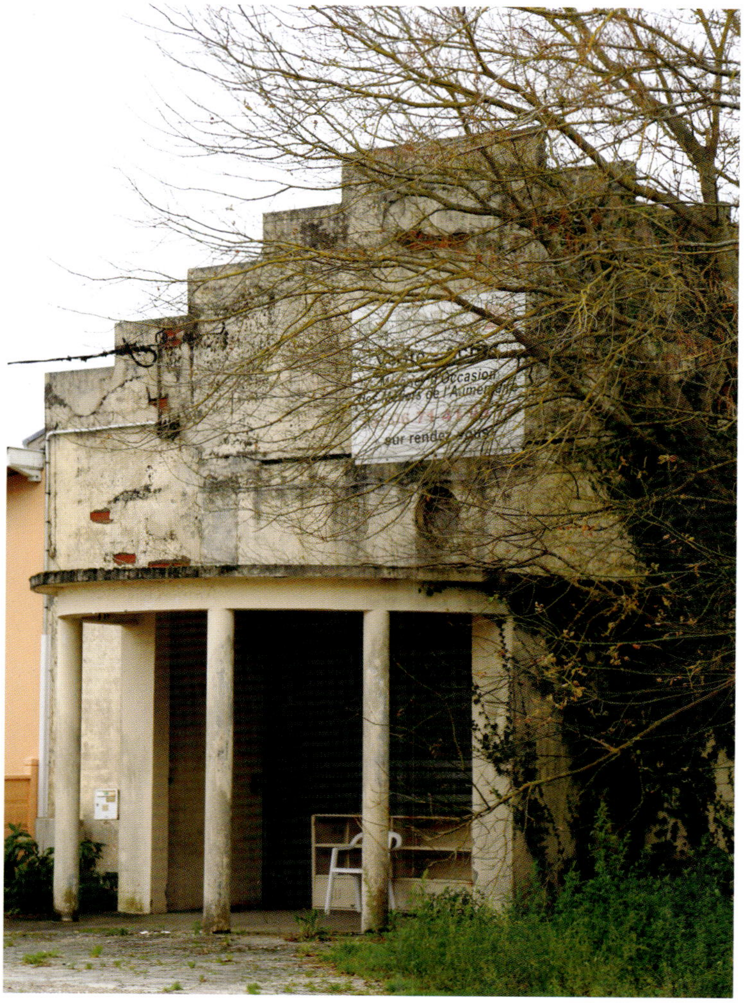

Vendaye-Montalivet – Rex – 2019

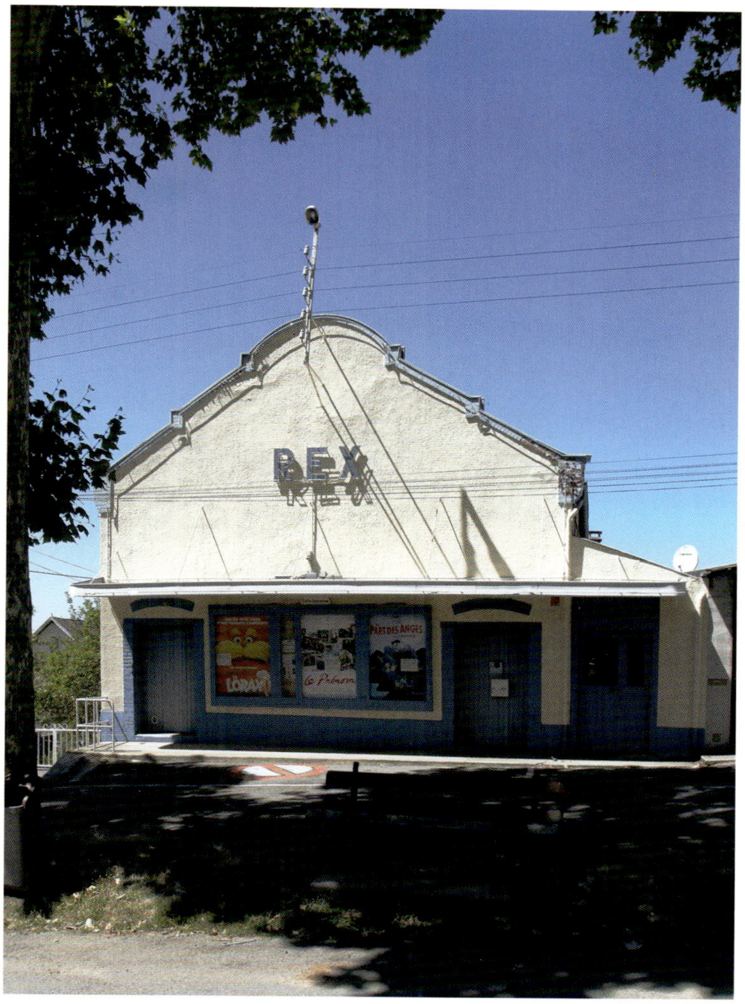

Saint-Léonard-de-Noblat – Rex – 2012

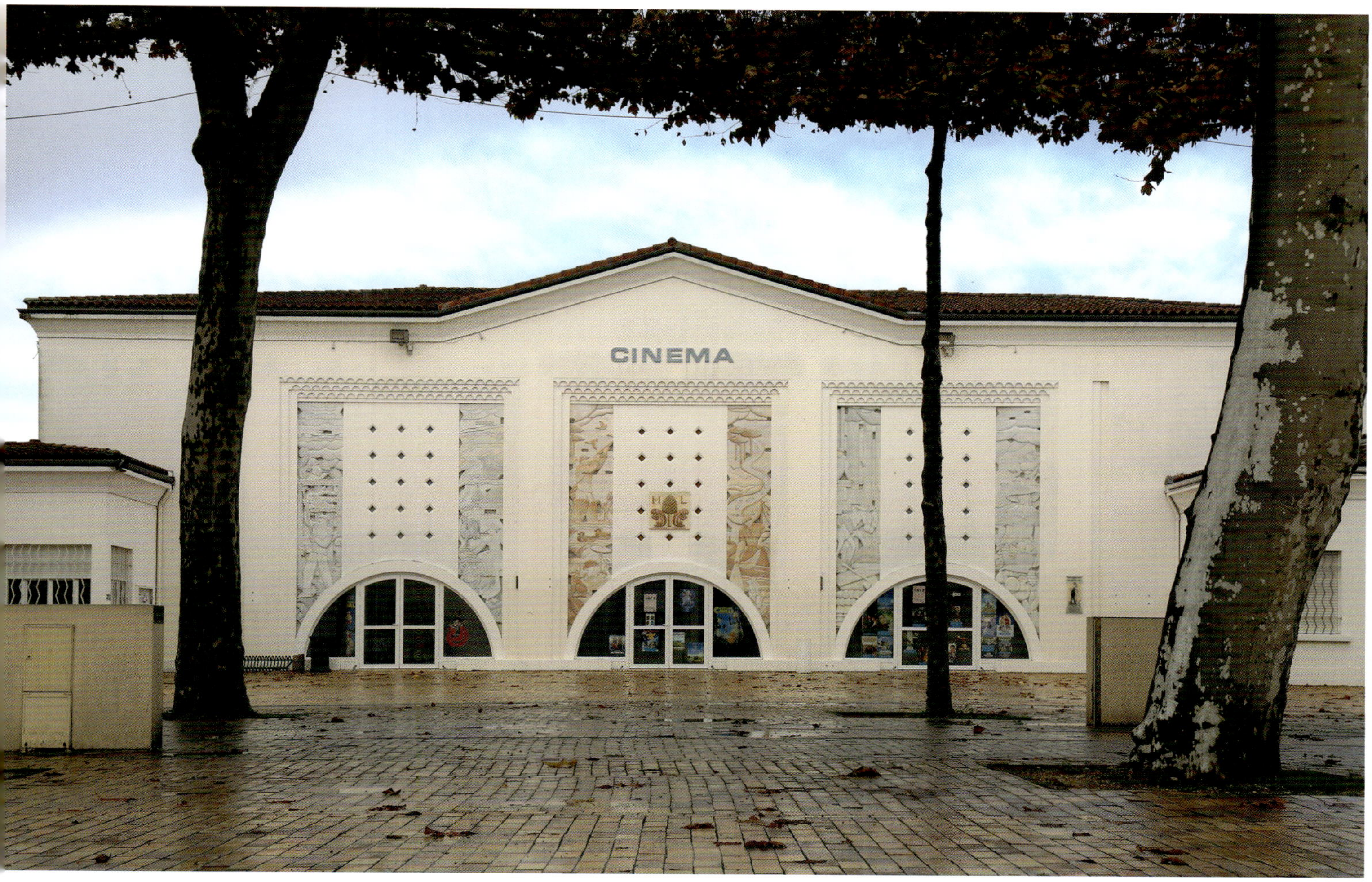

Morcenx – Cinéloisirs – 2019

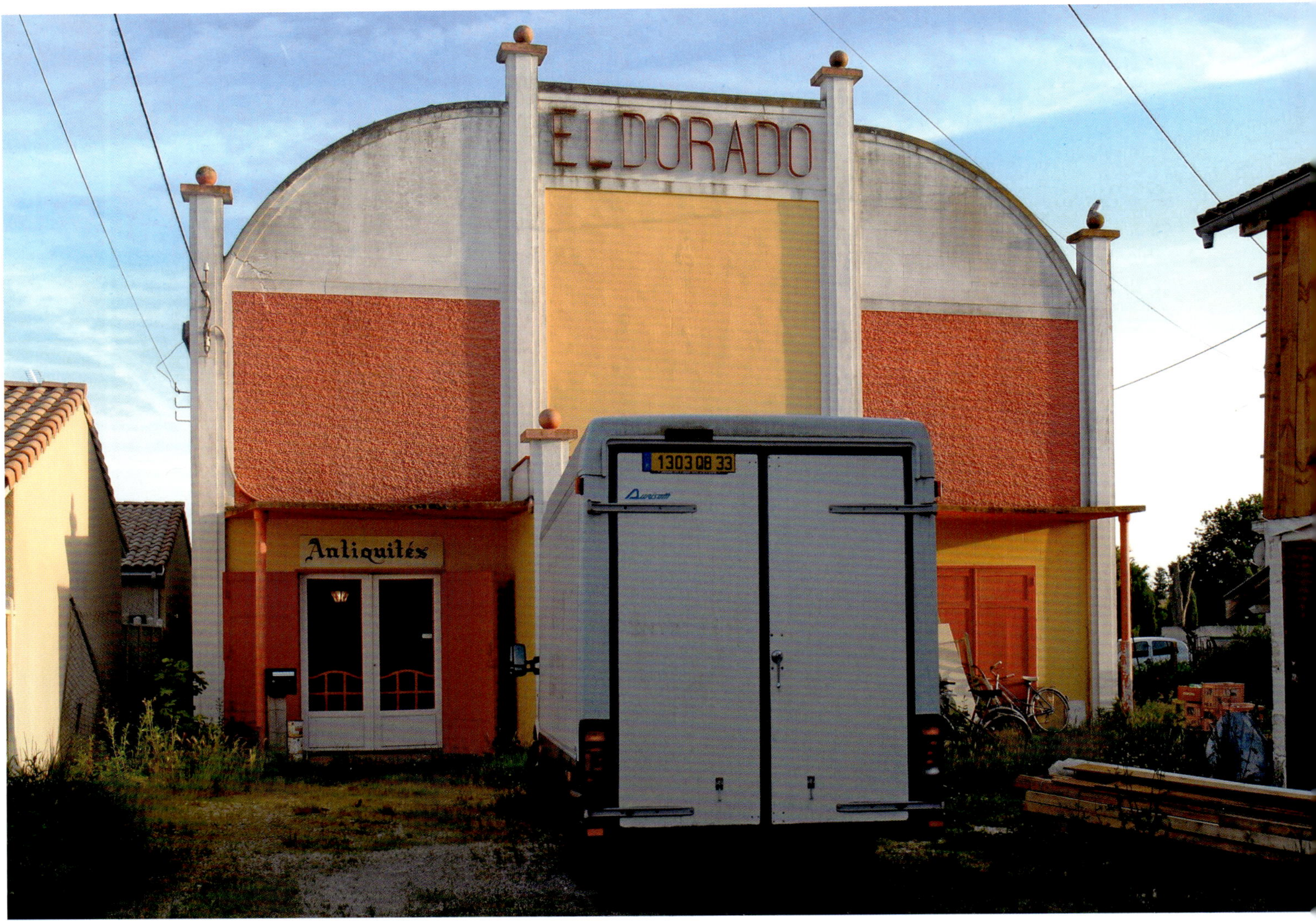

Gujan-Mestras – Eldorado – 2008

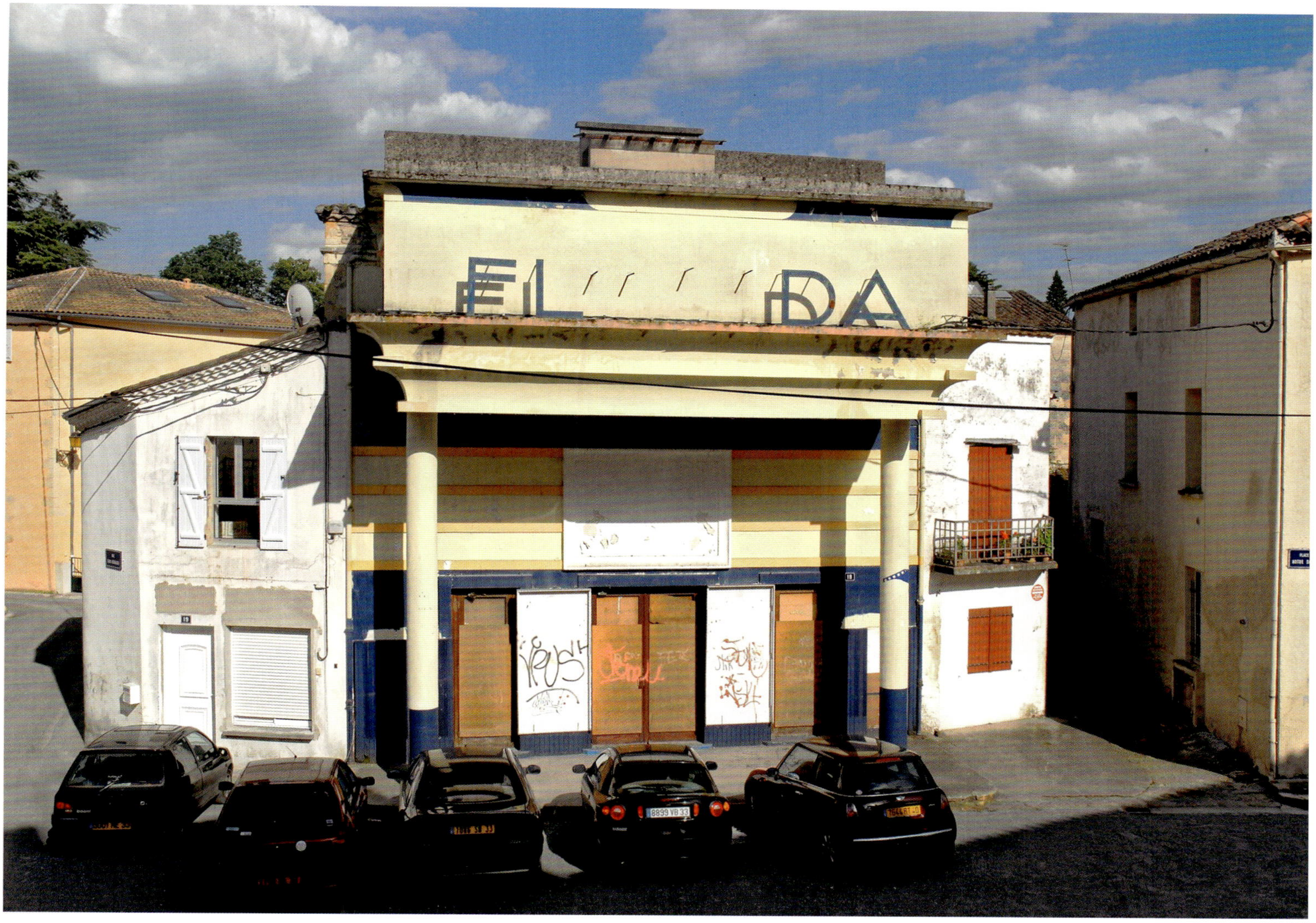

Langon – Florida – 2008

Langon, Florida. Audiences abandoned this cinema to its painful fate a long time ago. Only cars, tired of waiting for their owners, were hoping to go inside and find them … through a hidden entrance? Illuminating the theatre in the morgue-like half-light with their powerful headlights one last time before it's extinguished for ever.

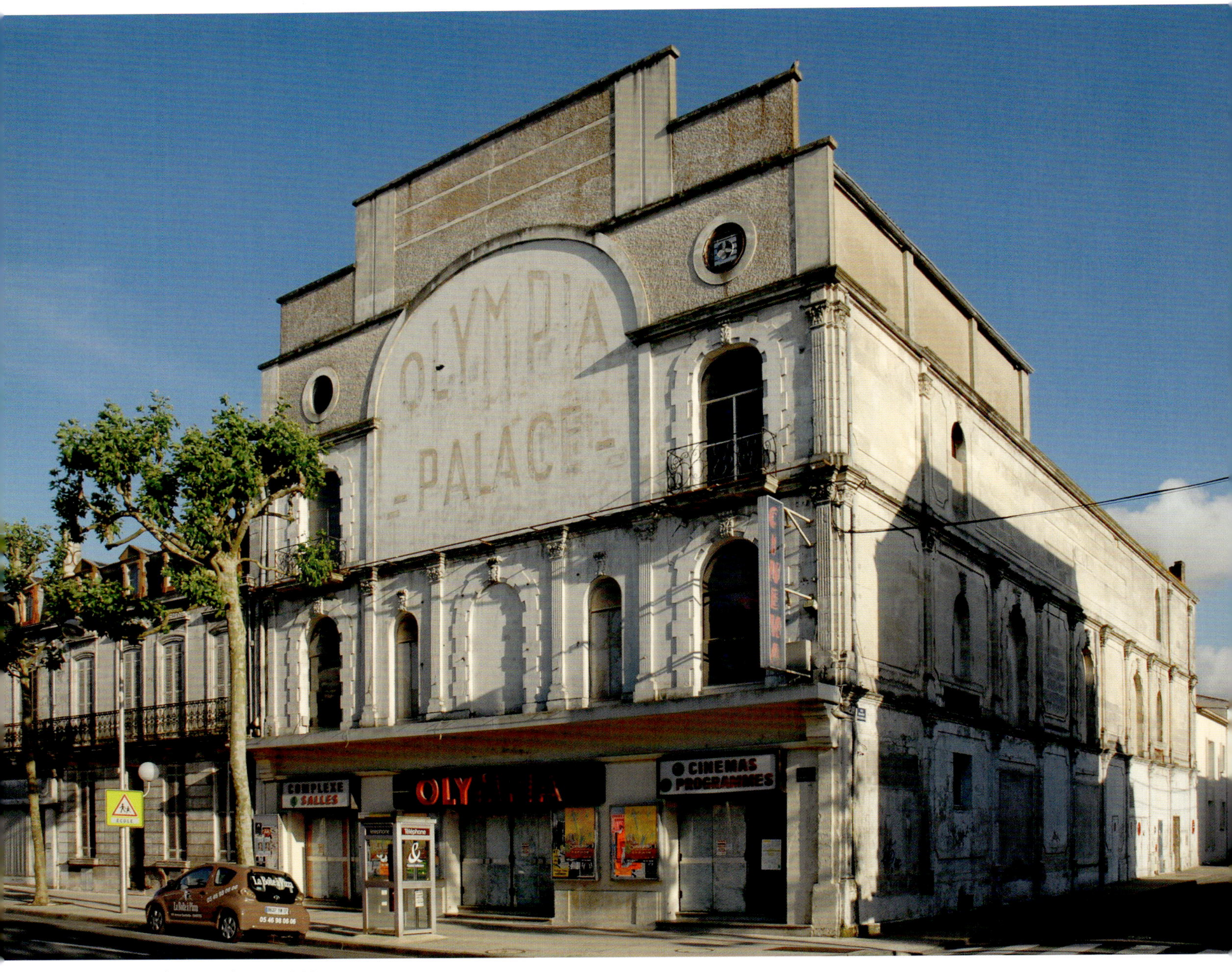

Saintes – Olympia Palace – 2008

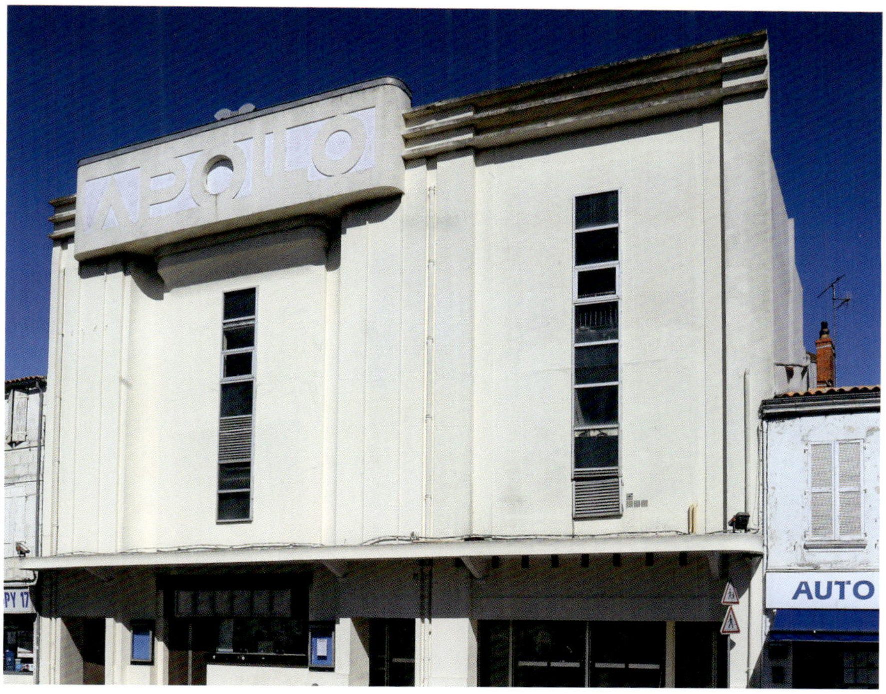

Rochefort – Apollo – 2016

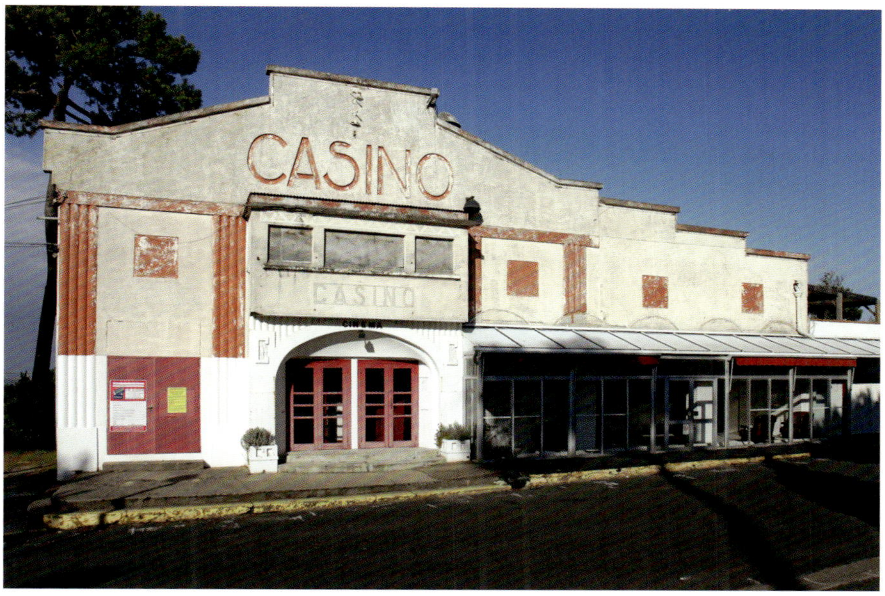

Saint-Trojan-les-Bains – Casino – 2014

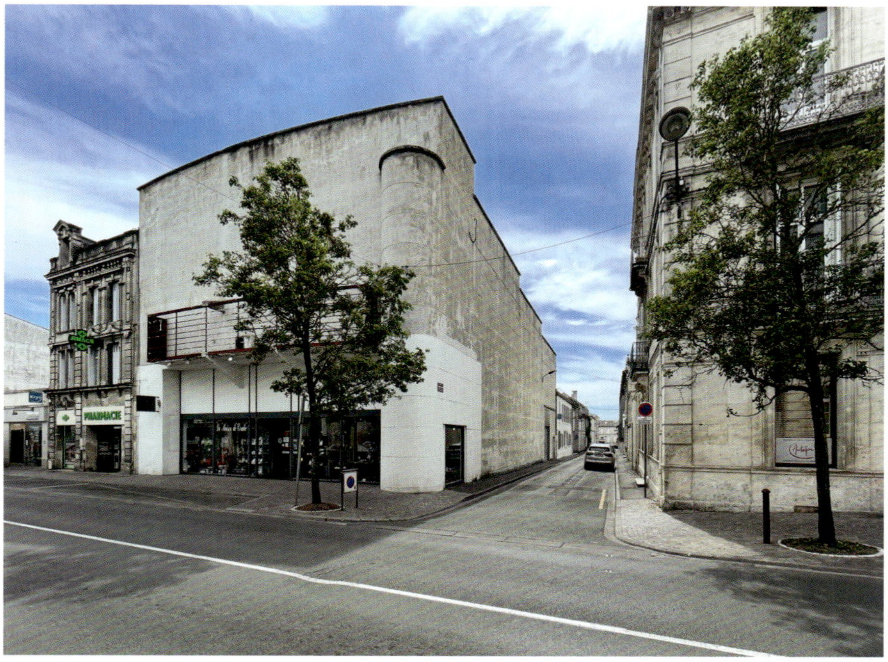

Cognac – Marignan – 2022

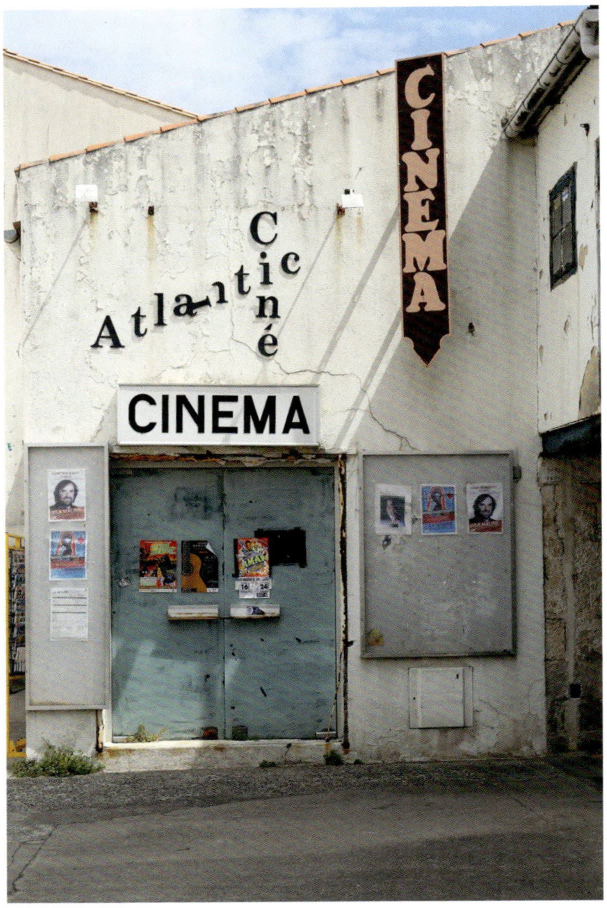

Saint-Martin-de-Ré – Atlantic Ciné – 2016

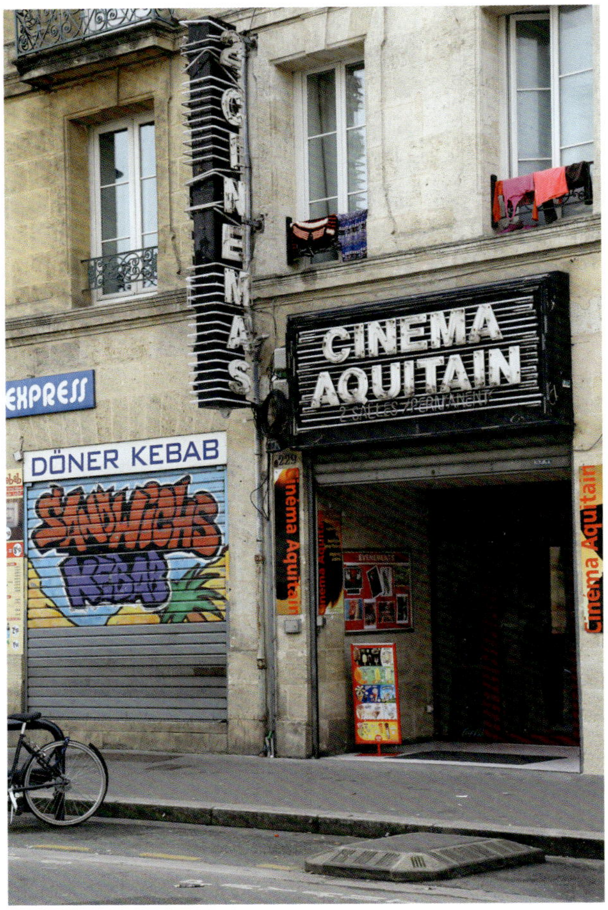

Bordeaux – Cinéma Aquitain – 2019 (destroyed)

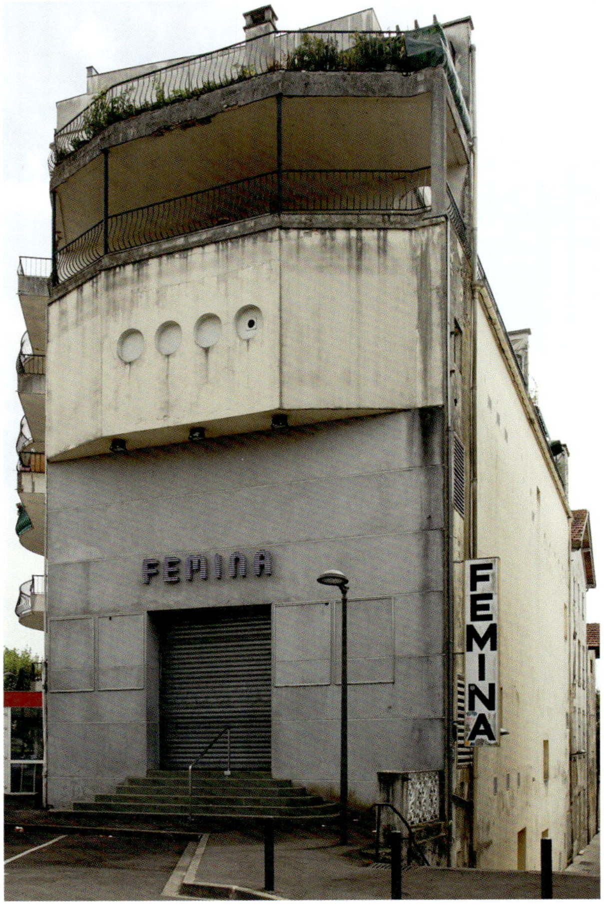

Dax – Femina – 2012

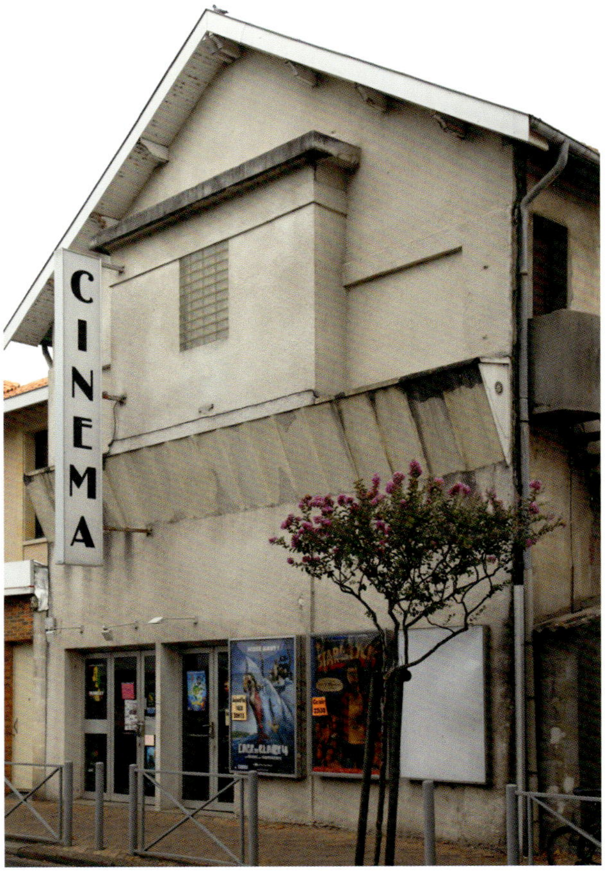

Andernos-les-Bains – Rex – 2012

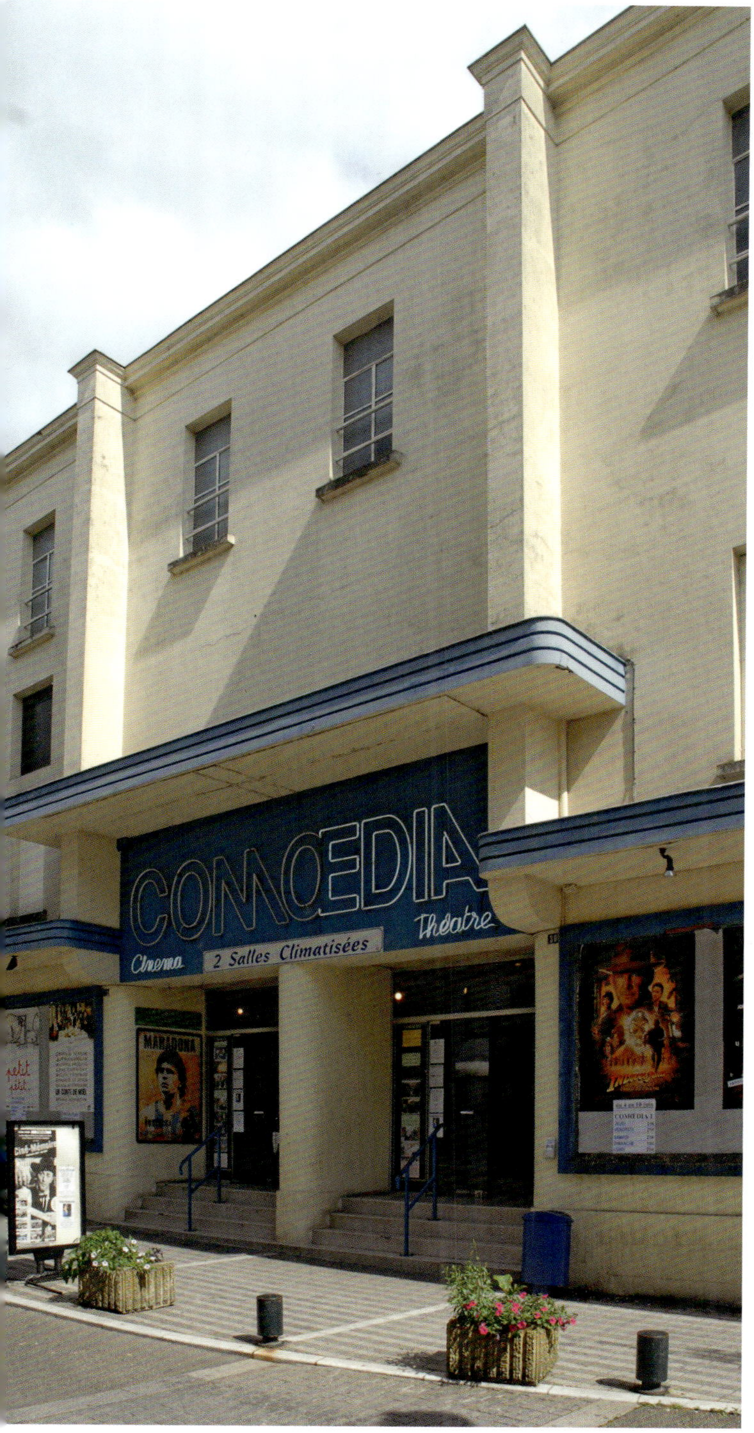

rmande – Comœdia – 2008

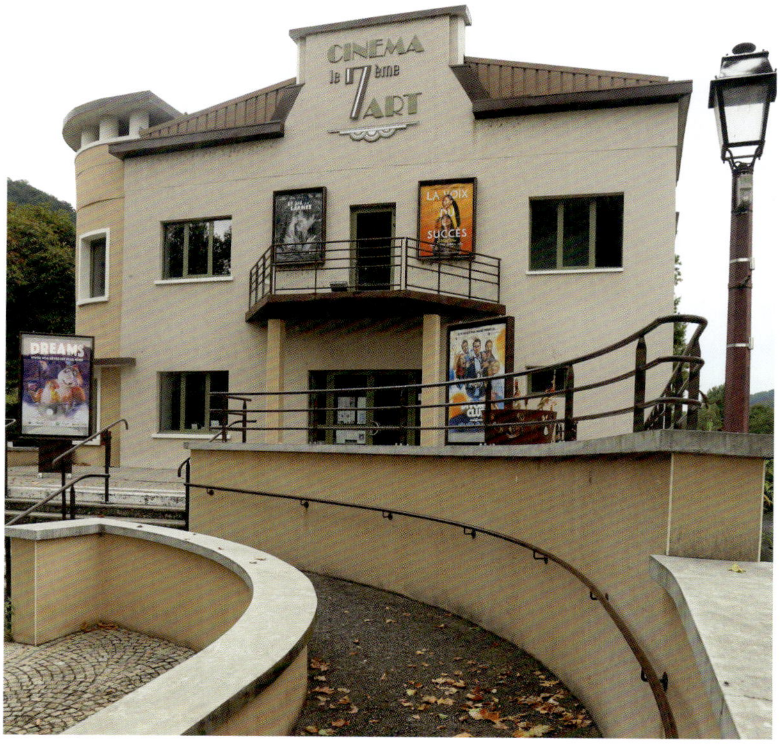

Bort-les-Orgues – Le 7ème Art – 2020

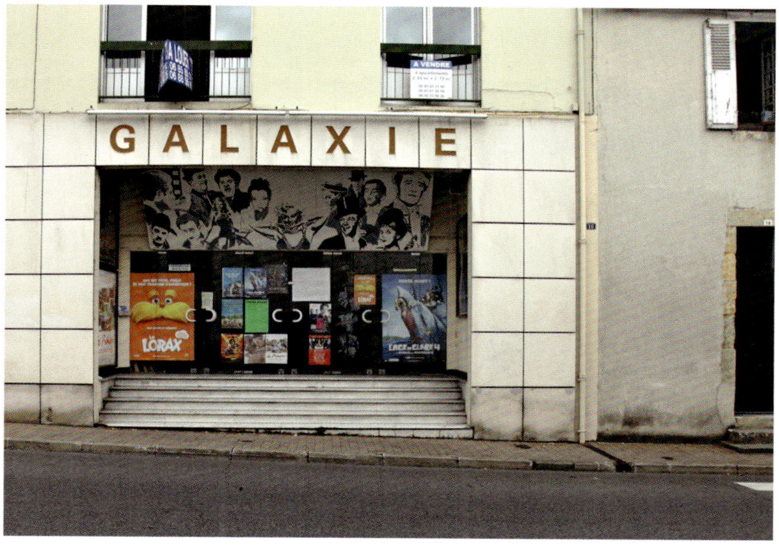

Aire-sur-l'Adour – Galaxie – 2012

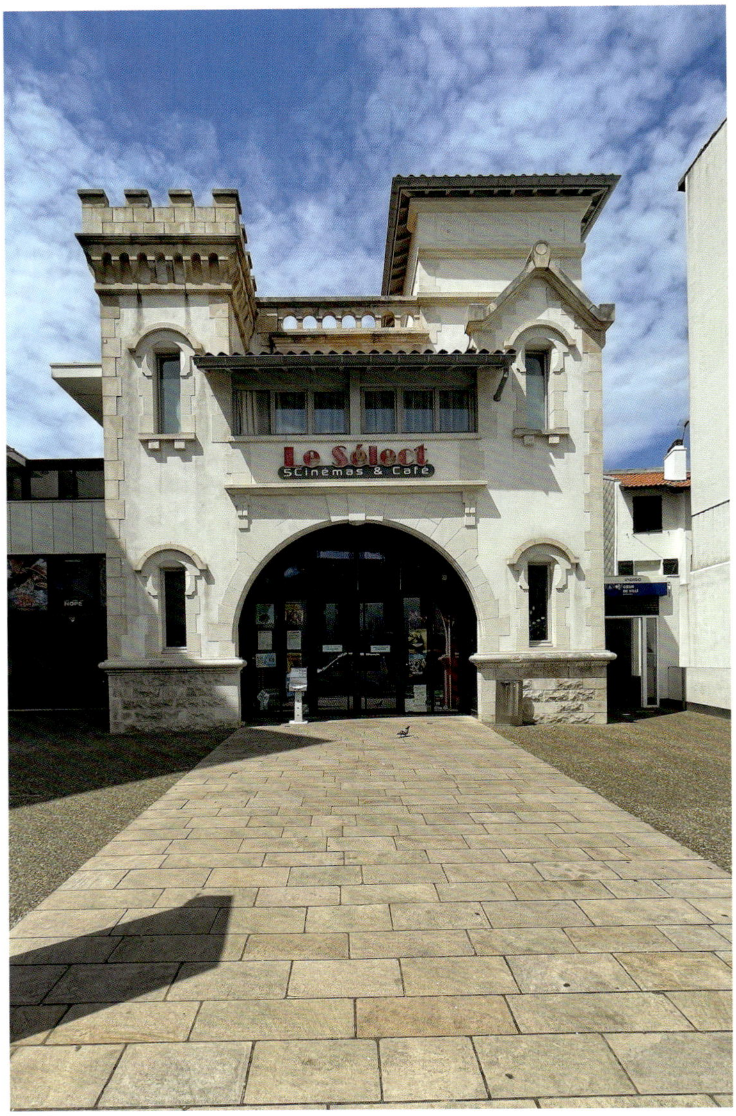

St-Jean-de-Luz – Le Sélect – 2022

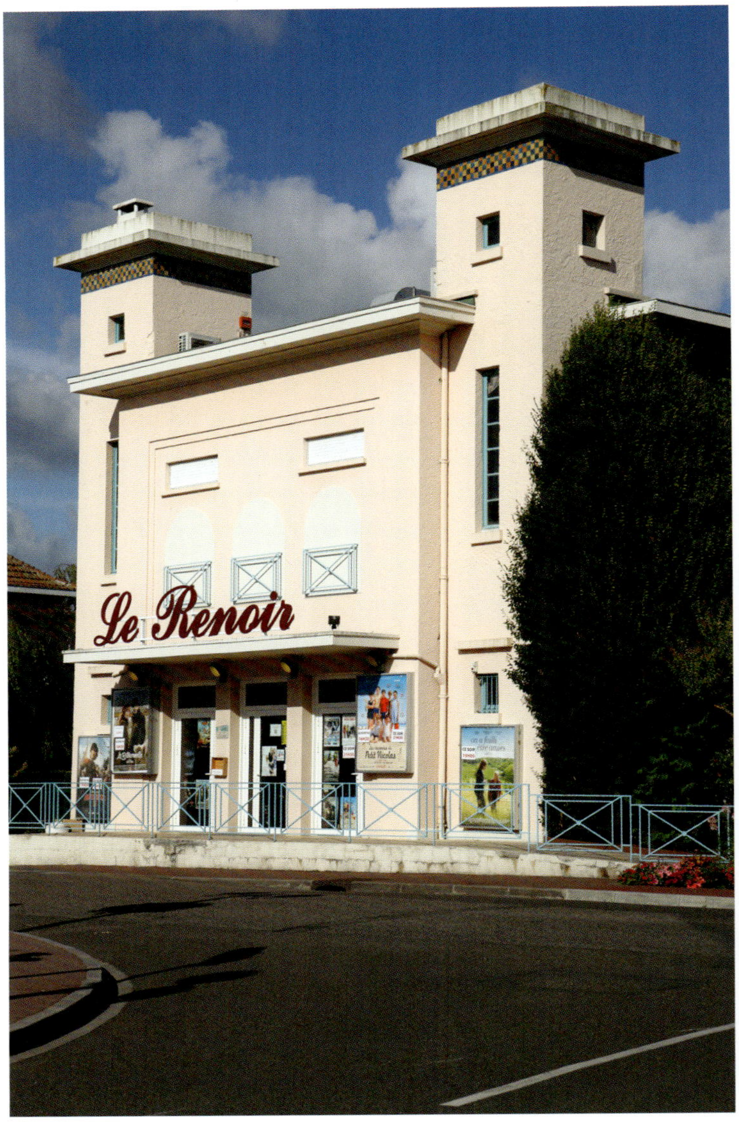

Biscarosse – Le Renoir – 2014

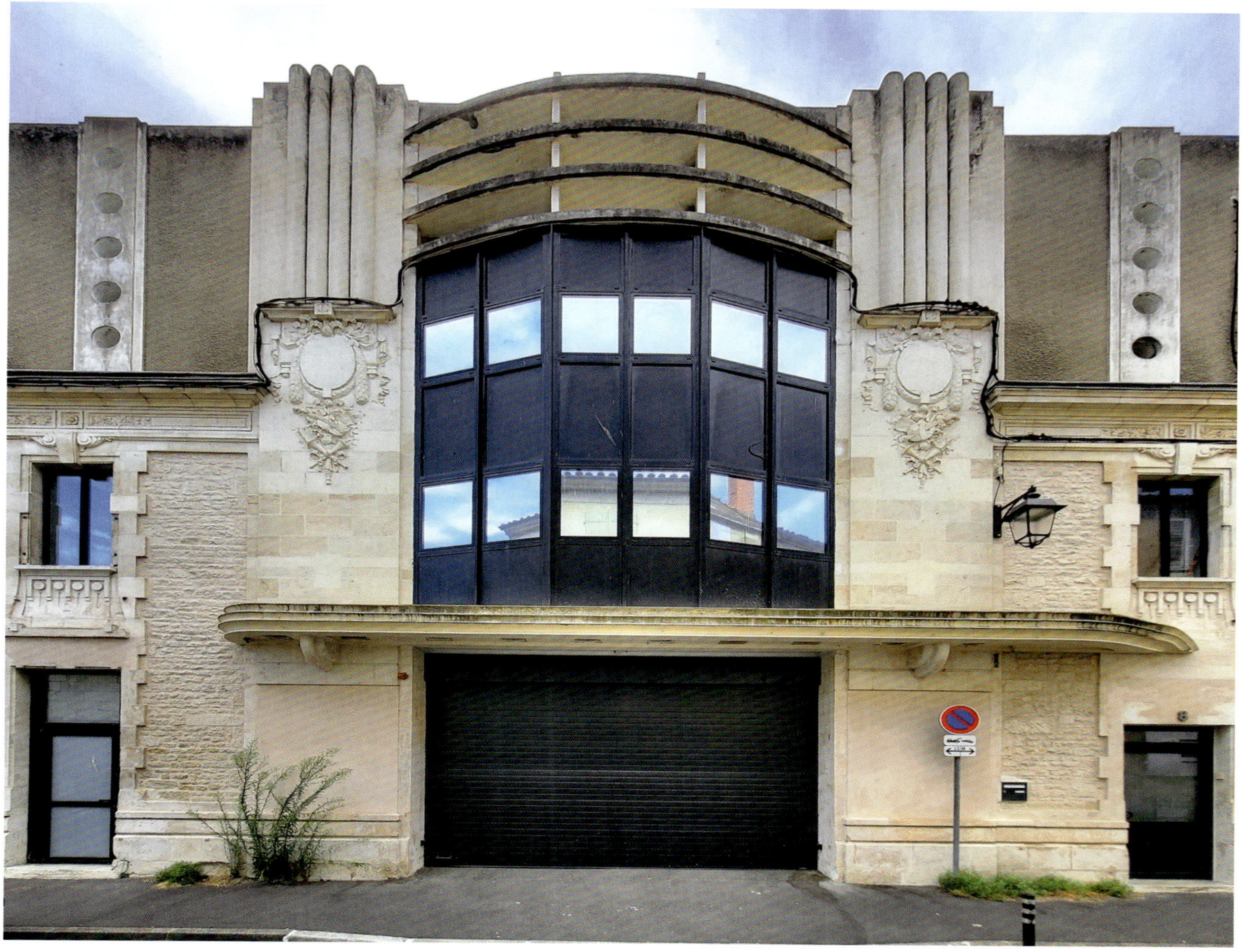

Niort – Eden – 2022

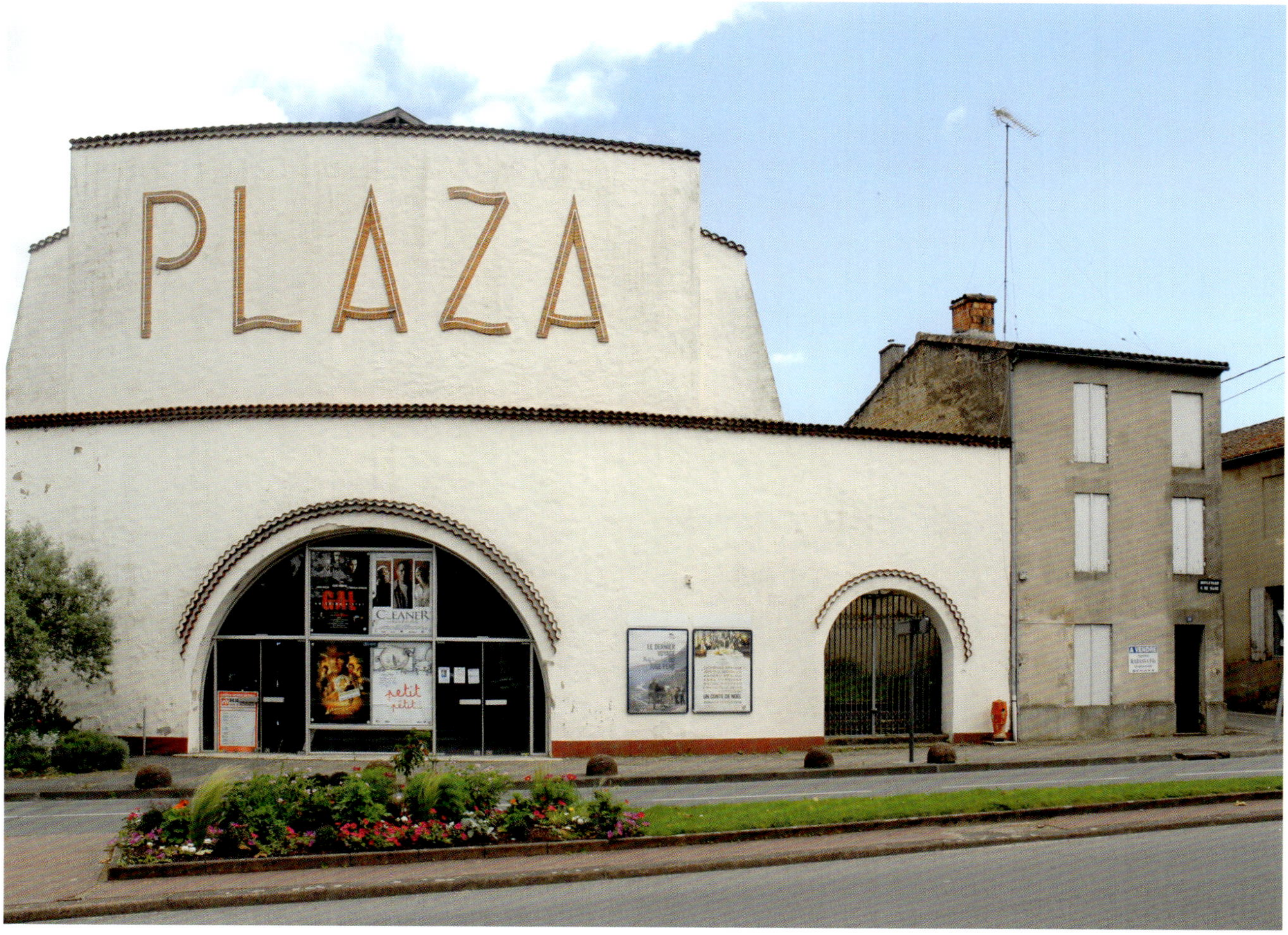

Marmande – Plaza – 2008

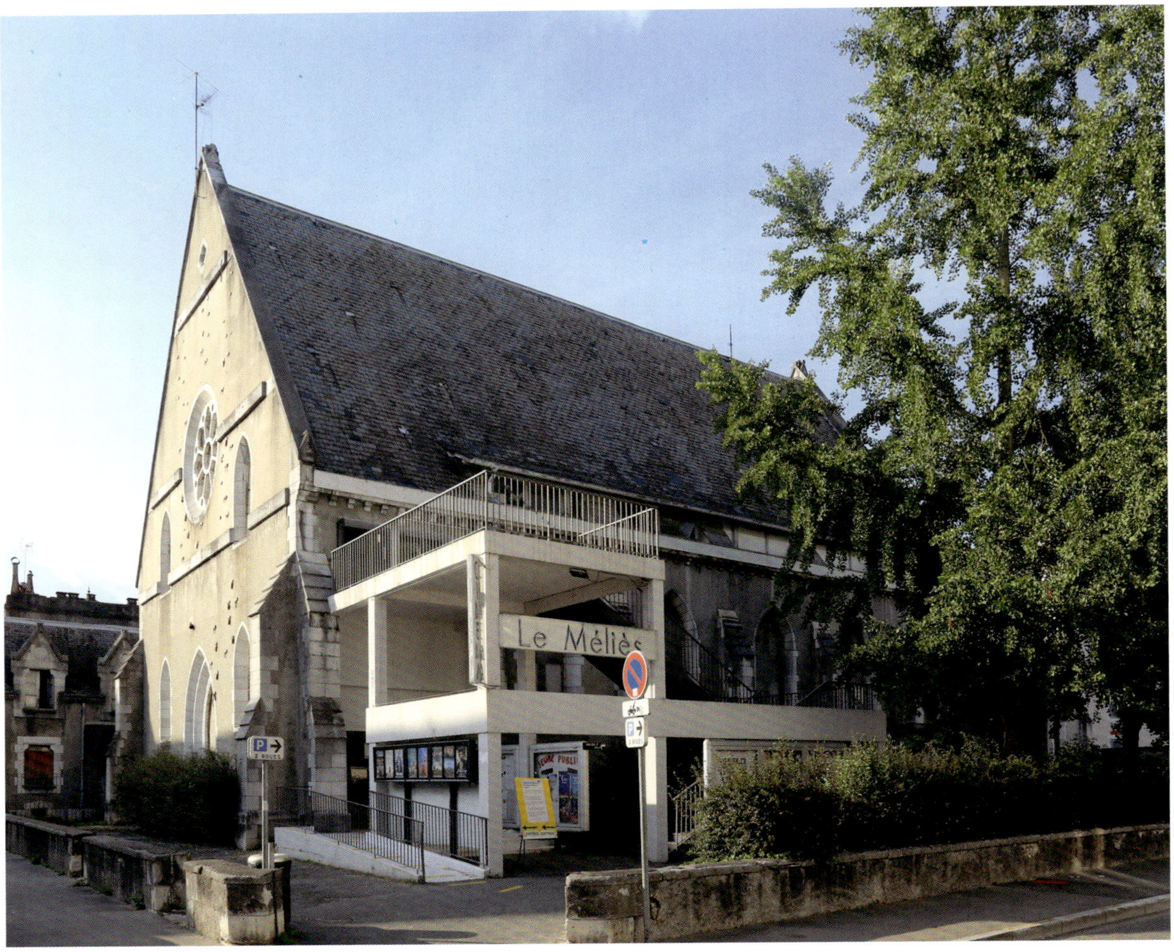

Pau – Le Méliès – 2021

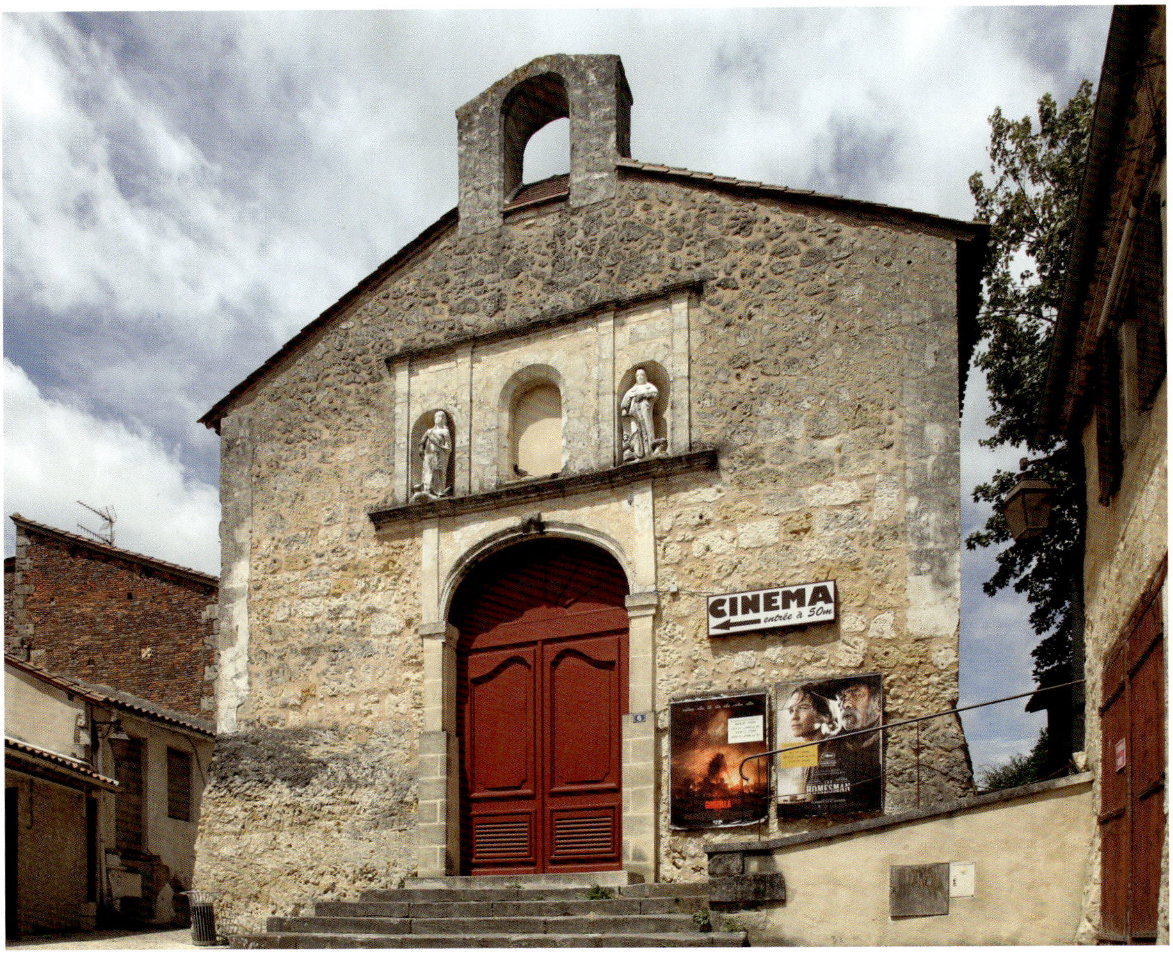

Mussidan – Notre Dame – 2014

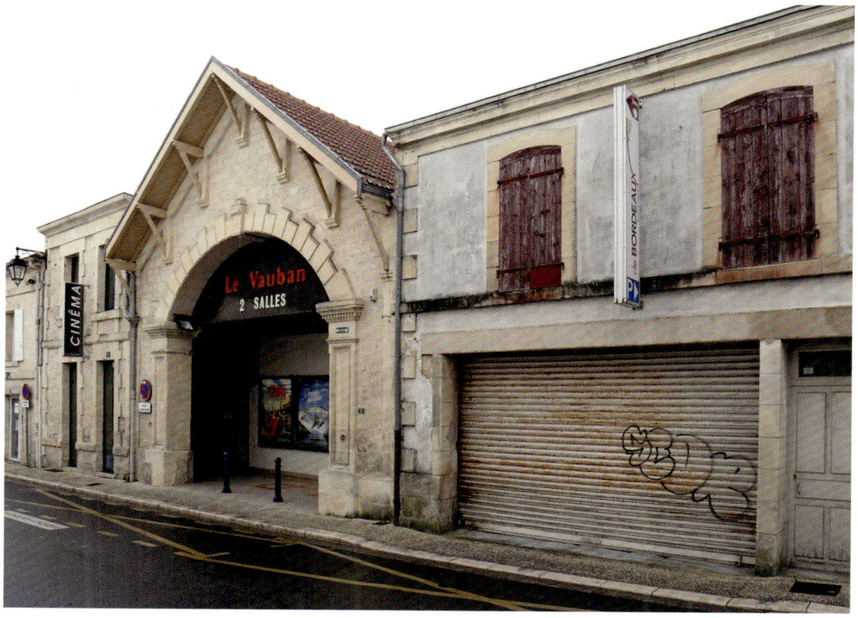

Pons – Le Vauban – 2019

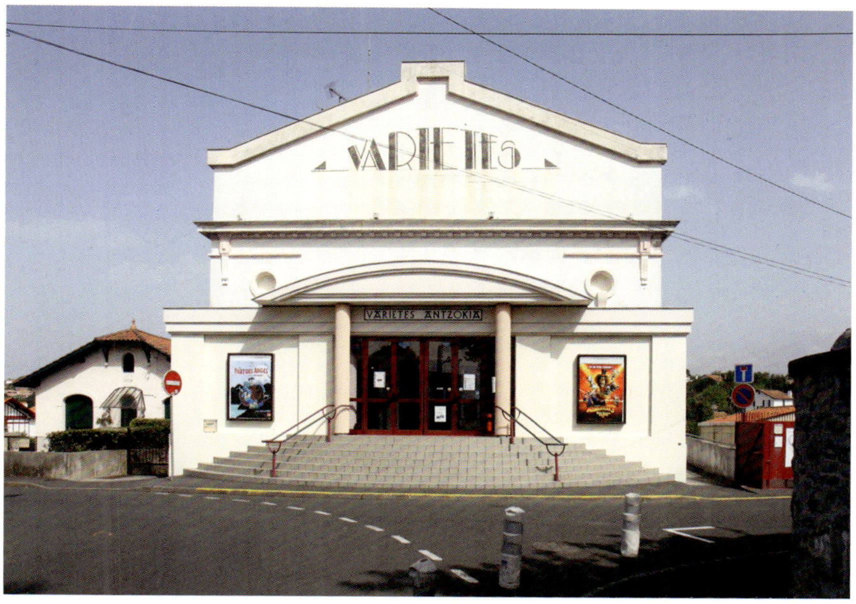

Hendaye – Variétés – 2012

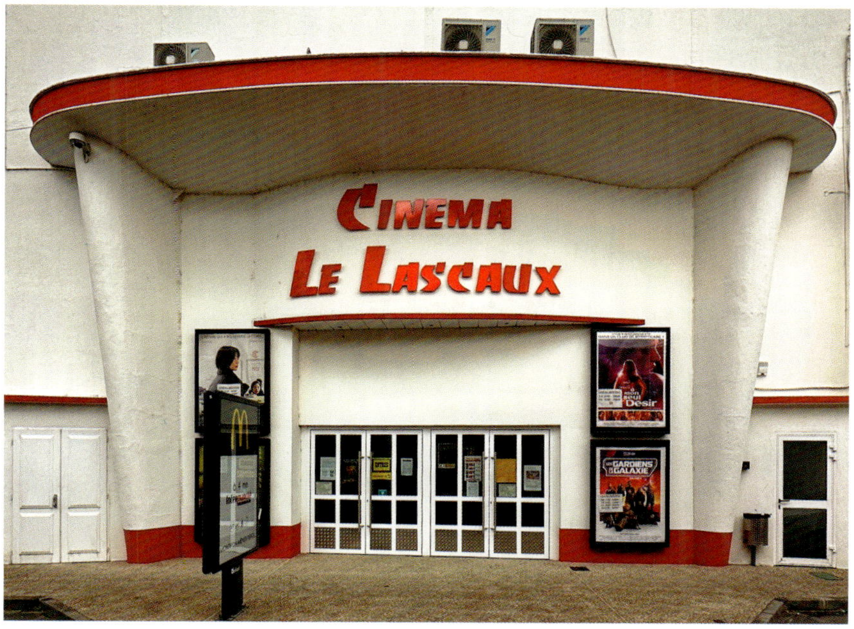

Montpon-Ménestérol – Le Lascaux – 2023

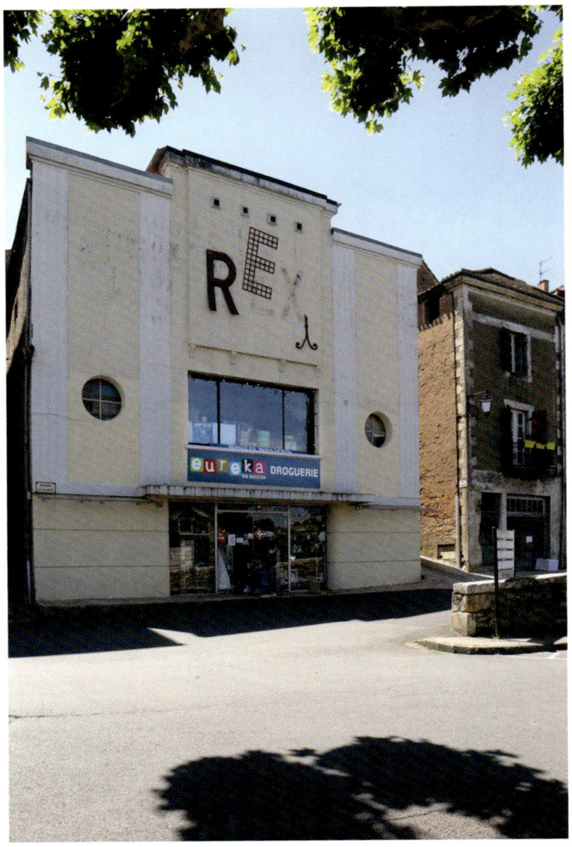

Belves – Rex – 2021

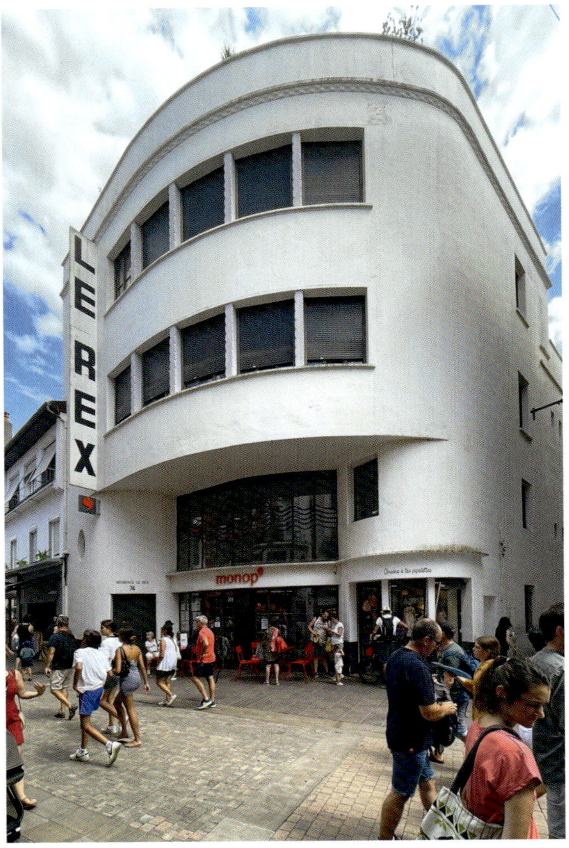

Saint-Jean-de-Luz – Le Rex – 2022

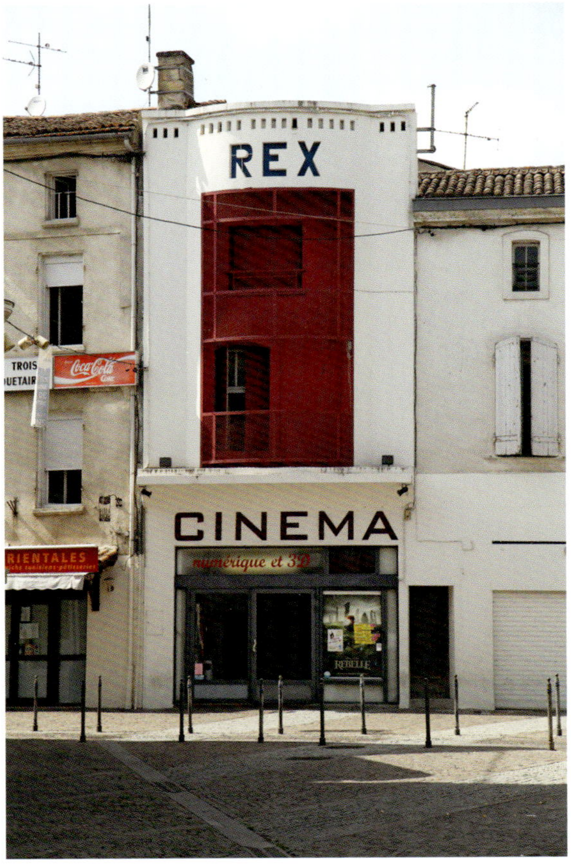

La Réole – Rex – 2012

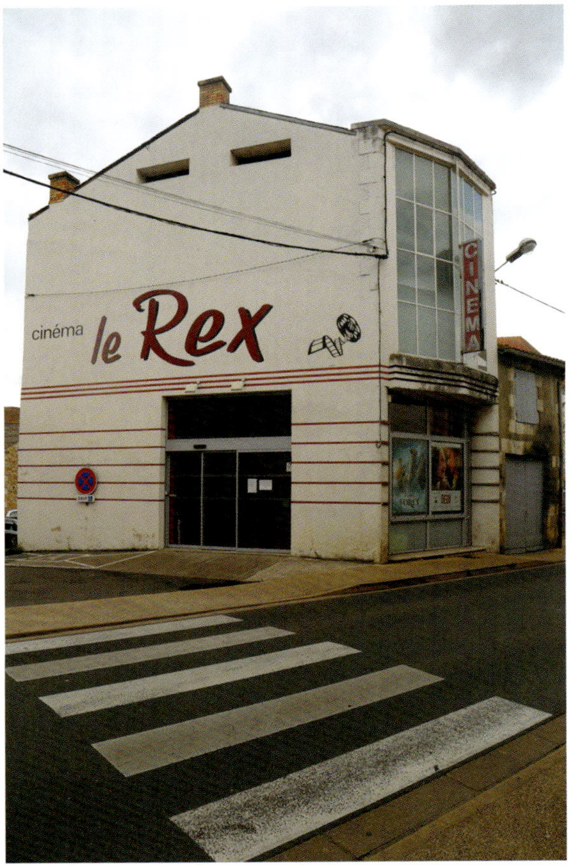

Chauvigny – Le Rex – 2020

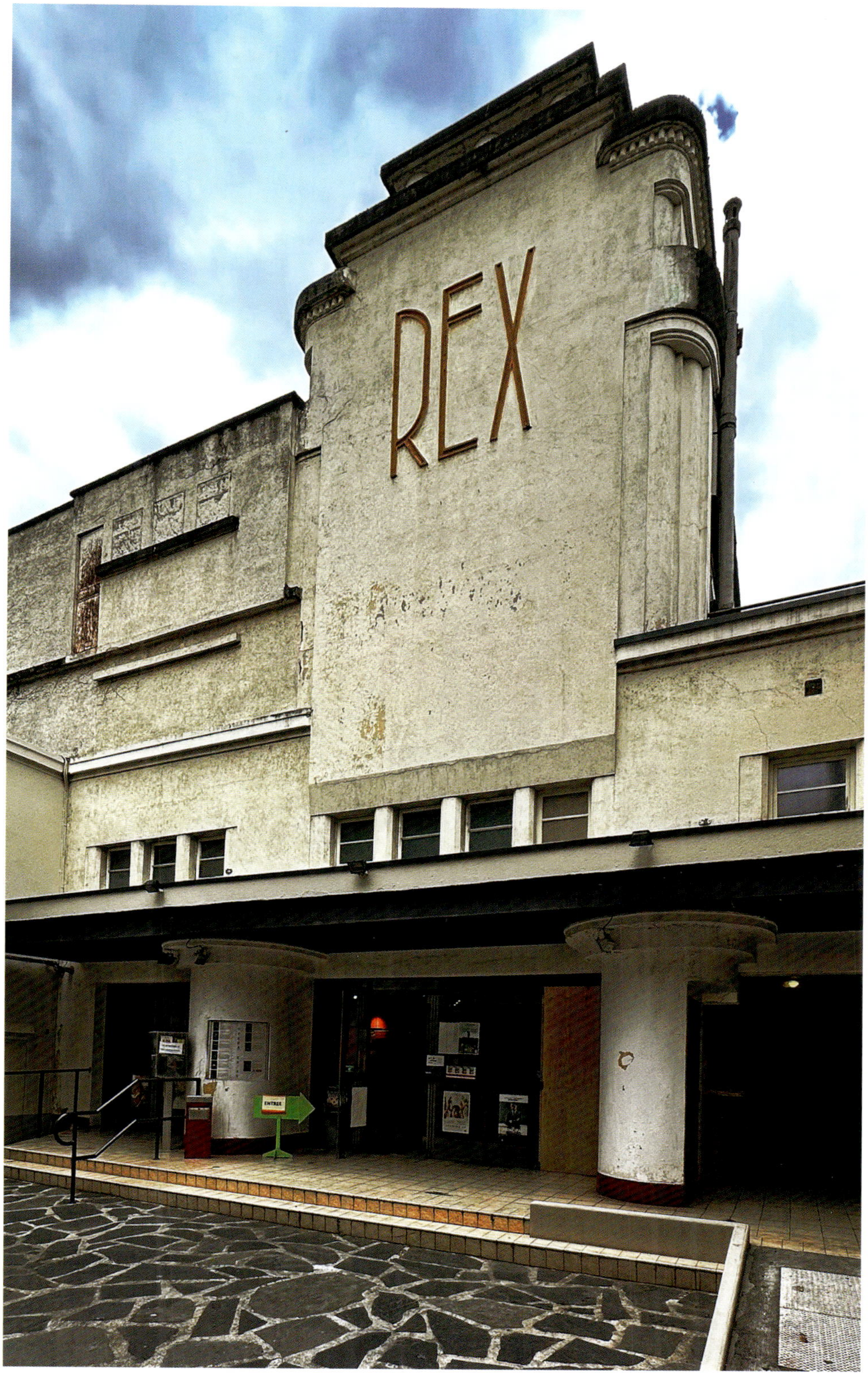

Brive-la-Gaillarde – Rex – 2014

Brive-la-Gaillarde, Rex. Built by architect C.-J. Villiéras, the Rex opened in 1936. The reinforced concrete infrastructure with its refined Art Deco geometric shapes is reminiscent of the ocean liner style with decks and portholes. In 2005, the cinema was listed in the inventory of historical monuments.

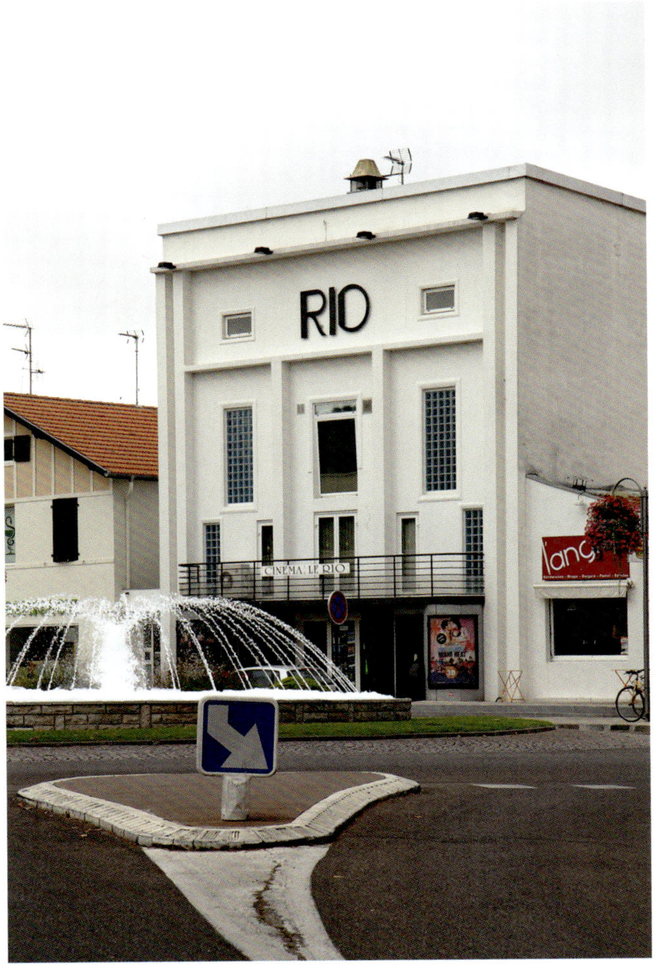

Cap Breton – Rio – 2012

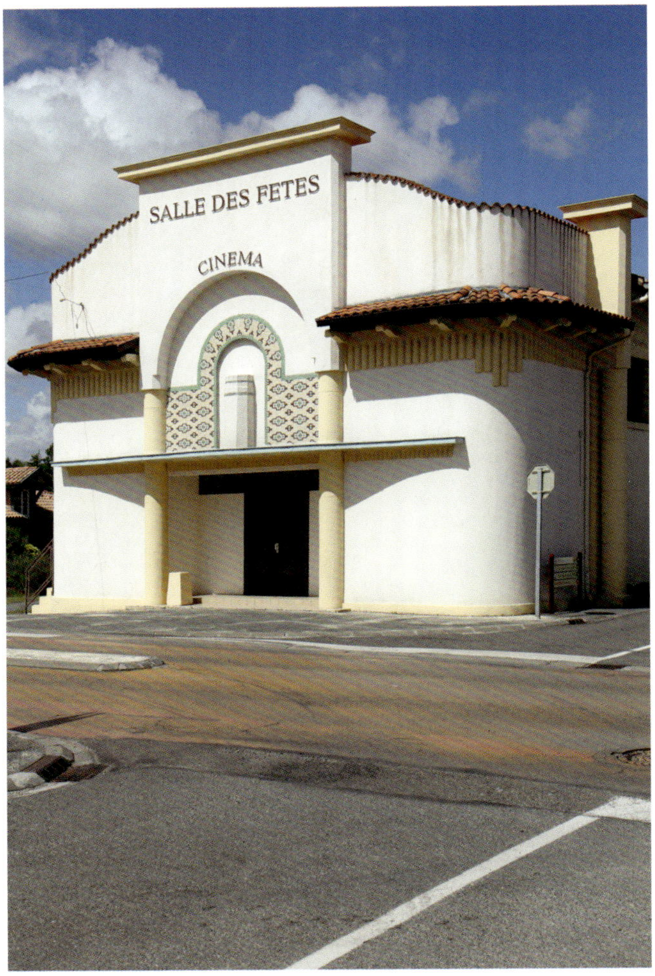

Linxe – cinéma – 2014

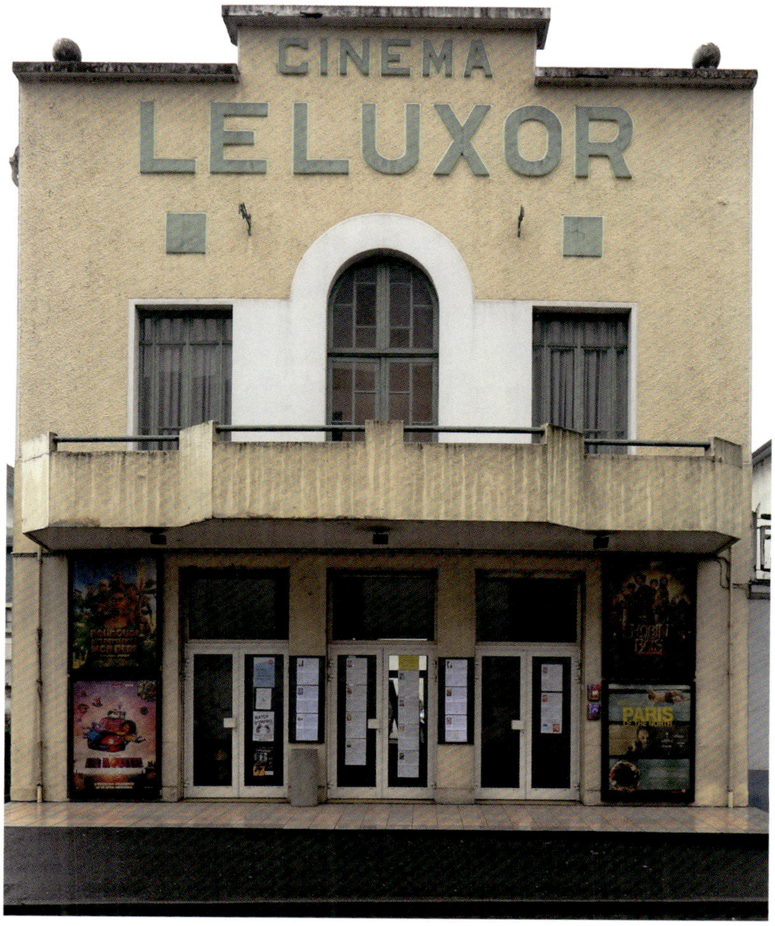

Oloron-Sainte-Marie – Le Luxor – 2015

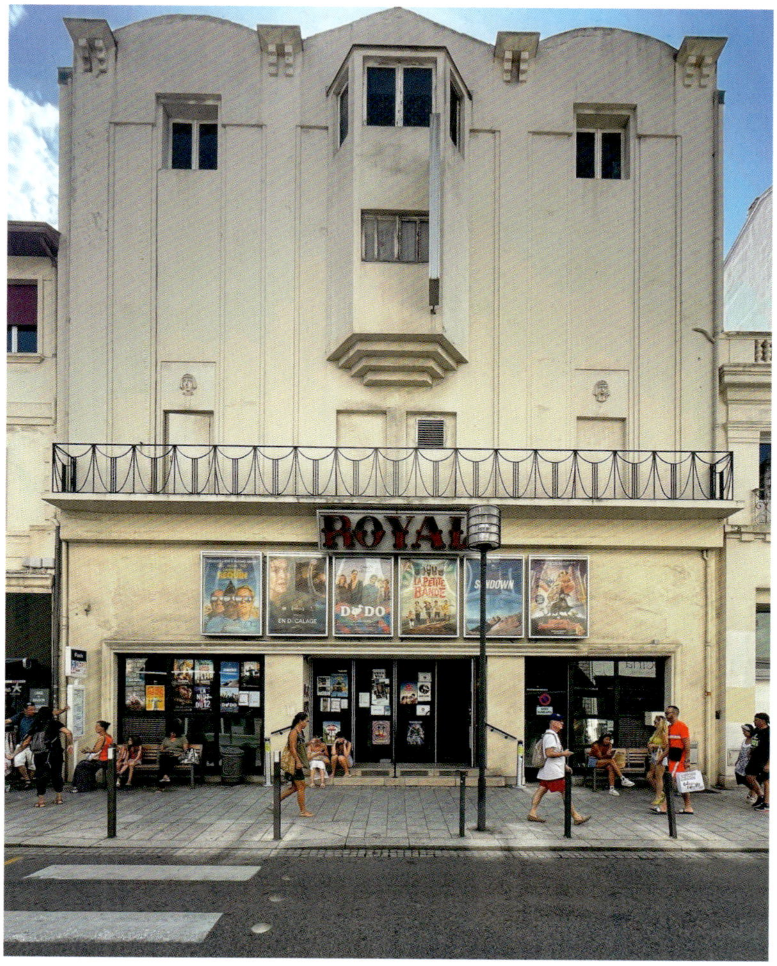

Biarritz – Royal – 2022

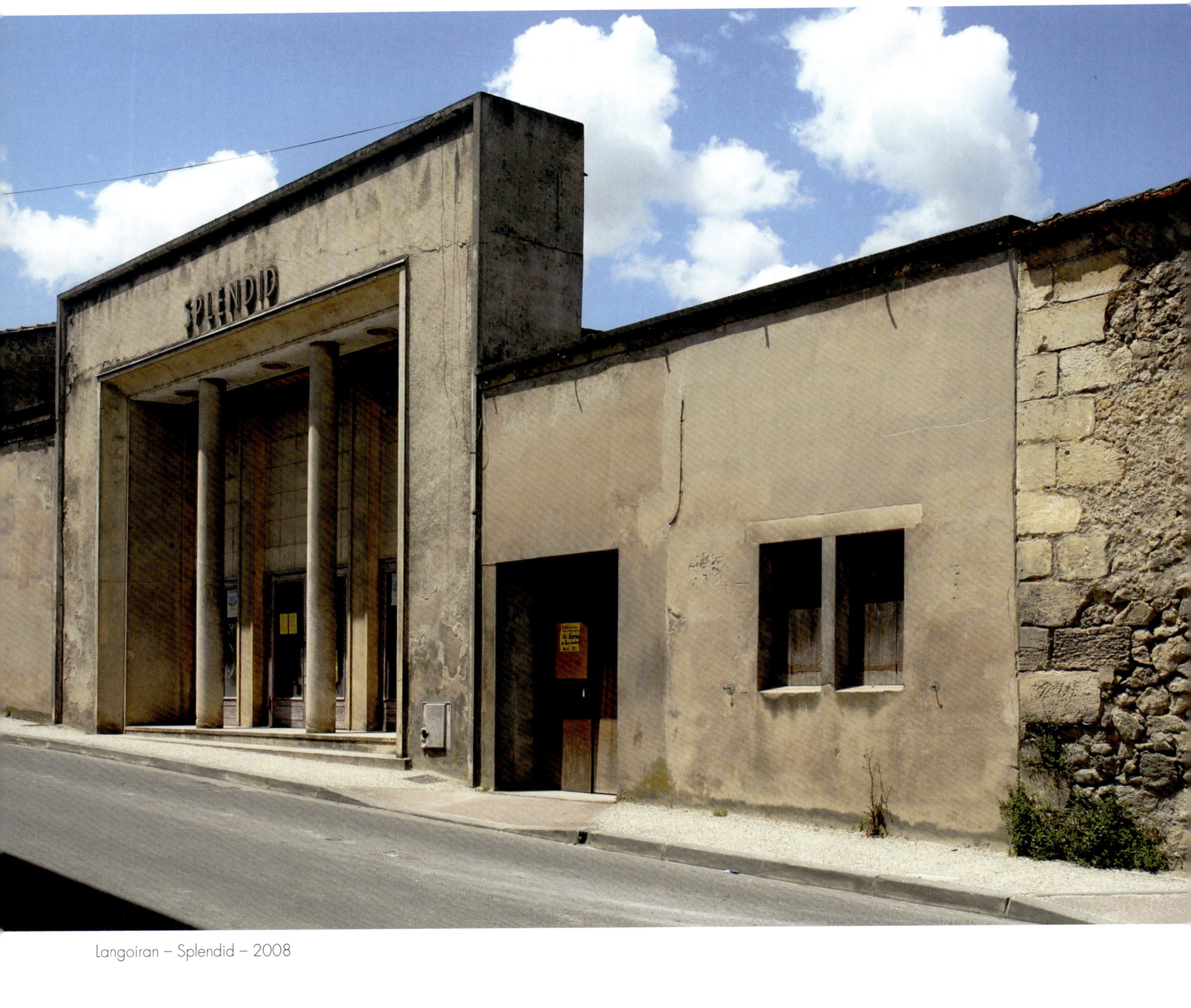

Langoiran – Splendid – 2008

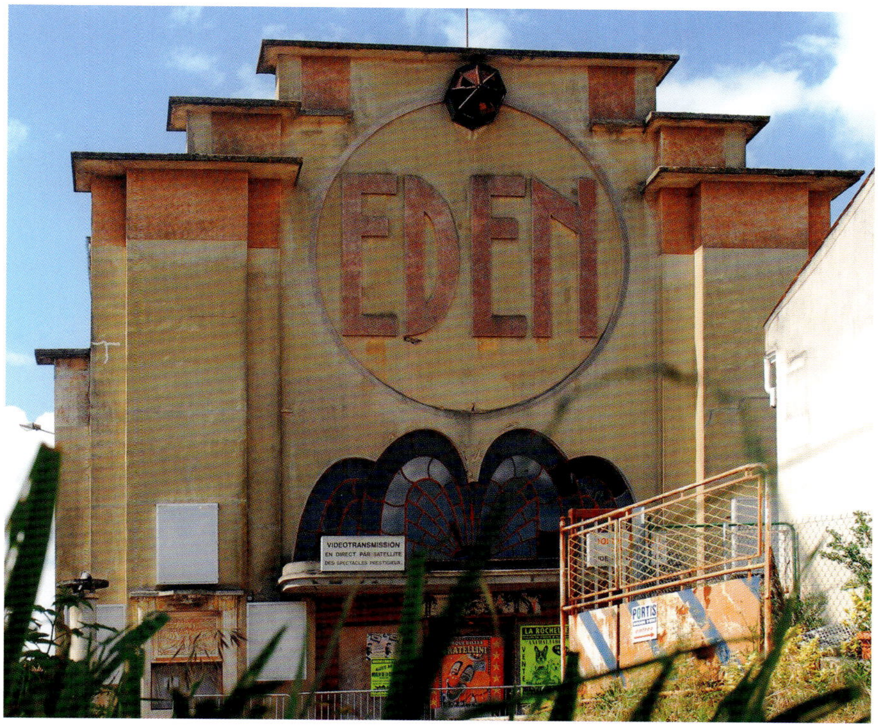

2008

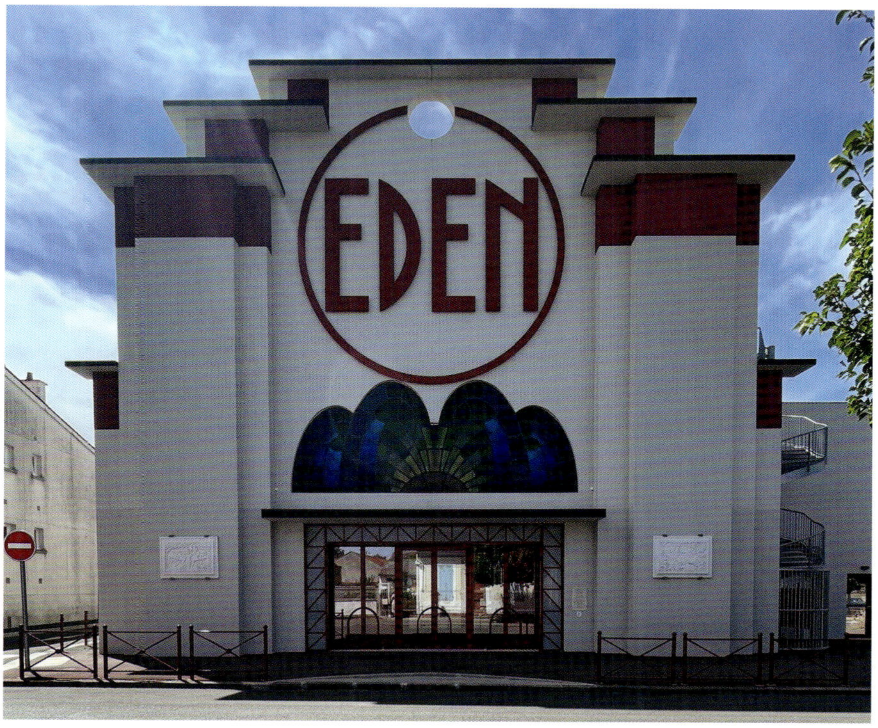

Saint-Jean-d'Angely – Eden – 2022

Saint-Jean-d'Angely, Eden. The Eden cinema, with its sublime Art Deco architecture, opened in 1931. In 2004, as often happens, the building fell victim to dilapidation and procrastinating local authorities and began a slow agony. Depredation, negligence and fire in 2014. The main façade collapsed and as a result the cinema disappeared from the landscape. An identical Eden opened in May 2018, rebuilt with a varied programme. In this turmoil, the cinema has lost the charm of passing time, but lives again rather like an orphaned child in search of its soul. Perhaps it will regain the original allure as it ages.

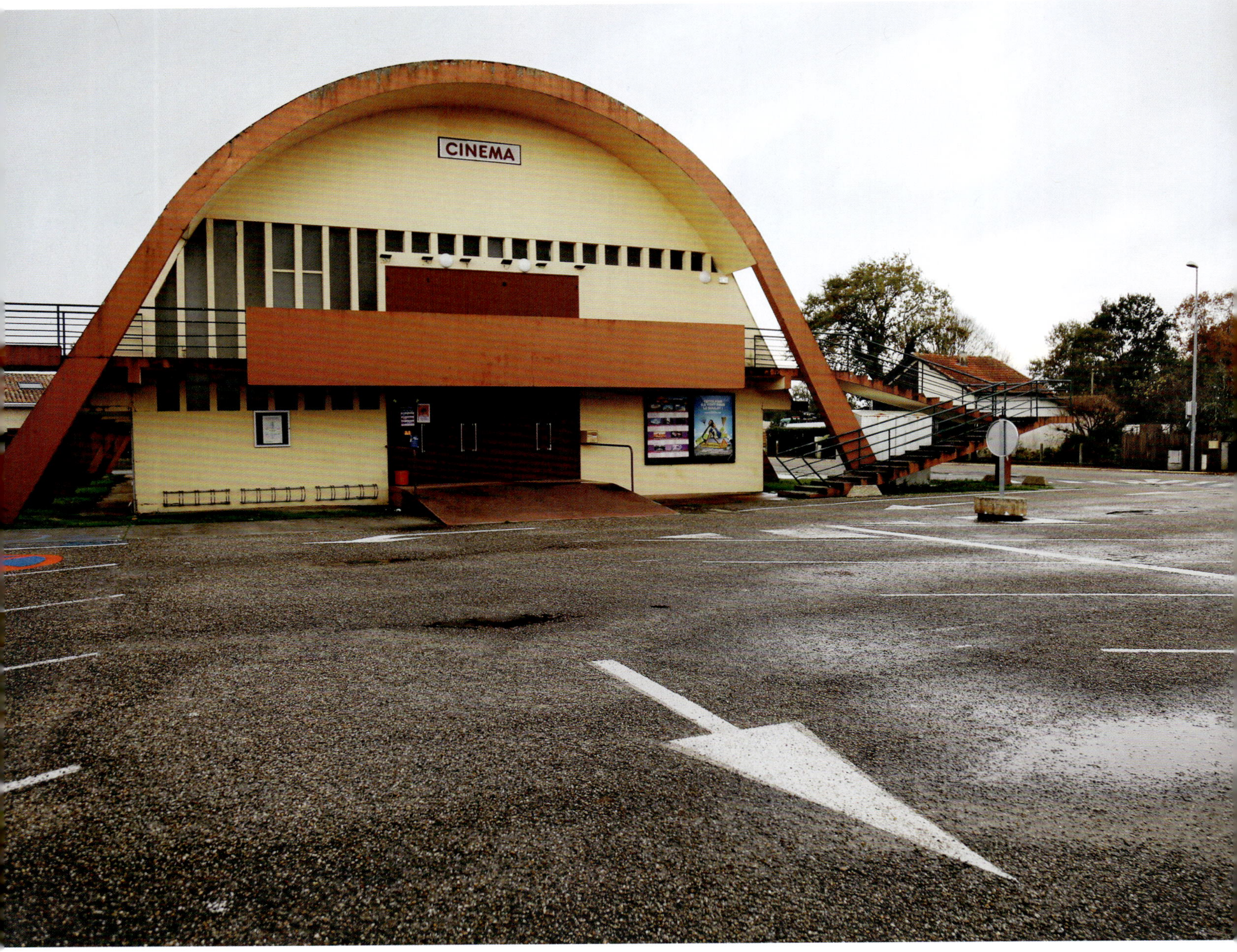

Hourtin – Lou Hapchot – 2019

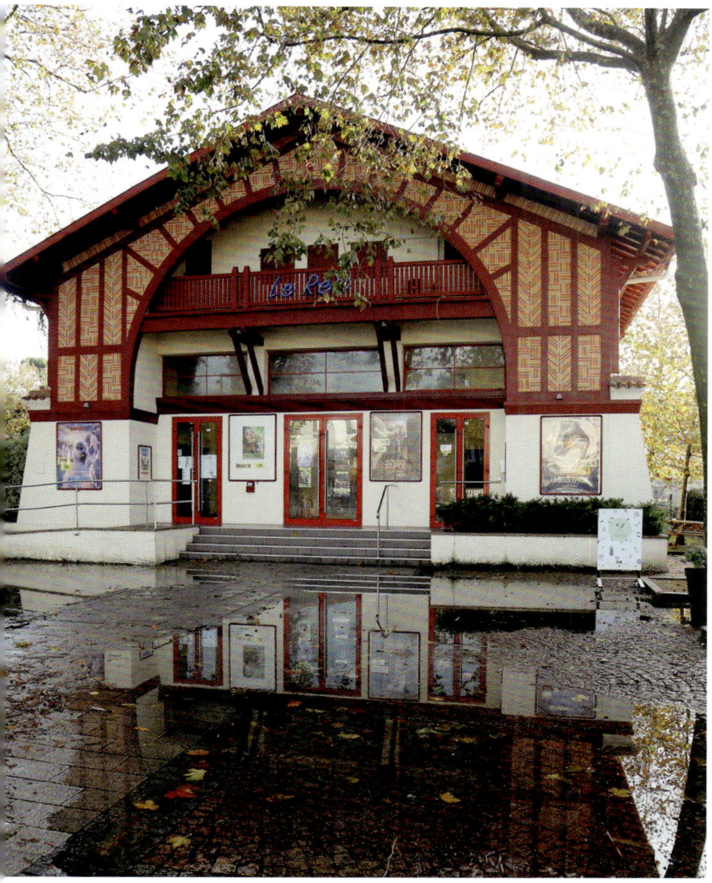

ssegor – Rex – 2019

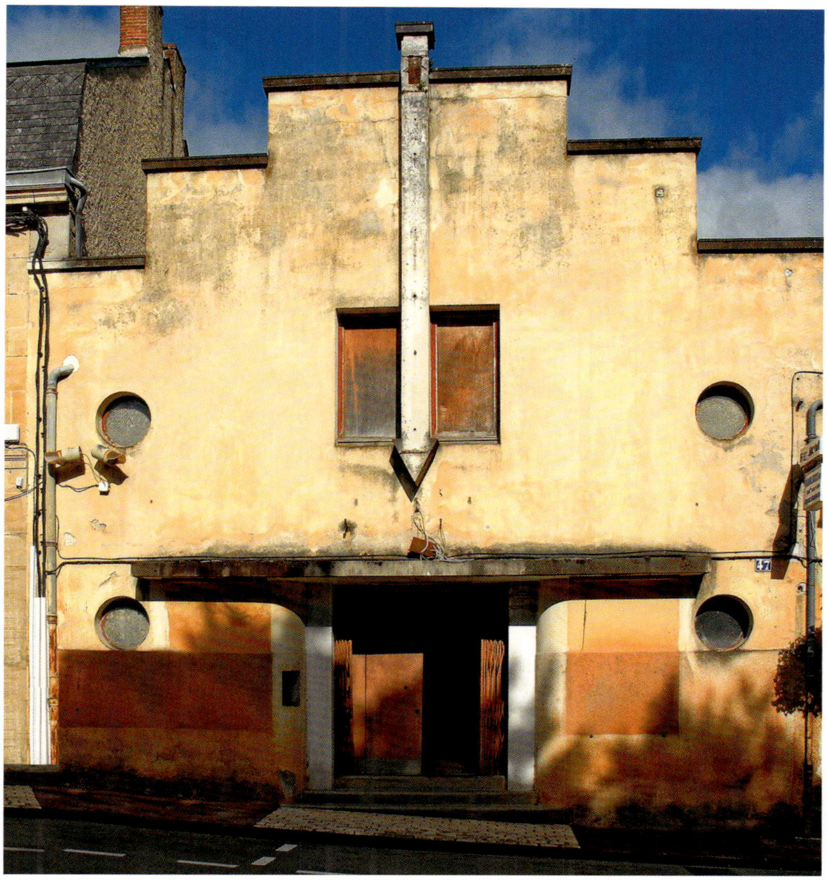

Thiviers – Rex – 2009

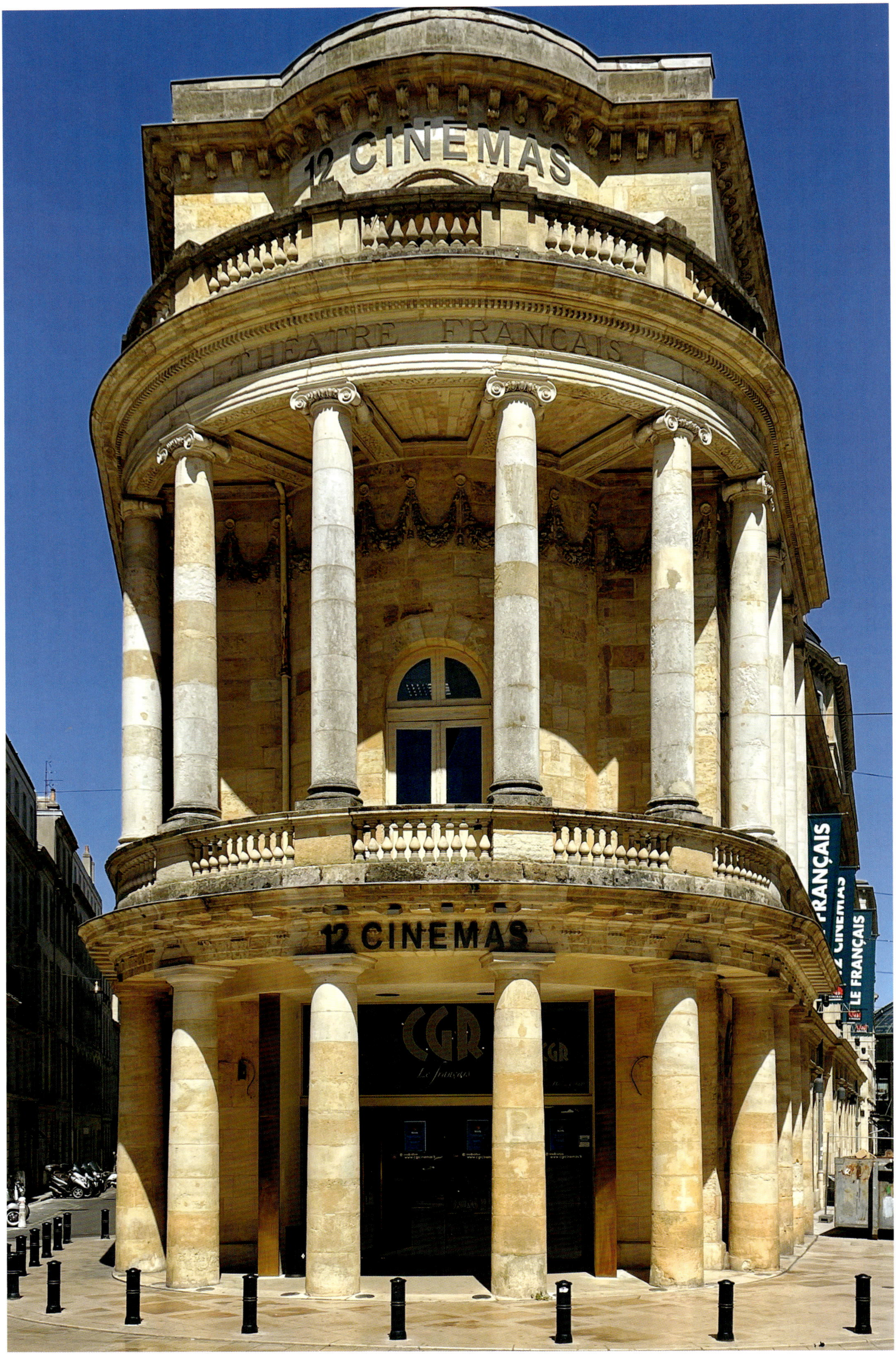

Bordeaux – Le Français – 2022

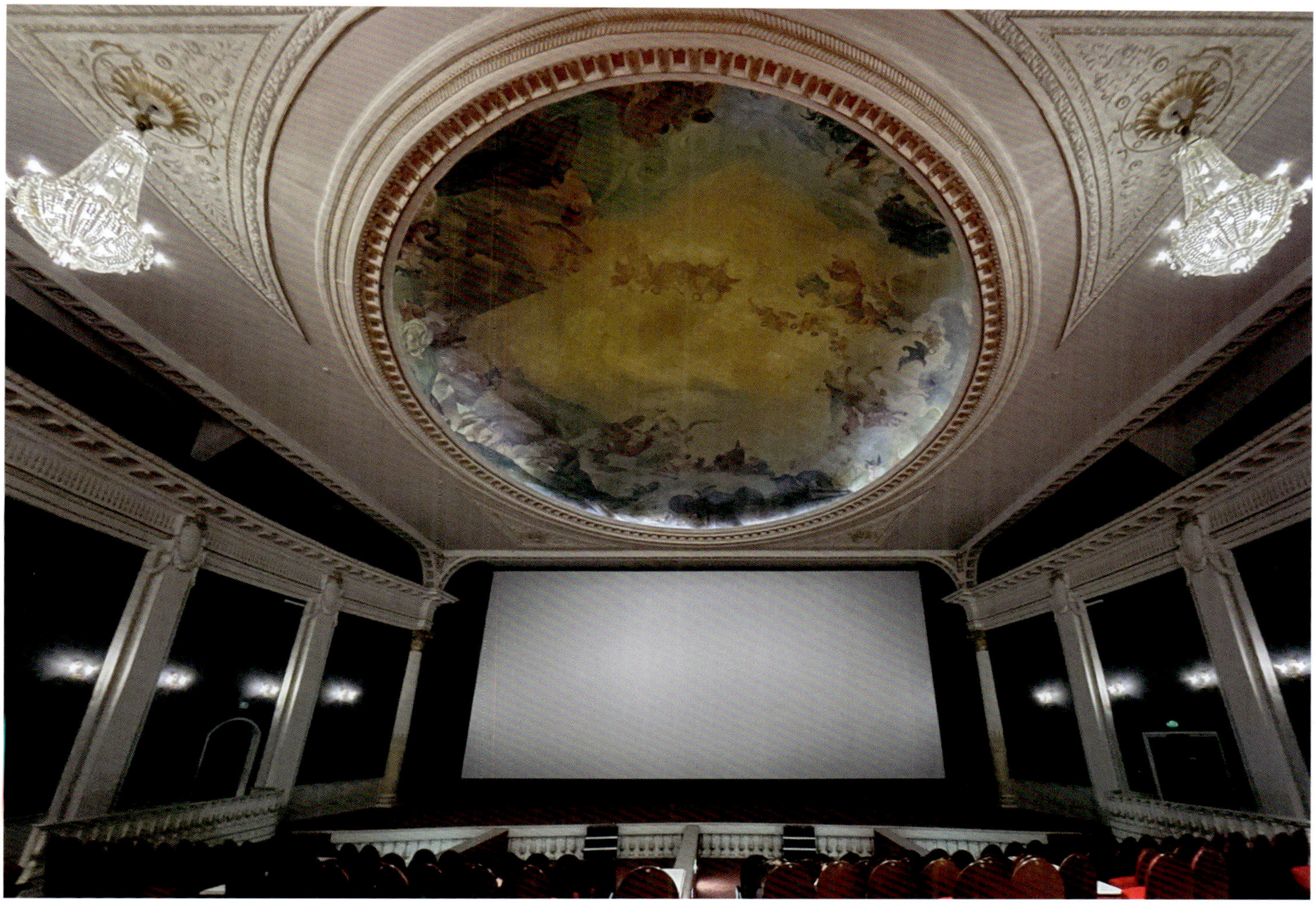

Bordeaux – Le Français – 2022

Bordeaux, Le Français. In Bordeaux beautiful theatres have become memories. The opening of Le Français in 2010 in an elegant former 19th-century theatre is seen as a true cinematic renaissance. The listed main hall is as fine a spectacle as any masterpiece that might be projected on its screen.

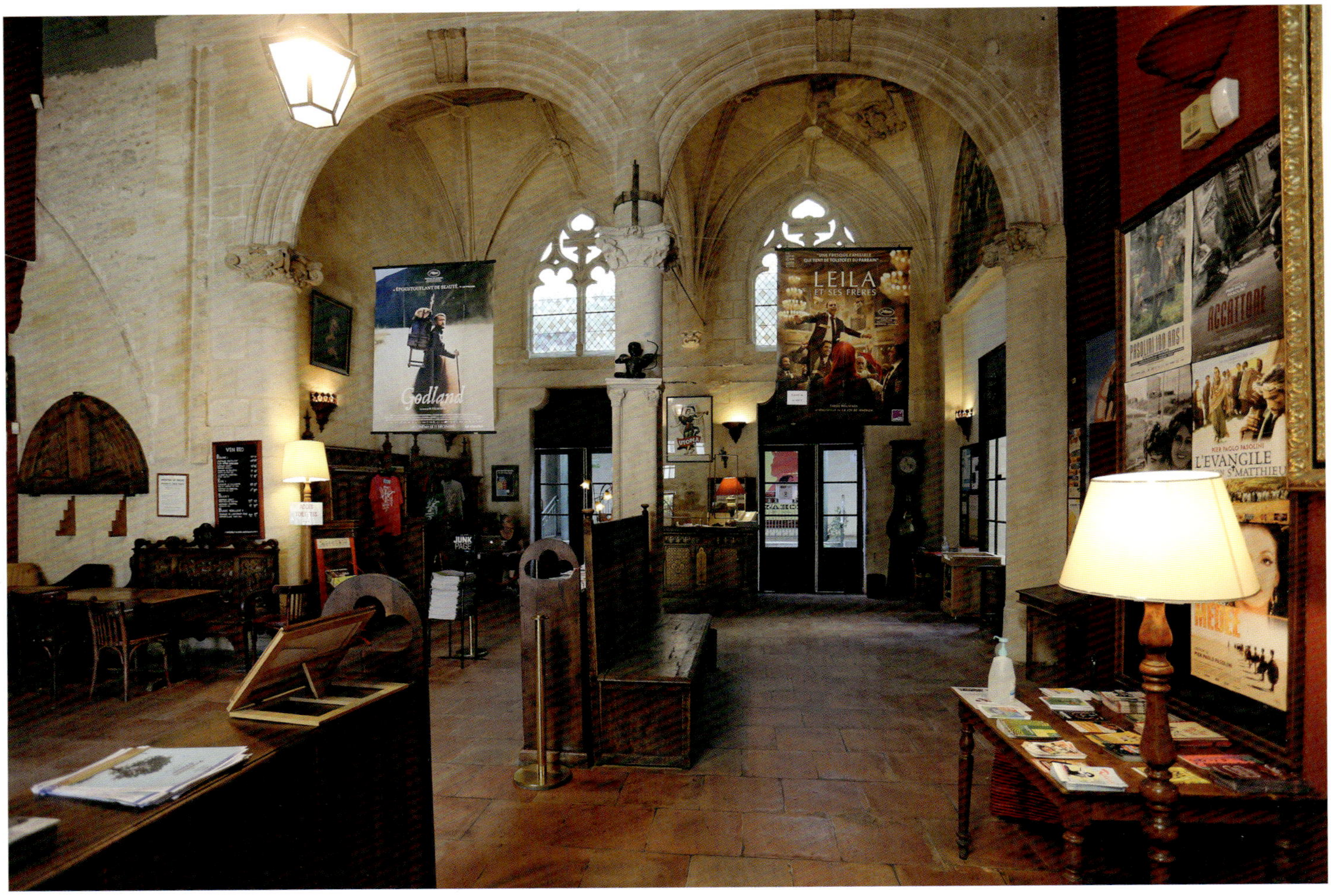

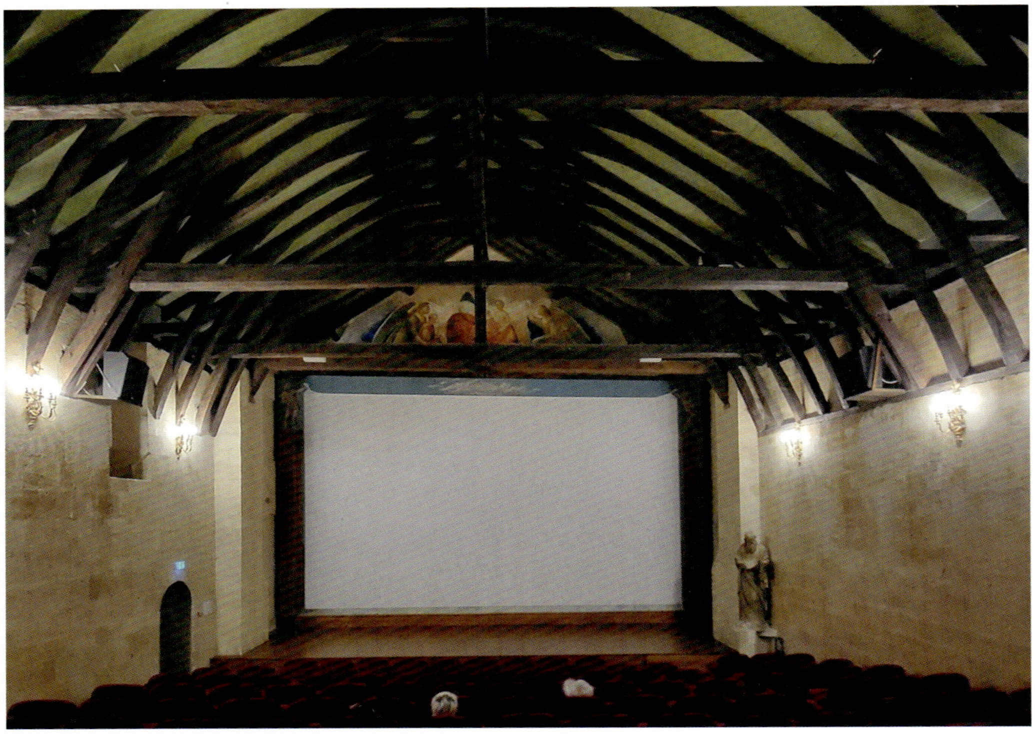

Bordeaux – Utopia – 2022

Bordeaux, Utopia. The Utopia cinema, a five-screen complex, opened in 1999 in the former Saint-Siméon church. The building, dating from the 14th to 16th centuries, had been disused since the French Revolution. Utopia cinemas are now found in six cities.

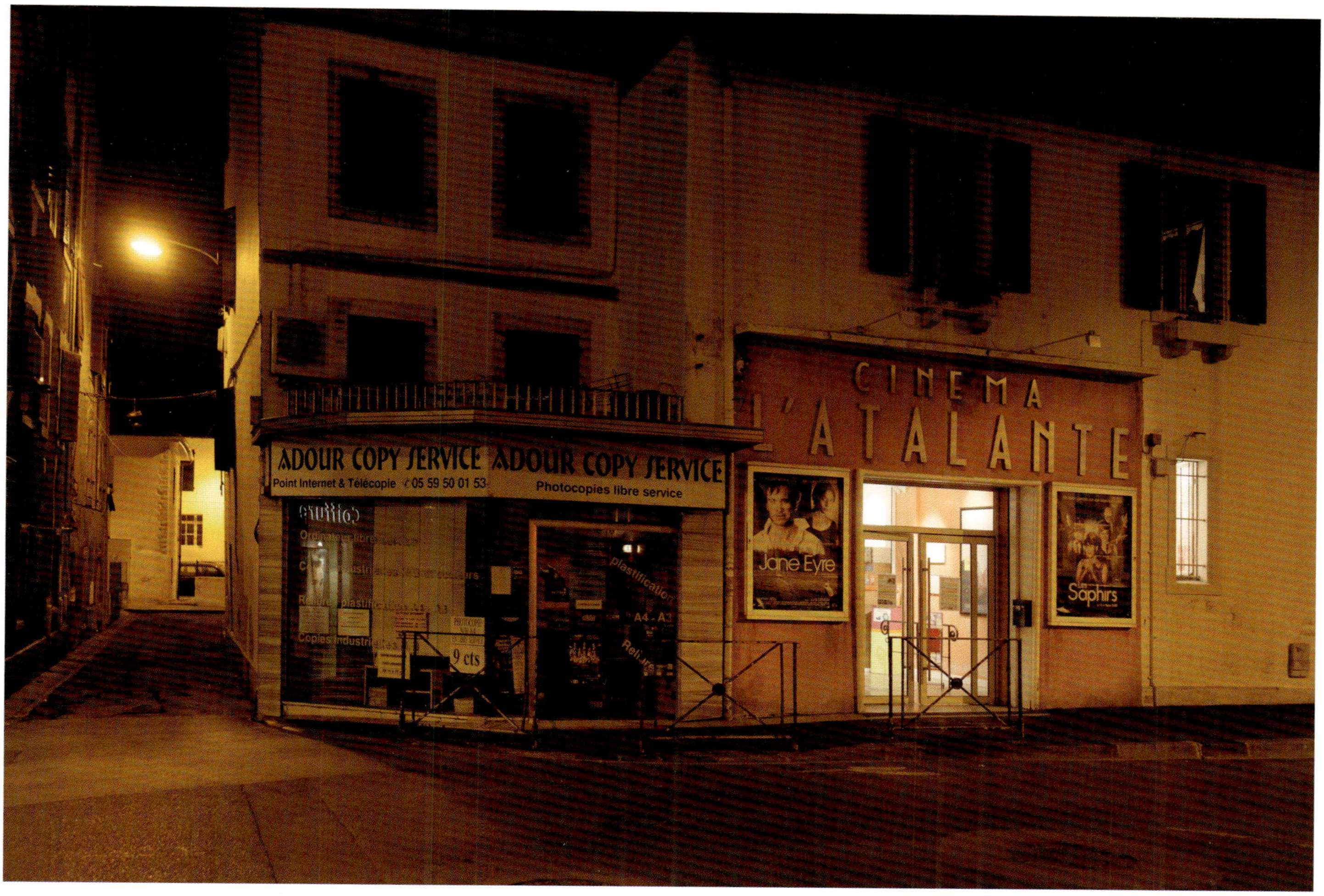

Bayonne – L'Atalante – 2012

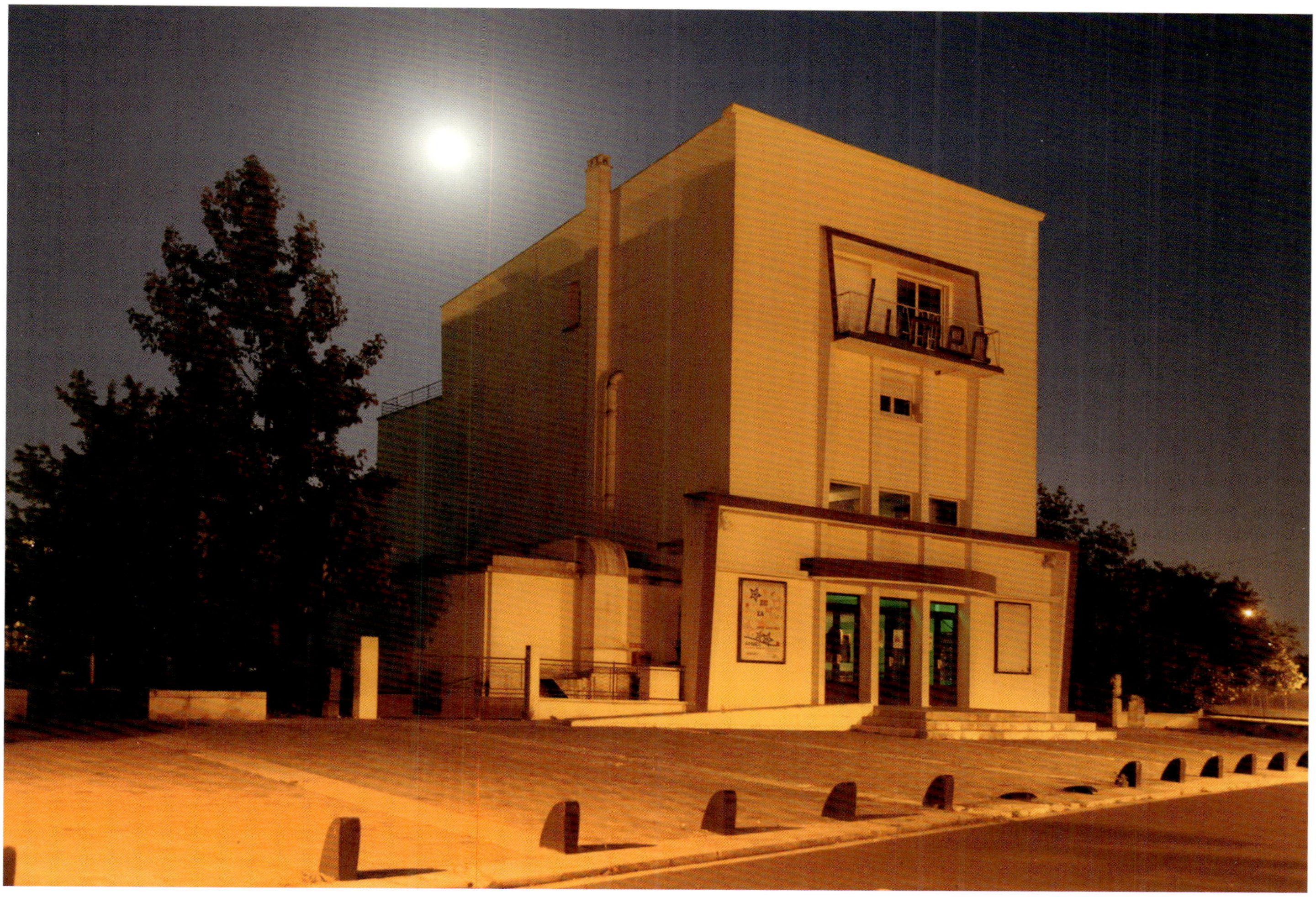

Ambès – Lumen – 2014

OCCITANIA

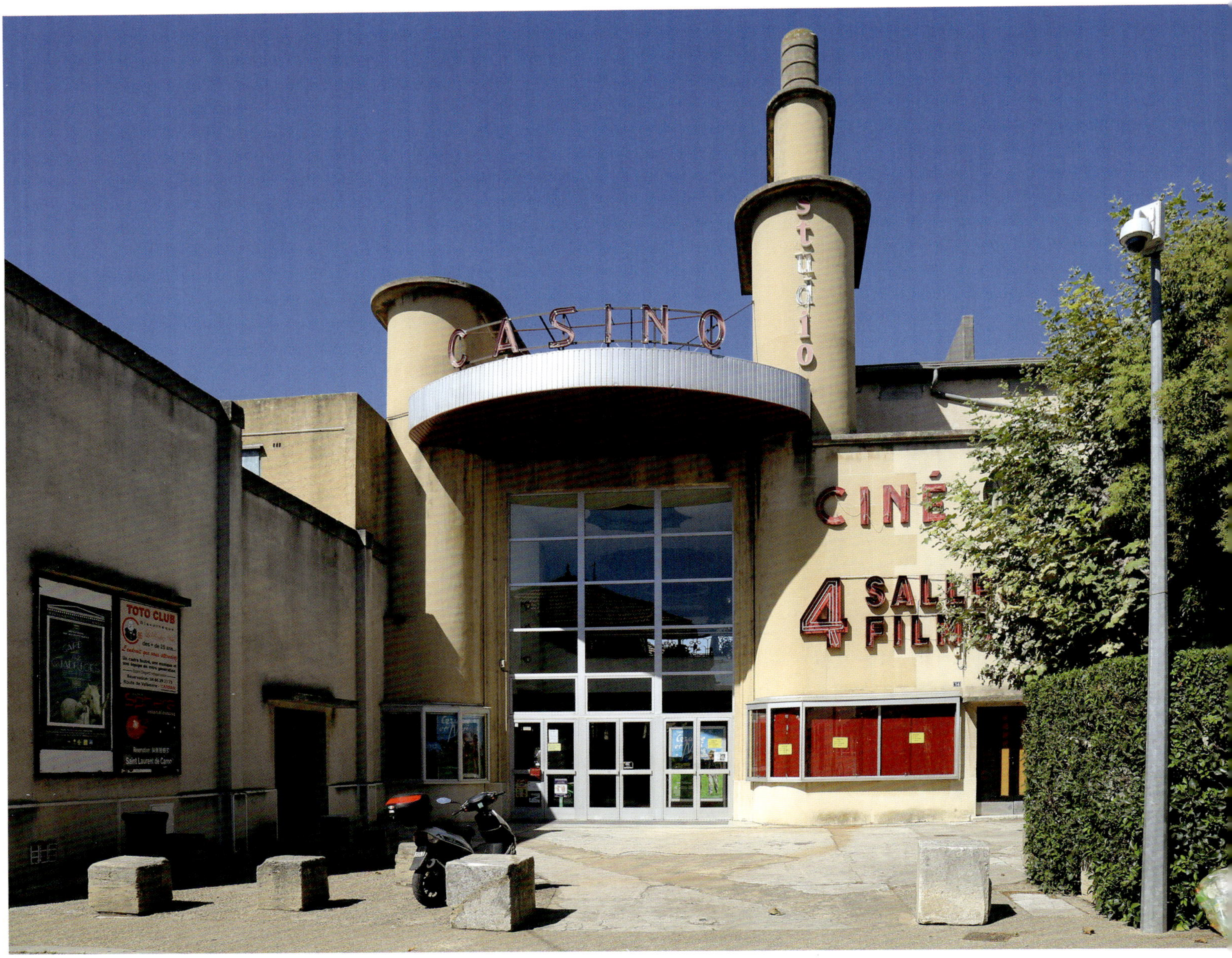

Bagnols-sur-Cèze – Casino – 2016

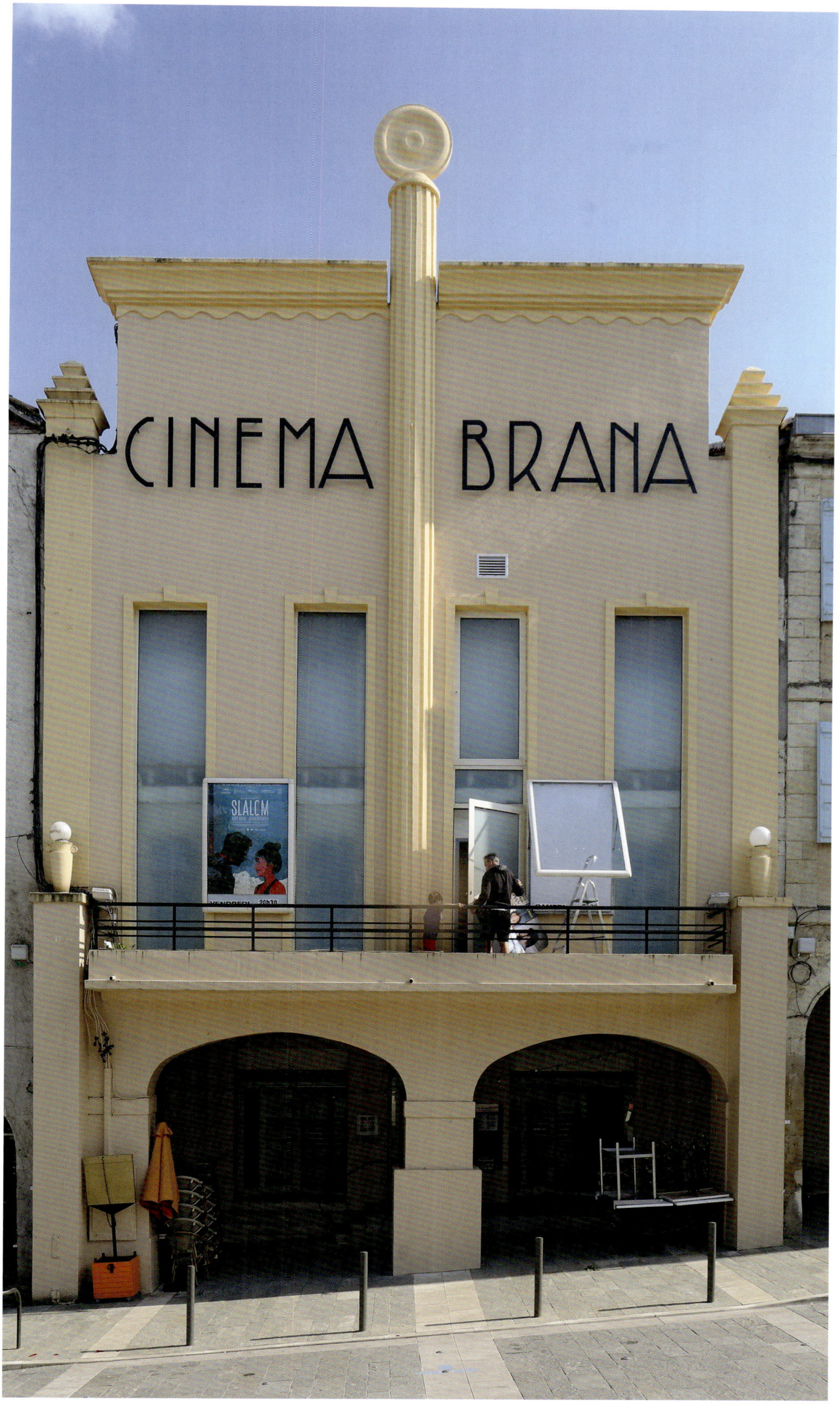

Vic-Fezensac – Cinéma Brana – 2021

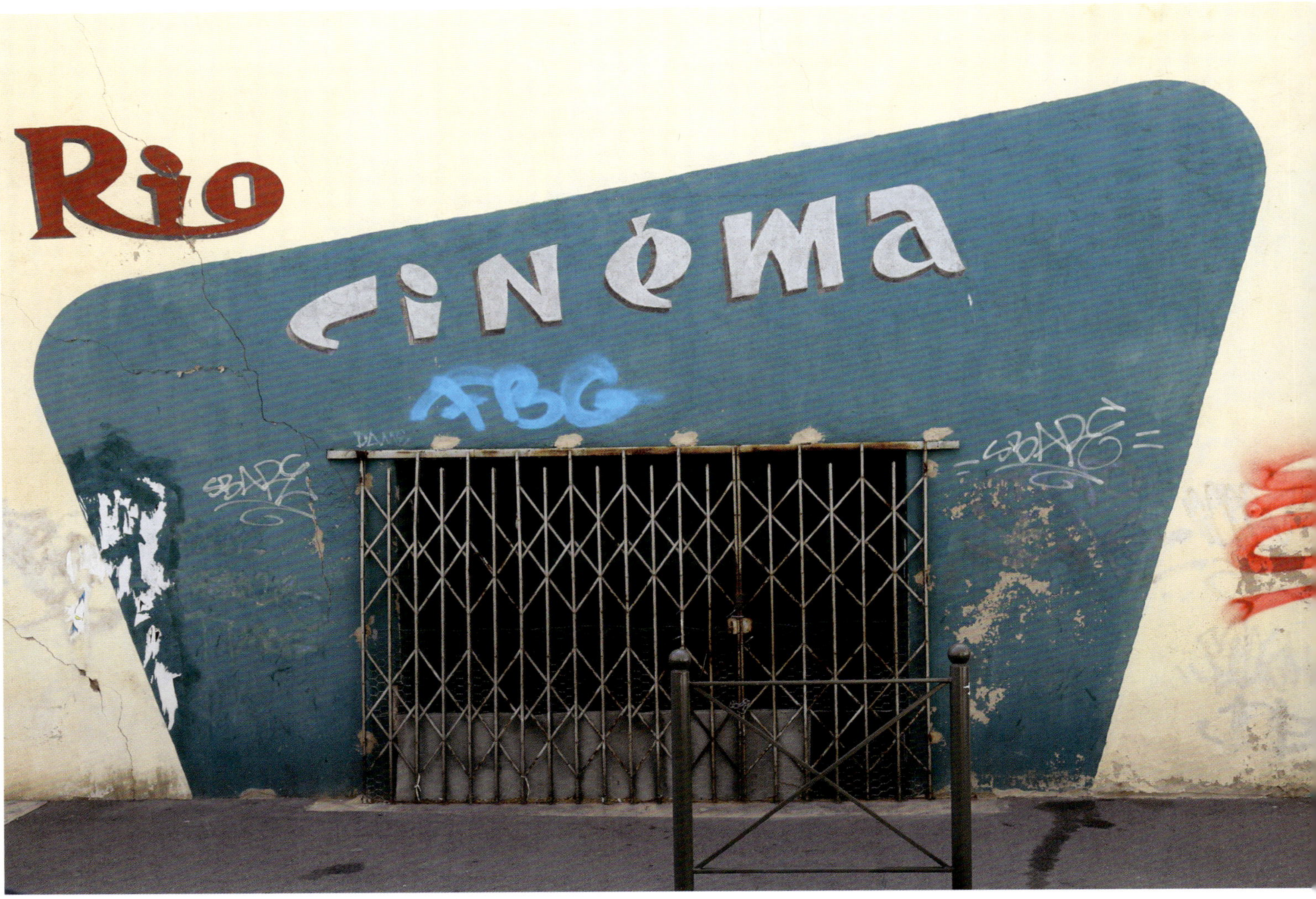

Sète – Rio – 2015

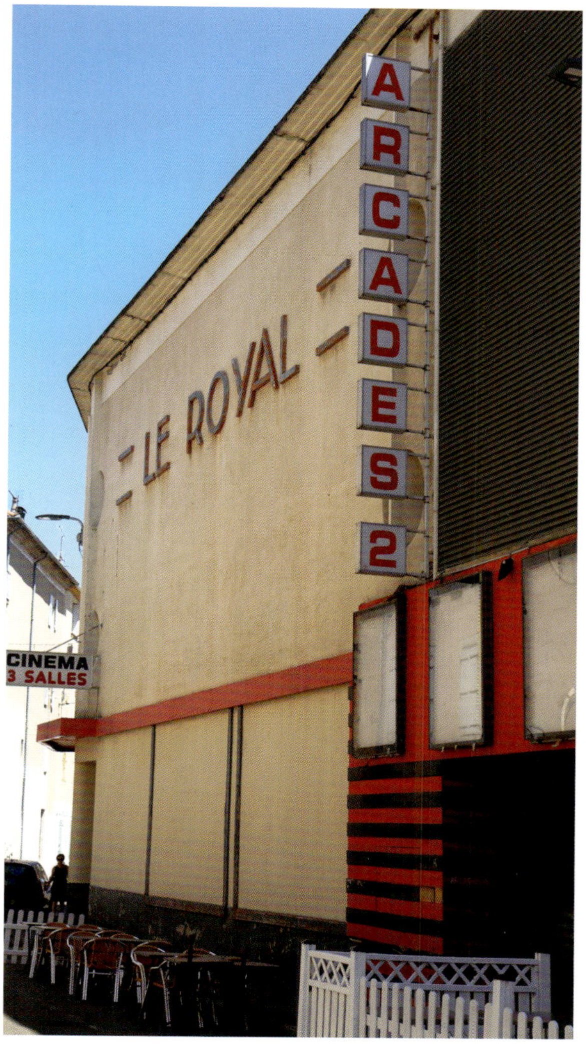

Alès – Le Royal – 2021

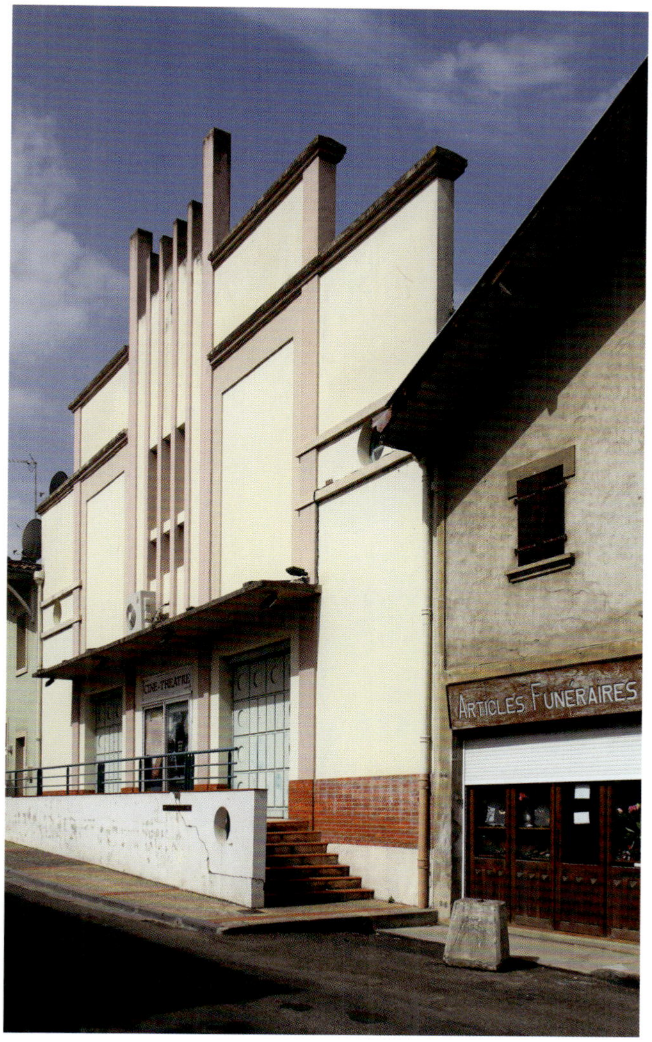

Nogaro – Ciné 32 – 2012

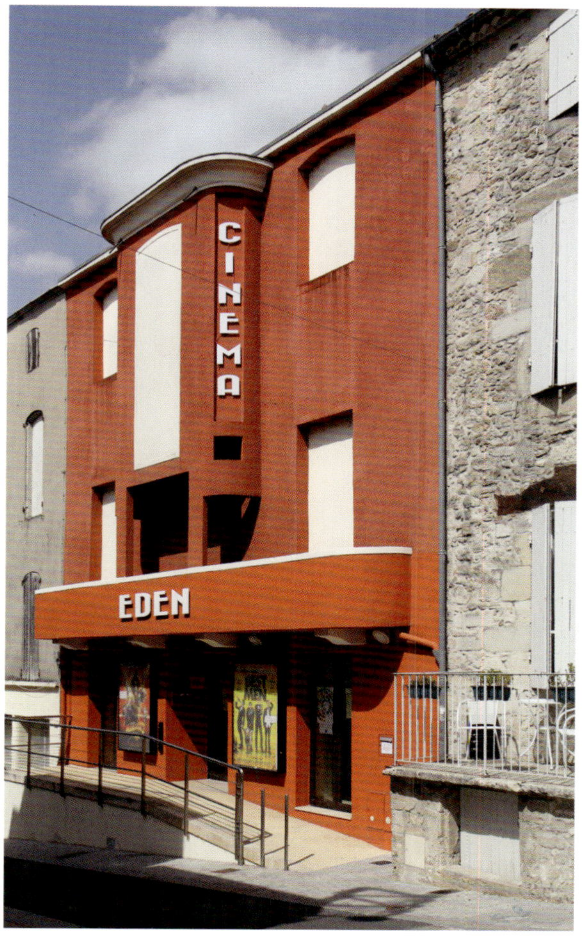

Monségur – Eden – 2012

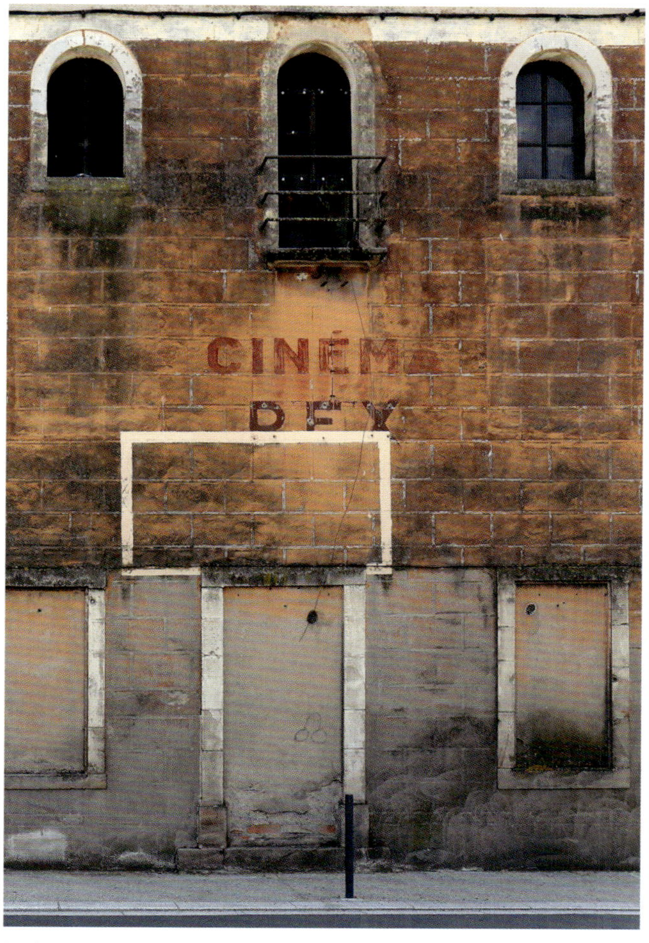

Réalmont – Rex – 2021

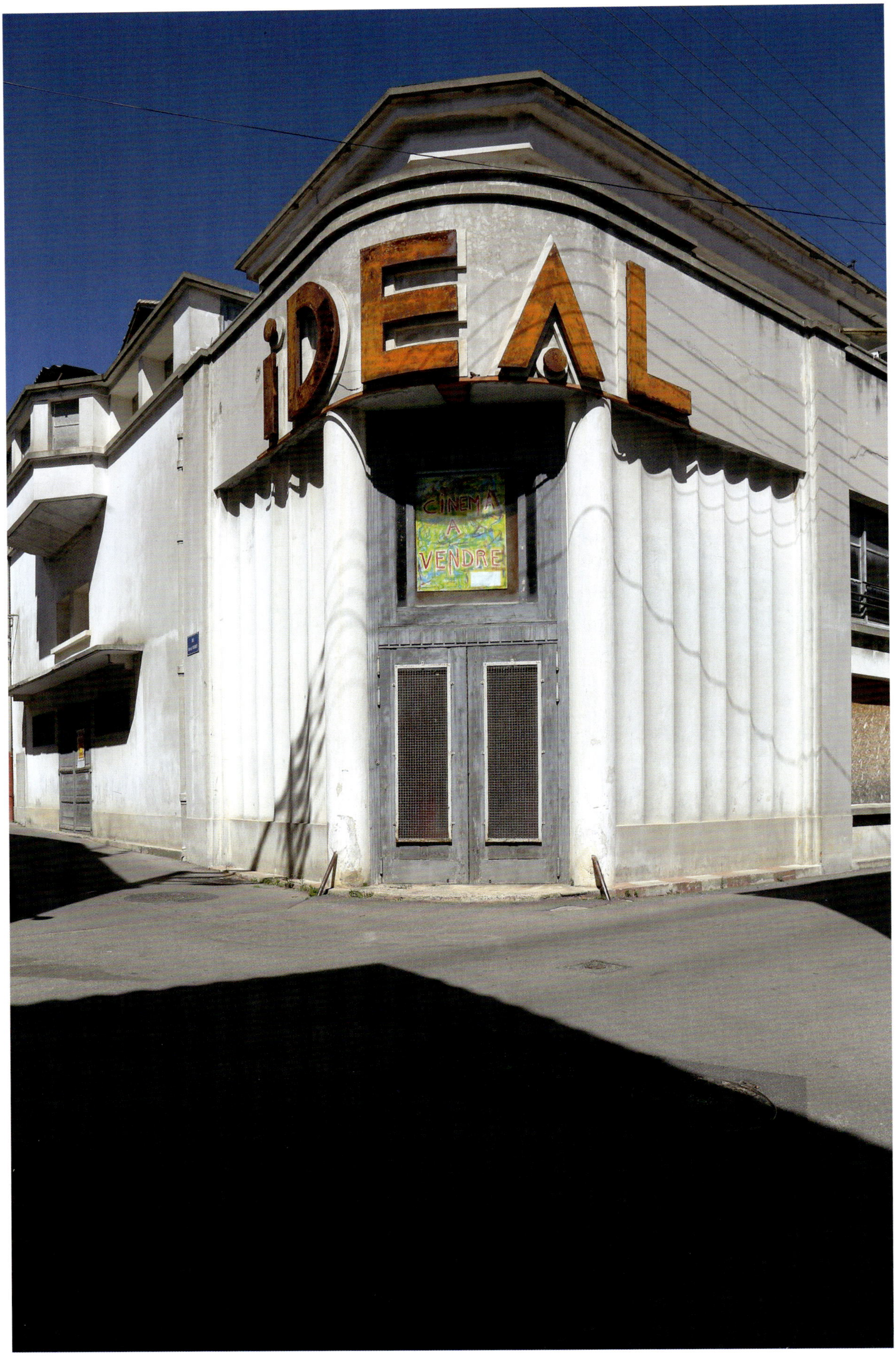

Lézignan-Corbières – Idéal – 2017

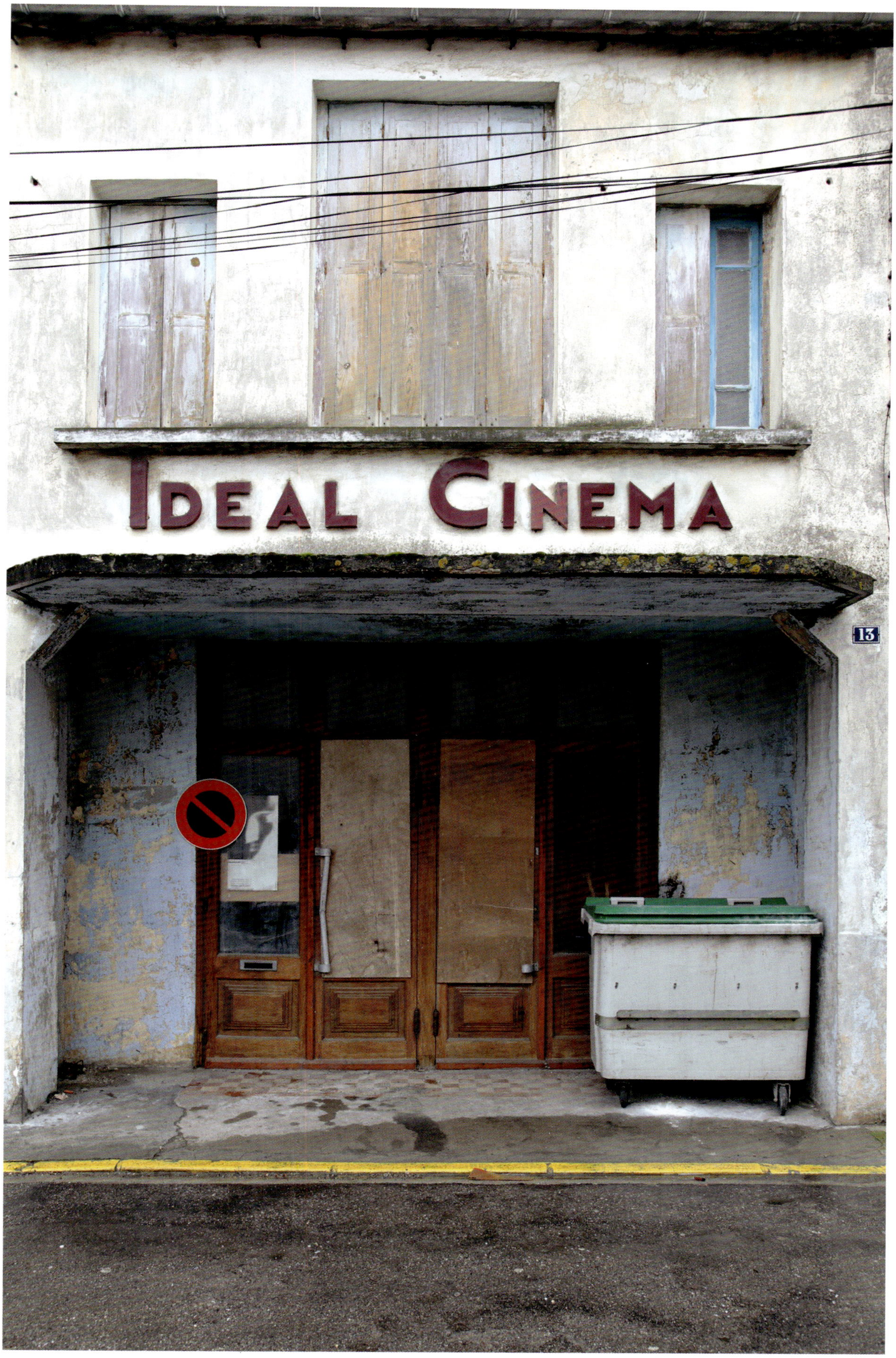

Bram – Idéal Cinéma – 2010

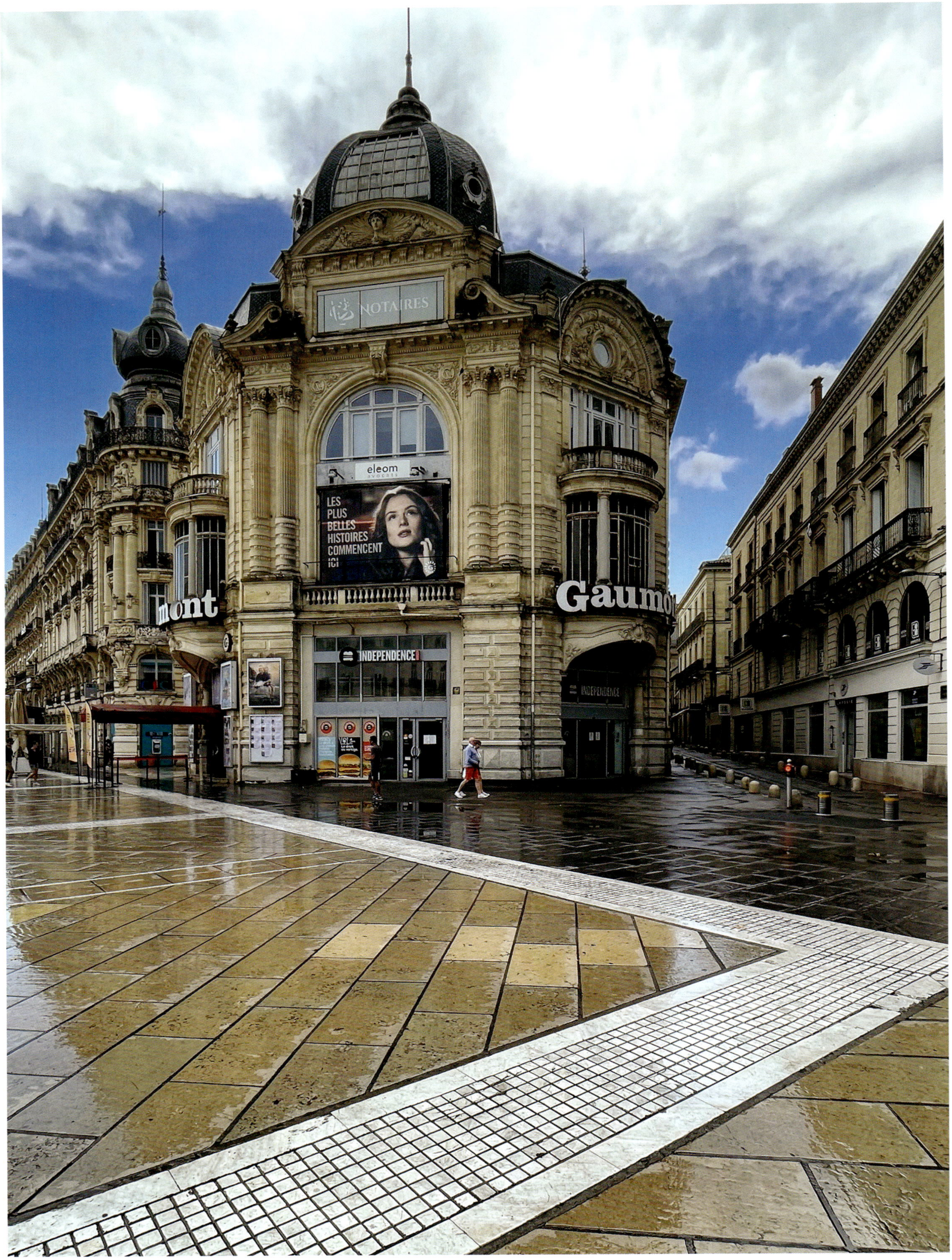

Montpellier – Gaumont – 2022

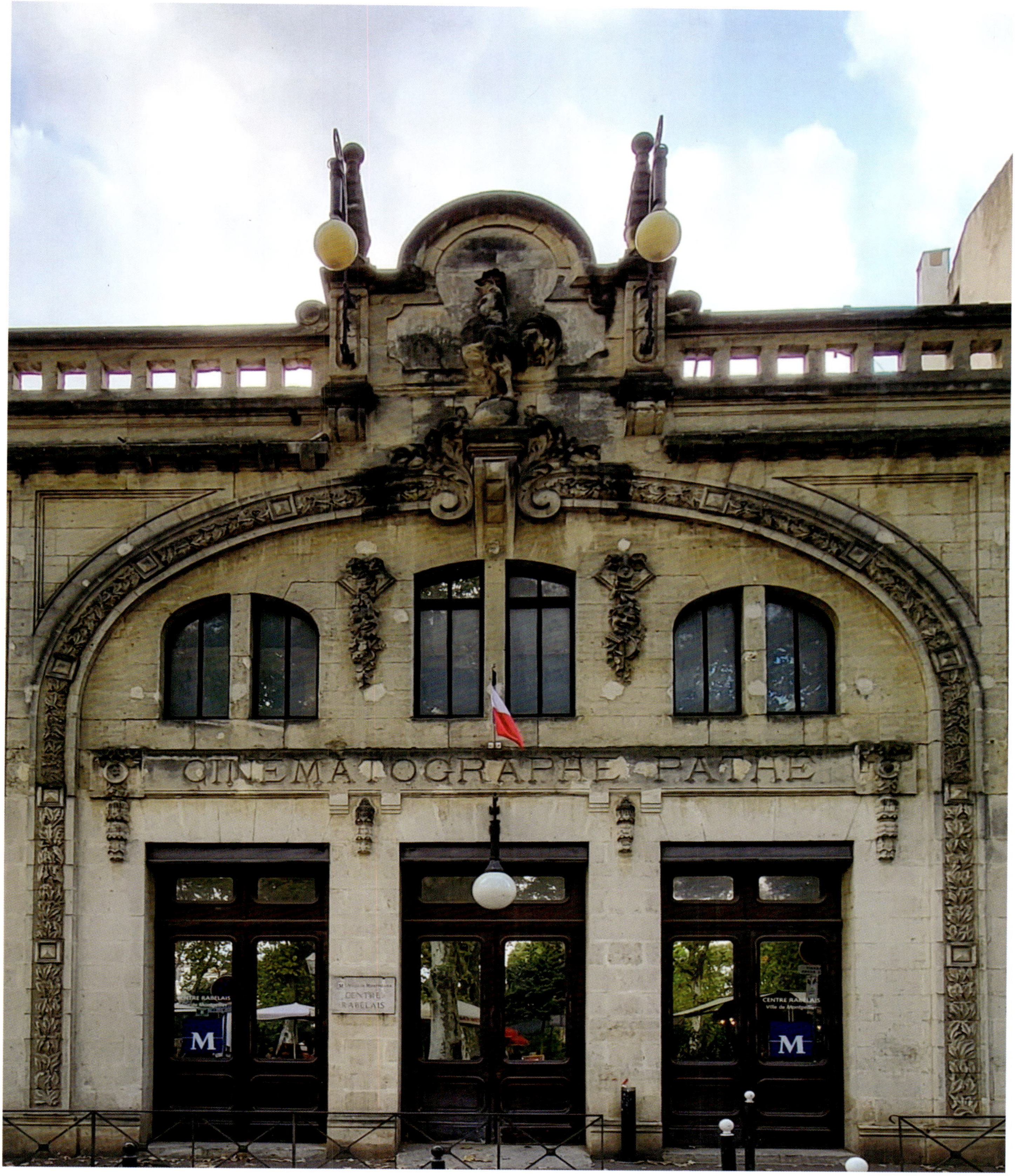

Montpellier – Cinématographe Pathé – 2022

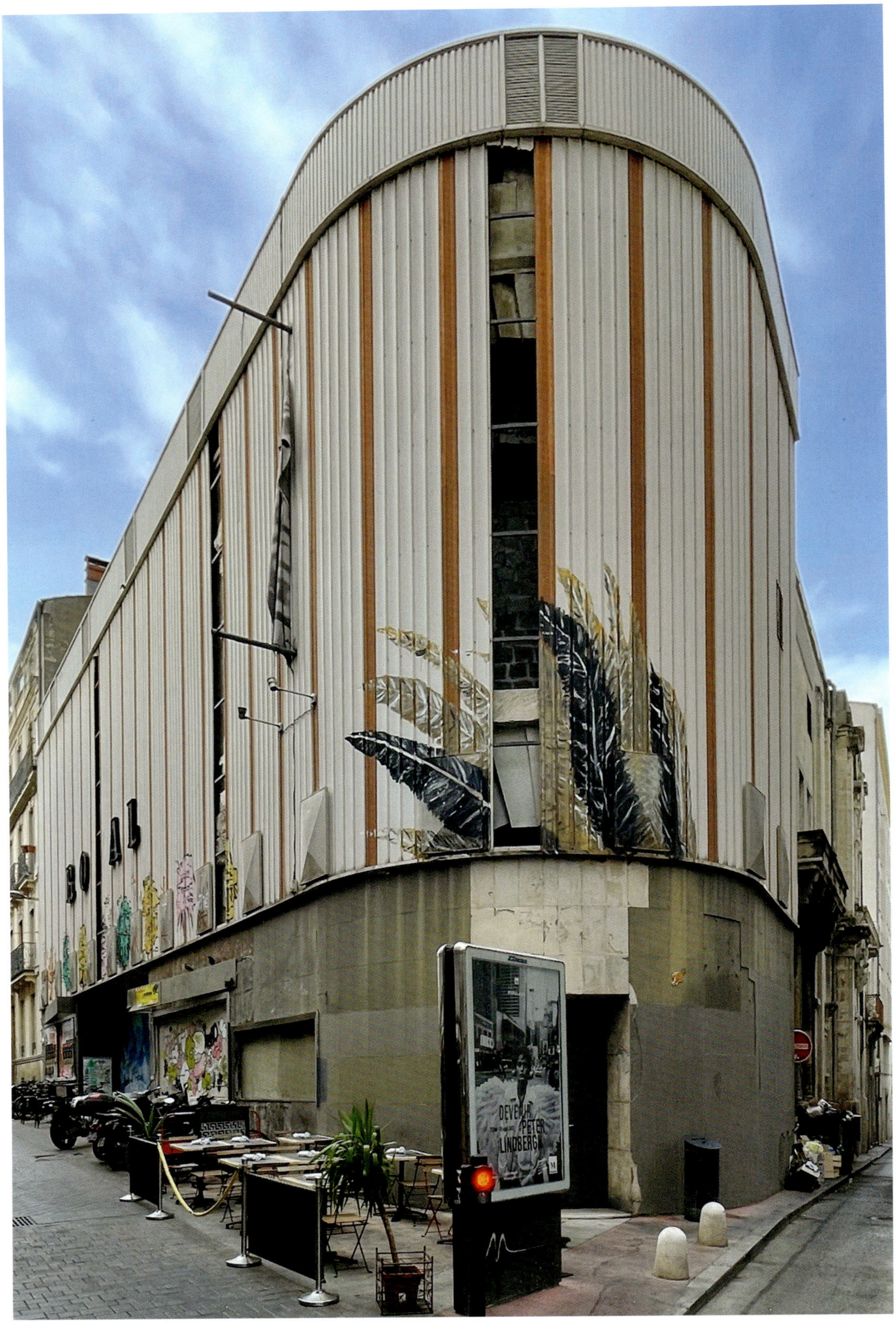

Montpellier – Le Royal – 2022

Montpellier, Le Royal. Starting out as an Italian-style theatre in the 19th century, Le Royal became a cinema in 1923. When it closed in 2015 it was soon used as a squat by young people dreaming of a better, more generous world, open to alternative forms of creation. The building was definitively closed and walled up in 2019. If it had to die, this cinema surely deserved a royal funeral rather than an unofficial one.

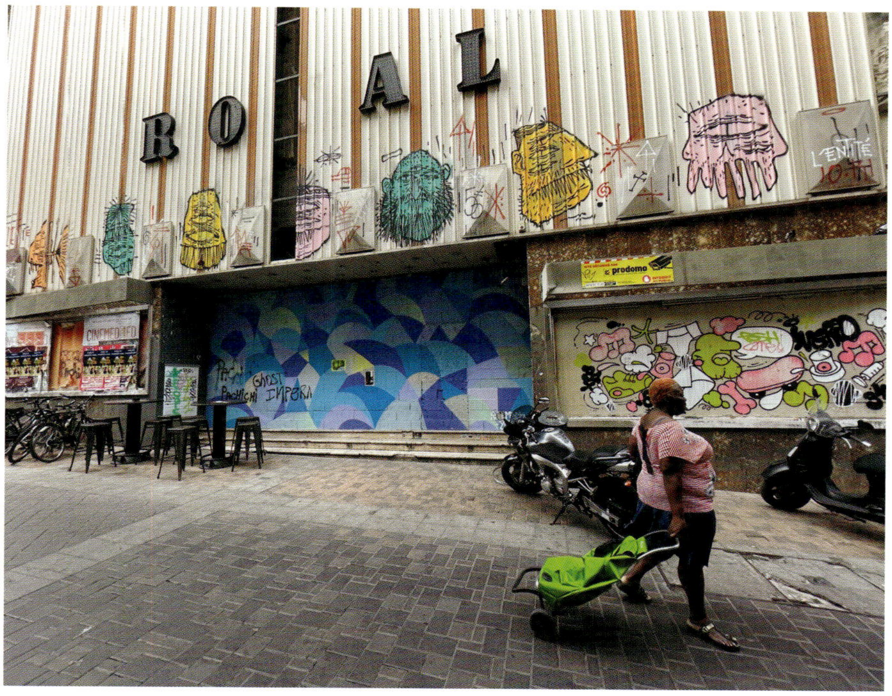

Montpellier – Le Royal – 2022

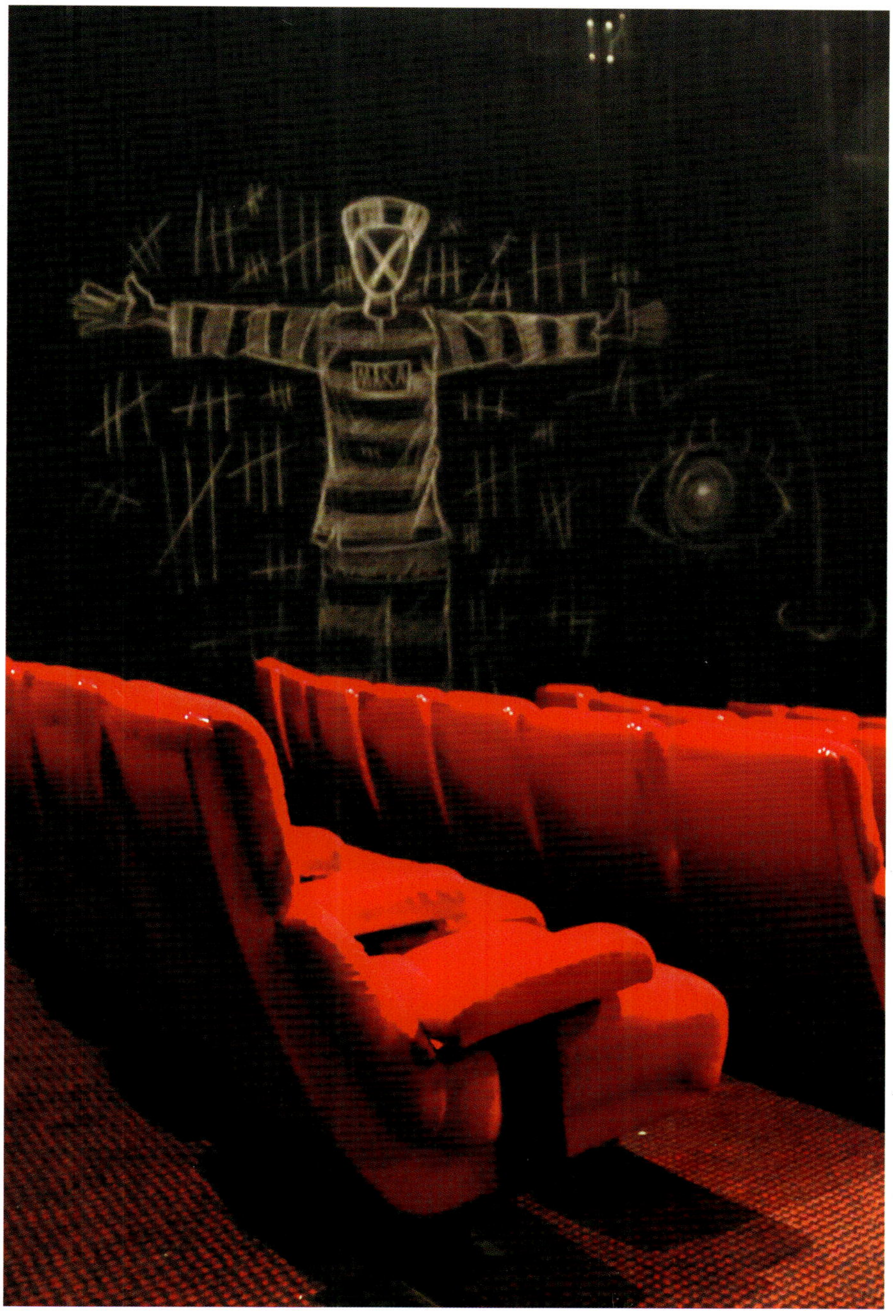

Montpe lier – Le Royal – 2017

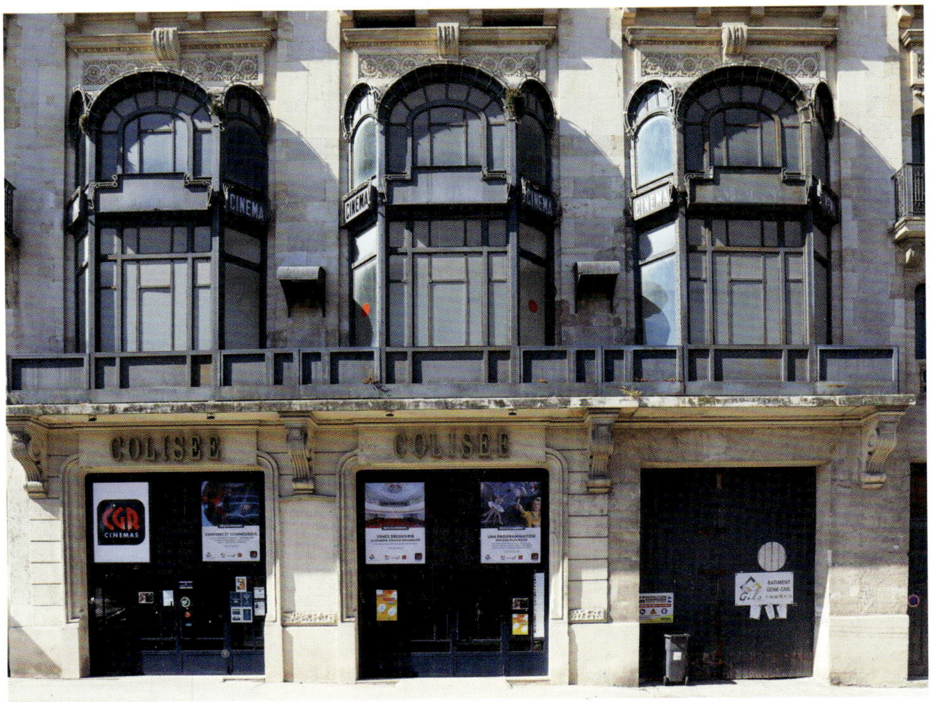

Carcassonne – Le Colisée – 2022

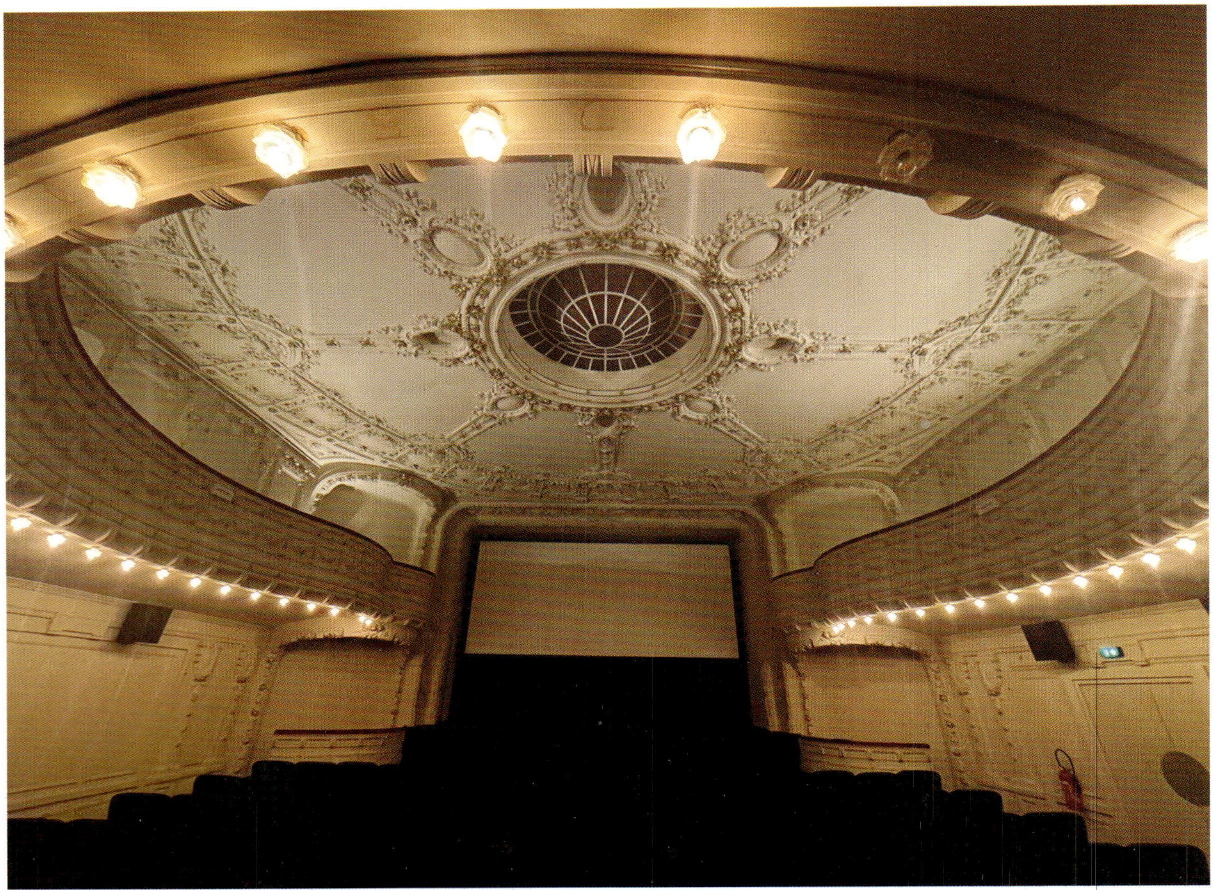

Carcassonne – Colisée – 2022

Carcassonne, Colisée. First a community hall, then a theatre, this Art Nouveau building became a cinema in 1932. Discover its sumptuous glass roof by looking up at the ceiling rather than at the screen. The roof, considered one of the most beautiful in the world, was renovated in 2021.

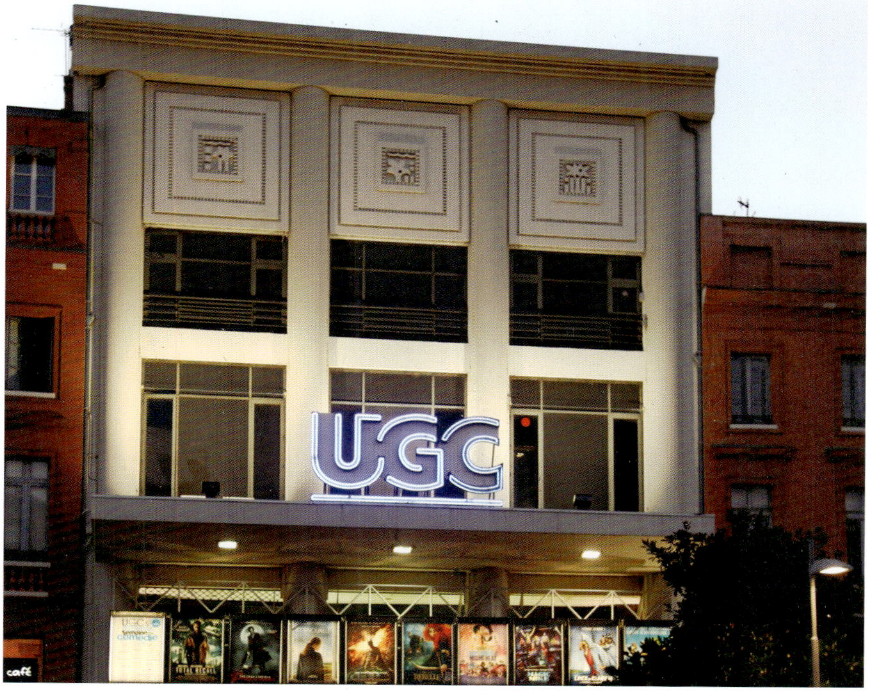

Toulouse – UGC – 2012 (destroyed)

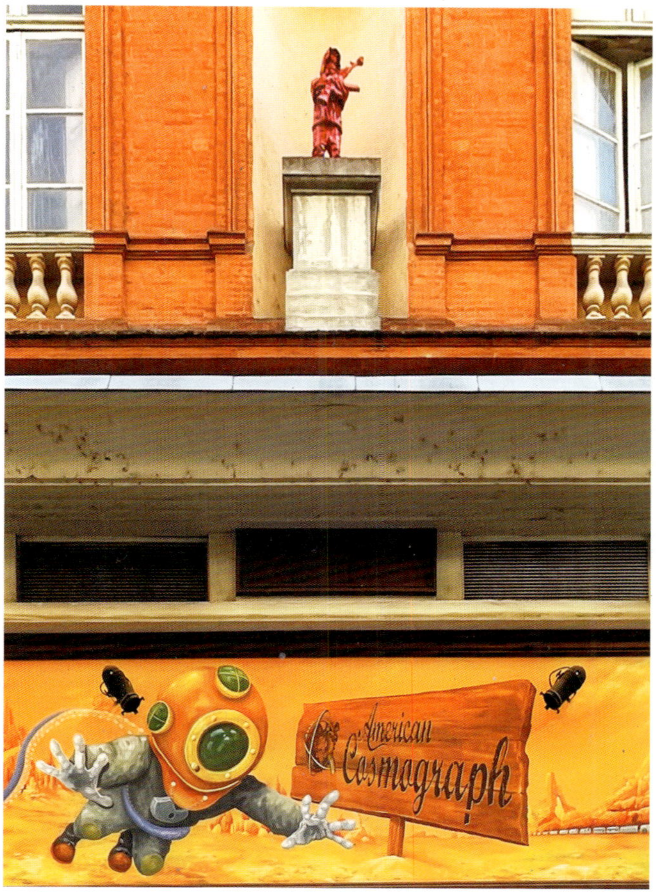

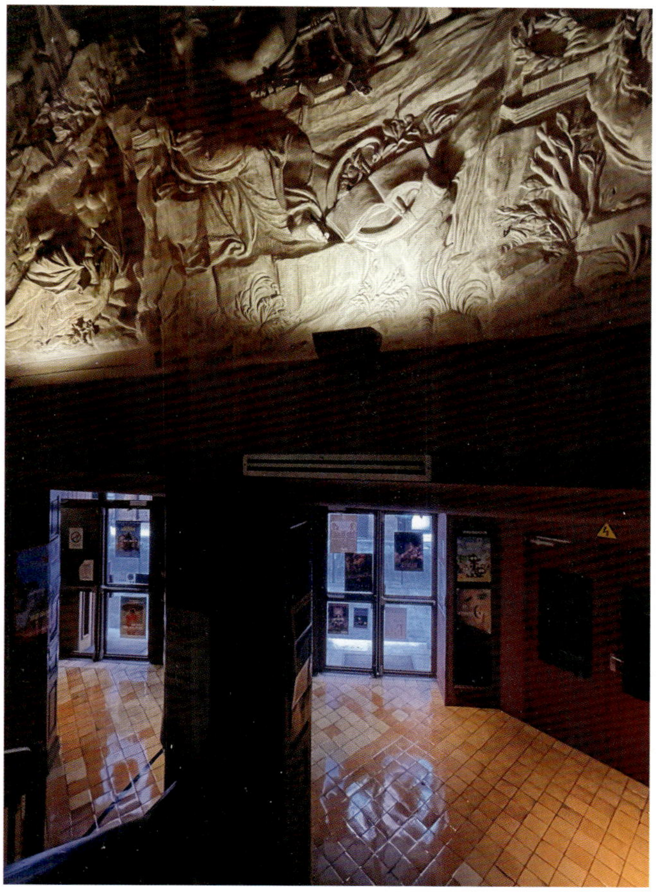

Toulouse – American Cosmograph – 2022

Toulouse, American Cosmograph. This was originally a tennis court which in 1687 became Toulouse's first opera house. Its function changed in the 19th century: political meeting hall, theatre, hotel and a café-restaurant. In 1907 it was converted into a cinema, after many changes of name and ownership, and finally regained its original name: American Cosmograph.

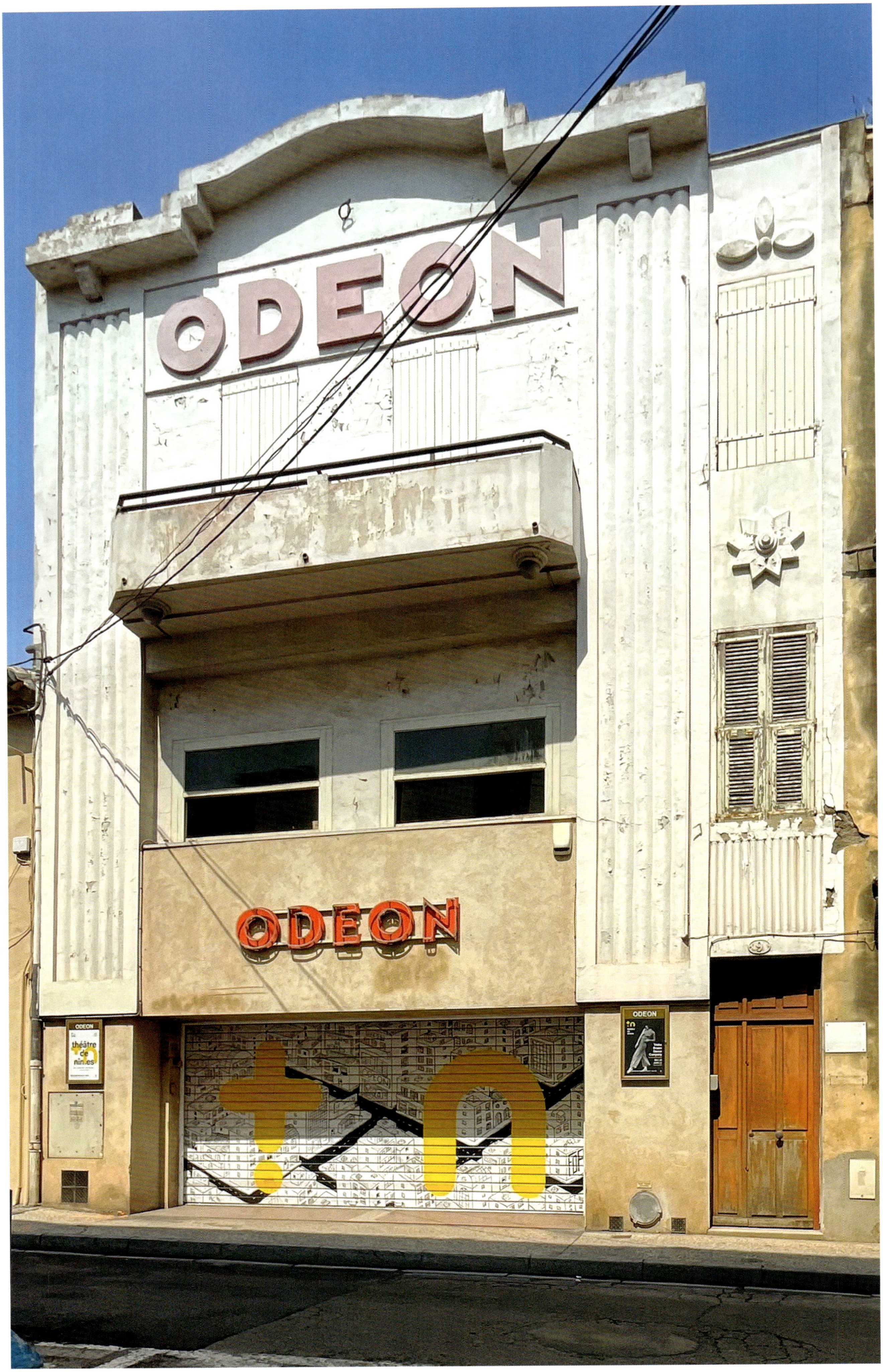

Nîmes – Odéon – 2022

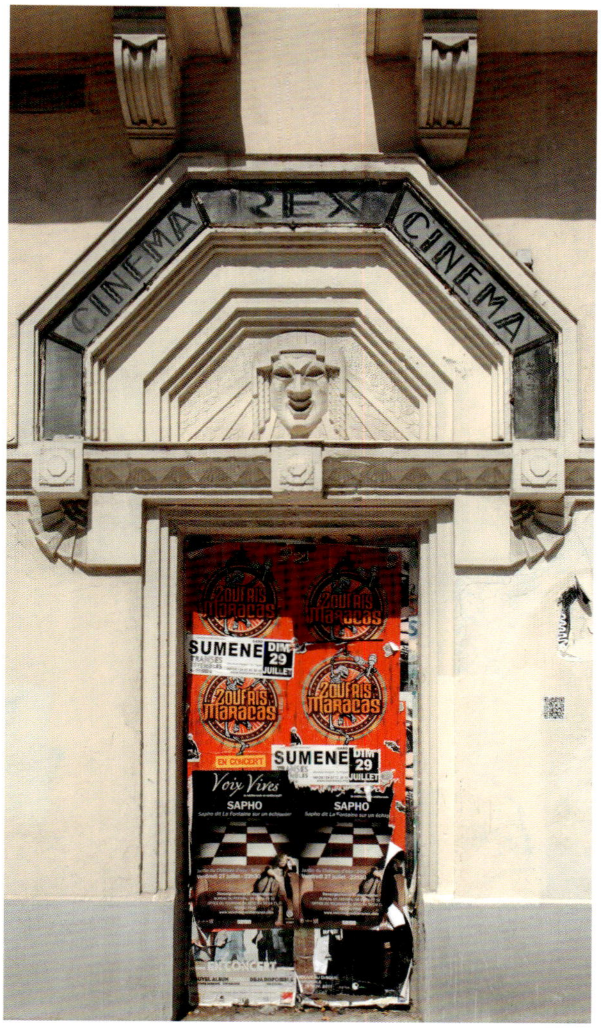

Montpellier – Rex – 2012

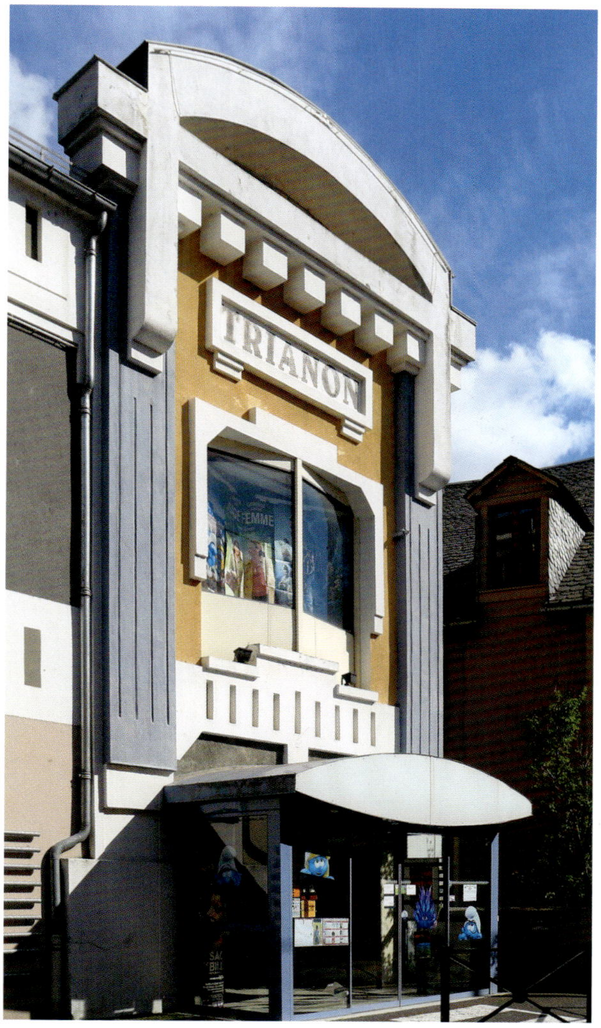

Marvejols – Trianon – 2017

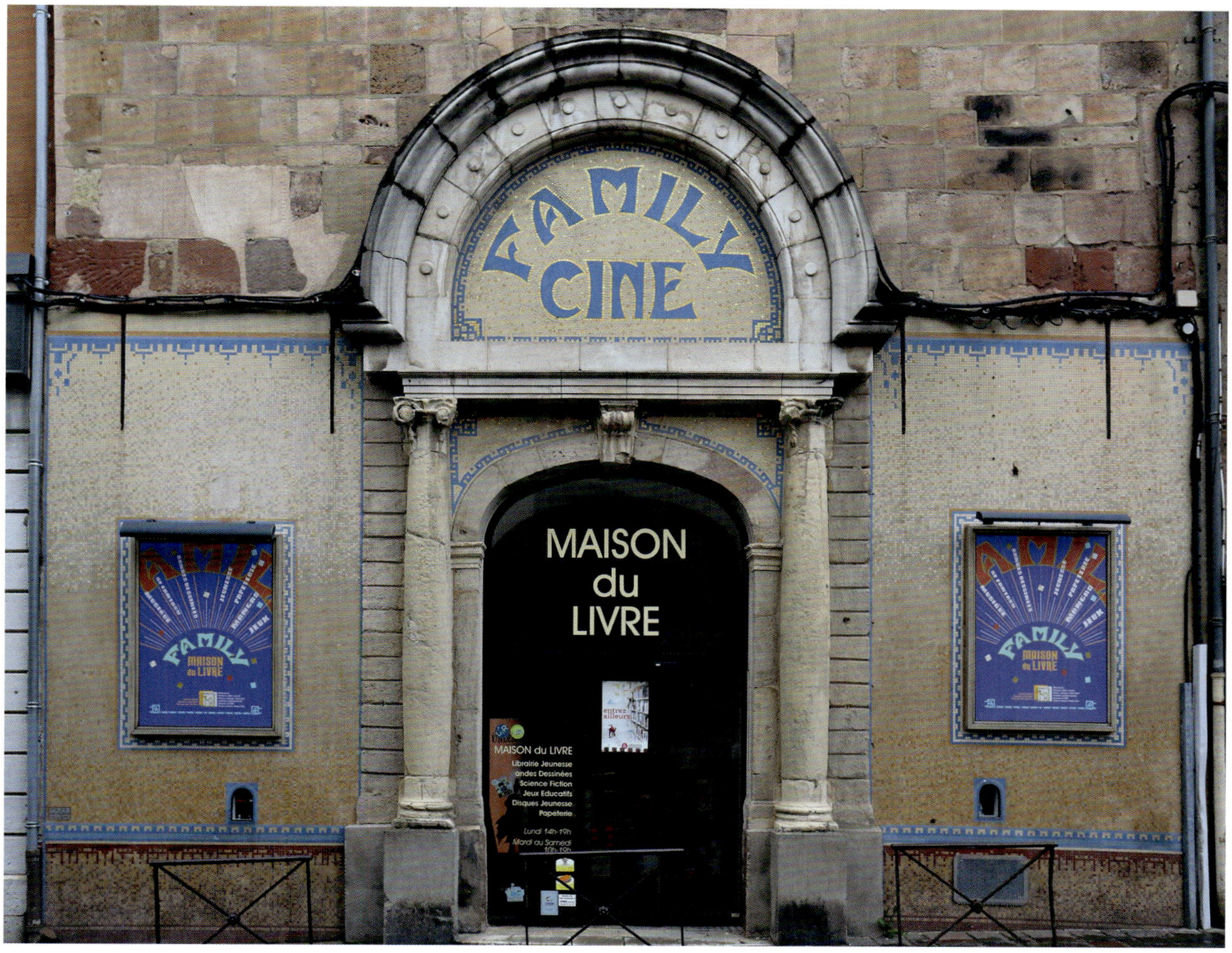

Rodez – Family Ciné – 2015

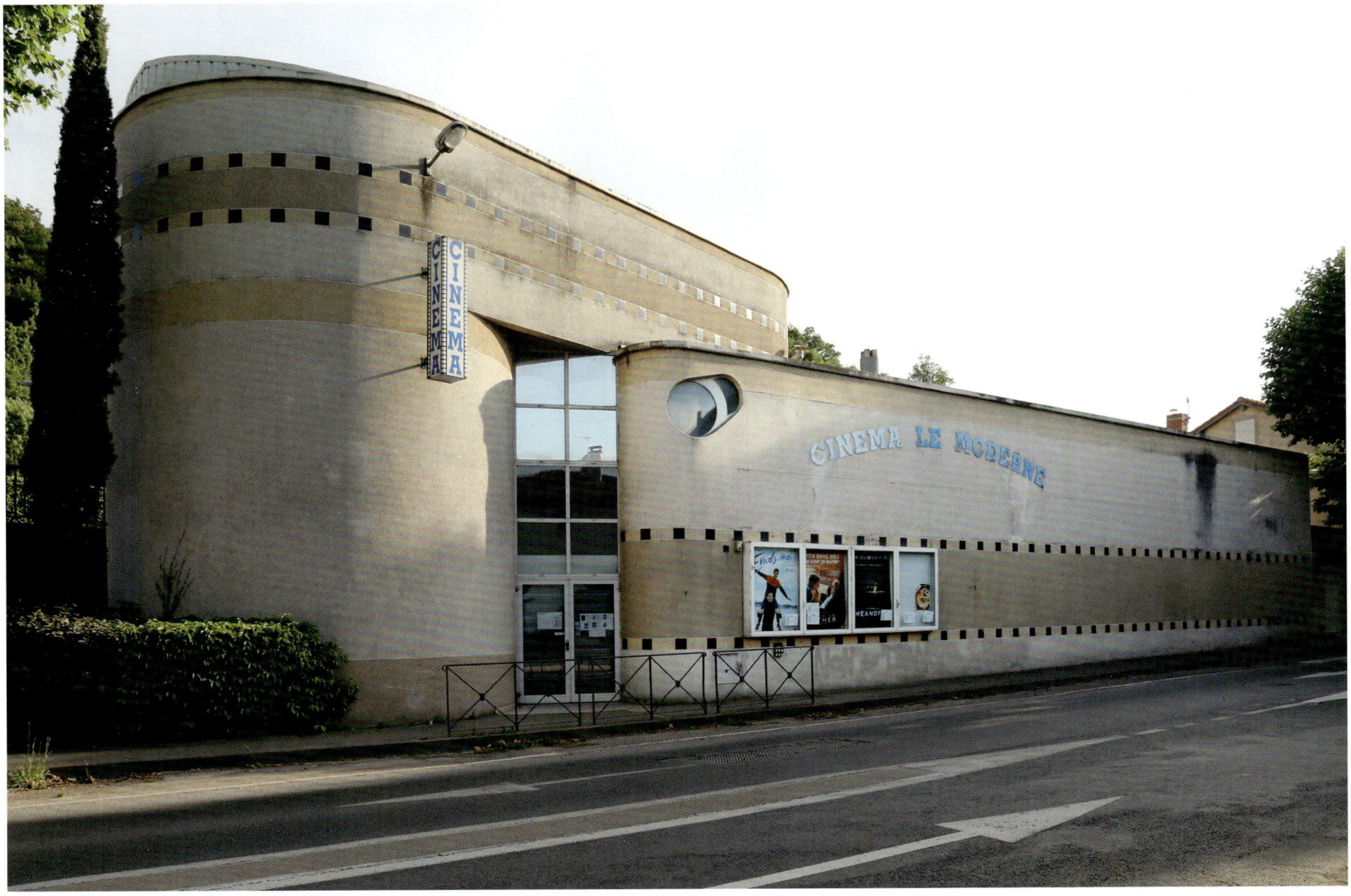

Saint-Affrique – Le Moderne – 2021

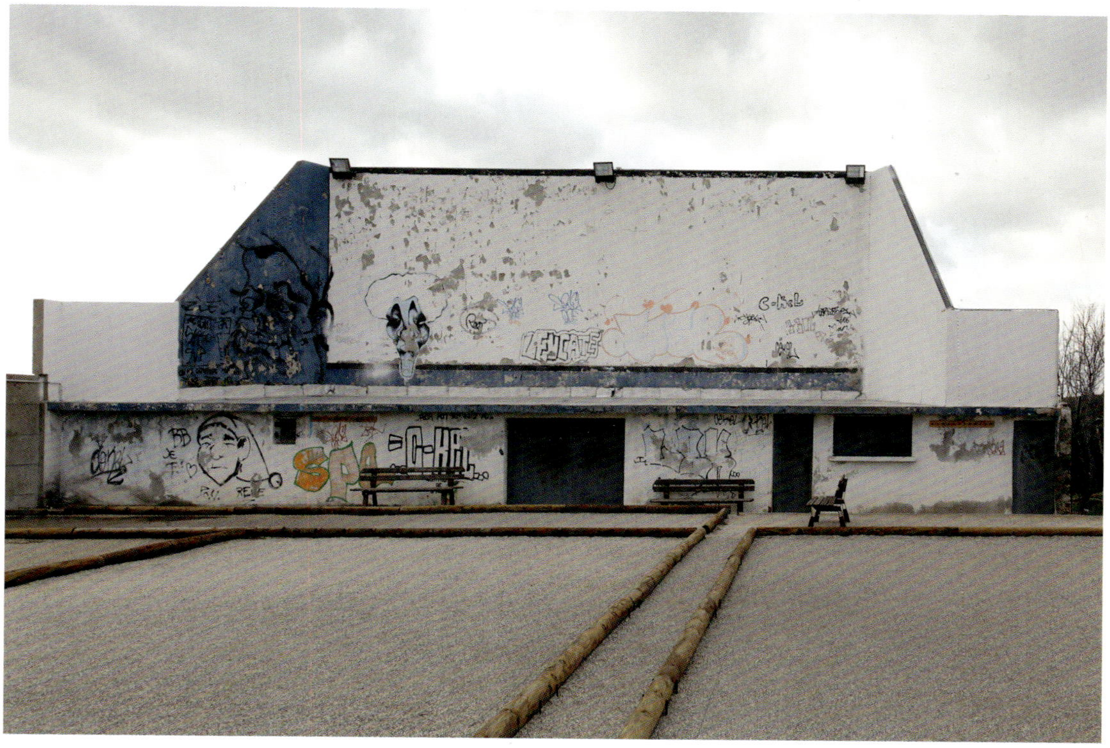

Leucate – Cinéma en plein air – 2010

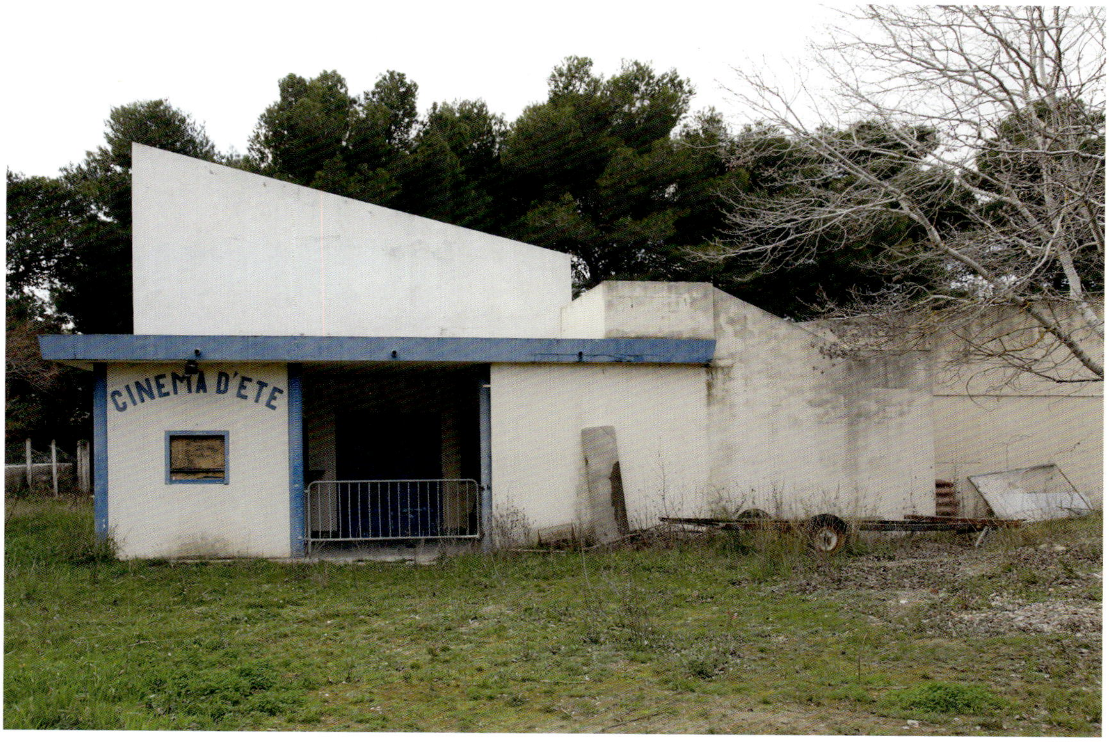

Leucate Plage – Cinéma d'été – 2010

Leucate, Cinéma d'été. The discreet old-fashioned charm of a vanished world. Sitting with plenty of people around you, waiting for nightfall, watching the stars shining, even counting them: a kind of innocent happiness. The sound not always audible, the projection sometimes a bit blurred, in no way detracts from the pleasure of watching a semi-successful film. The ambiance makes each projection a masterpiece. But soon forgotten by our memories less tuned to the relaxed rhythms of the past.

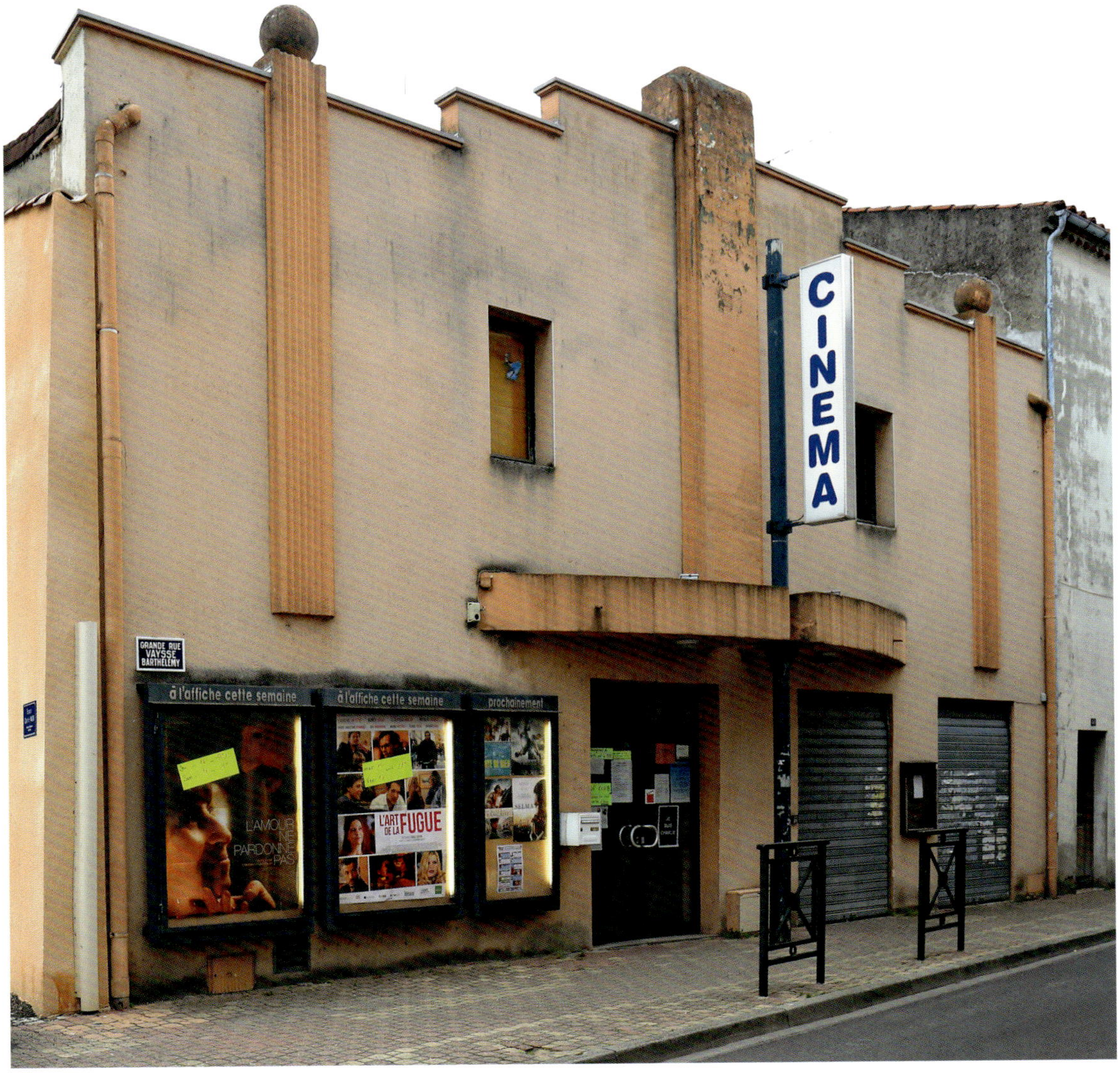

Quillan – Le Familia – 2015

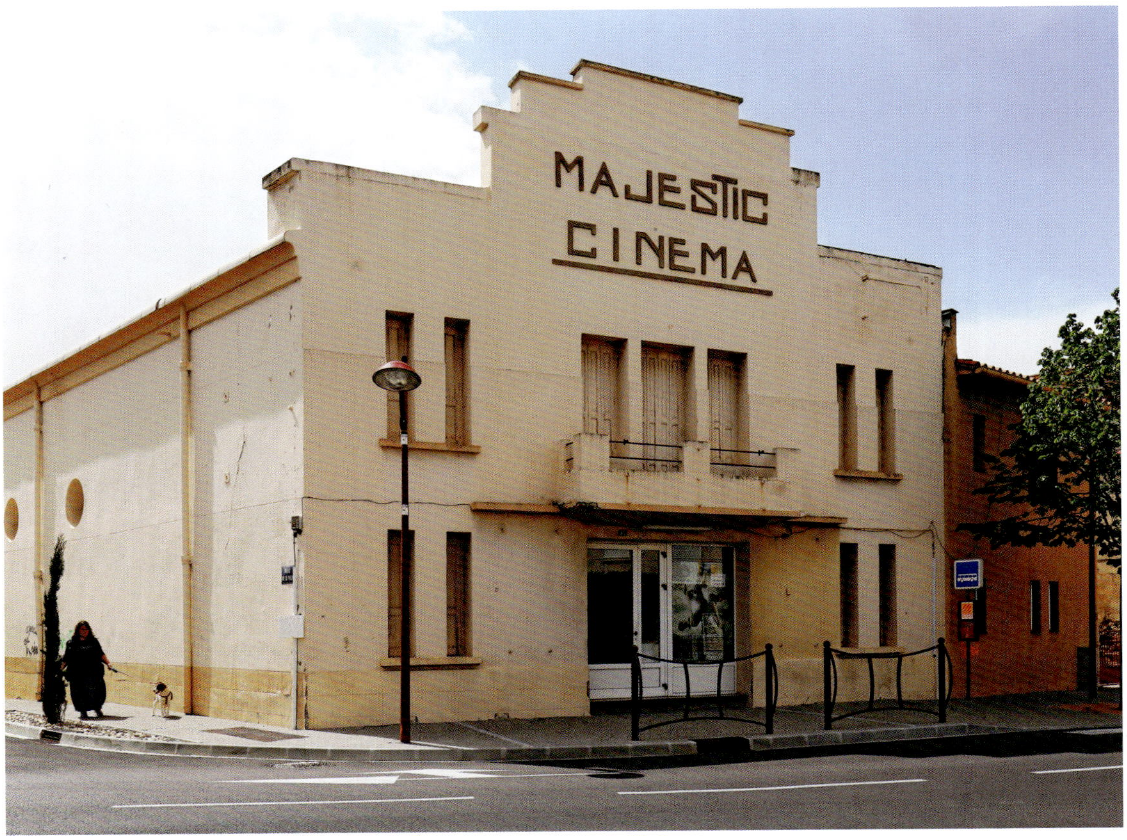

Le Boulou – Majestic – 2015

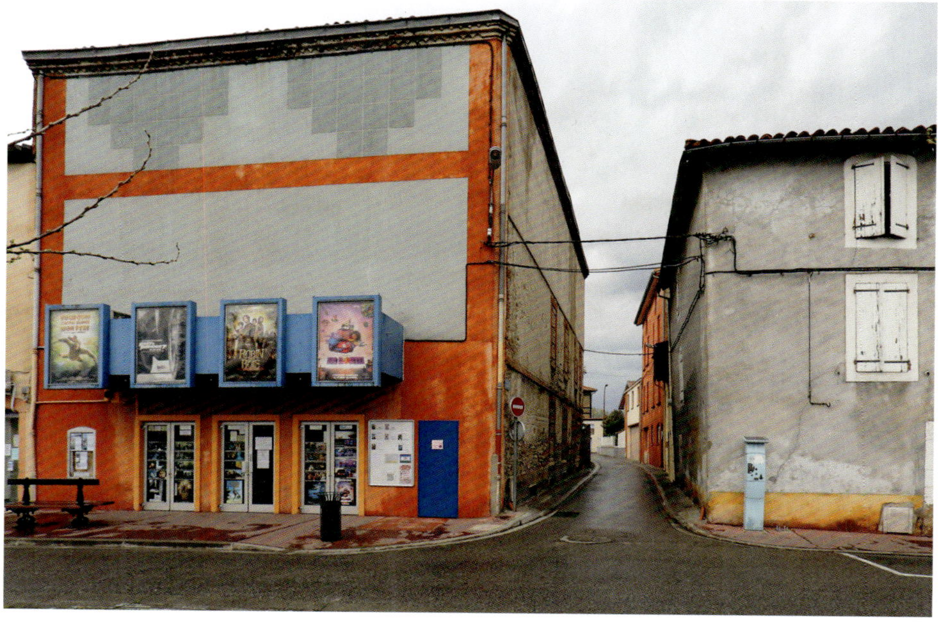
Pamiers – Rex – 2015

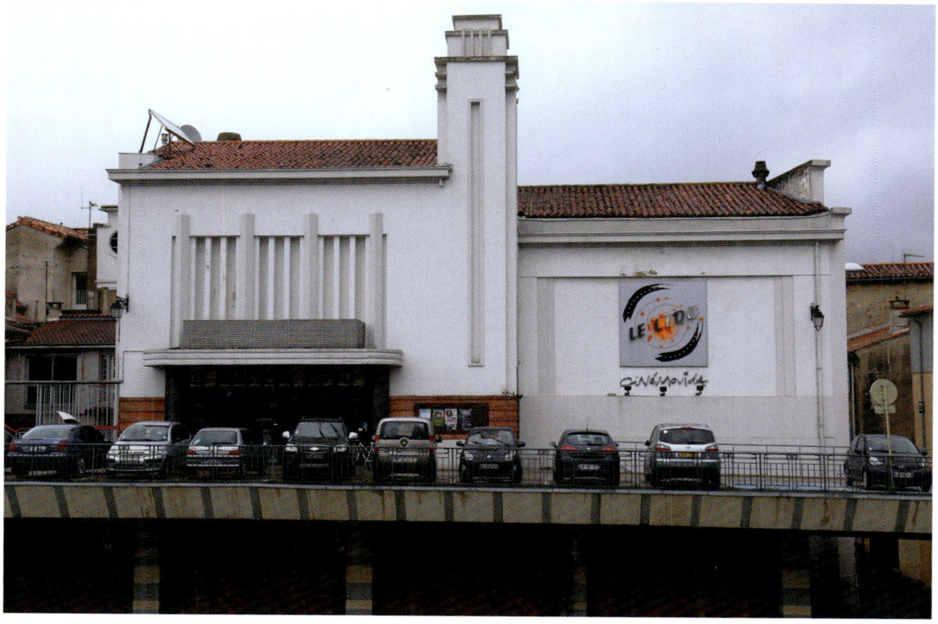
Castres – Lido – 2015

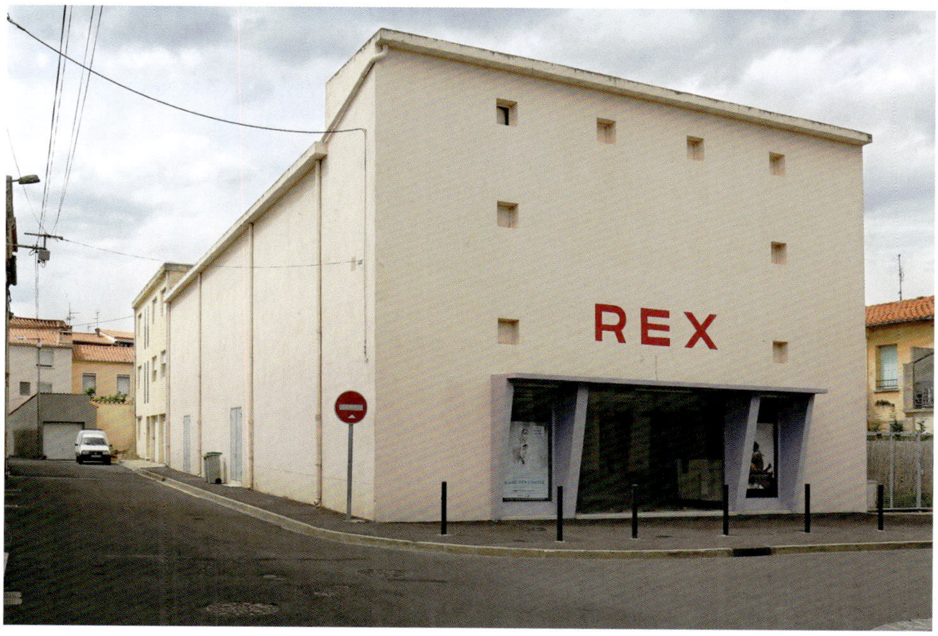

Ille-sur-Têt – Rex – 2015

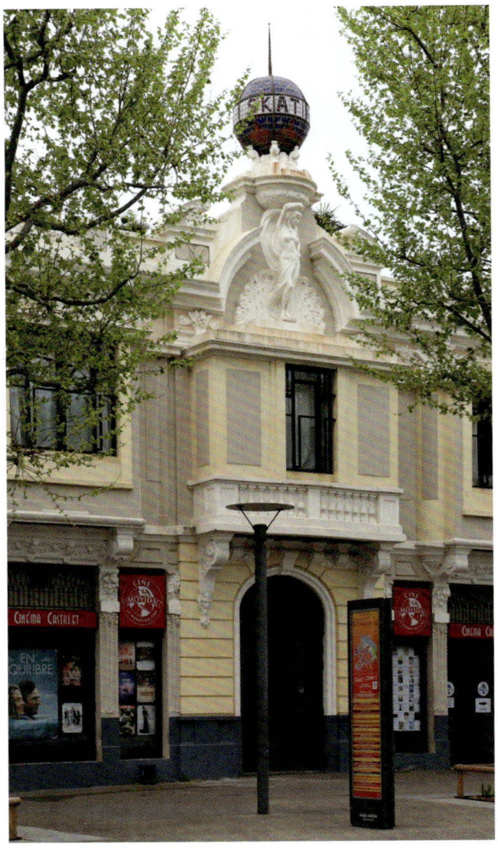

Perpignan – Le Castillet – 2015

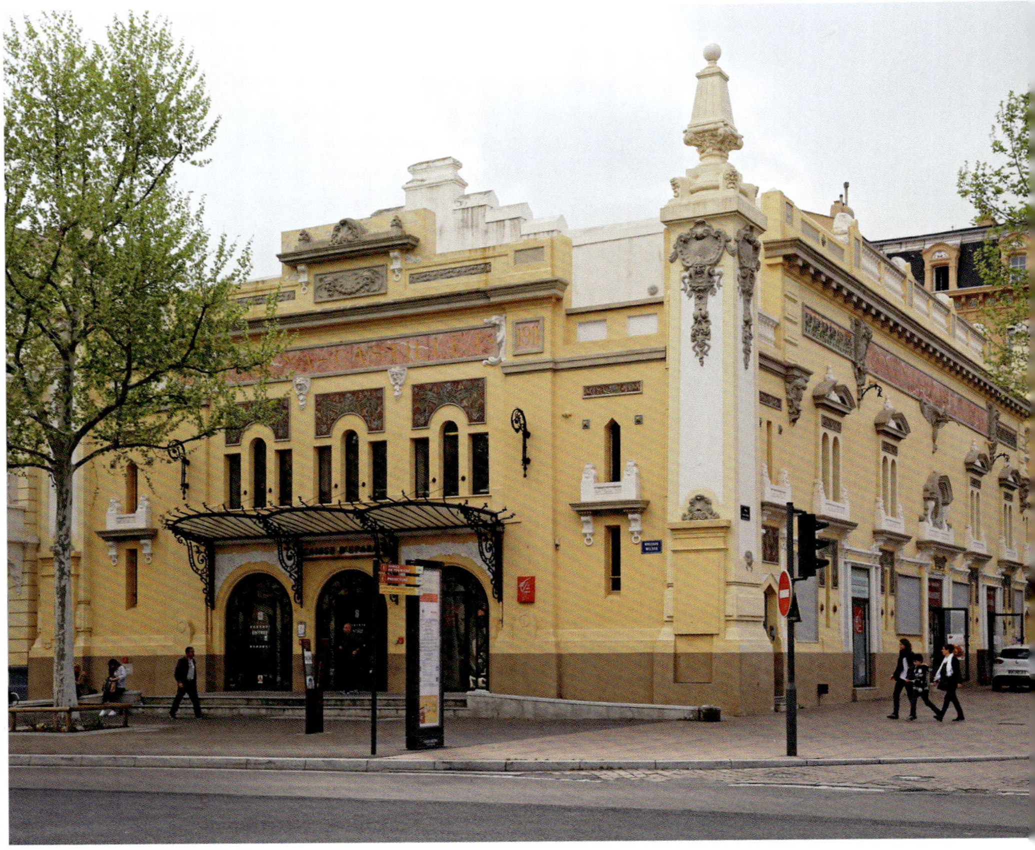

Perpignan – former Castillet – 2015

Perpignan, Le Castillet. Designed to become a cinema, Le Castillet opened in 1911 with a 1,100-seat theatre. Its architecture, inspired by 19th-century theatres with sculptures and friezes in polychrome earthenware in the spirit of Art Nouveau, aroused violent feelings of rejection when it opened. Today the Castillet is listed as a 20th-century heritage site.

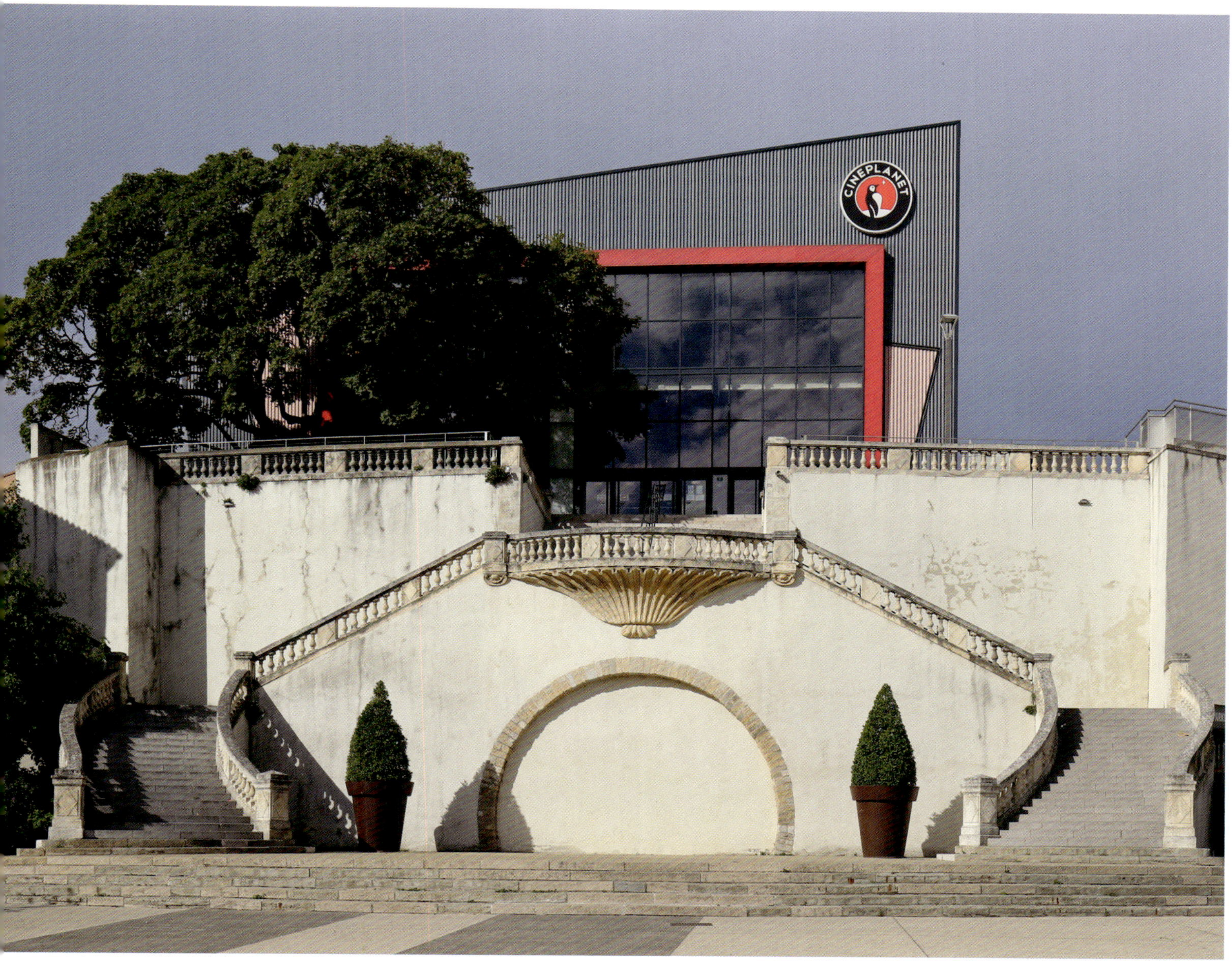

s – Ciné Planet – 2021

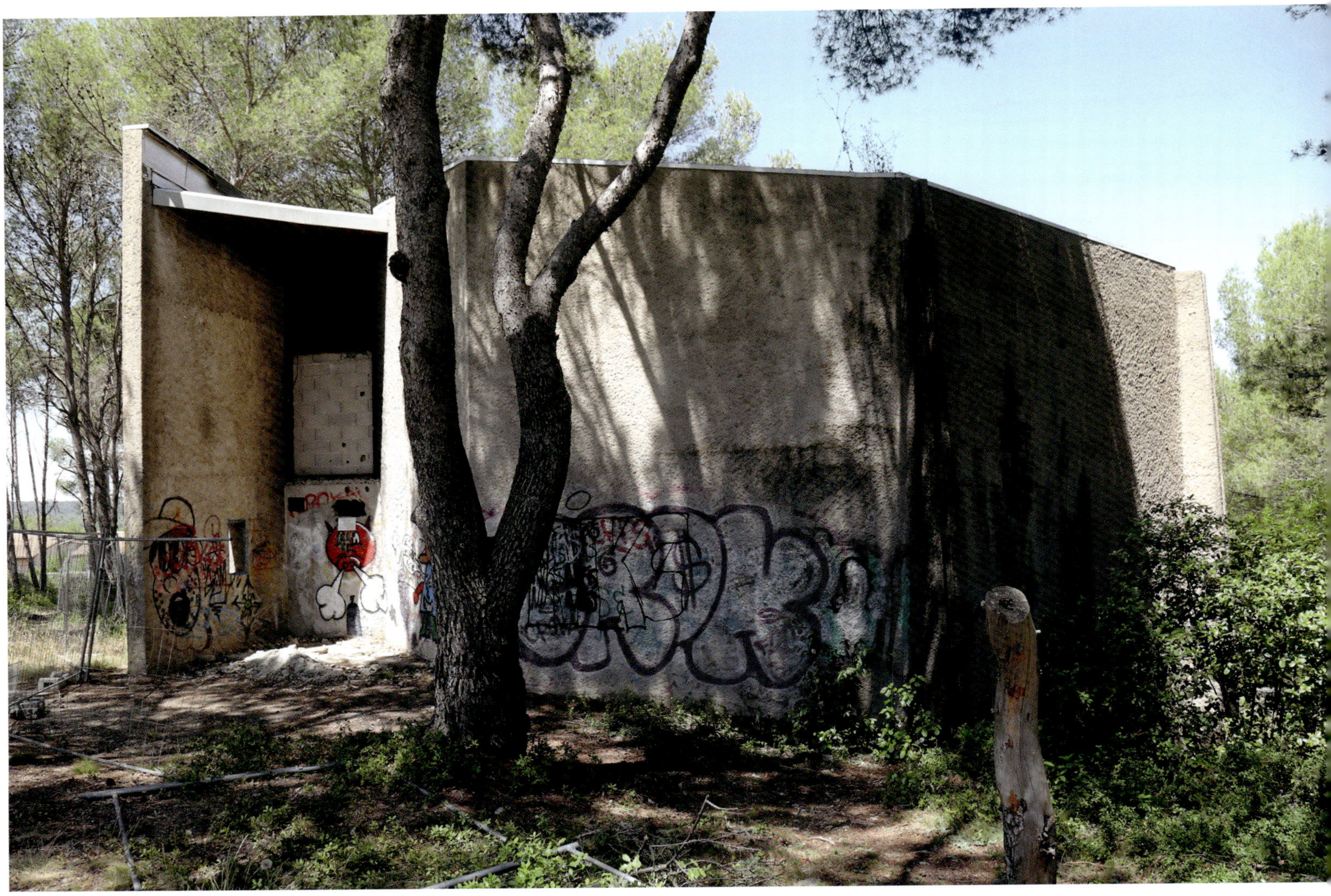

Castelnau-le-Lez – Panrama – 2021

Castelnau-le-Lez, Panrama. Panrama is a cinematographic process invented by Philippe Jaulmes (1927–2017), in which films are projected onto a hemispherical cinema screen. This visual technique gives the audience the impression of being at the centre of the action. The director of the Géode did not choose his invention, however, prefering the Omnimax, a version of the Imax. Yet one cinema based on his concept was built in Castelnau-le-Lez. Now a listed monument, it seems to be dozing before falling asleep for eternity.

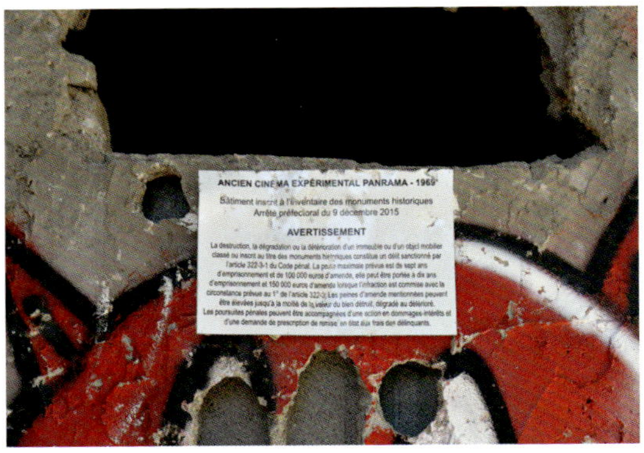

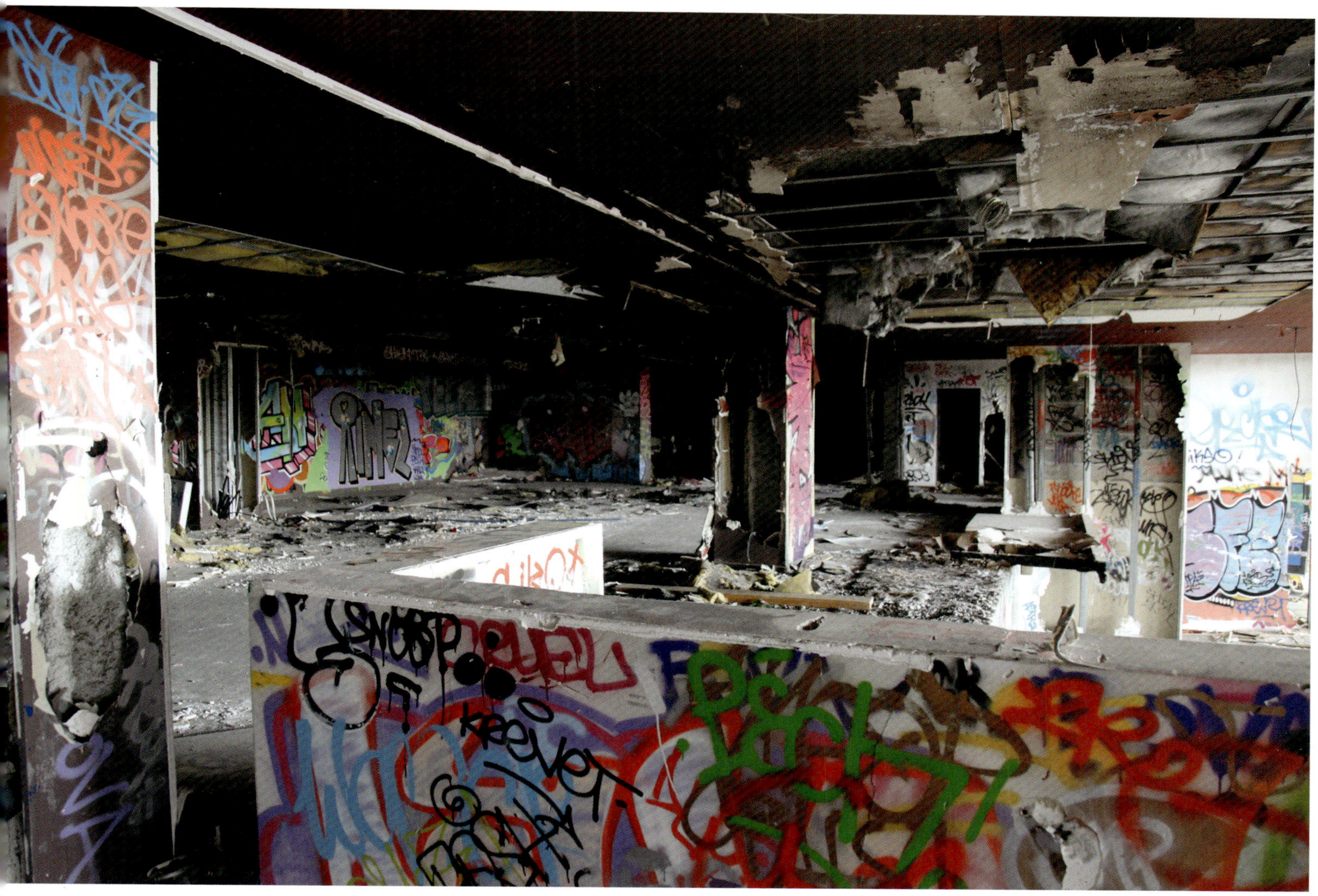

issargues – Majestic – 2010

Caissargues, Majestic. The Majestic multiplex, with its eight screens and 1,480 seats, closed its doors at the end of 2002. Inaugurated in 2000, it had only survived for two years. A first in the world of multiplexes. A fairly short life for a cinema with a construction budget of 7 million euros. In some towns they congregate, observing each other maliciously, killing the central old-fashioned cinemas in their path with discount prices and American-style car parks. The Majestic is the first victim of this debauchery of multiplexes ready to devour each other in an over-developed market that accounts for nearly half of global audience figures.

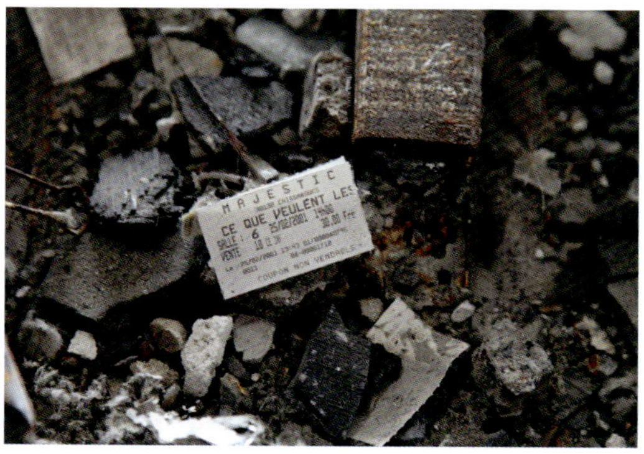

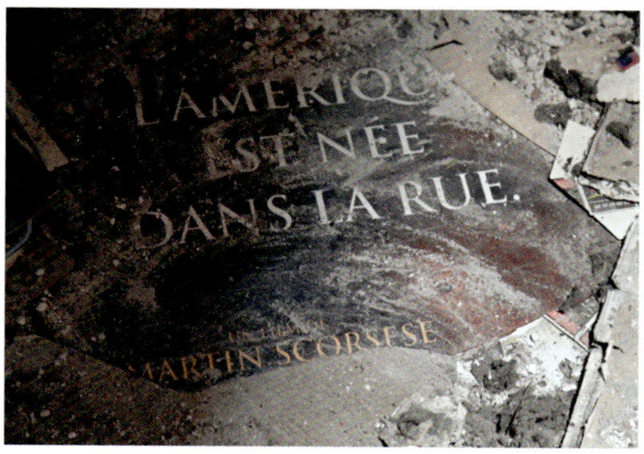

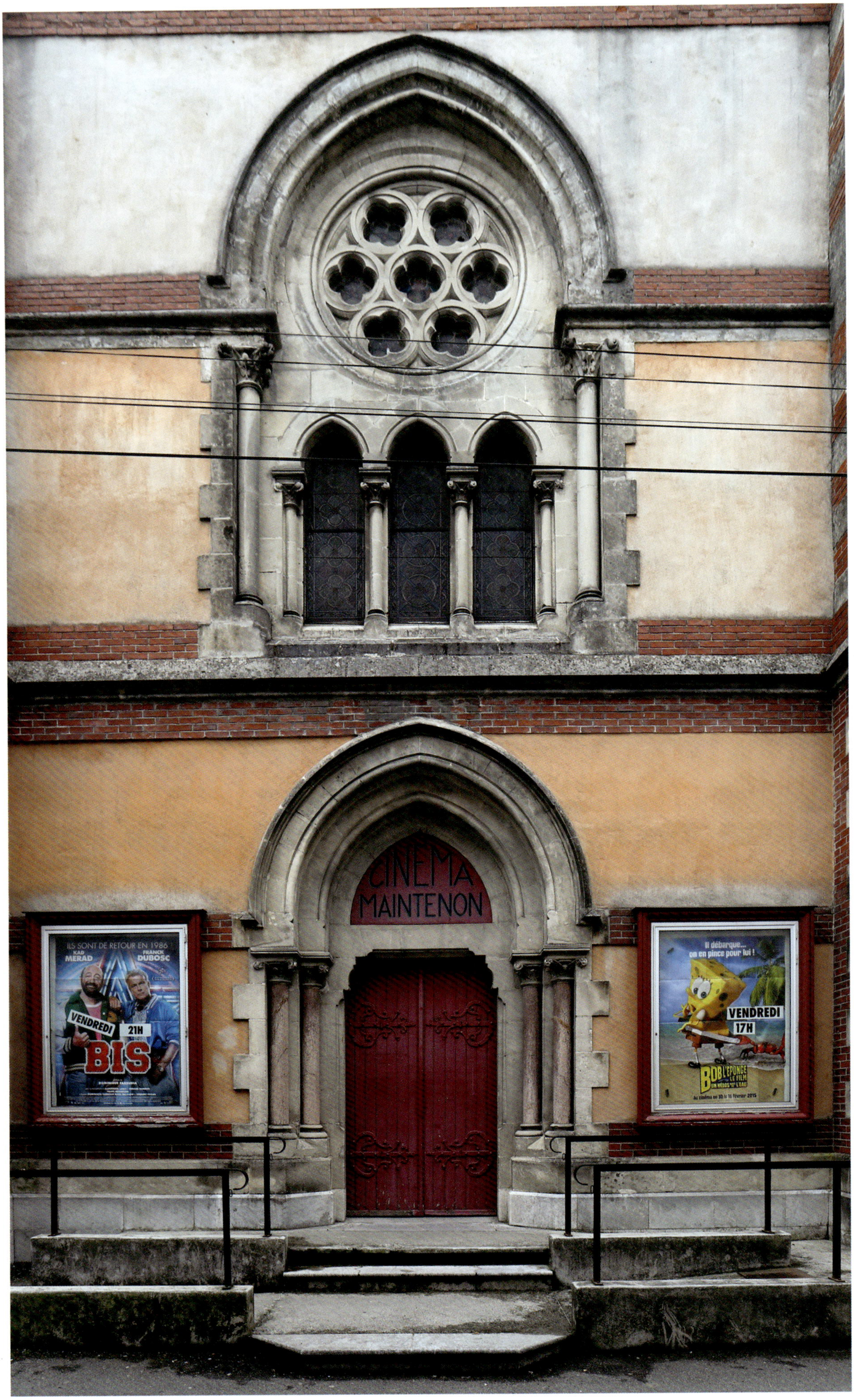

Bagnères-de-Bigorre – Le Maintenon – 2015

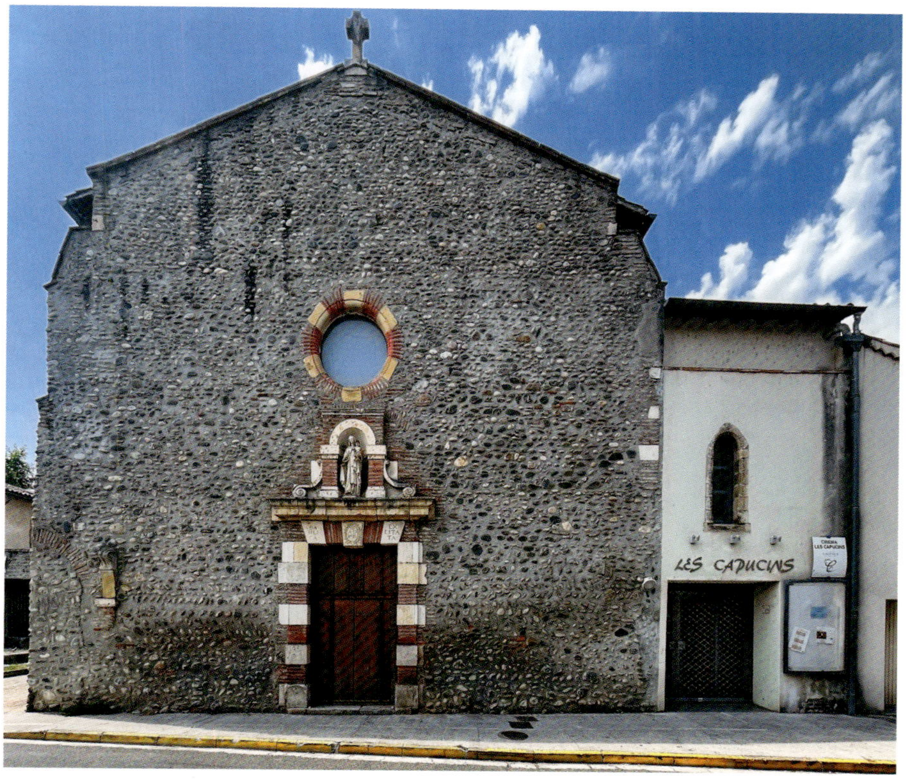

Cazères – Les Capucins – 2022

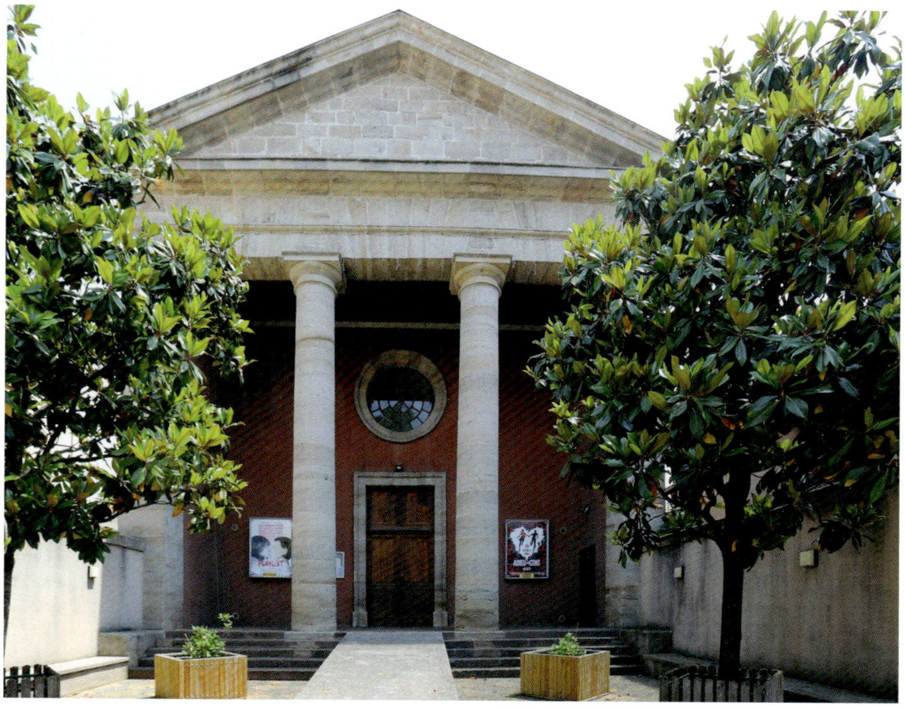
Camarès – Le Temple – 2021

Camarès, Le Temple. In 1983, unable to maintain it, the Protestant community of Camarès donated its temple. The place of worship became a cinema, open three times a week. The downside is that the community assumes the losses, a great incentive for the 1,000 inhabitants of this Aveyron town.

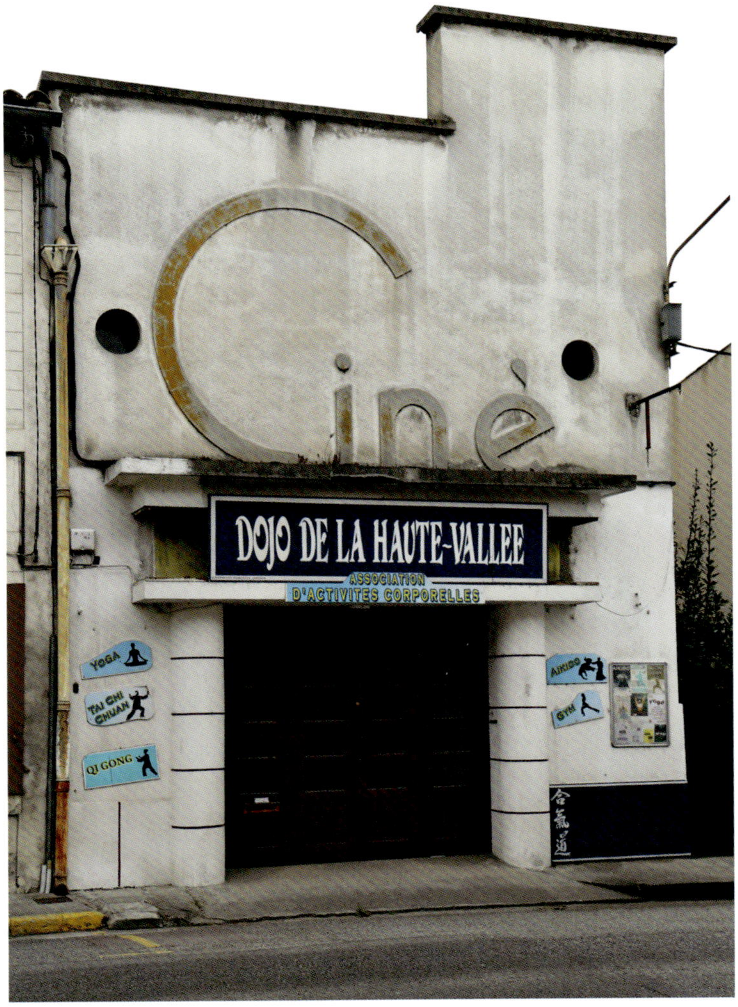

Limoux – Ciné – 2015

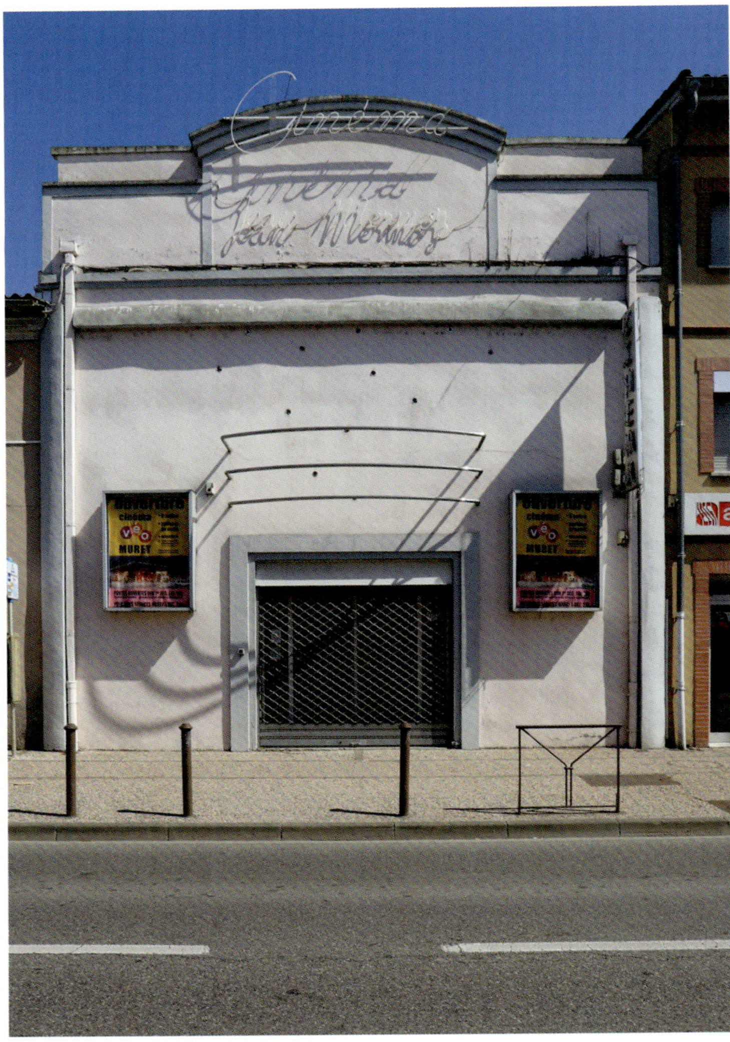

Muret – Mermoz – 2015

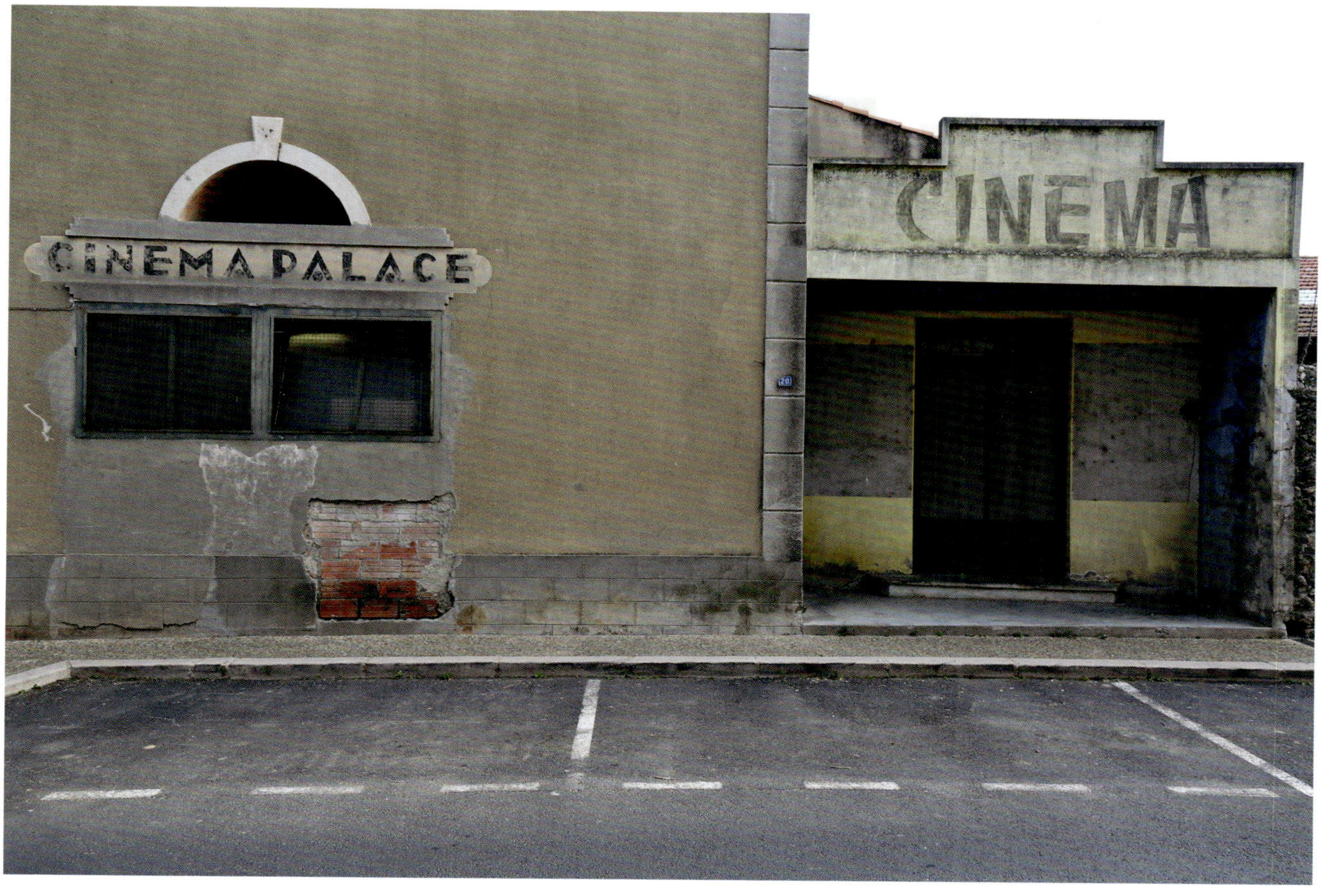

Cessenon sur Orbe – Cinéma Palace – 2015

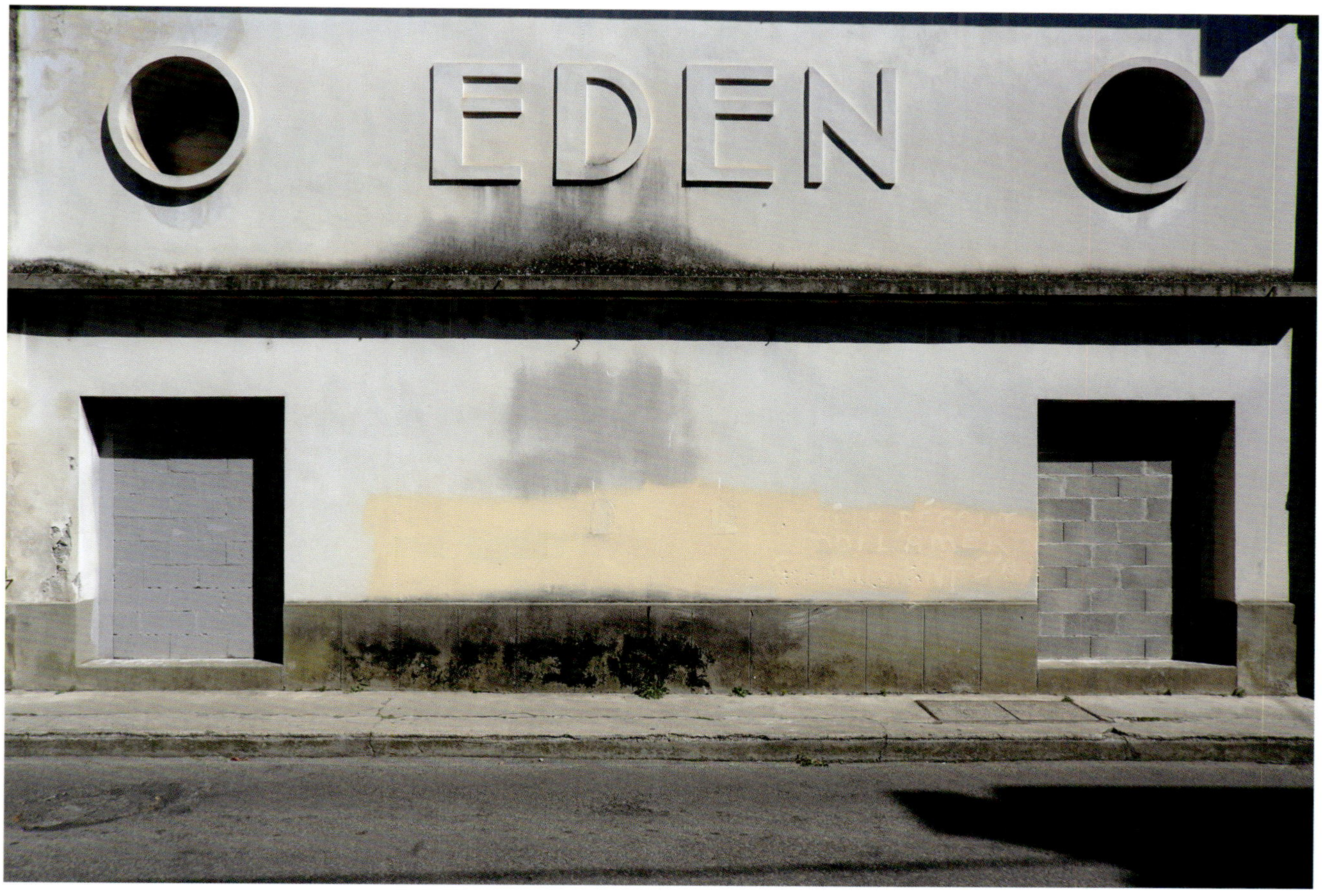

Ganges – Eden – 2016

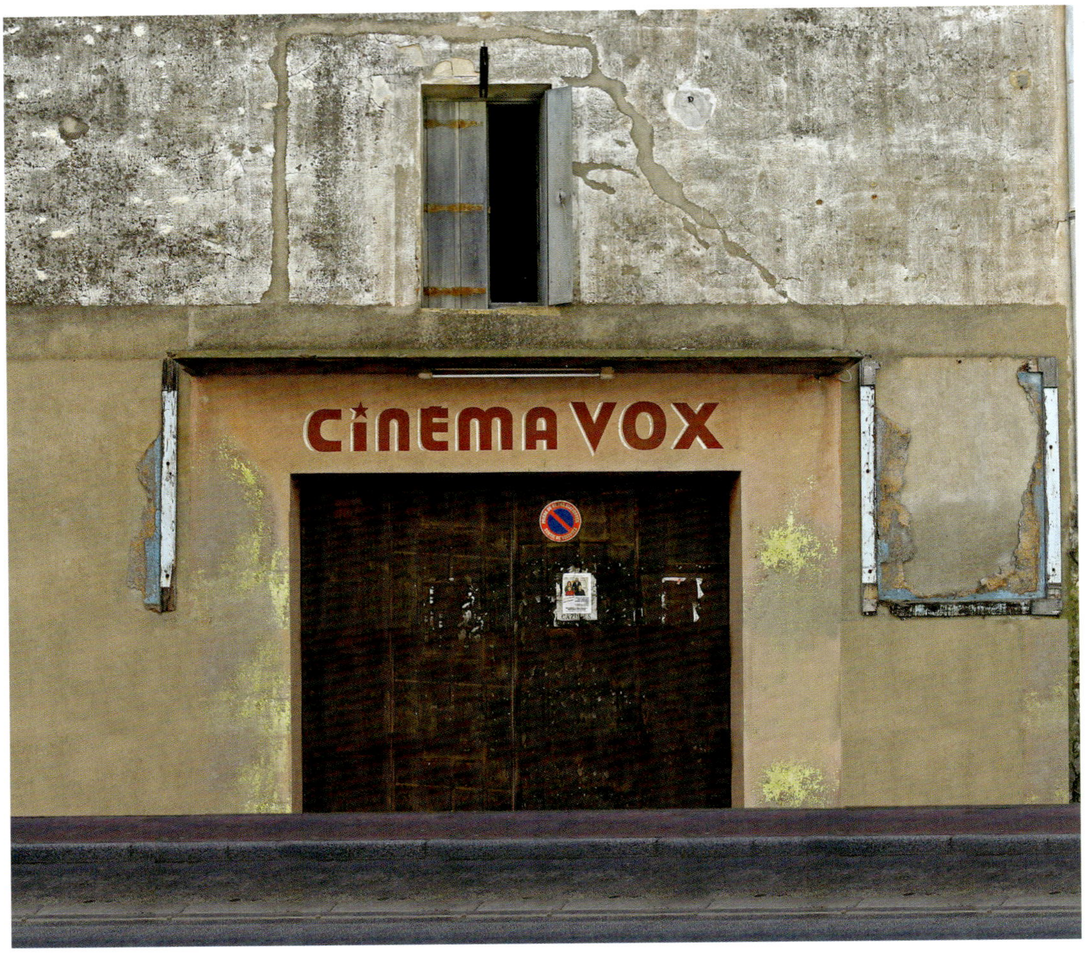

Cazouls-les-Béziers – Cinéma Vox – 2015

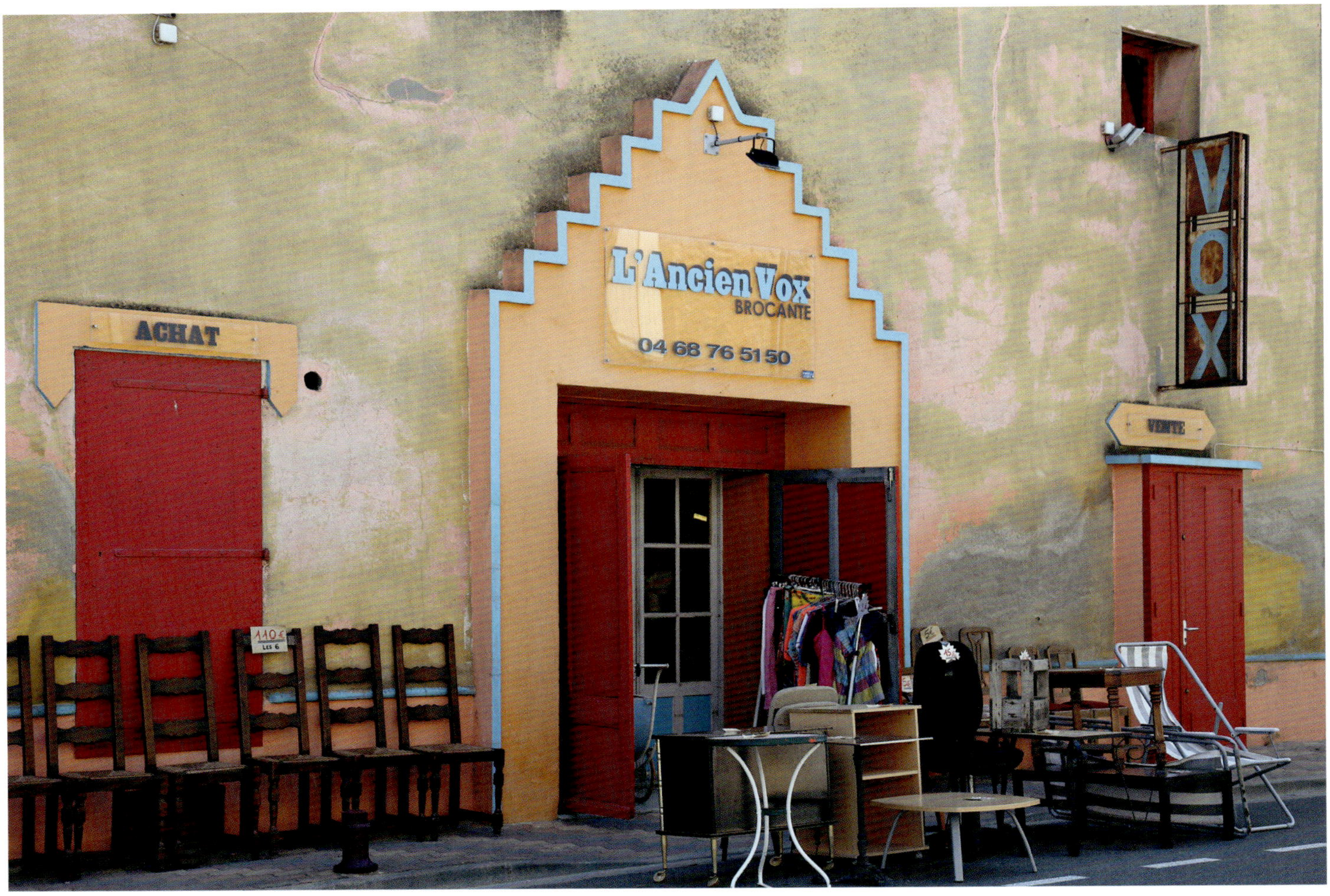

Rieux-Minervois – L'Ancien Vox – 2021

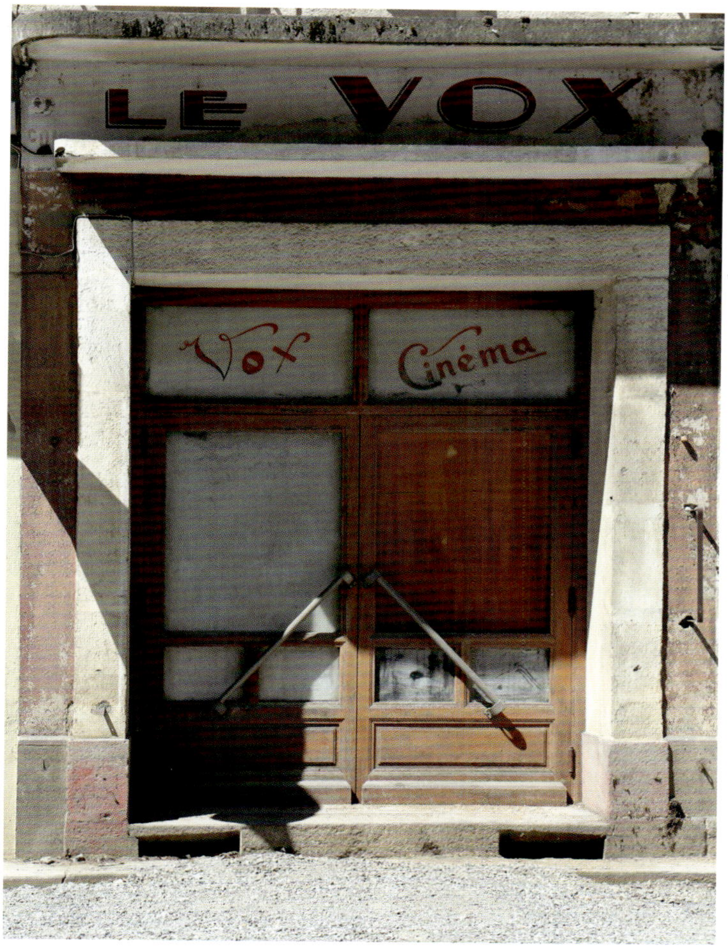

Brassac – Le Vox – 2017

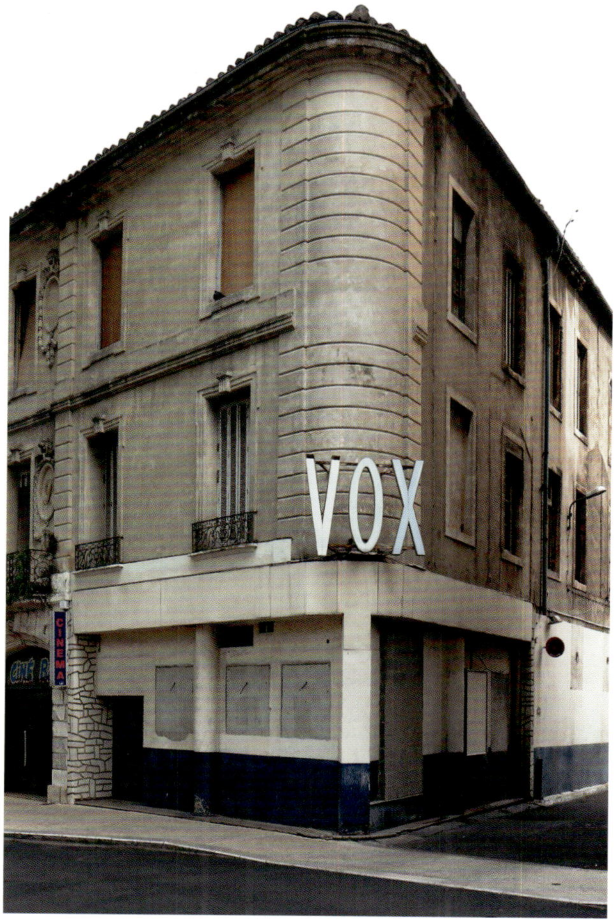

Nïmes – Vox – 2017

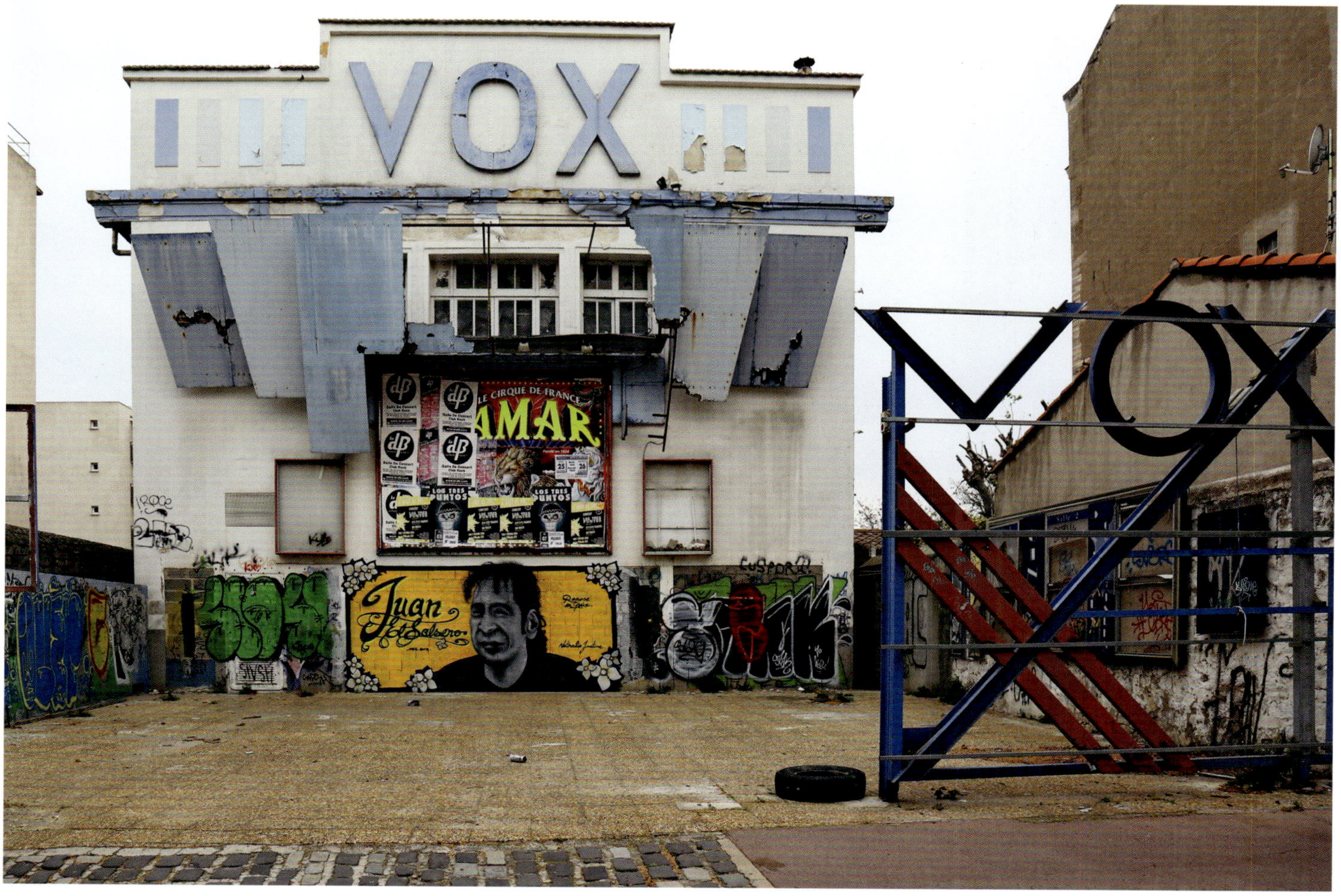

Narbonne – Vox – 2015 (destroyed)

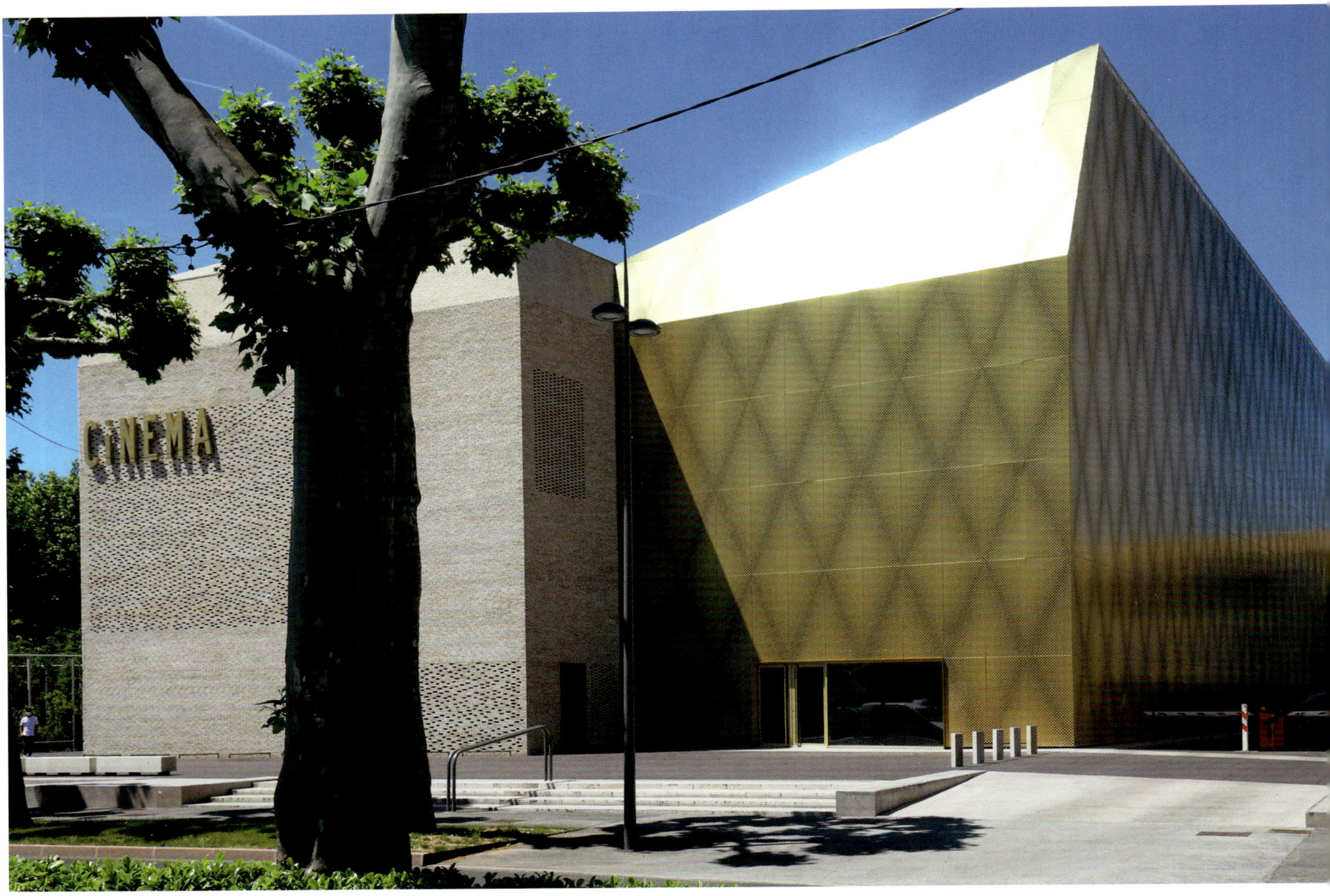

Cahors – Le Grand Palais – 2021

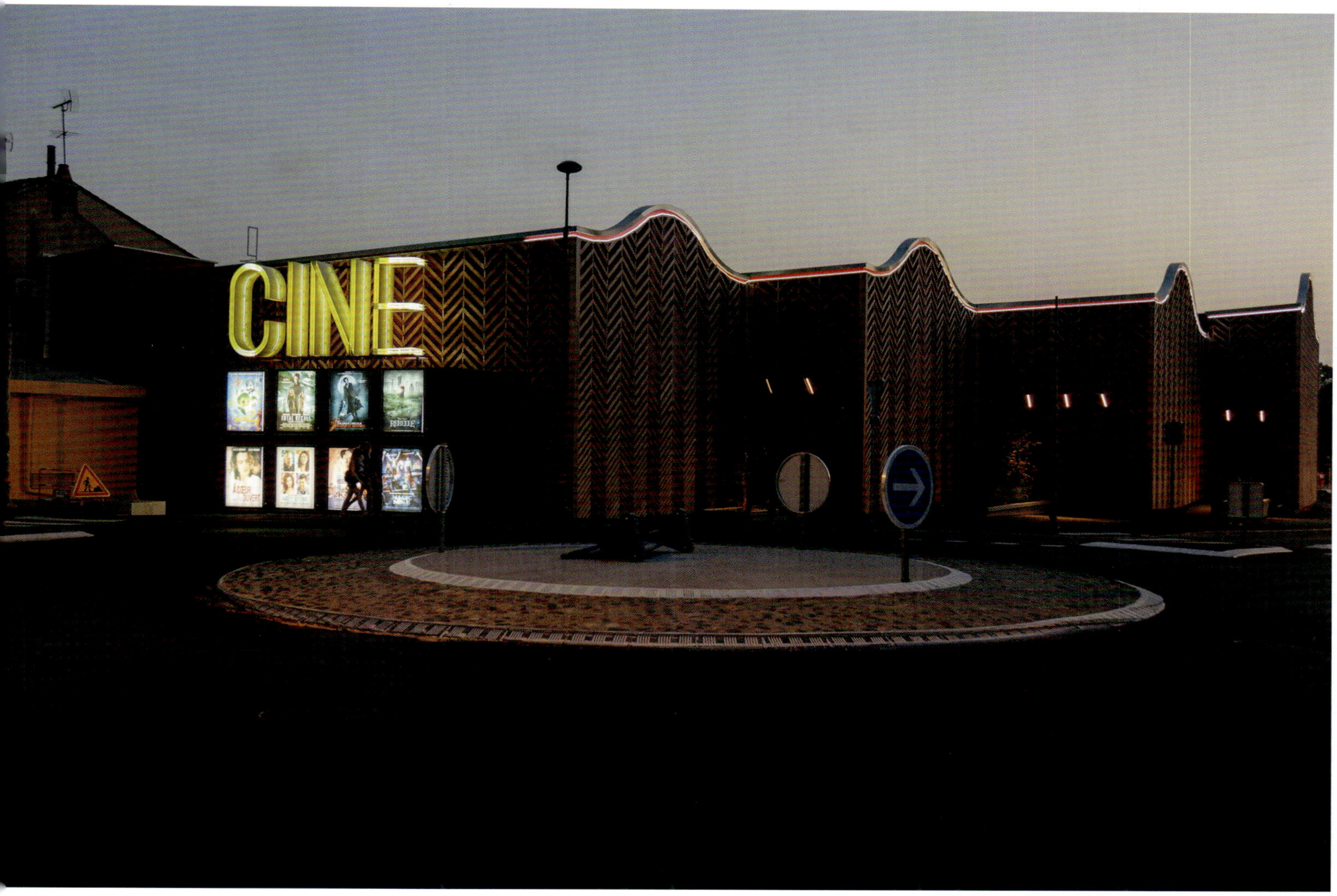

h – Ciné – 2012

PAYS DE LA LOIRE

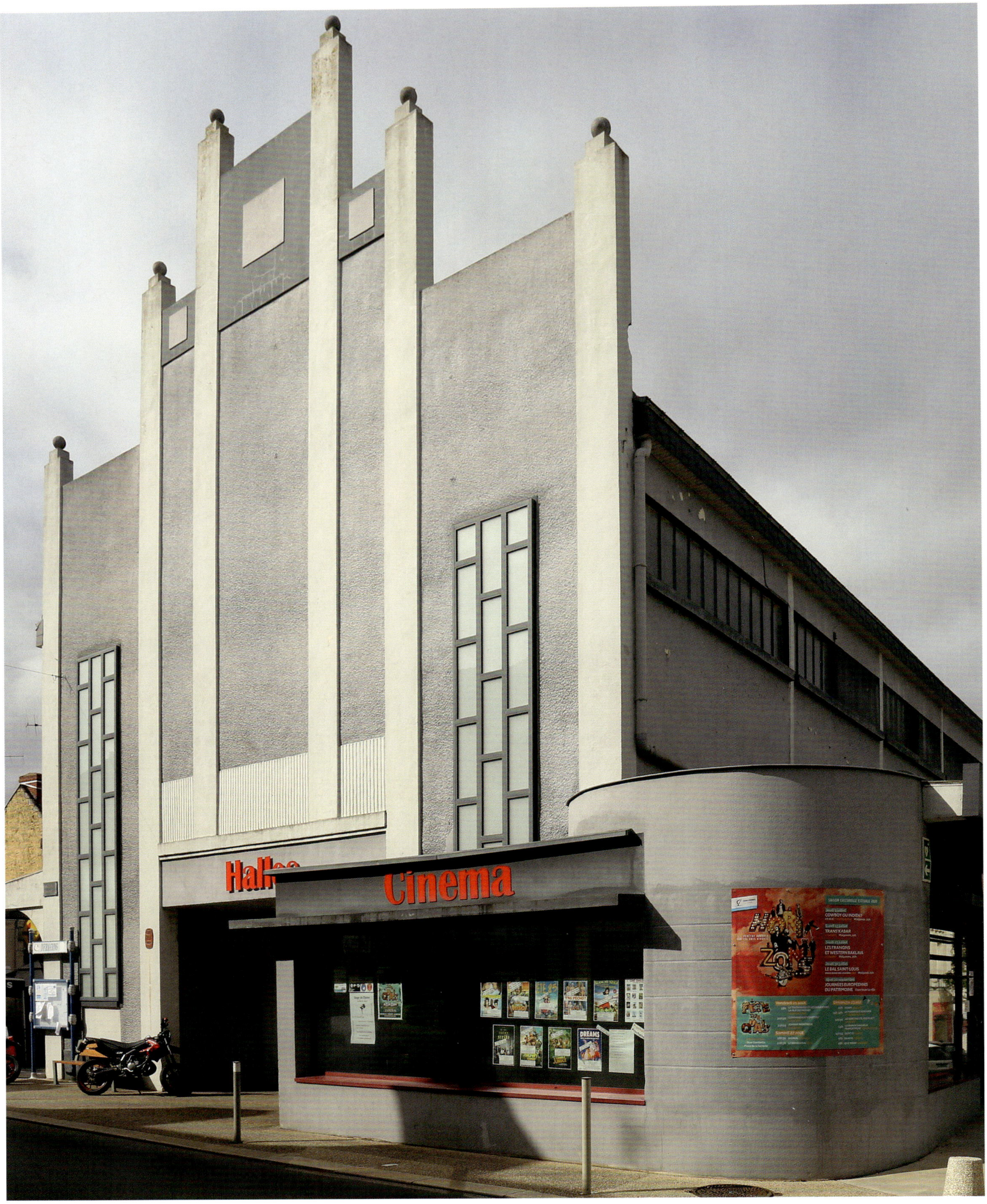

Chalonnes-sur-Loire – Espace cinéma – 2020

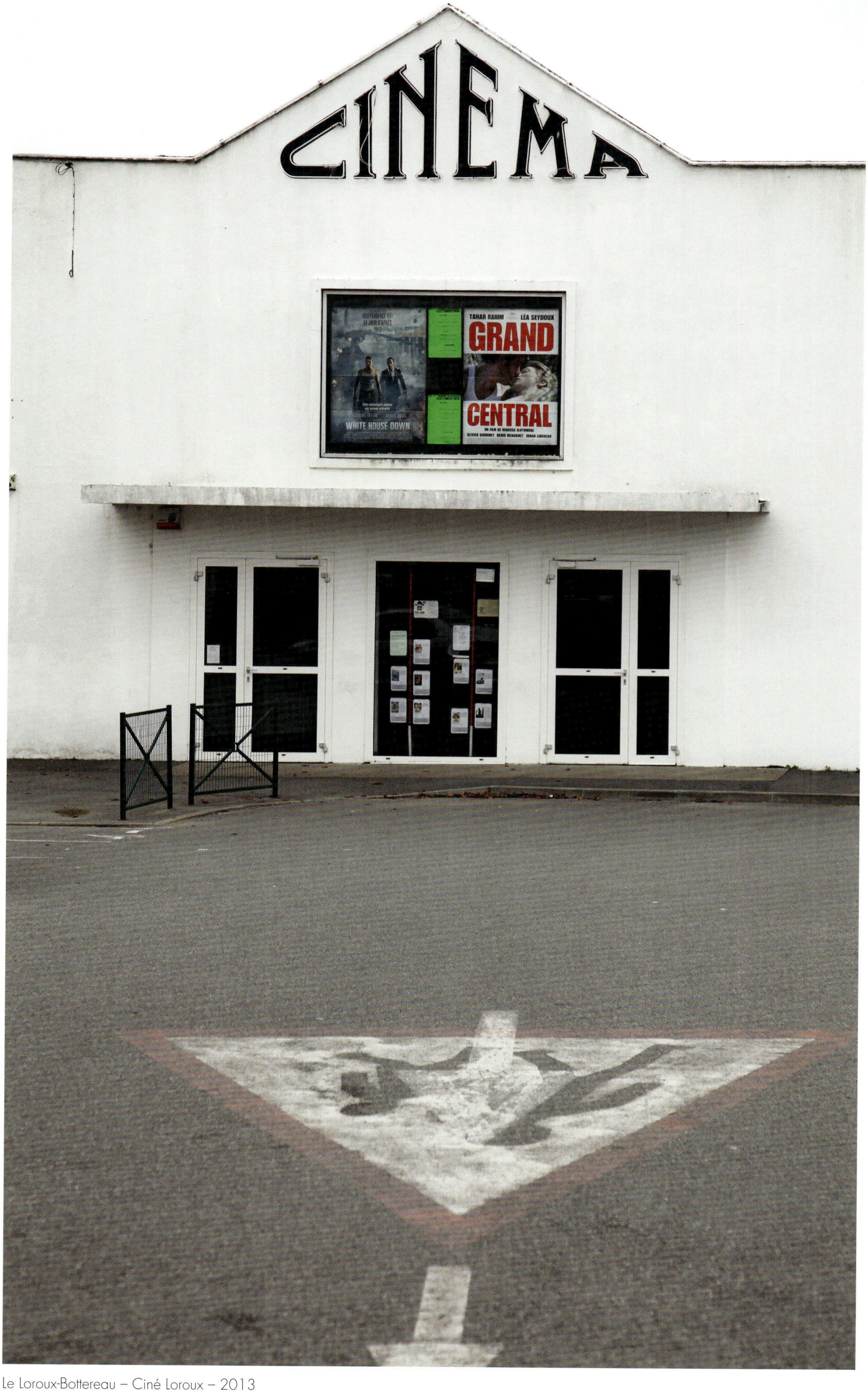

Le Loroux-Bottereau – Ciné Loroux – 2013

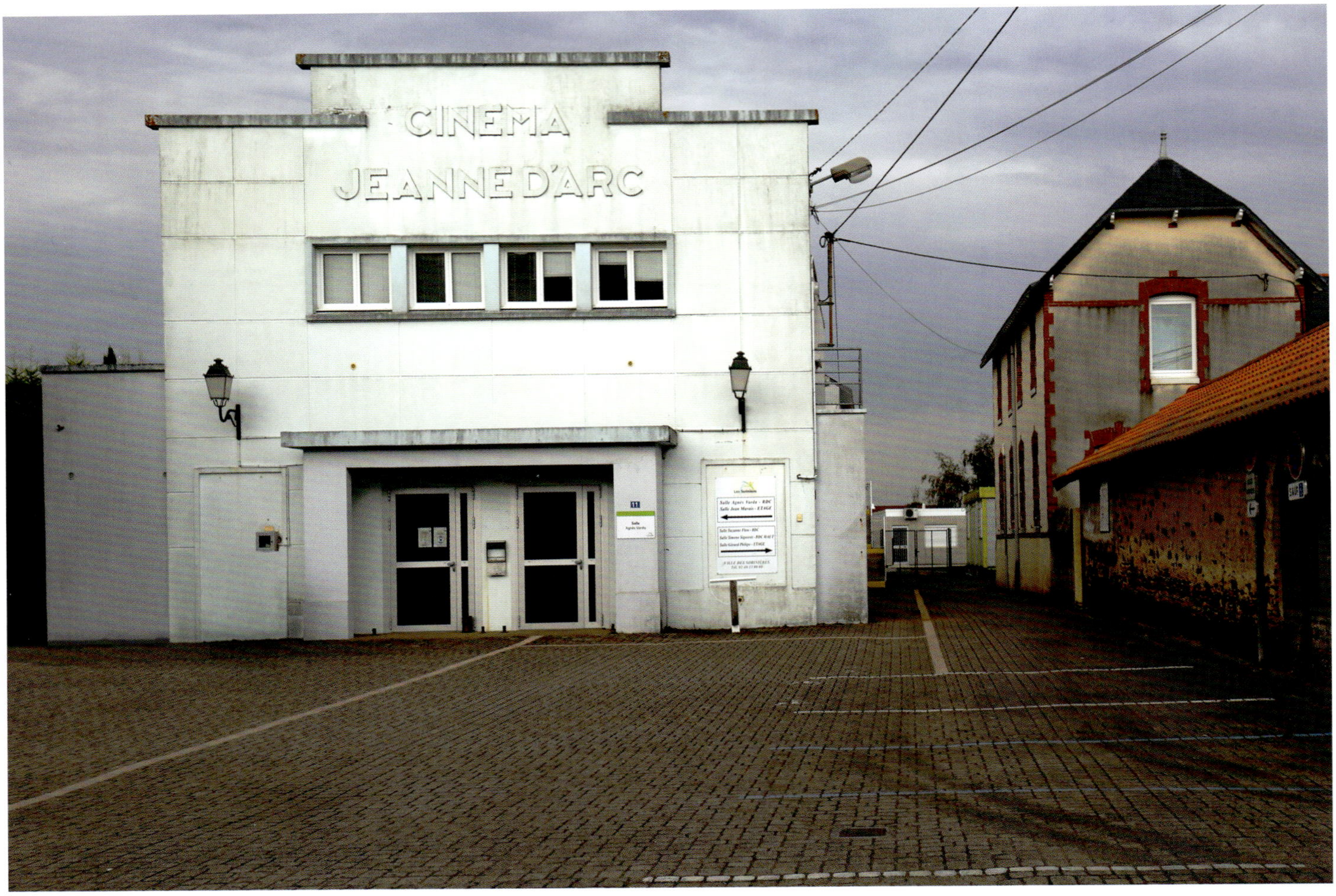

Les Sorinières – Cinéma Jeanne d'Arc – 2020

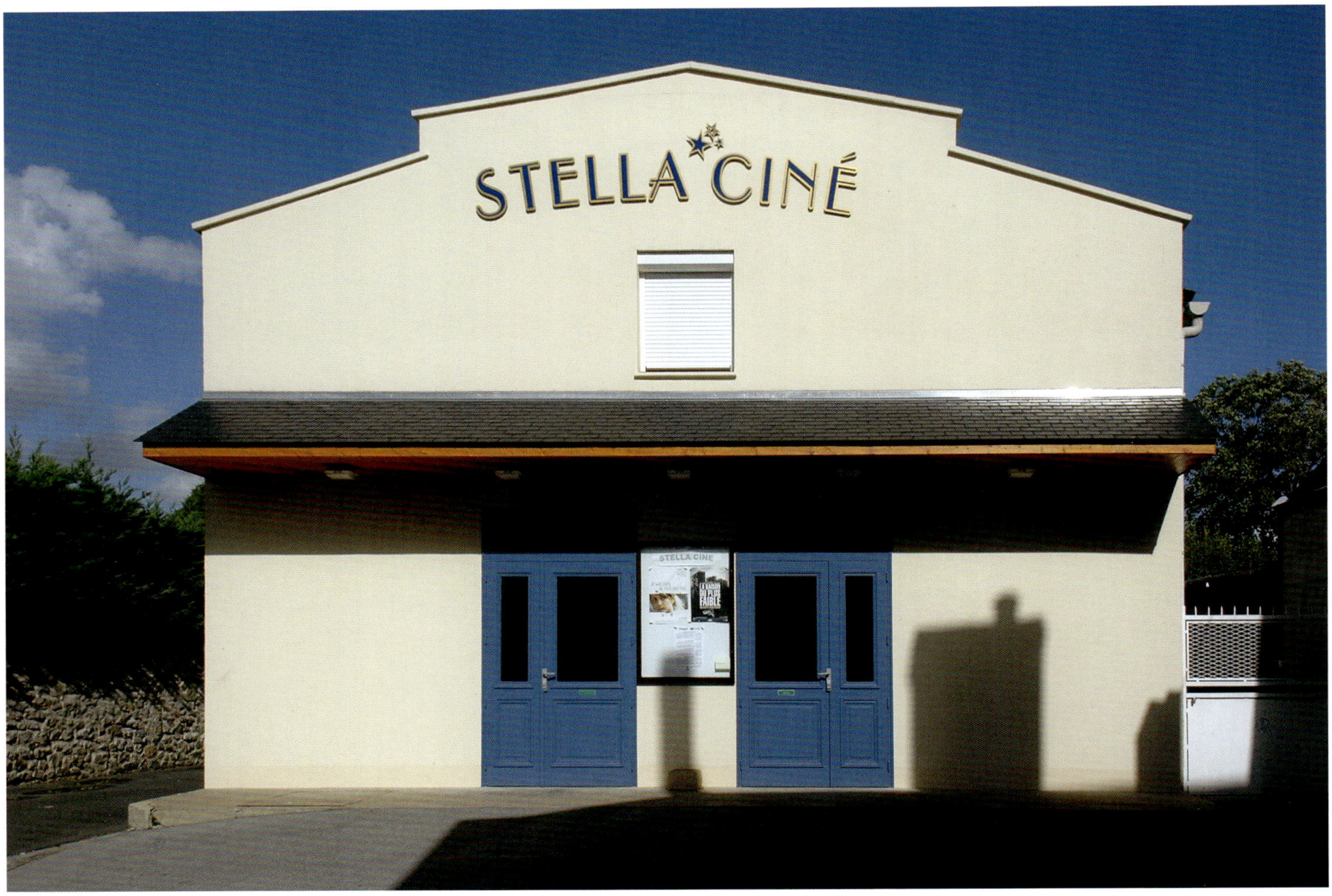

Baugé – Stella – 2006

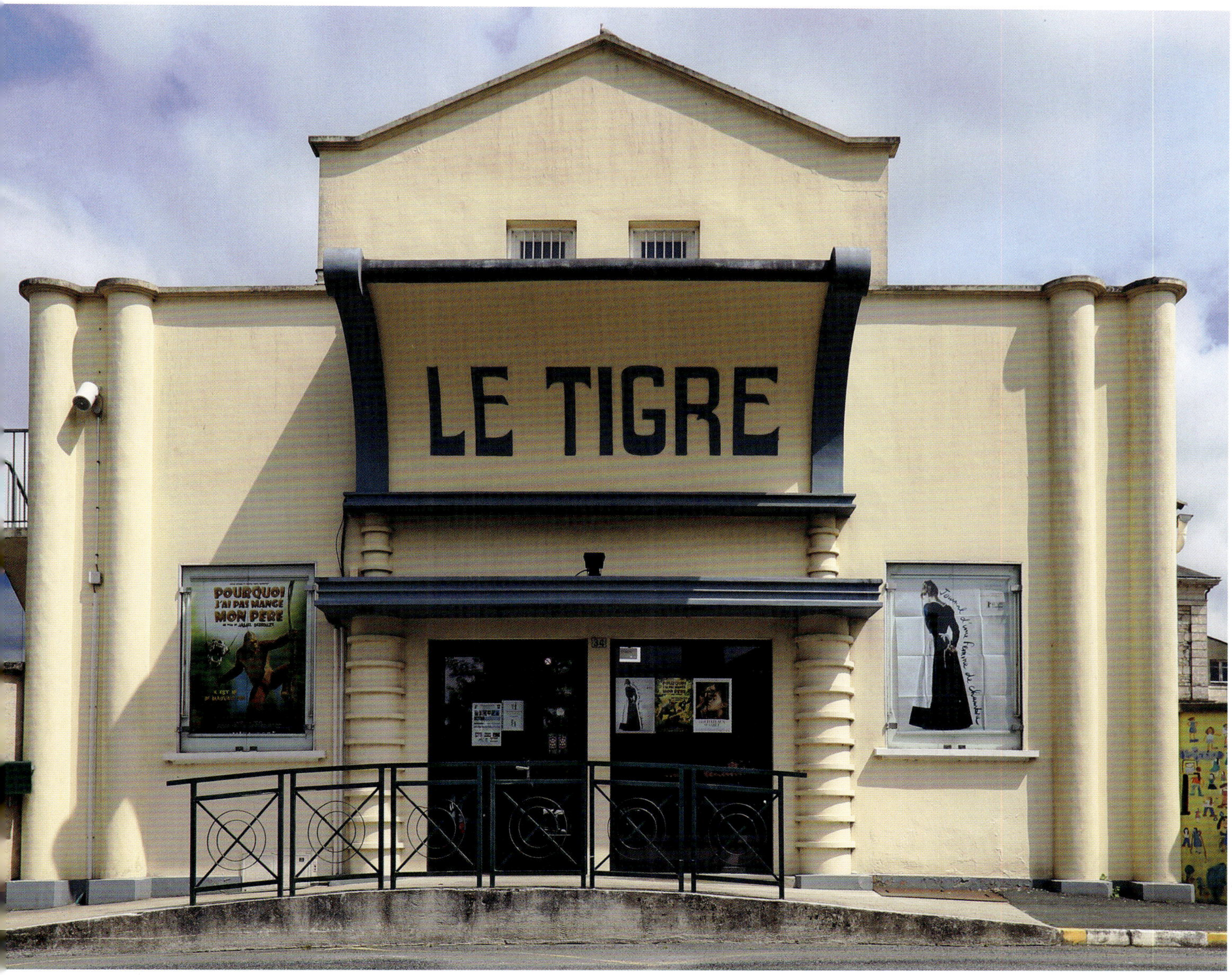

Sainte-Hermine – Le Tigre – 2015

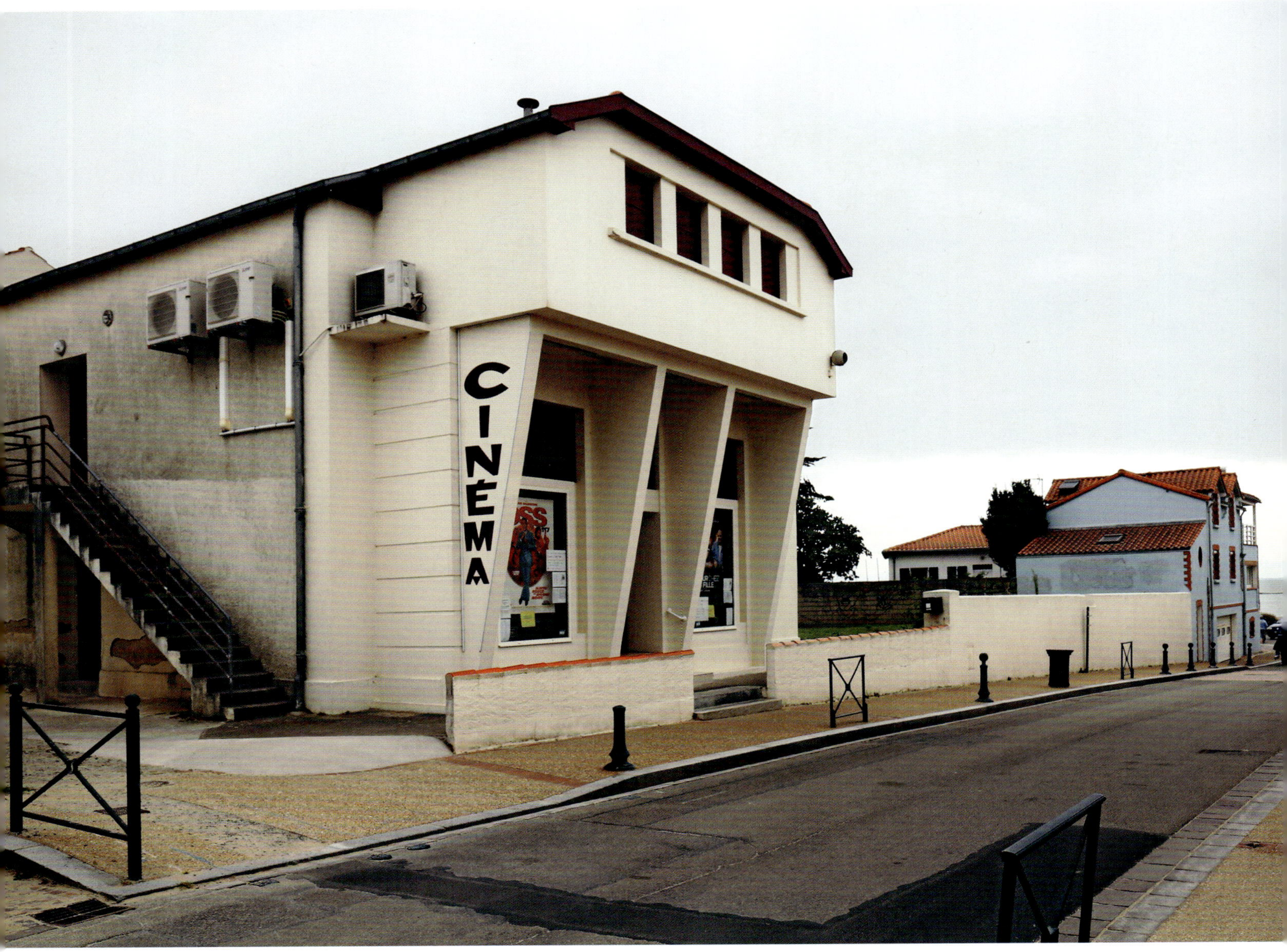

La Bernerie-en-Retz – Jeanne d'Arc – 2021

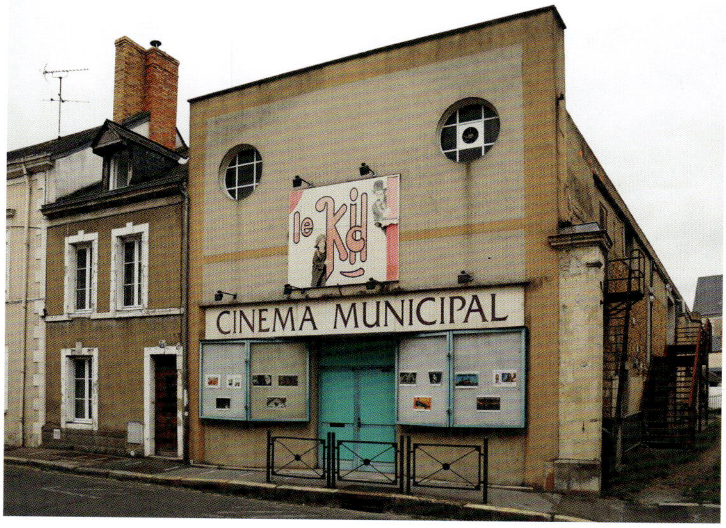

La Flèche - Le Kid - 2021

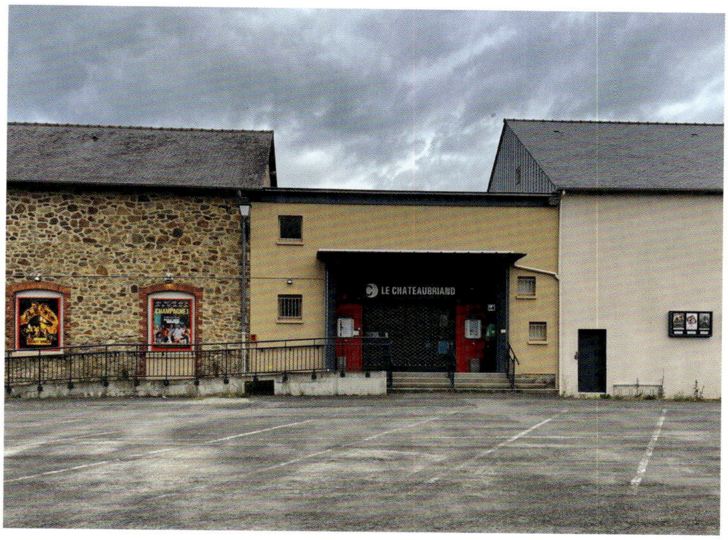

Combourg – Le Chateaubriand – 2022

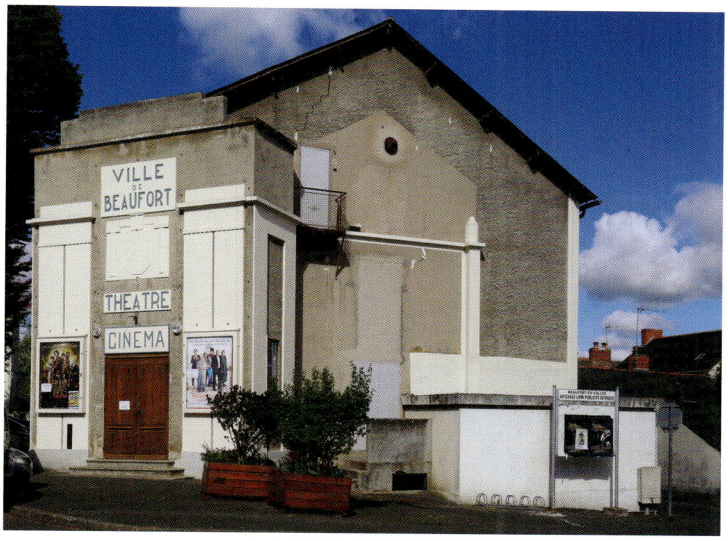

Beaufort-en-Vallée – Cinéma municipal – 2015

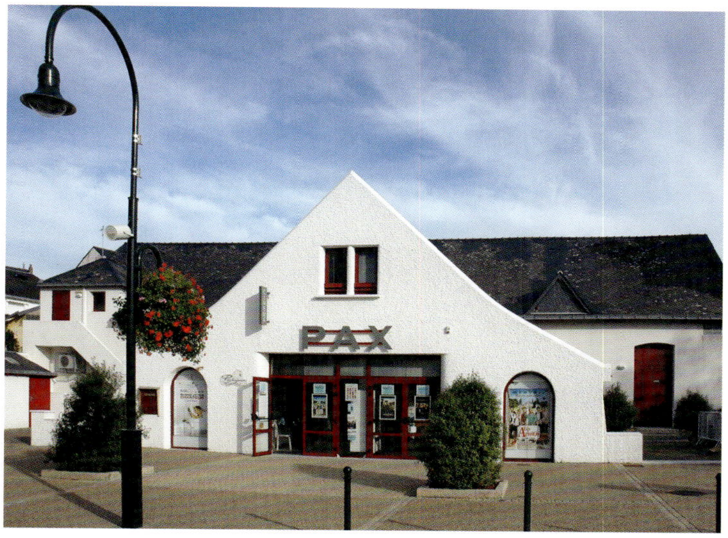

Le Pouliguen – Pax – 2006

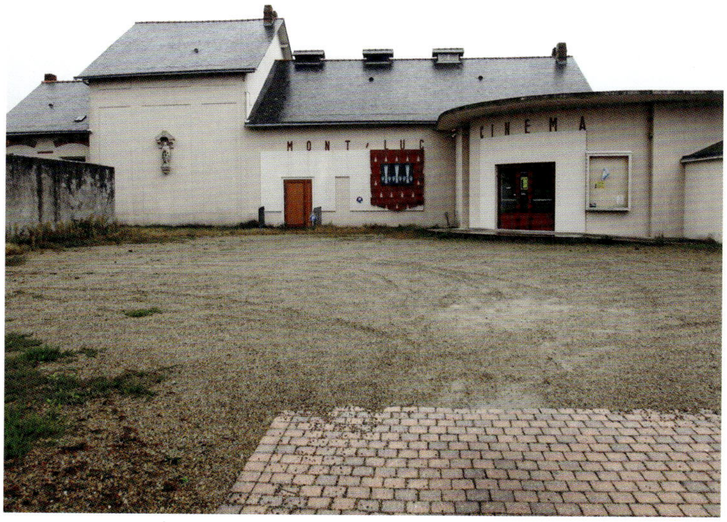

Saint-Étienne-de-Montluc – Mont–Luc – 2019

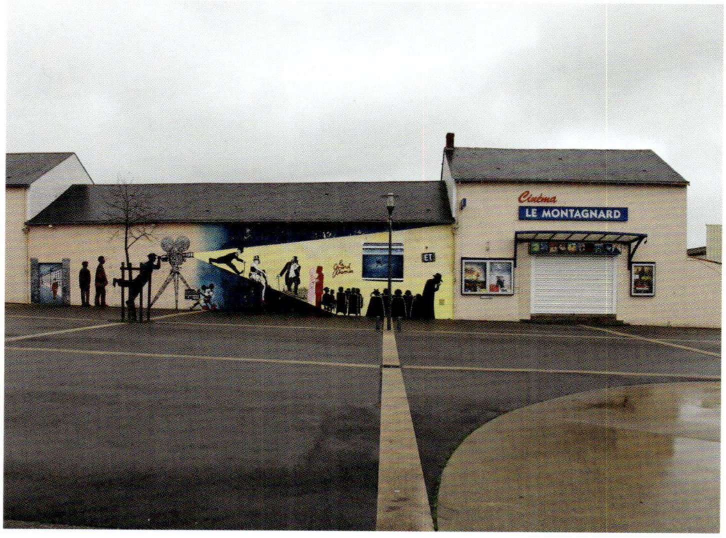

La Montagne – Le Montagnard – 2017

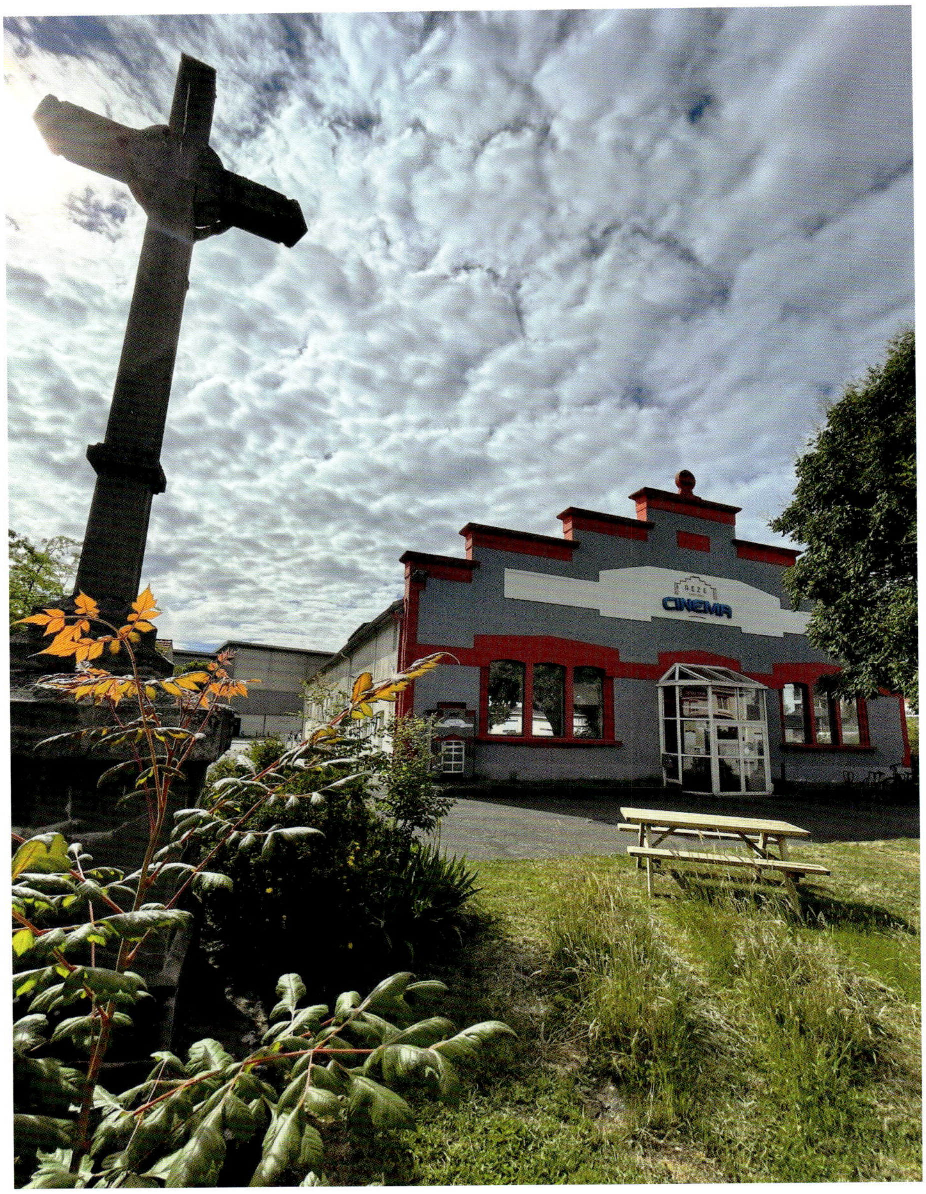

Rezé – Saint Paul – 2022

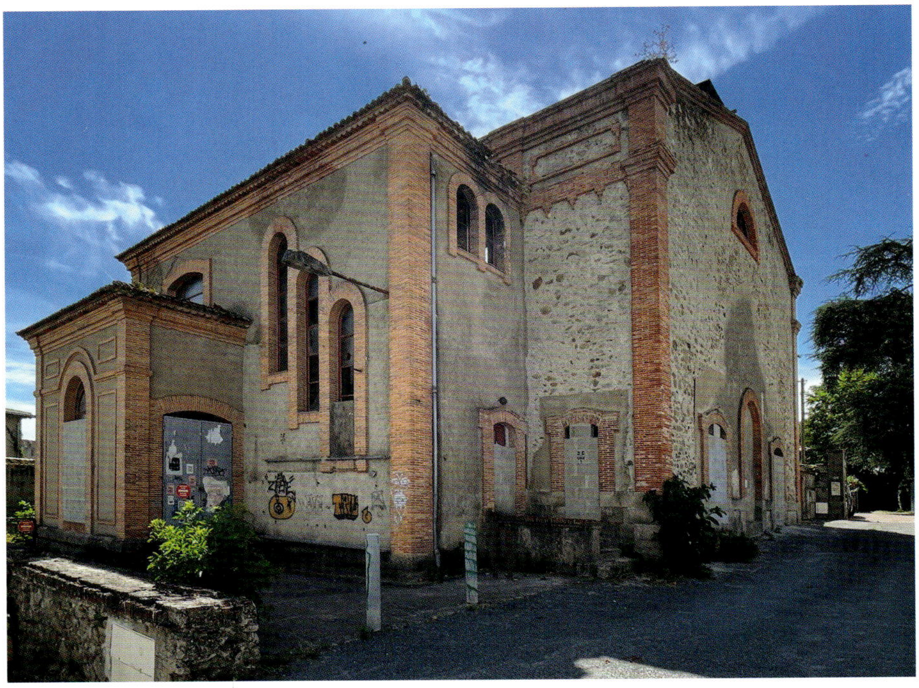

Clisson – former Tivoli cinema–theater – 2022

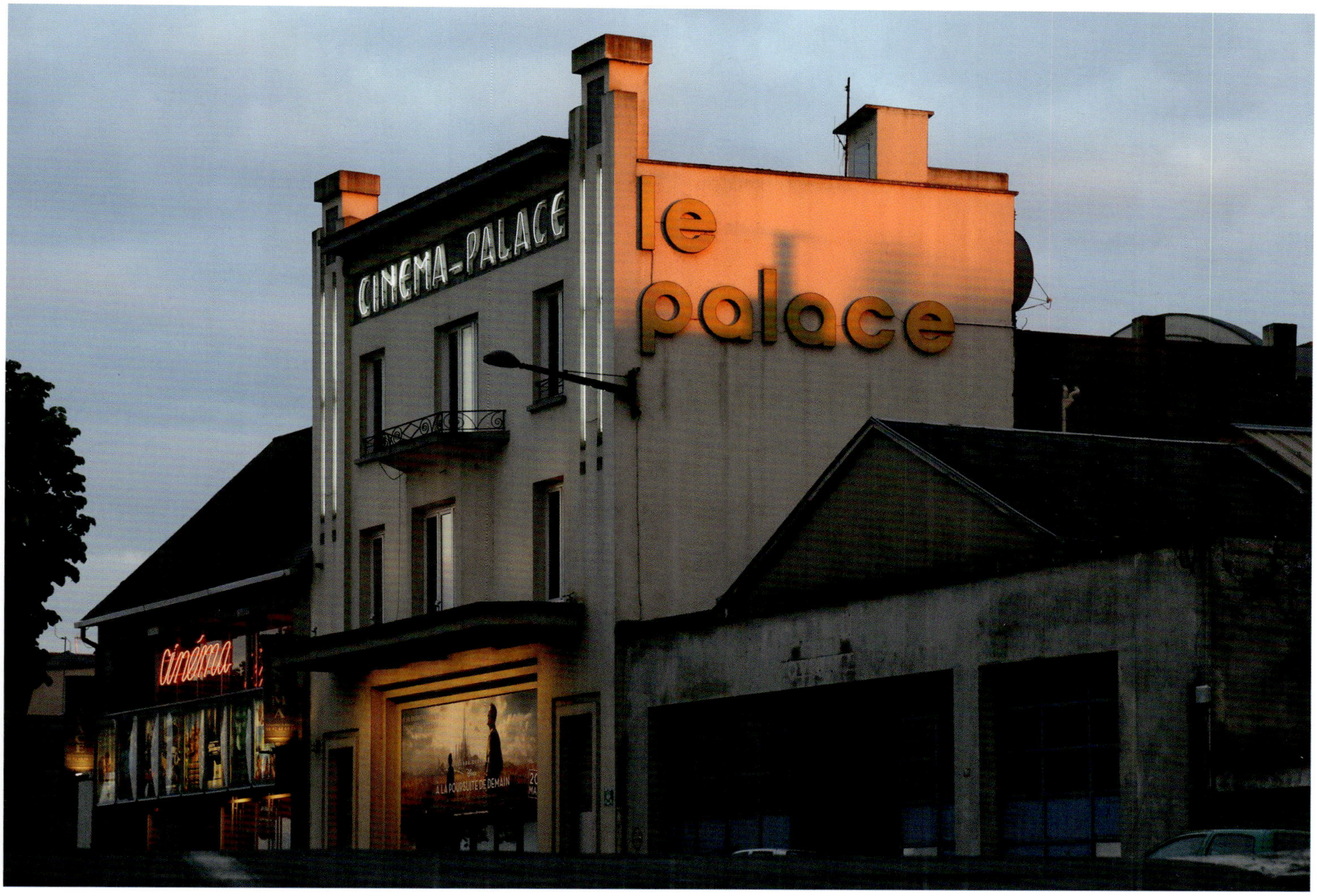

Saumur – Le Palace – 2015

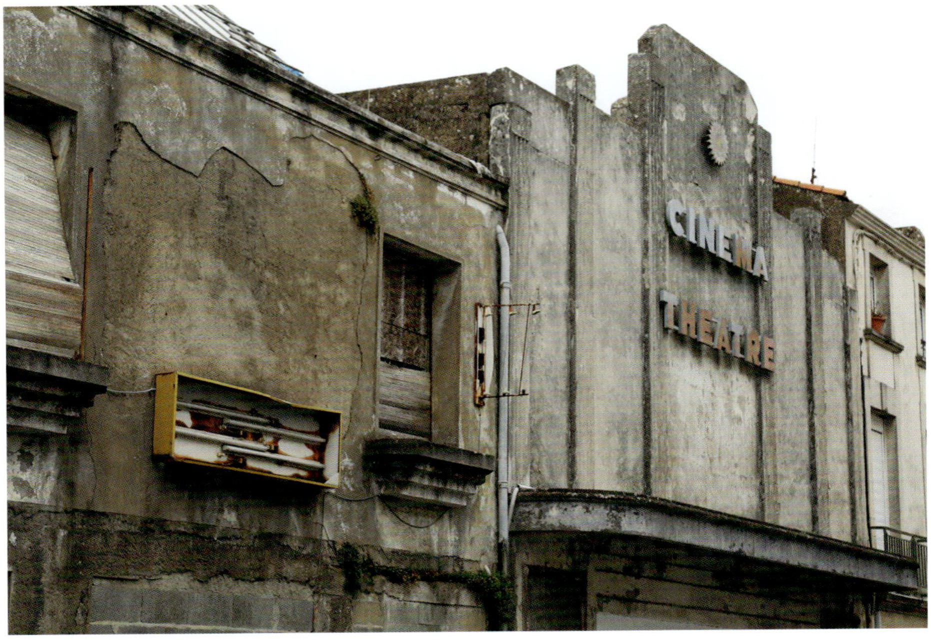

Paimboeuf – Le Familia – 2021

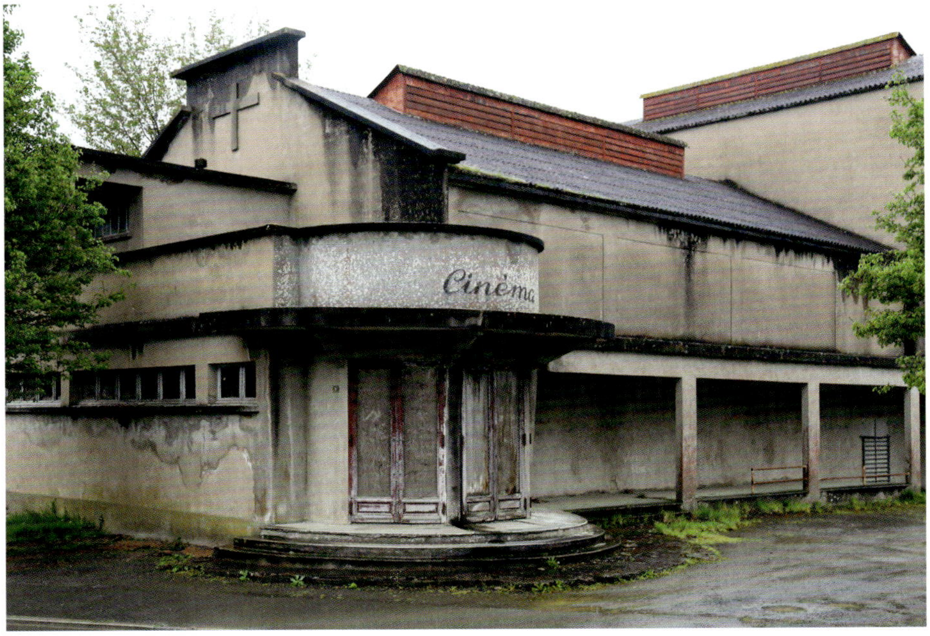

Derval – Saint-Sébastien – 2015, torn down

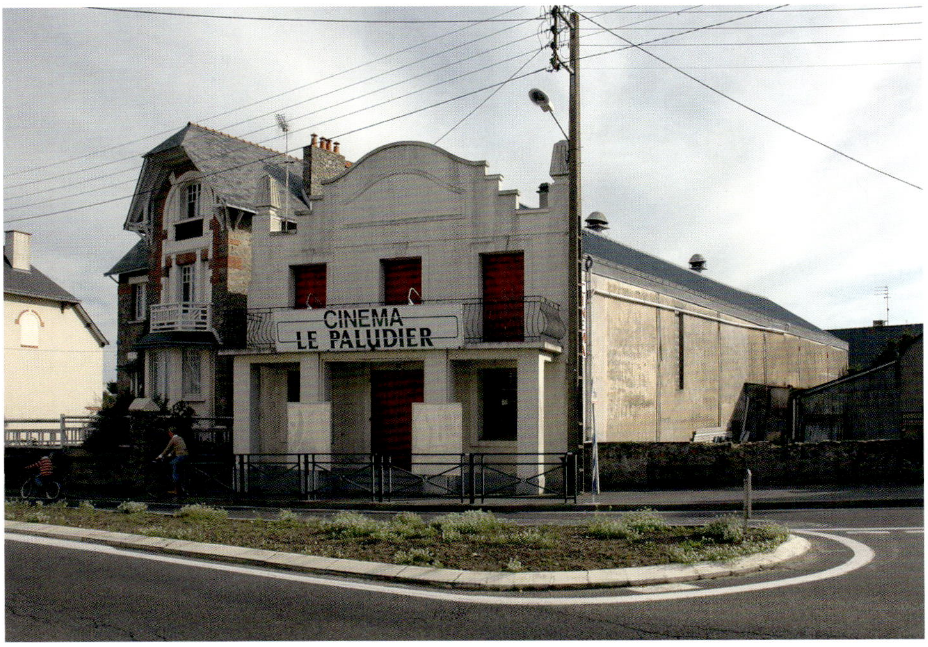

Batz-sur-Mer – Le Paludier – 2006

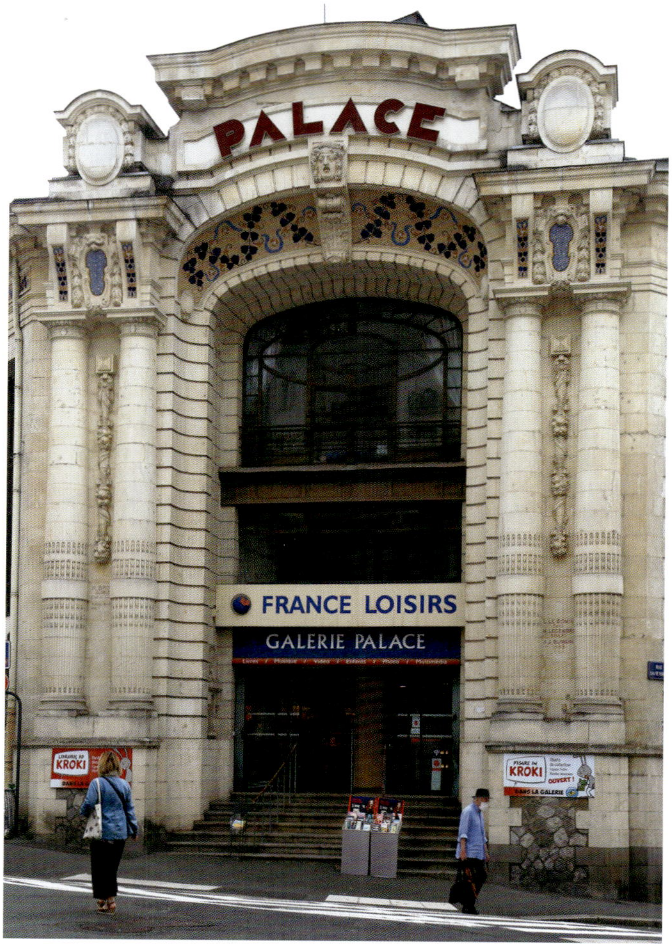

Angers – Palace – 2022

Angers, Palace. The cinema opened in 1922 under the name Familia: 1,200 seats with boxes and a monumental chandelier. It belonged to the Poulain chocolate manufacturer, owner of many venues, all with the same name. Taken over by Pathé, it became the Palace. The cinema disappeared in the early 1980s and turned into a shopping mall. The mosaic-decorated façade is unchanged.

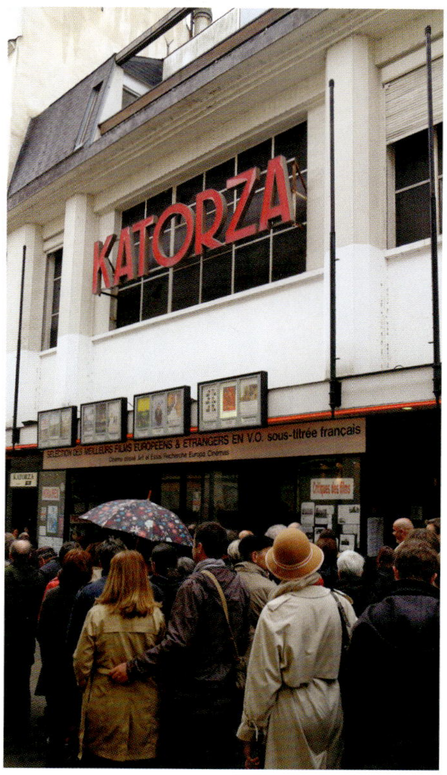

Nantes – Katorza – 2019

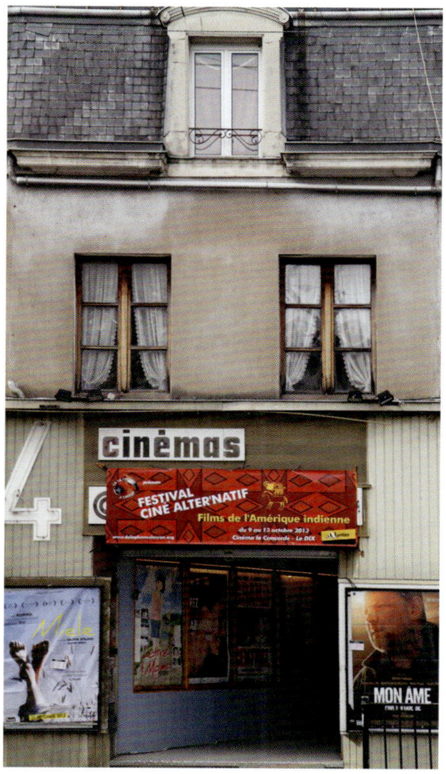

Nantes – Concorde – 2017

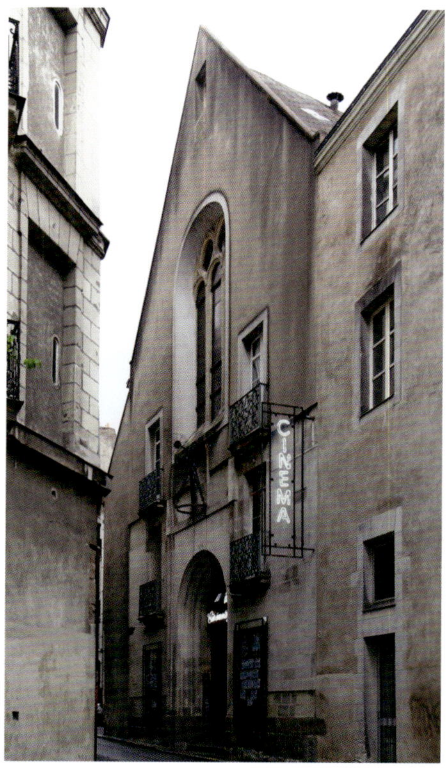

Nantes – Le Cinématographe – 2021

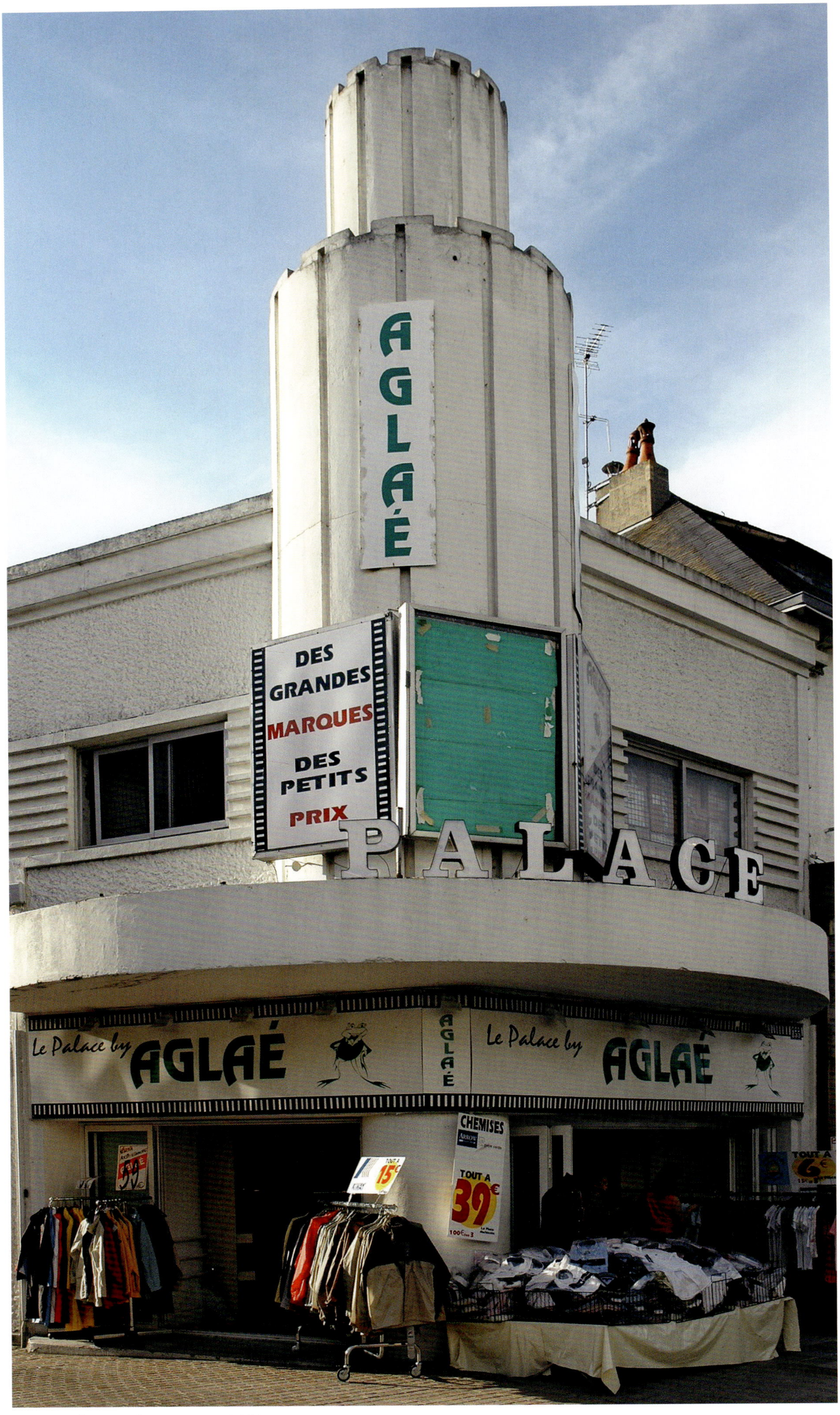

La Baule – former Palace cinema – 2006

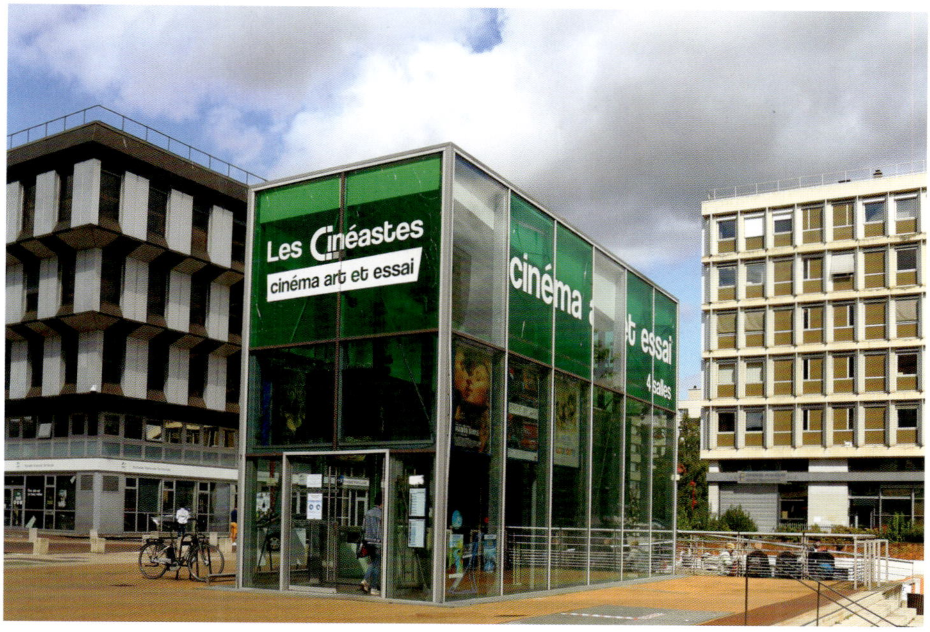

Le Mans – Les Cinéastes – 2021

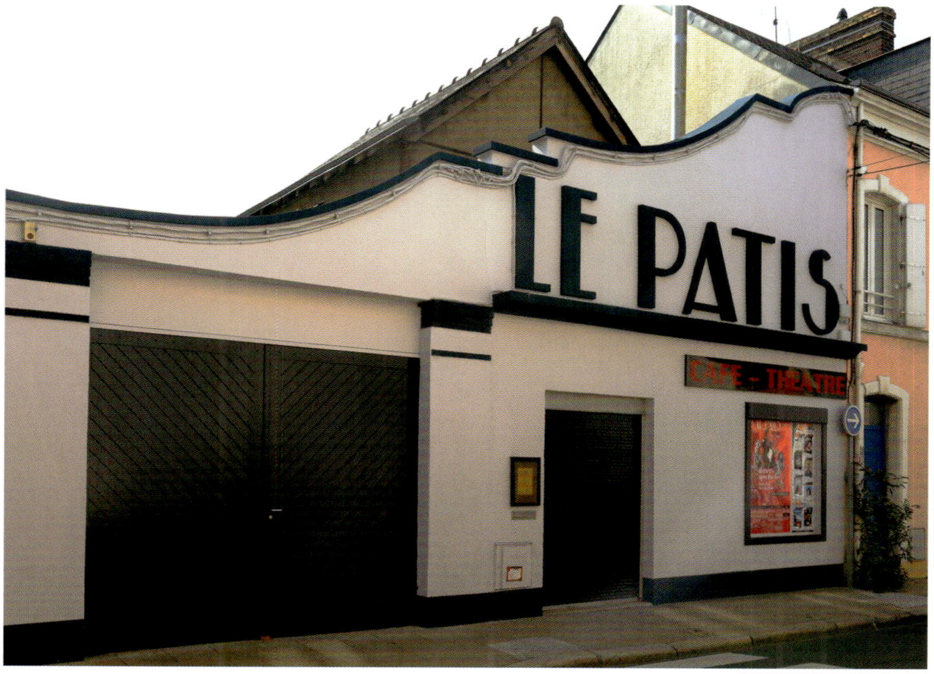

Le Mans – former Le Patis cinema –2020

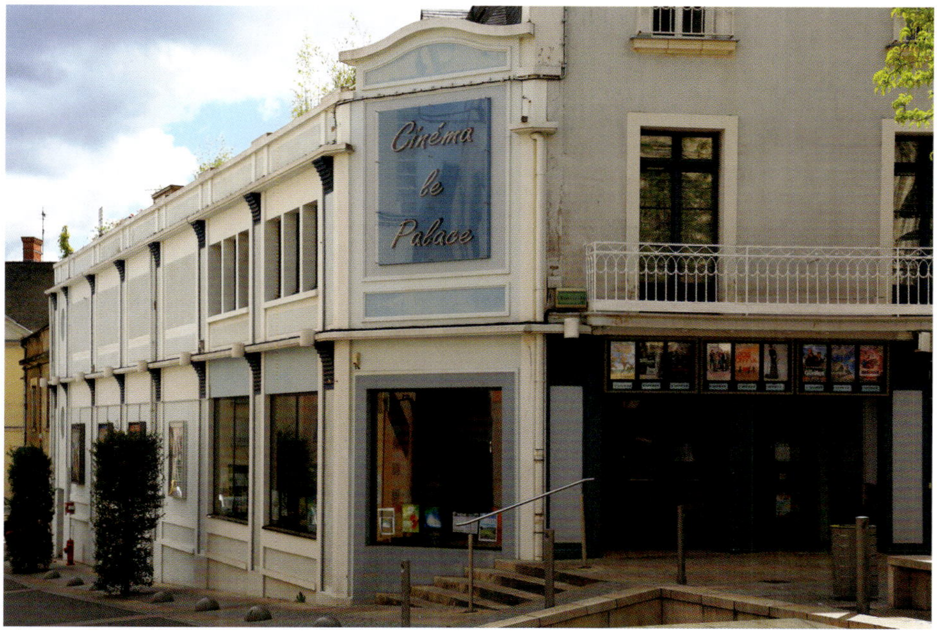

Château-Gontier – Palace – 2015

PROVENCE–ALPS–COTE D'AZUR

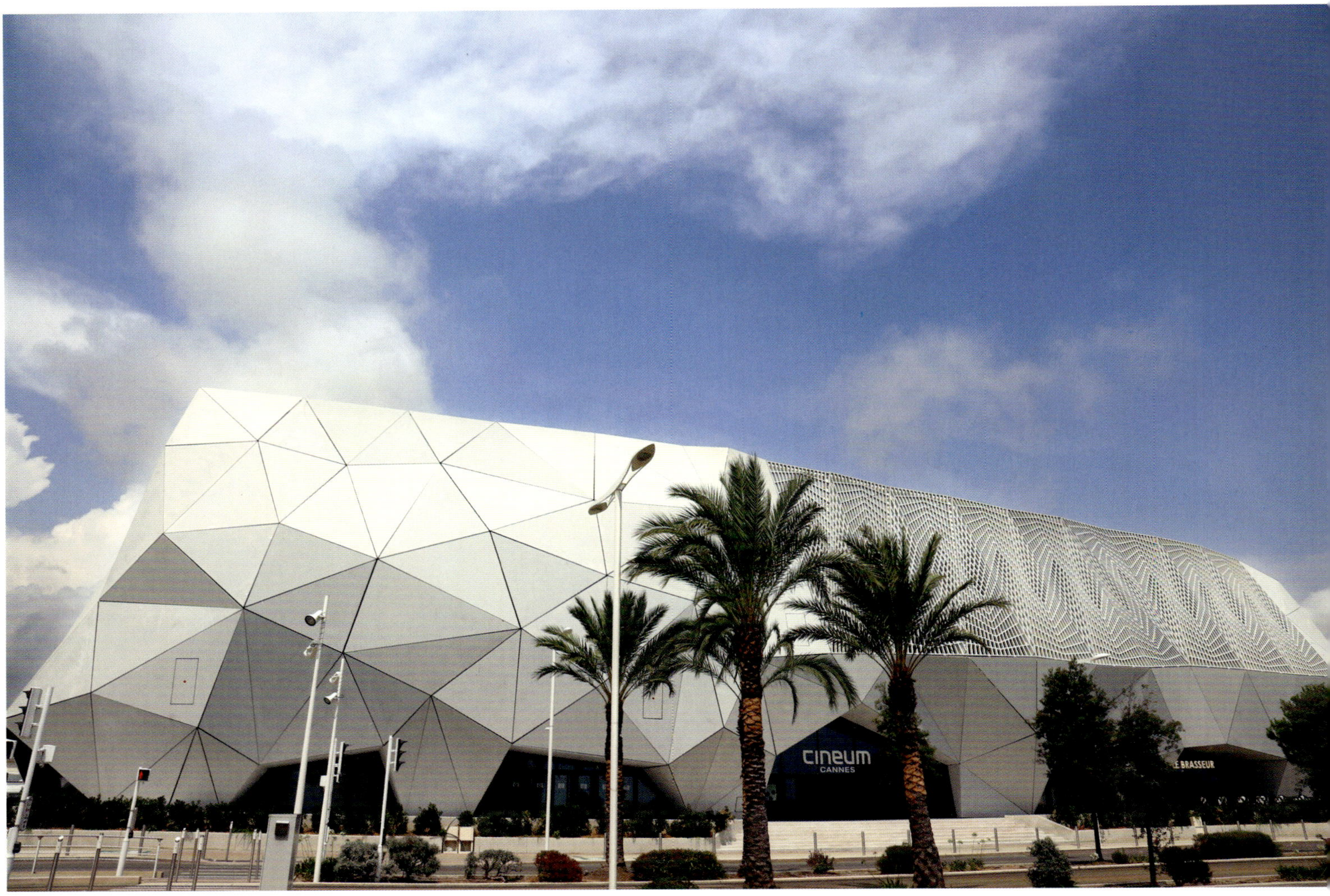

Cannes – Cineum – 2021

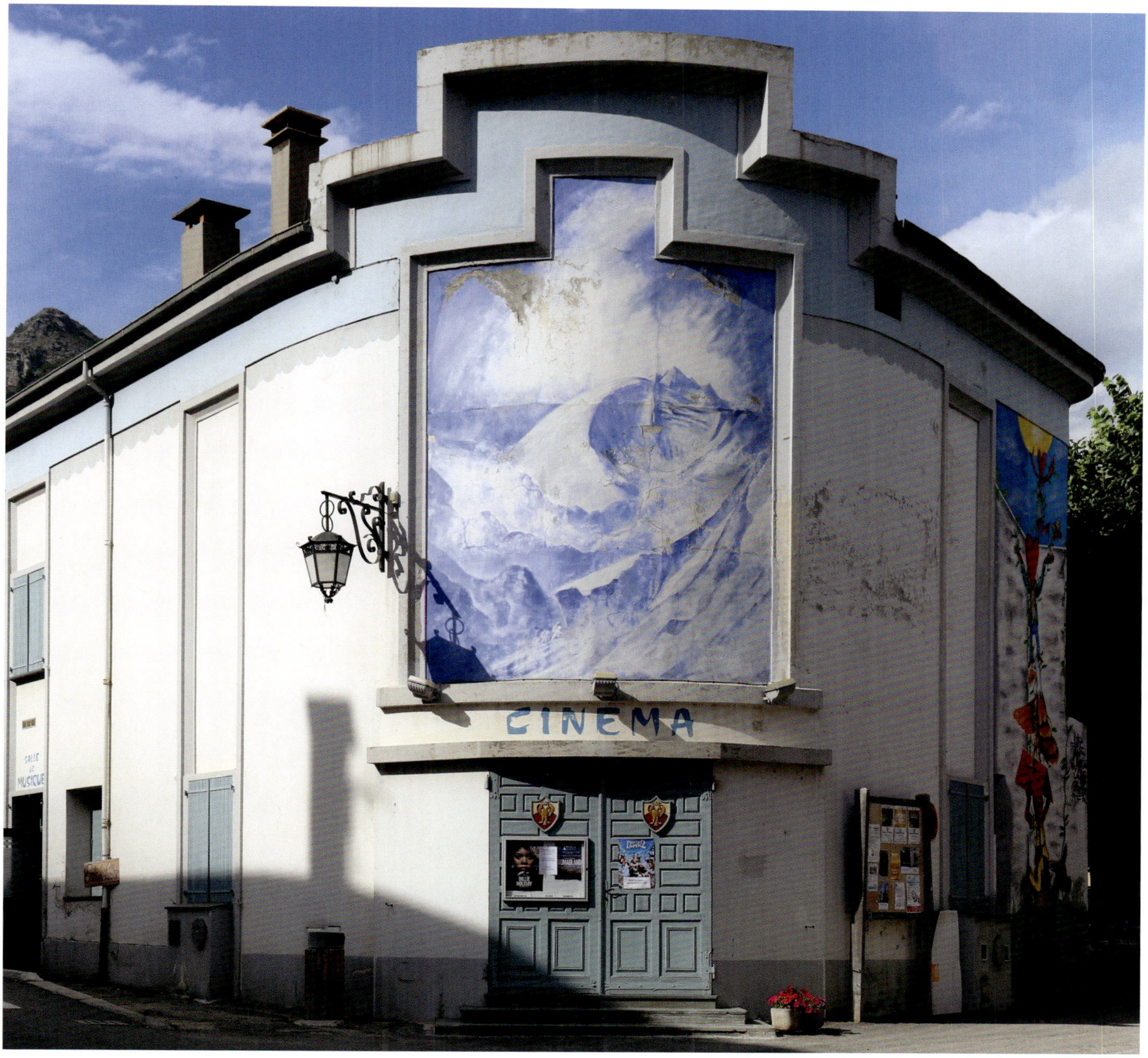

Tende – Le Bego – 2021

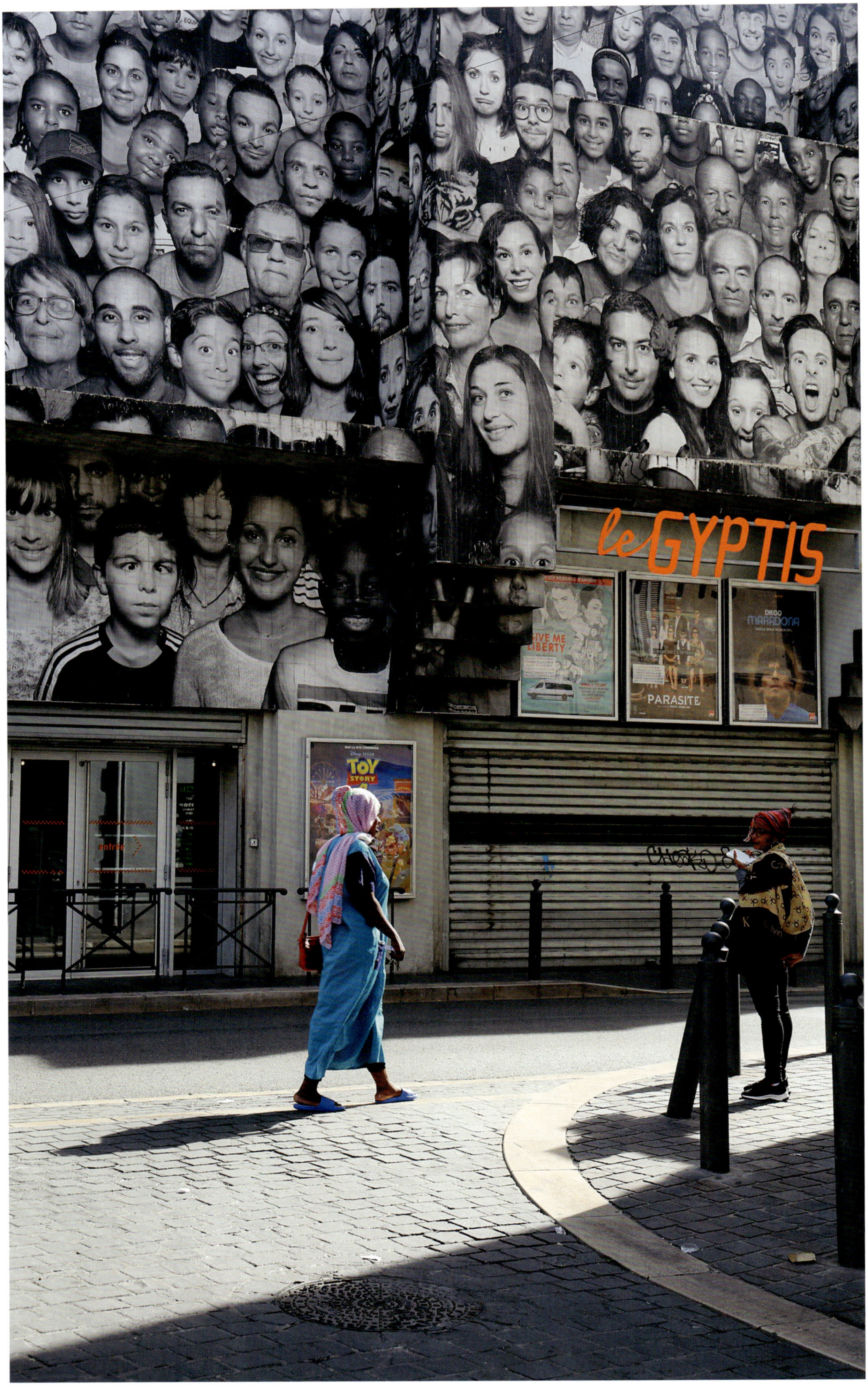

Marseille – Le Gyptis – 2019

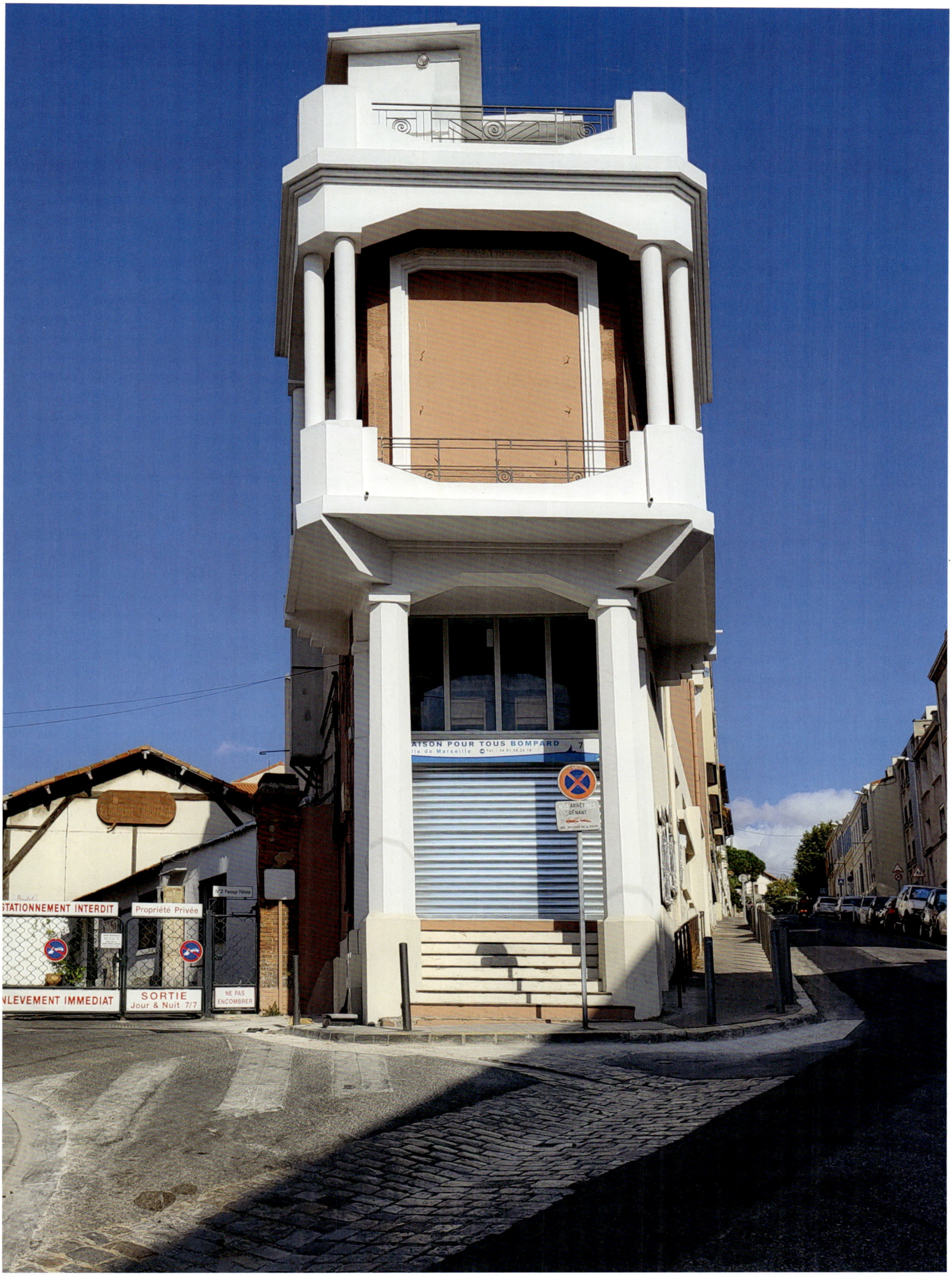

Marseille – Bompard – 2022

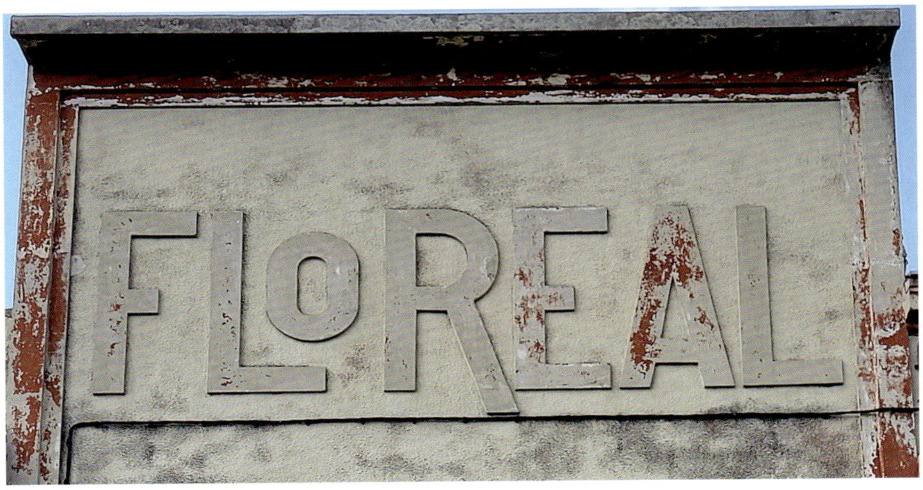

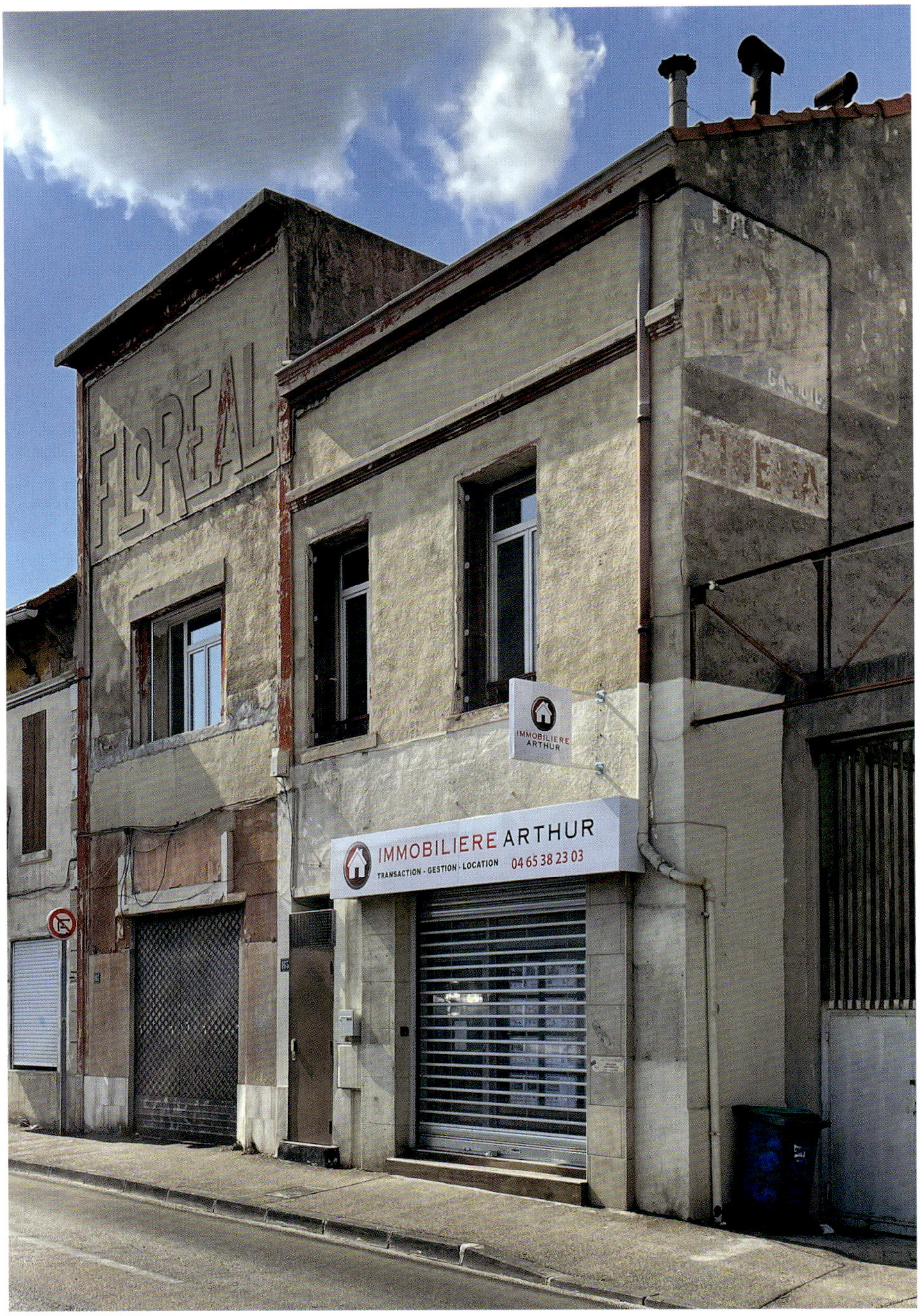

Marseille – Floréal – 2022

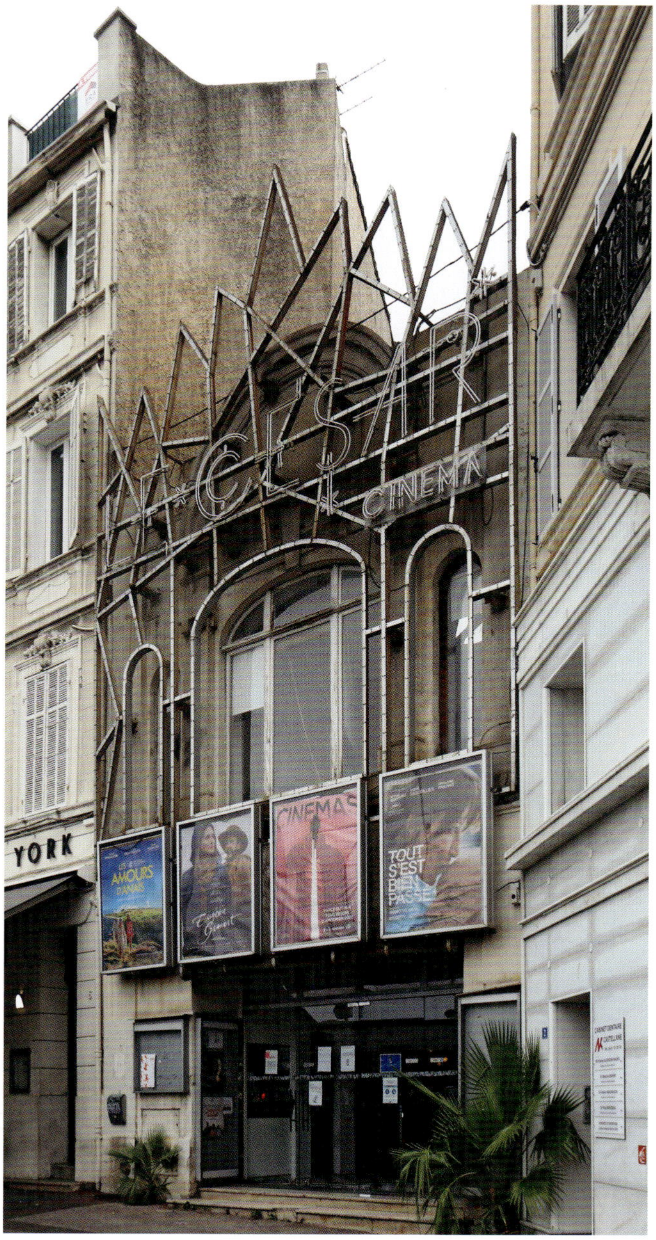

Marseille – Le César – 2021

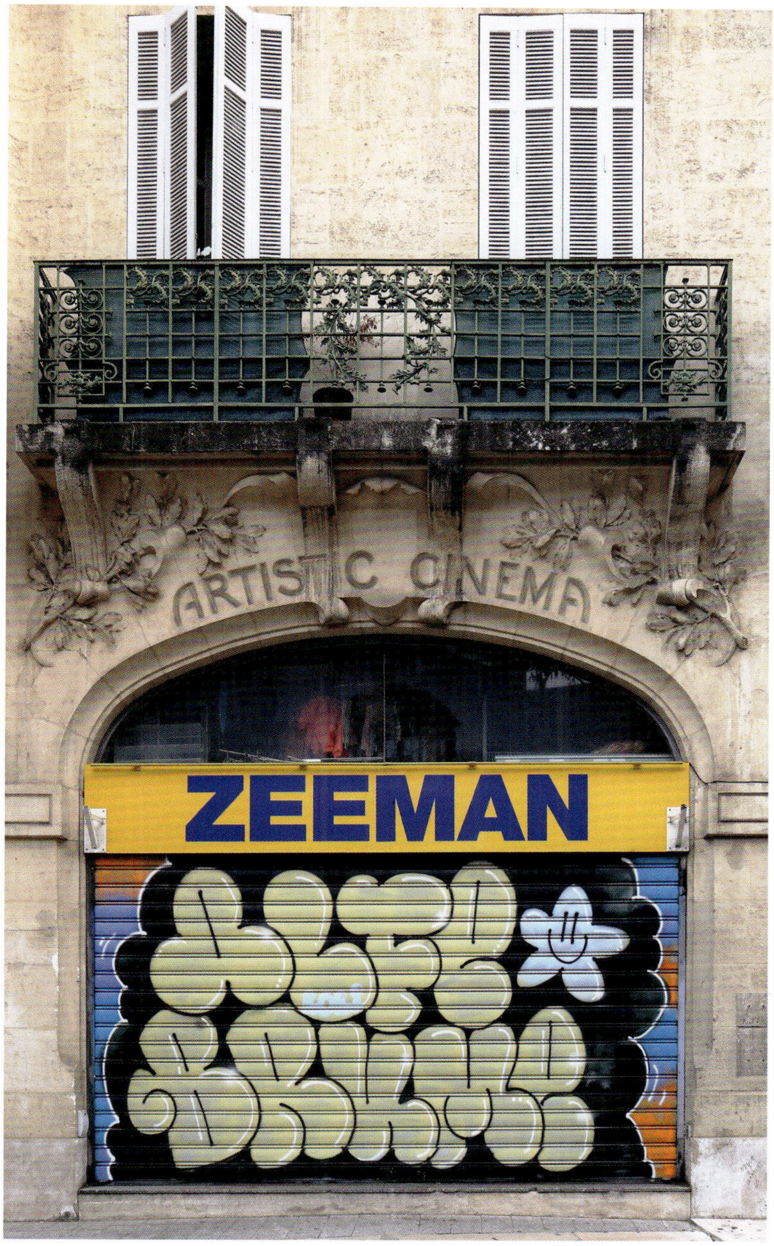

Marseille – Artistic Cinéma – 2021

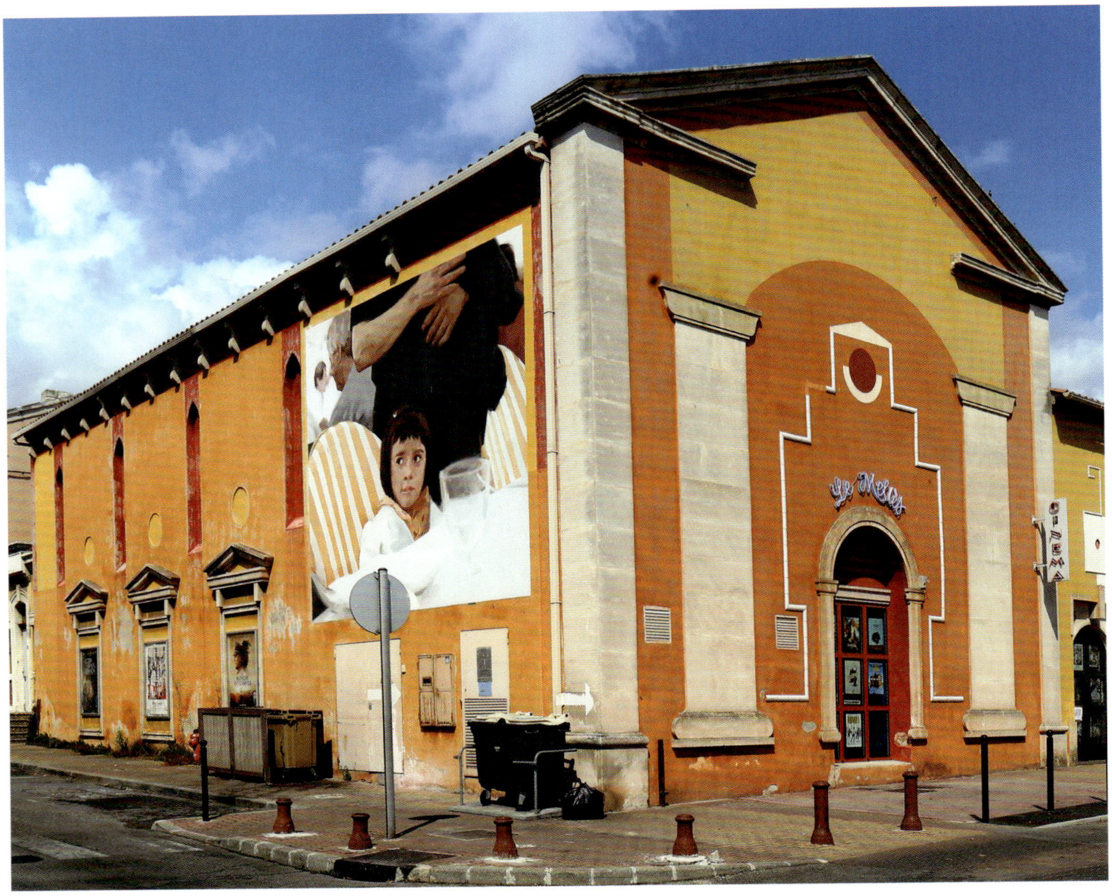

Port-de-Bouc – Le Méliès – 2022

Port-de-Bouc, Le Méliès. Before, the names of cinemas were meant to dazzle: Star, Majestic, Royal, Select ... Entering a movie theatre was like treading in the footsteps of the luckiest people in the world, the nobility of our time. Flamboyant luxury filled the gaze of the audience. Now, theatres are less majestic, smaller, and sometimes even foul-smelling. Over time, cinema has created other memories and likes to reminisce by paying tribute to those who developed it: Mélès, Renoir, Arletty, Truffaut ...

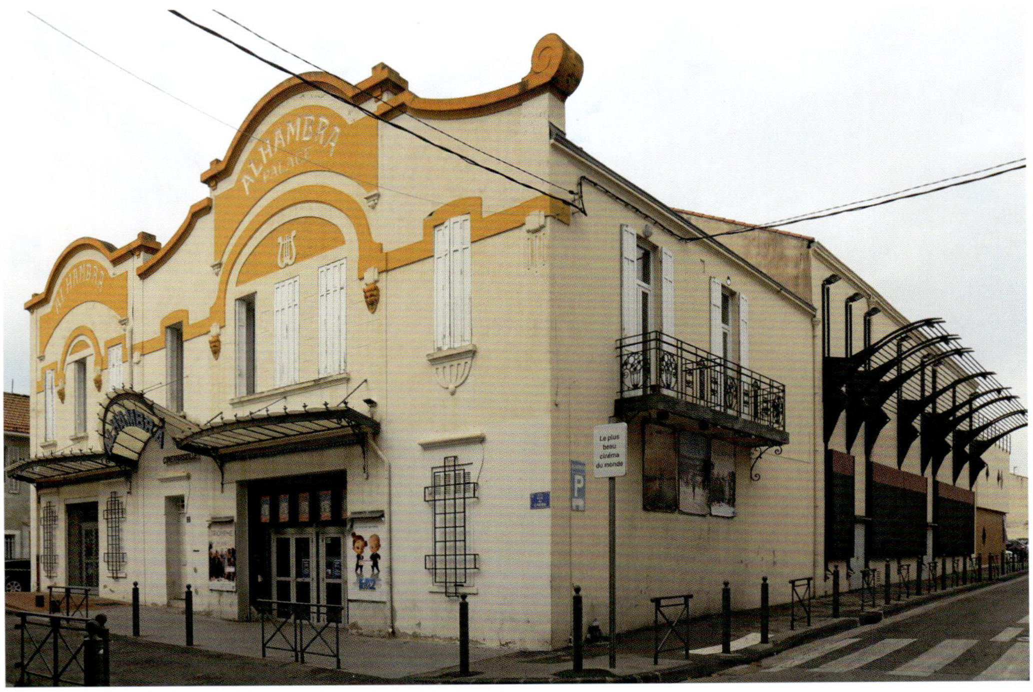

Marseille – Alhambra – 2022

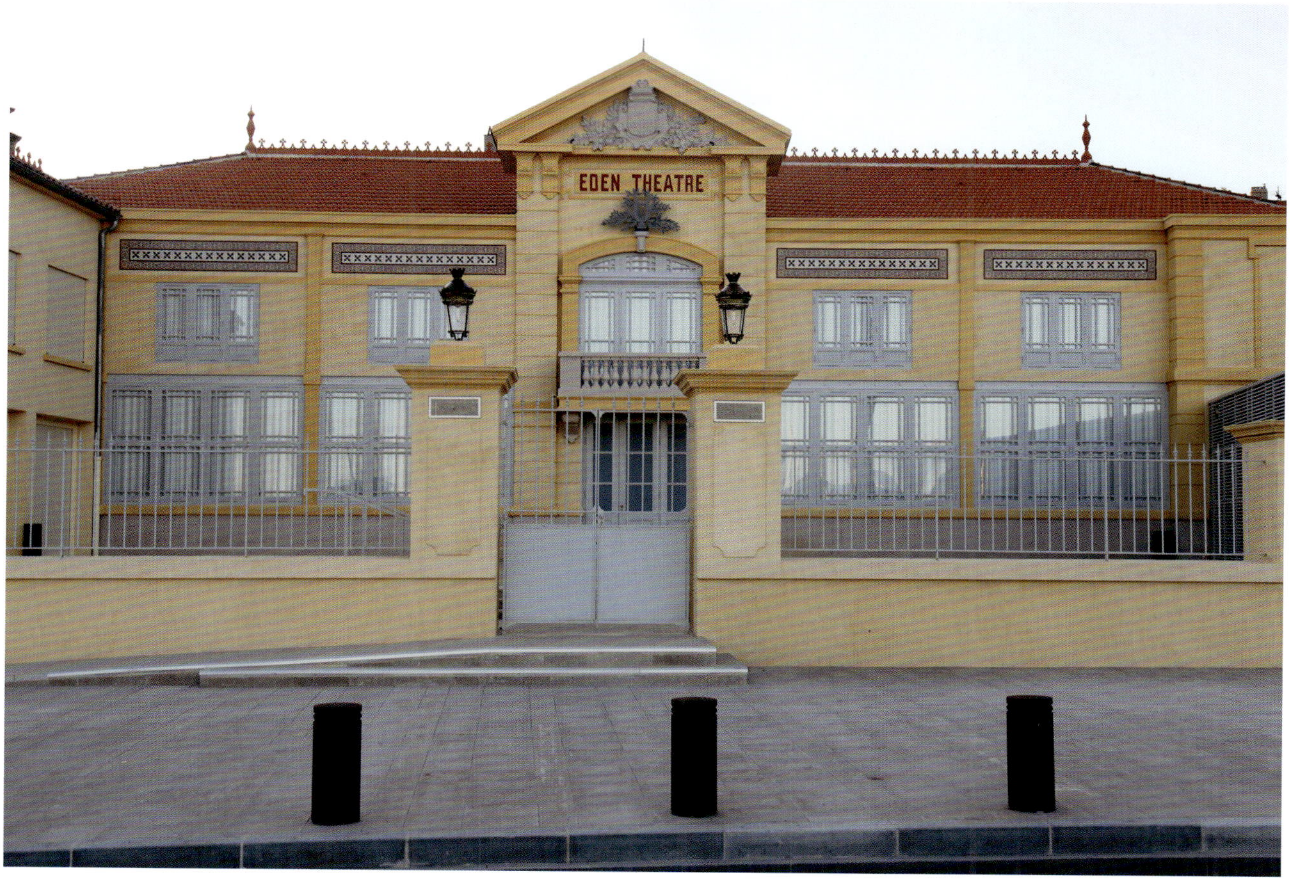

La Ciotat – Eden – 2014

La Ciotat, Eden. On 21 March 1899 the Lumière brothers presented 19 films at the Eden in La Ciotat, a cinema now thought to be the oldest in operation.

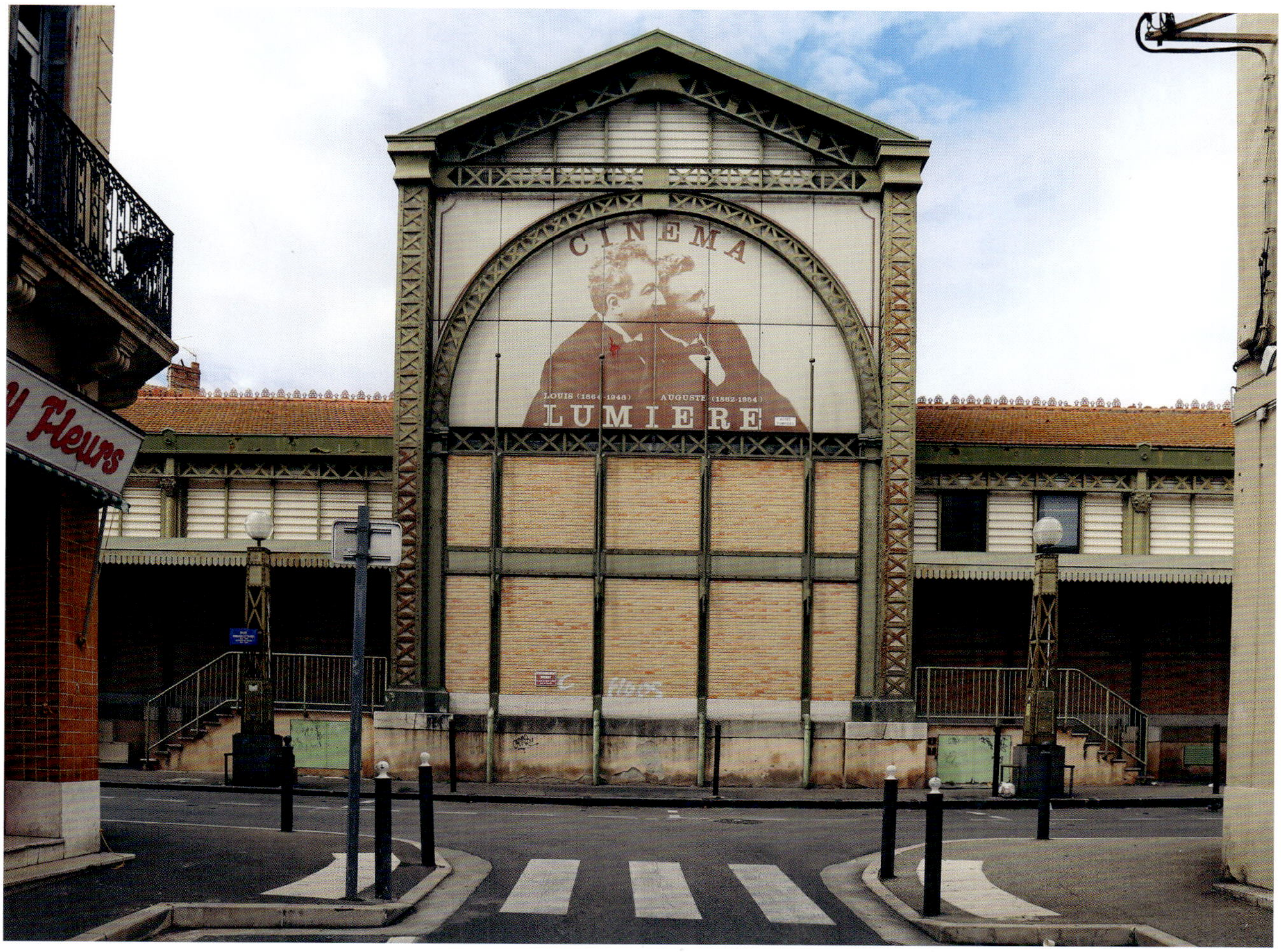

La Ciotat – Cinéma Lumière – 2021

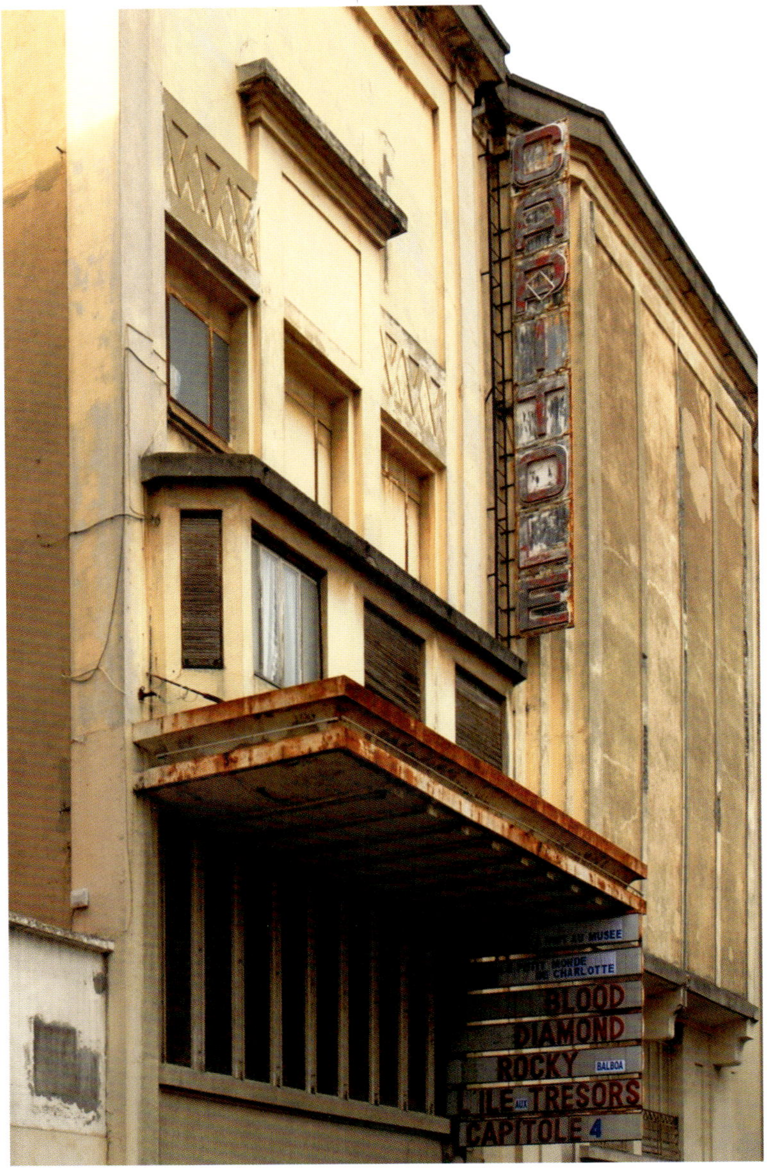

Avignon – Capitole – 2007

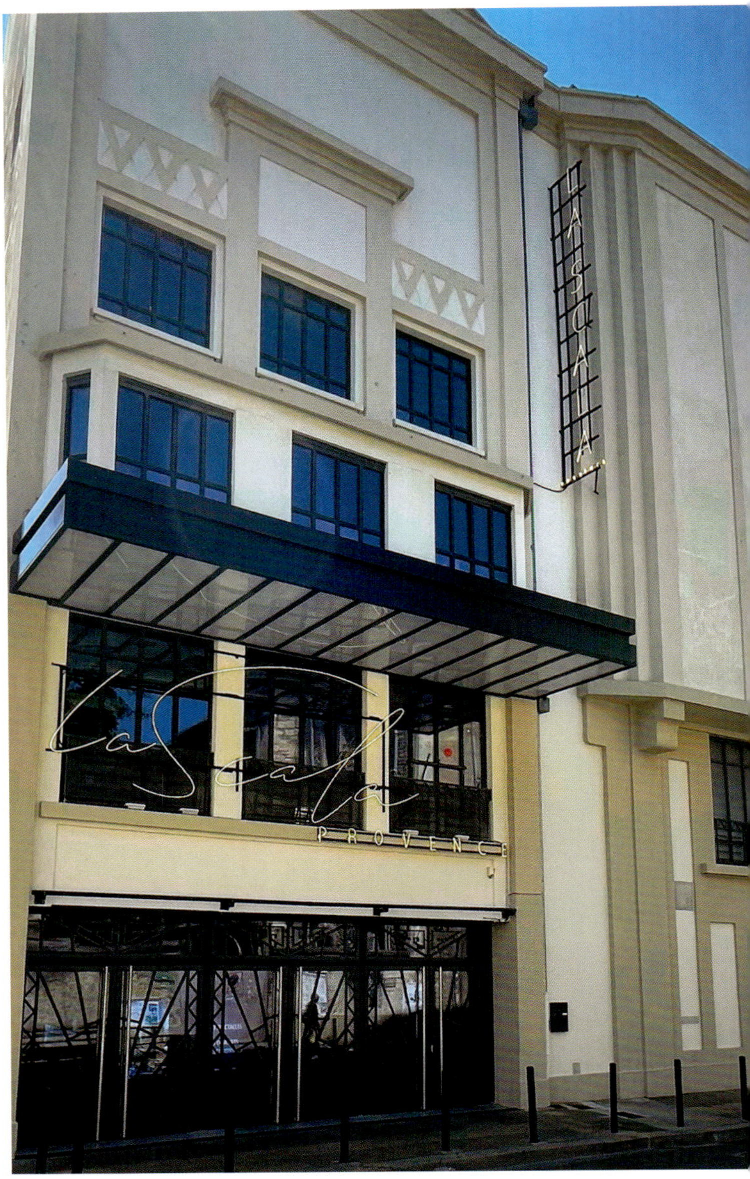

Avignon – former Capitole, today La Scala Provence théâtre – 2022

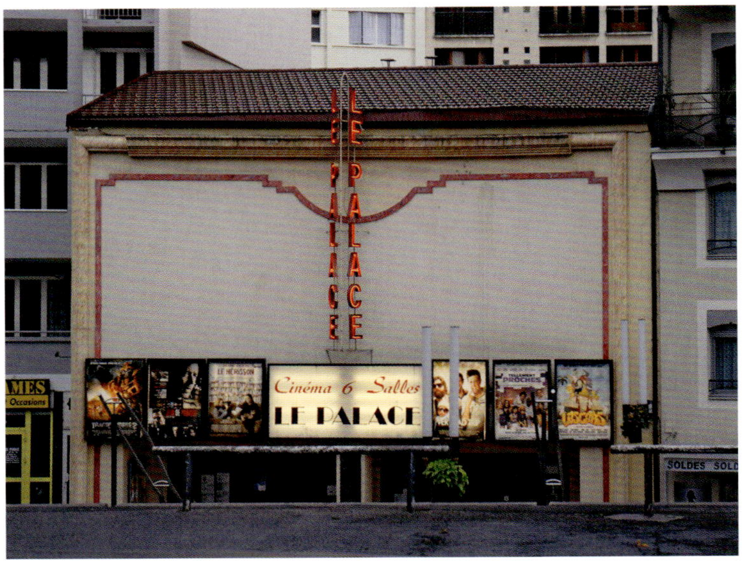

Gap – Le Palace – 2009

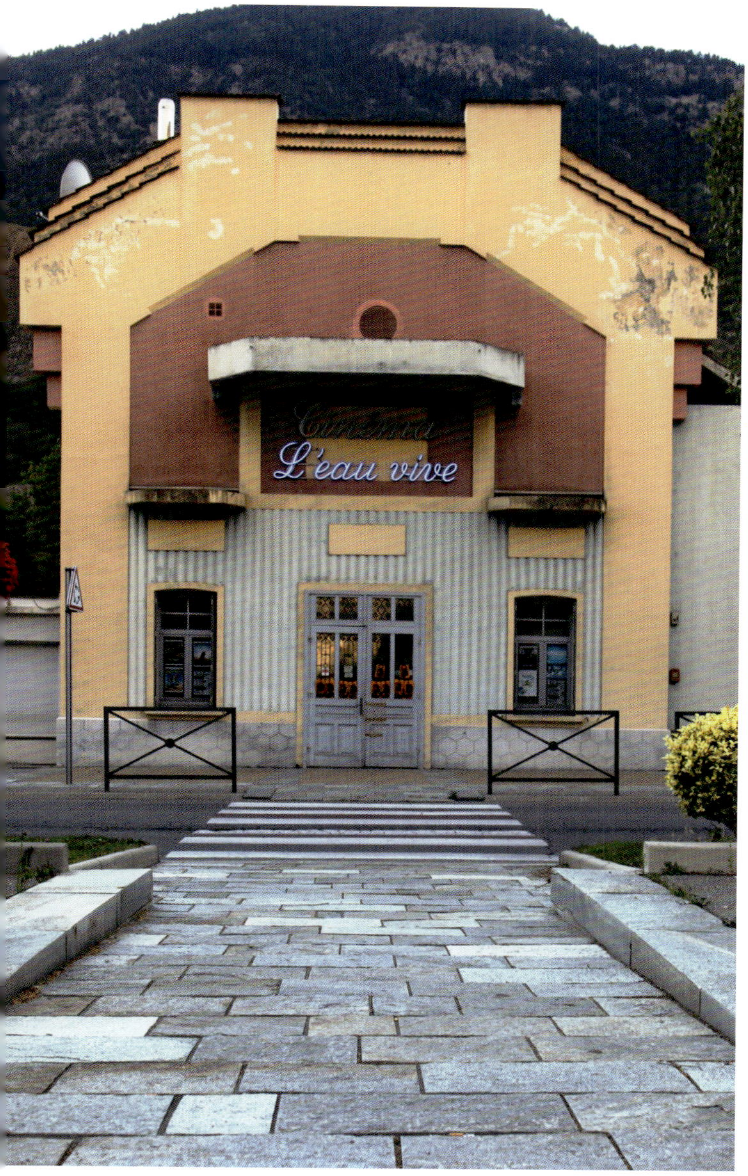

rgentière-la-Bessée – L'eau vive – 2013

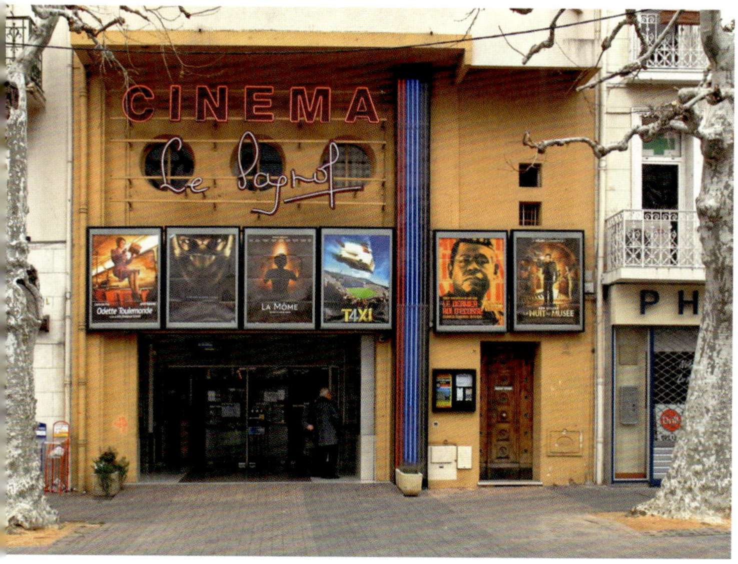

ɔagne – Le Pagnol – 2007

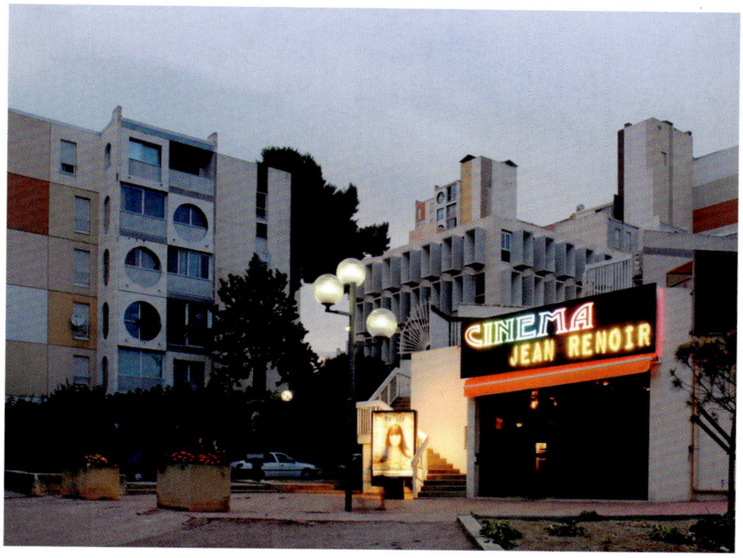

Martigues – Jean Renoir – 2009

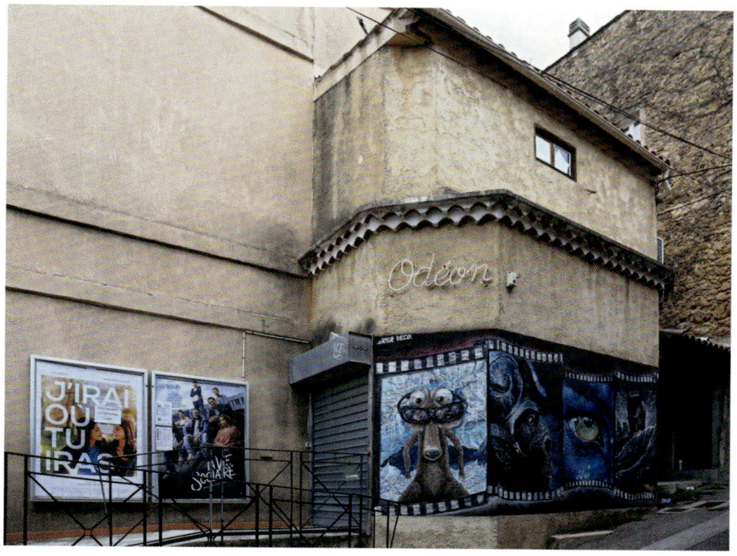

Barjols – Odéon – 2019

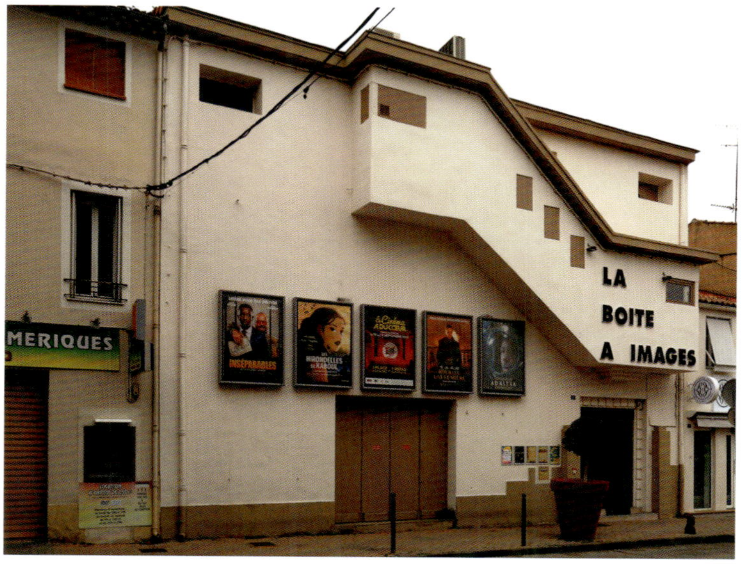

Brogmoles – La boite à images – 2019

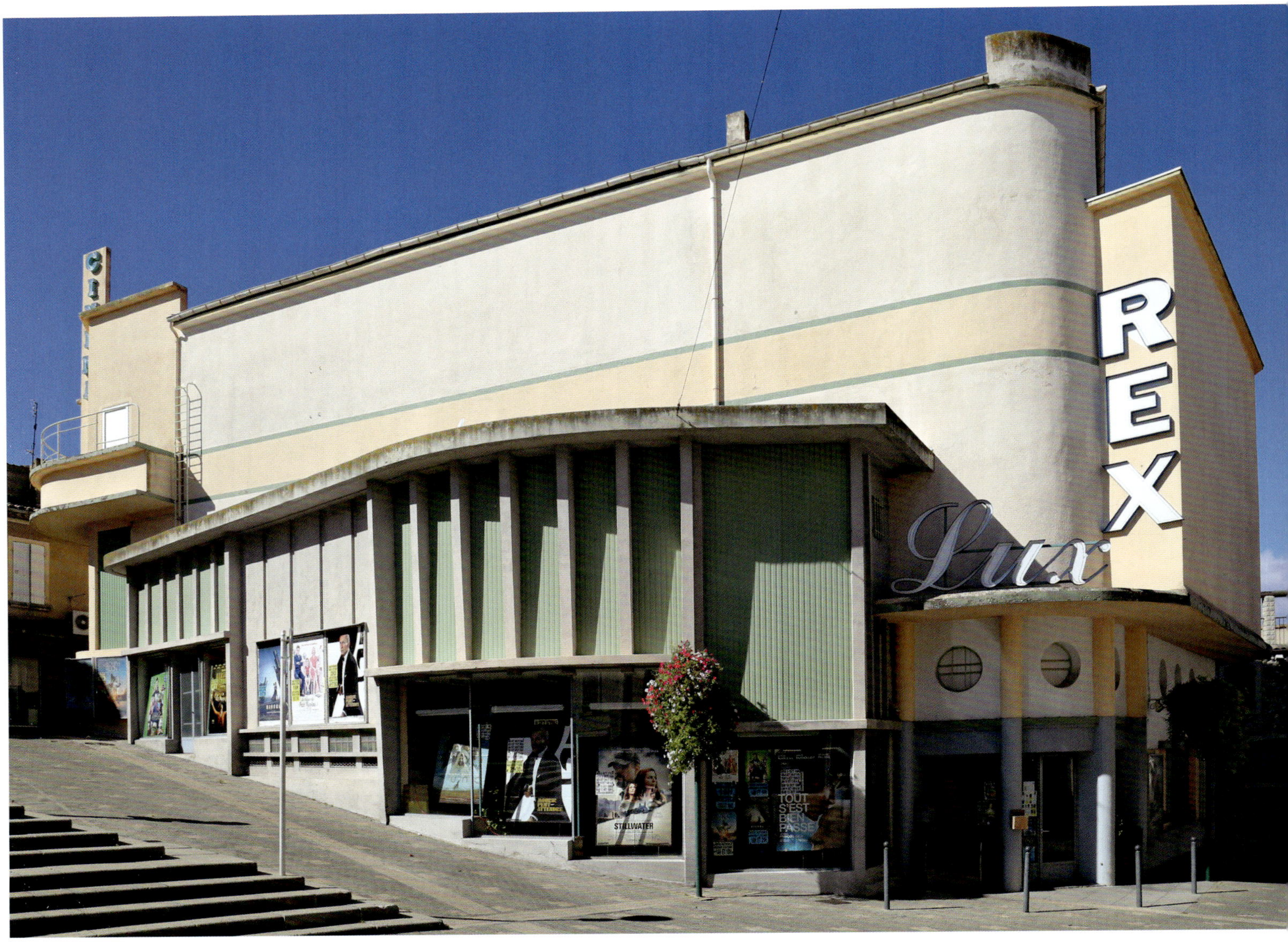

Valréas – Rex and Lux – 2021

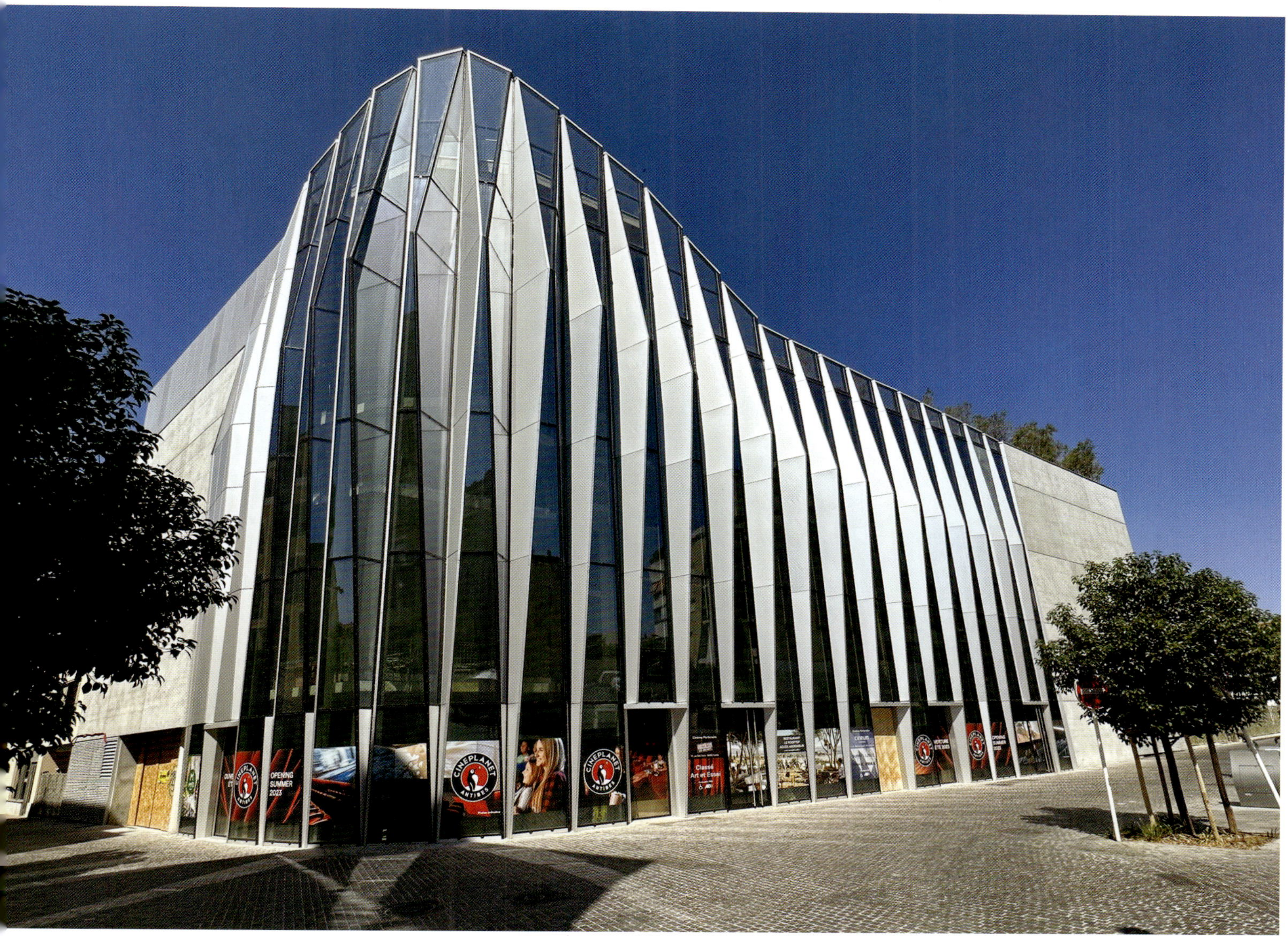

tibes – Cinéplanet – 2023

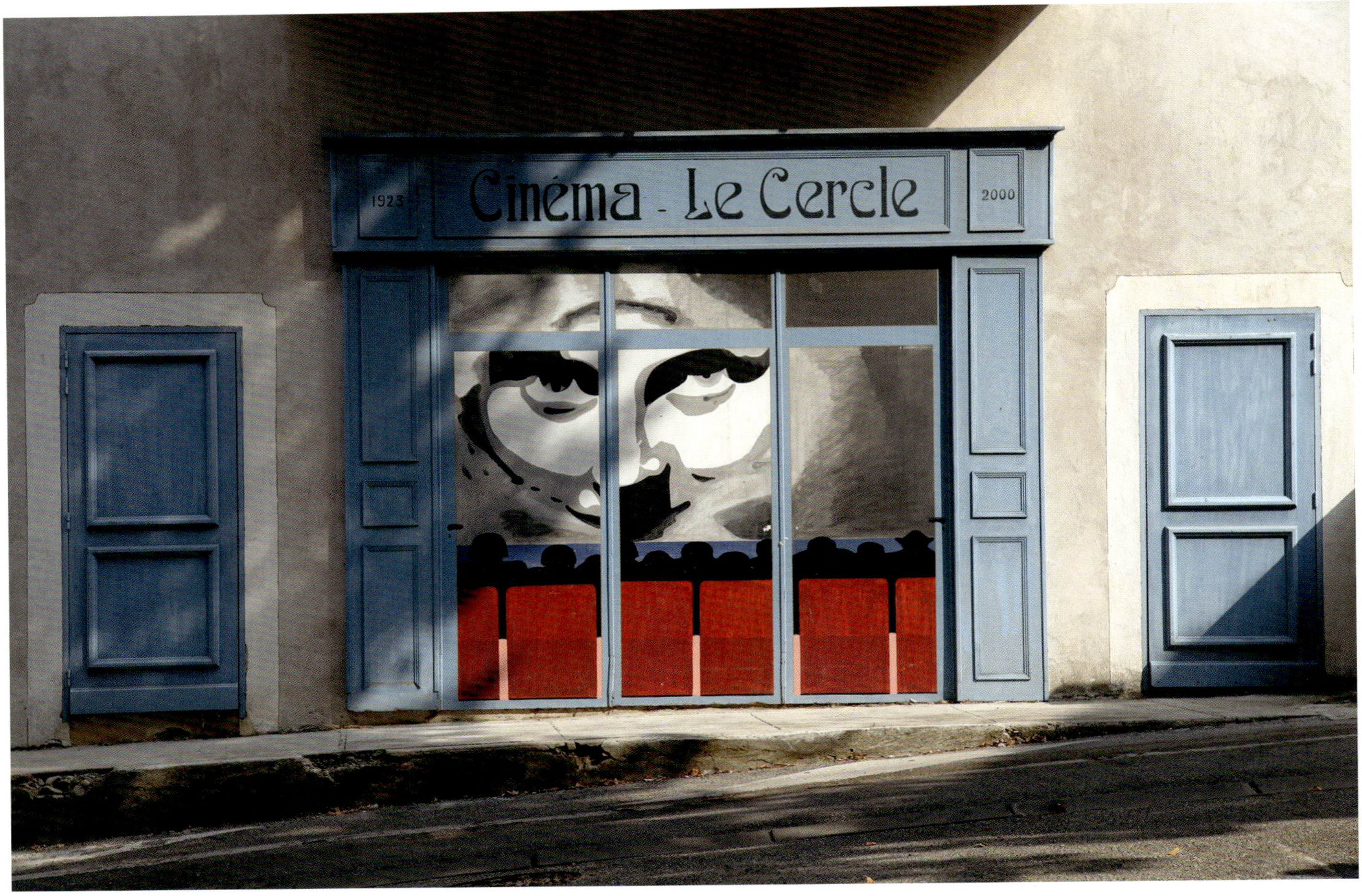

Bras – Le Cercle – 2013

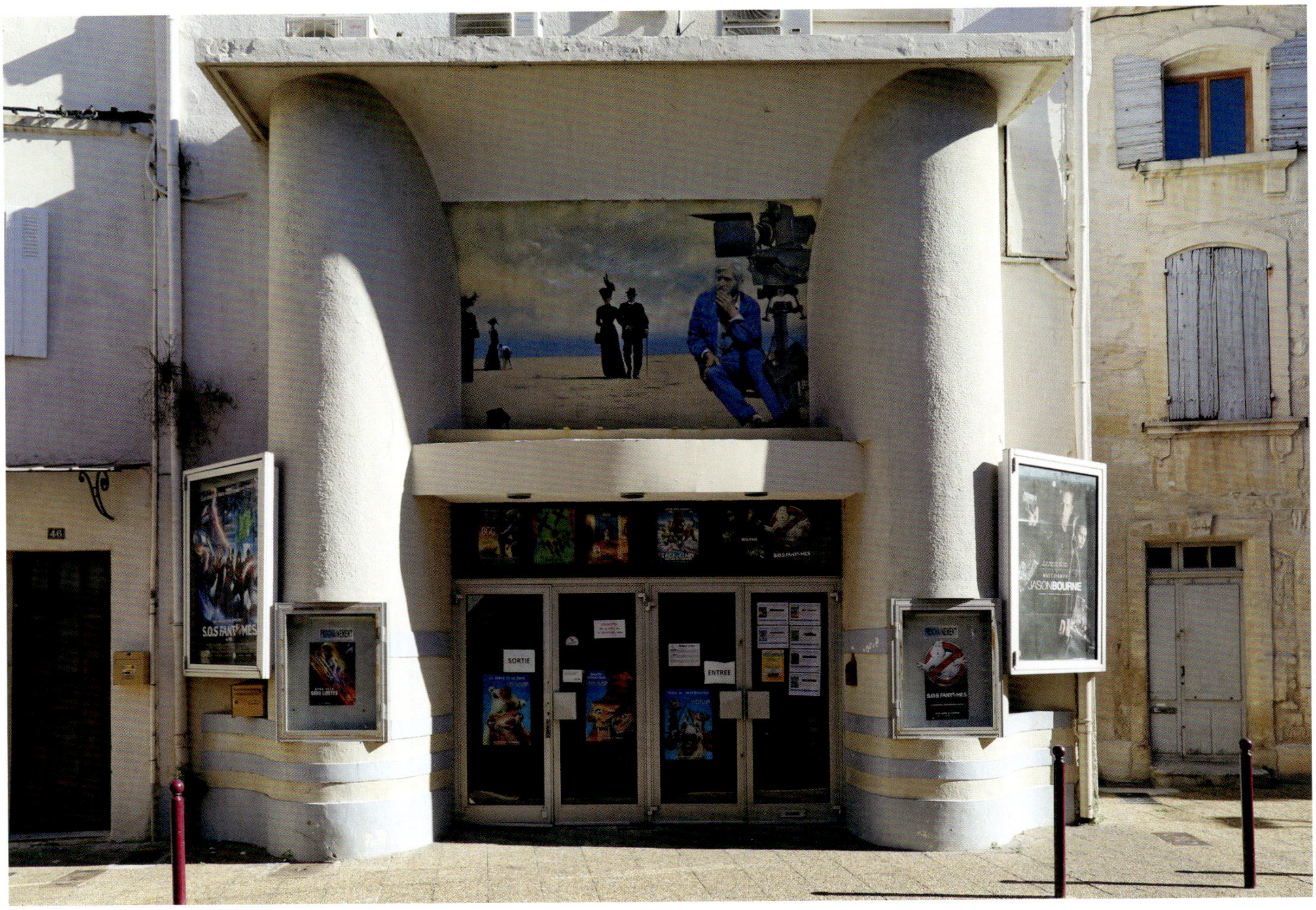

Tarascon – Rex – 2016

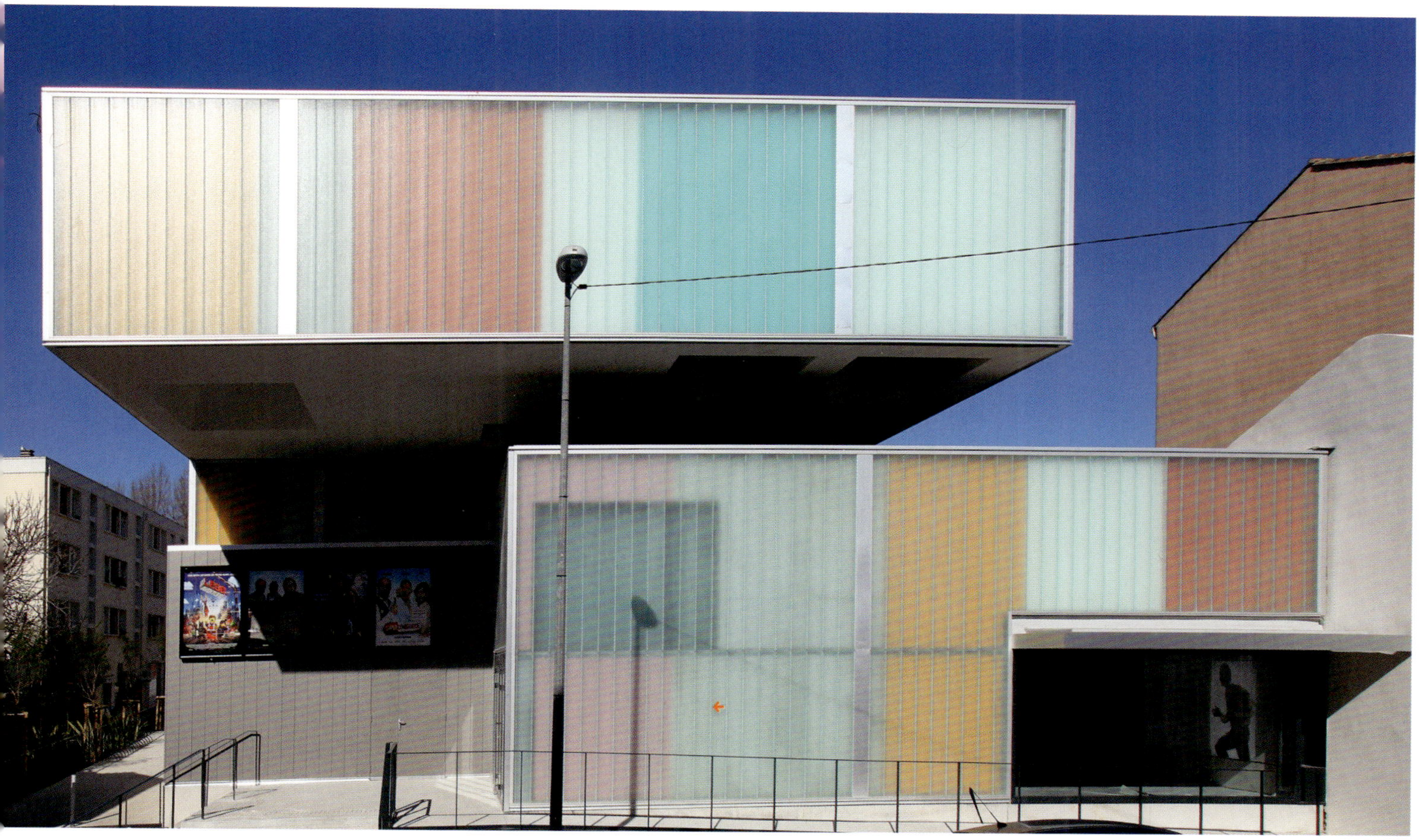

Six-Fours-les-Plages – Le Six n'étoiles – 2014

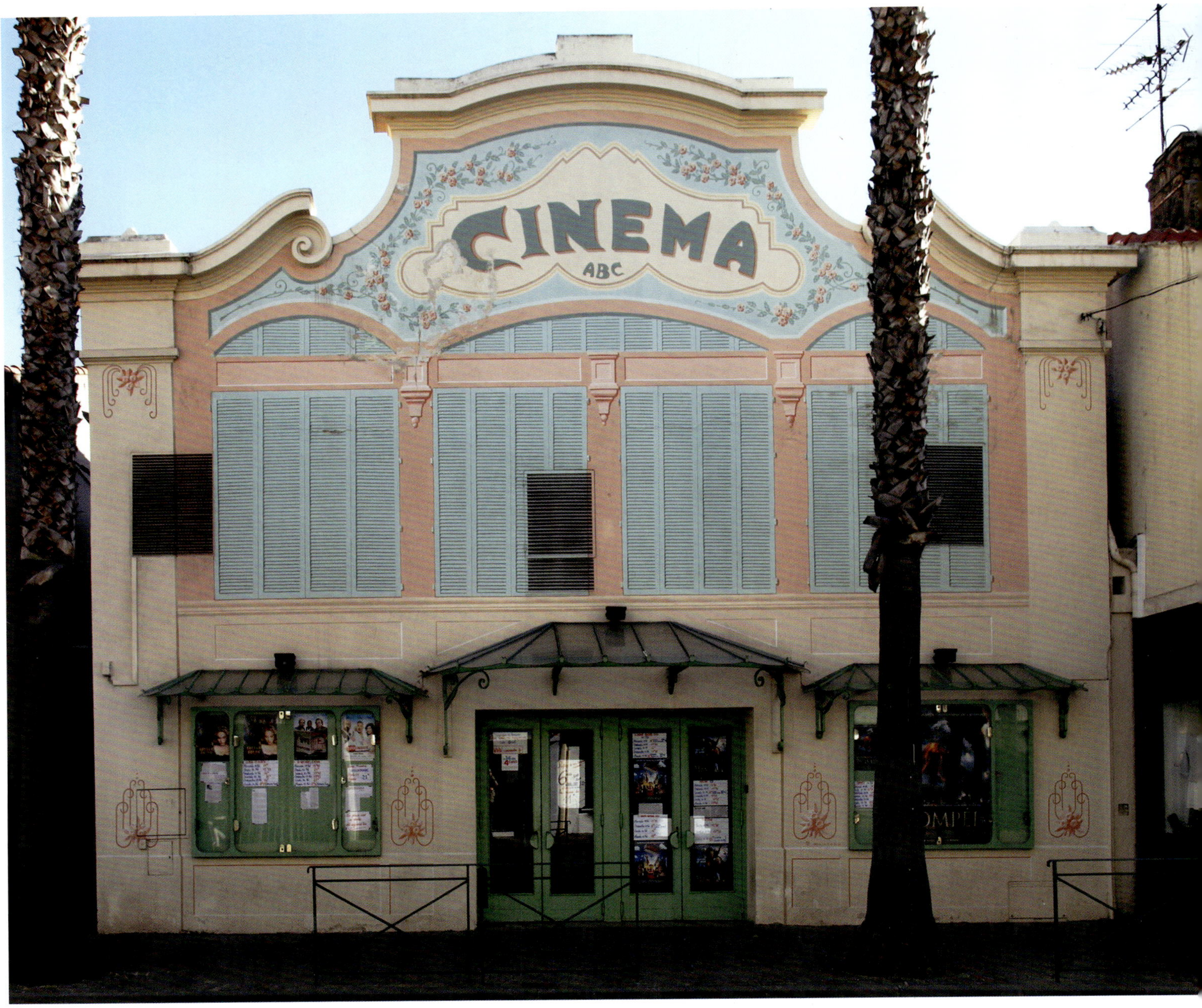

Sanary-sur-Mer – Cinéma ABC – 2014

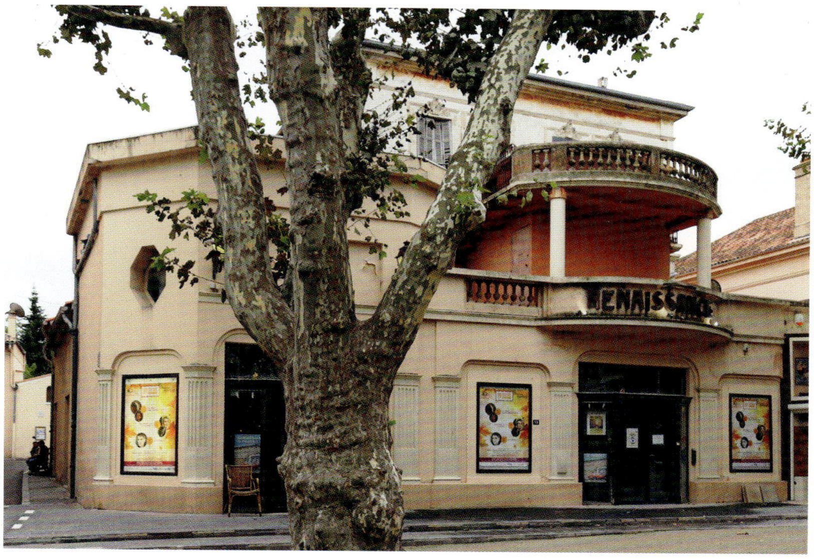

Saint-Tropez – Renaissance – 2020

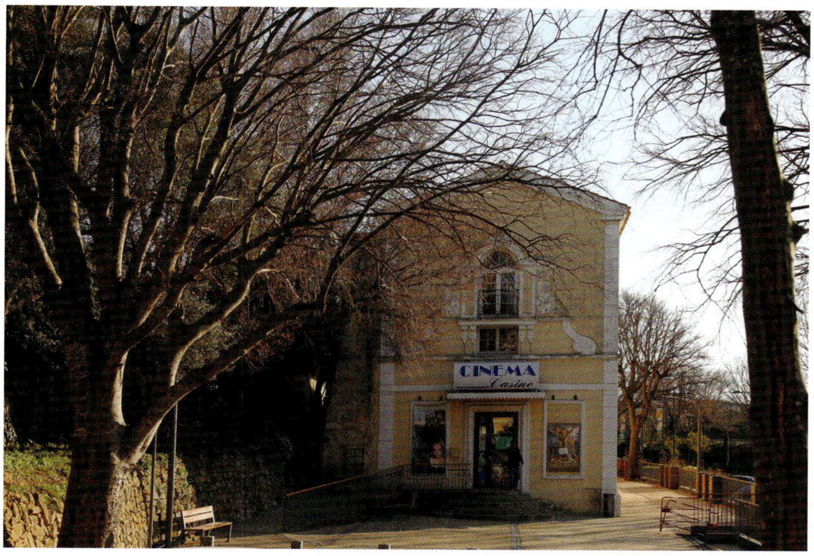

Saint-Cyr – Cinéma Casino – 2020

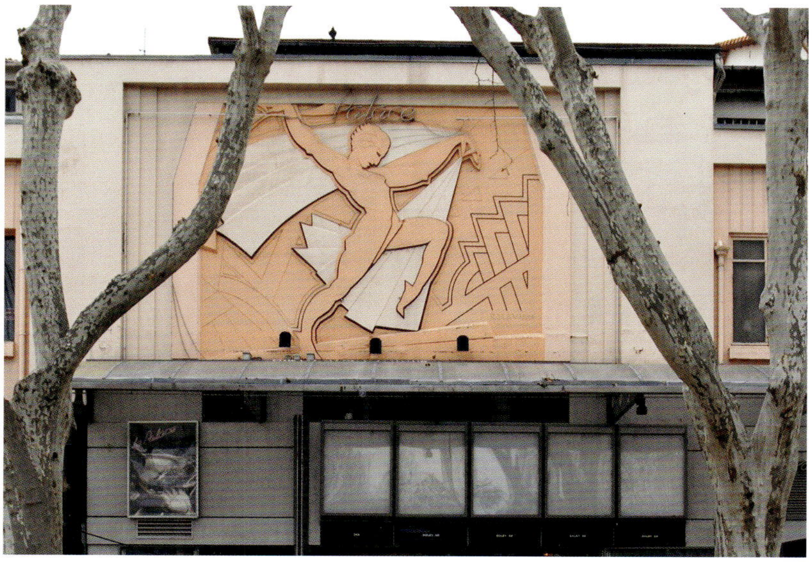

Avignon – Palace – 2015

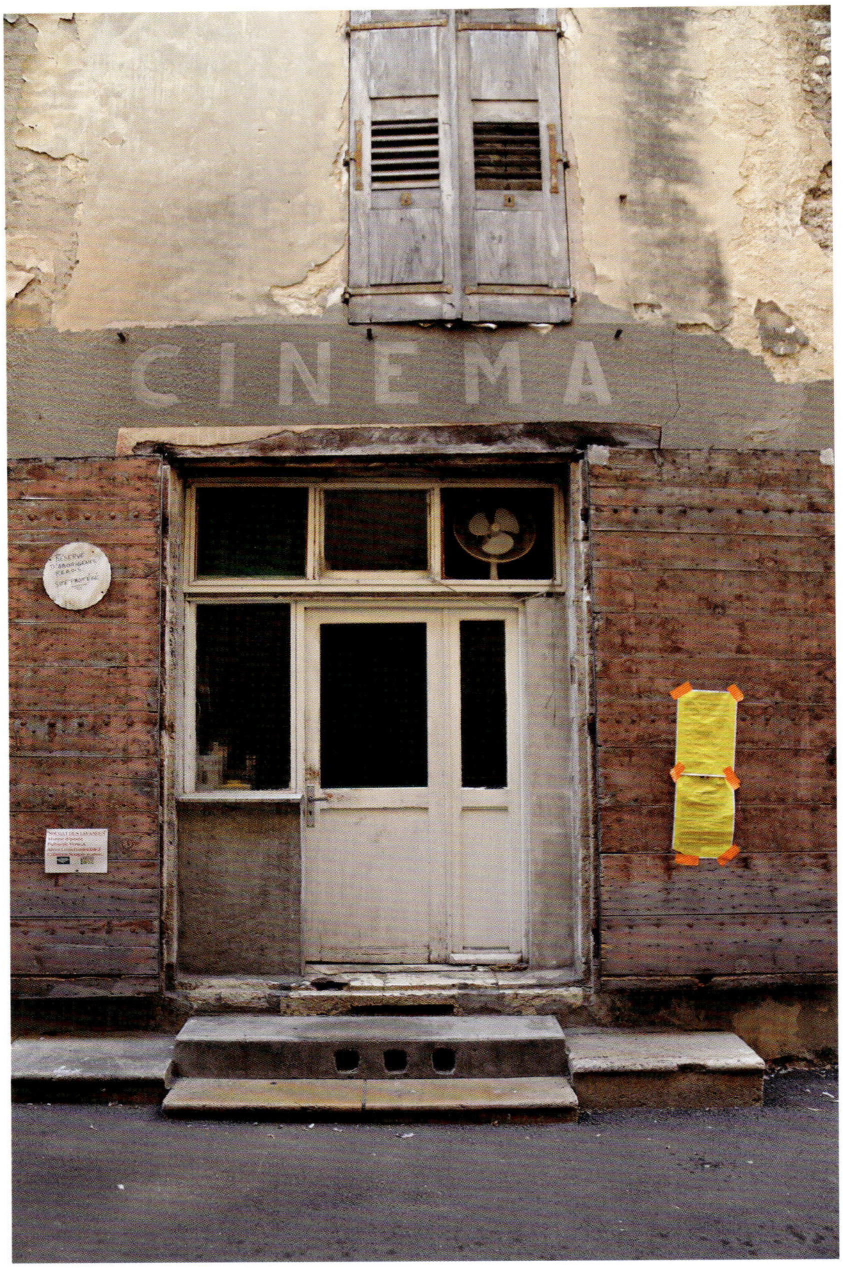

Riez – cinéma – 2019

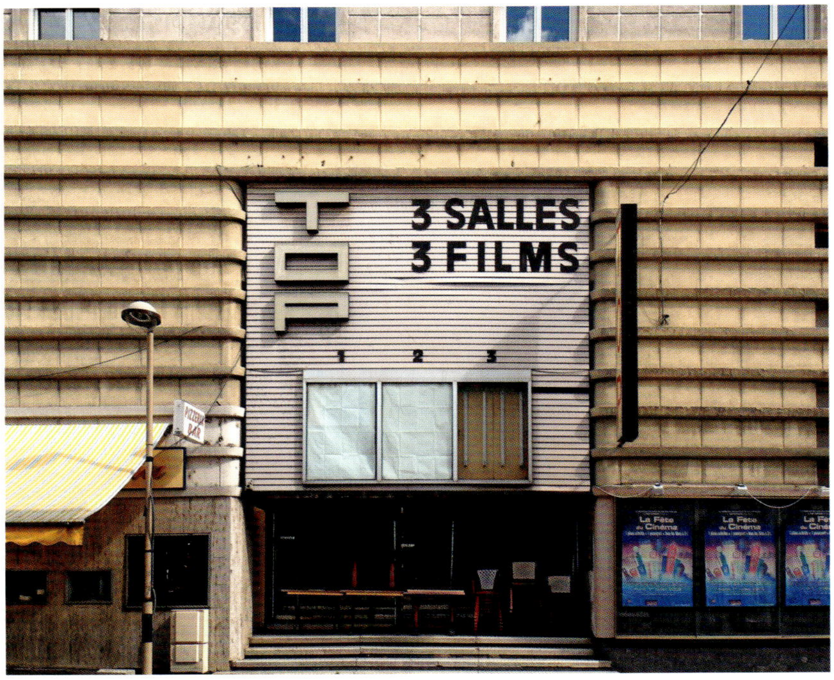

Digne-les-Bains – Top – 2009

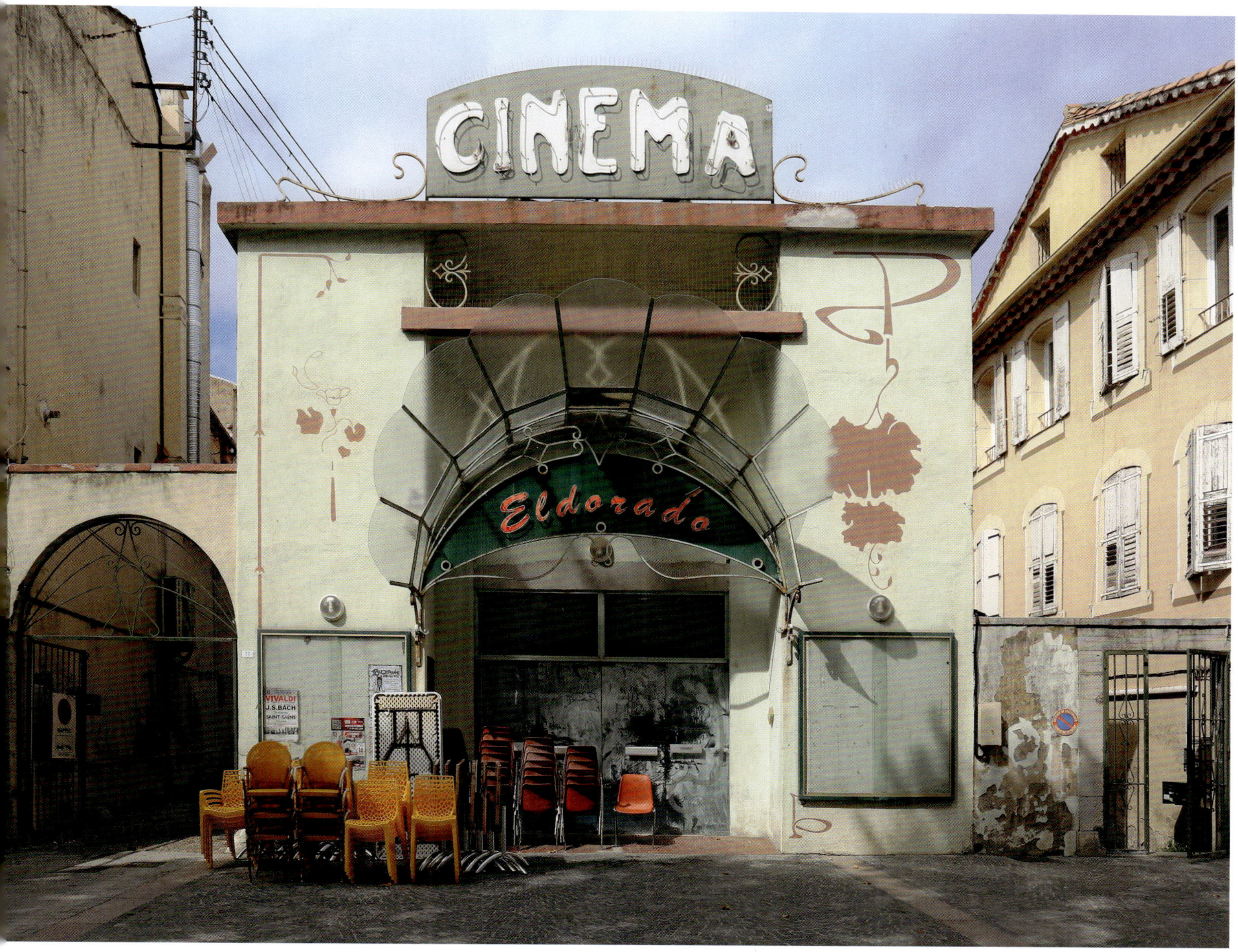

aguignan – Eldorado – 2019

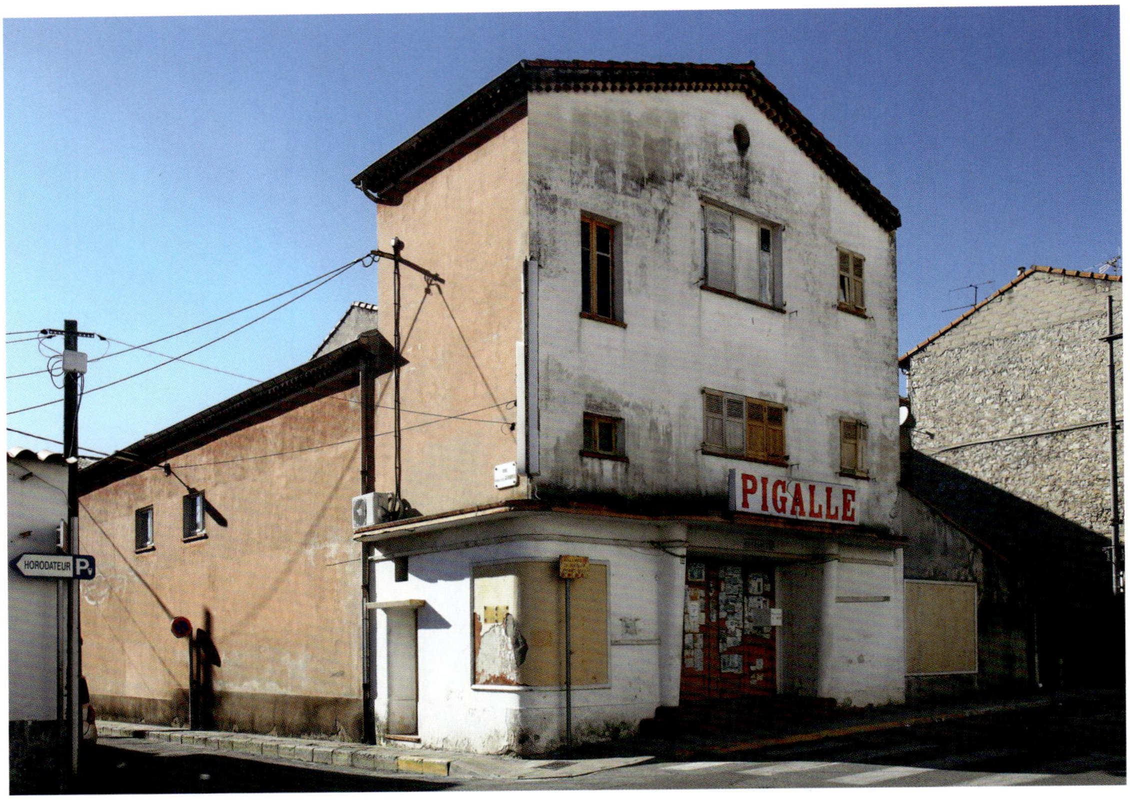

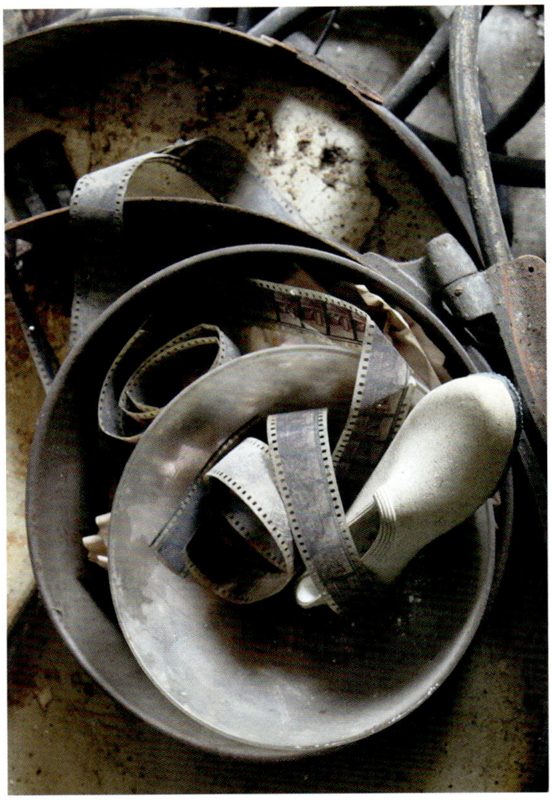

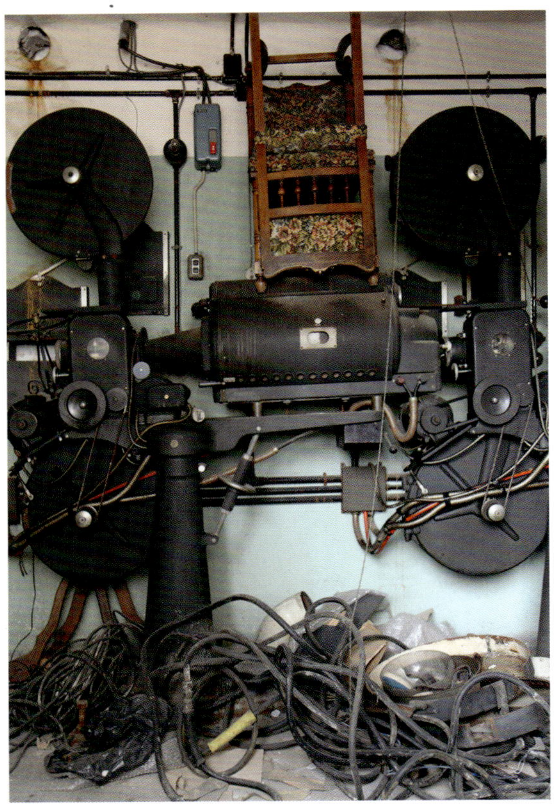

Vallauris – Pigalle

Vallauris, Pigalle. What remains of the Pigalle cinema? In 2008, a flea market installed in the body of the cinema proudly maintained the sign 'Pigalle', recalling the past. Over the years, memories faded and even the flea market disappeared along with the sign. The worn-down building, depressed by its past splendour, is slowly but surely fading away, leaving no sign of its previous life.

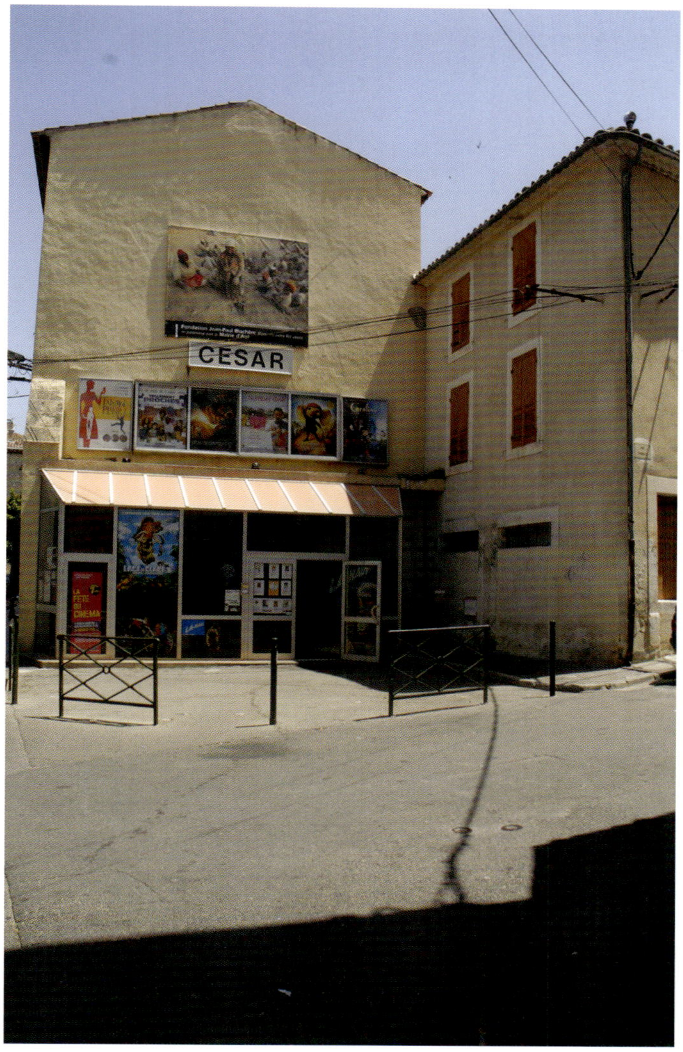

Apt – Ciné César – 2009

Apt, Le César. Le César is installed in the chapel of the White Penitents (listed as a historical monument). Inside, behind the screen, is a fresco and wooden panels sculpted by Jacques Bernus (1650–1728).

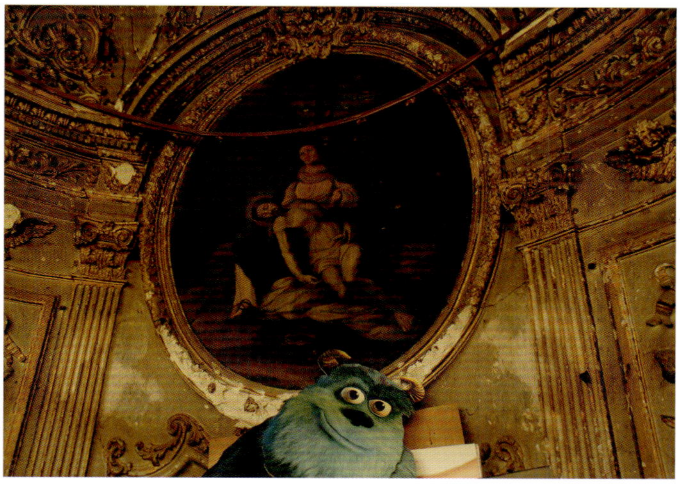

Apt – Ciné César

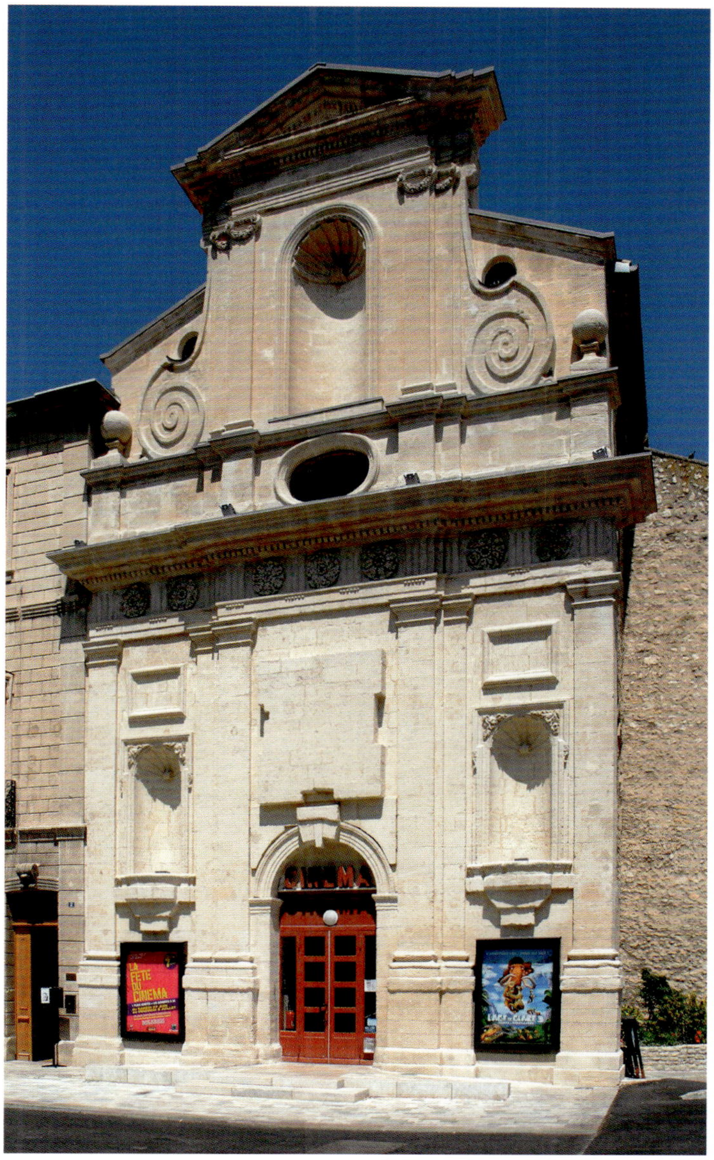

Forcalquier – Le Bourget – 2009

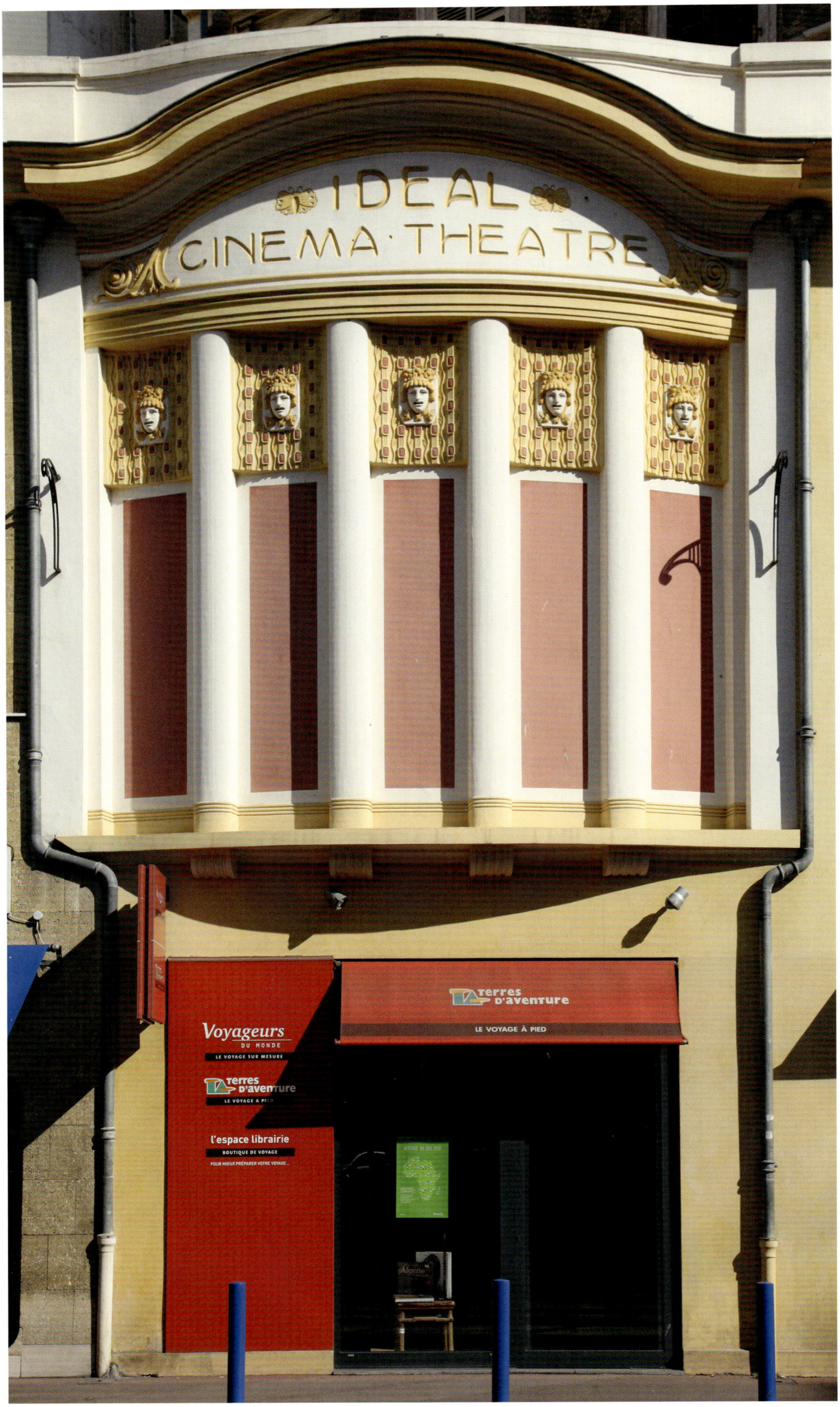

Nice – Idéal – 2010

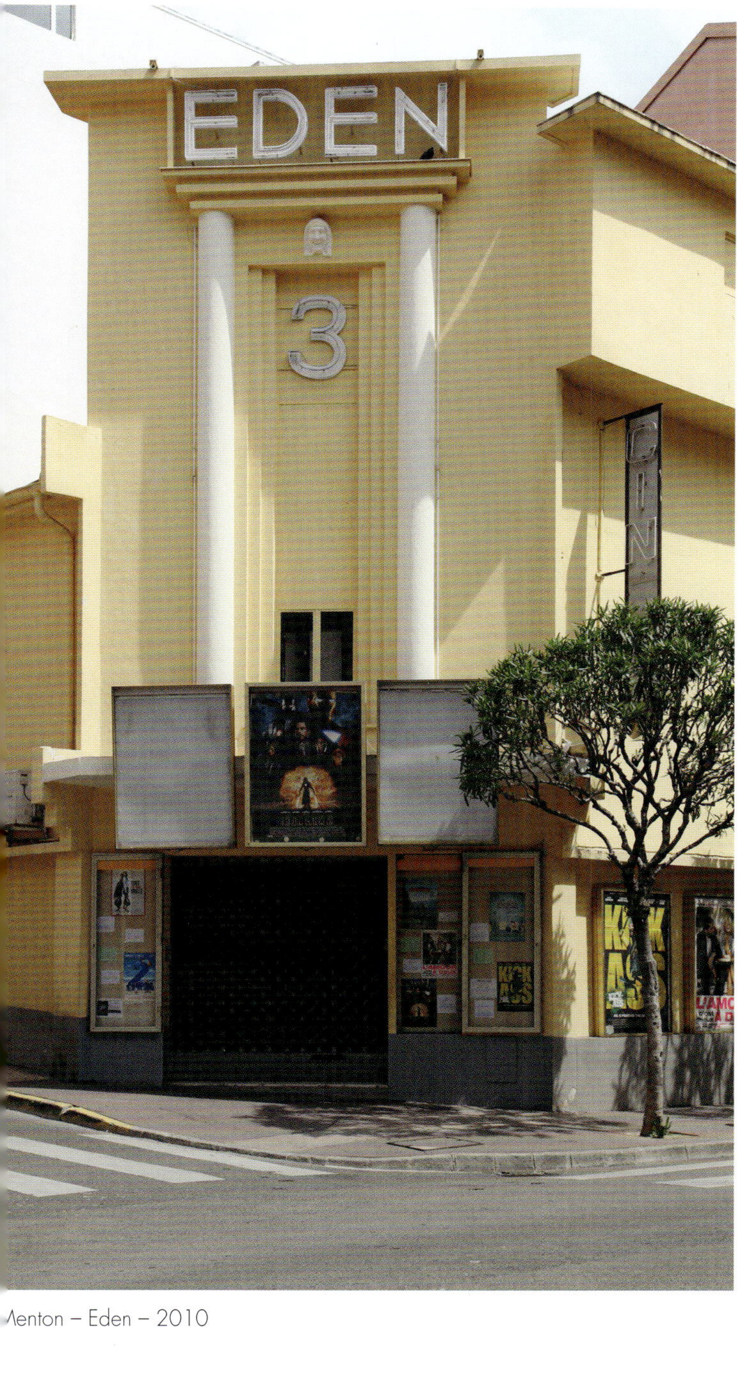

Menton – Eden – 2010

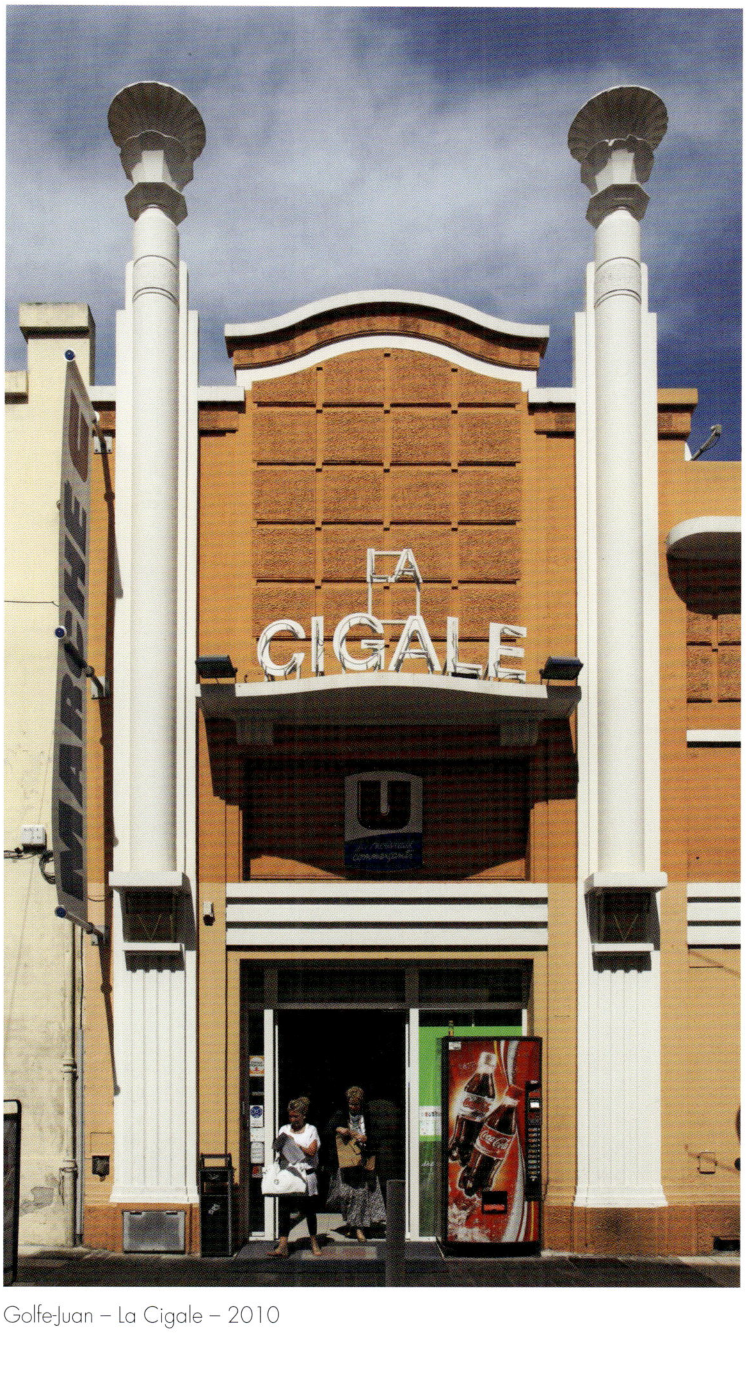

Golfe-Juan – La Cigale – 2010

GENEVA, SWITZERLAND

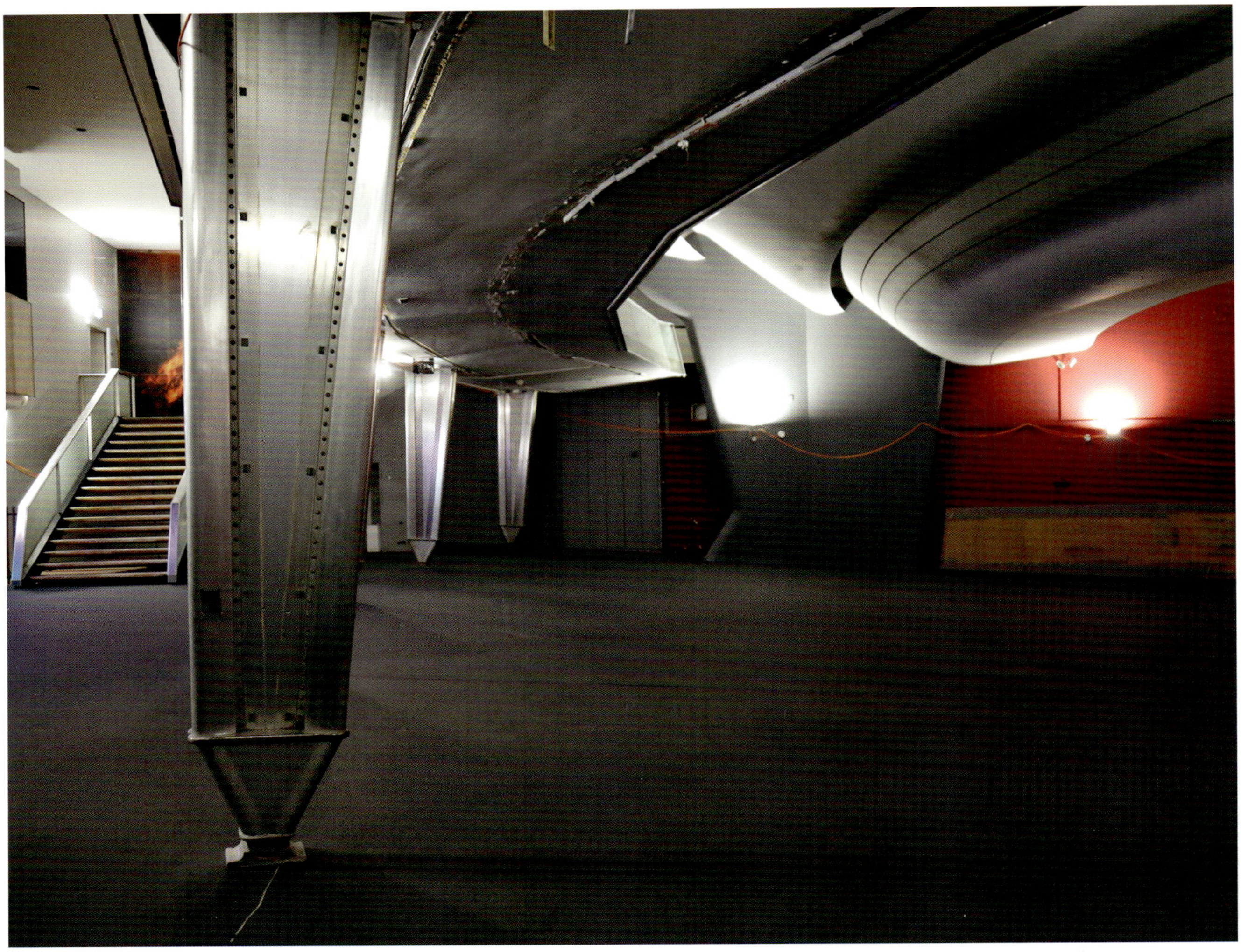

Geneva – Le Plaza – 2022

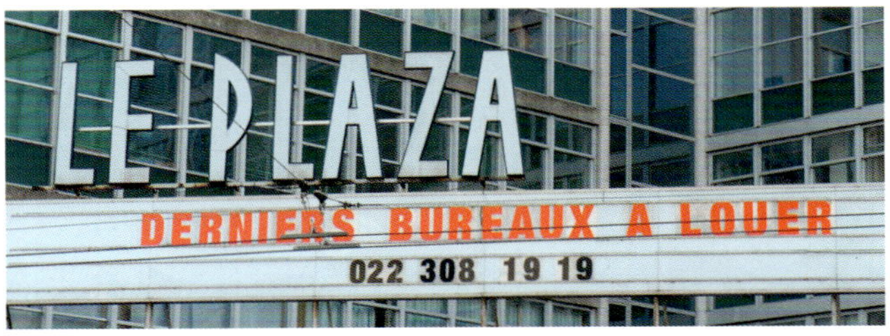

2013

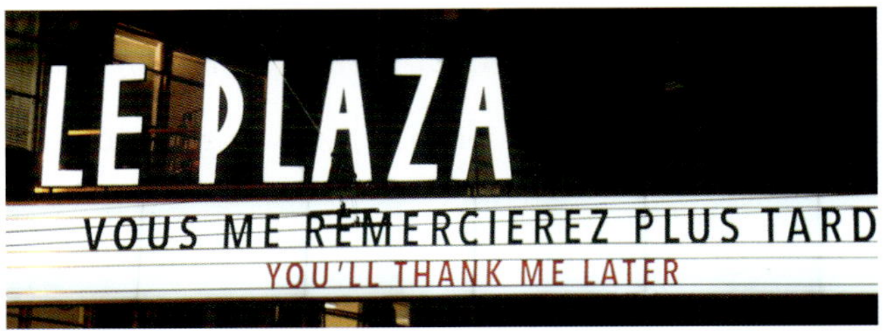

2021

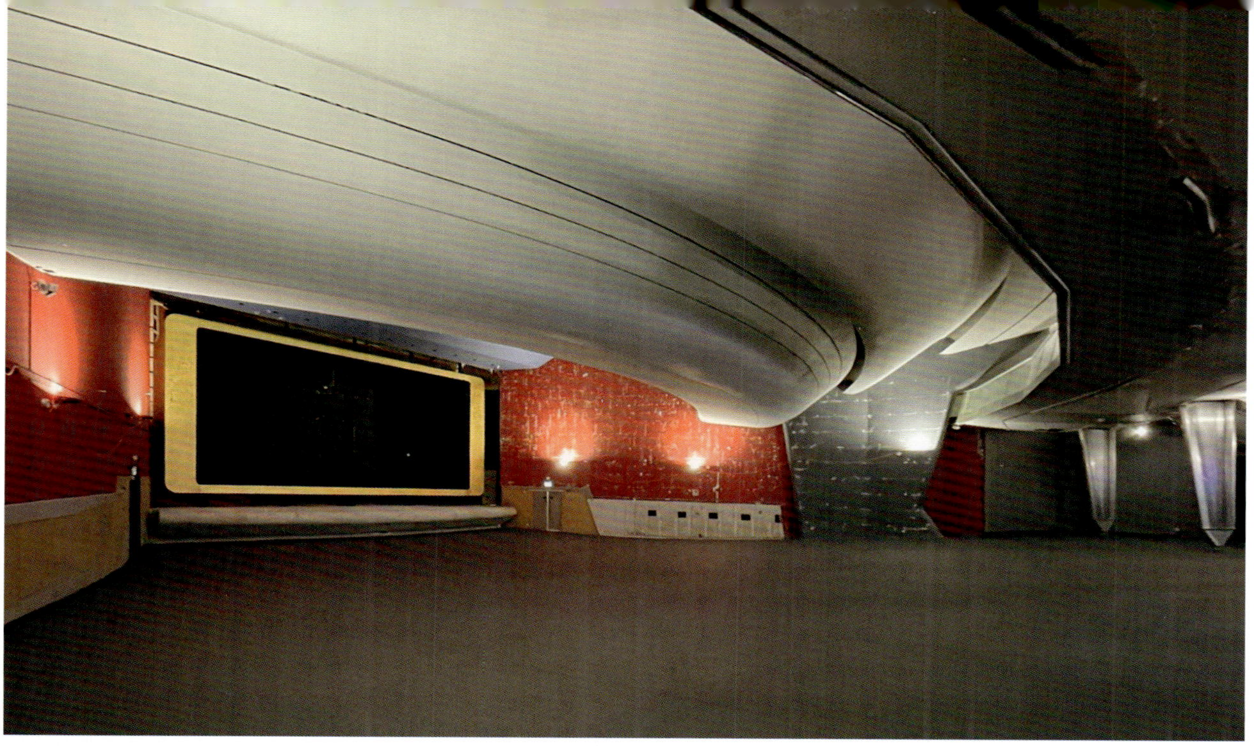

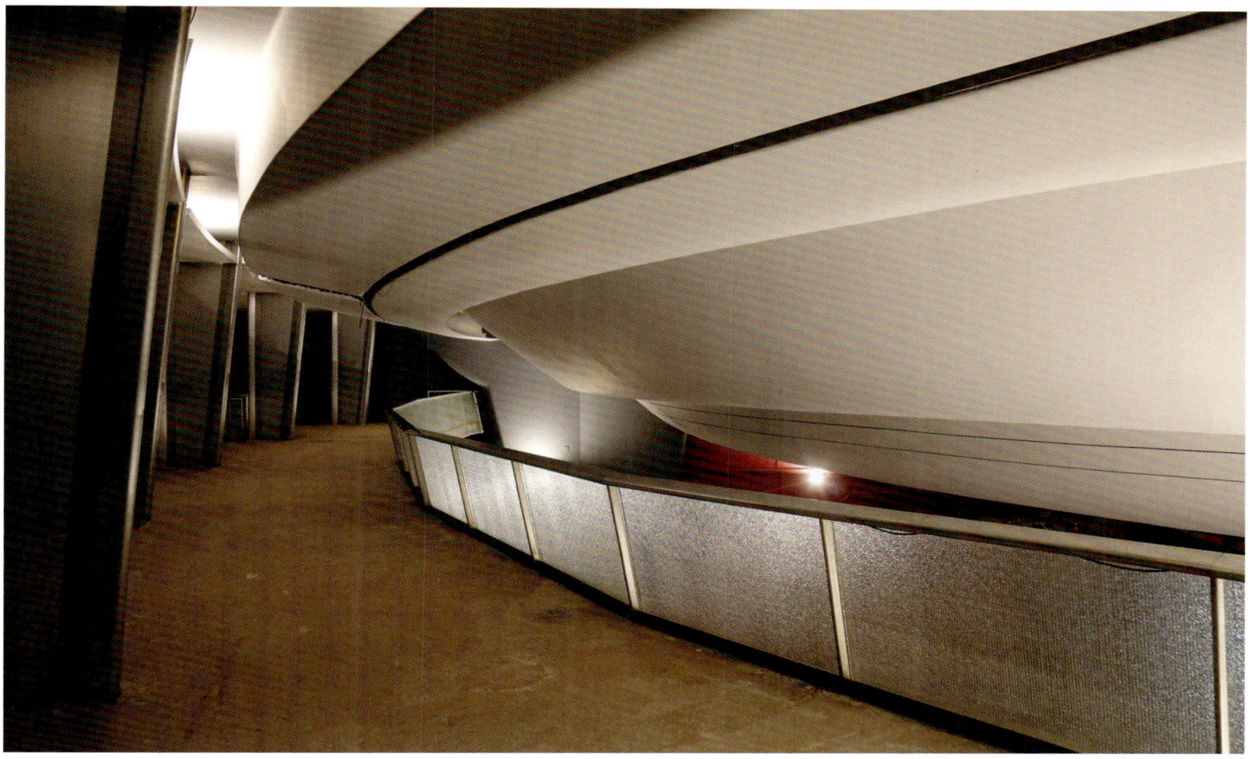

Geneva, Le Plaza. The Plaza, Geneva's most beautiful cinema, opened its doors in 1952. Built by architect Marc-Joseph Saugey (1908-1971), designer of the very audacious Manhattan cinema (now the Arditi Foundation Auditorium), the cinema easily thrived by showing masterpieces and forgetting the rest, before shutting down in January 2004. The abandoned building became the prey of real-estate speculators. Irresolutely listed as a historical building, it was soon downgraded, but an association formed to save this masterpiece. City authorities expressed only blameful indifference: all appeals were dismissed and the cinema was slotted for destruction. The bulldozers amassed in front of the entrance drooled with pleasure. Fortunately, a miracle occurred. The Hans Wilsdorf Foundation waved its magic wand, bought the entire building and decided to restore it according to the original plans, down to the last bolt. On 19 August, 2023, the Plaza was destroyed by a fire. The roof of the main hall collapsed in the flames. The opening has been postponed indefinitely. It was scheduled to reopen in the autumn of 2025.

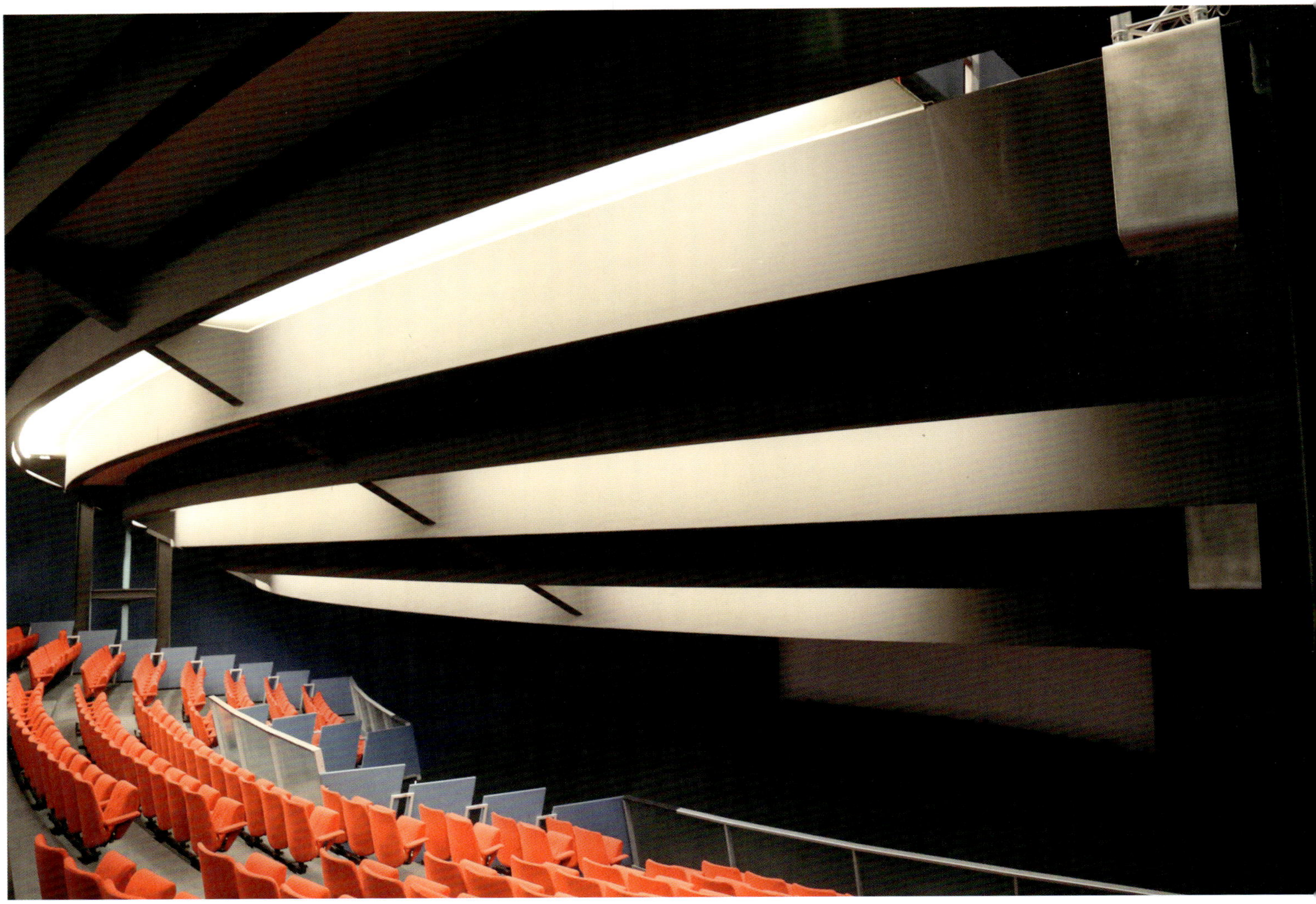

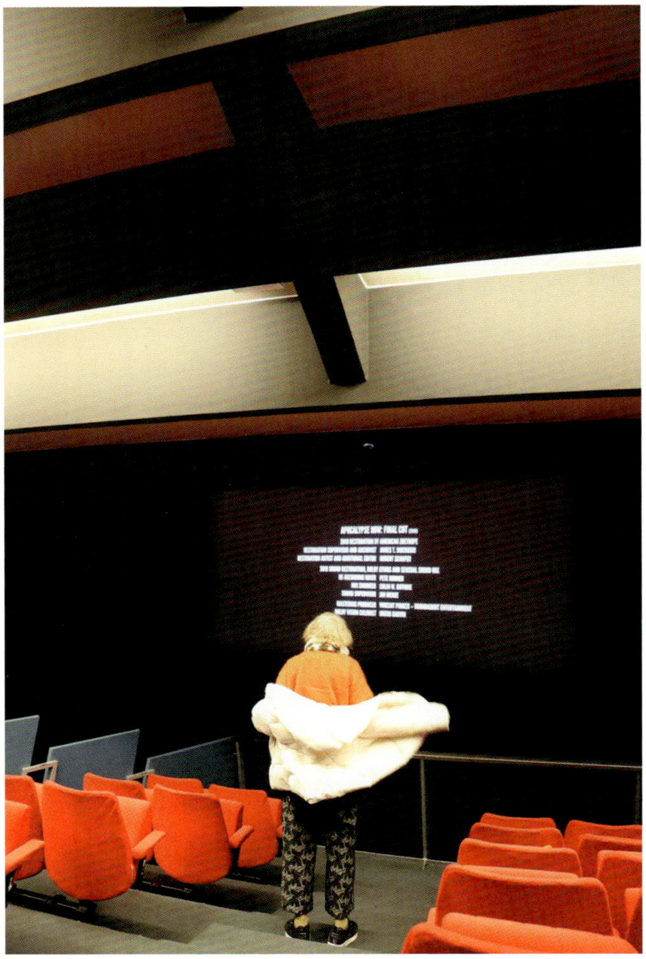

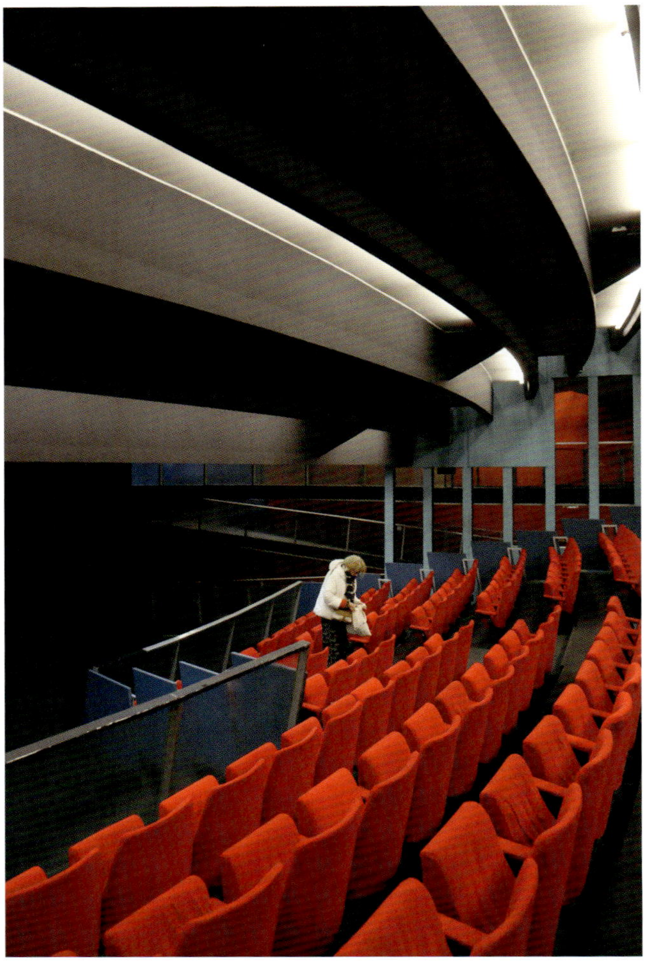

Geneva – Fondation Arditi – 2022

ACKNOWLEDGEMENTS

My thanks to my partner Elisabeth Christeler for her precious and constant assistance throughout this long adventure, as well as to Claude Richardet whose friendship, devotion and generosity have always been a source of support. My thanks also go to Bernadette Mermier and Michel and Olivier Oberson.

The End

THE AUTHOR

Born in 1942 in Geneva, Simon Edelstein has spent most of his life producing journalistic reports and documentaries for Swiss television. He has made a few future films for the big screen too. He is the author of two other books on cinemas: one is on cinemas in Switzerland and the other one is called 'Abandoned Cinemas of the World', both also released by Jonglez Publishing.

FROM THE SAME PUBLISHER

Atlas

Atlas of extreme weather
Atlas of geographical curiosities
Atlas of unusual wines

Photo Books

Abandoned America
Abandoned Asylums
Abandoned Australia
Abandoned churches – Unclaimed places of worship
Abandoned cinemas of the world
Abandoned France
Abandoned Italy
Abandoned Japan
Abandoned Lebanon
Abandoned Spain
After the Final Curtain – The Fall of the American Movie Theater
After the Final Curtain – America's Abandoned Theaters
Baikonur – Vestiges of the Soviet Space Programme
Chernobyl's Atomic Legacy
Forbidden Places
Forbidden Places – Vol.2
Forbidden Places – Vol.3
Forgotten Heritage
Oblivion
Unusual wines
Venice deserted
Venice from the skies

'Soul of' guides

Soul of Amsterdam– A guide to the 30 best experiences
Soul of Athens – A guide to 30 exceptional experiences
Soul of Barcelona – A guide to 30 exceptional experiences
Soul of Berlin – A guide to the 30 best experiences
Soul of Kyoto – A guide to 30 exceptional experiences
Soul of Lisbon – A guide to 30 exceptional experiences
Soul of Los Angeles – A guide to 30 exceptional experiences
Soul of Marrakesh – A guide to 30 exceptional experiences
Soul of New York – A guide to 30 exceptional experiences
Soul of Rome – A guide to 30 exceptional experiences
Soul of Tokyo – A guide to 30 exceptional experiences
Soul of Venice – A guide to 30 exceptional experiences

'Secret' guides

Secret Amsterdam
Secret Bali
Secret Bangkok
Secret Barcelona
Secret Belfast
Secret Berlin
Secret Brighton – An unusual guide
Secret Brooklyn
Secret Brussels
Secret Buenos Aires
Secret Campania
Secret Cape Town
Secret Copenhagen
Secret Dublin – An unusual guide
Secret Edinburgh – An unusual guide
Secret Florence
Secret French Riviera
Secret Geneva
Secret Glasgow
Secret Granada
Secret Helsinki
Secret Istanbul
Secret Johannesburg
Secret Lisbon
Secret Liverpool – An unusual guide
Secret London – An unusual guide
Secret London – Unusual bars & restaurants
Secret Los Angeles
Secret Madrid
Secret Mexico City
Secret Milan
Secret Montreal - An unusual guide
Secret Naples
Secret New Orleans
Secret New York – An unusual guide
Secret New York – Curious activities
Secret New York – Hidden bars & restaurants
Secret Paris
Secret Prague
Secret Provence
Secret Rio
Secret Rome
Secret Seville
Secret Singapore
Secret Sussex – An unusual guide
Secret Tokyo
Secret Tuscany
Secret Venice
Secret Vienna
Secret York – An unusual guide

Follow us on Facebook, Instagram and Twitter

Layout: Emmanuelle Willard Toulemonde – Translation: Sonny Alexander – Proofreading: Kimberly Bess – Publishing: Clémence Mathé

In accordance with jurisprudence (Toulouse 14–01–1887), the publisher is not to be held responsible for any involuntary errors or omissions that may appear in the guide despite the care taken by the editorial staff. Any reproduction of this book in any format is prohibited without the express agreement of the publisher.

© JONGLEZ 2023

Registration of copyright: September 2023 – Edition: 01

ISBN: 978-2-36195-610-3

Printed in Slovakia by Polygraf